ESSENTIAL GUIDE TO QUALITATIVE METHODS IN ORGANIZATIONAL RESEARCH

ESSENTIAL GUIDE TO QUALITATIVE METHODS IN ORGANIZATIONAL RESEARCH

Edited by

Catherine Cassell and Gillian Symon

⑤SAGE Publications
London ● Thousand Oaks ● New Delhi

First published 2004
Reprinted 2005, 2006

SAGE Publications Ltd
1 Oliver's Yard
55 City Road
London EC1Y 1SP

SAGE Publications Inc.
2455 Teller Road
Thousand Oaks, California 91320

SAGE Publications India Pvt Ltd
B-42, Panchsheel Enclave
Post Box 4109
New Delhi 110 017

British Library Cataloguing in Publication data

A catalogue record for this book is available from the British Library

ISBN-10: 0-7619-4887-2
ISBN-10: 0-7619-4888-0 (pbk)
ISBN-13: 978-0-7619-4887-2
ISBN-13: 978-0-7619-4888-9 (pbk)

Library of Congress Control Number available

Typeset by M Rules
Printed and bound in Great Britain by Athenaeum Press Ltd., Gateshead

This book is dedicated to our children,

Matt, Danny, Caitlin and Jamie.

They have been our best distraction from this work.

Contents

Notes on Contributors

John Benington is Professor of Public Policy and Management at Warwick Business School, Warwick University, and Director of the Institute of Governance and Public Management. His research interests are in public value, civic leadership, multi-level governance, and inter-organizational networks. His methodological interests are in action-research, co-research, and formative evaluation. Before becoming an academic he tried to practise what he now teaches. Fifteen years as a manager in the public and voluntary sectors taught him that things often work better in practice than in theory.

René Bouwen holds a PhD in psychology and is Professor of Organizational Psychology and Group Dynamics at the Catholic University in Leuven, Belgium. He is doing research on dealing with knowledge differences in organizations, innovation and change processes, group development and group effectiveness. Social change practices and multi-party collaboration are studied from a relational constructionist perspective.

John D. Brewer is Professor of Sociology at Queen's University of Belfast. He was Visiting Fellow at Yale University (1989), St John's College, Oxford (1992), Corpus Christi College, Cambridge (2002) and the Research School of the Social Sciences, Australian National University, Canberra (2003). He was elected a Fellow of the Royal Society of Arts in 1998 and an Academician in the Academy of Social Sciences in 2003. He is author and co-author of 13 books, including *Inside the RUC* (Oxford University Press), *After Soweto* (Oxford University Press), *Black and Blue: Policing in South Africa* (Oxford University Press), *Crime in Ireland 1945–95* (Oxford University Press), *Police, Public Order and the State* (Macmillan), *Anti-Catholicism in Northern Ireland 1660–1997* (Macmillan) and *Ethnography* (Open University Press). He is editor of *Can South Africa Survive* and *Restructuring South Africa* (both with Macmillan) and co-editor of the *A–Z of Social Research* (Sage).

Catherine Cassell is Professor of Organizational Psychology and Director of Research in the Management School at the University of Sheffield. Her research interests are in the areas of organizational change and development and managing diversity. Catherine has had a long term interest in issues of research methodology, particularly in relation to qualitative methods. She has collaborated with Gillian Symon over a number of years to produce books, articles and conference contributions about the use of qualitative methods in organizational research.

Elizabeth Chell is Professor of Entrepreneurship and Director of the Institute for Entrepreneurship, at the University of Southampton. Previously she held the Rory Brooks Chair of Enterprise at UMIST and the Chair of Enterprise, the University of Manchester. She has published extensively in entrepreneurship, organizational behaviour and research methods. Her latest book is *Entrepreneurship: Globalization, Innovation and Development* published by Thomson Learning, 2001. She has recently contributed an entry on the critical incident technique in *The*

Encyclopaedia of Research Methods in the Social Sciences edited by M. Lewis-Beck, A. Bryman and T. Futing Liao, Thousand Oaks, California: Sage. She is currently working on a revised edition of her 1991 research monograph *The Entrepreneurial Personality:Concepts, Cases and Categories* published by Routledge. Her current research interests focus on nascent entrepreneurship, women and science enterprise and technological entrepreneurship.

Chris Clegg is Professor of Organizational Psychology and Deputy Director of the Institute of Work Psychology at the University of Sheffield. He is a Co-Director of the ESRC Centre for Organization and Innovation, and Co-Director of the BAE/Rolls-Royce University Technology Partnership for Design. He currently chairs the Sociotechnical Specialist Group of the British Computer Society. He holds a BA (honours) in psychology from the University of Newcastle-on-Tyne and an MSc in business administration from the University of Bradford. He is a Fellow of the British Psychological Society, Fellow of the Royal Society of Arts, and a chartered psychologist. Chris's research interests are in the areas of new technology, e-business, work organization, information and control systems, sociotechnical theory and new management practices. He has published his work in a number of books and journals.

Louise Corti is an Associate Director and Head of the Qualidata and Outreach and Training sections of the UK Economic and Social Data Service based at the UK Data Archive, at the University of Essex. In the past she has taught sociology, social research methods and statistics, and spent six years working on the design, implementation and analysis of the British Household Panel Study also based at the University of Essex. She has authored a virtual tutorial for social research methods and published in the area of sharing and re-using qualitative data. She is interested in a broad range of methodological and data quality issues across qualitative and quantitative social research, and in the use of data in teaching and learning.

Kevin Daniels is Professor of Organizational Psychology at Loughborough University Business School. He received his PhD in Applied Psychology from Cranfield Institute of Technology. His research interests are concerned broadly with the relationships between emotion and cognition in organizations. He has published papers in journals such as *Human Relations, Journal of Occupational and Organizational Psychology, Journal of Management Studies, Organization Studies* and the *Strategic Management Journal*. He is an Associate Editor of the *Journal of Occupational and Organizational Psychology*.

Penny Dick is a Lecturer in Organizational Behaviour at Sheffield University Management School. She is a chartered occupational psychologist with a wide array of industrial experience. Her research interests and publications are in the management of diversity and organizational stress, particularly in emergency service settings.

Janet Fink is Lecturer in Social Policy at the Open University. Her research interests are centred on the turn in contemporary social policy and the intersections of family life and welfare discourses during the second half of the 20th Century. Her recent publications include the book *Rethinking European Welfare* (co-edited with Gail Lewis and John Clarke) and the journal articles 'Private lives, public issues: moral panics and the "family"' (*Journal for the Study of British Cultures*) and 'Europe's cold shoulder: migration and the constraints of welfare in Fortress Europe' (*Soundings*).

Yiannis Gabriel is Professor in Organizational Theory, Tanaka Business School, Imperial College, London, having taught previously at Bath University. He has a degree in Mechanical Engineering from Imperial College London, where he also carried out postgraduate studies in industrial sociology. He has a PhD in sociology from the University of California at Berkeley. His main research interests are in organizational and psychoanalytic theories, consumer studies, storytelling, folklore and culture. His latest book *Storytelling in Organizations*, looks into organizational folklore as a window into organizational culture and politics. Other publications include articles on computer folklore, organizational nostalgia, chaos and complexity in organizations, fantasies of organizational members about their leaders, organizational insults and research methodology using stories and narratives. He has been editor of the journal *Management Learning* and is associate editor of *Human Relations.*

Dorothy Griffiths is Professor of Human Resource Management and Deputy Principal of the Tanaka Business School at Imperial College, London. She has a degree in sociology from London and an MSc in the sociology of science and technology from the University of Bath. Her recent work has focused on gender, science and technology and on a critique of the concept of core competencies. With other colleagues she is currently working on the transfer of management learning to practice. She is an editor of *Feminist Review* and Chair of the Feminist Review Trust.

Claire Harris is a Research Associate at the Health Organizations Research Centre, University of Manchester Institute of Science and Technology. Her main research interests are cognition and emotion and organizational change. She is currently researching aspects of organizational change within the health care sector, in particular implementation of electronic patient records and changes in working time for junior doctors within the NHS. She is also a facilitator for the Leadership Through Effective Human Resource Management programme at UMIST. Claire has previously worked on a Health and Safety Executive funded project exploring the risks of stress from a cognitive perspective at the University of Sheffield and the University of Nottingham.

Jean Hartley is Professor of Organizational Analysis, Warwick Business School, University of Warwick, UK. She is also an ESRC Advanced Institute of Management Research (AIM) Public Service Fellow. Jean is responsible for the Local Government Centre's research programmes on organizational change, leadership and learning in public service organizations. She is the Research Director of the team monitoring and evaluating the Beacon Council Scheme (concerned with inter-organizational learning and corporate and service improvement). She has undertaken both formative and summative evaluations for government on programmes of service and organizational improvement and change in local public services. Her work on leadership includes developing a self-assessment instrument for political leadership. She has published three books and many articles on organizational psychology, public service improvement, and organizational change. She has written a number of articles on methods in organizational research, including case studies, employee surveys and co-research.

Frank Heller originally qualified in engineering followed by economics and psychology. He was Head of the Department of Management in what is now the University of Westminster, followed by a six year assignment as consultant to the International Labour Office and the

United Nations Special Program in Argentina and Chile. He was visiting Professor at the University of California at Berkeley and Stanford University, Hangzhou University China and the University of Santiago, Chile. He joined the Tavistock Institute in London in 1969 and founded the Centre for Decision Making Studies, of which he is a Director. The Centre is a European network of cross-national researchers who have carried out large programmes of investigation on the distribution of influence and human resource utilization in organizations in 14 countries.

Phil Johnson is a Principal Lecturer and Research Fellow in the School of Business and Finance at Sheffield Hallam University. He has undertaken and published research mainly in the areas of epistemology, methodology, management control, change management and business ethics. He has recently undertaken management research projects sponsored by ESRC and EPSRC. He has experience of the supervision of management research projects from first degree to doctorate.

Nigel King has a first degree in social psychology from the University of Kent at Canterbury, and a PhD from the University of Sheffield. He is currently a Reader in Psychology at the University of Huddersfield. His main research interests are: creativity, innovation and change in organizations; social and organizational psychological aspects of primary care; phenomenological and other qualitative approaches in psychology; paranormal beliefs and experiences. He is the author (with Neil Anderson) of *Managing Innovation and Change: A Critical Guide for Organizations* (Thomson Learning, 2002) as well as numerous book chapters and journal articles.

Mika Kivimäki, PhD, is a Professor of Occupational Health Psychology in the University of Helsinki and the Finnish Institute of Occupational Health, Finland. His current research interests relate to the role of psychosocial factors in the aetiology of cardiovascular disease, musculoskeletal disorders and depression.

Hannakaisa Länsisalmi, is Business Development Manager of Rautaruukki Group, a large international steel company. She is also a Research Fellow at the University of Helsinki. Her current research interests relate to innovation in organizations. She has worked previously as a business consultant at Accenture and the Finnish Institute of Occupational Health.

Andreas Liefooghe is an Organizational Psychologist at the Department of Organizational Psychology, Birkbeck, University of London. His main research interests are bullying at work, voice, discourse and power and the notion of morale and well-being at work. He uses a variety of methodologies in his work, with a main emphasis on qualitative methods.

John McAuley is Professor of Organization Development and Management in the School of Business and Finance, Sheffield Hallam University. He is Assistant Director (Research Coordination). His most recent research has been into the ways in which professionals in organizations respond to issues of change. He has published in the areas of change management, organization behaviour and the work of professionals. He has undertaken management and organizational consultancies in a wide range of public and private sector organizations. He has trained as a psychotherapist and uses insights acquired from this in developing understanding of behaviour in organizational settings.

Seonaidh McDonald is a Senior Research Fellow at Aberdeen Business School, Robert Gordon University. She has two main fields of interest. The first centres on a range of closely related strategic issues such as the management of change, organizational learning, innovation and knowledge management. She has an interest in studying the strategy making processes themselves as well as their content and outcomes. Her other area of interest is waste management. Her research in this field is also concerned with change, but focuses on the household rather than the organization. This work aims to understand, and to increase, public participation in domestic waste recycling schemes.

Kate Mackenzie Davey is a Lecturer in Organizational Psychology at Birkbeck College, University of London. She has published work on socialization, identity, value change, culture and bullying at work. She is interested in discursive and multi-method approaches to organizational processes especially the role of marginality in the individual–organizational relationship. Her current interests are in gender and perceptions of organizational politics, consultancy and contract work and the role of communication in organizations.

Stephanie Morgan is currently an Associate Lecturer at Birkbeck College, University of London, and Director of Crosslight IT Consulting Ltd. She has a BSc in psychology and an MSc in organizational behaviour, and received her PhD in organizational attachments in IT outsourcing at Birkbeck. Her current research interests and recent publications include issues around remote management, outsourcing transitions and technology related organizational change. Her focus on methodology includes the use of technology in research, longitudinal qualitative analysis, and the development of process models.

Gill Musson is a Lecturer and Researcher in OB/HRM at Sheffield University Management School. She has published in the areas of managing change in clinical and manufacturing contexts: the role of language in reflecting and structuring realities; and more recently on the dynamics of home based teleworking. She is co-author of *Understanding Organizations Through Language* (Sage, 2003), reflecting an overriding interest in language and meaning making and their role in organizational processes.

Sara Nadin is a Research Fellow at Sheffield University Management School. She has recently completed her PhD, the focus of which was the psychological contract in small businesses. Prior to commencing her PhD Sara worked on a number of projects concerned with change management and innovation in SMEs. As well as her specialist interest in the study of small businesses, her other interests include job design and research methods.

Nigel Nicholson is Professor of Organizational Behaviour at London Business School. He has been pioneering the application of evolutionary psychology to business in many writings including 'How hardwired is human behavior' for the *Harvard Business Review* (1998) and in his book *Managing the Human Animal* (Texere, 2000). Recent work includes an in-depth study of risk and decision-making among traders in the City of London. His current research focuses on leadership in family firms, and the role of personality in executive development.

José-M. Peiró, PhD, is Professor of Social and Organizational Psychology at the University of Valencia and Director of the Department of Psychobiology and Social Psychology. He served as President of the European Association of Work and Organizational Psychology and is currently President-elect of the Division 1 (Organizational Psychology) of the IAAP. He is also associate editor of the *European Journal of Work and Organizational Psychology*. He has published several books and articles on collective stress at work, burnout, work socialization, and organizational climate.

Anne Rees is presently a Senior Research Fellow in the School of Psychology at the University of Leeds. She received her MA in Linguistics from the University of Sheffield (1983). In addition to her interest in how ideas of the self can be assessed, she is engaged in research into effective psychotherapeutic treatments for depression and enduring and severe psychological disorders.

Michael Rowlinson is Professor of Organization Studies in the Centre for Business Management, Queen Mary, University of London. His research interests are in organization theory, critical management studies, and the emerging field of organizational history. His last book, *Organizations and Institutions* (1997), provides an overview and sociological critique of economic theories of organization, including game theory, agency theory, property rights and transaction costs. In a series of articles he has explored the tensions between organization studies and business history. He recently co-edited and contributed two articles for a themed section of the journal *Organization* (2002, 9(4)) on 'Foucault, management and history'. His current research, funded by the ESRC under the Evolution of Business Knowledge Programme, explores the relation between documentary corporate history and knowledge management, examining how companies use historical knowledge of the past in the present.

Fran Ryan is a chartered occupational psychologist with over 20 years' experience in organization and community work. She has a strong background in recruitment and development but now concentrates her work on two broad areas: participative strategic planning for organizations and communities, and participative organization design (where people redesign their organization to be optimal). She was co-author, with Robert Rehm (2002) of *Futures that Work*, and a contributing author to *People in Charge* edited by Robert Rehm (Hawthorn Press, 1999), a book about self-managing teams and organizations. She is currently researching the future conference at Oxford Brookes University.

Dalvir Samra-Fredericks is a Lecturer at Nottingham Business School and a visiting research fellow at the Management School, Keele University. Her research interest is in the nature of managerial elites' everyday rhetorical–relational dynamics, in particular, their linguistic skills, forms of knowledge and modes of rationalities for shaping strategic direction and simultaneously accomplishing identity and 'organization'. Associated interests arising from this are: extending the ethnographic approach to include recording 'real time' interactions and developing a critical pedagogy within management studies. She has recently published in *Corporate Governance, Journal of Management Studies* and *Management Learning*.

Jo Silvester is Professor of Occupational Psychology and Director of the Occupational Psychology Research Group at Goldsmiths College, University of London. She holds degrees from the Universities of London, York and Leeds and has lectured at the University of Leeds, the University of Wales Swansea, and City University London. Her main research interests concern how we judge competence in others – particularly in relation to employee selection and assessment – and the influence of stereotyping, culture and diversity. Her current work includes ESRC sponsored research into leadership and diversity in investment banking, and the psychological determinants of empathy in general practitioners. In addition, recent work has centred on developing fair selection procedures for parliamentary candidates; a project aimed at increasing the number of women and ethnic minorities who become MPs. Jo has published widely in the field of employee selection and assessment. She is an associate editor for the *International Journal of Selection and Assessment* and the *Journal of Occupational and Organizational Psychology*.

Chris Steyaert is Professor of Organizational Psychology at the University of St Gallen. After receiving his doctoral dissertation in Psychology from the Catholic University, Leuven (Belgium), he was attached to the Institute of Organization and Industrial Sociology, Copenhagen Business School, Denmark and to the Entrepreneurship and Small Business Research Institute (ESBRI), Stockholm, Sweden. He has published in international journals and books in the area of entrepreneurship and organizational innovation. His research themes include organizing creativity, diversity management and difference, language and translation, forms of performing/writing research and the politics of entrepreneurship and human organization.

David Stiles is a Lecturer in Strategy and Marketing at Cardiff Business School, Cardiff University, having completed a BSc in Bath University and an MBA and PhD at Cardiff. He previously worked as a strategist, economist and marketer in financial services and economic development. His research and consultancy work centres on strategy making and implementation in the private and public sectors. Major recent publications involve strategy in higher education and the police, joint ventures and culture in developing countries, and organizational image and identity. This includes the development and application of new methodologies in pictorial representation.

Gillian Symon is Senior Lecturer in Organizational Psychology in the Department of Organizational Psychology, Birkbeck College, University of London. Her main research interests lie in the areas of technological change at work and research practice. She and Catherine Cassell have collaborated over many years in producing articles, book chapters and conference papers that challenge traditional research practices in their discipline and seek to encourage both reflexivity in research and the use of innovative research methods.

Paul Thompson is Research Professor in Sociology at the University of Essex. He is author of many books using the life story/oral method, including *The Voice of the Past*, *The Edwardians*, *Living the Fishing*, *I Don't Feel Old*, and *Growing Up in Stepfamilies*. He is Founding Editor of *Oral History*. He was founding director of *Qualidata* and he is Founder of the National Life Story Collection at the British Library National Sound Archive.

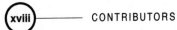

David Waddington is Reader in Cultural Studies at Sheffield Hallam University. His main research interests are: industrial relations, the policing of public order, and the sociology of mining communities.

Sue Walsh is a Senior Clinical Tutor on the Doctorate in Clinical Psychology course at Sheffield University and a consultant clinical psychologist in cognitive analytic therapy. Her academic and practitioner interests lie in the interface between clinical and organizational psychology.

Acknowledgements

It has been 10 years since we first set off on our quest to raise the profile of qualitative methods. In seeking to achieve this goal, we have been reliant on the expertise and commitment of our contributors. Our thanks go to all those who have given full and frank accounts of their own research practices in all our volumes, and who have unfailingly responded to the demands we have made of them. We also wish to thank Brian and Bill, for all their support, encouragement and affection.

Promoting New Research Practices in Organizational Research

Gillian Symon and Catherine Cassell

In editing our first volume of qualitative methods in organizational research (Cassell and Symon, 1994), we claimed that our aims were threefold and included: documenting the variety of qualitative methods available; providing accessible outlines of how to apply the methods in practice; and raising the profile of qualitative methods within organizational research. In a general sense, these aims have not changed, either with the second (Symon and Cassell, 1998a) or this third volume. Here, we aim to bring together many of the research approaches our contributors outlined in the earlier books, as well as providing introductions to other approaches not previously covered. Given this broad coverage, we felt entitled to call this an 'essential guide' and its production signals our last venture into this particular genre. Consequently, we felt that this introductory chapter would be a good opportunity to reflect back on our experiences over the years as proponents of 'qualitative' research, to discuss how our ideas have developed, and to debate how the field has changed over the years. Our experiences in this respect have inevitably been heavily influenced by our own disciplinary background as organizational psychologists. Psychology is a largely conservative field with respect to research methods (with some notable exceptions, for example, discourse analysis in social psychology). For those from other disciplines, our arguments may seem naïve or over-stated, however, within psychology, they can sometimes be seen as dangerously radical and the desire for change as completely misguided (Morgan, 1998). In describing these experiences, we have structured the chapter in relation to different issues we have confronted over the years: defining qualitative research and underlying research philosophies; publicizing alternative research methods and recognizing constraints in pursuing qualitative research; and strategies for influencing research practice.

DEFINING THE FIELD

When we set off on our mission to raise the profile of qualitative research in the organizational arena, we felt that the focus of our aspirations was unproblematic. We thought we knew what qualitative methods were. Over the years, our volumes (including this one), and various conference symposia we have organized, have retained the title of 'Qualitative Methods'. However, while this is a convenient label, one we feel people recognize and which is widely used, it is actually very problematic. In our first volume, we had already conceded that we could only really talk about 'characteristics' of qualitative research, without an overarching definition, because there was such a variety of methods that might claim this title and little consensus over a 'core' meaning. By 1998, we had come to the conclusion that to discuss 'qualitative' methods was something of a 'red herring' (Symon and Cassell, 1998b: 3) and that what was of importance in understanding particular research practices was to appreciate a variety of ontological and epistemological stances (such as are summarized in the meta-theories of Burrell and Morgan, 1979, and Alvesson and Deetz, 2000). While much (so-called) quantitative method might be underpinned by a positivist, normative or functionalist paradigm, qualitative methods might be informed by all possible epistemological positions, including those traditionally associated with quantitative methods (Gephart, 1999).

This difficulty in labelling raises a number of issues. Firstly, Dachler (1998), in a review of our first volume, emphasized that as long as 'alternative' methods were labelled qualitative in opposition to 'traditional' quantitative methods, they would always be perceived as an adjunct to quantitative research, rather than forming a distinct perspective based on different underlying epistemological assumptions and following different research goals. In our experience, quantitative researchers do not call their research 'quantitative'. They just call it research and 'qualitative' research may be viewed as something subsidiary. We may be creating a false dichotomy or simply not recognizing underlying value judgements by using these labels. Secondly, the use of such a broad label masks a very great variety of approaches, which perhaps should not be taken together as some sort of coherent whole. Their only shared characteristic might be that they do not seek to quantify phenomena. Even then, some researchers claiming to be engaged in qualitative research may go on to quantify their data (for example, counting frequencies of interview responses, and using statistical techniques to compare groups). This raises a third issue of 'can these researchers then be said to be engaged in "real" qualitative research?' In our reply to Dachler's review (Cassell and Symon, 1998), we emphasized the particular problems of this argument. If there is no agreed definition that might act as a 'gold standard' against which to make the judgement, then anyone who says they are conducting 'qualitative' research *is* conducting qualitative research. Despite our earlier description of the characteristics of qualitative research, we were reluctant to 'speak for' qualitative research, to claim a special prerogative or knowledge which allowed us to be the arbiters in judging whether research is 'truly' qualitative or not. We also were not seeking to privilege a particular epistemological standpoint, but rather to seek a 'level playing field' (Symon and Cassell, 1999: 396) for all kinds of research practice. This is, however, quite a relativist position, and therefore has its own problems. Hoshmand (1999) suggests that qualitative research should be specifically aligned with action research and critical hermeneutical traditions and that qualitative researchers should form a 'community' around these specific concerns. Indeed, her argument is that:

> Philosophical and procedural differences among qualitative approaches have made it difficult for qualitative researchers to forge a unified proposal and to establish the place of qualitative inquiry in psychology in particular and in the social sciences in general. (1999: 15)

Thus, we cannot gain credibility for qualitative research unless qualitative researchers show some sort of united front. We feel that this approach might well undermine the current variety of approaches taken to research, loosely termed 'qualitative', which are based in different epistemologies. An alternative approach would be to abandon the term 'qualitative' and seek instead some sort of common reflexive practice across research – such that all researchers seek to account for their practice and assumptions whatever they are. We discuss this further in the penultimate section of this chapter. However, Hoshmand does raise the important issue of the politics of research practice, to which we now turn our attention. In the rest of this chapter, we continue to use the phrase 'qualitative methods' to reflect accepted practice within the research community.

RAISING THE PROFILE AND POLITICIZING THE PROCESS ——————————————

One of our original aims in producing these volumes was to raise the profile of qualitative research. We felt this was somewhat achieved by simply documenting the range of methods available. Giving a method a title and reference point achieves some legitimacy for the research practice simply by allowing users to cite some credible source. Quite apart from our efforts, and judging by the number of textbooks available in the area, it is clear that qualitative methods have achieved an increased prominence since the 1990s. As well as the publication of our first volume, 1994 saw the first edition of the massive *Handbook of Qualitative Research* (edited by Denzin and Lincoln and also published by Sage). This brought together a range of writings, not confined to a particular discipline, and detailing underlying theoretical perspectives, research practices and specific techniques. Since then, numerous authors have sought to provide alternatives to the normative model that dominates research practice (for example, Flick, 2002; May, 2002; Ritchie and Lewis, 2003; Smith, 2003) reflecting a growing interest in the area. However, publishing textbooks does not guarantee any particular change in research practice. We are keen to see changes such as: the acceptance of qualitative approaches on their own terms and as a valued research practice; the publication of qualitative research in prestigious journals; the presentation of papers based on qualitative methods at conferences; and the provision of a thorough grounding in alternative methods in university research methods courses. Raising the profile is not enough, the research process itself can be perceived as an essentially political one, closely bound up with issues of identity, career progression and power. This has implications for the spread of alternative research approaches:

> The academic and disciplinary resistances to qualitative research illustrate the politics embedded in this field of discourse. The challenges to qualitative research are many. Qualitative researchers are called journalists or soft scientists. Their work is termed unscientific, or only exploratory, or entirely personal and full of bias . . . (Denzin and Lincoln, 1998: 7)

In Symon and Cassell (1999) we identified a number of different barriers to innovation in research practice which we suggested were interrelated and emanated from a variety of social-psychological processes. We specifically identified the issues below:

- getting research past epistemological gatekeepers (journal editors and reviewers, conference committees);
- conforming to journal editorial criteria and constraints of other presentations (set up with quantitative studies in mind);
- pressure to justify research methods according to inappropriate (normative) criteria;
- convincing organizations who associate quantitative methods with 'science' and 'truth'; and,
- researchers given little exposure to alternatives on training courses.

Thus we argued that it is not that qualitative research is inherently weaker or less rigorous but rather that judgements of 'good practice' in research cannot be made without reference to the social and political context. Our analysis of debates in such publications as *The Psychologist* (the magazine of the British Psychological Society), suggested to us that the difficulty in gaining acceptance of qualitative methods could be partly because of the value placed on research based on the natural science model, and because of the identity processes bound up with the role of 'scientist'. Where funding councils and other institutions may favour the supposed objectivity and rigour of 'science', then we must all be seen to be 'scientists'. Career and psychological investments may be made in that identity – particularly in psychology, which may have struggled to be accepted as a serious discipline over the last century.

The identification of these sorts of problems, leads us to conclude that if we are to continue to 'raise the profile' of qualitative research within this political context, then we have to pay attention not just to publicizing 'alternative' approaches in textbooks such as this, but also 'selling' them to research councils, journal editors and our colleagues. To this end, with our colleague, Dr Phil Johnson, we have recently received a UK Economic and Social Research Council grant[1] (as part of a recent research methods funding initiative) to review current practice in qualitative research and devise training in the area. We discuss this further in the next section.

INFLUENCING RESEARCH PRACTICE

Our intention has always been to influence research practice within our own discipline by producing these edited volumes. We hope that we can encourage others (academics *and* practitioners, Symon et al., 2000) to consider alternative methods of inquiry. We have argued that despite the recent developments in the concerns of work psychology, there has been little change in the underlying epistemological assumptions that influence how research is construed (Symon and Cassell, 1999). Other researchers have also suggested that a lack of reflection and creativity in this respect is stifling to the discipline (Anderson, 1998). In other words, quantitative studies driven by positivist concerns, are adopting an essentially conservative research strategy, concentrating on investigating minor variations of already established theoretical models (adding a variable here or there, trying the model out in a different context or with a different sample, etc). This is not contributing to a vibrant and innovative research community. Qualitative approaches and research adopting alternative epistemological perspectives hold out the promise of new insights by adopting a critical stance on accepted practices and approaching research topics with different objectives. As noted above, however, producing edited volumes is insufficient to bring about these changes. Other strategies we see as important include: exploring judgements of 'good' research practice; researcher reflexivity; and training, and we discuss each of these below.

Evaluation criteria

One of our research objectives within the ESRC project is to establish current perceptions of the 'worth' of qualitative research amongst: the editors of influential journals in the field; those sponsoring research (for example, research councils and charities); those working in UK public policy; practitioners (such as management consultants); and those training new researchers (for example, Directors of PhD programmes in UK universities). In interviewing various representatives of these groups, one of our aims will be to establish current assessment criteria, namely how do these individuals judge the quality of the research accounts they read? This issue has been a vexed question for many years within the area of qualitative research (Merrick, 1999). We have argued (Cassell and Symon, 2002) that qualitative research reports (particularly with respect to journal submissions perhaps) may be judged according to inappropriate criteria, for example applying positivist notions of reliability and validity to judge the quality of a postmodern analysis – and finding it, not surprisingly, wanting in these respects. Various authors have attempted to come up with criteria for assessing qualitative research specifically. For example, Yardley (2000) has suggested that good qualitative research should demonstrate:

- sensitivity to context – in terms of related theory, epistemological commitments of the research and socio-cultural context of data collection;
- commitment, rigour, transparency and coherence – in terms of researcher engagement with the study, completeness of the data collection and analysis, careful description of the research process and intellectual coherence of the arguments presented through the analysis; and
- impact and importance – in terms of the substance and worth of the work with relation to earlier theory and the specific issue being explored.

Criteria may differ considerably in the extent to which they seek to ape the concerns of quantitative research (for example, Lincoln and Guba, 1985; Stiles, 1993) or seek to establish alternative approaches to research evaluation (for example, Guba and Lincoln, 1989; Schwandt, 1996). Madill et al. (2000) and Johnson et al. (2003) suggest that different criteria may be suitable for different epistemological positions, while others have tried to formulate a general set of criteria which would be suitable for judging the quality of *both* quantitative and qualitative research (Salmon, 2003). The danger of the evolution of such criteria is that of 'methodologism' (Salmon, 2003): the mechanical application of 'validity' techniques without reflection, demonstrating an over-emphasis on procedure as a way of 'getting it right' which is more reminiscent of the concerns of 'traditional' quantitative research. In addition, there is the issue of the bewildering array of different lists of criteria now available. Overall, there may be too much attention being paid to producing lists rather than understanding the research process. The danger of not producing some sort of framework, however, is that judgements are prejudiced by subconscious and stereotypical ideas of what constitutes 'good research'. In psychology particularly, this is likely to be heavily influenced by a positivist paradigm specifically as this is the basis of training in the discipline. We are interested to see to what extent judgements of the quality of qualitative research amongst members of our research panels are informed by established criteria of the sort outlined above or pre-conscious stereotypes of acceptable practice. Our own view, as suggested above, is that reflexivity (the critical appraisal of one's own research practice) must be an important element of any sort of effective research practice.

Reflexivity

In 1998, we argued with Peter Dachler that we saw ourselves more as participants in a 'quiet revolution' than a 'radical transformation' of our discipline. Whatever our own epistemological commitments (which we describe in our own empirical work for example Cassell et al., 2000, and Symon, 2000), we did not particularly see the future as a work and organizational psychology entirely devoted to postmodernism. What we have argued we would like to see, however, is a more reflexive discipline (Symon et al., 2001). This recognition of the pivotal place of reflexivity in research practice is not new (for example, Woolgar, 1988), but seems to be of particular contemporary interest (for example, Holland, 1999; Alvesson and Skoldberg, 2000; Finlay, 2002; Johnson and Duberley, 2003). In a conference paper presented to the tenth European Congress of Work and Organizational Psychology in 2001, we suggested that critical appraisal of research practice within our discipline could operate within several different domains:

- Critical appraisal of our methodological practices, for example thinking about how the research should be designed or conducted in order to provide a convincing account; thinking about alternative interpretations of our results and how these might be refuted; thinking about the role we might have played in producing the results; reflecting on the choices that were made during the research process and reasons for them.
- Acknowledgement of and reflection on our epistemological commitments namely, while we can learn about the mechanics of particular research methods (such as have been outlined in the collections we have edited), what will also be of importance in understanding any research outputs or claims, will be our views on the nature of reality and knowledge. What are we doing when we pursue a research project, seeking a truth or giving an account, and how do we justify the claims we make as a result of our research, through reference to external sources such as mathematical formulae or through rhetoric and self-reflection? Lewis and Grimes (1999) suggest that researchers engage in multi-paradigmatic research, re-analysing data from different epistemological perspectives (they use Burrell and Morgan's meta-theory to structure this process) and thereby giving, they suggest, a more rounded perspective on the phenomenon of interest.
- Recognizing the influence of our disciplinary backgrounds on the knowledge we produce, i.e. we fit people into our (disciplined) way of thinking about the world. By creating some particular account, we deny other meanings and interpretations. Being reflexive in this way would entail reflecting on how the assumptions of our background discipline have prompted us to create a particular version of reality through our research. Why were we interested in these particular research questions? What disciplinary-based interpretative frameworks inform our accounts? What aspects of our disciplinary background lead us to dwell on certain aspects of the research context and not others? And from a more critical perspective, whose voices were allowed to be heard? In addition, viewing our research from the perspective of other disciplines may allow hitherto unseen insights to emerge.

We did not confine our description of this reflexive practice to 'qualitative' research necessarily (traditionally, reflexivity has been associated with qualitative research), nor to research emanating from more subjective research paradigms such as interpretivism or postmodernism. We would argue that encouraging reflexivity in research practice should be a very important aspect of future research training in general:

> . . . to make unexamined metatheoretical commitments, and remain unaware of their origins, amounts to an abdication of intellectual responsibility which results in poor research practices. (Johnson and Duberley, 2003: 1280)

Training

In Symon and Cassell (1999) we claimed that one of the barriers to the use of innovative research practices is that undergraduates and postgraduates are predominantly taught the procedures and concerns of positivist research only. Less attention may be paid to alternatives, and where these are included, they may be fairly limited in scope or taught through a positivist epistemology only. This may be particularly the case on psychology courses but also management and other courses of relevance to organizational research. For example, in a recent editorial the Chair of the Research Methods Division of the US Academy of Management has drawn attention to the emphasis on quantitative methodology training amongst management PhD students and has estimated that there are five times as many quantitative courses as qualitative ones (Boje, 2001). It is possible that the situation in Europe is less acute than that reported by Boje in the US. We are hoping as part of the ESRC grant to collect outlines of course syllabuses in the UK to gain an appreciation of the status of qualitative research training in management schools at least. However, the significance of the situation in the US for European organizational researchers is that many of the journals regarded as the most prestigious in the research community are US-based. Therefore, the biases of US research training are transmitted through the types of articles published in these prestigious journals.

In order to address the issue of training directly, we are proposing to produce some 'training' materials as one of the outputs of our current ESRC grant. The design of such materials, it is envisaged, will draw on the concerns raised by our research panels with respect to skill shortages, and examples of best practice found as a result of our research. For us, this raises the issue of what constitutes 'training'. As noted above, and in the books we have so far edited, we do not want to encourage the mechanical learning of methods and procedures (and the term training can sometimes imply this kind of learning). The books (including this one) are mainly indicators of the concerns of particular methods and examples of researchers' personal experiences. A thorough grounding would require a good grasp of the epistemological and ethical issues involved and experience with using the methods in various contexts. Part of learning would also involve reflecting on one's use of the method and individuals' experiences of participating in the research. In time, one might hope for insights to develop and modify the method. Ultimately, as an experienced qualitative researcher, one might expect to throw away the method book and draw on one's reflexive learning about the research process as a whole, one's own role in the research process and the act of engaging with others in exploring interesting issues. Any training materials we produce will certainly be positioned as only the start of a process of 'becoming a qualitative researcher'.

THIS VOLUME

It has often been argued that there are essentially three different kinds of qualitative research: participant observation, interviews, and document analysis. Even if reducible to these underlying forms, the variety of approaches documented in this volume demonstrates the rich diversity of 'qualitative' options available to researchers. Thus, there are many different forms of interviewing available: structured interviews such as the repertory grid, contextual interviews such as life histories, and focused interviews such as the critical incident technique.

In a similar vein, there are a variety of ways of analysing the data arising from such techniques of data collection, for example: structured techniques such as grounded theory and attribution analysis, which may concentrate on identifying content themes; and those which focus on language use specifically, such as discourse and conversation analysis. There are many approaches which advocate a combination of data collection techniques such as case studies and action research. Some 'methods' documented in this volume advocate particular kinds of attitudes towards and treatment of participants in the research (for example, co-research, action research, search conferences, critical analysis) which then have implications for how the research is conducted and interpreted. In these latter examples, we perhaps see more of a direct relationship between epistemology and method. However, this is not always the case: the same method may be used within different epistemologies. In some edited volumes, epistemology may be considered separately from research methods (for example, Denzin and Lincoln, 2000), however, here we wanted the research accounts to be more holistic. Consequently, and given our experiences over the years (documented above), we have encouraged contributors to this particular volume to consider reflexivity and epistemology in their accounts. Space restrictions constrained the extent to which they were able to do this, however, we feel readers are able to get a good feel for the assumptions and commitments driving the research described.

In respect of pursuing educational objectives, the variety of methods documented here certainly provides the researcher (academic or practitioner) with a range of options and opportunities for exploring diverse issues within the area of organizational research. The account of each method is necessarily too brief to give a complete grounding in the application of the methods described. However, each contributor has provided a list of additional reading at the end of their chapters so that interested readers can pursue the possibilities further.

CONCLUSION

Over the last 10 years we have sought to raise the profile of qualitative methods in organizational research through producing edited volumes such as this one. In the process, we have learnt a considerable amount about the research process and our views have changed as a consequence. We now consider the term 'qualitative methods' to be somewhat problematic; see acknowledging underlying beliefs about knowledge and research as important aspects of research practice; recognize the political context of conducting and disseminating research; and seek to encourage critical appraisal as an integral part of research training and practice. We hope to pursue our understanding of the field and continue to publicize alternative approaches through other projects.

However our views as to the usefulness of books such as these have not changed. We believe the contributors to these volumes have provided an invaluable service to both experienced researchers and practitioners wishing to pursue alternative approaches, and those starting out in organizational research, seeking to learn about the fundamentals of conducting research in an ethical and reflexive way. Taken together, these volumes illustrate the range and diversity of research approaches available, providing a comprehensive source of ideas for practice and encouraging the exploration of contemporary issues in organizational research in dynamic and innovative ways.

NOTE

1 ESRC Grant no. H333250006 'Benchmarking Good Practice in Qualitative Management Reseaerch'.

REFERENCES

Alvesson, M. and Deetz, S. (2000) *Doing Critical Management Research*, London: Sage.

Alvesson, M. and Skoldberg, K. (2000) *Reflexive Methodology: New Vistas for Qualitative Research*, London: Sage.

Anderson, N. (1998) 'The people make the paradigm', *Journal of Organizational Behaviour*, 19: 323–8.

Boje, D. (2001) 'Report from the division chair', *Academy of Management Research Methods Division Newsletter*, 16(2), Fall 2001.

Burrell, G. and Morgan, G. (1979) *Sociological Paradigms and Organizational Analysis*, London: Heinemann.

Cassell, C., Close, P., Duberley, J. and Johnson, P. (2000) 'Surfacing embedded assumptions: using repertory grid methodology to facilitate organizational change', *European Journal of Work and Organizational Psychology*, 9(4): 561–73.

Cassell, C. and Symon, G. (eds) (1994) *Qualitative Methods in Organizational Research: A Practical Guide*, London: Sage.

Cassell, C. and Symon, G. (1998) 'Quiet revolutions and radical transformations: a reply to H. Peter Dachler', *Organization Studies*, 19(6): 1039–43.

Cassell, C. and Symon, G. (2002) 'Expanding our epistemological boundaries', paper presented to the 26th International Congress of Applied Psychology, Singapore, July.

Dachler, H. P. (1998) 'Does the distinction between qualitative and quantitative methods make sense?', Review of C. Cassell and G. Symon (eds) 'Qualitative Methods in Organizational Research, *Organization Studies*, 18 (4): 709–24.

Denzin, N. and Lincoln, Y. (eds) (1994) *Handbook of Qualitative Research*, Thousand Oaks: Sage.

Denzin, N. and Lincoln, Y. (1998) 'Introduction: entering the field of qualitative research', in N. Denzin and Y. Lincoln (eds), *The Landscape of Qualitative Research*, Thousand Oaks: Sage, pp. 1–34.

Denzin, N. and Lincoln, Y. (eds) (2000) *Handbook of Qualitative Research*, second volume, Thousand Oaks: Sage.

Finlay, L. (2002) 'Negotiating the swamp: the opportunity and challenge of reflexivity in research practice', *Qualitative Research*, 2 (2): 209–30.

Flick, U. (2002) *An Introduction to Qualitative Research*, second edition, London: Sage.

Gephart, R. (1999) 'Paradigms and research methods', *Research Methods Forum*, volume 4 (Summer).

Guba, E. and Lincoln, Y. (1989) *Fourth Generation Evaluation*, Newbury Park, CA: Sage.

Holland, R. (1999) 'Reflexivity', *Human Relations*, 52: 463–83.

Hoshmand, L. (1999) 'Locating the qualitative research genre', in M. Kopala and L. Suzuki (eds), *Using Qualitative Methods in Psychology*, Thousand Oaks: Sage, pp. 15–24.

Johnson, P., Buehring, A. Cassell, C. and Symon, G. (2003) 'Evaluating qualitative management research: towards a contingent criteriology', working paper.

Johnson, P. and Duberley, J. (2003) 'Reflexivity in management research', *Journal of Management Studies*, 40 (5): 1279–303.

Lewis, M. and Grimes, A. (1999) 'Metatriangulation: building theory from multiple paradigms', *Academy of Management Review*, 24(4): 672–90.

Lincoln, Y. and Guba, E. (1985) *Naturalistic Inquiry*, Beverley Hill, CA: Sage.

Madill, A., Jordan, A. and Shirley, C. (2000) 'Objectivity and reliability in qualitative analysis: realist, contextualist and radical constructionist epistemologies', *British Journal of Psychology*, 91 (1): 1–20.

May, T. (2002) *Qualitative Research in Action*, London: Sage.

Merrick, E. (1999) 'An exploration of quality in qualitative research', in M. Kopala and L. Suzuki (eds), *Using Qualitative Methods in Psychology*, Thousand Oaks: Sage, pp. 25–36.

Morgan, M. (1998) 'Qualitative research: science or pseudo-science?' *The Psychologist*, 11: 481–3.

Ritchie, J. and Lewis, J. (2003) *Qualitative Research Practice*. London: Sage.

Salmon, P. (2003) 'How do we recognise good research?' *The Psychologist*, 16: 24–7.

Schwandt, T. (1996) 'Farewell to criteriology', *Qualitative Inquiry*, 2 (1): 58–72.

Smith, J. (ed.) (2003) *Qualitative Psychology: a Practical Guide to Research Methods*, London: Sage.

Stiles, W. (1993) 'Quality control in qualitative research', *Clinical Psychology Review*, 13: 593–618.

Symon, G. (2000) 'Everyday rhetoric: argument and persuasion in everyday life', *European Journal of Work and Organizational Psychology*, 9 (4): 477–88.

Symon, G. and Cassell, C. (eds) (1998a) *Qualitative Methods and Analysis in Organizational Research: A Practical Guide*, London: Sage.

Symon, G. and Cassell, C. (1998b) 'Reflections on the use of qualitative methods', in G. Symon and C. Cassell (eds), *Qualitative Methods and Analysis in Organizational Research: A Practical Guide*, London: Sage, pp 1–9.

Symon, G. and Cassell, C. (1999) 'Barriers to innovation in research practice', in M. Cunha and C. Marques (eds), *Readings in Organization Science – Organizational Change in a Changing Context*, Lisbon: ISPA, pp. 387–98.

Symon, G., Cassell, C. and Dachler, H.P. (2001) 'Towards a reflexive work and organizational psychology', paper presented to the 10th European Congress of Work and Organizational Psychology, Prague, May.

Symon, G., Cassell, C. and Dickson, R. (2000) 'Expanding our research and practice through innovative research methods', *European Journal of Work and Organizational Psychology*, 9 (4): 457–62.

Woolgar, S. (ed.) (1988) *Knowledge and Reflexivity: New Frontiers in the Sociology of Knowledge*, London: Sage.

Yardley, L. (2000) 'Dilemmas in qualitative health research', *Psychology and Health*, 15: 215–28.

Nigel King

The interview remains the most common method of data gathering in qualitative research, employed in various forms by every main theoretical and methodological approach within qualitative applied psychology. As such, it is impossible to provide a comprehensive account of the method within one relatively short chapter. Rather, my aim is to give an introduction to the variety of forms of qualitative research interview (and the assumptions that underly their use), before providing practical guidance on how to design and carry out a study using this method. The recommended texts detailed at the end should help readers deepen their knowledge of those aspects of the method of most relevance to their own work.

Types of research interview and their uses

The first question to address is that of definition: what types of interview can be considered qualitative? As is often the case with qualitative methods, terminology is a problem: the types of interview which fit this label are variously referred to as 'depth', 'exploratory', 'semi-structured', or 'un-structured'. I will use in this chapter the general term 'qualitative research interview'. This covers a range of approaches to research interviewing; however, all qualitative research interviews have certain characteristics in common. Kvale defines the qualitative research interview as; 'an interview, whose purpose is to gather descriptions of the life-world of the interviewee with respect to interpretation of the meaning of the described phenomena' (Kvale, 1983: 174). The goal of any qualitative research interview is therefore to see the research topic from the perspective of the interviewee, and to understand how and why they come to have this particular perspective. To meet this goal, qualitative research interviews will generally have the following characteristics: a low degree of structure imposed by the interviewer; a preponderance of open questions; and a focus on 'specific situations and action sequences in the world of the interviewee' (Kvale, 1983: 176) rather than abstractions and general opinions.

A key feature of the qualitative research interview method is the nature of the relationship between interviewer and interviewee. In a quantitative study using structured interviews, the interviewee is seen as a research 'subject' in much the same way as if completing a questionnaire or taking part in an experiment. The researcher's concern is to obtain accurate information from the interviewee, untainted by relationship factors. The interviewer therefore tries to minimize the impact of inter-personal processes on the course of the interview. In contrast the qualitative researcher believes that there can be no such thing as a 'relationship-free' interview. Indeed the relationship is part of the research process, not a distraction from it. The interviewee is seen as a 'participant' in the research, actively shaping the course of the interview rather than passively responding to the interviewer's pre-set questions.

Qualitative research interviews: methodological and epistemological distinctions

Qualitative research interviews vary in methodological features such as length, style of questioning, and participant numbers (group or individual). While most are carried out face-to-face, qualitative interviews can also be carried out by telephone, or via the internet (see Morgan and Symon, Chapter 3, this volume). There are important differences in the philosophical assumptions underlying approaches to interview methodology. The theoretical traditions from which qualitative methods have developed in psychology make widely varying claims about the nature of the material gathered through interviews, and the uses to which it legitimately can be put. Madill et al. (2000) suggest that qualitative methodologies can be classified on a dimension representing their epistemological positions. At one end are 'realist' approaches, which assume that the accounts participants produce in interviews bear a direct relationship to their 'real' experiences in the world beyond the interview situation. At the opposite end are 'radical constructionist' approaches. These see the account as a text produced in the specific setting of the interview, to be analysed in terms of the discursive strategies employed and resources drawn upon by the interviewee. No attempt would be made to make claims about the participant's personal experience.

This dimension is a very useful way of getting to grips with the differences between qualitative approaches, though as Willig (2001) points out, such categorization systems inevitably involve a degree of simplification of positions, and of the distinctions between them. Simplification is also unavoidable in classifying types of qualitative research interview for a short chapter like the present one. The following section can therefore only provide an outline of some of the main types, highlighting their key methodological features and epistemological assumptions.

REALIST INTERVIEWS

From a realist epistemological position, interviewees' accounts are treated as providing insight into their psychological and organizational lives outside of the interview situation. This necessitates a concern with the accuracy of accounts; researchers may compare interview findings with those obtained through other methods, such as documentary analysis or quantitative survey data – a process known as triangulation. Realist interviews may be rather more structured than some other qualitative interviews, because of the need to ensure that different participants' accounts and different types of data can be systematically compared.

PHENOMENOLOGICAL INTERVIEWS

Phenomenology is a major philosophical tradition which has had a substantial impact on the social sciences, and especially on the development of qualitative research methods. It is also a very diverse field, encompassing distinct strands which differ in important ways (Moran, 2000), making generalisations about phenomenological research methods difficult. Important strands within psychology include the hermeneutical-phenomenological approach developed at Duquesne University by Giorgi and colleagues (Giorgi, 1985), Moustakas' transcendental-phenomenological model (1994), and Smith's Interpretative Phenomenological Analysis – commonly referred to as 'IPA' (Smith, 1996).

One key feature of phenomenological methods is the emphasis placed on the need for the researcher to consciously set aside his or her presuppositions about the phenomenon under investigation – a process sometimes referred to as 'bracketing'. This, of course, means that the researcher must reflect on the presuppositions he or she holds, and remain alert to how they may colour every stage of the research process. Phenomenological interviews are often quite lengthy, and it is common for data collection and analysis activities to substantially overlap – the analysis of one interview informing the way in which the subsequent one is carried out, as the researcher seeks to deepen his or her understanding of the phenomenon. In terms of epistemology, phenomenological approaches may be seen to occupy the middle ground on the kind of dimension proposed by Madill et al. (2000). Such approaches recognize that the text produced in the interview situation is shaped by that context, but would not accept the radical relativist position that it bears no necessary relationship to the interviewee's wider experience.

SOCIAL CONSTRUCTIONIST INTERVIEWS

As with phenomenology, social constructionism is a broad movement within psychology (and other disciplines) which comprises of several theoretical and methodological strands (Burr, 1995). The common ground is a focus on the constructive nature of language; it is argued that language does not just describe the external social world and people's internal mental states, it actively constructs them through discourse in interaction. For example, when someone says they are 'feeling sad', this is viewed not as a description of an emotion inside the person, but as a discursive act within an interaction, aimed at achieving an objective – eliciting sympathy, disclaiming responsibility and so on.

Social constructionist interviews share common features with other types, including their loose structure, the use of probes to follow up points of interest, and the need for reflexivity on the part of the researcher. The epistemological position of social constructionism does, however, lead to certain characteristic features of interviewing in this tradition. Social constructionists see the text of an interview not as a means of gaining insight into the 'real' experience of the interviewee, but as an interaction constructed in the particular context of the interview. They would also hold as a central tenet the claim that every text has an indefinite number of possible interpretations, and no one interpretation can be seen as superior to others. Wood and Kroger (2000) argue that these assumptions necessitate an active style of interviewing, in which the interviewer seeks to present as wide a variety of contexts as possible, within which the interviewee can display the range of discursive practices available to him or her (see Dick, Chapter 17, this volume, for further description).

DESCRIPTION OF THE METHOD

This section will describe the main practical issues involved in using qualitative research interviews. While much of what I cover is generally applicable, the slant will be rather more towards phenomenological and realist interviews than discourse analytic ones. I will also not cover the analysis of interview data, as several chapters in the present volume provide accounts of particular analytical techniques. To help bring the issues to life, I will illustrate my discussion with examples from a project with which I have recently been involved.

A real-life example: evaluating the Calderdale and Kirklees Out of Hours Protocol for Palliative Care

This project was concerned with an innovation in services provided for people suffering from a terminal illness and being cared for at home. One recognized problem in supporting dying patients in the community is the provision of care outside of the normal working hours of GPs and District Nurses (Thomas, 2000). If a crisis occurs during the night or at the weekend, all too often out of hours staff are unaware of these arrangements and uninformed about the patient's situation. The Calderdale and Kirklees Out of Hours Protocol provided advice and set up a series of mechanisms to address the problems in this area of care. Our project examined practitioner experiences of the scheme, using semi-structured interviews. Epistemologically, we made realist assumptions to the extent that the accounts given by participants were taken to provide insight into their actual experiences of involvement in the scheme. Data were collected from 15 GPs, using telephone interviews, and from District Nurses through four area-based focus groups of 5 (a total of 20 participants across all groups). Interviews were taped and transcribed, and analysed using a variant of the template approach (see King et al., 2003, for full details of this project and the background to it).

Constructing and carrying out qualitative research interviews

The process of constructing and using qualitative research interviews can be split into four steps:

* defining the research question;
* creating the interview guide;
* recruiting participants;
* carrying out the interviews.

I will discuss the first three of these here, and look at the practical issues involved in carrying out interviews in the next section.

DEFINING THE RESEARCH QUESTION

Most of the issues involved in defining the research question have been raised in the introductory section of this chapter. To recap: the research question should focus on how participants describe and make sense of particular element(s) of their lives. The primary concern should not be to quantify individual experience, and the researcher should be wary of framing the research question in a way which reflects his or her own presuppositions or biases. There may of course be a number of research questions for any one study. The research question in this study was as follows:

> From the perspectives of General Practitioners and District Nurses, how effective has the Out of Hours Protocol been in improving the provision of out of hours care for community palliative care patients – in particular in the areas of communication, carer support, specialist medical support and drug/equipment availability?

Note that the question acknowledges a priori that certain aspects of participants' experiences would be the subject of particular attention. These were the four areas specified in the scheme documentation as the foci of the innovation; as such it is legitimate (indeed necessary) to highlight them in advance. Such a strategy would almost certainly not be appropriate in a phenomenological or discursive study.

CREATING THE INTERVIEW GUIDE

The qualitative research interview is not based on a formal schedule of questions to be asked word-for-word in a set order. Instead it generally uses an *interview guide*, listing topics which the interviewer should attempt to cover in the course of the interview, and suggesting probes which may be used to follow-up responses and elicit greater detail from participants. There are three sources for topics to be included in an interview guide: the research literature, the interviewer's own personal knowledge and experience of the area, and informal preliminary work such as discussions with people who have personal experience of the research area. The development of the interview guide does not end at the start of the first interview. It may be modified through use: adding probes or even whole topics which had originally not been included, but have emerged spontaneously in interviews; dropping or re-formulating those which are incomprehensible to participants or consistently fail to elicit responses in any way relevant to the research question(s). Interview guides vary in the level of detail and structure they include. Realist interview guides tend to be rather more structured and to define more topics for discussion than phenomenological or social constructionist interviews.

In the Out of Hours Protocol study, development of the interview guide was influenced by discussion with those involved in setting up the scheme, as well as our reading of relevant research literature. Initially we sought to devise a single guide appropriate to both professional groups, but this proved impossible because of the differences in the nature of their involvement with palliative care provision. We therefore produced separate (though related) guides for district nurses and GPs, both of which were modified in response to our experience of using them. Table 2.1 shows an extract from the final version of the district nurses' interview guide.

Table 2.1 Extract from the district nurse interview guide

Support issues

4 To what extent is the out of hours provision addressing the needs of the patients?

Probe: In what ways is it/is it not?

5 Do the patients have enough support?

Probe: Who provides support?
Probe: What else (if anything) could be done?

6 Do you feel that the patients and/or carers know who to contact in a crisis?

Probe: If YES, how? If NO, why not?

7 In your opinion, what – if anything – has been the effect of the protocol on continuity of care?

Ask each participant

13 Give an example (if you can) of a case where poor communication led to problems for a patient/carer.

14 Give an example (if you can) of a case where good communication halted potential problems.

A few points are worth noting in relation to the extract. Coming from a realist approach, the guide includes more information-seeking questions than it would if used in other traditions (for example, question 6), but these are followed up with probes to explore the interviewees' views and experiences in more depth. Questions 13 and 14 are designed to help participants focus on concrete examples, rather than abstracted generalities – an important principle in most qualitative interviewing approaches. Finally, it can be seen that it incorporates fully formed questions. Some guides just use topic headings, to encourage the interviewer to be responsive to the interviewee and avoid presuppositions. The danger of this format, especially for inexperienced interviewers, is that the inteviewer becomes too immersed in the interaction with the interviewee, and slips into a questioning style close to that of ordinary conversation, which may be too directive and closed (Willig, 2001).

RECRUITING PARTICIPANTS FOR THE STUDY

The recruitment of participants to a qualitative interview study will of course depend on the study's aims, and on its theoretical, epistemological and methodological position. Thus a researcher using a discourse analytic approach would probably use far fewer interviews than one taking a realist case study approach. This is in part a pragmatic matter; discourse analytic studies involve the analysis of text at a very fine level of detail, and therefore analysis takes much longer than it would if a similar volume of material was tackled using methods founded on realist assumptions. However, it is not solely a matter of research logistics. As noted in my summary of types of qualitative interview, the social constructionist position of discourse analysis views interview data as texts within which particular discursive practices and resources can be highlighted. This task does not require a large number of texts to ensure representativeness, as it is assumed that these practices and resources are shared within a social context (see Dick, Chapter 17, this volume, for further discussion). The relativist epistemology also means that gathering a large volume of cases cannot guarantee the credibility of a study, since we can never define all possible readings of a text, and no one reading should be 'privileged' over another. In contrast, a case study which is making realist assumptions about the interview data would want to be sure to include a sample representing important distinctions within the organizational population in relation to the change under investigation, and would assert that the analysis gains in validity by increasing the number of different viewpoints collected via interviews.

Notwithstanding the specific requirements of different methodological positions, there are some issues relating to sample definition and recruitment which are widely relevant. As suggested above, in deciding how many participants to recruit, the amount of time and resource available is a critical factor. It is very easy for an inexperienced qualitative researcher to seriously underestimate the time needed to undertake a study based on qualitative research interviews. It is worth noting that even an experienced transcriber is unlikely to be able to transcribe more than two one-hour interviews in a working day. Analysing such a transcript in any depth is likely to require at least the equivalent to two or three full days' work – often much longer. To these figures must be added the time taken to develop the interview guide and recruit participants, to carry out the interviews, and to travel to and from them, and to feedback findings (in verbal or written form) to participants and funding bodies.

In terms of criteria for recruitment, most qualitative studies set a premium on diversity, because (in varying manners and for differing purposes) they seek to show the range of ways that a phenomenon is experienced within the chosen context. Sometimes the range of participants sought is defined fully in advance, to encompass variations expected to be of theoretical and applied interest. On other occasions, there may be minimal a priori definition of participant characteristics, with people recruited to the study as features of potential interest are identified through the process of carrying out interviews and conducting preliminary analysis.

In the Out of Hours Protocol study, participants were recruited to cover the main geographical areas within Calderdale and Kirklees, from those responding positively to an invitation letter circulated to both professional groups. We tried to ensure variety in terms of a number of personal and organizational characteristics, such as practice size and location, tenure, and experience in palliative care.

As in any type of social scientific research, potential participants must be assured of confidentiality, and should be told clearly who the research is being carried out for and what it hopes to achieve. These points should be repeated at the start of the interview itself, and permission to tape-record the interview must be obtained. The interviewee should be told what kind of feedback about the study he or she will receive and at least a rough idea of when he or she is likely to receive it.

Practical issues in carrying out qualitative interviews

Flexibility is the single most important factor in successful qualitative interviewing. It is likely that a common opening question will be used to start all interviews in a study, but beyond that topics need not be addressed in the order in which they appear in the interview guide, or any other predetermined sequence. As an interviewer, you may allow them to be raised by the interviewee or introduce them yourself at points where they fit naturally into the course of the interview. Similarly, probes need not be used in any particular order, and may not be required at all if the interviewee introduces the areas concerned.

STARTING THE INTERVIEW

It is normally best for the interviewer to open with a question which the interviewee can answer easily and without potential embarrassment or distress. More difficult or sensitive questions should be held back until some way into the interview, in order to give time for both interviewer and interviewee to relax and feel they are getting to know each other. Requests for factual or descriptive information can be useful opening questions. In the Out of Hours Protocol study, we normally started the GP interviews by asking participants about their experience of working for and/or utilising deputising services.

PHRASING QUESTIONS

The way in which questions are asked during the interview has a major bearing on how useful the responses are likely to be. It is advisable to avoid multiple questions, such as; 'Why did you join the scheme, and do you think it has brought benefits to patients, carers and your practice?' This is in fact four questions, and in attempting to reply to them as a single question, the interviewee may give only a partial answer, or may just become confused as to what question they are supposed to be answering. It is best to ask questions singly and phrase them as simply as possible. Leading questions – 'So you felt that the scheme had improved inter-professional communication, did you?' – should be avoided, as they impose your own perceptions on the interviewee, who may agree out of a wish to please you, or just to be polite. In the example just given, it would be better to say: 'What, if any, impact did the scheme have on inter-professional communication?' This would not give a cue to the interviewee that you expect a certain reply.

You need to beware of assuming that the answer to a question is so obvious that it need not be asked. For instance, while promotion might well be a significant goal for most middle-managers in a large corporation, it would be wrong to assume that it would be so for any one manager. In a qualitative study you would need to ask whether, and to what extent, promotion was important to each individual participant. You should not tell the interviewee what his or her answers mean – 'So what you're really saying is . . .'; again, your perception may be wrong, but the interviewee may not feel able or willing to challenge the misinterpretation. It is, however, sometimes useful to repeat an answer back to the interviewee in order to seek clarification.

ENDING THE INTERVIEW

It is important that you avoid ending the interview on a topic which is difficult, threatening or painful. If possible the concluding questions should steer the interview towards positive experiences; in any event the interviewer should not pack up and leave immediately after probing the interviewee about some highly negative, distressing or personal experience or feeling. Sometimes it is useful to finish by giving the interviewee the opportunity to make any comments about the subject at hand which have not been covered in the rest of the interview.

'DIFFICULT' INTERVIEWS

Not all interviews will progress smoothly. Occasionally you will come away from an interview feeling dissatisfied with your own performance, or irritated, angry or upset by the interviewee. While it is impossible to specify all the ways in which interviews can be difficult, there are some situations where difficulties are rather more common than usual, and by being aware of these it is possible to have coping strategies to hand if and when they do occur. Some tips about how to deal with common types of 'difficult' interview are given below.

THE UNCOMMUNICATIVE INTERVIEWEE

There are some interviewees who seem unable, or unwilling, to give anything more than monosyllabic answers. The reasons for this vary widely: they may be defensive about the topic being discussed; they may be trying to get the interview over with as quickly as possible; they may think that brief answers are what you want ; they may just be habitually laconic. The risks of monosyllabism can be reduced before the interview begins by being quite clear about how much time you require – and that the interviewee has the time available – and by stressing the anonymity of all answers. If the interviewee is unresponsive despite such precautions, the first thing to check is that you are phrasing questions in as open a way as possible. If you are succeeding in framing questions in a very open manner, and still getting brief, shallow answers, a useful tool to use is silence. Instead of moving on to your next question when the interviewee provides another terse response, pause for a few seconds. Very often this will serve as a cue to the interviewee that you would like to hear more on the subject, and is less likely to annoy him or her than repeated probes of the 'Tell me more' type.

THE OVER-COMMUNICATIVE INTERVIEWEE

The opposite problem to that discussed above is the interviewee who repeatedly indulges in long-winded digressions from the interview topic. Some degree of digression should be tolerated; sometimes it can lead you to areas that are of genuine interest which you had not anticipated when compiling the interview guide. However, if it is clear that the interviewee is repeatedly straying far from your questions without adding anything of significant interest, you need to attempt to impose more direction. Of course, this should be done as subtly as possible, to avoid causing offence. It is also important to ensure that you are not resorting to leading questions in your eagerness to keep the interview within your control. A good strategy is to politely interrupt the digression at a natural pause or break and refer back to an earlier point made by the interviewee which was relevant to your research question: 'That's very interesting. Could we go back to what you were saying earlier about [. . .] as I'd like you to tell me more about that . . .'

THE HIGH-STATUS INTERVIEWEE

When interviewing people of high status (such as senior managers and professionals), who are used to being treated with a considerable degree of deference in most of their daily interactions, it is important to set your relationship with them at an appropriate level. If you are over-familiar, or appear to show off your knowledge in their domain, you may cause offence. Conversely, if you are overly nervous or submissive you are likely to be patronized. Either way, it might be difficult for you to obtain anything other than the most shallow, surface-level of answers to your questions. You need to be respectful – especially in regard to their areas of professional or expert knowledge – but at the same time confident of the worth of what you are doing and of *your* own expertise.

INTERVIEWS ON EMOTIONALLY CHARGED SUBJECTS

Perhaps the most difficult situation for an interviewer (particularly if inexperienced) to cope with is when the interviewee becomes visibly upset as a result of questioning. It is perfectly natural to feel uncomfortable in such circumstances, but it does not necessarily mean that you have been insensitive, or that the interview must be terminated. When an interviewee is finding an area difficult to talk about because of their emotional reactions to it, make sure that you give them the time they require to answer your questions. Be particularly careful to avoid non-verbal cues that might be taken as indicating impatience: looking at your watch, fidgeting and so on. If the person's distress is great, let them know that it is perfectly alright for them to leave the question altogether, or to return to it later if they feel able to. You will probably find that people will often want to come back to questions which address issues of real importance to them, and just need time to muster their feelings. For the interview to be abruptly terminated can be the most hurtful option of all.

THE WOULD-BE INTERVIEWER

Some interviewees persistently ask the interviewer questions about their own opinions, experiences and so on. While this can be a good sign, showing that rapport has been established, as the interviewer you need to maintain control over the situation. The main danger if you simply concur and state your views is that you may bias the interviewee's subsequent responses in the same way as can happen with leading questions. Probably the best strategy is to say to the interviewee that you will be happy to answer any of their questions at the end, but for now you would like to concentrate on their views.

By being aware beforehand of some of the ways in which problems can arise in interviews, and of techniques for handling them, you are less likely to be thrown out of your stride by a difficult interviewee. That said, there really is nothing to beat experience in gaining confidence and competence as an interviewer. Happily, novices almost always find that their skills improve rapidly over the first few interviews they carry out, especially if able to review what went wrong (and what went right) with a supervisor or colleague as soon as possible after an interview.

Reflexivity and the qualitative research interview

I have made several references above to reflexivity in qualitative research; here I will consider some of the ways it may be achieved in a qualitative interview study. (Inevitably, certain suggestions will be more applicable to some research traditions than others.) The term reflexivity refers to the recognition that the involvement of the researcher as an active participant in the research process shapes the nature of the process and the knowledge produced through it. Researchers must reflect on the nature of their involvement just as they consider the meaning of their participants' contributions. There are numerous suggestions in the literature as to how such reflection can be facilitated. They include strategies such as the following:

- Putting your presuppositions down in writing at the start of the study, and consulting this list at each stage of the research process.
- Keeping a research diary in which you record your own feelings about the process.
- Listening to some of your taped interviews with a focus on your performance as an interviewer.
- Where you are working in a team, organizing meetings periodically with the sole purpose of reflecting on each other's experiences of involvement in the study.

These are just a few of the ways in which reflexivity can be facilitated. It is important to remember that such techniques are only means to the end of developing a habit of awareness and critical thinking regarding your engagement with your research and its participants. They should never become simply mechanistic procedures you go through in order to 'prove' the quality of your work, nor should the encouragement of reflexivity be taken as a licence for self-indulgence.

ADVANTAGES AND DISADVANTAGES OF THE METHOD

Most of the main strengths and weaknesses of qualitative research interviews will have become apparent in the course of my description of the method. I will draw them together here, with special reference to the context of applied psychological research in organizations.

Advantages

Different types of qualitative research interview can be used to tackle different types of research question in organizations, making it one of the most flexible methods available. It can address quite focused questions about aspects of organizational life, for instance, specific decision-processes such as selection decisions. At the other end of the scale, qualitative research interviews can be used to examine much broader issues, in areas such as gender, organizational culture and the effects of unemployment.

The qualitative research interview is ideally suited to examining topics in which different levels of meaning need to be explored. This is something that is very difficult to do with quantitative methods, and problematic for many other qualitative techniques. One area where qualitative interviews may be of great use is in studying organizational and group identities in large organizations such as the National Health Service, where a complex pattern of organizational, work-group, professional and interpersonal loyalties exists.

Finally, the qualitative research interview is a method which most research participants accept readily. This is partly due to familiarity with interviews in general; however, equally important is the fact that most people like talking about their work – whether to share enthusiasm or to air complaints – but rarely have the opportunity to do so with interested outsiders. Feedback I have received suggests that interviewees commonly enjoy the experience, and in some cases find that it has helped them clarify their thoughts on a particular topic.

Disadvantages

As already emphasized, developing an interview guide, carrying out interviews, and analysing their transcripts, are all highly time-consuming activities for the researcher. Qualitative research interviews are also tiring to carry out, as they involve considerable concentration from the interviewer; I would certainly recommend a maximum of three hour-long qualitative interviews in a day, and two would be preferable. Interviews are also time-consuming for interviewees, and this may cause problems in recruiting participants in some organizations and occupations. The best recruitment strategy is probably to send a letter with basic details of the study's aims and what will be required of the interviewee, with a follow-up phone-call in which the researcher can explain his or her aims in more depth and answer any queries. A firm time and date for the interview should be fixed as soon as possible. Once people have made such a commitment, it is rare for them to subsequently drop out of the study.

A difficulty faced by many researchers using qualitative research interviews is the feeling of data overload as a result of the huge volume of rich data produced by even a moderate-sized study. In these circumstances, I would suggest that there are three directions in which the researcher can turn for help. Firstly, there are the original aims of the study. If the researcher feels that they are getting lost in a particular line of exploration, they should ask; 'Is this adding to my understanding of the topics I set out to study? If not, is it raising new and related topics which are of interest?' If the answer to both questions is 'no', then the researcher should change the direction of the analysis. Secondly, the inexperienced researcher can turn to literature describing other studies using qualitative research interviews, to provide examples of how problems in data analysis were tackled, including material outside their own area. Thirdly, personal networking is of great importance. If there is no one even sympathetic to qualitative methods in the researcher's own work environment, try looking more widely. As the number of researchers using qualitative research interviews grows, the opportunities for such networking increase.

NOTE

1   I would like to acknowledge my colleagues on this project, Keri Thomas, Dennise Bell and Nicola Bowes. The project was funded jointly by Calderdale and Kirklees Health Authority and the University of Huddersfield.

FURTHER READING

Recent years have seen continued growth in the number of publications on all aspects of qualitative interviewing. The suggestions below are offered as useful starting points for readers to deepen their knowledge of this diverse methodological literature.

S. Kvale (1996) *InterViews*, London: Sage. (Broad and thoughtful coverage of both theoretical and practical issues in qualitative interviewing.)

C. Moustakas (1994) *Phenomenological Research Methods*, London: Sage. (Good introduction to phenomenological approaches, and latter part provides helpful examples of interview-based phenomenological studies.)

M.Q. Patton (1990) *Qualitative Evaluation and Research Methods*, second edition, London: Sage. Chapter 7 has many useful suggestions for carrying out qualitative interviews – especially relevant to case study approaches.)

D. Silverman (ed.) (1997) *Qualitative Research: Theory, Methods and Practice,* London: Sage. (Part IV provides critical accounts of qualitative interviewing from different approaches.)

REFERENCES

Burr, V. (1995) *An Introduction to Social Constructionism*, London: Routledge.

Fetterman, D.M. (1989) *Ethnography: Step-by-Step*, Newbury Park, CA: Sage.

Giorgi, A. (ed) (1985) *Phenomenology and Psychological Research*, Pittsburgh: Duquesne University Press.

King, N., Thomas, K. and Bell, D. (2003) 'An out-of-hours protocol for community palliative care : practitioners' perspectives', *International Journal of Palliative Nursing*, 9 (7): 277–82.

Kvale, S. (1983) 'The qualitative research interview: a phenomenological and a hermeneutical mode of understanding', *Journal of Phenomenological Psychology*, 14: 171–96.

Madill, A., Jordan, A. and Shirley, C. (2000) 'Objectivity and reliability in qualitative analysis: realist, contextualist and radical constructivist epistemologies', *British Journal of Psychology*, 91: 1–20.

Miles, M.B. and Huberman, A.M. (1984) *Qualitative Data Analysis: A Sourcebook of New Methods*, Beverly Hills, CA: Sage.

Moran, D. (2000) *Introduction to Phenomenology*, London: Routledge.

Moustakas, C. (1994) *Phenomenological Research Methods*, London: Sage.

Smith, J.A. (1996) 'Beyond the divide between cognition and discourse: using interpretative phenomenological analysis in health psychology', *Psychology and Health*, 11: 261–71.

Thomas, K. (2000) 'Out of hours palliative care: bridging the gap', *European Journal of Palliative Care*, 7: 22–5.

Willig, C. (2001) *Introducing Qualitative Research in Psychology: Adventures in Theory and Method*, Buckingham: Open University Press.

Wood, L.A. and Kroger, R.O. (2000) *Doing Discourse Analysis: Methods for Studying Action in Talk*, London: Sage.

—— **Electronic Interviews in Organizational Research** ——

Stephanie J. Morgan and Gillian Symon

The increase in the use of computers and communications equipment has led to the possibility of using these new technologies in research. To date the majority of such studies have been based on the (cross-sectional) survey method, with closed questions and quantifiable results. The term electronic interviews has been used here to emphasize the use of open questions and an interactive approach, moving more towards forms of research such as face-to-face and telephone interviews. After clarifying the use of the term 'electronic interviews', and outlining current (limited) usage, we will describe an example based on our own e-mail study. A discussion of the strengths and weaknesses of this method will be offered, taking into account particular epistemological issues, and we will finish with a consideration of future possible developments.

WHAT ARE ELECTRONIC INTERVIEWS?

Electronic interviews are research studies that use electronic communication facilities to access and communicate with participants. The interviews can be held online, in real time, using the Internet or company intranets, or can be off-line, in asynchronous mode, using e-mail communications. Although focus groups can also be held using the Internet and world wide web (www), they will not be discussed in any great detail here as there are different issues surrounding their use (see Chen and Hinton, 1999). Online interviews can include the use of Internet forums, discussion groups, and chat rooms.

However we will not discuss research on Internet communities, as again there are very different issues involved (being more similar to ethnographic research, see Brewer, Chapter 25, this volume). The focus of this chapter is on the potential of e-mail for substituting or complementing face-to-face (f2f), one-to-one, qualitative interviews.

To generate interview style data using e-mail requires a *series* of communications (one list of questions would be more akin to an open-ended questionnaire). In electronic interviews, a number of e-mails are exchanged over an extended time period. Initially, a small number of questions are asked or a topic is raised and the participant will reply, offering their thoughts and opinions. The researcher will then need to respond specifically to those ideas, asking further questions or for clarification, raising linked issues, and generally 'opening up' the discussion. These communications may last for some weeks until the topic is exhausted or the participant shows signs of losing interest. The aim is to use the asynchronous, time-delay nature of e-mail to facilitate reflexivity in communication, enabling reflection and consideration. As time and self-disclosure have been shown to positively influence relationship formation (Walther, 1996), a more in-depth research relationship can also be developed.

Giving participants the opportunity to reflect in this way and construct their position can increase their 'role' in the research process (Smith, 1996). Indeed, it could be argued, that the increased reflexivity allowed for by using e-mail could facilitate taking the social construction of research seriously. It may lead us to abandon the concept of an essential 'self' (Davies, 1998) and increase our potential to reflect upon the relative and constructed nature of our research, such that we shift to a more transparent collective endeavour (Michael, 1996). The issues surrounding this will be discussed in more detail later as concerns regarding the possible increased reflexivity but reduced control of this method will vary depending upon the researcher's epistemological stance.

PREVIOUS STUDIES

Electronic interviews, particularly over the Internet, have been used in a variety of studies aimed at investigating Internet use and online behaviour (Paccagnella, 1997; Parks and Floyd, 1996). They have been used successfully to conduct research with those who are difficult to access, such as drug dealers (Coomber, 1997). The method is being used increasingly in educational research, to assess the use of distance learning and, in particular, the experience of disabled students, for whom technology may be of special benefit (Mann and Stewart, 2000). The use of such technology can also enable speedy multinational research, although there is always the danger that speed and ease of use lead to a lack of consideration with respect to cultural differences.

In organizational studies, published research has so far been limited to assessing how managers and staff use e-mail (for example, Romm and Pliskin, 1997), and the impact of communication technology on communications, decision making and team working (see El-Shinnaway and Markus, 1997; O'Mahoney and Barley, 1999; Platt and Page, 2001). There is little written about the use of electronic interviews as a research tool in this area. However, with the increased use of e-mail in organizations, the method has the potential to access a broad range of extremely busy people. Indeed, in many organizations, people operate in transient ways, travelling the globe, working on a number of different sites, or carrying out shift-work, so arranging appointments can be difficult. Furthermore, in some organizations e-mail has become the standard method for communication – for some even the *preferred* method of communication – suggesting that research using this method may be more acceptable than alternatives.

AN ORGANIZATIONAL EXAMPLE: OUTSOURCING TRANSITIONS

This section describes the practical issues involved in designing and conducting electronic interviews, illustrating these with a discussion of our own preliminary experience in using this method. We begin with a brief outline of the background to the research.

Background and rationale

The research was part of a longitudinal study on commitment and identification within systems houses (companies whose employees develop programs for and manage operations of other companies' computer systems). In particular we were interested in the experience of staff who had been through a process of 'forced outsourcing', where their department and skills are transferred to a systems house. Their contract of employment is taken over on a tupe (transfer of undertaking, protection of employment) contract and attempts are made to integrate them into the new company.

The potential participants worked for an international systems house and were scattered across Europe. Some of the staff had difficulties expressing themselves clearly in English and some worked shifts, making contact through other qualitative research methods more difficult. There were also some participants in England who expressed interest in keeping up regular communications after a first face-to-face interview. This offered the potential of following people through time on a more regular basis, without extensive travelling or high telephone costs, and in many ways fitting in more naturally to their norms of communication. The participants could reply in their own time, whether during the day or at night. We were given lists of the e-mail addresses of newly transferred employees. All of these were invited to participate.

Research design and process

INTRODUCTION AND INSTRUCTIONS

It is particularly important to ensure that the participants fully understand right at the start how the research will progress. Mann and Stewart (2000) highlight the need to offer 'advance organizers' to clarify the research procedure as it is not so easy to clear up misunderstandings in early e-mail contacts. We also wanted to ensure participants understood that the research really was confidential, and that they did not *have* to take part. Of course, on the other hand we wanted them to reply, so we tried to explain the benefits of the research, to others and to themselves. All this had to be done in fairly simple English; therefore we had everything checked by two non-English contacts in the organization. Finally, we felt that participants should have an option to contact us by another method if they wanted to so we gave them a contact telephone number.

MESSAGE FORM

Our initial e-mail opened the communication with a few open-ended questions. Participants could use the 'reply with quote' function and fill in their answers easily. They could then just 'send' the e-mail and delete it from their computer if they wished. We followed up the participants who replied, with additional questions based on their responses to the first e-mail. Not all of them replied back but we did manage to develop a 'rapport' with a small number of people, and we exchanged a few e-mails to discuss their experiences in more depth. It is important to reply to individual messages specifically based on their content, rather than send general 'second stage' questions.

> For example, to the question:
> How did you feel when it was announced that you would be outsourced?
> The participant replied:
> Shocked, I thought we would be the last ones to go!
> Our reply began:
> That's really interesting, and useful to us, to know you were shocked even though you were aware these things were going on. Can you tell us what the impact was of that surprise element?

We then opened up a discussion regarding the atmosphere in the organization and why some departments deemed themselves safer than others.

The aim was to simulate the empathy and reflective questioning found in relational interviews, although extra care needs to be taken in the wording of responses and in supporting the participants' ideas. In particular it is important to thank the participant for responding, offer feedback such as summarizing to show you understand, and show explicit support for their ideas. At the same time, it is helpful to adapt your language style to that of the participant and maintain a friendly tone. Mann and Stewart (2000) found that participants needed additional encouragement and positive feedback using e-mail.

Timing has also been shown to be important in this form of communication. A speedy response indicates a positive attitude (Walther and Tidwell, 1995), suggesting the researcher should check regularly and reply quickly. At the same time a delay from the participant (which may be frustrating to the researcher) should not be taken as a bad sign, as they may be busy or, indeed, taking time to reflect.

SECURITY

Computer viruses are an increasing problem, and some people are unwilling to open e-mails from strangers. We had hoped to reduce this problem, and conform with ethical guidelines, by requesting that the HR department send an introductory e-mail to all staff. However problems still arose because the central 'firewall' (part of the main computer system that controls access to and from other computers, in particular e-mail and internet access) had been set to high security due to a new virus, and was bouncing even standard e-mails. This is unusual, but must be taken into consideration when discussing access via this method.

ETHICS OF E-MAIL RESEARCH

E-mails can be intercepted, and if stored on the company mainframe, accessed by certain privileged staff. Regulations regarding e-mail monitoring at work are confusing and still under review (Crichard, 2001), but many companies do monitor e-mails, partly for their own protection. We were concerned that staff might feel they *had* to reply, would not reply for fear of 'eavesdropping' and/or that they would only say positive things in case these e-mails were read by others. We took extra care to ensure they knew confidentiality and anonymity were important considerations for us. To help with this we e-mailed the staff from a home computer (giving them a personal air, and the knowledge that there was no 'big brother' at our end checking the contents).

MAINTAINING INTEREST

This is a particularly difficult aspect of electronic interviews. In our case it was not thought through clearly in advance how we were going to keep people communicating, and as noted above, many dropped out after the first set of questions. There is very little to stop people simply not replying, or forgetting to reply, except for a reminder e-mail or using other modes of communication. Mann and Stewart (2000) outline some methods for keeping participants involved, but much will depend on the research question and whether it is interesting to the participants, as well as the researcher's skill in involving participants in the research.

It may sometimes be useful to supplement the e-mail contact with other methods, to maintain interest and to aid disclosure. The richest information that we received on an initial e-mail was from a participant with whom we had first spoken on the telephone. It has been shown that self-disclosure can help to build rapport, and Mann and Stewart (2000) emphasize the importance of 'online listening'. This 'listening' needs to be expressed in the 'text' and often requires a skilful choice of words. They recommend taking particular care in wording replies and questions, and being alert to changes in tone and response timescales. Respondents will need frequent and explicit assurances of the usefulness and relevance of their input, and a constant reminder that what they 'say' is important to you. In some cases, respondents may find it easier to divulge personal information to a 'disembodied' researcher, and there is evidence of increased self-disclosure in some circumstances (Joinson, 2001) meaning more information may be gained than when working face to face.

DEBRIEFING

All the participants were sent a personal e-mail (not a reply) thanking them for their help and asking them to contact us whenever they wanted to in the future.

Analysis

In principle, analysis can continue as with any interview data (see relevant chapters in this volume) however, Mann and Stewart (2000) highlight particular issues with analysing data gained electronically. If one accepts this may be a new way of transmitting meaning there may be differences in responses (as yet unknown), which we need to take into consideration. In particular, discursive approaches might not be possible due to the differences in communicative form. However, there is a potential advantage in that there is nothing 'lost' in transcription, as there is no need to transform the data, and indeed some non-verbal aspects are explicitly presented in the body of the e-mail text. It was decided that in this case we would use hermeneutic interpretive analysis (Alvesson and Skoldberg, 2000), as that is being used for the face-to-face interviews also being conducted, and enables access to meanings in context (see also Lindlof, 1995). It is not intended to give the details of the analysis here, as the purpose of this chapter is to assess electronic interviews as a form of data collection. However, the repeated nature of the communications does mean that analysis can be carried out explicitly during the interviews and areas of uncertainty (which may be missed in an interview) can be picked up, for example:

> From the management I know they were hoping I could bring some different thinking within this group. Kind of a hard job to deal with . . .

Note here the use of three dots, which we felt may indicate that there was more to say on the subject, or that it was particularly difficult to express. These aspects of e-mail communication can be picked up and raised in the response. A balance is needed though, as to pick up on fine detail too often may make the participant feel that even more care and thought has to go into the response, or they may decide to withdraw.

Progress

So far we have only run a small pilot, but the response rate has been quite good compared to postal methods. In a few cases a relational form of communication was enabled, and, even in the shorter communications, the wording and tone gave us a great deal of information and enabled us to raise further questions which generated more rich data in the follow-up. Other researchers have achieved a depth of analysis using this method (see Mann and Stewart (2000) for a review) and we suspect there may be a number of ways we could improve our study to gain more depth. In future studies we will be more careful to explain the ongoing nature of the research, to make more use of 'repeated' interviews, and to use more active 'online listening' techniques.

EVALUATION AND EPISTEMOLOGICAL ISSUES

Studies of the use of electronic interviewing tend to compare this form with face-to-face research. Although this comparison is ubiquitous (Giese, 1998), it is perhaps unfair, as at first glance it is more akin to telephone or postal research. However, the comparison raises some useful epistemological issues so we will adopt this strategy to facilitate further discussion. We suggest that electronic interviews should be considered as neither better nor worse than other methods, but rather as a unique approach.

Kvale (1996) highlights that interviewing is above all about the relationship between the researcher and the participant. In electronic interviewing the relationship is in many ways 'disembodied' – distanced by time and space – and de-contextualized. Can a new type of relationship be developed that leads to new forms of knowledge generation or must we accept a minimal interaction? To assess this requires discussion of both epistemology (forms of knowledge and ways of accessing it) and ontology (subject matter or nature of reality), both of which are of course interlinked. Indeed one's view of the utility of electronic interviews may vary depending on one's epistemological stance. In this chapter we have two key areas to consider: the nature of the interview itself and the data that result, and the nature of communication technologies. We will discuss them in turn.

Interviews and interview data

Fontana and Frey (1998) highlight the broad range of interviewing styles carried out in practice, and note that even 'unstructured' qualitative interviews vary widely. At least some of this variance is due to the influence of varying schools of psychology (Chirban, 1996). There are many ways in which one can slice up the epistemological chart (see Alvesson and Deetz, 1999; Denzin and Lincoln, 1998; Henwood, 1996). Positioning on realism or relativism, subjectivity or objectivity, will strongly influence one's approach to research and to interview data. For simplicity we will reduce these issues to whether the interviewer leans more towards a positivist or a constructionist epistemology and request that those working (or perhaps oscillating) somewhere along the continuum, bear with us.

Those leaning towards the positivist end may carry out qualitative interviews as a shift towards deepening understanding, perhaps before developing a questionnaire. From this perspective, electronic interviews may be viewed positively as a way of ensuring all participants are asked the same question in the same way without any interference from researcher error or interviewer effects. The chief concern about the method would be reliability and validity. The data may not be reliable as the respondents have had time to reflect and look at previous communications, influencing their response. There may be problems with accessing an objective 'truth' because of this. The data may not be valid as sampling is likely to be skewed and there may be other issues with the communication medium as yet unknown. A disadvantage of electronic interviews from this perspective would be the (possibly) reduced potential to check and clarify 'true' meanings with the respondent.

From a more social constructionist perspective, the interviewer and the interviewee may be perceived as involved in the joint construction of a version of 'reality'. There is a shift away from the 'masculine' paradigm of 'subjects' and 'objects' to developing a closer relationship between interviewer and respondent (Oakley, 1981). The power dynamics between researcher and interviewee are highlighted. From this perspective, a potential benefit of electronic interviews may be the reduced cues to status differences enabled by computer-mediated communication. On the other hand, the interaction between the interviewer and respondent is considered key to the research process. If we use ourselves as research instruments to try to achieve empathy with and an understanding of the other, and the respondents' reactions to the researcher are fundamental to their definition of the situation and their (joint) construction, then might the disembodied nature of electronic communication be too great a disadvantage? The evidence for a build-up of intimacy or richness of information exchanged between researcher and respondent is mixed (see Mann and Stewart (2000) for a review). To consider the reasons for this we need to assess the nature of electronic forms of communication.

The nature of electronic communication

There are a number of ways in which the use of electronic communication may have a bearing upon the interview process. We have already highlighted that the nature of the interaction may change: we are no longer face to face and a range of additional signals that enable us to develop a relationship may have been lost. These differences could be said to be epistemological, in that they may impact upon the nature of knowledge, and certainly upon how we acquire it, or ontological, in terms of influencing the subject matter or 'reality' that we are trying to access. We will consider what may be changed due to the use of this medium in three areas:

- social cues;
- power and democracy; and,
- temporality.

SOCIAL CUES

Some theories suggest that the absence or reduction of social cues inherent in electronic media means that e-mails and intranets are unsuitable for certain forms of communication, particularly ambiguous or relationship building forms (Schmitz and Fulk, 1991). Gorden (1980) outlines four types of non-verbal signals that are generated in face-to-face interactions. Although these cues are clearly missing from electronic forms of communication, some aspects of these are explicitly included in e-mail texts, either by use of emoticons or by stating mood, posture (sigh), and so on. The issue of media richness is controversial (Mann and Stewart, 2000; Walther et al., 2001). There is evidence that socio-emotional content *can* be found in e-mail messages, and that equivocal tasks can be handled by e-mail due to the ongoing nature of communication and time for reflection inherent in the medium. Walther (1996) argues that uncertainty reduction and self-disclosure, important elements of relationship building, merely take longer using e-mail. However, there is evidence of a form of 'swift trust' and 'hyperpersonal' relationships even in short-term groups (Joinson, 2001). It has also been suggested that people develop new social processes and new 'strategies of visibility' (Paccagnella, 1997) to make up for the limitations of electronic communication. However, this type of research tends to focus on effects of the medium on constructs such as intimacy, affection and social attractiveness, rather than about the *quality* of the communication, which is important to qualitative researchers.

Research is continuing in these areas, and certainly one needs to be aware of potential differences in response when using this method. At a practical level, Sallis and Kassabova (2000) suggest poor e-mail readability can lead to considerable ambiguity, suggesting care should be taken to develop a clear style. For the moment, we will agree that e-mail communication is a simplified register and a hybrid of oral and written communication (Murray, 1995, in Selwyn and Robson, 1998), which if managed with sensitivity could lead to a rich new form of information exchange.

POWER ISSUES AND DEMOCRACY

It has been suggested that, due to the lack of social information, electronic research can transcend race, gender and age (Selwyn and Robson, 1998), leading to democratization or equalization through computer mediated communications (Sproull and Kiesler, 1990). However, it has also been shown that many cues are still available using this medium. For example, the very style and nature of language used in the texts is a social cue and attributions will be made (Hayne and Rice, 1987). In organizations, people are probably aware of the status of individuals using e-mail (for example, Mantovani, 1994). For research purposes, participants will already know the interviewer is a researcher, and that carries with it much detail regarding likely social class and educational level. Although some suggest that research using this method is potentially non-coercive and anti-hierarchical (Paccagnella, 1997), there remain issues around the researcher-participant power relationship. This is not helped by the potential low security of electronic interviews. Care should be taken to ensure participants do not feel their responses may be made public or that the researcher is being intrusive (for example, by sending an excessive number of reminders). There may be differences in the reaction of participants to the use of e-mail rather than other methods. For example, Moon (1998) highlights differences in impression management when using e-mail, and Walther (1996) suggests that the sender will tend towards an optimized self-presentation and the receiver towards an idealized perception. How these perceptions impact upon research and whether the processes change by context or over time is not really known. We would certainly argue that the power issue between researcher and participants still needs to be carefully managed, and that consideration should be given to respondents' perceptions of the research process and method.

TEMPORALITY

The ability to communicate across time boundaries, regardless of whether the individual is actually 'there' is a key strength of this method, however there are some issues related to this. Some suggest that spontaneity is very important in interviews (Kvale, 1996) and this may be lost with electronic interviews. Whilst this method could increase reflexivity, especially as it also gives the respondent time to look at previous communications, it is uncertain whether all respondents actually *do* this, often e-mails are responded to in a speedy stream of consciousness. There is some evidence that people become more self-aware and can focus more because of the reduction in distractions, leading to increased reflexivity. Indeed it has been suggested that the need to express emotions explicitly in electronic communication may itself lead to heightened self-awareness (Joinson, 2001). This potential increase in reflexivity, for both parties involved, may be considered to be a very positive aspect of the medium for some social constructionists because it makes the socially constructed nature of 'reality' more transparent.

This temporal and spatial distancing also means contextual information is lost. We do not know, in many cases, where the person was when they replied, and, unless they tell us, what circumstances they are in, or what mood. In organizational research this may mean we do not understand the organization, culture, climate, structure, or where this person 'fits in'. These may or may not be important depending on the research question, and it could be argued that they are aspects often ignored in research anyway (Johns, 2001). We suggest, therefore, that this is not entirely an issue belonging to electronic interviews, and that the lack of apparent context with this medium can be a trigger to *put the context back* – to investigate this explicitly both through the interviews and in other ways.

CONCLUSION

Our research suggests that electronic interviews can be useful within organizational research, particularly in populations where e-mail is an accepted form of communication. Sample issues then become less of a problem, and it can be a useful way to overcome some access barriers.

One's epistemological stance will influence one's views on the strengths and weaknesses of the method, with those researchers who believe that building a rapport is important perhaps finding this method unsatisfactory. Other researchers, however, have demonstrated that a rich exchange of information is possible using electronic communications, and it may depend very much upon the research question and the researcher's skills in engaging and maintaining participants' interest. Researchers should note Parks and Floyd's (1996) finding that relationships that start on the net rarely stay there. Many net-friends use additional forms of communication and this may be necessary in research also, depending on the depth of relationship required for the study. In many studies, one is looking more for a rapport sufficient to sustain the interview process, rather than a long-term relationship, therefore the issue may be less important. In our view, the greatest advantages of this method may be the increased reflexivity allowed to all parties and the potential to (re)-negotiate meanings and genuinely co-construct the research process.

The issue of how well one can access meanings with this relatively new mode of communication does require further research. We do not yet understand what impact increased reflexivity and an oral-text register may have upon the meanings participants offer us in this form of research. We may need to accept that it can be hazardous to aim for a real-life 'truth' with any method, but that perhaps we *can* learn about a changing symbolic universe (Paccagnella, 1997) within organizations. The emphasis may need to be on awareness of the possibility for misunderstanding, the impact of reduced organizational and interactional context and the implications of the electronic context. We may need to be more aware of the links between our research findings, personal identity, and broader social changes epitomized in this mode of communication, which empties out time and space and offers new mechanisms of symbolic tokens (Giddens, 1991), perhaps changing the very 'object' of research.

In future, technological advances, such as broadband and voice-based e-mail communications, may alter again the form of communication. Moon (1998) found that voice input reduced the degree of impression management and suggests that certain voices may be more or less likely to lead to response bias. This highlights the importance of assessing all aspects of this rapidly changing form of communication. The possibility, for example, of being able to 'plug-in' to merger 'discussions' (if allowed) through such systems (Mann and Stewart, 2000) open up exciting new modes of organizational research.

Qualitative interviews themselves vary by depth, structure and time, so electronic interviews will also vary. Perhaps rather than continually comparing them with face-to-face interviews we should consider them as a new symbolic form of 'oral-text' exchange, with strengths and weaknesses that should be considered in relation to the research purpose, as with any other method.

FURTHER READING

An increasing amount of research relevant to this subject is available on the Internet, although it is worth checking the quality as not all are peer reviewed. The following are useful websites and papers for those wishing to do some background reading. In particular, we would recommend Mann and Stewart (2000) for a thorough introduction to the subject.

P. Chen and S.M. Hinton (1999) 'Realtime interviewing using the world wide web', *Sociological Research Online*, 4 (3): http://www.socresonline.org.uk/socresonline/4/3/chen.html

N, Illingworth (2001) 'The Internet matters: exploring the use of the internet as a research tool', *Sociological Research Online*, 6 (2): http://www.socresonline.org.uk/6/2/illingworth.html

A.N. Joinson (2001) 'Self-disclosure in computer-mediated communication: the role of self-awareness and visual anonymity', *European Journal of Social Psychology*, 31: 177–92.

C. Mann and F. Stewart (2000) *Internet Communication and Qualitative Research: A Handbook for Researching Online*, London: Sage.

NOTE

Our thanks go to all those people and organizations participating in this research, and to the ESRC for funding.

REFERENCES

Alvesson, M. and Deetz, S. (1999) *Doing Critical Management Research*, London: Sage.

Alvesson, M. and Skoldberg, K. (2000) *Reflexive Methodology: New Vistas for Qualitative Research*, London: Sage.

Chen, P. and Hinton, S.M. (1999) 'Realtime interviewing using the world wide web', *Sociological Research Online*, 4 (3): http://www.socresonline.org.uk/socresonline/4/3/chen.html

Chirban, J.T. (1996) *Interviewing in Depth: The Interactive-relational Approach*, Thousand Oaks: Sage Publications.

Coomber, R. (1997) 'Using the Internet for survey research', *Sociological Research Online*, 2 (2): http://www.socresonline.org.uk/socresonline/2/2/2.html

Crichard, M. (2001) 'E-mail monitoring-1: eavesdropping at work – is it legal?', *Computer Law and Security Report*, 17(2): 120–1.

Davies, B. (1998) 'Psychology's subject: a commentary on the relativism/realism debate', in I. Parker (ed.), *Social Constructionism, Discourse and Realism*, London: Sage.

Denzin, N.K. and Lincoln, Y.S. (eds) (1998) *Strategies of Qualitative Inquiry*, Thousand Oaks: Sage.

El-Shinnaway, M. and Markus, L. (1997) 'The poverty of media richness theory: explaining peoples' choice of electronic mail vs voice mail', *International Journal of Human Computer Studies*, 46: 443–67.

Fontana, A. and Frey, J.H. (1998) 'Interviewing, the art of science', in N. Denzin and Y. Lincoln (eds), *Collecting and Interpreting Qualitative Materials*, Thousand Oaks: Sage.

Giddens, A. (1991) *Modernity and Self Identity: Self and Society in the Late Modern Age*, Cambridge: Polity Press.

Giese, M. (1998) 'Self without body: textual self-representation in an electronic community', *First Monday*, 3(4): http://www.firstmonday.dk/issues/issue3_4/giese/index.html

Gorden, R.L. (1980) *Interviewing: Strategy, Techniques and Tactics*, Homewood, IL: Dorsey.

Hayne, S. and Rice, R. (1997) 'Attribution accuracy when using anonymity in group support systems', *International Journal of Human-Computer Studies*, 47: 429–52.

Henwood, K.L. (1996) 'Qualitative inquiry, perspectives, methods and psychology', in J. Richardson (ed.), *Handbook of Qualitative Research Methods for Psychology and the Social Sciences*. Leicester: BPS Books, pp.25–40.

Johns, G. (2001) 'In praise of context', *Journal of Organizational Behavior*, 22: 31–42.

Joinson, A.N. (2001) 'Self-disclosure in computer-mediated communication: the role of self-awareness and visual anonymity', *European Journal of Social Psychology*, 31: 177–92.

Kvale, S. (1996) *InterViews: An Introduction to Qualitative Research Interviewing*, Thousand Oaks: Sage.

Lindlof, T.R. (1995) *Qualitative Communication Research Methods*, Thousand Oaks: Sage.

Mann, C. and Stewart, F. (2000) *Internet Communication and Qualitative Research: A Handbook for Researching Online*, London: Sage.

Mantovani, G. (1994) 'Is computer-mediated communication intrinsically apt to enhance organizational democracy?', *Human Relations*, 47: 45–62.

Michael, M. (1996) 'Constructing a constructive critique of social constructionism: finding a narrative space for the non-human', *New Ideas in Psychology*, 14 (3): 209–24.

Moon, Y. (1998) 'Impression management in computer-based interviews: the effects of input modality, output modality, and distance', *Public Opinion Quarterly*, 62 (4): 610–22.

Oakley, A. (1981) 'Interviewing women: a contradiction in terms', in H. Roberts (ed.), *Doing Feminist Research*. London: Routledge & Kegan Paul, pp. 30–61.

O'Mahoney, S. and Barley, S.R. (1999) 'Do digital telecommunications affect work and organization? The state of our knowledge', *Research in Organizational Behavior*, 21: 125–61.

Paccagnella, L. (1997) 'Getting the seats of your pants dirty: strategies for ethnographic research on virtual communities', *Journal of Computer Mediated Communication*, 3: http://www.ascusc.org/jcmc/vol13/issue1/paccagnella.html

Parks, M.R. and Floyd, K. (1996) 'Making friends in cyberspace', *Journal of Computer Mediated Communication*, 1 (4): http://jcmc.huji.ac.il/vol1/issue4/parks.html

Platt, R.G. and Page, D. (2001) 'Managing the virtual team: critical skills and knowledge for successful performance', in N. Johnson (ed.), *Telecommuting and Virtual Offices: Issues and Opportunities*, Hershey, PA: IDEA Group.

Romm, C.T. and Pliskin, N. (1997) 'Playing politics with e-mail: a longitudinal conflict-based analysis', in A. Lee, J. Liebenau and J. DeGross (eds), *Information Systems and Qualitative Research*, Proceedings of the IFIP Conference, London: Chapman and Hall.

Rosenfeld, P., Booth-Kewley, S. and Edwards, J.E. (1993) 'Computer-administered surveys in organizational settings', *American Behavioral Scientist*, 36: 485–511.

Sallis, P. and Kassabova, D. (2000) 'Computer-mediated communication: experiments with e-mail readability', *Information Sciences*, 123: 43–53.

Schaefer, D.R. and Dillman, D.A. (1998) 'Development of a standard e-mail methodology: results of an experiment', *Public Opinion Quarterly*, 62: 378–97.

Schmitz, J. and Fulk, J. (1991) 'Organizational colleagues, information richness, and electronic mail: a test of the social influence model of technology use', *Communication Research*, 18: 487–523.

Selwyn, N. and Robson, K. (1998) 'Using e-mail as a research tool', *Social Research Update*: http://www.soc.surrey.ac.uk/sru/SRU21.html

Smith, J.A. (1996) 'Evolving issues for qualitative psychology', in J.T.E. Richardson (ed.), *Handbook of Qualitative Research Methods for Psychology and the Social Sciences*, Leicester: BPS Books, pp 189–201.

Sproull, L. and Kiesler, S. (1986) 'Reducing social context cues: electronic mail in organizational communication', *Management Science*, 32: 1492–512.

Walther, J.B. (1996) 'Computer-mediated communication: impersonal, interpersonal, and hyperpersonal interaction', *Communication Research*, 23 (1): 3–43.

Walther, J.B., Sovacek, C.L. and Tidwell, L.C. (2001) 'Is a picture worth a thousand words? Photographic images in long-term and short-term computer-mediated communication', *Communication Research*, 28 (1): 105–34.

Walther, J.B. and Tidwell, L.C. (1995) 'Nonverbal cues in computer-mediated communication, and the effects of chronemics on relational communication', *Journal of Organizational Computing*, 5 (4): 355–70.

4 — Life Histories

Gill Musson

This chapter provides some background to the development of the life history technique, its epistemological traditions, and an analysis of its relevance to organizational research, together with some empirical examples of its application in case studies drawn from research. The chapter concludes by evaluating the usefulness of the approach, summarizing the circumstances in which it might best be used, and providing some recommended reading.

THE LIFE HISTORY APPROACH

Life history method focuses on the ways in which individuals account for and theorize about their actions in the social world over time. The subjective interpretation of the situation in which people find themselves, past or present, is its cornerstone. It is predicated on the fundamental assumption that 'if men [sic] define those situations as real, they are real in their consequences' (Thomas, 1966: 300). As such the method prioritizes individual explanations and interpretations of actions and events, viewing them as lenses through which to access the meaning that human beings attribute to their experience. The method is useful for gathering information about changes in the material and social networks within which people construct their lives.

Life history method is firmly rooted in an interpretive epistemological perspective, and specifically in the symbolic interactionist paradigm which views human beings as living in a world of 'meaningful objects' – not in an environment of stimuli or self-constituted entities. In this epistemological tradition, the world is socially produced in that knowledge and 'meanings are fabricated through the process of social interaction' (Blumer, 1969: 540; see Hammersley, 1989 for a detailed exposition of symbolic interactionism). Through the processes of symbolic interaction, different groups come to create and maintain different worlds, but these worlds are not presumed to be static. Rather, they are fluid and dynamic, colliding and overlapping, continually being created and re-created, changing as the objects that compose them are changed in meaning. Thus, the reflexivity of human beings is central to this perspective and it is this process of reflexivity, how human beings theorize and explain their past, present and future, which the life history method seeks to capture.

BACKGROUND TO THE METHOD

Various psychologists have defined self-identity as a life story. For example, McAdams (1989: 161) defines life histories as 'an internalized narrative integration of past, present and anticipated future which provides lives with a sense of unity and purpose'. As such the life history method provides a fundamental source of knowledge about how people experience and make sense of themselves and their environments, allowing the actors to speak for themselves. In some circumstances the voices may then be interpreted, but the process of interpretation will always attempt to reflect the actors' perspective, rather than simply that of the researcher. This is not to say that the approach accepts the account of the individual as some kind of unproblematic version of an objective 'truth'. Rather, the method is predicated on the assumption that 'all perspectives dangle from some person's problematic. Views, truths and conceptions of the real can never be wholly ripped away from the people who experience them' (Plummer, 1983: 57). But neither does the method seek to deny that people exist within particular structural and institutional constraints. Instead, it specifically locates itself in the nexus between deterministic structures and individual agency, between those factors that might be described as relatively objective, and the subjective interpretation of the individual (Casey, 1993; Elder, 1981). Ontologically, it recognizes the dialectical relationship between these two processes: that human beings, through their actions, impose themselves on and create their worlds, but they do so in a world which presents itself as already constituted through a network of typifications. These typifications – for example, group norms, group meanings, group language – express the systematic and coherent 'rationality' or 'grammar' of the context, and thus reflect, and in turn constitute, the culture or system of shared meaning in which the individual is located. In sum, the approach views 'the individual, embedded in a network of relationships and statuses, as the irreducible unit of analysis' (Mathews, 1977: 37).

But it would be a mistake to view life histories as totally individualistic. Of course they reflect the experiences of the individual through a given period of time, but because lives move resolutely through history and structure they can also provide an understanding that extends beyond the individual and into the wider context of organizations, institutions, cultures and societies. As Thompson (in Bertaux, 1981) points out, a life history cannot be told without constant reference to historical change: social or organizational. In a period when constant change is perceived as the norm and much organizational and management research is devoted to trying to understand it, life histories can provide a useful window through which to widen our understanding of the change process within organizations. The method can avoid the common research error which Becker (1966: xiii) noted three decades ago but which still holds true today: that process is an 'overworked notion' in research, in that researchers often talk a lot about ongoing processes whilst using methods which prevent them from uncovering the very processes which they seek to identify.

The life history method also recognizes the collusion of the researcher in the research process. It does not presume that the researcher is some impartial, value-free entity, unproblematically engaging in the research process to produce objective accounts of a reified truth. Rather, the approach recognizes that the researcher also brings implicit and explicit theories to the research situation, and the task of the researcher includes surfacing these in the struggle for balance between theory in the researcher's head and theory employed by the people in the research situation.

The explicating of the researcher's basic assumptions and theoretical frameworks is a central aspect of the validity of the method. In addition, validity is achieved through the congruence of research explanations with the meanings with which members construct their realities and accomplish their everyday activities. Part of the methodological rigour, then, entails allowing the explanations of the researcher to be subjected to the scrutiny of organizational members to see whether these accounts resonate with and inform the members' own understandings of their subjective experiences. Even though the concepts and categories used in this process might be allowed to emerge from the data (see Glaser and Strauss, 1967 for a full discussion of grounded theory, and Länsisalmi et al., Chapter 20, this volume), they must best interpret the particular material by retaining the meaning of the actors involved. In this sense, the concepts and constructs developed in a particular life history will be context specific.

APPLICATION OF THE METHOD IN ORGANIZATIONAL ANALYSIS

Some of the specific benefits of applying this method are, first, in understanding how organizations' function involves understanding the ambiguities, uncertainties and problematics that individuals experience and resolve on a daily basis. Allowing people to explain for themselves the experience of contradictions and confusions, moments of indecision and turning points, can illustrate graphically how organizational socialization processes are accomplished, for example, and consequently illuminate our understanding of how individuals and organizations function, more than methods which reduce experience to abstracted definitions and moribund descriptions.

Second, the technique allows the researcher access to the network of typifications, or interpretive schemes, which individuals bring to their roles in particular organizations. This may be particularly relevant if the research question involves understanding the motivations and influences which powerful organizational leaders, or specific groups, bring to bear on organizations (see, for example, Bloor and Dawson, 1994). The method can expose the manner in which entrepreneurs or founders come to hold their particular beliefs and versions of rationality, and how they impose these definitions on others.

Finally, the organizational literature is replete with studies of organizational culture but very few studies actually give specific advice about how to conduct a cultural analysis that captures the complexity and dynamism of cultural processes. Life history method can provide this. As Jones points out, 'the world of formal organization can be viewed as a network of typifications, as a particular form of language that has been produced historically through the rational and expressive acts of its population' (1983: 154). This organizational language, or grammar of action, provides the basic rules for organizational activity. In this sense, this grammar of action *is* the organizational culture. Understanding how this language is constituted, through gathering organizational life history data, can give students an analytic handle on the cultural composition of organizations. This understanding should include the recognition that organizational languages or grammars are constituted in three main ways (Jones, 1983), each of which is central to the way organizational lives develop.

First, organizations, like individuals, do not exist in a vacuum. The constitutive rules or grammars of action of an organization reflect a rationality embodied in the wider environment(s) of which the organization is a part. These rules are embodied in the language of the organization, and are reproduced through it. For example, the language of health care organizations in the UK now includes an economic discourse, which was introduced externally, but which now influences and informs the activity of all health care organizations. Second, organizational languages are constituted collectively, and represent and reproduce a collective memory of events (see Middleton and Edwards, 1991 for a detailed exposition on memory as a socially constituted activity). These collective memories, which provide recipes for action, are expressed through all aspects of the organization, including repertoires of myths and stories, but also the more concrete organizational forms of structure, technology, systems and procedures. Third, the constitution of an organizational grammar of action is an ongoing process. Changes in that grammar, which arise from and through the interplay and tension of shared and competing interpretations of organizational members, are reflected and reproduced by changes in the organizational language. For example, the introduction of economic rules and discourses in the UK health care environment could not be accommodated within the existing meaning structures of some health care organizations (see Cohen and Musson, 2000), and therefore the organizational grammar of these organizations changed to accommodate these new meanings. These changes were reflected in the language, which in turn served to reproduce these new meaning structures and provide new recipes for action, in an iterative process.

DATA COLLECTION AND ANALYSIS

As will be evident by now, the life history technique takes talk as data, as the 'disclosing tablet' that reveals how people are constituted by, and in turn serve to constitute, organizational realities (Forester, 1992). Although talk can take many forms, for example in written texts such as organizational reports, correspondence or diaries of organizational members, it is primarily through semi-structured or unstructured interviewing that life history data are commonly collected (see King, Chapter 2, this volume, for a discussion of interview techniques).

Asking people to talk about their life histories in order to unearth their understandings entails listening to their stories. People do not tend to express their experiences, or describe their sense making processes, in terms of succinct, abstract generalizations. Such generalizations and inferences at once remove the richness that a story preserves. Researchers need to understand that people construct narrative accounts as part of the sense making process, and as a way of preserving and communicating information, and that they do this through the telling of stories (see Gabriel and Griffiths, Chaper 10, this volume). It is the researcher's task to draw from life history narratives the principles on which the stories are founded, not the task of the storyteller. However, simply in terms of time constraints, it would be nonsense to suggest that researchers simply go into organizations and ask people to tell them whatever story pops into their head at that particular time. Obviously, the research question, and the specific phenomena that are of interest, will help the researcher to structure the facilitation of the storytelling process by asking appropriate questions (see for example Casey, 1993).

In the research described in the next section, I directed the storytelling process to a large extent by asking individuals to tell me about when and how their understanding of the purpose of the organization shifted. However, I accepted as central to them the story that they gave me in response to this question. These stories differed from focusing on the history of an individual's marital difficulties, to telling me a story about an individual patient and the way she was treated by the GPs in the practice. Both these stories gave me data about the culture of the organization and the way in which organizational members made sense of the past and the present. Likewise, I asked people to tell me about their lives in previous organizations and how they had experienced these; what they had found rewarding, constraining or difficult to make sense of, and how this differed in their current organization. Again, the open-ended structure of the narratives allowed people to introduce subjects of major importance to them.

Having obtained the data, the researcher is left with two analytical problems. The first involves what to do with the mass of data. The second involves the fundamental problematic around surfacing taken-for-granted assumptions. Basic assumptions are notoriously inaccessible in that they exist at a level whereby people are commonly unable to articulate them, even though their behaviour might be in accordance with the rules that they embody (Garfinkel, 1967; Schein, 1985). Jones (1983) suggests that researchers can deal with both these problems through a process of setting up a series of oppositions: first, within members' accounts; second, between members' accounts; and third, between members' accounts and the researcher's constructions of the situation. During this iterative process, the researcher will develop constructs and concepts which expose and describe the theoretical frameworks of individuals, at the same time as subjecting these to the theoretical orientation developed by the researcher. The object is to retain the integrity of the data whilst seeking to confront its internal logic and thus explain the relationship to taken-for-granted assumptions. The researcher should involve members as much as possible in this process by taking the ensuing theoretical explanations back to them for comment. The carrying out of this complex process is best illustrated through the description of empirical work contained in the next section.

SOME EMPIRICAL EXAMPLES

The examples referred to in this section are taken from doctoral work on how general medical practitioners (GPs) in the UK experienced and understood the 1990 health care reforms which impacted on their daily practice (Musson, 1994), *directly* linking for the first time their clinical activity, and the ability to document that activity, to the financial reward that they receive. It would be tempting at this point to indicate that life history method was a well thought out, predetermined approach at the start of the doctoral research, but this would not reflect the truth of the situation. It is much more the case that during the in-depth research with six general practices carried out over two years it became more and more apparent that the life histories of key actors were significant in the way the changes were construed, understood and experienced, and that allowing people to tell something of their life histories illuminated the sense making process. The original planned method involved using a variety of techniques including participant observation, semi-structured interviews, group discussions and analysis of documentation. This was eventually supplemented with informal interview data that focused specifically on collecting individual life histories. As Plummer (1996: 54) notes, this reflects a 'less formal life history strategy' of triangulated data collection, mixing participant observation, formal and informal interview data and field notes, rather than the more traditional method of encouraging people to write their own life history, or to record specific life history interviews over a period of time.

What follows are some extracts where life history data were able to enhance the understandings surfaced by the other methods. These extracts will also be used to describe the oppositional process outlined in the previous section. The extracts are necessarily short, but hopefully comprehensive enough to demonstrate how the method is useful in organizational analysis. They include actual quotes from the research data wherever possible.

Example 1: oppositions within members' accounts

In this three-doctor practice, Dr A was the senior partner and had practised single handed for many years before being joined by the other two doctors relatively recently. The practice was managed and run by him, organized like clockwork, with efficient, comprehensive systems and detailed procedures in place to support every activity. All of these systems had been devised by Dr A who had commented in a life history interview that 'I would have preferred to be an accountant but my family pressurized me into medicine.' He saw no connection between this thwarted desire and the way he ran the practice, and of course, there is no way of knowing in a concrete sense how these views originated. Nevertheless, he felt that 'all businesses should be organized like this whether they sell cars or offer a medical service'. But what is perhaps of more interest here is that the information systems manager, recently employed as a result of the information requirements of the NHS reforms, viewed the practice as having 'too much emphasis on systems and information management'. When I asked her what she, as information systems manager, meant by this statement, she replied 'because it has no soul', and proceeded to tell me a story about the previous practice in which she had worked, which 'had a much greater emphasis on individual patient care, although it was very badly organized but it provided a better service for patients'. Her story illustrated that she was making sense of her past and present experiences by setting up an opposition between care tailored to individual patient needs and delivered by 'really caring doctors', and the more population oriented care delivered by 'this system'. Analysis of her account revealed two basic assumptions: first, that patients experienced better care in the previous practice despite the disorganization; and second, that there was something about systematized care delivery that precluded an individual patient orientation.

Both of these assumptions could be challenged to a large extent by the data on disease management and referrals gathered from both these practices as part of the research (Musson, 1994), although quality of care is notoriously difficult to measure in any meaningful way. But this would be to miss the point. What the analysis revealed was the political antagonism that this person held about the new information requirements in general practice activity, and the ambiguity and contradictions which this invoked because these new information requirements were the source of her employment. This opposition was further exacerbated because she was very ambitious and 'keen to succeed', but she was doing so in an area of activity that challenged the political ideas that she had long held about good delivery of care. Moreover, her life history revealed that she had come from a background where 'women don't have proper careers' and that 'doing this job causes me lots of problems at home'. Still, she viewed the job as 'my chance to make my mark'. In sum, Dr A's life history helped to reveal how the norms, values and practices prevalent in the organization of the practice had come about, and the information systems manager's life stories illustrated the oppositions, contradictions and ambiguities she faced in making sense of her daily activity.

Example 2: oppositions between members' accounts

The following data are drawn from research in another practice that took part in the project. The practice had very recently employed a practice manager as a response to the new legislation, despite being very strongly opposed to the principles and practices of the reforms. At the time of the research the practice manager was experiencing some difficulties in 'fitting into the practice – I'm like a square peg in a round hole.' The scale of these difficulties can be demonstrated through describing a relatively minor, but significant, incident about whether her office door should be left open or closed. Since her arrival, the practice manager had left the door between her office and the reception area, which housed the rest of the office staff, open throughout the day. The reception staff, for whom she was responsible, interpreted this action as 'spying on us', and resented what they perceived as her interference in the way they carried out their work. She, on the other hand, felt that she was 'only doing my job by making sure everything's running smoothly and that I'm available if needed – I see that as my responsibility.' At first glance these can seem like very superficial disagreements, easily explained as interpersonal difficulties. But they actually embodied the different, and competing, assumptions deeply held by the various members of the practice, and which made up the network of typifications that served to structure their realities. Some of these typifications are discussed below.

Prior to the arrival of the practice manager, this three doctor, seven staff practice had prided itself on its very flat structure and its 'caring family' ethos. This family structure reflected the desire held by all the doctors, but particularly Dr B, to create a caring, cohesive, collective loyalty within, and to, the practice, which 'also includes the patients – we wouldn't have a practice without the patients.' This family orientation was reflected in the stories which staff told about the practice's past. For example, 'Dr B has been like a father to me' was how one receptionist described her relationship with the founder, whilst another told stories about 'all the support I received from here when I was going through my divorce – support that you'd expect from your family.'

The structure worked in the sense that relations based on the personal rather than the hierarchical evolved, together with the view that nobody was much higher or much lower in importance than anybody else. This was uncommon in general practice and these relations were manifested and reinforced in a variety of ways. For example, the use of first name terms for doctors, staff and patients conveyed friendship, and therefore reinforced the notion of relationships of equality. Similarly, many practice discussions were organized around issues unconnected with the usual functions of general practice. One such discussion took place about the political implications of the Gulf War, for example, reflecting the commonly shared political views held in the practice, and reinforcing the notion of the practice as a liberal, egalitarian organization. However, in reality the doctors held the locus of control, and an unspoken rule had evolved over many years which embodied the implicit knowledge that the doctors' views and therefore their authority were never really to be questioned. This contradiction was managed through a high level of trust and mutual respect which existed in the 'family' prior to the new legislation and the employment of the practice manager.

This family orientation and related structure were accompanied by a high value on clinical expertise and autonomy, but a very low value on management principles and techniques. The latter were seen as secular activities, potentially damaging to the sacred clinical orientation of the practice (Laughlin, 1991). Despite this, the doctors hired a management consultant to control and direct the appointment of a practice manager in response to the new reforms, again reflecting the value placed on expertise. The person appointed came from a highly bureaucratic background with a lot of experience in the wider NHS system. She was charged with implementing the reforms, which required the reorganization of much practice activity, but she was largely denied the power to do so, and struggles over the modification of organizational realities and practices ensued. These struggles became evident in organizational language. For example, 'she even talks differently to us – I know that she's got to look at the financial side but that's the only language she knows' was a typical comment found in stories about her effect on the practice. This reference illustrates how the economic discourse, the language of patients as profit and loss, began to surface in daily discussions about service provision. Similarly, the following example shows how this discourse served to restructure the realities of other members of the practice.

Prior to the practice manager's appointment, tetanus injections had been administered on a 10 yearly basis on the grounds that '10 years is a clinically justifiable time gap.' This had always been done on an ad hoc basis, whenever a patient's clinical profile suggested that it was necessary. The practice had not purchased the injections directly because 'there was no clinical advantage in buying it ourselves and we didn't want to be involved in anything purely for financial gain.' This quote refers to the financial saving which the practice could have made through direct purchase, because wholesale costs were significantly lower than the retail price that the practice could reclaim. After much debate, the practice manager did persuade the practice to purchase the vaccinations wholesale on the assumption that there would be no direct effect on the clinical decision to offer or administer the vaccination. However, shortly after the practice began purchasing the vaccine, the practice manager persuaded the doctors and nurses to adopt a system whereby a patient's tetanus status was checked as a matter of routine, and an injection offered on a five yearly basis for which the practice received a significant financial benefit under the new legislation. One of the nurses explained the rationale behind this change of heart as follows: 'when the PM pointed out just how much tetanus did earn I was converted – well people still die of tetanus anyway, not many but they do, and this way we might eradicate it . . . I said it was immoral at first, we'd always opted for the 10 year rather than the five year gap, and we shouldn't do it, but . . . it's still not quite a money spinner but . . .' This quote was typical of many which illustrated the internal rationalization processes evident in coming to terms with oppositions created by clinical changes that were essentially economically driven.

Example 3: oppositions between members' accounts and the researcher's construction of events

This section continues with the data described in the previous section to illustrate how the researcher can confront the accounts of organizational members with other theoretical interpretations. Of course, I have been doing this to some extent throughout the previous two examples, since it is impossible for researchers to report data objectively: description and analysis are intricately entwined. However, this section reports on my practical involvement in confronting the members' explanations of events, and the basic assumptions and oppositions that they contained. It is difficult to be succinct about this part of the process within the confines of this chapter, partly because it is very complex, but also because in this instance it was a very emotional experience for everybody involved (see Musson, 1994 for a detailed account).

By the end of the practice manager's first year, conflict, which was normally suppressed in the practice, had begun to bubble to the surface in a way which nobody knew how to handle, and the organization was in crisis. In an attempt to resolve rapidly deteriorating relationships, the doctors called an evening meeting between themselves and the practice manager, to which the researcher was invited, 'to talk honestly to each other'. The meeting took place in a very emotionally charged atmosphere and the talk centred very much on disagreements about specific and relatively minor issues, and after three hours little progress had been made. Listening to this conversation, and in the light of the interview data already gathered, the following four interrelated factors seemed central to me about how the situation had developed thus far. These factors formed my theoretical construction of the situation.

First, the practice manager had been appointed to deal with the reforms that the doctors, and the rest of the practice, would have very much preferred to ignore. In this sense her marginalization began even before she started working in the practice. Second, her appointment not only symbolized the encroachment of these reforms, but also ruptured the highly valued flat 'family' structure. Third, the practice manager had a worldview, a fundamental value system, and norms about appropriate ways of organizing which were very different from those of the doctors. For example, her long experience in hierarchical organizations, whose norms she had internalized, were in direct opposition to those of the doctors. In addition, her political views on issues such as unemployment, for example, which she described as coming from years of experience of living amongst people who 'sponge off the system', were different from the beliefs held by other people in the practice. And finally, the power differential, although unacknowledged and submerged, prevented her from 'succeeding in my terms in putting things right round here'. Although she struggled to enforce the norms that fitted her particular version of reality, she did not have the power to do so to any large extent, but she did have sufficient power to become an extremely disruptive force even though this was not her intent. The resulting struggles were focused around minor issues, such as the open door, but they were actually manifestations of these much deeper oppositions and differences.

At this point I was invited to give my view of the situation and offered a diagnosis that included these theoretical interpretations. I was surprised that none of the actors had considered these possible interpretations because they seemed obvious to me. But I recognized that they were, at least in part, a product of being relatively detached from the situation and having access to data denied to others (life history data for example), and the time to ponder over it. My feelings about the response to my interpretation were at once positive and negative. My explanation was described as 'very valuable – it's shed some light on the problem' and its validity did seem to be accepted by all the actors who 'had not thought of it like that before even though it makes such sense to me now'. From this perspective I felt that some measure of enlightenment had been achieved through confronting the oppositions held between the key players. However, the meeting finally ended after four hours on a dismal note, because as Dr B said at the time, 'I don't see what we can do to resolve the situation because we're coming from such different ideas.' Indeed, the situation was never amicably resolved, but space precludes any further discussion here.

EVALUATING THE METHOD

Life history method is best used in circumstances where the researcher seeks to understand the complex processes which people use in making sense of their organizational realities. In addition to addressing questions of socialization, career development, and managerial style, the method can be used to give voice to otherwise unheard accounts. Organizational research often has a managerial focus, but organizations are made up of many diverse groups of people, the voices of which are rarely heard in research (Casey, 1993).

The method can be used either in conjunction with others, or as a technique on its own. However, my own preference is for using a variety of methods together so that they complement each other, providing, at least potentially, a more fertile data set. For example, participant observation (see Waddington, Chapter 13, this volume) can be combined with life history data to provide a richer, more holistic picture than perhaps either method could furnish on its own. Similarly, discourse analysis can be applied to data generated through life history method to strengthen the analysis (see Dick, Chapter 17, this volume).

The major problem of using the method is that it is immensely time consuming for both the researcher and the actors involved. Gathering and analysing life history data commonly involves the researcher in many hours of data collection, and analysis can be an uncertain process requiring a high tolerance of ambiguity over considerable periods of time. Although the resulting accounts might read as if the data collection and analysis were planned, linear and unproblematic, this does not reflect my experience. Other problems associated with this kind of research include the emotional repercussions that can result (see Musson, 1994), and reporting data that compromise neither the richness of the stories nor the actor's anonymity. These are factors that the life history researcher must be prepared to face.

FURTHER READING

The text by K. Plummer (1983) *Documents of Life: An Introduction to the Problems and Literature of the Humanistic Method,* London: Allen and Unwin, should be read by anyone considering using the life history method. Plummer has also written an edited version of Chapter 5 of the above book, entitled 'Life story research', in J.A. Smith, R. Harré and L. Van Langenhove (1996) (eds), *Rethinking Methods in Psychology,* London: Sage, which focuses on the key practicalities of life history research.

Kathleen Casey (1993) has written a very interesting book on her life history research with three distinct groups of women teachers: Catholic nuns, secular Jewish women, and African American women, *I Answer with My Life: Life Histories of Women Teachers Working for Social Change,* London: Routledge.

The chapter by Jones (1983) 'Life history method', in G. Morgan (ed.), *Beyond Method: Strategies for Social Research,* Beverley Hills, CA: Sage, is powerful, practical and very readable.

REFERENCES

Becker, H.S. (1966) 'Introduction to "The Jack Roller" by Clifford Shaw', in H.S. Becker, *Sociological Work* (1971), London: Allen Lane.

Bertaux, D. (1981) *Biography and Society,* Chicago: University of Chicago Press.

Bloor, G. and Dawson, P. (1994) 'Understanding professional culture in organizational context', *Organization Studies,* 15 (2): 275–95.

Blumer, H. (1969) *Symbolic Interactionism,* Englewood Cliffs, NJ: Prentice-Hall.

Casey, K. (1993) *I Answer with My Life: Life Histories of Women Teachers Working for Social Change,* London: Routledge.

Cohen, L. and Musson, G. (2000) 'Entrepreneurial identities: reflections from two case studies', *Organization,* 7(1): 31–48.

Elder, G. (1981) 'History and life course', in D. Bertaux (ed.), *Biography and Society,* Chicago: University of Chicago Press.

Forester, J. (1992) 'Fieldwork in a Habermasian way', in M. Alvesson and H. Willmott (eds), *Critical Management Studies,* London: Sage.

Garfinkel, H. (1967) *Studies in Ethnomethodology,* Englewood Cliffs, NJ: Prentice-Hall.

Glaser, B.G. and Strauss, A.L. (1967) *The Discovery of Grounded Theory: Strategies for Qualitative Research,* New York: Aldine.

Gramsci, A. (1980) *Selections from the Prison Notebooks of Antonio Gramsci*, ed. and trans. Q. Hoare and G.N. Smith, New York: International.

Hammersley, M. (1989) *The Dilemma of Qualitative Method: Herbert Blumer and the Chicago Tradition*, London: Routledge.

Jones, G.R. (1983) 'Life history method', in G. Morgan (ed.), *Beyond Method: Strategies for Social Research*, Beverley Hills, CA: Sage.

King, N. (1994) 'The qualitative research interview', in C. Cassell and G. Symon (eds), *Qualitative Methods in Organizational Research: A Practical Guide*, London: Sage.

Laughlin, R.C. (1991) 'Environmental disturbances and organizational transitions and transformations: some alternative models', *Organization Studies*, 12 (2): 209–32.

Mathews, F. (1977) *Quest for an American Sociology: Robert E. Park and the Chicago School*, Montreal: McGill-Queens University Press.

McAdams, D.P. (1989) 'The development of narrative identity', in D.M. Buss and N. Cantor (eds), *Personality Psychology: Recent Trends and Emerging Directions*, New York: Springer-Verlag, pp 160–74.

Middleton, D. and Edwards, D. (eds) (1991) *Collective Remembering.* London: Sage.

Morgan, G. (1986) *Images of Organization.* Beverley Hills, CA: Sage.

Musson, G. (1994) 'Organizational responses to an environmental disturbance: case studies of change in general medical practice'. PhD thesis, University of Sheffield.

Pettigrew, A.M. (1987) 'Context and action in the transformation of the firm', *Journal of Management Studies*, 24 (6): 649–70.

Plummer, K. (1983) *Documents of Life: An Introduction to the Problems and Literature of the Humanistic Method*, London: Allen & Unwin.

Plummer, K. (1996) 'Life story research', in J.A. Smith, R. Harré and L. Van Langenhove (eds), *Rethinking Methods in Psychology*, London: Sage.

Schein, E.H. (1985) *Organizational Culture and Leadership*, London: Jossey-Bass.

Thomas, W.I. (1966) in M. Janowitz (ed.), *Organization and Social Personality: Selected Papers*, Chicago: University of Chicago Press.

⑤ ── Critical Incident Technique ─────────

Elizabeth Chell

The Critical Incident Technique (CIT) was first used in a scientific study almost a half century ago (Flanagan, 1954). The significance of this time span is that then the assumption of a *positivist* approach to social science investigations was largely unquestioned. It was the dominant paradigm in the social sciences as it was in the natural sciences. However, the CIT has been developed further as an investigative tool in organizational analysis from within an interpretative or phenomenological paradigm (Chell, 1998; Chell and Pittaway, 1998; Pittaway and Chell, 1999). This means that there are two variants of the CIT each to be applied as appropriate.

In this chapter I shall present some background about the use of CIT, followed by a description of my own usage of it. This will be illustrated by means of a detailed case example of its use within an interpretive paradigm.

BACKGROUND TO THE METHOD ──────────────────

Following Flanagan (1954), researchers used CIT in occupational settings, and it was here that the validity and reliability of the method was established (Andersson and Nilsson, 1964; Ronan and Latham, 1974). Much of the research focused on managerial and employee performance and the identification of less tangible factors that might affect it (McClelland, 1976, 1987; Spencer, 1983). The use of CIT within social constructionism emerged in the early 1990s (Chell et al., 1991; Chell and Adam, 1994a, 1994b; Chell and Pittaway, 1998; Pittaway and Chell, 1999; Wheelock and Chell, 1996). Additionally, it has been used to identify the context of emotionally laden critical events (Chell and Baines, 1998), from which experiential learning takes place (Cope and Watts, 2000). This chapter applies the method to a series of related incidents that dramatically affected an entrepreneur's business and personal life.

Flanagan defined the Critical Incident Technique as:

> [A] set of procedures for collecting direct observations of human behaviour in such a way as to facilitate their potential usefulness in solving practical problems and developing broad psychological principles . . . By an incident is meant any specifiable human activity that is sufficiently complete in itself to permit inferences and predictions to be made about the person performing the act. To be critical the incident must occur in a situation where the purpose or intent of the act seems fairly clear to the observer and where its consequences are sufficiently definite to leave little doubt concerning its effects. (Flanagan, 1954:327)

The studies reviewed by Flanagan (1954) assumed that reality was tangible and specified occupational groups in defined situations. Observations were deemed to be factually correct if a number of independent observers made the same judgement. Thus, fundamental to the method is the ability to classify the critical incidents. Ideally, it is desirable to observe a comprehensive set of incidents from which a classification system is derived. This presents the analyst with objective criteria for application to a fresh study. As the classification has been arrived at inductively it can never be assumed to be fully comprehensive. The outcome of Flanagan's research was a set of descriptive categories – 'critical requirements' – of effective combat leadership. By the use of expert observers whose independent judgements were compared, the essentially subjective nature of this process was converted into an objective set of criteria, which could be rigorously applied to further groups.

The 'behavioural event interview' (BEl) developed by David McClelland and colleagues was derived from the Flanagan Critical Incident method. It was known that measurable skills like verbal fluency and cultural knowledge did not predict the performance of diplomats. Hence the objective was to develop a means whereby the less tangible aspects of behaviour, specifically 'soft' skills and competencies, could be identified. The interviewees were asked to identify the most critical incidents they had encountered in their jobs and to describe them in considerable detail. The interview transcripts were content analysed to identify behaviours and characteristics that distinguished superior from average job performance. Cross validation tests were also used. The outcome of this work was the development of a Job Competence Assessment process to identify 'soft skills', which predict performance in more than 50 professions (Spencer, 1983).

In the 1990s, CIT was developed within a qualitative, social constructionist (Chell et al., 1991) or grounded theory (Curran et al., 1993) framework. For example Chell et al. (1991) sought to distinguish behavioural differences between business owners of small to medium sized enterprises (SMEs) across a range of business sectors. The specified activity was business development. The interviewee identified critical incidents that affected development. Thus the *outcome* was the nature of business development (measured in terms of growth indicators) whilst the inputs were behaviours carried out by the interviewee in relation to the identified incidents. Research questions were what incidents in the opinion of the business owner shaped behavioural and business outcomes, and how did s/he handle those incidents? Could the behaviours by which s/he handled the events be construed as evidence of entrepreneurship?

A study that focused upon inter-regional comparisons in locations in the north-east and south-east of England was carried out, the aims and objectives being to examine the interaction between business and household and the implications for each (Wheelock and Chell, 1996). Micro-business owners could select 'domestic' incidents if he/she wished in order to explain business development activity or inactivity. Some of this work is reported in Chell and Baines (1998).

Pittaway's study of the social construction of entrepreneurial behaviour (Pittaway, 2000) applied the CIT to a study of restauranteurs and café owners in Newcastle (UK). The data were analysed and profiles of entrepreneurial behaviours from two 'benchmark' cases were used for purposes of interpretation of the sample (Chell and Pittaway, 1998; Pittaway and Chell, 1999). The method yielded a rich data set.

Cope and Watts (2000) explore the learning process of entrepreneurs in relation to the parallel processes of personal and business development. They discuss the impact of critical incidents on the developmental history of the business. They show that entrepreneurs often face prolonged and traumatic critical periods or episodes that are emotionally laden. Further, they demonstrate that the incidents result in higher level learning, and conclude that entrepreneurs need support to interpret critical incidents as learning experiences. The case discussed in the ensuing pages has many of these features, and is derived from the study with Susan Baines and Jane Wheelock outlined above.

COMPARISON WITH OTHER QUALITATIVE METHODS

CIT may be used in case study research but is more often used in multi-site studies. The question arises as to whether other methods, for example participant observation and unstructured or semi-structured interviews, might not be more effective as research tools.

The CIT has in common with participant observation and the unstructured interview the fact that they are all examples of qualitative techniques used to 'get closer to the subject' (Bryman, 1989). However, participant observation has a number of disadvantages. Covert participant observation raises ethical issues (for example of deception), it focuses upon the 'here and now' and it presents difficulties of recording observations. CIT is overt in that the subject is aware of being interviewed. Once assurances have been given of confidentiality and anonymity, the interviewee usually relaxes and is able to recount his or her story. One disadvantage is that the accounts are always retrospective; however, the fact that the incidents are 'critical' means that subjects usually have good recall. Moreover, unlike the unstructured interview, there is a focus, which enables the researcher to probe aptly, and the interviewee to 'hook' their accounts. As is the case with participant observation, CIT is context-rich, but unlike participant observation the context is developed entirely from the subject's perspective. Some things can be checked. It is therefore usual to use documentary sources to check factual statements, and if possible to interview at least one other significant person. Further where the CIT is used across multiple sites the researcher can look for evidence of commonalties in themes, that is, 'incidents' that increase generalizability[1]. A further advantage of the CIT is that the analysis enables the researcher to relate context, strategy and outcomes, to look for repetition of patterns, and thus to build up a picture of tactics for handling difficult situations. This gives first hand evidence of the relationship between context and outcome.[2]

DETAILED BREAKDOWN OF THE METHOD

The method, as developed by the author, assumes a phenomenological approach. It is intended through the process of a largely unstructured interview to capture the thought processes, the frame of reference and the feelings about an incident or set of incidents, which have meaning for the respondent. In the interview the respondent is required to give an account of what those incidents meant for them, their life situation and their present circumstances, attitudes and orientation.

This same approach may be used with the in-depth case study, as well as the multi-site investigation. Thus, this method assumes an alternative definition to that of Flanagan.

The critical interview technique is a qualitative interview procedure, which facilitates the investigation of significant occurrences (events, incidents, processes or issues), identified by the respondent, the way they are managed, and the outcomes in terms of perceived effects. The objective is to gain an understanding of the incident from the perspective of the individual, taking into account cognitive, affective and behavioural elements.

There are six distinguishable aspects of the method:

1　introducing the CIT method and getting the interview under way;
2　focusing the theme and giving an account of oneself as researcher to the respondent;
3　controlling the interview, by probing the incidents and clarifying one's understanding;
4　concluding the interview;
5　taking care of ethical issues;
6　analysing the data.

Introducing CIT

Once the researcher has gained access s/he should explain succinctly what the nature of the critical incident interview is, and outline the purposes of the research and any possible benefits, particularly where there may be practical and/or policy implications. It is wise to raise issues of confidentiality at this juncture and to give assurances as necessary. This type of interview gives the respondent an opportunity to take 'time out', to reflect upon a number of key issues and events. For this reason it is often enjoyed and viewed by the respondent to be more like a conversation. Thus, establishing a rapport of trust and confidence is important. Conducting the interview where the respondent is uncomfortable or tense does happen but should not be due to the interviewer's presence. Handling feelings is an important skill.

In some instances the respondent appears not to be able to identify any critical incidents. This may be puzzling; as it seems difficult to comprehend that nothing of substance appears to have been happening. Clearly there is an ethical issue in respect of how the interviewer then handles the interview. The interview should not be 'forced', although it may well be more difficult for the interviewer to explore the apparent non-events and lengthy periods of absence of incident with the respondent in a way that yields useful information.

Focusing the theme

The interviewer must focus the respondent's attention and be able to explain succinctly the CIT in the context of the topic to be discussed. The interviewer must be ready for a respondent who will deny that 'anything has happened'. One ploy is to get respondents to think about the sequence of events that have transpired over the past (say) five years by means of a visual aid – a double-arrow-headed line on a single sheet of paper. The respondent is encouraged to mark the position of the 'here and now' and work backwards, marking critical events along its length. This visual aid serves several purposes; it focuses attention, enables the interviewee to relax, jogs the memory and enables the researcher to get a sense of the nature and chronology of any critical events.

The interviewer will then ask the respondent to 'select three events'. S/he may indicate that all incidents have been either negative or positive. The interviewer must accept this initial statement as reflecting the respondent's frame of reference. The interviewee will commence his/her story by recounting one of the events. Some events may be interwoven both in time and in the mind of the respondent therefore the interviewer must listen carefully and probe appropriately to ensure that he/she has fully grasped the essential details.

Controlling the interview

Generic probes seek answers to the following types of question:

What happened next?
Why did it happen?
How did it happen?
With whom did it happen?
What did the parties concerned *feel*?
What were the consequences – immediately and longer term?
How did the respondent cope?
What tactics were used?

Such generic probes are translated into specific questions, which relate to the context, language and rapport of the specific interview. For example, some interjections by the interviewer may seek *clarification:* 'And he came in as a partner?' They help control the flow of the interview and keep the interviewer alert. They also give a breathing space to the respondent to gather her/his thoughts. In highly critical incidents with high emotive content the interview could become a monologue. This is not desirable as the interview may ramble and lose focus. This militates against gaining a genuine understanding by elucidating the nature of the context, which gives the words their particular meaning. Thus the interviewer may seek *further information* until they are satisfied that they *do* understand. It is important, however, that the interviewer does not dominate the discussion or interrogate the respondent; a balance must be struck.

Concluding the interview and taking care of ethical issues

The interview tends to come to an end naturally as the respondent concludes their account. Usually the interviewer will simply thank the respondent for their time and energy in giving such a complete and vivid account of the incidents in question. It may be that the researcher aims to give feedback in a short report or a business seminar. Certainly the researcher must leave the impression that the interview was valuable and that any revelations will be treated with strict confidentiality. Such issues must be addressed before the researcher departs. It is also a morale booster and valuable for the research if the interviewer can leave with a genuine and realistic feeling that s/he will be welcomed if s/he returns.

Analysing the data

The analytic process is likely to be based on a grounded approach; alternatively the researcher may have developed or adopted a conceptual framework, which he/she wishes to test. Grounded theory assumes that the researcher abandons preconceptions and through the process of analysis, builds up an explanatory framework through the conceptualization of the data. Thus there emerge categories of behaviour, context and the strategies adopted for dealing with it. The evidence of patterns of categorical behaviours builds up within a transcript and also in the body of transcripts to enable a theory to be developed. Only after the accumulation of a considerable body of material can the theory move from the substantive to the level of formal theory. An extant conceptual framework, on the other hand, suggests a set of preconceived categories – a coding frame – for which evidence may be sought in the data. Such a framework may not only be tested but also extended using the CIT methodology.

The unit of analysis may be the individual, the group or team, but the CIT allows for the focus to shift, for example, to the organization, the industrial sector or the location. Thus, for example, one may explore overarching concepts like 'climate', 'culture', 'style', and so on by examining the categorical data across the sample as a whole.

A research project has aims and objectives from which central themes are deduced. For example, if the central theme is *business development*, then the coding technique works by first identifying the central idea, in this case business development. This forms the core category. The link between the core category and its subcategories is by means of relational concepts: the conditions in which the action took place, the strategies adopted for dealing with the phenomenon, and the outcomes of the action. The conditions that obtain may be, for example, the need to establish a client base, or to firm up relations with suppliers or to strengthen the top management team. The next step is to identify what strategy the interviewee adopted in order to achieve the particular outcome. The case study shows that the interviewee's initial strategy was to take on a business partner. The CIT enables the coder to examine how this was handled and what the outcome was.

To examine how this was handled is to identify *what events took place*. Thus the critical event identified by the coder in the case to follow is: setting up a business partnership. Further analysis seeks to identify what the *properties* of this event were. In the case these were the quality of the relationship, the individual's performance, the change in business fortunes, and so forth. But how much detail is needed? The answer to this question will clearly depend upon the aims and objectives of the project. However, where further detail is required the *dimensions of properties* are identified. Thus, a relationship may be categorized as close or distant, sad or miserable, firm or fickle, and so on; the individual's performance as effective or ineffective, persistent, insightful or whatever; the business performance as declining, expanding, rejuvenating, plateauing and so on.

Each event adds evidence in relation to the central theme. The business development theme raises the question of *how* the incumbent conducts his/her business. The categories that might suggest themselves are, for example, naively, deviously, opportunistically, and so on. Thus the subcategories may code at a level of considerable detail.

CASE STUDY: A BUSINESS OWNER'S ACCOUNT OF INCIDENTS IMPACTING HIS BUSINESS ACTIVITIES, THEIR CONSEQUENCES FOR HIS FAMILY AND SUBSEQUENT BUSINESS BEHAVIOUR[3]

Objective

The objective was to focus upon the internal dynamics of the micro-business household and to examine the interaction between business and family, with particular reference to entrepreneurial behaviour.

Method

The CIT was conducted at the family home where the business owner also located his business. Both the business owner and his wife were present and both responded to the interviewer's questions.

Background to the case study

Prior to setting up his present micro-business 'Bernard' owned three other small businesses in the service sector. The events, which unfolded, were dramatic and critical both to the demise of those businesses and the establishment, structure and size of the emergent micro-business. Although this is a complex case in which much of the detail has had to be omitted, it illustrates how the critical incident technique may be used to reveal the particular construction placed on events, how incidents were handled and what the consequences were: that is, the context of action, the tactics, strategies and coping mechanisms adopted, and the outcomes, results or consequences of actions, and the new situation with which they are faced.[4] The discussion is presented from the business owner's perspective of a series of negative incidents that impacted upon his business activities (and indeed his domestic and personal life).

The critical incidents which 'Bernard' identified were

(a) bringing in a business partner;
(b) taking up a leasehold property;
(c) fraudulent behaviour of seven staff; and
(d) the asset stripping and loss of the business at the hands of a less than honest solicitor.

In describing these incidents Bernard also highlighted other associated problems.

Focusing the interview initially

The interviewer briefly explained the purpose of the interview and then asked the interviewees if they would give an account of the development of the business over the preceding five years, focusing upon anything that had happened, which they believed had changed its fortunes for either good or ill. To aid this process, the interviewer presented an A4 card containing a double arrow-headed line running centrally along its length. She then asked the interviewees to mark chronologically along its length the significant events that had occurred. The events were labelled on the card, and a brief account of what took place was given. This is an important first stage because the interviewer must be absolutely clear in her mind what in general terms has happened, and in what sequence. Thus the interviewer sought clarification of the respondents until she was clear, and then asked them to select and name three of the incidents for more detailed discussion.

Controlling the interview thereafter

The speech of the interviewees was recorded in detail and punctuated occasionally by probes that refocused attention. For example,

What was the situation with your (business) partner at this time?
Are those figures turnover figures?

The interviewer continued to use probes related both to the details of the situation being described, and, to the central theme (business development) being discussed. For example,

Do you want to make a lot of money?
So all these ideas and the running of your business – what's it all for?

About halfway through the interview, evidence that a relaxed relationship of trust had been established was shown in this quip by the interviewer: 'So what do you do when you're not working – apart from cutting the grass and hitting Bill?' Laughter ensued and the interview continued.

Concluding the interview and taking care of ethical issues

Towards the latter stages of the interview, the discussion broadened out, and refocused briefly on the present business. Owing to his (indeed the whole family's) dire experiences during the failure of the previous businesses, a new business was set up using the latest technology and avoided as far as possible dependence on others. The interview was concluded on a light-hearted note.

The key ethical issues were ensuring that all persons and details were sufficiently well disguised to assure anonymity. In the project as a whole the question of whether the business owner or the couple should be interviewed together or separately, or indeed whether to interview only the business owner and not include the spouse, was addressed. It was decided that where a spouse was involved in the business in some capacity, then it was appropriate that they be included in a joint interview. In the case being presented, both spouses were interviewed together. Indeed, although the daughter was not present, her feelings were discussed as being relevant to the judgement to restructure business activities in such a way as to minimize the impact on the family.

Detailed examination of the incidents: partnership and fraud

Bernard and Bill had worked together before but not as business partners. Initially a reputable firm of accountants bungled the setting up of the business partnership. Subsequently Bill's performance came under question as he tried to switch his attention from one business to another. Turnover dropped and Bill was offered a managing directorship with another company. 'So now he was leaving the ship'. He was given a two year contract with the company which according to Bernard, he then

> . . . decided he would do a management buy-out . . . Up until then he'd felt rather guilty about the state he'd left us in and we were really backs against the wall. And he then came on the phone drunk at night wanting the remainder of his money. But we'd paid him back and starved ourselves of cash . . . and the next thing that occurred . . . we think [was that] he'd been to bed with the manageress and as a result of that seven of them were involved in fraud . . . we had the police in . . . But they couldn't prove who'd actually done it the result was seven members of staff left, and we lost two and a half thousand pounds worth of turnover . . . So now we'd got losses [in all three businesses] . . . that's

> when the home pressure was at its most . . . we started to look at the options [with our accountants] and clearly one of the options was to bin it. Er, but you're very reluctant to do it cos it's like chopping your arm off, in a way, it's still painful . . .

It is not difficult to discern in this brief abstract the different types of information, which are given in the course of the interview: contextual and tactical information and outcomes are all apparent. So too is affective information. Occasionally, of course, what might appear as context could also be construed as an outcome. For example, the initial discussion of Bill's involvement in the business was interpreted as contextual information; it elucidates Bill's decision to join another company, which developed into the disastrous attempt to defraud the company. The outcome of this incident was the dismissal of seven staff, a loss of turnover and the undermining of Bernard's business affairs.

Landlord, accountant and solicitor

In the midst of this crisis the renegotiations of rental on the leasehold of a property blew up. After 18 months, the landlord

> . . . sacked his solicitor and the next thing was he fabricated an invoice and faxed us at half past four on a Friday afternoon . . . We either pay seventeen and a half grand tomorrow . . . or he's going to put the bailiffs in. . . . We had a conflict of interests with our accountants . . . so we decided . . . to go for (a solicitor). He was up in twenty minutes. He arrived on the scene said don't worry about it . . . I'll teach this landlord a lesson . . . What you need to do is tomorrow morning be at court . . . Incidentally what's in the company? . . . We suddenly sort of sat there and said we wished we'd done this before, just such a relief that you know someone is helping us . . . We got down to the court, and just before going in I said, look Mr Black you still haven't told me how much this is going to cost me. And he said, well you'll just have to trust me, won't you? And as soon as he said that I thought, God I've been had. So he said, well you can walk away if you like . . . well I mean I couldn't do that . . . and cutting a long story short, he robbed us of the company . . . He took thousands of pounds out in fees, he flogged the company to his mate, asset stripped it and they're now trading, and we got nothing . . . He screwed the paperwork up, didn't serve notice on the landlord . . . He cleared off to Australia for his holidays. The bailiff's came up . . . the landlord broke in with two heavies . . . So emotionally it was like devastating.

Bernard complained to the Institute of Chartered Accountants (ICA) and also got his MP involved but to no avail.

> So, you can imagine what that was like . . . there's a lot of bitterness, resentment, anger that comes out of that . . . [It] was like three years ago now . . . [Joan's attitude was] good riddance. My attitude is – this is wrong . . . I feel impotent that I can't deal with this . . .

This second set of incidents is presented largely in the interviewees' own words. It commences with an account of the situation facing them (context) and then proceeds to the tactics adopted by the couple in an attempt to manage their affairs ('so we decided . . .'). Interspersed throughout the account of what happened next is a description of their feelings, followed by a statement of the outcome of the incident. Next, an account of what happened further is given, again followed by an outline of Bernard's tactics (he complained to the ICA). This is rounded off by an indication of further outcomes including attendant feelings: 'now I feel impotent'. During the course of these revelations, the interviewer probed in order to seek clarification. The interviewees were forthcoming throughout. In many cases, however, the interviewer would need to probe rather more by following up leads and asking more questions. In the next excerpt of the CIT interview, the flow is much more interactive, with the interviewer checking out her understanding, and posing questions in order to clarify.

Controlling the interview

Once the overall story had been given, the interviewer probed for any additional information and reflection. In this excerpt, Bernard discusses the effect on the family and then he reflects on the cause – Bill, who had put the business into jeopardy.

Interviewer: Do you blame it on him or . . . ?
Bernard: No, cos I blame myself.
Interviewer: Was he partly responsible?
Bernard: We could have coped with him, we could have coped with the fraud, no problem, and we could have coped with them together. What we couldn't cope with was the lot. We couldn't cope with him, the fraud, the leasehold property deal, that's what brought us down, it was a combination of all those.

Bernard reflected further on the effect that these incidents had had on him, for example, how he'd lost respect for institutions and other systems of authority and how his attitude and feelings in respect of the new business had changed

Joan: It was quite amazing how one's mistakes have such a knock-on effect – that was the frightening thing.
Interviewer: What was the mistake?
Joan: Bill.
Interviewer: Did you have any doubts about Bill?
Joan: No . . . I thought Bernard was getting a bit bored . . . and wanted to do something . . . I actually thought Bill would be the motivational tool . . . we knew the downside but we didn't look at that – but you don't when you're on the crest of a wave.
Interviewer: So how do you cope with stress?

Bernard then described help that he got from a reflexologist.

Bernard: It was almost like physical venom. It was almost like being sick. It sounds awful, but it was almost solid, and I felt this terrific badness . . . coming out, and at the end of it she said, now think of something nice. And I did . . . so she helped me enormously.
Joan: You went and thumped Bill and that helped as well didn't it?

Bernard actually described this event in detail and how the family felt about it. Interviewer: 'Did it make you feel better?' The answer was in the affirmative from both spouses!

DISCUSSION

Analytical issues

The above excerpts from a transcripted interview with a business owner and his wife are heavily edited. In describing in detail four critical incidents the respondent painted a context out of which arose his present business – a micro-business which he runs from home. His motivation to develop that business had been dashed, and he has operated with extreme caution when it was a question of with whom he would do deals. Given this and his entrepreneurial nature (Chell et al., 1991) the research made it possible to construct a coherent explanation as to why such an individual was operating on such a small scale.

Reading through the transcript, one has to disentangle the chronology of events. In the case, they overlapped in time and as the respondent points out, it was having to cope with all four that added to the criticality. In analysing these incidents, it is important to note the type of incident. They were: a problem with the business partner, rental of a leasehold property, and fraud perpetrated by employees and a dishonest solicitor. This finding can be extended by asking: 'Are such incidents typical of the development activities of micro-businesses in the business services sector?'

A further observation is the timescale and duration of the incidents. In the case it was over a two-year period. Being unable to get along with one's business partner is not untypical. As with a marriage, severing the ties may be difficult and it is during the period of separation that the real damage is done. The business partner Bill, we are told, did not fit in, became aggressive and is alleged to have become involved in fraud. Whilst we have not got the whole story (nor could we have!) we have sufficient detail of the nature of this incident to be confident about its detrimental effect. Both spouses appeared to be taken in by Bill, believing him to be a useful addition who would give a growth spurt to at least one of the businesses. What we do not know is how Bernard handled Bill, or indeed if he was frozen out of this close knit husband and wife team (Chell and Baines, 1998).

The incident over the leasehold and the 'crooked landlord' appeared to be sheer bad luck. But was it? Bernard's 8-year-old daughter had said, 'Daddy why do you deal with these people?' and he commented, ' . . . you make your own work . . . '. In other words, people create their own luck; they can create a situation that increases the probability of a particular outcome. In this case, by associating with people who tended towards dishonesty the likelihood of one of them 'doing him' was thereby increased. As a consequence of this glimmer of self-awareness Bernard changed his lifestyle, his business activity and his friends. Other outcomes of this case were that Bernard addressed the issue of the impact that such events were having on his family. He set up a much smaller scale operation, which relied less on other people and rather more on new technology. He and his wife increased their leisure and time spent at home.

Phenomenological approach

This method enables a focused discussion around issues under investigation and it facilitates the revelation of those issues, which are of crucial importance to the interviewee. This was evident in the case where incidents unfolded showing a strong negative relationship to the development of the business. The actual incidents could not have been anticipated. The choice of what incidents to recount is under the control of the interviewee. The skilled interviewer will attempt to ensure that there is thorough coverage.

The CIT enables the issues to be viewed in context and is also a rich source of information on the conscious reflections of the incumbent, their frame of reference, feelings, attitudes and perspective on matters which are of critical importance to them. Bernard, for example, recounted how they were cheated of their company and what that felt like. Both he and his wife were able to put the incidents in perspective, for example, as they contemplated their 'knock-on effects': how 'frightening' this all was. The information revealed using CIT enables a fine-grained analysis and detailed explanation of the behaviour of the incumbent and the outcomes of behavioural and managerial processes. Whilst other methods may also enable the researcher to achieve this, the advantage of the CIT is that the linkage between context, strategy and outcomes is more readily teased out because the technique is focused on an event, which is explicated in relation to what happened, why it happened, how it was handled and what the consequences were. An unstructured interview does not require the respondent to focus in this way.

Whilst phenomenology assumes the uniqueness of individual consciousness, the interpretivism CIT enables the researcher to gain insights both into particular cases and across a sample of cases. For example, if the subset of cases is self-employed women with children, single parents, business owners at start-ups, and so on, then typical issues raised by the particular subset may be identified. Is there a common set of problems? In the case study outlined above, the questions arise: are problems with business partners typical or rare? Do problems with other relationships typically occur, for example with subordinates?

Even where an extant conceptual framework is adopted, there is scope not only to test but also to extend theory. Thus the CIT enables inductive theory development by adopting a grounded theory approach (Strauss and Corbin, 1990). Further, the CIT is particularly useful for comparative work. Case studies may be built up of specifiable organizational contexts, critical incidents, the strategies adopted to handle them and the outcomes. This compares with clinical work in the sense that, whilst cases are examined individually, patterns of behaviour may be discernible that may inform theory, policy and practice. It can, however, be used where there is more than one interviewee, as was true in the above case study (compare Yin, 1994: 32–45). Further, as pointed out by Schultz and Hatch (1996), taking a multiparadigm approach, there are similarities and differences between the aims and the types of data that may be revealed from each paradigm. Both expose patterns that yield insights into the workings of human nature in interaction with others.

Ethical issues

Subjectivity and personal interpretation of matters of crucial importance to individuals increases the likelihood of ethical considerations. There are confidentiality issues, which must be respected as respondents may name other people and/or their businesses putting them in a light which may constitute slander, or in some cases hint at criminal activity. In such cases a strict code of ethics and a procedure for handling tape-recorded and transcripted material is essential in order to protect all parties and the integrity of the research process.

The security of individual researchers is a consideration where the interview is to be carried out at the interviewee's home or in a context or location where common sense would suggest caution.

Methodological issues

GENERALIZABILITY

A view may be taken that research which is not based on large quantitative sample surveys, is insufficiently generalizable to be of value in the creation of organizational knowledge for academic or policy purposes. Qualitative researchers are challenging this view. The heterogeneity of populations of organizations and of their owner-managers suggests that smaller samples tightly controlled for structural and other relevant dimensions are likely to have greater explanatory power than could be revealed by a large scale survey, although of course the latter may be useful for other purposes. In organizational behaviour, understanding the detail of the processes and behaviours is paramount and a technique such as CIT enables such an objective to be accomplished.

RELIABILITY

The CIT interview is not easy to conduct well. It requires a skilled and mature researcher who can manage the respondent, directing the interview to achieve clarity of understanding and who can handle the expression of emotion including distress. Of course not all respondents will reveal negative incidents and here the interviewer must be able to probe sensitively and not be carried away by the wave of success which the respondent may be putting across. In other words the interviewer must under all circumstances try to establish a rapport of trust, honest and open exchange. In the above case study, the interviewer probed with relevant questions, first to ensure her understanding, and secondly to ensure that the account did not become a monologue. Thus the interaction between interviewer and interviewee can help control the pace, add light relief and steer the interview so that it remains focused. Further, the interviewer should reflect upon their role as interviewer, the style adopted and the way the interview was conducted.

An added difficulty of conducting the interview well is attempting to ensure that all critical incidents have been captured. Indeed as has been pointed out, some interviewees do not always appear to be able to identify a single incident. Should this arise, the interviewer needs to deal with it skilfully and ethically. Clearly in an inductive situation, whether all incidents have or have not been identified cannot be 'proved'. Techniques such as the arrow diagram help assure this part of the process. However, critics evaluating this method might argue that it is difficult to test for reliability (compare, Andersson and Nilsson, 1964). There are several things that can be done in order to improve reliability. For example, the possibility of conducting more than one interview with the subject should always be considered. Time, budget and access considerations are likely constraints. The key issue is whether additional interviews are likely to improve reliability and should they be conducted under the same circumstances? Would it be desirable were the same incidents to be discussed with a 'relevant other'? Clearly the answer to this question is a matter of judgement. For example, it is likely to be resisted by an employer in relation to an employee and spouses in relation to each other. However, the point is that one is trying not to find a 'single truth' but to understand the respondent's perspectives and actions. The reliability therefore is largely built into a quality interview process in which there is coherence. It may still be thought desirable to triangulate the results with other sources of data, particularly where there may be tangible evidence.

CONCLUDING REMARKS

The creation of management knowledge has relied upon the scientific method for the earlier part of this century. Phenomenology was considered to be an approach associated with esoteric areas of sociological or cultural anthropological enquiry (Burrell and Morgan, 1979). Now management researchers recognize the need to identify and explain processes, which go on within organizations. There is no textbook answer to what is a dynamic process and real life is messy; the people immersed in those situations and circumstances are trying to make sense of them (Weick, 1995). Their accounts are partial; but partial or not, biased or not, such accounts constitute *their* reality, and, arguably, it is the way they view the world which shapes their future actions. How if those closest to the events have only a partial view which they may not have clearly articulated, can we as researchers hope to collect valid data by use of extensive survey techniques? How can we hope to gain a genuine understanding of the persons involved in an organizational drama if we do not know anything of the context? The case of Bernard illustrates graphically this point. Had we not known about his previous business undertakings and the circumstances surrounding their unfortunate demise we would not be able to understand him and his present business activity.

Some critics have been known to question the integrity of qualitative researchers: 'how do we know that they haven't made it up?' Such a criticism misses the point; the point is that the qualitative researcher can only present an interpretation of the events recounted to them. The value of this approach is that it yields genuine insights into the processes, which shape behaviour, and as a coherent account it has face validity. Furthermore, the integrity of research is maintained by either permitting public access or disseminating sufficiently widely so enabling wider debate and critical appraisal.

Finally, an advantage of adopting the CIT is that it permits a degree of replication. Whilst the individual firm's circumstances may be unique, the type of incident, the context, strategy and outcomes as a pattern of related activities may in general terms be apparent in other businesses. The relationship between these actions and activities is *contingent*. This contrasts with the nature of the relations assumed within the positivist paradigm. There the relation is causal. CIT enables the development of case based theory grounded in actual critical events that shape future actions. The insights gleaned and the conclusions drawn not only facilitate the development of theory but also policy. In combination with the application of grounded theory (Strauss and Corbin, 1990), CIT is capable of extending our theoretical understanding and our ability to explain organizational behaviour.

NOTES

1 Current developments in methodology pursue multiparadigm enquiries that combine both functionalist and interpretivist paradigms. The method known as *interplay* enables the researcher to identify data that highlights similarities and differences revealed by the two methodologies (Schultz and Hatch, 1996). This is one approach that enables the identification of both *pattern* that is generalizable and *essence* that is contextually specific. The CIT is likely to be a useful tool for the development of such a methodological approach (Cope and Watts, 2000; Chell and Allman, 2003).

2 'Outcomes' is a difficult concept. In the context of the application of the CIT method, the discussion indicates a consequence that has been identified by the interviewee. Such

consequences do not have a necessary causal relation with context and strategy, rather these are contingent relations. None the less, in building up case evidence modelled on the operation of a 'clinic', the categorization of outcomes linked to context and strategy facilitates the identification of a meaningful pattern of behaviour.

3 The case study material was collected and developed from a research project funded by the Economic and Social Research Council (ESRC) grant number R00234402. I would like to acknowledge the particular assistance of Dr Sue Baines and Dr Alison Abrams for their part in the data collection process and subsequent discussion of the particularities of the case. The sample of business owners included: sole female; sole male; husband and wife; joint male; joint female; and joint non-related male and female.

4 Although beyond the scope of the present study, cases such as this show that experiential learning has taken place. The subject has reflected on his experience and modifies his future decisions and actions accordingly.

FURTHER READING

There are no other texts that describe how the Critical Incident Technique may be used but the following readings show how the CIT has been used for particular kinds of research. They principally concern entrepreneurship/organizational behaviour issues, however, there is also a literature stream for the hospitality industries sector that uses the CIT in a slightly different way.

E. Chell (2003) 'The critical incident technique', in M. Lewis-Beck, A. Bryman and T. Futing Liao (eds), *The Encyclopaedia of Research Methods in the Social Sciences*, Thousand Oaks, CA: Sage (forthcoming).

E. Chell, J.M. Haworth and S. Brearley (1991) *The Entrepreneurial Personality: Concepts, Cases and Categories*, London: Routledge.

E. Chell and L. Pittaway (1998) 'A study of entrepreneurship in the restaurant and café industry: exploratory work using the critical incident technique as a methodology', *International Journal of Hospitality Management*, 17 (1): 23–32.

J. Cope and G. Watts (2000) 'Learning by doing: an exploration of experience, critical incidents and reflection in entrepreneurial learning', *International Journal of Entrepreneurial Behaviour and Research*, 6 (3): 104–24.

J.C. Flanagan (1954) 'The critical incident technique', *Psychological Bulletin*, 51 (4): 327- 58.

L. Pittaway (2000) 'The social construction of entrepreneurial behaviour'. PhD dissertation, University of Newcastle upon Tyne, UK, especially pp.220–30, 233–40, 245–60, 270–6.

REFERENCES

Andersson, B.E. and Nilsson, S.G. (1964) 'Studies in the reliability and validity of the critical incident technique', *Journal of Applied Psychology*, 48 (1): 398–403.

Bryman, A. (1989) *Research Methods and Organization Studies*, London and New York: Routledge.

Burrell, G. and Morgan, G. (1979) *Sociological Paradigms and Organizational Analysis*, London: Heinemann.

Chell, E. (1998) 'The critical incident technique', in G. Symon and C. Cassell et al. (eds), *Qualitative Methods and Analysis in Organizational Research – A Practical Guide*, London: Sage, pp.51–72.

Chell, E. and Adam, E. (1994a) 'Exploring the cultural orientation of entrepreneurship: conceptual and methodological issues'. Discussion Paper No. 94–7, School of Business Management, University of Newcastle upon Tyne.

Chell, E. and Adam, E. (1994b) 'Researching culture and entrepreneurship: a qualitative approach'. Discussion Paper No.94–9, School of Business Management, University of Newcastle upon Tyne.

Chell, E. and Adam, E. (1995) 'Entrepreneurship and culture in New Zealand'. Discussion Paper No.95–8, Department of Management Studies, University of Newcastle upon Tyne.

Chell, E. and Allman, K. (2003) 'Mapping the motivations and intensions technology oriented entrepreneurs', *R & D Management*, 33 (2): 117–34.

Chell, E. and Baines, S. (1998) 'Does gender affect business performance? A study of microbusinesses in business services in the UK', *International Journal of Entrepreneurship and Regional Development*, 10(4): 117–35.

Chell, E., Haworth, J.M. and Brearley, S. (1991) *The Entrepreneurial Personality: Concepts, Cases and Categories*, London: Routledge.

Chell, E. and Pittaway, L. (1998) 'A study of entrepreneurship in the restaurant and café industry: exploratory work using the critical incident technique as a methodology', *International Journal of Hospitality Management*, 17 (1): 23–32.

Cope, J. and Watts, G. (2000) 'Learning by doing: an exploration of experience, critical incidents and reflection in entrepreneurial learning', *International Journal of Entrepreneurial Behaviour and Research*, 6 (3): 104–24.

Curran, J., Jarvis, R., Blackburn, R.A. and Black, S. (1993) 'Networks and small firms: constructs, methodological strategies and some findings', *International Small Business Journal*, 11 (2): 13–25.

Flanagan, J.C. (1954) 'The critical incident technique', *Psychological Bulletin*, 51 (4): 327–58.

Glaser, B. and Strauss, A. (1967) *The Discovery of Grounded Theory*, Chicago: Aldine.

Haworth, J.M., Brearley, S. and Chell, E. (1991) 'A typology of business owners and their firms using neural networks', *Entrepreneurship and Regional Development*, 33 (3): 221–35.

McClelland, D.C. (1976) *A Guide to Job Competency Assessment*, Boston: McBer & Co.

McClelland, D.C. (1987) 'Characteristics of successful entrepreneurs', *Journal of Creative Behaviour*, 21 (3): 219–33.

Morgan, G. and Smircich, L. (1980) 'The case for qualitative research', *Academy of Management Review*, 5 (4): 491–500.

Pittaway, L. (2000) 'The social construction of entrepreneurial behaviour'. PhD dissertation, University of Newcastle upon Tyne, UK.

Pittaway, L. and Chell, E. (1999) 'Entrepreneurship in the service firm life cycle', Proceedings of the eighth annual CHME Hospitality Research Conference volume 1 (April 7–9): 203–19, University of Surrey, UK.

Ronan, W.W. and Latham, G.P. (1974) 'The reliability and validity of the critical incident technique: a closer look', *Studies in Personnel Psychology*, 6 (1): 53–64.

Schultz, M. and Hatch, M.J. (1996) 'Living with multiple paradigms: the case of paradigm interplay in organizational culture studies', *Academy of Management Review*, 21 (2): 529–557.

Spencer, L.M. (1983) *Soft Skill Competencies*, Scottish Council for Research in Education.

Strauss, A. and Corbin, J. (1990) *Basics of Qualitative Research: Grounded Theory Procedures and Techniques*, London: Sage.

Weick, K.E. (1995) *Sensemaking in Organizations*, Thousand Oaks, CA: Sage.

Wheelock, J. and Chell, E. (1996) *The Business-owner Managed Family Unit: An Inter-Regional Comparison of Behavioural Dynamics*, Ref. No R000234402, London: Economic and Social Research Council.

Yin, R.K. (1994) *Case Study Research: Design and Methods*, second edition, Thousand Oaks, CA: Sage.

6

—— **Repertory Grids** ————————————————————————————

Catherine Cassell and Susan Walsh

The repertory grid technique stems from the personal construct psychology (PCP) proposed by George Kelly (1955). It is a well-used technique within psychological research although, traditionally, repertory grids have predominantly been analysed using quantitative techniques. In this chapter, we focus on how repertory grids can be analysed in a qualitative way, indeed we argue that this is more appropriate given their underlying constructivist epistemology. First, we outline the principles of Kelly's personal construct psychology and review the use of repertory grid technique in organizational research. We then describe a study we conducted using repertory grid technique, and finish by evaluating the advantages and disadvantages of using repertory grids in a qualitative manner.

KELLY'S PERSONAL CONSTRUCT PSYCHOLOGY ————————————————————————

Kelly believed that individuals act like scientists, continuously striving to make sense of their world and their place within it. A key notion within PCP is that the individual is an inquiring person (Bannister and Fransella, 1977). This implies that the unique principle that governs human behaviour is the need for meaning which includes the need to make sense of the world. In order to do this individuals develop constructions (or theories) of themselves and their world. These constructs change as we experience events that confirm or disconfirm previous predictions we have made based on our existing construct system. Kelly therefore adopts an explicit ontological and epistemological stance. The repertory grid is located within the philosophy of constructivism, namely we all create and make sense of our own worlds. Salmon (1978) suggests that Kelly's psychology is all about the sensemaking process, about how we come to know what we know, and how we live out that knowledge. She suggests that the central feature of it all is the 'absence of any single, final version of reality' (Salmon, 1978: 43).

In seeking to understand the processes of personal sensemaking it is recognized that our constructs develop through negotiations with others. Kelly also stresses that our construct system is often unarticulated or implicit, and the exploration and elaboration of these systems is therefore a key theme. This philosophy shapes how both researcher and the researched are perceived. As Salmon (1978) suggests:

> One consequence of his particular view of construct systems as *personal* is the emergence of both the researcher and any subjects he [sic] may be working with, as salient personal figures. From a Kellyan standpoint, the convention of a non-person, black box of an investigator, and a group of subjects described only by some crudely defined common denominator, is totally inappropriate. (1978: 41)

The key point here is that in Kelly's personal construct psychology there are a set of significant principles about human behaviour and the undertaking of research which are represented within the repertory grid technique.

THE REPERTORY GRID TECHNIQUE IN ORGANIZATIONAL RESEARCH

The basic tenets of personal construct psychology provide the rationale for the repertory grid technique, which is a technique for accessing an individual's personal constructs. Gammack and Stephens (1994) suggest that although there are variations to repertory grid techniques, they all contain three basic stages:

1   The elicitation of elements, identifying the entities in the area of construing to be investigated.
2   The elicitation of constructs, identifying the distinctions which can be applied amongst these elements; and
3   The construction of a matrix (grid) of elements and constructs (1994: 76).

The technique provides a way of accessing an individual's unique set of personal constructs, and therefore enables the researcher to access an individual's view of reality (Gammack and Stephens, 1994).

Up until the 1960s the great majority of repertory grid studies had a clinical focus (Easterby-Smith et al., 1996), however during the last 20 years the technique has been increasingly used in organizational psychology. Jankowicz (1990) outlines the numerous ways in which PCP has been applied to business practice. He argues that repertory grids have been applied to a wide range of areas, for example job analysis (Smith, 1986); employment selection (Anderson, 1990); induction training (Stewart and Stewart, 1982); risk analysis (Gammack and Stephens, 1994); and training evaluation (Easterby-Smith, 1980). Additional areas in the work psychology field are: graduate careers (Arnold and Nicholson, 1991), transition (Fournier and Payne, 1994); introduction of new manufacturing practices (Parker et al., 1994); and gender differences in performance evaluation (Dick and Jankowicz, 2001). He suggests that this diversity in applications reflects the flexibility of the technique. This extensive range of applications is not surprising given the relative advantages that repertory grids have over other methods of data collection. Easterby-Smith et al. (1996) point out that the value of repertory grids includes the following:

> The fact that perceptions of nebulous relationships can be written down rigorously by someone who is not a trained psychologist, is itself significant. The visual representation helps to focus the analysis and makes communication about them easier. It also involves verbalizing constructs which would otherwise remain hidden . . . . at a personal level it may be a way of generating self-insights. Most importantly, the grid provides a representation of the individual's own world; it is not a model imposed by an outsider. As such the individual can explore the world for him/ herself. (1996: 6)

Hence it would seem that the use of repertory grids engenders reflexivity: the ability to think about one's own thinking (Bourdieu, 1990). This is an advantage that we would argue has potentially been undermined by the over-quantification of grid data. Where repertory grids have been used in organizational psychology research, quantitative methods of data analysis have traditionally been utilized. The increasingly sophisticated computer packages available have focused on looking for statistical similarity between constructs through forms of factor and cluster analysis, or on construct groupings through principal components analysis for example. However the danger of the developments in statistical analysis that accompanies grid data is a move away from the central point of concern: understanding how the individual makes sense of the world. As Bannister (1985) suggests, the grid has become

> a Frankenstein's monster rushed away on a statistical and experimental rampage of its own, leaving construct theory neglected, stranded high and dry, far behind. (1985: xii)

This poses problems for a technique that is used within an interview setting and essentially has a qualitative focus on language (Easterby-Smith et al., 1996). Our approach to data analysis fits in with that of Gammack and Stephens (1994) who remind us that the grid is most meaningfully grounded within Kelly's PCP as a 'conversational technology' (1994: 76). The value of the grids to the study reported here lies in providing significant cues and clues in the respondent's own language about the ways in which performance is evaluated and assessed within their own working world. The background to the study is outlined below.

BACKGROUND TO THE RESEARCH

The two authors of the chapter were approached by a number of senior women in the UK publishing industry who were keen to commission a piece of research to investigate the barriers to women's progression within the publishing industry. This group were explicitly concerned with generating qualitative data about the issues. They felt that there was already a wide range of quantitative information about women's position but that more detailed research was needed that could potentially address some of the more subtle covert barriers that prevented women from reaching the top. It was felt that a study was needed which explored the interrelationships, if any, between cultural aspects of an organization, and an individual's internal sense of themselves.

The situation of women in publishing is an interesting one in that, despite the roughly equal number of women and men who enter publishing, it is clear that beyond a certain grade that equivalence disappears. A large-scale quantitative survey carried out by Tomlinson and Colgan (1989) identified that women within publishing were under-represented at the top tiers of the industry and that 'men are more than twice as likely to become managers, and more than five times as likely to be a company board director' (1989: 9).

The aims of the research were to: explore the covert barriers to progression within the publishing industry with a particular emphasis on the experience of women; to identify aspects of organizational culture which impacted on the success of women; and to describe how men and women viewed their own opportunities for achieving success. Previous research using repertory grids has demonstrated that a person's self-concept is often viewed as a crucial influence on their career decisions and other behaviours (Arnold and Nicholson, 1991). Therefore a way of examining personal experiences was particularly pertinent to this research given the key issue of how women see themselves and their opportunities within the publishing industry. The repertory grids were used to map participants' perceptions of themselves and others within the organizations in relation to organizational success. The method was chosen for its sensitivity in assessing an individual's view of the world: in this case their view of their organization and their place within it. The explicit comparison between oneself and others is a key element of the repertory grid. We would expect such a comparison to be particularly important in a work context.

THE RESEARCH

Four publishing companies took part in the study: two from the trade sector and two from the information/education sector. Sixty employees were interviewed (15 participants from each company: 9 women and 6 men). The researchers chose a range of interviewees on the basis that their job descriptions covered a range of roles and responsibilities. Each interview lasted approximately an hour and was conducted during work time. During the initial stages of the interview (lasting about 10–15 minutes), respondents were asked a variety of open-ended questions about: their career history; their experiences of working with the firm; their views about the company, its values and environment and their own role within it; and their views of any equal opportunities policies. The individual's responses were recorded in note form by the researchers.

The second stage of the interview involved eliciting a number of constructs from interviewees using the repertory grid technique. Eleven elements were used that represented those who took on key roles in a participant's personal or professional life. These were: a competent management at work; an incompetent manager at work; my closest friend; my line manager; a female work colleague; my mother; my father; an important person in the hierarchy at work; a male work colleague; someone who supports me at work; and myself. Interviewees were asked to bring to mind an individual who fitted in to each of those categories. Interestingly the only category any of the participants had problems with was that of an 'incompetent manager at work'. A number of individuals told us that there were no incompetent people in their organization. When that was the case we suggested that they choose a manager who they respected a little less than other managers to fit in to that category. A separate individual was chosen for each element.

These elements were then presented in varying triad combinations and interviewees were asked to characterize how two of the individuals were similar in some respect of their work behaviour, but different from a third. The triads were presented in varying combinations 10 times to each interviewee. These combinations were standardized so that each interviewee addressed the same combinations at the same stage of the interview. The constructs that the interviewees generated were then written onto the grid. Any comments the interviewee made during the elicitation process were noted. Once the grid was complete interviewees moved into stage three of the interview process. Here issues that emerged in the grid were followed up with a particular emphasis on what behaviours individuals thought were important to do a good job and what behaviours they felt led to success in the company. Specifically individuals were asked to mark on the grid using a scale of 1 to 7 the extent to which they felt a particular behaviour was important to them doing a good job, and the extent to which they thought each behaviour led to success in the company. Therefore any discrepancies between the two could be identified. An example of a completed repertory grid is shown in Table 6.1.

In practice this is a deviation from the way in which repertory grids are usually conducted. After the grid has been constructed it is usual to ask the interviewee to rate all the elements

Table 6.1 An example of a completed repertory grid

In control	√	X					Out of control
Accessible		X	√				Untrustworthy/Impersonal
Mild in views			X		√		Dominant and forceful
Self-confident	√				X		Lacking in confidence
Concerned with people around them		X		√			No concern with the impact of their actions
Ambitious in career	√			X			Not ambitious
Impulsive, ill-considered					√	X	Objective and calm
High academic achievement		X	√				Solid, down to earth
Consistent achiever	√	X					Inconsistent achiever
Immense ambition		√		X			Comfortable with themselves

X The extent to which this behaviour is important for me to do a good job
√ The extent to which this behaviour is important to be successful in the company

on each of the constructs. We deviated from this traditional procedure in this research because we were keen to identify any potential discrepancies between men's and women's views of effective performance as outlined above. As you can see from Table 6.1, the interviewee feels that in order to do a good job he needs to be 'concerned with the people around him', but this is not a behaviour that is necessarily rewarded by the company. The opposite can be said for 'confidence' and 'ambition', two constructs that are seen to be important for success in the company, but that the interviewee perceives as not that necessary to do a good job.

A total of 562 constructs were generated from the 60 grids. Each repertory grid in itself is a rich source of data, consequently the first stage of analysis involved the researchers in the process of 'immersion' (King, 1994) where we read and studied the grids numerous times in order to familiarize ourselves with the data and look for meaningful patterns, for example within organizations. At the second stage in order to analyse the grid data we began by generating categories in line with the processes of grounded theory (Glaser and Strauss, 1967; Henwood and Pidgeon, 1992; Länsisalmi et al., Chapter 20, this volume). We referred to these categories as themes. In this approach the themes do not emerge from some pre-existing theoretical concerns, but rather from the data themselves. This is consistent with Kelly's PCP and the general philosophy underlying repertory grid technique. Each construct was examined in turn to generate the initial set of themes, within which each construct could be placed. The themes were then altered or regrouped as a result of the process of splitting or splicing themes where appropriate. The next stage of the analysis involved the researchers discussing the construct theme allocations together, to see whether any alternative interpretations could have occurred. One of the aims of this discussion was to assess the extent to which the data were trustworthy or credible, that is did the allocation of a construct to a particular theme make sense? In discussing these allocations, making sense of the meaning of constructs was enhanced by having access to the comments made by interviewees as part of the interview process.

Where it was felt that a construct could fit into more than one category, then it was dual categorized. The aim of this process was to make the data more manageable, through reducing it so that we could look for similarities and differences within the constructs generated by men and women. Initially separate sets of categories were generated from the data for the male and female interviewees to enable us to examine whether certain issues emerged as being more pertinent to one particular group. When trying to look at the themes that emerged in this way, there was considerable overlap, so it seemed more appropriate to generate a set of themes for the participants as a whole. The 562 constructs were therefore divided into a set of 40 themes that covered both male and female responses. Examples of themes were *ambition*; *work/home split*; *confidence*; and *approachability*. Examples of two of these themes are shown in Table 6.2.

Table 6.2 An example of the categorization of constructs into themes

Theme	Construct examples
Ambition	Drive/less apparent sense of drive
	Immense ambition/comfortable with themselves
	Fiercely ambitious/career not driving force
	Unambitious/Ambitious
	Wanting to be recognized/not ambitious
	Socialist/ambitious
	Ambitious/satisfied with current achievements
	Clearly ambitious/content where you are
Work/home split	Job is whole life/has other priorities e.g. domestic
	Loyal to family/loyal to firm
	Family put first/profession put first
	Career oriented/family oriented
	Family focus/work, professional focus
	Family as priority/work as priority

Each construct was allocated to a particular theme. For example the theme *ambition* contains constructs such as 'ambitious/satisfied with current achievements' and 'clearly ambitious/content where you are'. By counting the number of constructs entered into each theme we could indicate the issues that were mentioned the most by the interviewees. Clearly this raises an issue of how we were using numbers in that we were assuming that because a construct was used by a larger number of interviewees it had more salience to the respondents as a whole. We made this assumption because we needed to make some claims about how men and women experienced aspects of the culture and what differences, if any, there were between the different groups. Therefore there was a need to aggregate data in this simple way. But where does this leave us epistemologically? We would argue that by counting which were the most common constructs used we were not necessarily deviating from Kelly's constructivist approach, in that the main focus was still on how the individuals concerned constructed and made sense of their working world. However it could be argued that aggregating responses to be able to say things about groups does deviate from Kelly's stance. This would however render much of the work done using repertory grids outside of the individual clinical setting as a similar deviation. As well as counting we also looked at the different constructs that were in each particular theme and made some interpretation that became our findings. For example we saw at this stage that most of the responses in the theme of 'work/home split' came from women, and that they had numerous different ways of referring to the tensions that emerged from trying to combine a family life with a publishing career, some of which are outlined in Table 6.2.

The next stage involved looking at the responses that individuals had given in answer to the two questions about the prerequisites for organizational success and how the individual saw them. By looking at the grids we could see where individuals felt discrepancies occurred between their views and the views they perceived within the company more generally. However it is important to note that we did not give a numerical value to these discrepancies, as we felt this would not be coherent with our overall constructivist approach. Rather we noted the constructs on which the discrepancies were more likely to occur. The findings of the data analysis are outlined in the next section.

FINDINGS FROM THE RESEARCH

The rich findings covered a number of areas: the culture of the publishing industry; barriers to women's progression in the workplace; and different constructions of success. These three areas represent the research questions that formed the basis for this study. The repertory grid data and the interview data were taken together to produce the findings. In this sense, part of the role of the construct elicitation process is to create a conversation around the pertinent issues.

The culture of the publishing industry

Analysis of the repertory grids and the interviews suggested that the cultures of the four separate organizations, despite having some similarities, were really quite different. In particular there were clear differences between trade and information/educational.

Interviewees in all the organizations were keen to point out that the outsider's view of the publishing industry, as a whole, was often quite inaccurate. The common view was that those outside the industry often saw it as a very glamorous area to work:

> It's not glamorous, outsiders just don't understand, there's a lot more to it than people expect, it's a lot more technical than you think, people have an image of publishers swanning about, it's not like that, there's a tight budget for a start.

A number of interviewees suggested that outsiders often had no conception of the complex processes that occurred during the production of a book. Indeed one theme that emerged from the repertory grid analysis – which covered a number of constructs that nearly all interviewees commented on in the interviews – was the extent to which the industry had changed over the last 10 years to a more business oriented and market focused culture:

> Publishing is about making sound commercial decisions about what people need and want . . . It used to be a gentleman's profession, but now we've had to tighten our act up – we need to publish things quickly and cheaply.

This change was experienced by those who had worked in the industry for a long time as creating a far more pressurized work environment, despite the fact that individuals often had clearer targets to achieve. The issue of constant change was very important, and being able to deal with change and implement it successfully as a manager often emerged as a construct within interviewees' repertory grids.

Another major theme that emerged from the repertory grid data within each organization was the commitment that individuals were expected to have towards their jobs and publishing as a whole. The notion of a 'workaholic culture' was raised frequently. In general, publishing personnel were seen as extremely committed to their work, indeed a number of interviewees talked of loving their work:

> You get bitten by the bug, people love it and are very dedicated . . .

One interviewee suggested that the whole industry was dependent on the fact that individuals loved their work and as a consequence were prepared to work numerous extra hours in order to do their job effectively. Others suggested that generally the pay was not very good, so people would not be there if they did not find the work so attractive. The emphasis on commitment and workaholism clearly has implications for equal opportunities which are discussed in more detail later.

Barriers to women's progression

A consensus amongst interviewees was apparent in that all agreed that there were no obvious cases of discrimination against women within their organizations. Issues to do with equal opportunities for women were rarely recognized as important, mainly because they did not emerge as problematic within everyday working life. Additionally, within the sample of 60 interviewees there were no clear differences in career aspirations between men and women. There was no evidence to suggest therefore that women did not want to climb the career ladder in the publishing industry, though some individuals set their sights higher than others. Despite the lack of overt barriers to success there was a clear sense from many of the interviewees that barriers did exist to hinder women in the achievement of their career ambitions. These barriers were perceived as difficult to see and outline, but were nevertheless, highly significant.

The most pertinent issue to the female interviewees related to issues around having children, and how that was perceived as fitting into their working lives. The theme of work/home split contained more constructs than any other theme, by far the majority coming from women. Each of the organizations was seen as having good human resource policies in relation to women. Women were seen to be encouraged to develop through management training, and a range of policies were available for women who wanted to take time out to have children. Despite the existence of such policies many of the women interviewed experienced a clear conflict between the existence of such policies and the cultural assumptions about having children that existed within the organization. In two of the organizations it was suggested that taking maternity leave was frowned upon. Indeed one male interviewee described his organization as having 'a culture of restricted fertility', where despite positive policies 'people know that having babies is frowned upon'. Women with children were perceived as less effective workers, and as women who came back after leave could find themselves in worse jobs, they were also effectively punished. These data came from the comments that were made towards the end of the repertory grid interviews when interviewees were reflecting upon the content of the grid they had produced.

Profiles of career success

As part of the repertory grid process interviewees were asked which constructs were important for success in their organization. There were some interesting differences in the constructs highlighted by men and women. The most prominent factor mentioned by women was the significance of managing the work/home, public/private split. This re-affirms the centrality for women workers of juggling home and work commitments. The next theme linked in to the difficulties associated with balance. This factor was labelled the ability to be organized, efficient, be able to prioritize and meet deadlines. The third most significant theme was ambition and having the drive, determination and will to succeed. The role of decisiveness was also identified and was linked with the ability to make decisions, accept responsibility and take the initiative. Other key factors were approachability, being able to appear to be in control, and trust and honesty.

Looking at how men rated their constructs, the most important factor for success was ambition, drive and determination. Men had a very clear perception that it was the individual's own abilities, skills and commitment to the job that would produce success. Trustworthiness and honesty were also seen as significant factors, in particular being reliable to others was seen as important. Strategic thinking and the need to take a business approach (as opposed to taking a bureaucratic approach) were described as vital. Having the right kind of personality, being extroverted and outgoing was seen as useful in your career. Finally having experience and knowledge about the industry and the task in hand was important.

The importance of these two profiles was that an overarching theme in the analysis was that women needed to maintain a strong (but hidden) link with home/family commitments, and that women were more strongly embedded in the world of the relationship. They therefore saw the successful management of this dynamic as the key determinant of potential success.

EVALUATION OF THE TECHNIQUE

There are a number of advantages of using the repertory grid technique, both in this and other contexts. The most obvious advantage is that the interviewer has access to how the individual is construing and making sense of their own world, in their own words. Within this context for example, it would be difficult to see how we could have accessed such in-depth accounts about how performance was evaluated without the construct elicitation process. As Kelly suggested, the technique of construct elicitation encourages the emergence of the implicit, which is not always easily recognized, one of the main benefits of the technique. Therefore the technique offers insights to a rich source of data, in this case not just about evaluations of performance, but also about how individuals construed the meaning of work in their everyday lives.

Additional advantages emerge from the way that the process of construct elicitation engenders reflexivity on behalf of the interviewee. That is, the interviewee has the opportunity to reflect on their own assumptions, in this case, about how performance was assessed within their company and the differential assessment of performance between women and men. As part of the 'conversational technology' the interviewer also had the chance to expand in more detail on the individual's constructs and to identify the ways in which they fit together to form a construct system. A further advantage that the repertory grid has is that it enables the researcher to challenge and clarify their own views and understanding of the situation as described by the interviewee. We frequently took this opportunity within the interviews, particularly at the time when they were reflecting on what they needed to do a good job, compared to what they felt their company rewarded. These reflections often allowed us to clarify our own developing understanding of the publishing industry, and the various elements of the different organizational cultures.

Other advantages emerge from the nature of the grid itself in that it provides a very structured form, both for eliciting and presenting data. As Harri-Augustein (1978) suggests, within the grid meaning is embodied and displayed within a relatively simple format. This means that the process is engaging for interviewees. Whilst conducting the interviews we found that the interviewees were keen to see how the grid was developing, and how it all fitted together. The process of unfolding meaning was one in which they were keen to engage.

There are however a number of problems with using repertory grids, some of which we encountered in this study. The first is that, on a couple of occasions, individuals found it difficult to understand what the technique was about. It is a fairly complex technique for individuals to grasp. In feeding back the results to the funding body, although they felt that the technique was very interesting and creative, at times we felt they were trying to push the results beyond what we felt were appropriate epistemological limits, by making grand claims about the data which we felt were inappropriate. This is not just necessarily a problem for this particular qualitative technique. A key advantage of the grid is in the representation of individual constructs, yet inevitably in the analysis the researcher wants to claim some patterns, as we have earlier about differences between women and men for example. Some authors have criticized the grid on this basis. Harri-Augustein (1978) for example argues that the process by which the description of meaning from a grid is arrived at tends to be reductionist, with constructs categorized together in convenient ways to make a whole. This is an issue we highlighted earlier with reference to counting the number of constructs. We tried to offset this by referring to the underlying epistemological basis of the technique when we presented our findings. However this is clearly something to which the researcher needs to give some attention.

Another issue is that the elicitation of constructs needs to be handled in a sensitive manner. Therefore there is a need for researcher skills in this area. We would also argue that the researcher needs to be familiar with the underlying philosophy behind Kelly's theory in order to use the technique in an appropriate manner. One additional issue is that this form of research also produces a vast volume of data, in the form of elements that need analysis. However this is similar to the use of any other qualitative technique, and can be addressed by carefully applying some of the analysis techniques outlined elsewhere in this book. Overall we felt that the quality of insightful data produced from the study by far offset the disadvantage of the complex data analytic processes required.

Repertory grids, as used in this study, can play an important part in understanding how people make sense of their experiences in the workplace. Through the processes of exploration and elaboration, the constructs used as part of sensemaking start to emerge. In our experience the greatest contribution of the repertory grid is through its role as a conversational technology providing the stimulus through which the researcher and the researched can discuss often complex issues. It is therefore not surprising that the technique, originally designed as a therapy tool, has been used so widely within organizational research, and still continues to maintain its popularity. Although the most widespread uses of the technique often rely upon quantitative analysis, we would argue that an in-depth qualitative analysis of a repertory grid has much to offer.

FURTHER READING

The classic text on how to construct a repertory grid is D. Bannister and F. Fransella (1977) *A Manual For Repertory Grid Technique*, London: Croom-Helm. Other texts that look specifically at how repertory grids can be used with reference to organizational research are V. Stewart and A. Stewart (1982) *Business Applications of Repertory Grid*, London: McGraw Hill and Jankowicz's (1990) chapter in G. Neimeyer and R. Neimeyer (eds), *Advances in Personal Construct Psychology*, volume 1, New York: JAI Press. An alternative route into finding more about what lies behind the repertory grid is to look at texts on personal construct theory, for example V. Burr and T. Butt (1992) *Invitation to Personal Construct Psychology*, London: Whurr, or the classic Donald Bannister and Fay Fransella text: *Inquiring Man: the Psychology of Personal Constructs*, London: Croom Helm (1986). Examples of the application of repertory grids to various research questions in organizational research can be found in some of the papers in the reference list below.

REFERENCES

Anderson, N. (1990) 'Repertory grid technique in employee selection', *Personnel Review*, 19 (3): 9–15.

Argyris, C. and Schon, D.A. (1977) *Organizational Learning: A Theory of Action Perspective*, London: Addison-Wesley.

Arnold, J. and Nicholson, N. (1991) 'Construing of self and others at work in the early years of corporate careers', *Journal of Organizational Behaviour*, (12): 621–39.

Bannister, D. (1985) 'Introduction', in N. Beail (ed.), *Repertory Grid Techniques and Personal Constructs: Applications in Clinical and Educational Settings*, London: Croom-Helm.

Bannister, D. and Fransella, F. (1977) *A Manual for Repertory Grid Technique*, London: Academic Press.

Bourdieu, P. (1990) *The Logic of Practice*, Cambridge: Polity Press.

Dick, P. and Jankowicz, A.D. (2001) 'A social constructionist account of police culture and its influence on the representation and progression of female officers: a rep. grid analysis in a UK police force', *Policing: An International Journal of Police Strategy and Management*, 24 (2): 181–99.

Easterby-Smith, M. (1980) 'The design, analysis and interpretation of repertory grids', *International Journal of Man-machine Studies*, 13: 3–24.

Easterby-Smith, M., Thorpe, R. and Holman, D. (1996) 'Using repertory grids in management', *Journal of European Industrial Training*, 20 (3): 2–30.

Fournier, V. and Payne, R. (1994) 'Change in self-construction during the transition from university to employment: a personal construct psychology approach', *Journal of Occupational and Organizational Psychology*, 67: 297–314.

Gammack, J.G. and Stephens, R.A. (1994) 'Repertory grid technique in constructive interaction', in C.M.Cassell and G. Symon (eds), *Qualitative Methods in Organizational Research: A Practical Guide*, London: Sage Publications.

Glaser, B.G. and Strauss, A.L. (1967) *The Discovery of Grounded Theory: Strategies for Research*, New York: Aldine.

Harri-Augustein, E.S. (1978) 'Reflecting on structures of meaning: a process of learning to learn', in F. Fransella (ed.), *Personal Construct Theory 1977*, London: Academic Press.

Henwood, K.L. and Pidgeon, N.F. (1992) 'Qualitative research and psychological theorizing', *British Journal of Psychology*, 83 (1): 97–111.

Jankowicz, A. (1990) 'Applications of personal construct theory in business practice', in G. Neimeyer and R. Neimeyer (eds), *Advances in Personal Construct Psychology, vol. 1*, New York: JAI Press.

Kelly, G.A. (1955) *The Psychology of Personal Constructs: Volumes 1 and 2*, New York: Norton.

King, N. (1994) 'Qualitative interviews', in C.M. Cassell and G. Symon (eds), *Qualitative Methods in Organizational Research: A Practical Guide*, London: Sage Publications.

Parker, S.K., Mullarkey, S. and Jackson, P.R. (1994) 'Dimensions of performance effectiveness in high-involvement work organizations', *Human Resource Management Journal*, 4 (3): 1–22.

Salmon, P. (1978) 'Doing psychological research', in F. Fransella (ed.), *Personal Construct Theory 1977*, London: Academic Press.

Smith, M. (1986) 'A repertory grid analysis of supervisory jobs', *International Review of Applied Psychology*, 35: 501–12.

Stewart, V. and Stewart, A. (1982) *Business Applications of Repertory Grid*, London: McGraw-Hill.

Tomlinson, F. and Colgan, F. (1989) *Twice as Many, Half as Powerful? Report of a Survey into the Employment of Women in the United Kingdom Book Publishing Industry*, London: Polytechnic of North London/Women in Publishing.

7

— **Cognitive Mapping in Organizational Research** ——

Seonaidh McDonald, Kevin Daniels and Claire Harris

Cognitive mapping is a term applied to many methods. Behind the term lies a bewildering range of approaches, which make different assumptions about method, methodology and even epistemology. Cognitive maps have been developed from, for example, company documents (Barr et al., 1992), interview transcripts (Laukkanen, 1994), card sorting (Daniels et al., 1995), semi-structured questionnaires (Markoczy, 1997), standardized repertory grids (Hodgkinson, 1997) and through interactive computer software (Cropper et al., 1992). As the use of the cartographic metaphor suggests, many forms of cognitive mapping are concerned with pictorial representation of data (for example, Huff, 1990) but even this is not always the case (for example, Laukkanen, 1998). Given that there are many kinds of cognitive mapping methods used by researchers from a variety of backgrounds, it is then hardly surprising that cognitive mapping methods have been put to many uses. A number of edited works, most notably Huff (1990), have appeared which give good coverage of the range of methods employed under the broad heading of cognitive mapping (for example, Eden and Spender, 1998).

In this chapter, we will try to outline some of the important debates that feature in the cognitive mapping literature. We will also present two, quite different, examples of cognitive mapping which will help demonstrate some of the range of possible applications of mapping in management research.

IMPORTANT DEBATES

Historically, cognitive mapping methods have been developed in order to investigate, and to depict, thinking. It is a well-established principle that individuals store, retrieve and use information from memory in a structured manner (Anderson, 1983). Further, the structure of this information influences decision-making, reasoning, judgement, predictions about future events, categorization of phenomena and communication (Daniels and Henry, 1998). These 'information structures' are known variously as cognitive models, scripts, belief structures, knowledge structures and mental models amongst other terms (Walsh, 1995). Here, we shall use the generic term 'mental model' (Johnson-Laird, 1989) that subsumes all other terms, which have more specific meanings. Cognitive mapping has grown out of a need to capture and articulate these mental models.

However, researchers disagree about the extent to which various forms of cognitive maps actually represent mental models, or whether, as we argue below, they need represent mental models at all. This basic problem is manifest in the literature through a series of inter-linked but differently articulated debates.

In her well-known five-fold classification, Huff (1990) classifies methods according to the level of interpretation they require by the researcher to get from the raw data to the finished map (see Figure 7.1). On the one extreme, she places maps that simply report 'manifest content' (Berelson, 1952) where, '. . . verbal expression is taken as a direct indication of mental activity' (Huff, 1990: 14). These include maps that, for example, present word counts of common terms used by an individual, making the assumption that concepts used often are more significant. Next, she describes methods that are concerned with describing the taxonomies we use to understand a concept. This includes maps that define meaning through contrast (for example, how similar or different one concept is to another) or through categorization (a laurel is a kind of tree, a tree is a kind of plant). Huff's third category of maps contains methods that are designed to show the causal reasoning between two concepts. Between this category and the last, there is a significant increase in the complexity of the maps, as well as the number of uses that they might have. The penultimate family of maps is described as 'strategic argument maps'. These include tools that can depict the paths of decisions in the past or of strategic options in the future. The final group of maps in Huff's classification are maps that seek to explore value and meaning systems by inferring links between the linguistic patterns observed and the underlying 'schemas, frames and perceptual codes' (Huff, 1990: 16) that we use to interpret new experiences by comparing them to what we already know.

Huff notes that each successive category often requires the researcher to have a larger interpretive input. Clearly the first category of maps requires little or no researcher interpretation as the data can be allowed to speak directly. The fifth category requires what Huff describes as 'the greatest leap from text to map' (1990: 16).

Closely linked to this problem of how much of any given map is the 'voice' of the researched and how much is researcher interpretation, is the debate around how maps should be aggregated across individuals, and consequently whether maps aggregated across individuals can be thought representative of collective cognition (Bougon et al., 1977; Schneider and Angelmar, 1993; Nicolini, 1999).

Another manifestation of this same debate about whether a map constitutes a direct representation of thinking is the problem of whether researchers make use of primary or secondary data (Fiol, 1994). There are a number of studies that draw on secondary data such as minutes of meetings, company reports and other such organizational documents as raw data to derive cognitive maps (Huff and Schwenk, 1990; Barr et al., 1992). Other researchers feel that only primary data such as the transcripts of interviews undertaken for that study and dealt

Attention, association and importance of concepts (word counts, contiguities of concepts)	Dimensions of categories and cognitive taxonomies (card sorts, repertory grids)	Influence, causality and system dynamics (influence diagrams)	Structure argument and conclusion (decision trees)	Schemes, frames and perceptual codes (combination of methods used for 2, 3 and 4)

Increasing interpretive input from researcher

Figure 7.1 Huff's generic families of maps
Source adapted from Jenkins, 1998

with in the context of the company at the time could be considered to represent cognition (for example, Johnson, 1999).

Another facet of this debate, particularly relevant to this book, concerns the use of structured quantitative methods versus unstructured or semi-structured qualitative methods for the production of cognitive maps. Some researchers have approached the problem of how to make maps that are as faithful to cognition as possible by trying to eliminate bias that may be introduced through the role of the researcher. They have done this by making use of methods that require all participants to assess a standardized pool of concepts using Likert-type scales. Additionally, it is argued that since such methods afford the use of larger sample sizes that they will increase the replicability of findings (for example, Hodgkinson, 1997, 2001, 2002). Others argue that an increase in quantification and standardization in terms of research instrument will not *necessarily* equate to a more exact replication of cognition (for example, Daniels and Johnson, 2002) and can limit research to the preconceived ideas of the researcher and hence introduce a different kind of bias whilst sacrificing richness in the data.

Given the multitude of methods and the varied backgrounds of those employing the methods, it is not surprising that much has been written concerning the proper use and analysis of cognitive mapping methods. Neither is it surprising that a number of different terms have been applied to the methods often described as cognitive mapping methods – one such being cause (or causal) mapping. We raise these debates to make the reader aware of the arguments that need to be addressed before using cognitive mapping. We do not attempt to solve these debates for the reader, since the nature of the solution is often appropriately rooted within the research questions and the research approach adopted within a given study (Daniels and Johnson, 2002).

Mapping conventions

In the following sections of this chapter, we illustrate two applications of mapping methods. Although assumptions behind these methods are quite different, both of them make use of mapping techniques that are drawn from Huff's third category: maps that show causal reasoning. Further, both examples make use of Decision Explorer® software and the mapping conventions that it supports.

The map that follows (see Figure 7.2) is an example of output from Decision Explorer®. It is made up of concepts (blocks of text) and links (arrows). The numbers have no significance in this map other than to represent the order that the concepts were typed in. Concepts express the ideas or issues of the map. They are usually quite short and need not be proper sentences. They can be typed in a number of 'styles' to represent different themes or ownership, for example. Styles are shown in different colours or fonts and the printed map will have a key showing all the styles used. Some of the concepts (see for example 1,368) have one phrase separated from another by an ellipsis (. . .). These phrases are 'poles' of the concept, and the ellipsis can be read 'rather than'. The idea of an opposite pole lends a great deal of meaning and power to the map. As an example, consider a concept that reads 'have a Scottish Parliament'. If the concept owner supplies 'being integrated with the UK' as the negative pole for this concept, you realize that a Scottish Parliament represents fragmentation of governance in the map. On the other hand, another person may have offered 'being controlled by a foreign power' as a negative pole to the same concept. This would lead to an

Figure 7.2   An example of a cognitive map

entirely different understanding of the concept. Asking people whose ideas you are mapping to clarify a negative pole is a good check that you understand what they mean by the words they have offered as concepts.

The arrows that are drawn between the concepts are read as 'may lead to' in the direction that the arrow is pointing. Arrows that have minus signs next to them (see for example the link between 1,371 and 1,365) signify that the first part of the concept (emergent pole) at the tail of the arrow will lead to the second part of the concept (opposite or contrasting pole) of the concept at the head of the arrow. In other words, it leads to the explicit or implicit negative pole. The map is often drawn in a roughly hierarchical way, with the sense, or lines of argument running from the bottom to the top of the map.

This very simplistic set of conventions can help to represent and then analyse and develop very muddled, difficult and interwoven issues or ideas. These techniques are covered in more detail in Eden et al. (1992). The conventions that are discussed here refer specifically to those used by the Decision Explorer® software, but mapping can equally be done manually, independently of this software (Bryson et al., 1995). The examples that follow both use these mapping techniques, but for different purposes and in different phases of enquiry.

Jenkins (1998) identifies three phases involved in mapping: surfacing, mapping and analysis. In reality, these phases will be at least overlapping and in some cases deliberately combined (for example, Jones and Eden, 1981) into one interactive process. This is certainly the case in our second example. Here the surfacing, mapping and to some extent, the analysis, are combined. The mapping is done in real time with and by the interviewees (see Figure 7.3). In the first example, the researcher employs a different approach, using maps for data management and then to construct the research narrative (see Figure 7.4).

By choosing illustrations of different assumptions about mapping, operationalized by the same tool, we hope to show the range of uses to which mapping methods can be applied irrespective of the theoretical or meta-theoretical perspective of the researcher.

Figure 7.3 A mapping research process

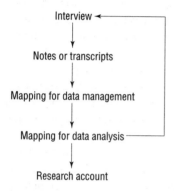

Figure 7.4 A mapping research process

USING MAPPING IN QUALITATIVE RESEARCH IN ORGANIZATIONS

The method presented in this section makes use of the Decision Explorer® software to operationalize a qualitative approach to organizational research. Here the researcher is not trying to represent cognition, but rather to manage research data and ideas. The aim of this research project was to understand the effect of 'slack' (excess capital, labour, capacity and other types of resources) on innovation in organizations (for example, Nohria and Gulati, 1997). The researcher used theoretical sampling techniques (Gummesson, 1991) to identify companies that had innovation as a central and crucial goal. Some competed in industries that have a high rate of change (for example, software) and some represented ultra-high technology sectors (for example, defence). Sampling stopped once theoretical saturation had been reached. In all, six companies were included in the study.

Data were collected from each organization through a series of in-depth interviews with key figures. The interviews were in two parts. The first part was unstructured, allowing the managers to talk about their immediate concerns related (sometimes loosely) with innovation. The second part was semi-structured, where the interviewer returned to salient parts of the narrative to explore them in more detail, or asked the managers to reflect on particular issues which were prominent in the academic literature, or had been raised in earlier interviews. These interviews were taped, with the permission of the interviewees and then transcribed verbatim.

Mapping for data management

Up to this point, this project was conducted like any other qualitative study. However rather than moving straight from the transcripts to a data analysis process, the raw interview data were developed into a series of maps like the one shown in Figure 7.2. The maps that were built from each interview reflected the conversation that took place between the researcher and the interviewee by depicting the lines of argument. It is important to reiterate that these maps were not meant strictly to represent the mental model of the interviewee, although the process does attempt to retain both the language and the sensemaking of the interviewee.

The data is still represented from the interviewee's point of view at this stage, but may include the voice of the researcher in the conversation that was developed, or issues from the literature that influenced the formation of the research questions. Equally it may contain the voices of other people (mentors, dissonant voices, sources of influence) as introduced or 'reported' by the interviewee. In more ethnographic work, or when using a case study approach, it is possible to include observations of company conventions, body language or any other facets of the conventional research diary. These may be simply woven into the map, or can be explicitly signalled through the use of different colours or fonts for concepts. What is important is that the map can capture the conversation with all of its contradictions, meandering threads, underlying priorities and contextual explanations in a way that linear prose never can. We have moved from a linear narrative of what was *said* in an interview to an exploration of what was *meant* by preserving, making explicit and depicting the complexity of an interviewee's own reasoning.

Mapping for data analysis

The maps were then analysed both visually and by using the software's built-in tools. When a map is complete, it is often possible to detect distinct clusters of concepts in it (Eden et al., 1992). Sometimes these are obvious through simply looking at the map, but Decision Explorer® can also perform a 'cluster analysis', searching for concepts that are linked together in a group but more loosely linked with the rest of the map. Another type of analysis that can help to highlight themes in the map is 'domain analysis', which searches the map for the most highly linked concepts. It counts both arrows leading into and out of each concept and then ranks concepts according to how highly linked they are. Concepts with many links may represent issues that are particularly important to the interviewee or project. They may be concepts that are very influential in terms of being closely connected to many other issues discussed, be considered 'pivotal' in some way, or are simply mentioned by many people. These, and further, analysis techniques are discussed in more detail in Eden and Ackermann (1998).

The maps in this study showed, for example that some people returned to particular issues many times in the course of their interview, creating densely linked areas in their maps. Others told stories, or concentrated on detailing their beliefs about the future, generating linear, hierarchical sections of map. The emerging themes in each map were colour coded and it quickly became obvious which issues were most important to each interviewee and each organization. This process also helped to identify the similarities and differences between the maps. These techniques helped to surface a number of themes within the data about the kinds of 'slack' that interviewees believed was having an impact on innovation within their organizations (McDonald, 2003). These could be fed back into the interview process to inform the next iteration of the research.

Benefits of cognitive mapping for qualitative research

This method has been designed because moving between raw data and the development of the themes and categories that form the basis of the qualitative theory building process can be extremely difficult. The method suggested here is aimed at crossing the divide between data and theory in a way that can be easily grasped and used by researchers with varying experience.

The analysis process is similar to many of the familiar 'categorization' techniques used in social science. It has one important advantage over 'cut and paste' techniques in that it simultaneously allows the preservation of all the detail of the map as a context for any concept, and the ability to 'collapse' the map to show only the high level 'routings' through the map. Thus the researcher can easily switch back and forth between what is effectively a representation of a conversation and the surfacing theoretical structure. This is not only an enormous help in the sensemaking process, but also prevents the meaning of concepts drifting as they are forever tied into their original context.

As well as being able simultaneously to represent conflicting viewpoints, the other particular strength of this technique is that it represents issues and statements that are interlinked, interrelated, interdependent and even tangled. In contrast, the attempt to construct linear text forces the researcher to choose an organizing framework in advance of writing. This may be time (in the case of an interview transcript), or reasoning, or theme, for example. Sometimes simply not having to choose a starting point and being able to 'start in the middle' can make beginning the writing process more accessible. Liberation from more 'traditional' forms of predetermined order also means that mapping has the advantage of recording nuance and complexity very quickly compared with prose.

USING COGNITIVE MAPPING TO ELICIT MENTAL MODELS OF EMOTION AT WORK ——————

In this second example, we describe a method used to explore mental models of emotional experience at work. Here, semi-structured methods based upon principles of cognitive representation are used to elicit representations of participants' mental models. Again this was done by making use of maps which show causal reasoning (see Figure 7.1), but this time we chose to develop a visual card sort technique (Daniels et al., 1995) with the explicit intention of eliciting mental models. The visual card sort is a technique that enables rapid, open-ended elicitation of mental models.

Developing the interview schedule

The current research utilized a semi-structured interview, with theoretically derived prompts to maximize elicitation of concepts thought to be important to the current research. These prompts were developed from a review of the relevant literatures intended to capture the main features and processes by which emotions develop at work (Harris et al., 2002). Since we sought to examine differences in mental models of different emotional experiences at work, the interview schedule gave the participant enough discretion to explore their beliefs in an unstructured manner, although the interview schedule also enabled the probing of 'deeper' level information, identified from the literature review and which may not have been elicited through a fully unstructured approach.

The interview schedule progressed as follows:

STAGE 1 – EMOTION

The participants were first asked to describe a specific emotion they had experienced at work over the previous two weeks.

STAGE 2 – PRIMARY JOB CONDITIONS

Working from the emotion identified in Stage 1, participants were then asked to describe what it was about their work that caused the emotion.

STAGE 3 – SECONDARY JOB CONDITIONS

Participants were then asked to describe the causes the work features directly related to the named emotion.

STAGE 4 – COPING

Participants were then asked to explain in turn what they and their managers could do to: enhance the emotion or causes of the emotion if positive (for example, happiness); or decrease the emotion or its causes if negative (for example, frustration). Participants were then asked about changes to work or organizational processes that would enhance the positive emotion or its causes, or decrease the negative emotion or its causes.

STAGE 5 – CONSEQUENCES

Last, participants were asked to explain both the immediate and long-term consequences of their emotion and other concepts already elicited.

By accessing thoughts directly from the participants and allowing them to sort their own concepts, the final maps displayed a more detailed approximation of thinking than could be gained through researcher defined concepts in surveys. By drawing on theories of the development and consequences of emotion, it was assumed that the interview prompts would enhance recall of emotion-related mental models (Anderson, 1983).

As an interviewer, it was necessary to facilitate the cognitive mapping process; helping the respondent retrieve, verbalize and construct their interpretations. Although evidence suggests that people do store knowledge in a structured manner, some of the information and associations may be so deeply ingrained that they may take the form of taken-for-granted assumptions and deeper held beliefs. Using laddering techniques it is possible to facilitate retrieval and verbalization of concepts. Similarly by utilizing a semi-structured interview protocol it is also possible to enhance recall and to reduce the possibility that the resultant maps represent demand characteristics of the situation rather than an approximation of cognition.

Sorting and mapping

Sorting and mapping is specific to the type of cognitive mapping method chosen for the research. The current research utilized a variant of the visual card sort. The procedure is shown below (see also Figure 7.3):

STEP 1

Following each stage of questioning in the schedule, responses were written onto 'Post-it'™ notes and then passed to the participant to check their accuracy.

STEP 2

The participant was then asked to arrange the 'Post-it'™ notes on the table to show how they were or were not causally related to the concepts already elicited. This occurred after each level of questioning.

STEP 3

As the participant explained the links, the interviewer sketched a map of the concepts showing the direction of linkages.

STEP 4

The participant was shown the map and asked to check that it accurately represented their views after each set of concepts had been added.

Coding the maps

Because the method generated maps unique to each participant, it was necessary to code the map data to facilitate analysis. Here we used template analysis, which involves producing a list of codes (a 'template') representing themes identified in the data (King, Chapter 2, this volume). Here, the levels of questioning themselves were used to guide the initial coding protocol (King, Chapter 2, this volume). In the work stress literature, there exist several categorization schemes for coding job conditions associated with emotions, coping and outcomes associated with stress and emotional experience (Harris et al., 2002). We used some of these existing categorization schemes as initial templates. However the coding protocol was refined through several iterations of data coding following Huff and Fletcher's (1990) recommendations to modify coding protocols as more experience is gathered with the data. In order to ensure reliability within the coding process, the data were coded independently by the interviewer and a second member of the research team. Disagreement was measured and resolved through discussion (Harris et al., 2002, provide a fuller explanation).

Analysing the maps

The emotions elicited were initially grouped into three categories:

1   pleasant emotions such as happy;
2   low activation emotions such as bored; and
3   unpleasant emotions such as anxiety.

Based on concepts and links elicited from at least 30 per cent of each sub-sample corresponding to each emotion category, aggregate maps were produced for each class of emotion (see Figure 7.5 for an example). The aggregate maps revealed that there were consistent similarities between respondents in the job conditions and outcomes associated with different kind of emotional experience at work. The method was able to detect differences in attribution of the causes and consequences of emotions at work and these differences were consistent with the literature on emotional information processing indicating the validity of the method (Harris et al., 2002).

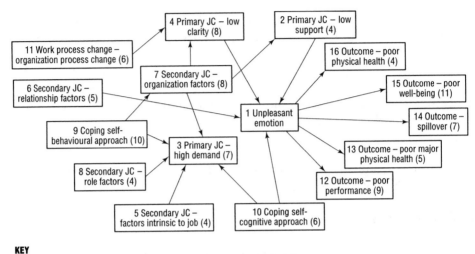

KEY

Primary JC	Primary job characteristics – proximate cause of emotion
Secondary JC	Secondary job characteristics – distal cause of emotion
Self cope	Things respondent can do to alter emotion or job characteristic
Manager support	Things manager can do to alter emotion or job characteristic
Work process change	Things that can be changed in the process to alter emotion or job characteristic
Outcomes	Influence of emotion on performance, well-being and physical health

Figure 7.5 Unpleasant emotion aggregate map (number on left of concept indicates order in which concept was elicited)

Source: Adapted from Harris et al., 2002

CONCLUSION

We began this chapter by noting the evolution of cognitive mapping as a means of studying how people represent and use information in real organizational settings. As mapping methods have evolved, so has our knowledge of what different methods are capable of doing. Only a sub-set of methods might really approximate the content and structure of participants' mental models – or 'map cognition'. The second method described in this chapter is an example of a method that is more explicitly cognitive. However, as illustrated in the first application described, mapping as an approach is not constrained merely to represent the structure and content of mental models.

There are many advantages and disadvantages to using various mapping methods. For the more cognitively oriented methods, mapping methods allow researchers to study topics that are inherently cognitive (such as examining factors which produce divergence and convergence of mental models). However we emphasize that care should be taken to ensure any conclusions are appropriate for the form of mapping used. It is also often necessary to collect other forms of data with some of the more cognitively oriented methods – as researchers try to understand ways in which mental models develop, or the consequences of those mental models. Collection of additional data adds further complexity to the design, execution and analysis of such research. Amongst the more reflexive approaches, with less emphasis on representation of mental models, data from multiple sources of information (for example, documentary data, interviews, observations) and multiple participants can be directly included in maps. This makes more reflexive mapping approaches useful for case study and ethnographic research.

The ability to represent complex and rich information without imposing a linear structure is an advantage of many mapping methods. That the representation is often pictorial allows data to be presented in a format in which the researcher can examine detailed relationships in the data without losing sight of the overall arrangement of the data, and vice versa. Since simple conventions are often used to develop maps, participants' maps can often be constructed by participants themselves, as in the second example. This enables researchers to check the accuracy of responses during mapping. Methods that build upon the language used by participants during data collection also allow the researcher to stay close to the participants' perspectives during analysis. This is important whether researchers wish to represent their subjects' cognition, or simply seek to follow a grounded approach to their data. Certainly, mapping methods may allow researchers greater ease in conveying to participants that their perspectives are important to the research. Although the collection and analysis of mapping data can be very time consuming, even compared with other qualitative methods, we have generally found that participants engage with many of these methods readily and sustain their interest throughout their contribution to data collection (for example, Brown, 1992).

It is certainly not the case any more that mapping methods need be used only for cognitive research in organizations. As the first example shows, mapping methods can be used as a tool for any form of qualitative research. We suggest that the applications of mapping methods seem, in many ways, to be constrained only by the imagination of the researcher.

FURTHER READING

The Banxia website (*www.banxia.com*) provides more information about the Decision Explorer® software as well as a comprehensive bibliography of cognitive mapping literature. For a general overview of mapping approaches, we would recommend Huff (1990). Eden and Spender's (1998) edited collection covers a good range of issues relating to mapping in organizational settings. Eden et al.'s (1992) contribution to the *Journal of Management Studies* special edition on cognitive mapping and Eden and Ackermann's (1998) book on mapping as part of strategic development are both helpful on the practical analysis of maps. For more insight into the debate about quantitative versus qualitative approaches to mapping, please see Daniels and Johnson (2002), Hodgkinson (2001) and Hodgkinson (2002). Readers wishing to consider how best to compare maps should also see Daniels et al. (1994). Both Nicolini (1999) and Walsh (1995) deal more generally with the notion of cognition in organizations and how researchers might approach it.

NOTES

Author order was decided by drawing lots. Each author has made an equal contribution to the chapter.

The authors would like to thank Jenny Brightman for her comments on an early draft of this chapter.

REFERENCES

Anderson, J.R. (1983) *The Architecture of Cognition*, Harvard University Press.
Barr, P.S., Stimpert, J.L. and Huff, A.S. (1992) 'Cognitive change, strategic action, and organizational renewal', *Strategic Management Journal*, 13: 15–36.
Berelson, B. (1952) *Content Analysis in Communications Research*, Glencoe, IL: Free Press.
Bougon, M.G., Weick, K. and Binkhorst, D. (1977) 'Cognition in organizations: an analysis of the Utrecht Jazz Orchestra', *Administrative Science Quarterly*, 22: 606–39.
Brown, S.M. (1992) 'Cognitive mapping and repertory grids for qualitative survey-research – some comparative observations', *Journal of Management Studies*, 29: 287–307.
Bryson, J., Ackermann, F., Eden, C. and Finn, C. (1995) 'Using the 'oval mapping process' to identify strategic issues and formulate effective strategies', in J.M. Bryson (ed), *Strategic Planning for Public and Nonprofit Organizations*, second edition, San Francisco: Jossey Bass.
Cropper, S., Eden, C. and Ackermann, F. (1992) 'Exploring and negotiating collective action through computer-aided cognitive mapping', *The Environmental Professional*, 15: 176–85.
Daniels, K., de Chernatony, L. and Johnson, G. (1995) 'Validating a method for mapping managers' mental models of competition', *Human Relations*, 48: 975–91.
Daniels, K. and Henry, J. (1998) 'Strategy: a cognitive perspective', in S. Segal-Horn (ed.), *The Strategy Reader*, Oxford: Blackwell.
Daniels, K. and Johnson, G. (2002) 'On trees and triviality traps: locating the debate on the contribution of cognitive mapping to organizational research', *Organization Studies*, 23: 73–82.
Daniels, K., Markoczy, L. and de Chernatony, L. (1994) 'Techniques to compare cognitive maps', in C. Stubbart, J.Meindl and J.F. Porac (eds), *Advances in Managerial Cognition and Organizational Information Processing*, vol. 5, pp. 141–64. Connecticut: JAI Press.
Eden, C. and Ackermann, F. (1998) *Making Strategy: the Journey of Strategic Management*, London: Sage.
Eden, C., Ackermann, F. and Cropper, S. (1992) 'The analysis of cause maps', *Journal of Management Studies*, 29: 309–24.
Eden C. and Spender, J-C. (eds) (1998) *Managerial and Organizational Cognition: Theory, Methods and Research*, London: Sage.
Fiol, C.M. (1994) 'Consensus, diversity and learning in organizations', *Organization Science*, 5: 403–20.
Gummesson, E. (1991) *Qualitative Methods in Management Research*, London: Sage Publications.
Harris, C., Daniels, K. and Briner, R.B. (2002) 'Using cognitive mapping for psychosocial risk assessment', *Risk Management: An International Journal*.
Hodgkinson, G.P. (1997) 'The cognitive analysis of competitive structures: a review and critique', *Human Relations*, 50: 625–54.
Hodgkinson, G.P. (2001) 'The psychology of strategic management: diversity and cognition revisited', in C.L.Cooper and I.T. Robertson (eds), *International Review of Industrial and Organizational Psychology* (vol. 16), Chichester: Wiley, (2001).
Hodgkinson, G.P. (2002) 'Comparing managers' mental models of competition: why self-report measures of belief similarity won't do', *Organization Studies*, 23: 63–72.
Huff, A.S. (ed.) (1990) *Mapping Strategic Thought*, Chichester: Wiley.
Huff, A.S. and Fletcher, K. E. (1990) 'Key mapping decisions', in A.S. Huff (ed.), *Mapping Strategic Thought*, Chichester: Wiley.
Huff, A.S. and Schwenk, C.R. (1990) 'Bias and sensemaking in good times and bad', in A.S. Huff (ed.), *Mapping Strategic Thought*, Chichester: Wiley.
Jenkins, M. (1998) 'The theory and practice of comparing causal maps', in C. Eden and J-C. Spender (eds), *Managerial and Organizational Cognition: Theory, Methods and Research*, London: Sage.
Johnson, P. (1999) 'A study of cognition and behaviour in top management team interaction', PhD thesis, Cranfield University.
Johnson-Laird, P.N. (1989) 'Mental models', in M.I. Posner (ed.), *Foundations of Cognitive Science*, Cambridge, MA: MIT Press.
Jones, S. and Eden, C. (1981) 'Modelling in marketing: explicating subjective knowledge', *European Journal of Marketing*, 15: 3–11.

King, N. (1998) 'Template analysis', in G. Symon and C. Cassell (eds), *Qualitative Methods and Analysis in Organizational Research*, London: Sage.

Laukkanen, M. (1994) 'Comparative cause mapping of organizational cognitions', *Organization Science*, 5: 322–43.

Laukkanen, M. (1998) 'Conducting causal mapping research: opportunities and challenges', in C. Eden and J-C. Spender (eds), *Managerial and Organizational Cognition: Theory, Methods and Research*, London: Sage.

Markoczy, L. (1997) 'Measuring beliefs: accept no substitutes', *Academy of Management Journal*, 40: 1228–42.

McDonald, S. (2003) 'Innovation, organizational learning and models of slack', Proceedings of the 5th Organizational Learning and Knowledge conference, Lancaster University.

Nicolini, D. (1999) 'Comparing methods for mapping organizational cognition', *Organization Studies*, 20: 833–60.

Nohria, N. and Gulati, R. (1997) 'What is the optimum amount of organizational slack? A study of the relationship between slack and innovation in multinational firms', *European Management Journal*, 15(6): 603–11.

Schneider, S.C. and Angelmar, R. (1993) 'Cognition in organizational analysis: who's minding the store?', *Organization Studies*, 14: 347–74.

Walsh, J.P. (1995) 'Managerial and organizational cognition: notes from a trip down memory lane', *Organization Science*, 6: 280–321.

8 — The Twenty Statements Test

Anne Rees and Nigel Nicholson

> I am an independent-minded person; I am committed to personal improvement; I am competitive; I am gentle; I am good at many things, brilliant at none; I am an entrepreneur; I am inconsistent; I am enthusiastic; I am not very gregarious; I am deceptive in business dealings; I am fair; I am intolerant of superiors; I am a risk taker; I am excited by personal business; I am not motivated by a career pattern; I am a planner; I am not materialistic; I am a sportsman; I am easy to get on with; I am a family orientated person.

These are the 20 self-identifying statements made by one of our respondents – rich data indeed. Viewed holistically, these definitions are a self-portrait the individual offered by making conscious choices about what really mattered to him about himself – a 'desert-island-discs' of the personality. Although our aim here will be to demonstrate the potential of the Twenty Statements Test (TST) as a qualitative research tool which can also yield codable and quantifiable assessments, a significant implicit assumption of our methodology is that each response gains meaning from the others. The example above, at one level, tells an irreducible story, yet what respondents provide when they complete the TST is not a straightforward reflection of some underlying 'truth'. We shall argue that such self-identifications make explicit how individuals mediate their social environment in different, more or less adaptive ways. Additionally, by using the methods we shall describe, themes can be extracted so as to allow for meaningful comparison with others, or of the same self over time. Therefore, a further aim is to describe the three-part rating system we developed to capture as much as possible of what was psychologically valid about these employees' self definitions. This chapter aims to persuade the reader that the TST can be a powerful alternative or addition to standard psychometric techniques, offering the possibility of quantifiable assessment hand-in-hand with rich qualitative freely elicited material.

THEORETICAL BACKGROUND

The TST was developed within a symbolic interactionist perspective, a framework with a pedigree of writing and research (usually case-based ethnographies) extending long before the instrument itself came into use. This theoretical perspective locates the self as a crucial element in the analysis of social behaviour, with identity dependent upon symbolic mediation for its interior meanings and control of action. Agents are seen as framing their actions in terms of internalized social definitions and self-reflections. Within the broad spectrum of adherents to symbolic interactionism, some would resist any methodology that constrains the forms of interpretable behaviour or expression to be collected. Others have taken a more eclectic approach, and it was in the latter spirit that Kuhn looked for an empirical means of assessing the self in society, and began the first work on the TST in the late 1940s.

The first time the current version of the TST was used was in 1950 when students at the University of Iowa completed it as part of a study of the effects on the self-concept of unfavourable evaluations by others. The study documented the initial administration of the TST, conceptual categories for coding, and scoring techniques. The instrument was used extensively in the 1950s and 1960s, and is comprehensively reviewed in Spitzer et al.'s manual, *The Assessment of the Self* (1973).

Individuals think of themselves in terms of what they do and how they do it, whether this is 'mother', 'designer', 'athlete' or whatever. They also identify themselves in terms of values and moral attitudes, which locate the self within a shared cultural frame of norms and constructs, and provide a symbolic system for action. Therefore the aim of measurement is to allow sufficient statements to be made for individuals to articulate the most salient aspects of the symbolic system they apply to themselves. An underlying assumption is that the 'self' depends on 'others' – self classifications have to be culturally shared if they are to be a feature of an individual's social behaviour with others. Related to this is the idea that the individual is not just a passive agent, responding to external stimuli, but that the process of self-identification helps to determine which objects are given attention, what interpretations are made of them, and what behaviours they elicit.

GENERAL DESCRIPTION OF THE METHOD AND ITS ANALYSIS

In its early days, the TST was used in the USA in varied settings with differing populations, in order to test various hypotheses. It was also used in different formats. In most instances, a maximum of 20 statements was requested, with an overall mean of over 15 statements per respondent. The standard format for instructions was:

> In the spaces provided below, please give twenty different statements in answer to the question, 'Who am I?' Give these answers as if you were giving them to yourself, not to somebody else. Write fairly rapidly, for the time for this part of the questionnaire is limited. (Kuhn, 1950)

Categorizing the statements

As described in Spitzer et al. (1973: 15ff.), many different procedures were developed for classifying statements on the TST, mostly falling into a 'specific category approach' or a 'total domain approach'. The latter classifies every statement available, whereas the former only classifies specific types of statement. The originator of the total domain approach was McPartland, who in 1965 devised a fourfold comprehensive schema of 'referential frames'. This system recognized that statements made in response to the question 'Who am I?' reflect the different relationships people have with their objective world; his classification of self definitions places any statement in one of four mutually exclusive categories:

- category A: conceptions of the self as a physical structure in time and space ('I am six feet tall'), termed 'physical';

- category B: the self identified in terms of position within social roles and structures ('I am a psychologist'), termed 'social';
- category C: as a social actor abstracted from social structure ('I am not very self confident'), termed 'reflective';
- category D: conceptions of the self as abstracted from physical being, social structure and social action, that is to say, non self-identifying statements ('I am a human being'), termed 'oceanic'.

All statements defining the self can be fitted into one of these four categories, although special classes may have to be constructed for ambiguous statements.

For most individuals, the majority of statements fall into a single class, A, B, C, or D, which suggests that these four categories may be used not only to describe responses, but also *respondents*. On the available evidence, Spitzer stated that seven out of 10 respondents could be clearly characterized by self definitions of one of the four types. Through the use of the TST in the USA in the 1950s, researchers came to the conclusion that the vast majority of Americans were firmly anchored socially, because respondents from different research populations gave statements falling mainly in the B category, and could therefore be characterized as 'social selves'.

Since the work reported here, apart from our own studies, the TST as a tool for characterizing personality has languished, while more standardized and conventional scaling approaches to identity constructs have thrived, largely as a result of the increased analytical sophistication available through highly accessible software packages. Yet one could argue this is more of the same, in terms of paradigm predominance, and fails to get at the qualitative richness we know to be the distinctive essence of experienced identity. Perhaps it is in response to this deficit that once again researchers have started to look again at the TST as an instrument of choice – uniquely combining a structured approach with maximal response openness.

One recent highly practical use was by Coover and Murphy (2000) who examined the interaction between self and social context, and concluded that academic success was predicted by more complex self-identities than by self-esteem as measured in the TST. More theoretically, Bettencourt and Hume (1999) found that values, emotions and personal relationships were more often used in group identity representations than in personal identity representations, in their investigation of the cognitive content of social group identity. The TST has also been used to show how some self-perceptions can be dysfunctional; Jennings et al. (1986) used the measure to identify self-reflective individuals to test the relationship between ideal-self discrepancy and anxiety. In an organizational context, Locatelli and West (1991) with a modified form of the TST, along with other instruments and techniques, collected images of organizational culture, concluding that the TST yielded the richest and most useable data. However, another organizational study was carried out by Walker et al. (1996) in which they completed a qualitative versus quantitative comparison of an organization's culture, using a modified form of the TST ('This company is . . .') for the qualitative assessment. They found each method produced similar cultural themes.

APPLICATION OF THE REFERENTIAL FRAMES METHOD

Our own initial research with the TST focused on the changes in self identity which accompany the career entry of a group of graduate entrants into a large technically based organization (Arnold and Nicholson, 1991; Nicholson and Arnold, 1989a, 1989b, 1990). In developing our methodology for the research, we sought measures which would reflect transformations in aspects of self identity over the course of the entry transition. We assembled a battery of methods for this purpose, including repertory grids, interviews, and standardized questionnaires. Many of these methods tend to bias towards stability ('retest reliability' in testing jargon), and we wanted to be sure that, even over a short period of time, we would include instrumentation highly sensitive to subtle shifts in identity, through which we would be able to test differential predictions about personal change.

We hypothesized that, over time, there would be an increase in frequency and saliency of occupational self-identifications; for example, reference to their specialist roles in engineering, computing or marketing, and increasing endorsement of organizational values and norms. We also expected a decreasing proportion of C-type/reflective statements, and an increase in B-type/social statements. We were especially attracted by the possibilities the TST offered for revealing degrees of change in free-floating reflective constructions versus more socially anchored self perceptions through this period of early career role adoption and professional identity development.

The group of 97 graduate entrants was made up of 33 1982 entrants, all of whom completed the TST within two weeks of joining the organization, and a further 16 (four from each of four departments) who had joined the organization in each of the years 1978 to 1981. Of the 97 who completed the standard TST in autumn 1982, 94 completed it again a year later, 32 women and 62 men. We felt that an atmosphere of trust, developing over the course of intensive interviews, was important for the successful administration of an instrument such as the TST, which requires respondents to be unconstrained in their choice of self definitions. Individuals completed the form in privacy, and then handed it to us for analysis. Confidentiality was assured and guaranteed by a system of unique codes. At the first phase, respondents produced an average of 19.7 responses; and at the second phase, 19.5 responses. This yielded a total of 3,774 statements to classify and analyse.

RATING SYSTEM

The system we used for rating statements was multi-level, providing three classifications: response type (referential frame); for C-mode/reflective statements only, we constructed our response content level (the SICV – Skills, Interests, Character and Values System); and response value (self evaluation). The purpose here was to evolve a system of rating which could tell us in a standard form something about the *content* of people's responses. The authors developed the system after many iterations with the data and ad hoc rating trials, before it was fully developed for test by independent raters. The earliest systems we used proved unwieldy with too many overlapping categories, with which we failed to achieve a reasonable level of reliability. Returning to this issue some time later, another social psychologist joined us as a rater, using the system as described below. All three of us trained together for one week, using six protocols for the purposes of illustrating categories. The second author took on the role of arbiter for the independent ratings of the other two.

Our primary system was the A–B–C–D method, described above. Spitzer et al. (1973) suggest that all statements can be placed in A, B, C, or D, apart from statements which (a) relate to completing the instrument itself; (b) indicate that the question itself has been rejected or misunderstood; or (c) are intended to trivialize the exercise. We used an 'uncodeable' category for all such statements, 3 per cent of the total.

We predicted that most of the new graduate entrants, at the point of entry into the organization, would be modal category C, demonstrating definitions of self not relating primarily to social structure, occupation or organization. We were particularly interested in respondents' shifts over time from their own baseline levels, described below.

To demonstrate better the range of responses typically produced, and some of the analytical problems they pose, we give an actual example of a completed TST protocol, followed by a brief interpretive commentary. So that the reader can get the full flavour of this employee's self-description, we show responses from both phases, one year apart. A common progression through respondents' 20 statements was two or three A- and/or B-type statements, and the bulk of their self-descriptions as C-type/reflective statements (54 of the 97 at phase one took this form). In the case illustrated in Table 8.1 below, the slight shift from 19 C-mode statements at the first phase to 18 after a year was a fairly typical pattern for these graduate entrants.

Clearly, this 24-year-old woman, working in the organization for three years in a technical capacity, demonstrates some stability in self-description over the year. Six of her 20 statements remain unchanged, almost word for word. On balance her self-image is positive, although both sets of responses indicate some ambivalence in self-presentation.

Table 8.1 The most common pattern of response: a slight shift away from reflective

	Phase 1	Phase 2
1	I am married [B]	I am married [B]
2	I am broad-minded [C]	I live in (name of place) [A]
3	I am friendly [C]	I am social [C]
4	I am interested in the environment [C]	I am career minded [C]
5	I am of a nervous disposition [C]	I am outgoing [C]
6	I am not very self-confident [C]	I am not very self-confident [C]
7	I am fairly intelligent [C]	I am always considering alternatives [C]
8	I am outgoing [C]	I tend to worry [C]
9	I am ambitious [C]	I am moderately ambitious [C]
10	I am not always articulate [C]	I am moderately materialistic [C]
11	I am a worrier [C]	I enjoy travelling [C]
12	I enjoy the arts [C]	I tend to be discontented [C]
13	I am not a sportswoman [C]	I am cautious about acting on new ideas [C]
14	I enjoy living in (name of place) [C]	I like to be popular [C]
15	I am interested in travel [C]	I am efficient (generally) [C]
16	I am close to my parents [C]	I enjoy the theatre [C]
17	I am moderately efficient [C]	I am very happy with my home [C]
18	I enjoy socializing [C]	I enjoy an intellectual challenge [C]
19	I can be lethargic [C]	I sometimes over-react [C]
20	I tend to jump to conclusions [C]	I try to be perfectionist [C]

Twelve of the 97 respondents gave responses more or less equally distributed across the physical, social and reflective categories. Again, this pattern was more typical of people who had worked in the organization for several years, and demonstrates a striking stability of self definition, partly due to the high level of physical and social description. But even reflective definitions tended not to change over time. Typically, we found that people identifying themselves as equally A-, B- and C-mode made no negative evaluations, projecting an unproblematic, objective, 'this is how others see me and this is how I am' image. These individuals were closest to Zurcher's (1977) 'mutable selves'.

Reliability of referential frame scoring

Agreement between the two female postgraduate raters on the primary cut made on this rich qualitative data, the referential frames A-B-C-D + uncodeable category, was 94 per cent, in line with the level of agreement reported for various studies by Spitzer et al. (1973). However, agreement in some cases fell to 12 or 14 out of the 20 statements given. Clearly, even on this primary A-B-C-D cut, some sets of responses proved much easier to code than others, typically those involving conventional single phrase self-descriptions. The minority of respondents who provide more extended multi-phrase and qualified expressions presented more difficulties. However, the general rule adopted for multiple single responses ('a keen sportsman and supporter of the arts') was to code the first clause only, though there may be the need for some flexibility in applying this rule.

In general, we achieved less reliability on the first-phase responses given by new entrants. One reason for this was that they tended to use more complex linguistic constructions. Second, they expressed more uncertainty about their current working state. Table 8.2 shows a case that illustrates a degree of ambivalence, a 21-year-old man who had entered a technical environment within the previous two weeks. Our purpose in selecting this case is also to demonstrate some of our difficulty in resolving competing interpretations.

The disagreements here nearly all arise from ambiguity between the social (B) and reflective (C) classes, a confusion most often generated by responses which add some qualification to stated membership of a social class or grouping. Where there is such qualification, we work on the principle that the statement is primarily reflective rather than social: although 'I am a student' would be (B) social, 'I have many of the trappings of a student' is a (C) reflective statement. The use of the word 'patriot' in statement 14 illustrates a different kind of ambiguity. Rater 2 understandably classified this as a B-type response, on the implicit reasoning that it connoted a distinct set of social attitudes. But even though patriotic attitudes might turn out to be associated with particular social groups (for example, a political party or interest group) 'patriot' itself denotes no identifiable social role or grouping. Thus beliefs and values clearly anchored in social norms and associated with social categories are reflective unless the respondent's social position is the explicit frame for them. Again, Rater 2 chose to use the 'uncodeable' class for the first two statements, feeling that they were too ambiguous to code, whilst Rater 1 decided that they were in the reflective category, since they seemed to carry overtones of an identification which was situation-free but significant to this individual.

By the time he completed the TST a year later, this man demonstrated less uncertainty, identifying himself more consistently within the work context, and making more B (social) 'other-orientated' statements. In consequence, we achieved higher agreement on his second-phase responses.

Table 8.2 Resolving competing interpretations: ambiguity between social and reflective classes

		Rater 1	Rater 2
1	I am an Englishman at heart	C	uc[1]
2	I am half foreign by ancestry and it does affect me	C	uc[1]
3	I am a Christian still learning what it means to be one	C	C
4	I am a loyal friend	C	C
5	I am sometimes almost medieval in my moral judgements	C	C
6	I enjoy being a host and sharing with people	C	C
7	I am uncertain of my future	C	C
8	It does not worry me that I do not know what is coming	C	C
9	I have many of the trappings of a student	C	B[2]
10	I have not yet become a working man	C	C
11	I am a liberal intellectual	C	C
12	I am sceptical about many new ideas	C	C
13	I am a democrat	C	C
14	I am a patriot	C	B[2]
15	Even though I have finished studying I feel like a historian	C	B[2]
16	I am a would-be playwright	C	C
17	I am an actor	B	B
18	I am a runner at heart, even though I am not training at present	C	B[2]
19	Many of my choices are still dictated by social pressures	C	C
20	I am fairly self-sufficient, and do not depend on any particular person	C	C

[1] Uncodable.
[2] Competing interpretations.

ADDITIONAL CODING METHODS

The overwhelming preponderance of C type responses convinced us of the need for finer analysis of the content of the reflective data. For this purpose, we initially took Kuhn and McPartland's (1954) 'inclusive categories' as a basis for sub-dividing identity-related constructs:

1 ideological beliefs (individuals' explanations of the cosmos, life, society – and their part in them);
2 interests (approach and avoidance with respect to social objects);
3 ambitions (status and role intentions, anticipations and expectations about positions in social systems);
4 self-evaluations (varieties of pride or self mortification over the way individuals imagine they appear to others who matter to them).

It was apparent that the fourth of Kuhn and McPartland's categories was not exclusive of the others; for example, one could reflect on one's ambitions in a spirit equally of self-derogation or pride. Therefore we set aside self-evaluation as a completely orthogonal classificatory dimension, which we shall discuss shortly. The remaining three we augmented to make up a fourfold system of:

1   skills and abilities;
2   interests and needs;
3   character and behavioural style;
4   values and beliefs.

We then analysed responses in terms of the scales, traits and dimensions commonly found in psychometric instruments in each of these areas, collapsing categories where discrimination proved difficult.

Table 8.3 describes the rating scheme in detail, and gives typical examples of constructs and their antonyms in each of the system's 31 categories. Readers should note that responses can receive a plus or a minus score for a given category according to whether respondents explicitly state it or its antonym as a self-description.

Self evaluation

Our third method of classification was based upon implicit self-evaluative content. This method completes the triangle of three complementary analytical approaches: response type (referential frame), response content (the SICV – Skills, Interests, Character and Values System), and response value (self-evaluation). The obvious application of the last of these would be for the TST to be sensitive to the psychological health or adaptive state of the subject, as measured conventionally by such constructs as self-esteem, ego-strength, self-efficacy, stress and well-being. We adopted a simple threefold coding: 3 = positive, 2 = neutral and 1 = negative.

Agreement on 2,983 statements was 83 per cent for negative, 62 per cent for neutral and 77 per cent for positive evaluations. The low agreement neutral was largely due to one rater's reluctance to use a negative rating: disagreements were nearly always in the same direction. Taking just the reliably rated C-type statements, 57 per cent at phase one and 55 per cent a year later were positive; 23 per cent and 24 per cent were neutral; and 20 per cent and 21 per cent were negative. This further demonstrates stability over time: the proportion of negative statements is an indication of the openness of self-disclosure.

Even this response value rating proved to have its difficulties. Our guidance for raters is again to maintain a holistic orientation: look at the whole range of an individual's responses as a meaning-imbued context, within which there are likely to be clues about the evaluative intent in an ambiguous response. The neutral category should be used where there are conflicting indicators or ambiguities for other reasons, and in all other cases where the respondent's intent cannot be clearly discerned. In view of this overriding consideration, one approach to coding for self-evaluation is, as recommended by Spitzer et al. (1973), to ask respondents to evaluate their own statements. This method can be used interactively with individuals for all the systems we have described, if appropriate to the context and purpose.

THE TST AND THE STUDY OF PERSONAL CHANGE

One aim has been to describe the three-part rating system we developed to capture as much as possible of what was psychologically valid about these employees' self-definitions. Along the way, we have selected data to illustrate the degree of shift or stability in employees' self-

Table 8.3 The Nicholson-Rees SICV (Skills, Interests, Character and Values) system for categorizing TST reflective statements

---

(i)   Skills, abilities, attainments

01   *Cognitive skills*: being intelligent, quick-witted, good memory, analytical; (antonyms) slow
02   *Social skills*: persuasive, negotiating, relating to others, impression management, verbal fluency, approachable, being well liked, tactful, perceptive; (antonyms) tongue-tied, aloof, tactless
03   *Technical skills*: good at languages, computing, report writing, numerate, knowledgeable, experienced; (antonyms) poor/bad at specifics
04   *Organizational skills*: administrative skills, methodical, accurate, tidy, persevering, finishes, meets deadlines, decision-making, conscientious; (antonyms) scatterbrained, sloppy, unpunctual
05   *Adaptive*: independent minded, self-sufficient, innovative, problem-solving; (antonyms) non-creative, lacking initiative, perfectionist
06   *Achieving*: good at job, effective, successful, able, professional; (antonyms) ineffective, failure
07   *Fortunate*: lucky, privileged, wealthy, high status, non-specific 'talented'; (antonyms) unlucky

---

(ii)   Interests, needs, motives

08   *Need for achievement*: like challenge, competing, achieving, ambitious, determined; (antonyms) non-competitive, unambitious
09   *Need for power*: like controlling, assertive, dominant, argumentative, overbearing; (antonyms) modest, democratic, passive
10   *Need for affiliation*: needing and being interested in other people, liking groups, conforming, in love; (antonyms) only a few intimates, being a loner, liking solitude
11   *Need for growth*: interest in/need for development, learning, growth, interested; (antonyms) not wanting to change
     [NB use this category to denote desires/motives; use 19 where outlook or style are implied]
12   *Arts, sciences, entertainments*: likes, hobbies, interests in literature, music, sciences; (no antonym)
13   *Work orientation*: career minded, committed, involved; (antonyms) family more important than job [family orientated, use 10]
14   *Physical, active*: sporty, keen to keep fit, active, athletic; (antonyms) unfit, sedentary, overweight

---

(iii)   Character, style

15   *Outgoing*: lively, easily bored, flirt, humorous, friendly, sociable, trendy, attractive; (antonyms) reserved, quiet, serious, sober, studious
16   *Conceptual*: abstract, theoretical, analytical (types, not skills), critical; (antonyms) practical, scientific, logical
17   *Confident*: self-confident, arrogant, complacent, direct, straightforward; (antonyms) shy, uncertain, awkward
18   *Impulsive*: risk-taking, hasty, romantic, restless, spendthrift; (antonyms) considered, unadventurous, patient
19   *Open to experience*: open-minded, tolerant, expectant, keen to travel, change-oriented, complex; (antonyms) opinionated, obstinate, cynical, suspicious
20   *Caring*: considerate, helpful, sensitive (to others), good listener; (antonyms) self-centred, nasty to people
21   *Well-being*: happy, optimistic, satisfied, relaxed (mood); (antonyms) pessimistic, depressed, anxious, frustrated
22   *Self application*: energetic, hardworking, fit, a worker, persevering, involved, enthusiastic, busy, proactive; (antonyms) lazy, cowardly, easily tired, unmotivated

Table 8.3   *cont.*

23   *Emotional:* changeable, moody, shows feelings, easily hurt, a worrier, nervous; (antonyms) calm, steady, relaxed [type]

24   *Reliable:* good, decent, loyal, trustworthy, sincere, honest; (antonyms) moral self condemnations [neutral = other self statements]

25   *Introspective:* self-critical, self-aware; (antonyms) ignorant about self, unaware of what I want

(iv)   Values, beliefs

26   *Religious:* Christian, member of named religious group; (antonyms) atheist, agnostic

27   *Political:* right-wing, liberal, radical, conservative; (antonyms) apolitical

28   *Ethical:* humanistic, environmentalist, other value statements; (antonyms) no moral beliefs

29   *Psychological:* statements of belief about human nature

(v)   Others

30   *Miscellaneous:* habits, customs, tastes: vegetarian, nail-biter

31   *Expectations:* planning to emigrate, get married

identification over one year in their work environment. As we have stated, repertory grids were also used with these graduate entrants (Arnold and Nicholson, 1991), from which one of the major findings was how stable their self-concept proved to be over the year, even for those who had just entered the organization. Through the TSTs, we expected to find evidence of subtle changes in self-identity. Although the great majority of individuals were still in the reflective mode at phase two, the percentage of B-type responses had increased. We interpret this as evidence of a shift, particularly amongst new recruits, towards greater stability within explicitly structured situations, often in relation to work. However, the reader has seen from several examples how stable self-definition remained.

EVALUATION

The measure's capacity to reflect the salience of facets of identity is a critical feature favouring the TST over other instruments. The open-ended format allows individuals to determine the type and order of response, and gives them the opportunity to define their personal constructs. This is a special advantage over conventional techniques. Another is its ability to reflect the extent to which individuals locate and evaluate themselves within the social system. These internalized aspects of the self based on social relationships and role identities are largely inaccessible to fixed response self-concept measurement. We found that 28 of the 32 women (or 88 per cent) made a statement about being 'a woman', 'female', 'girl', 'career woman', 'a business woman', or 'an independent woman' within their first three statements, whereas only 22 of the 62 men (36 per cent) identified themselves as 'male' or 'a man' in their first few statements. In a technically based organization, and in these specific occupational groups, gender is of greater salience to women, but for men is more thoroughly internalized and therefore not articulated. We do not know of any other measure that would have brought this difference out so clearly, because none other would offer equal scope for individuals to define their own identities. Apart from gender for women, occupational and family membership categories were highly salient for this sample of young people.

Projective measures have long been used in clinical practice as diagnostic aids, and found wide acceptance in other applied fields, especially to derive indices of achievement, affiliation and power motivation (McClelland, 1961, 1987). Sentence-completion and draw-a-person techniques (Loevinger, 1976, 1987) have had similar applications, with similar claimed advantages over quantitative methods. These are all valuable techniques, but present analytical difficulties, such as prior investigator interpretation, creating unpredictable demand characteristics, or eliciting responses which may vary on many dimensions, highlighting familiar problems of reliability and validity. As we have seen, the TST does not completely avoid all these difficulties, but it does have the twin virtues of openness and transparency: openness in that a single direct stimulus instruction produces a specified number of discrete but unconstrained responses; and transparency in the face validity of the task, which elicits self-descriptions directly. Of course, respondents may still wonder what the investigator will do with the material, or how it will be interpreted, but this can be more openly shared, without invalidating the data, than in conventional projective tests.

In some research settings one might imagine classifications being conducted collaboratively with respondents. This method would be especially useful in instructional contexts, where, for example, one wanted to explore with a group of students or managers the meanings and implications of their self images, or of the specific social environment of interest. In career guidance, the method could be imagined as a useful adjunct to the assessment of opportunities and choices. It is also apparent that the TST can be a powerful tool in clinical practice, where a counsellor or therapist wishes to explore with clients the salient constructs they apply to themselves.

In published research, the A-B-C-D method of rating is usually the system exclusively used to quantify results, though, as we have demonstrated here, there are further riches to be extracted by additional analytical frames. In our own research we are undertaking extended analysis and evaluation of reflective statements, to reveal their psychological content. Ours is very much a developing system, and we hope that others will be encouraged to use the methodology, and offer suggestions for its extension.

FURTHER READING

Epistemological underpinnings

The current literature provides several examples of the TST used in research. However, to understand the theoretical strands underlying the symbolic interactionist approach, we recommend that readers return to early pioneering work in the field. The strand originating in William James's (1890) work was that the self can be viewed as an entity that is 'known' (the 'me' or the object of knowledge) and also as the 'knower' (the 'I' or the agency) (see Berkowitz (1988)). The philosopher Charles Sanders Peirce (1839–1914) (see Brent (2000)) insisted that knowledge is inferential and tripartite, requiring three elements, a sign, the object signified, and the interpretant. Another theoretical strand of importance derives from the work of C.H. Cooley, who proposed that how one is perceived by significant others determines one's view of the self, and that people are accurate in perceiving how they are perceived by others (see Cook and Douglas (1998)). These three original sources will help the reader to integrate different theoretical perspectives on how our ideas of our selves are constructed.

REFERENCES ——————————————————————————

Arnold, J. and Nicholson, N. (1991) 'Construing of self and others at work in the early years of corporate careers', *Journal of Organizational Behaviour*, 12 (7): 621–39.

Berkowitz, L. (ed.) (1988) *Advances in Experimental Social Psychology*, vol. 21: *Social Psychological Studies of the Self: Perspectives and Programs*, San Diego, CA: Academic Press, Inc.

Bettencourt, B.A. and Hume, D. (1999) 'The cognitive contents of social-group identity: values, emotions, and relationships', *European Journal of Social Psychology*, 29 (1): 113–21.

Brent, J. (2000) 'A brief introduction to the life and thought of Charles Sanders Pierce', in J. Muller. and J. Brent. (eds), *Peirce, Semiotics, and Psychoanalysis. Psychiatry and the Humanities*, vol. 15, Baltimore, MD: Johns Hopkins University Press.

Cook, W.L. and Douglas, E.M. (1998) 'The looking-glass self in family context: a social relations analysis', *Journal of Family Psychology*, 12(3): 299–309.

Coover, G.E. and Murphy, S.T. (2000) 'The communicated self: exploring the interaction between self and social context', *Human Communication Research*, 26 (1): 125–47.

Jennings, P.S., Holmstrom, R.W. and Karp, S.A. (1986) 'Personality correlates of reflectivity', *Psychological Reports*, 59 (1): 87–94.

Kuhn, M.H. (1950) 'Mutual derogation', unpublished manuscript.

Kuhn, M.H. and McPartland, T.A. (1954) 'An empirical investigation of self attitudes', *American Sociological Review*, 19: 68–76.

Locatelli, V. and West, M.A. (1991) 'On elephants and blind researchers: methods for accessing culture in organizations', MRC/ESRC SAPU memo no. 1281.

Loevinger, J. (1976) *Ego Development*, San Francisco: Jossey-Bass Inc.

Loevinger, J. (1987) *Paradigms of Personality*, New York: W.H.Freeman & Co.

McClelland, D.C. (1961) *The Achieving Society*, Princeton, NJ: D van Nostrand Company, Inc.

McClelland, D.C. (1987) *Human Motivation*, Cambridge: Cambridge University Press.

McPartland, T.S. (1965) *Manual for the Twenty Statements Problem (Revised)*, Kansas City, MO: Department of Research, Greater Kansas City Mental Health Foundation.

Nicholson, N. and Arnold, J. (1989a) 'Graduate entry and adjustment to corporate life', *Personnel Review*, 18 (3): 23–35.

Nicholson, N. and Arnold, J. (1989b) 'Graduate early experience in a multinational corporate', *Personnel Review*, 18 (4): 3–14.

Nicholson, N. and Arnold, J. (1990) 'From expectation to experience: graduates entering a large corporation', *Journal of Occupational Behaviour*, 12: 413–29.

Spitzer, S., Couch, C. and Stratton, J. (1973) *The Assessment of the Self*, Iowa City, IA: Sernoll Inc.

Walker, H., Symon, G. and Davies, B. (1996) 'Assessing organizational culture: a comparison of methods', *International Journal of Selection and Assessment*, 4: 96–105.

Zurcher, L.A. (1977) *The Mutable Self: A Self Concept for Social Change*, Beverly Hills, CA: Sage.

Qualitative Research Diaries ————————————

Gillian Symon

We are familiar with the concept of diaries as either calendars in which we record planned future activities or an autobiographical account of events, thoughts and feelings we have experienced, usually recorded on a daily basis. The growing interest in conducting diary studies *as a research method* has tended to be from within a positivist paradigm, focusing on quantified measurements. In contrast, this chapter aims to encourage *qualitative* diary research by offering some practical design and implementation guidelines, as applied to organizational settings.

USES OF DIARIES IN RESEARCH ——————————————————————————

> The diary is the document of life par excellence, chronicling as it does the immediately contemporaneous flow of public and private events that are significant to the diarist. (Plummer, 1983: 17)

Diaries can be used to investigate a wide range of subjective phenomena. Respondents may be asked to record: reactions and feelings; specific behaviours; social interactions; activities (namely activity logs for example, Sonnentag, 2001); and/or events. The diary study allows access to this ongoing everyday behaviour in a relatively unobtrusive manner, which allows the immediacy of the experience to be captured, and also provides accounts of phenomena over time. Some claim it allows 'hidden' behaviours and events to be revealed for example, violence in the workplace (Leadbetter, 1993).

In organizational settings diaries are most often utilized in research into shift work or stress. Typically, in the case of shift work, respondents may be asked to monitor feelings of overload, eating patterns and mood before and after a change in shift schedule to establish disruptive effects and stabilization periods (for example, Williamson et al., 1994). In stress research, respondents may be asked to identify stressors, evaluate the intensity of the stress impact, and record measures of other concurrent physiological and emotional experiences, thus allowing the description of variations in stress responses over time, links between stress responses and other 'symptoms', and the identification of 'everyday' stressors (namely daily hassles, for example, Kenner et al., 1981). A more recent application is the study of violations of the psychological contract (Conway and Briner, 2002), where the recording of violations is then linked to (quantitative) ratings of affective reactions and general mood.

More unusually, diaries may be used as an intervention tool. In the occupational stress area, for example, respondents use 'stress logs' to monitor physiological symptoms of stress over time, the results of which can be analysed to identify patterns and formulate coping strategies (for example, Ross and Altmaier, 1994). Diaries have also been utilized as a training tool for managers (for example, Jepsen et al., 1989), allowing them to reflect on their work habits and work towards more effective personal strategies, for example, better time management.

DIARY DESIGNS

Diary studies, like interviews (King, Chapter 2, this volume), have the advantage that most respondents are familiar with the concept and are aware of what 'keeping a diary' means. However, diaries used for research purposes may look very different from the kind of personal diaries individuals may keep.

Most (published) diary studies use structured and quantitative measures (namely questions requiring yes/no answers or ratings) and the emphasis is on repeated measures of phenomena specified by the researcher. Diaries as intervention tools, however, tend to adopt a more open-format response style allowing respondents to recount feelings about personally meaningful events. Thus, Burt (1994) asked a sample of students to keep a diary where they were required simply to recall events of the day in an idiosyncratic way in order to investigate how daily recall of events related to measures of stress and anxiety. An interesting aspect of this study, from the point of view of this chapter, is that Burt required all the respondents to summarize their daily responses using seven provided codes (for example, 'thoughts, feelings and emotions', 'problems and hassles' etc. (1994: 333). All further (quantitative) analysis conducted by Burt was carried out using these codes. While ethical considerations are clearly important here, there also seems to be some waste of potentially insightful material. Of course the author's objective was to test hypotheses and from a positivist perspective this requires standard (quantitative) measures of phenomena. Hence, Stewart (1967), despite having conducted a large diary study, dismissed the material as unreliable because she judged the respondents were interpreting categories of activities in different ways. Indeed, from within a positivist paradigm, this issue is very problematic. However, from alternative perspectives, these concerns are less of an issue, given the rejection of a realist position and the acceptance of the relevance of individual accounts (for example, Woolgar, 1996). The 'problem', therefore, does not lie with the method but rests on the epistemological assumptions of the researcher. Thus, in line with the key characteristics of qualitative approaches to research (Cassell and Symon, 1994), 'qualitative' diaries may not pre-specify activities, events, attitudes or feelings but allow the respondent to record subjective perceptions of phenomena of relevance to themselves at that point in time. The objective of the researcher is to understand the respondent's reactions, descriptions, and so on from the respondent's perspective and within the context of their own worlds.

There are far fewer published instances of researchers adopting alternative (namely non-positivist) less-structured approaches to their diary design and analysis. Exceptions include the 'illness diaries', used by Stensland and Malterud (1999) within an action research framework (see Heller, Chapter 28, this volume) to investigate ongoing patient symptoms. In this particular study, the GP and the patient designed the diary together and patients were free to record both their symptoms and also their reactions to these as they wished. This document acted both as a communication tool and a prompt to further reflection and discussion. Plowman (2002) has used diaries in her PhD research to investigate the role of the organizational change agent. Her respondents made a weekly entry based on a series of four very open 'guiding questions' (for example, 'What happened this week that really made an impact on you?'). This allowed her to explore more of the informal practices of change and encouraged the respondents in some self-reflection on their role. Finally, Lindén (1996) reports the use of diaries to investigate psychosocial issues in the working lives of professional actors. The actors were asked to keep autobiographical diaries which they then brought to regular meetings of all the actors taking part in the research. Each week, one individual would read out their diary which would then form the basis of a group discussion. In this way, the researchers sought to challenge the supremacy of the author's (or the researcher's) voice and bring out alternative 'readings'.

DESIGN CONSIDERATIONS

I have suggested below some questions the aspiring diary researcher should ask themselves before and during their diary study. It is, of course, impossible (and probably not desirable) to provide step-by-step instructions – all contexts are different and the researcher and their respondents need to decide what is desirable and feasible in any particular situation. However, these questions may at least provide a starting point. I illustrate these questions through a discussion of my own qualitative diary study, which took place within a case study of the development and implementation of IT workstations in a public service organization (pseudonym DTA). In the early stages of this research, I was focusing on the development team and was interested in identifying what activities constituted IT development work.

What are you interested in finding out and do you need a diary study to do this?

The research objectives (What is the phenomenon of interest? What do you want to investigate?) should come well before considerations of methodology. If you are clear about why you want to conduct a diary study in particular, the design of the study and the analysis will be much easier.

OBJECTIVES OF THE DTA DIARY STUDY

I felt that the literature on the work of technical experts concentrated too much on their (so-called) 'technical' work (for example, designing software, testing hardware, and so on) and I suspected a wider range of activities given the technicians' potential roles as organizational change agents (Keen, 1981). So I wanted to get a picture of the sorts of activities they were engaged in on a daily basis. I was also aware that many (supposedly trivial) decisions were made and unpredictable events occurred on a daily basis which could change the direction of the IT project and have future repercussions. I wanted to capture some of those moments, partly to capture the complexity of the technological change process as it happens but, also, because I was planning a longitudinal study and thought I might find these data useful in interpreting future events. Furthermore, I was interested in each individual's account of what was occurring – sometimes different perceptions of the same events.

Another important consideration in deciding to conduct a diary study was my relationship with the members of the development team. I had been involved in this research for several months before the diary study took place, and had established a fairly good relationship with (most of) the potential diary respondents. Consequently, I felt that

I *could* ask them to keep diaries for me (which can be quite an onerous task).

Who should fill it in?

The available literature on diary design, as it is predicated on the collection of quantitative data, assumes the need to gather a representative sample (Stone et al., 1991). However, the rather different underlying assumptions of alternative paradigms may suggest different strategies. The major consideration therefore might be to ask yourself, 'Who is *relevant*?' Additionally, most qualitative diaries are likely to be pen-and-paper and require a certain amount of discursive material from the respondent. This does have implications for the likely literacy level of participants (see Carp and Carp, 1981 for other demographic factors which might affect diary completion).

PARTICIPANTS IN THE DTA DIARY STUDY

For me, the group of participants was, to a great extent, predetermined, defined by their membership of the development team. However, this is not as unproblematic as it first appears. For example, who is a member of the development team and who is not? For the purposes of the larger study, I had already formulated a definition of 'the development team' which was more inclusive than many previous assumptions. Furthermore, it should be borne in mind that, over time, the constitution of the team can change. In my case, no-one joined or left mid-way through this particular diary study – but this eventuality should be considered in the design of any similar study. In all, 10 members of the development team kept individual diaries.

How often should respondents fill it in and over what period of time?

This rather depends on the objectives of the research project. Respondents could be asked to complete the diary at a particular specified time (for example, end of the day); after pre-specified events (for example, an organizational meeting); or at specific intervals throughout the day (for example, every two hours) (Parkinson et al., 1996). You should be aware of the context in which diary completion is taking place – for example, will the diary be completed during a time of organizational upheaval (which does not form part of your research interests) and what implications does that have for the reporting of events and attitudes? If the diary study is related to a particular organizational project, is there any specific stage of that project when diaries might prove most fruitful?

SCHEDULE OF DTA DIARY COMPLETION

Given my objectives, I expected a daily completion, at the end of the day, would be sufficient for most respondents. However, given the disparate roles of the team members, it was clear that some would be working full-time on the project while some would be also working on other projects. Consequently, in order to encourage completion and be sensitive to the demands on and different circumstances of the respondents, some respondents did not complete the diaries on a daily basis but as and when they were engaged in a (self-defined) 'relevant' activity.

I decided to conduct the study over a period of a month, which I felt was long enough in the context of this particular project to allow all the team members to have been engaged in a number of project relevant activities. This period covered the middle to end of one project phase and the beginning of the next, thus potentially including a variety of activities.

The most dedicated respondent in this case – the project manager – was commuting to and from work and filled in his diary on the train on the way home every day. He therefore had a specified time and place for completion which suffered from few distractions and rarely varied. I think this illustrates a more general point. While I did discuss with participants when they should complete the diary at the time of distribution, it might have been helpful if I had worked on specifying a *particular* time and place with them.

What questions should you ask and what is the best medium?

Again, this depends on the purpose of the research study. You should bear in mind that you will not be present to explain completion requirements (although, as suggested below, you should have spent some time with the respondents at the outset demonstrating the diary). Therefore the method of completion should be as self-explanatory as possible and the questions clear.

You (in collaboration with the respondents?) have to decide what degree of structure is required in the diary. Are there particular issues you want to see covered? Or is it particular events you are interested in? Can the respondents note any information they feel is relevant? Or do you want to orient them to specific aspects of the event, experience, and so on?

Most diary studies are pen-and-paper but you could consider dictaphones or computerized personal organizers (there are clearly cost issues here, including programming the personal organizers). When using booklets, it makes intuitive sense to keep response pages to one page so as not to overburden the respondent (one page looks less daunting) or cause omissions (when people fail to turn over the page).

DTA DIARY STRUCTURE

I did not want to assume what activities might constitute a 'day-in-the-life' of a systems developer and I wanted to understand the concerns of the participants from their perspective. So my diaries consisted of open-ended questions, as shown in Figure 9.1.

Each A4 page represented one activity. Requiring the respondents to note date and other participants in the activity meant that I could later match up accounts of events from the perspectives of different project team members. I was interested in the purpose of the activity in terms of how the respondent saw this activity as contributing to the overall project and what they were expecting to achieve. I asked about outcome to ascertain whether this was an ongoing activity and because I thought that might help me to link activities recorded here to future activities. Their evaluation of the activity I thought would give some indication of whether the purpose they had identified was achieved and some idea of *why* they regarded activities as successful or not.

Despite the fact that I had visited each of the respondents individually and explained the diary study to them, I still included a front page (see Figure 9.2) detailing how often they should complete the diary, how long they should take on the task and some examples of likely entries. In this latter case, I had to weigh up the disadvantage of unduly influencing the participants' responses against the advantage of giving the participants some guidance so they felt more comfortable with the task. In the end, I decided to provide the examples, and the respondents did provide examples which differed from those I suggested.

At the time of the diary study, my key contact within the organization was the user project

Date:

Activity:

Participants:

What is the purpose of this activity from your point of view?

Outcomes of the activity (e.g. problems solved, new activities revealed, activities completed, activities postponed/cancelled)?

Has this been a straightforward or a difficult activity? Why?

Figure 9.1   Page from DTA diary

\<Project name\> Project diary

At the end of each day, please spend 15 minutes describing your major activities over the day in relation to the \<project name\> project. The activities may include: a telephone conversation; writing a document; attending a meeting; discussion with colleagues; devising diagrams, etc. The nature and number of the activities will largely depend on your role in the project(s).

When describing these activities, please try to answer as fully as possible.

The completed record will be considered confidential.

Figure 9.2   Diary frontispiece

manager, who agreed to pilot the diary for me for a week. This exercise did forewarn me that at particularly busy periods, respondents might be less conscientious in regularly updating the diaries, so I was prepared to try to negotiate this point with individuals at the time of diary distribution. Otherwise, the user project manager did not report any problems in understanding the questions or completing the task.

How should the diaries be distributed?

A major concern in diary-based research is participant attrition. Quite apart from obvious ethical considerations, one way of retaining participants is to explain the requirements of the study as thoroughly as possible from the beginning, including the likely demands. In this way, the participants know what to expect and are not caught unawares or feel as if they have been deceived. Explaining the instructions very carefully is also of the utmost importance. You will not be at hand to advise your respondents (although you should leave a contact telephone number or e-mail address so that they can contact you with queries).

Explain the objectives of your research plan. Apart from being ethically appropriate, this allows respondents to understand properly the importance of regular and comprehensive completion (*if these factors are important to your study*). It may also be helpful to the participant to give some indication of the amount of time you would expect diary completion to take on a daily basis. This will give some idea of the time commitment required and also the depth of response sought (for example, an hour's writing every evening suggests quite a different kind of response than 10 minutes!).

DTA DIARY DISTRIBUTION
I already knew most of the members of the development team and either phoned them up directly to ask them to take part in the diary study or asked them in the context of some other contact (for example, an interview or a site visit). I visited each of the respondents individually (sometimes in pairs) to give out the diary and explain the requirements of the diary study. I explained that I was interested in understanding, in relative detail, the day-to-day work of system development. My impression was that they were very happy to 'help me out' with my project as long as it did not interfere too much with their everyday activities. Consequently

I 'sold' the diaries with that view in mind, bearing in mind that I did not want to alienate them by overtaxing their commitment to the research process. This may have had implications for individual attitudes to diary completion, and I summarize strategies for encouraging diary completion in the evaluation section p. 111.

What happens over the course of diary completion?

It has been suggested that the first week of diary keeping is most susceptible to attrition (Stone et al., 1991), and, consequently, it is a good idea to keep in particularly close contact with participants during this time. For example, phone up to check how their diary is progressing. This gives the respondents a chance to ask you any questions that might have arisen since your initial briefing. It has also been observed (Stone et al., 1991) that if respondents fail to complete their diary on one or two occasions they may assume that they are no longer appropriate for the study and give up. You may not be aware this has happened and it may be useful to reassure respondents at this point. Indeed, it is a good idea to keep in regular contact throughout the period of the diary study (say once a week if the diary is to be kept for a few months), thus avoiding the respondent feeling they have been abandoned or that you are no longer interested in them. However, the degree of contact must be a case for personal discretion – there should be no question of 'pestering' the respondent or 'forcing' them to complete their diary. If the respondents are sufficiently committed to the study itself then you should be able to rely upon self-motivation.

MONITORING DTA DIARY COMPLETION

Over the time-span of the diary study, I was regularly visiting the organization for other reasons. Consequently, I was often in touch with members of the development team and would enquire about their experiences of diary completion. Generally speaking, they would claim to be completing the diary regularly, although many pointed out that this was not always on a daily basis. Clearly, this was rather a casual form of monitoring and is certainly something I would have done differently with hindsight – leading me now to emphasize regular contact as an important component of the diary study research design.

What should I do when it is time to collect the (hopefully) completed diaries?

As suggested above, the diary study can be a serious commitment on the part of the respondent and this should not go unacknowledged. Participants are entitled to proper feedback about the study in which they have invested so much time and effort, and in the outcomes of which they may well have a vested interest. Spend some time with the participant discussing how they felt about completing the diary and any issues that arose during the study. This kind of information is also important to the interpretation of the responses. Once you have formed a view of the results of the overall study, go back to the respondents and discuss that interpretation with them: do they see it the same way? If not, why not? In essence, this approach is similar to the 'diary-interview diary' advocated by Zimmerman and Wieder (1977).

DTA DIARY COLLECTION AND DEBRIEFING

At the end of the month, I visited each respondent at work to collect their diaries and had a general discussion of their experiences around the following questions:

- how they had selected what activities to record (namely what constitutes a relevant project activity) and what was omitted;
- the ease (or otherwise) with which they were able to record activities;
- the degree to which they felt keeping a diary changed the activities under review;
- how often they recorded events; and
- the degree to which they found the diaries useful.

Most claimed to have recorded their major activities concerning the project, excluding phone calls or brief discussions between colleagues working closely together (although a few respondents *did* record this material). Respondents varied according to whether they thought recording the activities actually changed their perceptions of that activity or their methods of pursuing the activities. About half felt that the diaries had had no impact. However, three others reported that the process of keeping a diary made them more reflective (for example, 'made me consciously deliberate over shortcomings', 'made me use my time better') and gave them insight on their activities: '. . . you realize [in meetings] you didn't make a decision – so woolly it was a waste of time . . .'. The important thing to note about this debriefing material is that it is an *integral part* of the research study which aided my interpretation of the actual diary material.

What can I do with the responses?

This is something that might be most helpfully considered *before* designing the diary. Again this seems like an obvious point but often we find ourselves at the end of a research project with a mound of data by which we feel overwhelmed. The manner of analysing the data is largely dependent on the purposes of the research and the format of the diary, and it is not the purpose of this chapter to describe all potential forms of analysis. The case study outlined below gives one specific example. However, you could also consider a 'thematic' analysis (looking for common themes in the data either across instances with one individual or across individuals, see King, Chapter 2, this volume). Stakeholder analysis (for example, Burgoyne, 1994) might be helpful in comparing different perspectives from different individuals on the same event. You could also look for patterns and changes across time using, for example, event listing and time-ordered matrices (see Nadin and Cassell, Chapter 22, this volume).

DTA DIARY DATA ANALYSIS

All 10 diaries were returned. Given the open-ended nature of the task, it was hardly surprising to find considerable differences in response 'styles'. Some respondents made very brief entries, while others were much more expansive.

Each of the diaries was then transcribed as an 'activity diagram'. Figure 9.3 comes from the Project Manager's (PM's) diary and Figure 9.4 from the User Project Manager's (UPM's) diary. Figure 9.5 is from a recent recruit to the team. In all of the figures, only a subset of the material is reproduced here to ease presentation.

The major activities identified form the central 'bubbles', surrounding these are specific

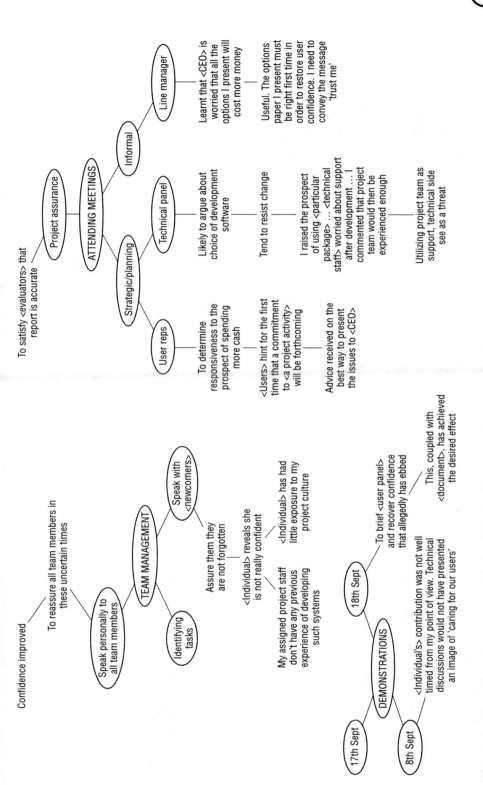

Figure 9.3 Diary of the project manager. Originally published as Figure 6.4 in Symon, G. (1998) *Qualitative research diaries*. In G. Symon and C. Cassell (eds) *Qualitative Methods in Organisational Research and Analysis*. London: Sage Publications. p 110.

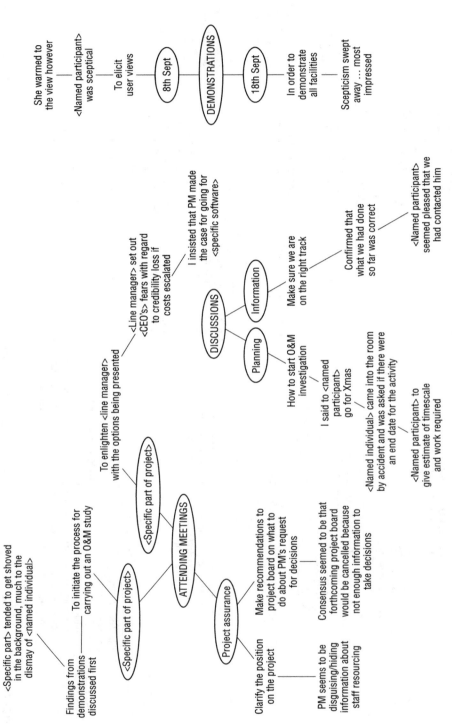

Figure 9.4 Diary of the user project manager. Originally published as Figure 6.5 in Symon, G. (1998) *Qualitative research diaries.* In G. Symon and C. Cassell (eds) *Qualitative Methods in Organizational Research and Analysis.* London: Sage Publications. p 111

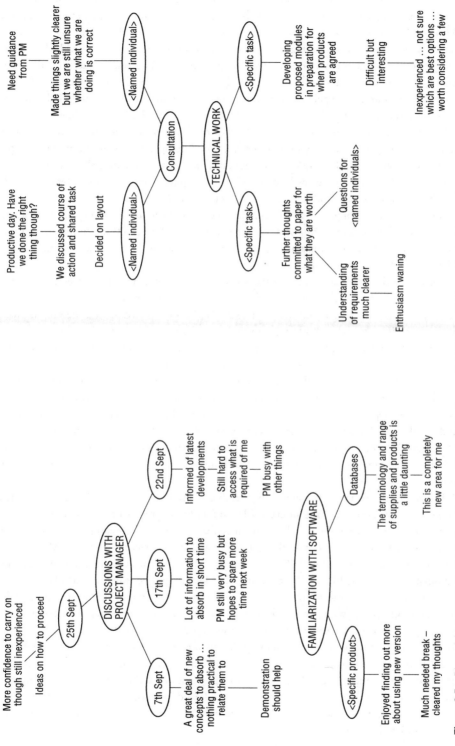

Figure 9.5 Diary of the new recruit. Originally published as Figure 6.6 in Symon, G. (1998) *Qualitative research diaries.* In G. Symon and C. Cassell (eds) *Qualitative Methods in Organizational Research and Analysis.* London: Sage Publications. p 112

instances of these activities.[1] In some cases, these are identified by date because I wanted to be able to look across the diaries and compare different perspectives on the same occasions. In other instances, distinctions were made by content or type (for example, meetings for the PM were distinguished as: strategic/planning; project assurance; 'informal'). These kinds of distinctions do not function as categories – in reading the diaries it was clear individual examples were often very distinctive and I did not want to lose any detail by grouping these together. The distinctions were sometimes common across individuals but more often idiosyncratic reflecting their different roles and experiences on the project. Spanning out from the bubbles are the perceived objectives and evaluations of the activities, with any additional comments.

I used very large sheets of paper for these transcriptions which allowed me to capture all the information from one diary on one sheet. I found being able to scan the whole month's work in one very helpful. This kind of diagrammatic form (or picture) allowed me to take in patterns and distinctions just by looking at it. And by putting two sheets side by side I could see where commonalities and distinctions lay between respondents.

While it is not the objective of this chapter to provide a discussion of my specific research project, I think it is illuminating in terms of explaining the research method to look more closely at some of the information I gathered. I found a lot of interest and relevance to the objectives of the research project.

Looking at the PM's diary, he construes many of the events he experiences and his own activities in political terms – more specifically, in terms of his need to manage the image of the project in a political environment, for example, 'receiving advice' at a meeting on how to present an issue to the CEO in the most effective light. He portrays system development as a political activity and presents himself as someone politically astute, thus establishing his credibility as a project manager in this particular environment.

The UPM's accounts mainly centre around issues of control – system development is depicted as an uncertain activity. For example, in both formal meetings and more informal discussions, he reports 'seeking to clarify the position on the project' and 'making sure we are on the right track'. Note the contrast between his account of the project assurance meeting 'PM seemed to be disguising/hiding information about staff resourcing' with the PM's account of the same meeting where he is seeking 'to satisfy [evaluators] that the report is accurate'.

Turning to the diary of the new team member, there is again a great deal of uncertainty portrayed in her account – she interprets her difficulties in terms of both her own lack of experience in this area and the lack of guidance from the PM. For example, on completing an activity 'Have we done the right thing though?' and after a meeting with the PM, 'still hard to assess what is required of me'. The system development project is portrayed as a difficult and unfamiliar activity. Indeed this team member left the project some months later.

Taking all three accounts together, system development comes across as a potentially dangerous enterprise, where any moment a carefully constructed image of control and expertise may be destroyed, with possibly serious repercussions for those involved.

I am aware that the diaries mean more to me than they will to the reader. This is because of my knowledge of the context – to some extent gleaned from other sources. In this particular case example, I used material from the diaries to inform my understanding and interpretation of the overall IT project (which I followed for about five years), in the context of other information I had gathered or to which I had access (for example, interviews, observations and documentation).

EVALUATING DIARY STUDIES

I have already referred to the many positive benefits of the diary study, which can be found in the immediacy of the account of events and feelings generated, and the degree of detail which can be recorded, which all contribute to an understanding of complex organizational processes. Additionally, the charting of events over time allows the identification of patterns and changes in respondents' accounts of these processes.

A potential drawback is the extent to which respondents are committed to recording events, reactions, and so on on a regular basis. I have suggested a number of ways in which respondents could be encouraged to provide 'full' accounts: by carefully explaining project objectives; by keeping in regular contact; by involving respondents in the design; by working on specifying a regular time and place for completion; and by ensuring the diaries are personally useful. However, one must also avoid the situation of 'forcing' respondents to provide 'answers' to 'questions' that are not really relevant. In my case example, some shorter diaries were probably an accurate reflection of the respondents' degree of involvement in the IT project. In this way, diaries may have the advantage over some methods in that they do not necessarily force participants to respond – depending, of course, on the particular design of the diary and the nature of the 'contract' between the researcher and the respondent.

This leads to another issue which I think should be considered in the design of diary studies: the degree of structure imposed on diary responses. One could argue that by providing specific questions I was influencing respondents' responses too much and structuring their accounts for them. Although the participants were free to define 'activity', even providing separate pages for each activity is an assumption on my part of some notion of (relatively) fragmented events. Reflexively, this illustrates for me the 'implicit theories' that the researcher brings to the research process. The diaries indicate some preconceptions on my part (for example, that activities can be regarded as separate events; and that activities have objectives and outcomes, and so on), some of which were challenged by the respondents themselves. It is, of course, possible to use much less structured materials (for example, a blank sheet for each day). In doing this, one may want to be careful about finding a balance between depicting participants' everyday experiences and fulfilling research objectives.

There are probably other disadvantages that could be described for the diary approach – and these will differ according to one's epistemological position. However, while I would not claim that my case study example is 'perfect' (and there are changes I would have made with hindsight), it certainly revealed for me the potential of the qualitative diary as a method of gaining insight into complex, ongoing organizational processes.

CONCLUSION

Stewart (1967) and Mintzberg (1973) concluded that diaries were inappropriate tools for gathering the kind of detailed information they were seeking. In this chapter, I have tried to illustrate that this conclusion was based on a rather restricted perception of potential uses of the diary method, and that the qualitative diary study can be a very useful and insightful information source.

While I have drawn on my use of a qualitative *activity* diary to demonstrate the potential of diary studies, there are many more psychological and organizational phenomena which might benefit from this kind of detailed, longitudinal approach. The guidelines provided here are not definitive but may act as a starting point for those unfamiliar with the method – particularly, perhaps, from a qualitative perspective. It is certainly my hope that more researchers and practitioners may be encouraged to explore the possibilities of diary studies in their own areas of interest.

NOTE

1 I have had to provide general terms in some instances in the figures to maintain anonymity.

FURTHER READING

There are few general reviews of the diary method – most accounts of diary studies are within reports of specific empirical studies in specific areas. These are usually medical/clinical or social applications such as eating habits, stress, alcoholism, and relationships. Those general reviews that do exist are usually oriented to the discussion of issues relevant to a normative (positivist) paradigm (namely one based on highly structured designs using quantitative measurements). One of the earliest discussions of the method as a research tool can be found in Allport (1942) *The Use of Personal Documents in Psychological Science* (New York: Social Science Research Council) and one of the latest is Bolger et al. (2003) 'Diary methods: capturing life as it is lived', *Annual Review of Psychology*, 54: 579–616. (Although this latter discusses design issues specifically, again it is largely written from a normative perspective.)

REFERENCES

Burgoyne, J. (1994) 'Stakeholder analysis', in C. Cassell and G. Symon (eds), *Qualitative Methods in Organizational Research: A Practical Guide*, London: Sage. pp. 187–207.

Burt, C. (1994) 'Prospective and retrospective account-making in diary entries: a model of anxiety reduction and avoidance', *Anxiety, Stress and Coping*, 6: 327–40.

Carp, F. and Carp, A. (1981) 'The validity, reliability and generalizability of diary data', *Experimental Aging Research*, 7: 281–96.

Cassell, C. and Symon, G. (1994) 'Qualitative research in work contexts', in C. Cassell and G. Symon (eds), *Qualitative Methods in Organizational Research*, London: Sage Publications. pp. 1–13.

Conway, N. and Briner, R. (2002) 'A daily diary study of affective responses to psychological contract breach and exceeded promises', *Journal of Organizational Behavior*, 23: 287–302.

Jepsen, L., Mathiassen, L. and Nielsen, P. (1989) 'Back to thinking mode: diaries for the management of information systems development projects', *Behaviour and Information Technology*, 8: 207–17.

Keen, P. (1981) 'Information systems and organizational change', *Communications of the ACM*, 24: 24–33.

Kenner, A., Coyne, J., Schaefer, C. and Lazarus, R. (1981) 'Comparison of two modes of stress measurement: daily hassles and uplifts versus major life events', *Journal of Behavioral Medicine*, 4: 1–39.

Leadbetter, D. (1993) 'Trends in assaults on social work staff: the experience of one Scottish department', *British Journal of Social Work*, 23: 613–28.

Lindén, J. (1996) 'Theoretical and methodological questions concerning a contextual approach to psychosocial issues of working life', *Science Communication*, 18 (1): 59–79.

Mintzberg, H. (1973) *The Nature of Managerial Work*, New York: Harper & Row.

Parkinson, B., Totterdell, P., Briner, R. and Reynolds, S. (1996) *Changing Moods: The Psychology of Mood and Mood Regulation*, Harlow: Longman.

Plowman, P. (2002) 'Personal communication', PhD thesis pursued at School of Development Studies, University of East Anglia.

Plummer, K. (1983) *Documents of Life: An Introduction to the Problems and Literature of a Humanistic Method*, London: George Allen & Unwin.

Ross, R. and Altmaier, E. (1994) *Intervention in Occupational Stress*, London: Sage.

Sonnentag, S. (2001) 'Work, recovery activities, and individual well-being: a diary study', *Journal of Occupational Health Psychology*, 6 (3): 196–210.

Stensland, P. and Malterud, K. (1999) 'Approaching the locked dialogues of the body: communicating symptoms through illness diaries', *Scandanavian Journal of Primary Health Care*, 17 (2): 75–80.

Stewart, R. (1967) *Managers and Their Jobs*, London: Macmillan.

Stone, A., Kessler, R. and Haythornthwaite, J. (1991) 'Measuring daily events and experiences: decisions for the researcher', *Journal of Personality*, 59: 575–607.

Williamson, A, Gower, C. and Clark, B. (1994) 'Changing the hours of shiftwork: a comparison of 8- and 12-hour shift rosters in a group of computer operators', *Ergonomics*, 37: 287–98.

Woolgar, S. (1996) 'Psychology, qualitative methods and the ideas of science', in J. T. E. Richardson (ed.), *Handbook of Qualitative Research Methods for Psychology and the Social Sciences*, Leicester: BPS Books. pp. 11–24.

Zimmerman, D. and Wieder, D. (1977) 'The diary-diary interview method', *Urban Life*, 5: 479–97.

10 — Stories in Organizational Research

Yiannis Gabriel and Dorothy S. Griffiths

We all like stories. Stories entertain and good storytellers and raconteurs command power and esteem. But good stories also educate, inspire, indoctrinate and convince. Teachers, orators and demagogues have long recognized their value. This chapter argues that stories also open valuable windows into the emotional and symbolic lives of organizations, offering researchers a powerful research instrument. It indicates how field research on stories may be conducted and how the material generated may be classified and analysed.

Organizational theory has been late in taking an interest in stories that people tell in and about organizations. The functions of stories for group cohesion or for relieving tedium and tension have been noted, but it is only recently that the importance of stories in organizational research has started to be recognized. In the first place, there is a recognition that organizations are not story-free bureaucratic spaces; storytelling is an important organizational phenomenon in its own right, which merits research attention. It is now becoming acceptable to talk of organizational lore which may be studied in ways similar to the study of folklore (Gabriel, 2000) . As the study of language, discourse and text assumed centre-place in their discipline, organizational theorists turned to stories, jokes and myths (Mitroff and Kilman, 1976; Pondy, 1983; Martin et al., 1983; Meek, 1988; Bowles, 1989), the stock in trade of ethnographers and folklorists, as vital ingredients of organizations. By collecting stories in a particular organization, by listening and comparing different accounts, by investigating how narratives are constructed around specific events, by examining which events in an organization's history generate stories and which ones fail to do so, we gain access to deeper organizational realities, closely linked to their members' experiences. In this way, stories enable us to study organizational politics, culture and change in uniquely illuminating ways, revealing how wider organizational issues are viewed, commented upon and worked upon by their members.

In telling a story, the requirement of accuracy is relaxed in the interest of making a symbolic point. Poetic licence is the prerogative of storytelling. At the same time, by shrouding a point in symbolic terms, stories are able to evade censors, both internal and external, and express views and feelings which may be unacceptable in straight talk. Criticizing one's superior may be frowned upon in most organizations, but a joke at his/her expense is less so. A story or a tale is a way of 'testing the water' to see whether others feel like the story teller, reading the same meaning into events. The teller of a joke or a story can always fall back on the defence 'It was only a joke/story!'

Stories in organizations are defined in different ways. Some definitions extend stories in different directions, seeking to encompass many types of meaningful text or discourse under the category of a story. A company logo, the shining surface of a car, a piece of graffiti and an academic textbook may then all be seen as stories. Gabriel has argued that such definitions do not do justice to the specific qualities inherent in stories understood in a narrower way.

He accordingly defines stories as

> narratives with plots and characters, generating emotion in narrator and audience, through a poetic elaboration of symbolic material. This material may be a product of fantasy or experience, including an experience of earlier narratives. Story plots entail conflicts, predicaments, trials and crises which call for choices, decisions, actions and interactions, whose actual outcomes are often at odds with the characters' intentions and purposes. (2000: 239)

Thus, stories are seen as emotionally and symbolically charged narratives; they do not present information or facts about 'events', but they enrich, enhance and infuse facts with meaning. This is both their strength and a potential weakness. For stories will often compromise accuracy in the interest of making a point or generating an emotion; they may focus on the incidental details, remaining stubbornly silent about what a researcher may regard as vital clues; they may contain inconsistencies, imprecisions, lacunae, non-sequiturs, illogicalities and ambiguities. Ultimately, the truth of a story lies not in its accuracy but in its meaning.

In this chapter, we shall argue that researchers who want to use stories as a research instrument must be prepared to sacrifice at least temporarily some of the core values of their trade and adopt instead a rather alien attitude towards their respondents and their texts. They must rid themselves of the assumption that quality data are objective, reliable, accurate and so on and must be prepared to engage with the emotions and the meanings which reside in the text. The very recognition that a narrative constitutes or is moving towards becoming a story rather than being a factual account depends on such an emotional engagement. Faced with distortions and ambiguities, researchers must resist the temptation of 'setting the record straight'; instead, they must learn to relish the text, seeking to establish the narrative needs, and through them the psychological and organizational needs, which distortions, ambiguities and inaccuracies serve. We shall argue that this is not merely a valid and useful way of doing research, but also a highly enjoyable one. We will also point out some of the ethical and epistemological difficulties which it raises.

The research strategy offered here is that of the researcher as a *fellow-traveller* on the narrative, engaging with it emotionally, displaying interest, empathy and pleasure in the storytelling process. The researcher does not risk alienating the storyteller by seeming to doubt the narrative or by placing him/her under cross-examination, but conspires to detach the narrative from the narrowness of the discourse of facts, guiding it instead in the direction of free-association, reverie and fantasy. Contradictions and ambiguities in the narrative are accepted with no embarrassment. Ambiguity lies at the heart of many stories, displaying an individual's ambivalent feelings or partial knowledge or understanding. While the researcher may ask for clarification of particular aspects of the story, the storyteller must feel that such clarification is asked in the interest of increased pleasure and empathy rather than in the form of pedantic inquiry.

THE USES OF STORIES IN SOCIAL RESEARCH

Compared to research based on more conventional methods, research using stories is still in its infancy; yet it is clear that there is no one dominant way of using them. In fact, existing research indicates a bewildering variety of possibilities and a multiplicity of inter-related research agendas which may be pursued, based on stories. These include viewing stories as elements of organizational culture (Allaire and Firsirotu, 1984; Mahler, 1988; Meek, 1988; Hansen and Kahnweiler, 1993), the study of stories (Bowles, 1989; Gabriel, 2000), the exploration of stories as a vehicle for organizational communication and learning (Wilkins, 1983; Wilkins and Martin, 1979; Boje, 1991, 1994), and the analysis of stories as an expression of political domination and opposition subverting management power (Rosen, 1985; Meek, 1988; Collinson, 1994; Gabriel, 2000). There has also been much interest in examining stories as performances involving a degree of improvisation and an interaction with an audience (Boje, 1991, 2001; Case, 1995) and also viewing them as narrative structures and studying them through different forms of discourse analysis. Generally, a researcher's methodology will reflect his/her theoretical interests and the uses to which the field material will be put.

SOME ISSUES OF METHODOLOGY

Should the researcher elicit stories?

Eliciting stories generates larger amounts of field material, the stories 'framed' for the benefit of the researcher. Different accounts of the same story may be compared as can the story profiles of different organizations in a relatively economical manner. The researcher knows when to switch his/her tape recorder on and off and may easily transcribe and process the material at his/her leisure later. This approach is favoured by many of the systematic researchers into stories (for example, Mahler, 1988; Gabriel, 2000). The main disadvantage of eliciting stories is that the researcher risks imposing his/her definitions of what is important or enjoyable. The stories are not encountered in their natural state, namely as part of organizational talk, but are presented and performed for the benefit of an outsider. They are part of the dyadic research discourse rather than of organizational discourse proper.

The alternative of collecting stories when and as they occur, is more time- and money-consuming and is part of a broader ethnographic approach. It has been used with notable success for studying humour (for example, Coser, 1959; Collinson, 1988; Gabriel, 2000) and is especially important if the emphasis lies on approaching stories as performance rather than merely as text. Boje (1991), who has made a notable contribution using this approach, observed that, within their organizational settings, stories are fragmented, terse, discontinuous, polysemic and multi-authored – most renditions omit large amounts of information which is taken for granted. Observers who are not familiar with such taken-for-granted information may miss the point or the catch or may not be aware that a story is actually being performed at all.

The researcher who pursues storytelling as part of a broader ethnographic project, without specifically seeking to elicit them, may be charged with pursuing research agendas hidden from their respondents. Besides ethical questions, this raises both practical and methodological questions. Does the researcher use a tape recorder? This risks intimidating or unnerving potential storytellers. The presence of a tape-recorder may inhibit organizational participants from telling tales which may not be factually backed up or which may compromise them with colleagues, subordinates and superiors. If no tape recorder is used, the researcher must rely on either hand-written notes or on recollection. Written notes have a less disturbing effect than tape-recorders but nevertheless slow down the storytelling and undermine the naturalness of the setting. It is often not possible to keep written notes if a story is told in a bar or a corridor. Recollection is not regarded as a very reliable method of recording research data. For the purposes of some types of research, recollection would be virtually useless. In the case, however, of stories, recollection is quite a legitimate method, especially if stories can be committed to paper, tape or electronic medium shortly after they were heard. Some stories may be remembered years after the researcher first heard them and occasionally their meaning becomes clearer after one has assumed a certain emotional and time distance from the narrative material. In spite of all these justifications, however, there is no denying that stories recorded, interpreted and analysed from recollection will bear the marks of the researcher's own conscious and unconscious elaboration and embellishment. Facets of the story which resonate with the researcher's desires, interests and research agendas are likely to be highlighted. Other features, which the researcher finds uninteresting, incidental or distasteful may be omitted or repressed.

The unit of analysis

While collecting stories, researchers must reflect on the fundamental unit of analysis of their research. This may be the individual story, the individual storyteller, specific incidents in an organization's history (for example, an accident or a crisis) or specific story themes (for example, the breaking of rules or meeting the organization's top leader). Alternatively a particular organization may be the unit of analysis either as a space where stories happen (how many stories, what types of stories, and so on) or as the topic of stories (namely what kind of stories are told *about* IBM).

As with many types of qualitative research, the unit of analysis with story-based research tends to be frequently redefined in the course of the research; yet, it cannot be disregarded altogether. If the unit of analysis is the individual, the research must focus equally on individuals who are good raconteurs and those who are not; by contrast, if the unit of analysis is the individual story, the researcher will spend more time with those individuals who will supply many stories. If the researcher wishes to explore a specific incident, he/she will seek to elicit accounts of the incident with direct or indirect means.

AN APPLICATION EXAMPLE

We shall now illustrate the use of stories in organizational research by outlining the results of a six-month field project carried out by one of the authors, entitled 'An exploration of organizational culture through the study of stories'.[1] The project was undertaken as a first attempt to investigate the nature of storytelling in organizations and to probe the deeper meanings and significance of stories, starting with a particular type of story, dealing with computers, and then moving on to collect other types of stories. Letters were sent out to 10 organizations requesting access and five of them responded positively. They represented a broad spectrum of organizations, including one of Britain's largest manufacturing companies, a research and publishing company, two district headquarters of a privatized utility, a hospital, and a consultancy unit attached to a university. Eventually, 126 individuals were interviewed by Gabriel and one assistant, yielding 377 stories. Four additional ad hoc interviews were conducted with computer analysts to obtain a sense of the type of stories favoured by computer-experts. These yielded a further 27 stories bringing the total database of stories to 404.

The interviews

The interviews were loosely structured, seeking to evoke stories the respondents had recently heard, or memories of critical events which were then presented as stories. Following an explanation of the research purpose (which included an explanation of the idea that through stories we often express our real feelings), the researchers asked a small number of questions:

1 'Do you see computers as your friends or as your enemies at the workplace?'
2 'Can you recall an incident which was widely discussed between yourself and your colleagues?'
3 'Are there any other incidents, not necessarily involving computers that were widely discussed?'
4 'Can you recall an incident that made you laugh/concerned/sad/proud, etc.?'
5 'Can you recall any practical jokes?'

Respondents were also asked to try and describe their organization in terms of one of a list of metaphors (which included family, well-oiled or creaky machine, castle under siege, conveyor belt, dinosaur, football team and so on.) and then asked to think of a critical incident which supported their preferred metaphor. The list of metaphors had been piloted with undergraduates being debriefed on their industrial placements and provided a light-hearted topic of conversation between the researchers and the respondents which naturally led to some stories.[2] All but a handful of interviews were recorded. During the interviews, brief hand-written notes were also kept to facilitate later transcriptions and analysis.

Table 10.1   Completed cardbox plus record

432	Authors: Emma Roberts (pseudonym)	
Org: Utility, Division 2		Type: comic, black humour
Theme: Lorry killed cat: driver then kills wrong cat		
Text: There was a chap driving a lorry and he hit a cat so he got out of the lorry and saw this cat on the side of the road and thought I'd better finish it off . . . smashed it over the head, got back in and drove off. A lady or chap phone the police and said I've just seen a lorry driver get out and kill my cat. So they chased after the van and found it and asked the driver whether he had killed the cat so he said he had ran over it and couldn't leave it like that . . . it's cruel so I finished it off. So they said can we examine your van and he said yes by all means so they examined the van and found a dead cat under the wheel arch. So it was the wrong cat [he had killed] sleeping at the side of the road.		
Emotions: amusement, mild disparagement		
Moral: Similar stories 842, 917, 923 Characters: cat, lady, lorry driver, police Quality: 10		
Key words: cat, lorry, mistake, killed, black humour		

PROCESSING

The interviews were then transcribed from tapes yielding 404 organizational stories, of which 159 involved computers. The stories were analysed with the help of a special version of a computer database package, Cardbox-Plus.[3] Each story was entered on a separate record with several distinct fields as in Table 10.1.

The software permits the selection of stories sharing specific qualities, or having particular words in common. For example, it instantly retrieves all stories which involve a disparaging comment about one's supervisor, or all comic stories involving computers or animals.

FINDINGS

Density of folklore

The number and quality of stories drawn from different organizations varies enormously. For example, 24 interviews at the manufacturing firm yielded 138 stories, whereas the same number of interviews at the research and publishing organization yielded a mere 48. This variation was not a product of the methodology but reflects, at least in part, the vitality and strength of folklore in different organizations. The research and publishing organization had an ethos of factual precision and accountability which seemed to inhibit the making of unsubstantiated claims and the spinning of elaborate stories. By contrast, the manufacturing company had many older participants who had known and worked with each other for a number of years and related many stories.

Types of stories

The classification of stories into different types of narratives was the hardest part of the processing.[4] Some stories instantly fell into a well-established type, such as comic or epic, or were hybrids of two or more types (for example, comic-tragic); yet, some were not easily classifiable in spite of several iterations. Several things eventually became clear. First, the same 'events' may feed different types of story. One particular event, involving the accidental explosion of a fire extinguisher gave rise to an epic, a comic and a tragic narrative (Gabriel, 2000). Second, certain narratives described events purely as facts, devoid of emotional or symbolic content. Such narratives were identified as 'reports' rather than 'stories', following a long-standing Aristotelean distinction.[5]

A third classification issue arose in connection with certain terse narratives with either a very thin plot or uncommitted emotional content; under certain conditions of repetition and embellishment these could yield fully fledged stories. Such narratives were classified as 'proto-stories'. There were 119 proto-stories among the 404 narratives in the database, the commonest of any type.

What then are the main story types and what are their principal qualities? The following classification is not exhaustive, although it covers the great majority of stories collected.

COMIC STORIES

These, as identified by Aristotle, involved 'deserved misfortune'. Their emotional qualities encompass amusement and mirth but also disparagement. The majority of these stories had a critical quality, namely were at the expense of an individual or group of individuals who appeared to deserve their misfortunes, for instance experts disparaging non-experts or vice versa. Specific groups in different organizations were targeted for special types of disparaging-comic stories, for example, lawyers at the manufacturing company or central management at the utility. Some comic stories focused on *practical jokes*.

EPIC STORIES

These stories focused either on achievement or on survival against the odds. Their chief emotional qualities were admiration, approval and especially pride. About one quarter of epic stories had comic qualities as well. In many cases the central character of these stories is a hero or heroine, worthy of admiration. Their plots emphasized achievement, success and victory.

TRAGIC STORIES

These stories focused on undeserved misfortune and tended to generate the classic mixture of horror and pity for the victim. These were variously mixed with bitterness, horror, guilt and anxiety. In the majority of these stories misfortune is not the result of accidental factors but the accomplishment of a villain. Tragic stories focused on insults, redundancies, bullying and harassment and can be sub-categorized into *gripes* and *traumas*.

ROMANTIC STORIES

These are stories which express gratitude, appreciation and love. Many of these stories involve gifts and acts of unsolicited kindness. These were often associated with feelings of affection but also nostalgia or self-pity. A special type of romantic story is the office or workplace *romance*. These are stories which focus on love affairs or love fantasies, without turning romantic attachments into occasions for disparagement or ridicule. Generally romantic stories construct the protagonist (individual, couple or even organization) as love object and include many nostalgic stories which celebrate the organization of old.

Distribution of stories across organizations

The distribution of story-types varied in the five organizations surveyed. Clearly, the methodology of the research was not geared at establishing the 'story-profile' of each organization, but, interestingly, comic stories were by far the most common story-type in the manufacturing company, yet entirely absent from one of the two utility branches. Romantic stories were found only in the hospital and the utility branch from which comic stories were absent. Epic stories were predominant in the other utility branch and the hospital. This finding suggest a line of inquiry which uses the organization rather than the individual story as the unit of analysis.

Thematic distribution of stories

In each organization, a small number of events generated a large number of the stories; for instance, the imbroglio over the introduction of a new information system, the disturbance during a Christmas party, an office romance leading to marriage, the death of a colleague, a practical joke involving a horse, were recounted by more than three interviewees in each case, with a minimum of prompting. Comparison of the different accounts reveal wide variations in matters of fact, substance and meaning. If one were to try and re-construct 'what actually happened' from these accounts it would be very difficult. The retired chief executive officer of the manufacturing company, a man of considerable public profile, had generated many stories within the company. With little prompting 11 such stories were collected, most of which present him as a 'hero' or at least as a leader admired by his 'troops'.

Raconteurs

The narrative ability of different individuals differed greatly as did their willingness to share a story with a stranger. There were some respondents who turned the thinnest material into meaningful stories through embellishment, timing and suspense, others who failed to bring to life vivid scenes which they had experienced, and yet others who reported events in a highly factual, 'objective' way, seemingly unwilling to sacrifice accuracy for effect. Characteristically, one respondent provided 14 high quality stories while several others provided no stories at all, in spite of considerable prompting.[6]

Most of those who related several stories seemed to have one or two preferred types of stories, for example jocular gripes, personal traumas, cynical jokes, romance, which accorded with their personality and their experience at work. There appeared to be a continuity or coherence in each narrator's repertoire of stories.

Narrative complexity and emotional richness

Very few of the stories collected combine the emotional, symbolic and narrative complexities of myths. Only 12 of the 404 stories exceeded 300 words when transcribed and only 30 had more than three distinct characters or groups of characters. Yet the emotions generated and communicated by these stories were quite powerful, and go some way towards reinforcing the view of organizations as emotional arenas (Fineman, 1993). In fact, the stories provide a fascinating window into a wide range of emotions which one may not normally associate with organizations. These included amusement, disparagement, pride, disapproval, relief, anger, pity, anxiety, reproach, sadness, satisfaction, affection, approval, nostalgia, derision, bitterness, horror, admiration, disappointment, panic, guilt, scorn and many others.

The emotional content of a story comprises: the emotions recollected by the narrator; the emotions which the story seeks to communicate to the listener; the emotions which the listener experiences while hearing the story; and the emotions which he/she later feels on recollecting it. Thus, a comic story which generates mirth and amusement to the teller may be based on events which at the time generated horror and panic, and are received with disgust by the listener. The complications resulting from any attempt to classify stories solely in terms of their emotional content are, therefore, formidable.

Story interpretation

One of the most interesting uses of organizational stories lies in their interpretation. On close scrutiny, stories reveal a wide diversity of meanings, some of which are relatively obvious and others more indirect or even unconscious. Here is a relatively straight-forward story:

> I used to work for a company where we had regular bomb practice. The security chief would hide a package with a sign saying 'BOMB', to see how quickly people got out of the building and how quickly his boys would locate the 'bomb'. They carried out this

exercise many times and were pleased with their response times. Until eventually the bomb was hidden under the mainframe, where it proved impossible to locate; for hours they searched all over the building, but nobody thought of looking under the machine! (Narrative 213)

This story, recounted light-heartedly over lunch by a computer executive (and recalled by one of the authors from memory later), generated much amusement. The storyteller invites the listener to speculate why the security staff failed to check under the mainframe. Was the machine seen as being above suspicion or was it a taboo object? Did the men perhaps fail to see the computer altogether, regarding it as a fixed part of the building? What made this a good story? Does the story try to tell us something more general about computers and organizations?

The meaning of the story (at least as far as the storyteller was concerned) is unlocked when we learn that it was recounted in response to a casual comment to the effect that to the non-expert, computers are mystifying and threatening. The story came as an amplification and embellishment of this rather trivial point, as if to say that even security men, hardened men who will go after bombs, share in the general malaise when confronted with computers. They did not dare touch the computer or even get close to it, as if that was the *real* bomb. And given that the teller was a man working constantly with computers, is the implication of the story not that computer experts are the real hard men of the organization, dealing with the truly dangerous objects? Such an interpretation may find some support in a subsequent story related by the same individual:

I had been doing consultancy for the launch of a US software product, called Soft-tool. With a name like this, you don't stand a chance, I told the manufacturers, you have to change the brand name. No luck, it was company policy to use the same name in all its geographic divisions. My job was to come up with a logo for this product, imagine now, 'Buy Soft-tool to increase your performance.' When they realized their gaffe, they changed the name to . . . Hard-tool! (Narrative 215)

This storyteller appears to equate masculinity with hardness and hardness with computers. (For more extensive interpretations of this story, see Gabriel, 2000.)

Some stories may be interpreted very extensively, like dreams, revealing rich combinations of meanings in many different layers. Like works of art, some stories permit different and even contradictory interpretations. How can we distinguish between valid and spurious interpretations? What corroborations may be offered to strengthen specific interpretations? Since the work of Barthes (1973) and postmodernist theorists, we have learnt that we read meanings not only in stories but in virtually any cultural artifact, from particular advertisements to blue jeans and from businessmen's grey suits to AIDS. Are all interpretations equally valid? We do not believe so. As Ginsburg (1980) has shown, interpretation lies at the heart of semiotic processes like forensic investigations, medical diagnoses, authentication of works of art as well as psychoanalysis. In all of these areas, one seeks to paint a general picture from individual signs or clues, like the primitive huntsman who pursues traces left by his prey, observing and interpreting every broken branch, every footmark and every disturbed bit of terrain as something leading to his prey. Interpretation is an art and a skill owing as much to tacit skills and know-how as to scientific method. Specific interpretations may not be proved or disproved by conventional scientific criteria. Yet, this does not make every interpretation equally meaningful or valid. An interpretation may be original, clever, perceptive, incomplete, misleading or even plain wrong.

We would argue briefly that there are four corroborating techniques which may be used to strengthen interpretations in virtually any field. First, the internal consistency of the interpretation. In a successful interpretation, the interpretation of parts is consistent with the interpretation of the whole, different signs or clues pointing in the same direction. Second, in strong interpretations specific outcomes are over-determined, namely not only different signs point in the same direction, but different mechanisms can be established leading to the same outcome. Third, strong interpretations, although not falsifiable on the grounds of individual pieces of evidence, do, nevertheless, make clear what evidence would lead to their refutation. Fourth, strong interpretations will generally address, account for and supersede less strong ones.

STORIES, MYTHS AND FOLKLORE

Some of the stories in the database have quite complex symbolic qualities, revealing strong emotions, expressing powerful unconscious fantasies. Their characters can be interesting, unusual or even brilliant even if they lack the towering presence of mythic heroes. The themes deal with everyday organizational realities. Looking at organizational stories as mythology inevitably leads to the conclusion that organizational mythology is mundane, lifeless, and unimaginative. Looking at them as folklore, on the other hand, highlights their vitality and invention. Folklore, unlike mythology, is the lore of ordinary people. Slang, jokes, traditions, proverbs and idiosyncrasies which are so alien to myth, all lie at the very heart of folklore (Dundes, 1965, 1980). It is perfectly possible and meaningful to talk of Xerox lore or the folklore of surfers and network-surfers without debasing the concept of folklore.

The researcher who looks for mythology in organizations is likely to be disappointed or may end up with a trivial view of mythology. By contrast, the researcher with an interest in folklore will find much fascinating material in organizations. As folkloric elements, organizational stories present many interesting possibilities. They offer a way of making comparisons between organizations opening many windows into the idiosyncrasies of each rather than providing access into human universals. Individual narratives also offer access to the specific wishes and dreams of each storyteller, their fantasies and their emotions, their symbolic and cognitive constructions.

SOME CONCLUDING EPISTEMOLOGICAL AND ETHICAL REFLECTIONS ON USING STORIES

An evident danger of story-based research is the risk of regarding stories as facts, especially if a storyteller insists that the events described in the story 'actually happened' or were actually witnessed by him/her. In many stories, the idea that something 'actually happened' or that it was 'witnessed with one's own eyes' is itself part of the poetic elaboration or story-work. Yet, as Aristotle pointed out, a literal untruth may be closer to the true nature of things than a literal truth which remains at the superficial and the mundane. Where literal representation accurately imitates the veil, the facade, the surface, poetry has transcendental qualities, reaching out towards the systematically hidden from sight, the enduring. It thus reveals a deeper truth.

The assumption that there exist deeper truths which are inaccessible to direct obervation is one shared by many contemporary approaches (including structuralism, hermeneutics and psychoanalysis) but it is opposed by positivism and empiricism. It can be a very fruitful but also dangerous assumption, through which stories may be used for the purpose of propaganda and deception. Stories are especially pernicious because of their memorable qualities. As every journalist knows, through selective presentation, editing, headlining and framing, a narrative may be put to work within virtually any overall story. This danger is ever-present in ethnographic research and does not imply any conscious malfeasance on the part of the researcher. Researchers who are pursuing a particular line of investigation may focus on those stories or story-interpretations which support their ideas and disregard or underestimate the importance of others. The ethical pitfalls of such approaches are evident.

The opposite difficulty, however, is to regard everything as narrative and to lose sight of the importance of actual events in organizations. Some postmodern approaches have tended to reduce everything, including organizations, to discourse and narrative – this tendency, which denies any difference between text and context, narrative and meta-narrative, fact and fantasy, views all social reality as mediated by language and existing through language. Numerous writers have challenged this approach, which has nevertheless acquired something of a succès de scandale (for example, Parker, 1995, Thompson, 1993). It seems to us that postmodern approaches have made considerable contributions to elucidating the role of language in organizing, structuring and occluding our understandings, without for one moment convincing us that everything *is* language. Between the Scylla of objectivism and the Charybdis of pantextuality, this chapter advocates the use of organizational stories as poetic elaborations on actual events, as wish-fulfilling fantasies built on everyday experience and as expressions of deeper organizational and personal realities. From this point, different researchers may make use of organizational stories to pursue different lines of inquiry – into organizational politics and resistance, into psychological injuries and discontents at work, into the dissemination of organizational knowledge or lore, into culture and symbolism, into interpretation or in the process of storytelling itself.

NOTES

1 This was undertaken with the aid of a grant from the Economic and Social Research Council (R 000232 627).
2 A different list of opening questions can been constructed, adapted to other research agendas. 'Are there any special characters in this place?' would be a suitable question if research interest lay more specifically in story characters.
3 Cardbox Plus (Version 4) is supplied by Business Simulations Limited, 30 St James's Street, London SW1A 1HB.
4 A detailed typology of organizational stories is offered by Gabriel, 2000. Each of the main story types constructs a different type of subject, as follows: the epic story constructs the subject as hero or heroic survivor, the tragic story as victim, the comic story as trickster or fool, and the romantic story as love object.
5 Aristotle must be credited with the first clear statement of the difference between stories and other narratives. He viewed stories as emotional-symbolic texts and used the term 'poetics' to describe the type of work that is involved in transforming facts into stories. By contrast, he viewed history as analytico-descriptive. While poetry is a discourse of meanings, history is a discourse of facts, causes and effects. He is also credited with the first convincing statement of

the distinction between comedy and tragedy, in terms of the emotions they generate. Both comedy and tragedy are poetic forms. See Aristotle *Poetics*.

6 When asked what stories they had heard or what incident had been discussed at the workplace, such individuals would say 'Nothing interesting ever happens here' or 'People only talk about work in this place'.

FURTHER READING

The systematic use of stories as a vehicle for the study of organizational processes only started about twenty years ago. An overview is provided by Gabriel (2000). Czarniawska Joerges (1995, 1997) gives a provocative account of organizations themselves as narratives – this is an approach which contrasts to the one taken in this chapter, but offers great insights into the nature of organizing when seen through the prism of storytelling. Boje's (1991, 1994, 2001) work has been very influential for authors, especially those interested in critical postmodernism.

Readers interested in stories as features of organizational culture can consult Allaire and Firsirotu (1984), Mahler (1988), Meek (1988), Hansen and Kahnweiler (1993).

The use of stories in analysing psychological processes, including fantasies, emotions, wish-fulfilment and defence is explored by Bowles (1989), Gabriel (2000), and Sandelands and Boudens (2000). The creative improvisatory qualities of storytelling is discussed by Weick (2001).

Stories as a feature of organizational communication and learning are discussed by Wilkins (1983), Wilkins and Martin (1979), and Weick (2001). Clark and Salaman (1996) discuss some of the uses to which they are put by management consultants and gurus. The influence of stories on action and strategy, especially in times of crisis or change is discussed by Boje (1991, 1994). Their political qualities, as tools of management control are discussed by Wilkins (1983), Martin and Powers (1983); as potential expressions of resistance and recalcitrance, Rosen (1985), Meek (1988), Collinson (1994), Gabriel (2000).

REFERENCES

Allaire, Y. and Firsirotu, M. E. (1984) 'Theories of organizational culture', *Organization Studies*, 5(3): 193–226.

Barthes, Roland (1973) *Mythologies*, London: Paladin Books.

Boje, D. M. (1991) 'The storytelling organization: a study of story performance in an office-supply firm', *Administrative Science Quarterly*, 36: 106–26.

Boje, D.M. (1994) 'Organizational storytelling: the struggles of pre-modern, modern and postmodern organizational learning discourses', *Management Learning*, 25 (3): 433–61.

Boje, D. M. (2001) *Narrative Methods for Organizational and Communication Research*, London: Sage.

Bowles, M. L. (1989) 'Myth, meaning and work organization', *Organization Studies*, 10(3): 405–21.

Case, Peter (1995) 'Representations of talk at work: performatives and "performability"', *Management Learning*, 26 (4): 423–44.

Clark, T. and Salaman, G. (1996) 'Telling tales: management consultancy as the art of storytelling, in D. Grant and C. Oswick (eds), *Metaphor and Organizations,* London: Sage. pp. 166–84.

Collinson, D. (1988) '"Engineering humour", masculinity, joking and conflict in shop-floor relations', *Organization Studies*, 9 (2): 181–99.

Collinson, D.L. (1994) 'Strategies of resistance: power, knowledge and subjectivity in the workplace', in J. Jermier, W. Nord and D. Knights (eds), *Resistance and Power in Organizations*, London: Routledge. pp. 25–68.

Coser, R.L. (1959) 'Some social functions of laughter', *Human Relations*, 12: 171–82.

Czarniawska-Joerges, B. (1995) 'Narration or science? Collapsing the division in organization studies', *Organization*, 2 (1): 11–33.

Czarniawska-Joerges, B. (1997) *Narrating the Organization: Dramas of Institutional Identity*, Chicago: University of Chicago Press.

Dundes, Alan (1965) *The Study of Folklore*, Englewood Cliffs, NJ: Prentice-Hall.

Dundes, Alan (1980) *Interpreting Folklore*, Bloomington, IN: Indiana University Press.

Fineman, S. (ed.) (1993) *Emotion in Organizations*, London: Sage.

Freud, S. (1910) *Observations on 'Wild' Psychoanalysis*, London: Hogarth Press.

Gabriel, Y. (2000) S*torytelling in Organizations: Facts, fictions, fantasies*, Oxford: Oxford University Press.

Ginsburg, C. (1980) 'Morelli, Freud and Sherlock Holmes: clues and scientific method', *History Workshop*, 9: 5–36.

Hansen, C.D. and Kahnweiler, W.M. (1993) 'Storytelling: an instrument for understanding the dynamics of corporate relationships,' *Human Relations*, 46/12: 1391–409.

Mahler, Julianne (1988) 'The quest for organizational meaning: identifying and interpreting the symbolism in organizational stories', *Administration and Society*, 20: 344–68.

Martin, Joanne and Powers, Melanie E. (1983) 'Truth or corporate propaganda: the value of a good war story', in L.R. Pondy, P.J. Frost, G. Morgan and T.C. Dandridge (eds), *Organizational Symbolism*, Greenwich: JAI Press.

Martin, Joanne, Feldman, Martha S., Hatch, Mary Jo and Sitkin, Sim B. (1983) 'The uniqueness paradox in organizational stories', *Administrative Science Quarterly*, 28: 438–53.

Meek, V. L. (1988) 'Organizational culture: origins and weaknesses', *Organization Studies*, 9 (4): 453–73.

Mitroff, I.I. and Kilman, R.H. (1976) 'On organizational stories: an approach to the design and analysis of organizations through myths and stories', in R. H. Kilman, L. R. Pondy and D. Slevin (eds), *The Management of Organizational Design*, New York: North Holland.

Nuttall, A.D. (1996) *Why Does Tragedy Give Pleasure?*, Oxford: Oxford University Press.

Parker, Martin (1995) 'Critique in the name of what? Postmodernism and critical approaches to organization', *Organization Studies*, 16 (4) 553–64.

Pondy, L.R. (1983) 'The role of metaphors and myths in organization and in the facilitation of change', in L.R. Pondy, P.J. Frost, G. Morgan and T.C. Dandridge (eds), *Organizational Symbolism*, Greenwich: JAI Press.

Propp, Vladimir (1984) *Theory and History of Folklore*, Manchester: Manchester Unvierstity Press.

Rosen, M. (1985) 'Breakfast at Spiro's: dramaturgy and dominance', *Journal of Management Studies*, 11 (2): 31–48.

Sandelands, L.E. and Boudens, C.J. (2003) 'Feeling at work', in S. Fineman (ed.) *Emotion in Organizations*, London: Sage. pp. 46–63.

Thompson, P. (1993) 'Postmodernism: fatal distraction', in J. Hassard and M. Parker (eds), *Postmodernism and Organizations*, London: Sage. pp. 183–203.

Weick, K.E. (2001) *Making Sense of the Organizations*, Oxford: Blackwell.

Wilkins, A.L. (1983) 'Organizational stories as symbols which control the organization', in L.R. Pondy, P. J. Frost, G. Morgan and T.C. Dandridge (eds), *Organizational Symbolism*, Greenwich: JAI Press.

Wilkins A.L. and Martin, J. (1979) 'Organizational legends' (Research Paper No. 521), *Stanford University Research Paper Series*, Palo Alto, CA: Stanford University.

(11)—— Pictorial Representation ——————————————

David R. Stiles

NUMBERS, WORDS AND PICTURES —————————————————————

Long after the words from newspaper columns have faded, what remains in the minds of millions after 11 September 2001 are images of passenger aircraft crashing into concrete and steel, tiny figures plunging to their certain deaths and devastated firefighters wandering lost amid smoke and rubble. As well as possessing an aesthetic quality, pictures enable users to communicate rapidly and universally, to record and summarize ideas, and influence the perceptions and behaviour of actors (Kotler, 1986). Given the qualitative power that such images convey, why are academics unlike the overwhelming majority of people so reluctant to embrace the pictorial form as a means of understanding their worlds?

Subjectivity in interpretation is one explanation for this, as are extreme variations in drawing ability, technical publishing difficulties and uncertainty about using the medium. Academic recalcitrance is compounded by the view that images are elusive and difficult to categorize. Another reason is that images are still regarded by the academic orthodoxy as a subjective, inferior or even eccentric form of data compared to words and numbers (see, for example, van Aken, 2000). Yet, digital technology has transformed pictures from an elitist knowledge domain protected by artists, photographers and graphic designers into a mass medium. This chapter explores how pictorial representation can provide researchers with a powerful and overlooked tool with which to develop more creative organizational strategies.

The origins and use of pictorial representation in organizations are explored, before providing a theoretical foundation for using image. This chapter then details methods developed by the author (Stiles, 1995), with glimpses following into the strategic use of pictorial representation in two real organizations. The last section discusses the advantages and disadvantages of the methods used. Overall, it is felt that images can be as valuable as words or numbers in exploring organizational constructs.

THE USE OF IMAGE IN QUALITATIVE RESEARCH —————————————————

Lately, an embryonic organizational research area has begun to emerge using image. In management, visual techniques have been developed to stimulate creative thinking and problem solving (Maddox et al., 1987; Russell and Evans, 1989; Checkland and Scholes, 1990; Majaro, 1991; Rickards, 1999; Henry, 2001). Some are also exploring organizational identity: the study of what an organization *is* or *appears to be* (Albert and Whetten, 1985). However, it is difficult to find a single picture within the expanding work on organizational identity. Instead, writers assume psychological perspectives (Ashforth and Mael, 1989; Hogg and Terry,

2000), psychodynamism/organizational learning approaches (Brown and Starkey, 2000), and intergroup relations theory (Brickson, 2000). Others explore impression or configuration management (Scott and Lane, 2000; Pratt and Foreman, 2000) and process frameworks (Gioia et al., 2000a). Many of these approaches use *realist* ontologies (assumptions about the social world we inhabit) and *positivist* epistemologies (assumptions about knowledge, or the way we understand that world) (Burrell and Morgan, 1979). Simply put, they aim to regulate or control organizations and consumers. As such, the organization is seen as a bounded entity capable of mechanical adjustment towards greater technical efficiency. The whole point is to maintain the existing system while permitting incremental adjustments and avoiding radical change. Human beings are seen as passive participants, lacking agency and self-will. Gioia et al. (2000a) recognize the shortcomings of these approaches and begin to discuss postmodern alternatives, but settle on a more conventional foundation.

More 'interpretivist' approaches explore feelings, emotions and values in order to 'understand the subjective experience of individuals' (Burrell and Morgan, 1979: 253). Such insights add greatly to our knowledge of how organizations work because they help explain more fully what underlies people's perceptions and actions. Berger and Luckman (1965) and Weick (1979) argue that people can experience the same reality in different ways, forming their own 'social constructions', 'constructs', or 'enactments' – shared perceptions that reconstruct reality and constitute the basic building blocks of meaning. I propose that tapping such embedded phenomena is integral to understanding organizations and deciding which strategies are likely to succeed. Moreover, I believe that such constructs are not just verbal, but also visual. Semiotic and visual sociologists (Chaplin, 1994; Emmison and Smith, 2000) challenge mainstream sociology by using visual forms, but emphasize the role of experts in analysing these. The approach here decentres the expert from the research process, focusing on images created and interpreted by ordinary people.

According to the dictionary, an *image* is 'A representation of the external form of an object', a 'figurative illustration' or a 'likeness' of something real or imaginary (Hawkins and Allen, 1991). It is a form of construct that can be either a mental representation or a more tangible physical representation of an object. Langer (1957: 145) distinguishes between an 'inner picture' and a 'fabrication'. The former is a subjective, projected record of a sense-experience mainly created for someone's own sake; the latter an impression communicated by a sender to an audience. Alvesson uses the term 'corporate image' to mean 'A holistic and vivid impression held by a particular group towards a corporation', partly because of the group's own sense-making processes and partly because of the communication of the corporation. This can be held by external audiences or by internal members of the organization (1990: 376–8). Gioia et al. (2000a) identify six different but related forms of image in the literature. Four of these definitions place organizational insiders at the centre of the construction and communication process. The remaining ones allow external stakeholders more agency in determining the organization's image. Gioia et al. believe identity and image to be separate, but closely linked: settling on identity as a self-reflective organizational concept and image in its construed external form. This study, however, sees image as synonymous with identity.

This results in a broad multi-dimensional concept. Image/identity is the entire process of expression and impression that defines the organization to its stakeholders: the result of conscious, unconscious and latent processes. Pictures, words and numbers are different *forms* in the expression of an image. They exist as elements of mental processes (inner pictures) and as more concrete representations (fabrications), such as drawings, paintings, photographs or movies. At one time, pictures were a society's sole means of recorded expression – such as in ancient Chinese pictograms. More recently, as human expression has become more sophisticated, words, numbers and pictures have developed as alternative but often complementary systems of meaning. For example, a picture of a relaxing seaside day could be enhanced by words such as 'sand', 'beach' and 'hot'.

Words, pictures and numbers can be described as *symbols* where they are an indirect, abstract representation typifying, representing or recalling something else to an audience (Hawkins and Allen, 1991). Here, they are a type of fabrication rather than an inner picture: a company logo, or a gold watch representing loyal service. This has led to a school of thought known as 'organizational symbolism', where the focus is on how managers communicate messages intentionally or unintentionally to others within their organization (Green, 1988). This chapter does not restrict the definition of image to communicated fabrications, but also includes inner pictures.

The images produced here are based on the use of a *metaphor*. In other words, one is invited to think of an object as though it *is* something quite different. For example, one might say that this book *is* a pot of gold, inviting you to dip into it from time-to-time, rather than trying to memorize its contents. The emphasis on imaginative knowledge rather than literality is important, because seeing things in new ways can help solve seemingly intractable problems. Morgan (1993) introduces organizations as cartons of yoghurt, sailboats and even spider plants in an attempt to help managers see beyond restrictive, customary ways of managing them. Similarly, strategists see organizations as 'cash cows', 'stars', 'dogs' and 'question marks' when deciding whether to invest in them or not (Johnson and Scholes, 2001: 285).

PICTORIAL REPRESENTATION TECHNIQUES

The techniques here depict the organization as a human personality. In the first stage of the study organizational members are interviewed individually. In stage two focus groups aggregate data, check and explore themes.

Individual interviews

In a face-to-face setting, respondents complete two 'warm-up' exercises to encourage them to draw and to think in visual terms. These involve drawing an imaginary human face. Creativity is then encouraged by inverting the image and drawing a more unusual humanoid (Edwards, 1981). The subject then completes a *free-drawn personality metaphor image* with minimal prompting:

> Imagine that you're trying to communicate with someone who can't read or write. Some people say that each place you work in has its own personality. I want you to imagine that your organization has its own personality and do a rough sketch to try to explain to this person who can't read or write what that personality looks like.

The communicatee is described as illiterate to encourage the respondent not to use words when drawing. Verbal interpretation of the drawing is made by the respondent, not by the interviewer, limiting the researcher's structuring to innocuous probes and non-verbal cues.

Interpretation of the verbal explanations is based upon Potter and Wetherell's (1987) discourse analysis approach. The researcher is looking for patterns across the transcribed data of all interviewees, where more than one respondent mentions the same thing (a consistency); or where a unique perception (a variability) appears in the text. The text and visual observations are presented in full in any final project report to allow the reader to make up his or her own mind, rather than stating categorically that a response means a certain thing.

Focus groups

Representative focus groups are subsequently held to

1 review and validate initial interview data;
2 determine 'realistic' and 'ideal' pictures of the organization; and
3 filter emerging suggestions on possible organizational strategies.

Focus groups also ensure that members are involved in the change process beyond initial interviews, helping to build acceptance of strategies.

A selection of face-to-face drawings is fed back into focus groups to determine whether one image best captures the organization and whether common themes prevail. These *pre-constructed personality images* allow the aggregation of personal constructs into common group constructs to ensure the continuity and grounding of data. Focus groups also allow a time dynamic to be incorporated into the process, with groups established months after the original interviews take place. Further iterations are also possible. For example, focus groups were replicated two years later for the Canadian case detailed in the next section, because it was felt that a change of leader might be influential.

Each pre-constructed image is multi-dimensional, because it reflects several organizational characteristics. The device can be quite powerful if the images are carefully selected to show a range of views. This means choosing five pictures, from an unfavourable depiction of the organization through a neutral view to a favourable one. Participants are presented with what is almost a 'pictorial Likert scale' from which to choose a consensus image. A summary of the discourse explaining each image is read out as each picture is revealed. Participants are then asked whether any of the five images reflect the character of the organization. Votes for each image assist in obtaining a majority view. Where no majority occurs, a split vote is registered. In either case, the full discourse is analysed, including rationales for consensus and dissensus images. Sessions are video taped to help identify separate speakers in later transcription. The group then produces a composite *free-drawn personality image* of its own. Drawings are facilitated to encompass the perceptions of all group members and verbal explanations are again discourse analysed.

The researcher does not need strategy generation in mind when using these techniques. Organizational psychologists, behavioural analysts, marketers and others will discover that pictures provide rich insights to enhance their understanding. Identifying an 'organizational personality' might be useful in surfacing latent tensions, to help deal with shared psychological problems (Semeonoff, 1976; Branthwaite and Lunn, 1985). Defining a common internal or external organizational image might help the marketer develop a campaign to promote a more desirable corporate image (Ziff, 1990).

PICTURES IN ACTION

Two 'live' case studies illustrate the use of pictorial representation in practice. These are university business schools in the UK and Canada, but the personality metaphor is sufficiently flexible and simple to use in any organizational setting. In fact, the author has applied it to financial services companies, call centres, tour operators, estate agents and many other organizations world-wide.

The aim here was to generate organizational strategies for the schools by examining images of the organization held by stakeholders (Scott and Lane, 2000). A dynamic view was ensured by an iterative process over three years, involving 76 face-to-face interviews with academics and 18 focus groups of academics, secretarial staff, undergraduate students, MBAs (Master of Business Administration students) and business people.

The discourse indicates that the interviewer successfully adopted a pacifying role, easing creative 'blocks' and calming apprehensions about drawing. To minimize anxiety and interviewer effect, the researcher left the room while drawing took place, although recording devices remained running. Transcription of an MBA student focus group proved problematic, because of different national accents. Videotape was useful here, allowing individuals to be identified and bodily movements examined.

The image in Figure 11.1 was most popular across UK groups. This was because of the perceived facelessness of the school, resulting in feelings of anonymity among internal stakeholders. A business suit jacket and jeans represented role conflict between business and academic demands and a perceptual gulf between old and young academics.

The image in Figure 11.2 was the favourite in Canadian focus groups. It showed a lack of strategic direction resulting from a change in leader and inherent academic-business role conflict through its clothing. Cautious optimism was embodied in a half-smile; but feet facing in opposite directions showed fragmentation and lack of interaction.

In the full report, all images and a large number of verbatim quotes are presented to provide richness and enhance understanding. Rather than being placed in appendices, the drawings are an integral part of the report. Editing is minimized to ensure readability, while the

Figure 11.1 Most popular pre-constructed personality image: UK school

Figure 11.2 Most popular pre-constructed personality image: Canadian school

interviewer's interaction is presented (shown here as 'DS') to reproduce the dialogue as closely as possible. The removal of text is shown by three full stops in succession. Individuals are not identified and focus group participants are allocated a designatory group letter and number (for example, F1 is the first member of the academic faculty group and S3 is the third member of the student group).

The strongest theme to emerge from both interviews and focus groups was that the two institutions were regarded as unhappy or neutral due to their leaders' management styles. One might think this inevitable in universities where, protective of their self-autonomy, academics resent any attempts to lead or manage them. However, at the UK school, antipathy seemed particularly strong. The leader was believed to be overly dominant in both strategic and operational decision making, abrasive in style and uncommunicative with internal members – creating unnecessary 'social distance' between him and others. One academic believed that the leader was:

[The purveyor of unhappiness lowering morale and things like that (DS: Right). But very big. (DS: Right). A long, thin, narrow neck, (DS: Right) because er emphasizing the distance between him and the rest of the organization in many ways it creates].

A long neck separating the head and body symbolized social distance for academic and MBA groups. In Figure 11.4 a mask of Janus from Roman mythology signified the dominance of the leader, superimposed upon an otherwise faceless entity. The figure's neck was also dotted to represent extreme thinness, with downward-pointing arrows showing a one-way flow of information, influence and communication. The relative powerlessness of the section heads was depicted by four carbuncles on the figure's shoulders; with the majority of academics at the bottom providing the research and teaching work to sustain the school. The character missed a shoe to show lack of movement/change, clenched one fist in frustration and waved 'goodbye' to symbolize exiting academics:

[F4: I mean we as individual lecturers and researchers and what have you, have no real power. We cannot within sections decide who is head of section. That comes from <names leader>, as devolved, sending it down through his system. OK, once it gets to

Figure 11.3   Face-to-face interview image: UK school

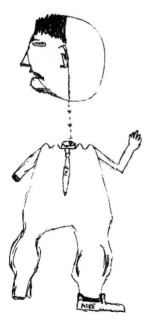

Figure 11.4   Academic focus group image: UK school

<names leader>, he is the decider when it comes to this Department] . . . [F3: Then you have got what we call the er the weak little spots of the place. Four little heads . . . Thin shoulders and big fat thighs, big muscularly thighs that keep it going].

Undergraduate and MBA students also emphasized this distance, with the leader's long neck and folded arms signifying lack of approachability. At the UK school, a feeling of disenfranchisement and restricted personal autonomy prevailed.

Lack of direction and fragmentation of academics were articulated more strongly in the Canadian school, because of the outgoing leader's perceived inconsistent management style. This was especially intense amongst contractual academics, who felt poorly treated in relation to permanent colleagues over teaching and research opportunities and contract renewal:

[That's me! (DS: A small figure?) Yes. (DS: Why?) Because I feel so small. Powerless. (DS: Right). And that's <names head of school>. <both laugh> He constantly says 'No'. (DS: Are you holding your hands up to your head?) Yes. (DS: Why, why's that?) 'Cos I'm losing my mind. I really am, I'm going insane. (DS: Why's that?) <interrupts> Because I'm totally frustrated . . . I think that the situations differ so much, depending on who you are. (DS: Right). You know, but this is *me*, and that's him. There's no question about it. (DS: Right. Right). And I'm getting smaller. (DS: You're getting smaller?) Oh, yes. Yeh. And he's getting bigger].

A year later a new organizational leader had generated a sense of 'cautious optimism' within the school. The organization was now believed to be at a critical juncture in terms of its strategic direction. According to MBA students, the choice was between the roads of mediocrity and success, with the figure displaying a simultaneous frown and smile. Positive factors were student talent and enthusiasm, with support for the new leader from most internal stakeholders. Rock-like obstacles on the road to success were the wider university bureaucracy, the deteriorating economy, overcompetitive students, diverse academic personalities and the outgoing leader:

[S1: Yeah, well I think it's at a crossroads, getting another dean]. [S2: Yep a new system, dean] . . . [S3: Hazy vision. <laughs>] . . . [S4: I think it's the blind leading the blind] . . . [S2: Uh, don't know which way we are going and which way they are going] . . . [S1: I

Figure 11.5   Face-to-face interview image: Canadian school

think it's the road meets resistance in a certain way, but if we want to make it what we want, then it's got to get over a lot of obstacles].

The concept of an image mismatch was evident in both organizations. Suits and ties created a degree of perceived respectability in both places; but also formality, conservatism and hierarchy. Canadian academics saw this mismatch as a conflict between business and academic roles, cladding figures half in business suits and half in academic regalia. UK academics also viewed the mismatch as a clash between internal and external perceptions of the organization. In other words, they believed that the school's projected professionalism was illusory:

[(DS: Why's he wearing a suit?) Oh, conventional. A grey suit. (DS: A grey suit?) It's done up as well – all three buttons. (DS: Why's that?) 'Cos that's what repressed, tight-arsed people do. (DS: Right) . . . Very besuited, very wants to be seen as a a manager, an accountant, or er someone of that sort. Greasy, yeh – Brylcreem. (DS: Right). That sort of thing. (DS: It it it's not a high-flying sort-of executive-type?) Oh, no, no, no! It's more like a glorified clerk. (DS: Right). Possibly slightly shiny bits on the suit. (DS: Right). Sort of a bit tatty].

Both institutions were depicted as male, although this was less strongly expressed at the UK school. This could be a simple description of the disproportionate number of male academics, but it was also felt to represent 'male' values, such as competitiveness and lack of emotional support for employees. Both organizations were seen as young/middle-aged, reflecting the time since establishment. The UK organization was seen as large/tall, whereas the Canadian one was medium, reflecting faculty size. Canadian academics also viewed each other as more intellectual than did UK academics.

Several pictorial characteristics were wholly unique to each institution. In the UK school, preoccupation with money and research, a lack of business world links and a feeling of size-based anonymity were mentioned frequently. High relative power to other faculties, a feigned

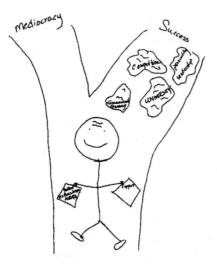

Figure 11.6 MBA students focus group image: Canadian school

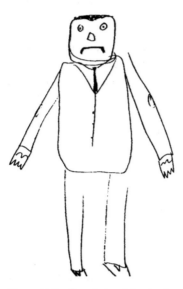

Figure 11.7 Face-to-face interview image: UK school

hi-tech orientation and a competitive environment were also referred to. The Canadian school was seen to have particular problems of recruitment and retention due to its geographical location. It also suffered from a lack of financial resources, and an inhibiting university bureaucracy. A lack of strategic direction resulted from a recent change of leaders, although there was cautious future optimism.

Overall findings

A summary of the pictorial exercises revealed organizational elements not identified using verbal research instruments. This is the acid test of using image. The top five constructs for each school are shown in Table 11.1 in order of descending frequency of mention (how many focus groups and interviews contained each characteristic). This shows how intensely and widely held each of these constructs are.

If strategy development is not the aim, one could be content with enhanced understanding of organizational identity. However, it is helpful to identify which of the organization's problems may be addressed and which are more difficult to change. For example, slow organizational response may be intrinsic to academic committees; but a lack of direction may be tackled with a well-defined strategic plan. The study developed written strategic objectives for each institution. Although these are confidential, they focus specifically on research, teaching, external target markets and human resource management.

Guidelines were also drawn to assist in internal and external image management. For the UK school, emphasizing and accentuating the organization's respectability/business orientation and its research orientation help mould a more positive impression. Challenging the perceived role mismatch in projected professionalism boosts the school's image, although only *real* changes in strategy are likely to alter perceptions in the long term.

Table 11.1 Example organizational characteristics, generated by pictorial exercises

Organizational characteristic	Frequency of mention	
	Focus groups	Interviews
UK school		
Unhappy/frustrating nature of organization	5	21
Respectability/business orientation	5	9
Maleness in faculty numbers and attitudes	4	28
Mismatch in appearance/role conflict	4	15
Research-orientation/preoccupation	3	7
Canadian school		
Watershed of cautious optimism	6	29
Lack of direction	6	8
Reasonably intellectual academics' nature	3	4
Slowness in response to external stimuli	1	11
Maleness in faculty numbers and attitudes	1	10

For the Canadian organization, a general feeling of cautious optimism showed initial support for the new dean. Anxieties concerning financial resources, salary inequities, economic instability, role conflict and the overall university bureaucracy were still prevalent. If the new leader were able to deal with these matters, further fragmentation, academic turnover and internal organizational conflict should be reduced.

CONCLUSIONS: THE POWER OF IMAGE

The unwary researcher should be aware of several potential problems with pictorial representation and how these might be overcome.

First, some people decline the invitation to draw pictures. Recalcitrant artists are more likely to be persuaded with widely understood metaphors such as personality than with unfamiliar ones such as cloud formations or motorbikes. Sometimes individuals claim they are image illiterate or lack drawing ability, although experience shows that this is often because of a reluctance to make creations public. Using warm-up exercises improves the chance of completing the exercise and the respondent can normally be put at ease with a few words of encouragement. If it helps, leave the room during drawing to minimize anxiety.

Others incorporate words into their drawings, contrary to instructions. Discretion must be exercised here, for it is normally better to accept minor encroachments than risk interrupting the creative process. In Figure 11.6, words are only used to clarify particular items. In Figure 11.5, the word 'no' increases the power of the drawing; although its removal would not alter the overall impression of the piece. In both cases, image is still the main means of communicating the idea.

A third set of problems concern interpretation. The researcher should not rely on his or her own 'expert' judgement of what the drawer is conveying because second-hand accounts invite misinterpretation. Analysing the drawer's own explanation also avoids accusations of reification – that one is treating the personality drawing itself as real. Transcribing, examining and presenting data using discourse analysis is very time consuming, because one is interested in interpreting all recorded interaction. Richness of data also risks revealing who the drawer is. For reasons of time and confidentiality, one might prefer to use content analysis or cognitive mapping (see Jones, 1985), although the richness of discourse analysis is preferred here.

The question also arises as to whether such methods reveal manifest or truly latent organizational constructs. Many pictorially stimulated constructs had not emerged during verbal questioning and participants were adamant that they had not thought of such things before. Ultimately, perhaps it is impossible to prove that what is being surfaced is truly 'latent'. However, the argument is stronger if pictorial techniques reveal new data *after* more orthodox verbal data are obtained.

Gioia et al. (2000b) warn of the dangers of using personal identity as a metaphor for organizational identity, which may mask important ontological differences between people as individuals and social participants. If individuals' drawings had been solely relied upon, the methodology might not have surfaced widely shared views. The solution here was for focus groups to aggregate constructs, using individuals' outputs as inputs into group processes and testing how widely shared they were. Holding focus groups after a significant period of time had elapsed also added an important temporal dimension. Of course, what is a 'significant' period depends upon the rapidity and intensity of change faced by the organization. Concerns about anthropomorphism should not deter the researcher. Indeed, personality metaphors generate insights precisely *because* they help respondents to associate the organization with an individual human.

While pictorial representation is not without its problems, it can be an illuminating alternative to more orthodox techniques. This is particularly so in strategy making, where tools such as SWOT (Strengths, Weaknesses, Opportunities and Threats) are often too familiar and inflexible to generate truly creative thinking. Images can be a novel, ice-breaking and insightful way of surfacing latent constructs. They reveal what words alone cannot, since they place participants in an unfamiliar situation: breaking down mindsets and challenging the reluctance to verbalize.

Ultimately, the true test of pictorial representation is in the field and the approach outlined here has generated creative organizational strategies. Whilst it is unlikely that more traditional academics will be convinced, it is hoped that more open-minded researchers will be tempted to explore alternatives to words and numbers.

FURTHER READING

Organizational research on pictures is embryonic, and there is little in strategic management. Morgan (1993) provides a good introduction to metaphors in organizational analysis and outlines social constructionist theory. Studies on organizational identity and identification have burgeoned recently and a special issue of *Academy of Management Review* (2000, 25 (1)) contains a number of relevant articles. Those by Gioia et al., Pratt and Foreman, and Scott and Lane are particularly recommended. Also worth reading is Strati's (2000) piece on photographic images of organizational life and Willmott's (1990) critique on the 'fetishism of identity'.

REFERENCES

van Aken, J.E. (2000) 'Gillian Symon and Catherine Cassell (eds): *Qualitative Methods and Analysis in Organizational Research: A Practical Guide*', *Organization Studies*, 21 (6): 1164–69.

Albert, S. and Whetten, D. (1985) 'Organizational identity', in L.L. Cummings and B.M. Straw (eds), *Research in Organizational Behaviour*, 7: 263–95.

Ashforth, B. and Mael, F. (1989) 'Social identity theory and the organization', *Academy of Management Review*, 14 (1): 20–39.

Alvesson, M. (1990) 'Organization: from substance to image?', *Organization Studies*, 11 (3): 373–94.

Berger, P.L. and Luckmann, T. (1965) *The Social Construction of Reality: A Treatise in the Sociology of Knowledge*, Harmondsworth: Pelican.

Branthwaite, A. and Lunn, T. (1985) 'Projective techniques in social and market research', in Robert Walker (ed.), *Applied Qualitative Research*, Aldershot: Gower.

Brickson, S. (2000) 'The impact of identity orientation on individual and organizational outcomes in a demographically diverse setting', *Academy of Management Review*, 25 (1): 82–101.

Brown, A.D. and Starkey, K. (2000) 'Organizational identity and learning: a psychodynamic perspective', *Academy of Management Review*, 25 (1): 102–20.

Burrell, G. and Morgan, G. (1979) *Sociological Paradigms and Organizational Analysis*, London: Heinemann.

Chaplin, E. (1994) *Sociology and Visual Representation*, London: Routledge.

Checkland, P.B. and Scholes, J. (1990) *Soft Systems Methodology in Action*, London: Wiley.

Edwards, B.R. (1981) *Drawing on the Right Side of the Brain: How to Unlock Your Hidden Artistic Talent*, London: Souvenir.

Emmison, M. and Smith, P. (2000) *Researching the Visual: Images, Objects, Contexts and Interactions in Social and Cultural Enquiry*, London: Sage.

Gioia, D.A., Schultz, M. and Corley, K.G. (2000a) 'Organizational identity, image, and adaptive instability', *Academy of Management Review*, 25 (1): 63–81.

Gioia, D.A., Schultz, M. and Corley, K.G. (2000b) 'Where do we go from here?', *Academy of Management Review*, 25 (1): 145–47.

Green, S. (1988) 'Strategy, organizational culture and symbolism', *Long Range Planning*, 21 (4): 121–29.

Hawkins, J.M. and Allen, R. (eds) (1991) *The Oxford Encyclopedic English Dictionary*, Oxford: Clarendon Press.

Henry, J. (ed.) (2001) *Creative Management*, second edition, London: Open University/Sage.

Hogg, M.A. and Terry, D.J. (2000) 'Social identity and self-categorization processes in organizational contexts', *Academy of Management Review*, 25 (1): 121–40.

Johnson, G. and Scholes, K. (2001) *Exploring Corporate Strategy*, sixth edition, Hemel Hempstead: Prentice Hall International.

Jones, S. (1985) 'The analysis of depth interviews', in Robert Walker (ed.), *Applied Qualitative Research*, Aldershot: Gower.

Kotler, P. (1986) *Principles of Marketing*, third edition, Englewood Cliffs, NJ: Prentice-Hall.

Langer, S. (1957) *Philosophy in a New Key*, Cambridge, MA: Harvard University Press.

Maddox, N., Anthony, W.P. and Wheatley, Jr., W. (1987) 'Creative strategic planning using imagery', *Long Range Planning*, 20 (5): 118–24.

Majaro, S. (1991) *The Creative Marketer*. Oxford: Butterworth Heinemann and Chartered Institute of Marketing.

Morgan, G. (1993) *Imaginization: The Art of Creative Management*, Newbury Park, CA: Sage.

Potter, J. and Wetherell, M. (1987) *Discourse and Social Psychology: Beyond Attitudes and Behaviour*, London: Sage.

Pratt, M.G. and Foreman, P.O. (2000) 'Classifying managerial responses to multiple organizational identities', *Academy of Management Review*, 25 (1): 18–42.

Rickards, T. (1999) *Creativity and the Management of Change*, Oxford: Blackwell.

Russell, P. and Evans, R. (1989) *The Creative Manager*, London: Unwin.

Scott, S.G. and Lane, V.R. (2000) 'A stakeholder approach to organizational identity', *Academy of Management Review*, 25 (1): 43–62.

Semeonoff, B. (1976) *Projective Techniques*, London: Wiley.

Stiles, D.R. (1995) 'The art of organizations: picturing UK and North American business school strategies in four dimensions', PhD thesis, University of Cardiff.

Strati, A. (2000) 'Putting people in the picture: art and aesthetics in photography and in understanding organizational life', *Organization Studies*, 21: 53–69.

Weick, K.E. (1979) *The Social Psychology of Organizing*, second edition, Reading, MA: Addison-Wesley.

Willmott, H. (1990) 'Subjectivity and the dialectics of praxis: opening up the core of labour process analysis', in David Knights and Hugh Willmott (eds), *Labour Process Theory*, Basingstoke: Macmillan.

Ziff, K. (1990) 'Focus group "art" reveals in-depth information', *Marketing News*, 3 September: 7, 20.

— **Group Methods of Organizational Analysis** ————

Chris Steyaert and René Bouwen

Studying group contexts, wherein people meet, talk and work, is probably the most natural method for gathering knowledge about social events and human interaction, especially in an organizational context. Throughout human history and in all places and circumstances people have gathered in groups to discuss what is going on and how to make sense out of it. The local village community, the United Nations taskforce on a special mission in the field, the project team in an engineering project – all meet to be informed. Meeting as a group is in all these cases the first step by which the social community keeps track of what is going on, and for all those involved it is the unique context in which meaning can be made out of the ongoing events. Members of small groups are 'natural' social research actors in that they are constructing, deconstructing and reconstructing the meaning of social realities. Although groups are natural contexts for study and have been a main research theme in social psychology and organizational behaviour (Guzzo and Dickson, 1996), it is surprising that the study *through* groups is less well known and used. This chapter revalues the group method as a research vehicle.

Our concept of social research includes all contexts where social actors meet to 'reconsider' the social reality they are building together. We will distinguish throughout this chapter between studying group contexts created explicitly by the researcher (such as setting up a focus group) and studying those that are already 'at work' in an organizational context (such as observing a work team). Furthermore, we will distinguish between using group methods for exploratory, generative and intervention purposes. Throughout the chapter, two specific uses of the group method will become illustrated, namely the classical group interview (a created group context) and the observation of a project group (an already 'existing' context).

A SOCIAL CONSTRUCTIONIST PERSPECTIVE ON GROUP CONTEXTS ————

Before entering into the description of different small group contexts for social research, we want to make explicit the social science paradigm we support. The choice of a research method, especially in the social sciences, is always steered by the epistemological and ontological assumptions of the researchers. It is therefore desirable to be explicit about those assumptions, because they will guide the conceptualization of problem issues, the concrete operationalizations of the research approaches and the states of the conclusions.

From our research experiences in two different but related fields, 'conflict in work settings' (Bouwen and Salipante, 1990) and 'organizational innovation and entrepreneurship' (Steyaert, 1995; Steyaert et al., 1996) we experienced the potential contribution of a 'social constructionist' approach (Gergen, 2001) for framing social research efforts. In those research projects we learnt that one can not talk about 'the' conflict or 'the' innovation as if there is a single social reality which can be defined in an unequivocal way. There are as many perspectives to a problem as there are actors. Actors define the issue by relating their definition to other definitions. There will never be a complete overlap among perspectives nor a definite understanding. There is a continuously ongoing negotiation relationship among the actors and in that sense the social reality is 'continuously in-the-making'. Since social constructionism emphasizes the relational qualities and the multiplicities of social realities, we find it an adequate theory to guide qualitative research in a group context. Also, the role of the researcher is mainly relationally constructed as we will illustrate in the chosen case examples below.

SIX GROUP FORMS FOR STUDYING ORGANIZATIONS

Different ways of using the group method

A very large variety of group contexts can be studied as a vehicle for generating data and interpretations about organizations on different levels. Some groups are created especially for research or intervention purposes. The researcher is then a major constituent of the group context. Other group contexts are 'natural' in the sense that they exist as work groups, teams or committees, which are part of the natural organizational environment. Thus, we can distinguish between 'natural' and 'created' group contexts. However, this distinction is not discrete, but should be seen on a 'continuum', where a researcher has more or less influence on the 'staging' of the group context.

A second dimension for distinguishing group contexts is the purpose of the convenor or the researcher. Is this purpose just the mere *exploration and description* of ideas? Is the purpose the *generation* of ideas and concepts by creating a stimulating interaction? Or is the group meeting intentionally set up to *intervene* in the experienced social reality? From exploration to intervention, there is an increasing influence of the coordinator or organizer of the group situation under study and also an increasing embeddedness in an existing organizational reality.

Combining both dimensions (natural/created and purpose), six generic group forms are distinguished which can be used for data collection and subsequent analysis and interpretation. Group interviews and focus groups ([1] in Table 12.1) are often considered as the most characteristic form for data collection. They have a long tradition in marketing research and in opinion survey. Even more often, this kind of group will be an existing or previously

Table 12.1 Different types of group method

Group setting/ purpose of research	Natural	Created
Exploration	Work-groups/Group observations (6)	Group interviews/Focus groups (1)
Generation	Work-team study/Group experiments/Role plays (5)	Group simulations/Group meetings (2)
Intervention	Team-building/Action research (4)	Project group/Taskforce analysis (3)

formed group (6) in the organization. In group experiments or simulations (2), the conditions are handled intentionally, and in the work-team study (5) a committee or group of representatives is formed to develop alternatives for action. In organization development projects, intervention work is often done within group contexts. The capacities for interaction and creativity are used to a fuller extent when the group context is used to generate new behaviour or new alternatives for action. Team-building efforts (4) seek to enhance the functioning of existing groups. In task forces (3), the group is created explicitly as an intervention device to decide upon and implement the intended changes.

This distinction of group forms is not exhaustive and there are many overlapping forms, but specification of group characteristics is important to typify the role of the researcher, the involvement of the group members and the kind of interaction that is aimed for. Taking all these aspects into account is essential in processing generated data and in making interpretations.

Previous work

With this scheme, it is possible to integrate methodological literature from different origins. Literature on group methods is rather scarce. Even one of the classics of the group method, the group interview, is poorly referenced or thinly discussed in handbooks on qualitative methodology (Marshall and Rossman, 1999; Strauss and Corbin, 1998). Furthermore, there has been a preference for the use of groups as a means of data gathering in applied contexts, such as marketing, personnel selection, training, group therapy, organizational development, applied social research, rather than for theoretical purposes.

Among the created group contexts, group interviews and focus groups (1) are the best known. Traditionally they have been very popular in marketing and consumer psychology, where consumers comment in a small group on a certain product or service (Templeton, 1994). Both Morgan (1997) and Bloor (2001) have written very useful and comprehensive monographs on focus groups as a qualitative research method, while Stewart and Shamdasani (1990) have placed the use and interpretation of focus groups within their theoretical contexts. Greenbaum (2000) and Krueger and Casey (2000) have produced practical guides, while we can mention also the handbooks by Greenbaum (1998), Edmunds (1999) and the so-called focus group kit, a series edited by Morgan et al. (with in 1998 a sixth volume). In social and organizational research, groups are thus more and more used to facilitate the conduct of research and for 'brainstorming' about social and organizational problems (for example, 'round tables' among personnel directors concerning unemployment; see Vaugh et al., 1996; Morrison, 1998; Bloor, 2001).

Creating groups for data collection in theory testing for organizational understanding is done in very different ways: experiments, simulations, role plays (2). In handbooks of experimental research, group experiments are rarely discussed. In organizational psychology, experiments have been used in the laboratory and the field, and as organizational simulations. Following Sackett and Larson (1990), experimentation has become one of the most used methodologies in the field of industrial and organizational psychology. Methodological considerations can be found in Sackett and Larson (1990), an example of organizational experiments in Litwin and Stringer (1968), and of organizational simulations in Rabbie and Van Oostrum (1984). Although the difference between group and organizational experiment/simulation is rather vague, typical group experiments are again lacking. Group simulations and role-playing have been used in the applied context for gaining human understanding, for example role-playing in conflict handling (Hare, 1985) and in educational and training situations (Eiben and Milliren, 1976). In the personnel context, group simulations and discussions are used during selection procedures and especially in assessment centres (Blanksby and Iles, 1990).

The gaining of information through groups for intervention activities has been used in team-building (Dyer, 1995) and in organizational development programmes (Lundberg, 1990). For learning purposes in particular (individual *and* organizational), the group (both the created [3] and the natural [4]) has been accorded a prominent place (Srivastva et al., 1977). But also within the context of action research, groups form the context where insights and new possibilities are generated on the collective level, as has been broadly explored in the 'appreciative inquiry' approach (Cooperrider and Srivastva, 1987) and in search conferences (Emery, 1996). In the group intervention context, a group is answering the questions: 'Where are we now, where do we want to go, and how do we bridge this gap?' The 'natural' interplay between the different voices is questioned, and the intervention aims at revitalizing the organizational dialogue that has become impeded or fixated.

Finally, the observation of groups for exploring (6) and generating (5) concepts and models of organizational processes has been used in organizational ethnography (Rosen, 1991), although groups do not have a privileged position compared to other kinds of observation contexts. This form is, in our view, the least known and applied, and is one of the forms we discuss in more detail.

A social constructionist approach to the group method

In this chapter we will document more in detail two types of group method: the classical form of group interview and the study of meetings for generating theory. We illustrate thus both a so-called 'natural' and created context, and both an exploratory and generative context.

How does a social constructionist view facilitate data generation and data-processing in these research illustrations of group method? First, the group interview or group discussion gives the opportunity to hear different accounts or voices at the 'same' time on the 'same' phenomenon or problem. Individuals are asked to tell their stories concerning the problem highlighted by the researcher. Each story can be aligned to or expand the story of another participant or can contrast a previous story. The aim is to catch in a condensed way the range of different voices. The group situation makes the differences and similarities between the different participants, and also the dynamics between the perspectives on a problem, directly visible.

Second, the observation of 'natural' group meetings goes one step further. It is comparable to the group interview in the way that organizational members give their view on the subject of the meeting. So, the natural mix of differences can be 'caught' there as well. But the researcher also comes in contact with the evolution of the different voices as they develop and emerge in a living social context, expressing the construction and deconstruction of shared meaning.

For us, using each of these different methods has been a tentative learning process. There is no single form of using a specific method, since it is a creative and context-bounded application. The methods will be presented by telling a short research story, documenting both *why it* was useful to use the group method and *how* the method was used.

The group interview: the context of small and medium enterprises (SMEs)

In answering the question 'why group interviews?', it is important to distinguish the group interview from the individual interview, and to describe why we started a three-year research project with the former method. In answering the question how to do group interviews, we discuss the following stages: preparation, application, analysis and integration of the group interview. Examples refer to group interviews carried out during a three-year research project on 'Consulting for growth and innovation in SMEs'.

WHY GROUP INTERVIEWS?

The general aim of this study was to understand the quality of the relationship between consultants and SME leaders in the light of the possibilities of consulting firms and the needs of the SMEs. The research project had three parts. The group interviews were carried out during the first part of the study, to explore the general accounts of SME leaders and consultants as to the quality of their cooperation. Furthermore, the group interviews could help us: to get a first impression of the field (together with some other exploratory individual interviews); to collect some general themes to aid in constructing questionnaires for the next research stage; and to confront the participants with some of our first thoughts (hypotheses if you will) which we brought to the research project. There was also a more pragmatic reason since two different intermediary representatives of SMEs proposed to the researchers to organize a group meeting: in one case with SME leaders, in the other with consultants.

PREPARING THE GROUP INTERVIEW

Two points are important: determining the size of the group and the number of interviewers (the 'who' level) and the preparation of the content (the 'what' level).

First, the general size of the group can be between six and 10 persons. This norm is used in marketing research (Morgan, 1997). Since we were interested in extended personal stories, a smaller number was more adequate and realistic. If possible, the participation of two researchers in the group interview will prevent a lot of problems, although it introduces fresh dilemmas: for example, how familiar are you with each other and with each other's interview style? Second, there has to be preparation on the content level on how open/structured the group interview will be. In our case, a list of guiding topics was prepared by one of the researchers, more as a security to fall back on than as a set of fixed questions we had to go through. We preferred an open research situation, in which all participants could tell their documented and critical story. For an overview of types of questions, we refer to Spradley (1979) in his discussion of the (individual) ethnographic interview.

CONDUCTING THE GROUP INTERVIEW

Here we discuss the flow of the group interaction (the 'how' level). Two roles were distinguished and divided among the two researchers. One researcher focused on the content level, the other on the procedural and process level. The first used the list of topics to invite participation. An example of such a topic is 'the short-term versus long-term outcome of the consultancy', which resulted in the following question: 'Are achievements by the consultant necessary in the short term?' Closed and tentative questions should generally be avoided. For example, the question: 'Don't you think it is important for the cooperation between SME and consultant that a relationship of confidence exists?' introduces a fundamental idea which frames the participants' comments as well as focusing them on 'the profile' of what the researchers seem to expect. Here the researcher wants to control and work more with 'his or her' data instead of being open to the 'data' the participants bring to the encounter. We would expect such a closed question at the end of the group interview or reformulate it as an open question: 'What are important features of the relationship between SME and consultant?'

The second interviewer made interventions in order to stimulate and steer the process and interaction between participants by asking structural and process 'questions'. In contrast to individual interviews, the group process requires extra focus as the group dynamics steers to a large extent the interview process (rhythm, alternation between participants, depth, group-think, dominant and silent participants, and so on) more than the interviewer. These questions are not on a content level, but the researchers try at the same time to structure the ongoing dialogue and to stimulate the interviewees in telling their story, their opinion, their ideas. Concrete examples of structural questions are: 'asking for clarification and illustration', 'reformulating the account of a person' or 'contrasting two opinions and inviting other participants to comment on these' or 'adding a third opinion', 'reminding of the time schedule', etc.

Through structural questions, the interviewer steers the interaction by focusing on the ongoing communication patterns; he or she is following the discussion with the following questions in the back of his or her mind: is it clear to the others or to myself what a person says? Are participants more or less equally active in the conversation? Are we respecting the available time? Are participants diverging too much or 'jumping around'? Experience and skills concerning 'conducting meetings' and 'time management' can be very helpful here to the group facilitator.

Through process questions, the interviewer focuses on the involvement and personal ease of the participants. This requires that the interviewer is an active listener and makes interviewees feel at ease, with the aim of building trust and creating an open climate. One should not forget that this group interview can be often the first one interviewees are involved in: they feel uncertain about what is going to happen and whether their contribution will be appreciated.

In the beginning of or even before the group discussion, the interviewer can 'test the water' and see how people 'feel' about the group interview. Interviewers often start by asking everybody to introduce themselves as a kind of 'ice-breaker'. Furthermore, the beginning of an interview is an ideal point to clarify one's own role and to illustrate how one is going to conduct the interview, for instance: 'I see my role as to give everybody an equal chance to participate in this discussion. Sometimes I will interrupt persons when I feel that other persons remain too much in the background.'

During the interview, the moderator can be confronted with some 'typical' situations such as the following:

1   One person is dominating the discussion and giving his or her reaction on every single thing the others say. Here a process intervention can be needed by confronting the participant while not losing his or her involvement: 'I appreciate very much your ideas and reaction, but I would suggest that we listen first to the other participants and, afterwards, I will ask you to give your reactions.'

2   Everybody is speaking at the same time. Here a structural intervention can be used by remaking a short 'contract' with the participants on how to run the discussion: 'I see that everybody has a lot to say on this topic, but I think that we should go around in a more systematic way.'

3   Sometimes the group discussion can 'flag' and reach a dead end. How can one then reinvigorate the group? This can be the moment to bring in a new content topic or theme. By a structural intervention, the interviewer can make a summary of what has been said so far, and test if persons find it necessary to continue this 'chapter' or if they agree to address a new one. The advantage is that participants are involved as well in how the interview is conducted. A process intervention can also be useful: 'I see that we are a bit out of inspiration, maybe it is useful to take a small break.' Here the moderator focuses on the involvement of the participants.

4   One person remains quiet during the interview and gives no comments unless the facilitator asks this explicitly. How can one encourage this person without making him or her feel even more uncomfortable? Through a process intervention, the interviewer can repeat his or her appreciation for every opinion even if this is very equal to or very different from the opinions of others. Here it is important not to ask directly for participation but to keep some space open so that the quiet participant can decide if he or she wants to intervene.

In general, it is important that an interviewer is able to manage his or her own action space, and keep it open enough so that he or she can be flexible in making content, structural and process interventions. Finding the right balance requires a learning process from the group interviewer which should be adapted to the specific group process as well. It is important not to talk too much during the group interview (as in the individual interview), but when the moderator sees/feels the discussion is going in the 'wrong' direction, he or she must not hesitate to make a facilitating intervention. Then it is as important to 'do something' as to clarify 'why one is doing this or that'. If participants understand the perspective behind the interviewer's concrete interventions, there is more chance that they will 'follow' him or her in steering the group interaction.

ANALYSIS OF THE GROUP INTERVIEW

The interviews were tape-recorded and afterwards transcribed into a copy of more than 60 pages (for each interview). Permission for tape-recording was asked from all participants. There was no video taping, since our intention was to explore general themes, and not to undertake an in-depth analysis of this group process.

The analysis took two forms. First, a classic 'content analysis' was carried out by one of the researchers (see, for example, Strauss and Corbin, 1998), leading to the first typology of possible relationships between SMEs and consultants. Second, the analysis of the group interview was seen in the light of the other data already collected and was obtained by integrating it into the larger project.

A FIRST EVALUATION

The group interview is similar to the individual interview in many ways. It can have multiple formats and the principles of good questioning are much the same (for example, the type of questions, the danger of closed questioning).

However, the following elements can be considered as distinctive. First of all, the key interaction is not between the interviewer and interviewee, but between the participants. Also other (social) processes are involved. One concerns the public character of the stories participants bring in. Another concerns the group processes which steer the general outcome of the interview. This requires insights into group dynamics and the ability to facilitate the process rather than the content.

Finally, one of the main outcomes of the group interviews, which only became clear afterwards, was that within the research team, which consisted of two researchers from different universities and from different academic backgrounds, a joint research experience was created. This made discussion of our own research process possible and helped us to understand our different perspectives. Indeed, as a research team, we also meet and discuss in order to research (or learn from) our own research process.

The project group study: the context of innovation

Through the next story, we want to describe and document the use of observation and analysis of group meetings and group discussions in their 'natural context'. On the one hand, the distinctive contribution of the group study will be illustrated in relation to the larger organization case study which consisted of the use of interviews, questionnaires, the study of documents and feedback sessions as well. On the other hand, we will describe more practically how we learnt to use this application of the group method. The case study from which examples will be given was part of a three year research project with the general aim of understanding the organizational processes underlying the implementation of innovation. It is one of seven longitudinal case studies which were set up for this research project. The researcher attended 18 project meetings as a participant observer. Besides the observation and analysis of this long sequence of group meetings, 28 interviews, an organizational climate survey, 100 pages of documents and a two-day feedback session were all part of the 'data collection'.

WHY GROUP STUDY?

Besides the epistemological considerations for using a project group study, more pragmatic reasons were involved. In the context of innovation, where project groups are the focus of the innovative activities, group observation becomes advantageous compared to other methods for understanding how organizations innovate differently. Our aim was not to study project groups as such, but to understand how the organizational innovation process develops by observing group meetings. As teamwork becomes more and more crucial for the well-functioning and effectiveness of all kinds of firms, increasing numbers of researchers will be confronted with studying groups at work with the aim of describing and understanding the whole organization.

PREPARING AND FOLLOWING THE GROUP MEETINGS

The preparation of and the participation in one actual meeting is not very demanding. During the meeting the researcher took notes both of what was said and by whom. He also made non-verbal observations (who came in late, silences, laughs, and so on). There was no tape-recording as the amount of data would have become too vast.

This research activity can be seen as an evolutionary task. The important step for the researcher at this stage is to get integrated and accepted in the social system of a firm and the particular project group. It takes some time before you as a researcher get invited spontaneously to the next meeting. Get a copy of the notes and summaries of the participants, or get a phone call from the secretary to inform you that the meeting has been postponed (it happened once that the observer was present but that the group was not!). It is not easy to get accepted, but step by step people get used to the idea of the presence of a stranger, and also on certain occasions people discuss the role of the researcher. In the firm the researcher even got a nickname.

COMING BACK TO THE RESEARCH TEAM

We would call the period after the participation in the meeting more important than the participation itself. On returning to the research team, the first thing the researcher did was check his notes, completing and rewriting them. Second, the researcher discussed with colleagues what he had been up to, asking the very general question of what had happened there, in the context of the research question. This discussion of first impressions and ideas constructs a narrative of the observed events and already constitutes an initial interpretation of the data.

Besides this informal reception of the returning researcher, the research team itself had its weekly meetings through which the innovation project was steered. This is one of the main ways of making this kind of group study fruitful, or at least surviving it. Pettigrew (1990) has emphasized teamwork in longitudinal field research. The role and influence of the research team for the observant researcher is valid on many levels:

1   Support: the researcher follows the emotional life of this group in evolution. Furthermore, the researcher does not see where this investment is leading him or her. Is there going to be a valuable outcome for the research? This creates a lot of uncertainty (should I go on with this or not?) which can be shared through coming back into the research team.

2   Distancing (Rosen, 1991): the team gives researchers another reality, which helps them to distance themselves from their participation. This is not only important emotionally; there is also a change of perspective, which is necessary for interpreting the data. Following Pettigrew (1990), teamwork helps the researchers balance detachment and involvement in the field. It also inhibits any tendency to overidentify with particular interpretations or interests when analysing the data.

3   Consensual validation: in analysing and discussing this case together, different perspectives and interpretations are added to the interpretations which the researcher originated.

ANALYSIS OF THE MEETING DISCUSSIONS

Analysis is carried out in four related steps. The first is writing the story as explained. The story is a mix of 'actual sayings', descriptions of (inter)actions, and interpretations (everybody giving their opinion). This story is written after the concept analysis and the construction of meaning configurations (step two) in order to document a more general interpretation of this meeting, for example the interaction between group and group leader.

In the second step, concepts are formulated using the method of interpretive grounded theory (Steyaert, 1995). In practice, this means that the field notes (or interview transcripts) are analysed part by part. A part of the text is taken and 'interpreted' by deriving a concept, for instance 'recycling problem definition', 'continuous evaluation' or 'the facilitating role of the project manager'. This results in a long list of concepts which are related to each other and integrated in so-called meaning configurations.

In the third step, the outcomes of the group study are compared to and integrated with the outcomes of the interviews and the study of documents. Here, the research team works towards an integrated case study. The research team uses a more 'holistic' interpretative style which can, however, be documented in more detailed parts of the analysis. Coming to an understanding of this complex sequence of events involves a circular consideration of both the whole and its parts (see Steyaert, 1995).

The fourth step consists of going back to the firm. Based on this set of analyses, an extensive report was written to present our descriptions and interpretations of the organization development project and was transmitted to all members of the project team. Furthermore, the supervisor and the researcher participated in a two-day residential seminar with the project team, where they gave an introductory presentation based on the report. This had a double aim. First, it was seen as a further step of analysis, based on co-inquiry. As researchers we have many questions like: Do they recognize our interpretations? Are they meaningful to them? Can they use them? What interpretations do they have? Can we agree on some interpretations? Here as a researcher you validate your findings with the direct participants, but it is also an exercise in communicating your findings and in exploring their usefulness. Second, this was a (well-elaborated) feedback exercise, which this group had been doing many times (what have we been doing?), and which helped in finding the future path.

A FIRST EVALUATION

Using the group method within this case has been very fruitful. First, it gave the opportunity to do a longitudinal study in vivo based on a partial integration of the researcher in the social system of the firm. The richness and depth of understanding would not have been reached on the basis of interviews alone. Second, it gave the opportunity to study the interaction of multiple parties at one and the same moment, and to focus on the dynamics of organizing: one can literally see the organization-in-the-making. Third, the researcher could observe persons in different situations, not only in the interview situation. It gave the opportunity to focus on the relation between what people do and what people say they do; also, the researcher could 'see' how people make sense of situations (in interviews) based on the meetings in which the researcher had participated.

This kind of group research method is quite complex and asks a lot of maturity of the researcher. First, it is a kind of selective form of organizational ethnography, making use of focused observant participation (see Czarniawska-Joerges, 1992). The researcher only goes now and then to the organization to participate in what can be regarded as 'significant moments' for the research problem. Although this can be seen as a minimal form of organizational ethnography, it asks for the same qualities as the organizational ethnographer. The researcher needs to build up a trust relationship and to define and redefine his or her role as the process goes on. Second, the researcher needs to be able to integrate different research methods into one overall case study. Third, he or she needs to have the courage to invest in a long-term affiliation with a particular firm with an uncertain and open end. The 'success' of this research investment is largely dependent on the learning process the researcher is going through during the study.

COMPARING AND CONTRASTING THE ILLUSTRATIONS

In Table 12.2, the group interview and the project group study which we illustrated, are compared and contrasted.

Table 12.2 Comparison between group interview and project group study

	Group interview	Project group
Goal of the research	Exploration of the problem or phenomenon	Theory generation
Social constructionist focus	Different voices on the same subject	Interplay between the voices
Background	Content and theme analysis	Interpretive grounded theory
Context of use	Marketing and consumer studies	Social interaction and communication, conflict
Data generation	Loosely coupled opinions/ideas	Theme-orientated perspectives
Analysis	Emerging themes	Concepts and meaning configurations
Main point	Content/Context	Process/Context
Role of the group	Stimulating ideas	Representing variety of perspectives on the problem
Role of the researcher	Discussion leader/Group facilitator	Observing participant
Data collection/ analysis relationship	Mostly separated	Co-inquiry

From a social constructionist perspective, both approaches allow the possibility of considering the multiplicity of perspectives, but with different accents. They are partly rooted in different methodological backgrounds, since the group interview goes back to content analysis while the project group study has affinity with interpretive grounded theory. Although the context of use is not restricted to one area, in the past this has actually been the case.

In the group interview, the main data are loosely coupled ideas/opinions, emerging from questions and given research themes. Through content analysis, several themes and exploratory insights emerge. Mostly the relationship between data collection and analysis is separated, although sometimes a new group interview is conducted in order to confront the group members with the findings from the previous groups. In the project group study, the data resemble mostly theme–orientated perspectives, which are based on interpretive grounded theory principles processed as interpretive grounded concepts and integrated in meaning configurations. Data collection and analysis are interwoven. Moreover, the participants not only generate data, but are involved in interpreting these as well.

The group functions as the main arena of research for studying the larger organizations, but the role of the group can again be accentuated differently. In the group interview, the group is there to stimulate ideas, and it is expected that the group process itself, as opposed to the cumulation of individual interviews, will stimulate the quantity and the quality of the ideas. For the project group study, the group represents the variety of perspectives on the theme as this evolves throughout the development of the project. The group here gives the possibility of seeing the different parties and logics within a firm 'at work'. Most generally, these types can be characterized differently, as respectively content- and process- oriented, since in the group interview the main outcome is the ideas and their diversity, while in the project group study, the focus is on the process of interaction. For both group methods, it is important to see the generated data as part of the organizational context. The role of the researcher asks for research competencies besides skills in group functioning and group dynamics. This requires process skills respectively for leading the group discussion and for building up a long-term integration as a participant observer.

Although Table 12.2 gives an overview of the core features of the group interview and the project group study, Table 12.3 presents a list of the main strengths and liabilities of both types as we evaluate them from working with these different uses of the group method.

Table 12.3 Comparison of strengths and weaknesses between the group interview and the project group study

	Group interview	Project group
Strengths	Different opinions at the same time Dynamics between different perspectives Easy to organize	Research *in vivo* and on a longitudinal base Depth of understanding Interaction between perspectives is accessible as well as their 'natural' evolution
Weaknesses	Less control over the outcome since the impact of the group (process) is quite high Difficult to guide Easier with two 'interviewers'	Difficult to analyse Long-term investment Need for support and distancing Easier when the researcher is part of a team

CONCLUSION: EMERGING CHOICES

In choosing and using the group method, it is important to consider three main interrelated choices. First, the group method, as it has been demonstrated here in practice, was not used in isolation but was embedded in the development of a larger research project, where other methods were used as well. The emergent question here, therefore, is what other methods should be added? Without going into the discussion on triangulation, our stories revealed that the research questions as well as the practical possibilities guided us in the continuous 'designing' of the research trajectory, and in implementing the group as a research vehicle. However, if organizations are increasingly seen as networks of social interaction, the choice of working in group contexts will become more and more self-evident.

The second choice considers the purpose for which you are going to use the group method. Two contexts are explored: do you prefer to work with existing groups or to create your own groups? And for what purpose do you want to use the group method: for a general exploration, for generating new concepts and models, or for stimulating new action and intervention?

The final choice concerns your role as 'researcher'. Several distinctive competencies in using both qualitative research and the group method have been mentioned. This raises special concerns for the education and training of the social science researcher. The choice can indeed be made between 'inquiry from the inside' and 'inquiry from the outside' (Evered and Louis, 1981). Do you opt for an experiential involvement, for an open and unstructured research scenario (no fixed set of data, no a priori categories in analysis, multiple levels of interpretation and integration), and do you have the intention to understand a particular situation? In particular, the question concerns the choice between the complex and holistic site of social interaction in vivo and the simplified and fragmented focus on isolated individuals – isolated from others (as in interviews, questionnaires) and from their context (as in experiments, simulations).

The creativity of the researcher using qualitative methods is crucial in the whole of the research project and especially critical in the analysis phase to obtain some added value. Quantitative analysis works with weighting precoded categories. Qualitative research, in essence, is the creative development of concepts which can capture the richness of the data generated. In group meetings this richness is very high, and therefore for some people and some purposes they are maybe too complex and chaotic. But is it not precisely in group life that the natural complexity and diversity of social life is revealed? The challenge for social science is to develop approaches which can address instantly the ongoing complex interaction while the social reality is being negotiated and renegotiated. Maybe then the social scientist can finally live up to the very pressing and demanding needs of present-day society, in a variety of contexts all over the world, to contribute substantially to urgent social tasks in conflictual environments.

FURTHER READING

M. Bloor (2001) *Focus Groups in Social Research*, London: Sage.
H. Edmunds (1999) *The Focus Group Research Handbook*, Lincolnwood, IL: NTC Business Books.
T.L. Greenbaum (2000) *Moderating Focus Groups: a Practical Guide for Group Facilitation*, Thousand Oaks, CA: Sage.
D.L. Morgan (1997) *Focus Groups as Qualitative Research* (Qualitative Research Methods Series, Vol. 16), Thousand Oaks, CA: Sage.
D.L. Morgan, R.A. Krueger and J.A. King (eds), *Focus Group Kit* (vols 1–6), Thousand Oaks: Sage.

REFERENCES

Blanksby, M. and Iles, P. (1990) 'Recent developments in assessment centre theory, practice and operation', *Personnel Review*, 19 (6): 33–44.
Bloor, M. (2001) *Focus Groups in Social Research*, London: Sage.
Bouwen, R. and Salipante, P. (1990) 'The behavioural analysis of grievances: episodes, actions and outcomes', *Employee Relations*, 12 (4): 27–32.
Cooperrider, D.L. and Srivastva, S. (1987) 'Appreciative inquiry in organizational life', *Research in Organizational Change and Development,* (1): 129–69.
Czarniawska-Joerges, B. (1992) *Exploring Complex Organizations*, Newbury Park, CA: Sage.
Dyer, W.G. (1995) *Team Building: Issues and Alternatives*, Reading, MA: Addison-Wesley.
Edmunds, H. (1999) *The Focus Group Research Handbook*, Lincolnwood, IL: NTC Business Books.
Eiben, R. and Milliren, A. (1976) *Educational Change: A Humanistic Approach*, La Jolla, CA: University Associates.
Emery, M. (1996) *The Search Conference: A Powerful Method for Planning and Organizational Change and Community Action*, San Francisco, CA: Jossey Bass.
Evered, R. and Louis, M.R. (1981) 'Alternative perspectives in the organizational sciences: "inquiry from the inside" and "inquiry from the outside"', *Academy of Management Review*, 6 (3): 385–95.
Gergen, K.J. (2001) *Social Construction in Context*, London: Sage.

Greenbaum, T.L. (1998) *The Handbook for Focus Group Research*, Thousand Oaks, CA: Sage.

Greenbaum, T.L. (2000) *Moderating Focus Groups: A Practical Guide for Group Facilitation*, Thousand Oaks, CA: Sage.

Guzzo, R.A. and Dickson, M.W. (1996) 'Teams in organizations: recent research on performance and effectiveness', *Annual Review of Psychology*, 47: 307–38.

Hare, A.P. (1985) *Social Interaction as Drama*, Beverly Hills, CA: Sage.

Krueger, R.A and Casey, M.A. (2000) *Focus Groups: A Practical Guide for Applied Research*, Thousand Oaks, CA: Sage.

Litwin, G.H. and Stringer, R.A., Jr (1968) *Motivation and Organizational Climate*, Boston, MA: Division of Research, Harvard Business School.

Lundberg, C.C. (1990) 'Surfacing organizational culture', *Journal of Managerial Psychology*, 5(4): 19–36.

Marshall, C. and Rossman, G.B. (1999) *Designing Qualitative Research*, Thousand Oaks, CA: Sage.

Morgan, D.L. (1997) *Focus Groups as Qualitative Research (Qualitative Research Methods Series, Vol. 16)*, Thousand Oaks, CA: Sage.

Morgan, D.L., Krueger, R.A. and King, J.A. (eds) *Focus Group Kit.* (Vols. 1–6), Thousand Oaks: Sage.

Morrison, D. (1998) *The Search for a Method: Focus Groups and the Rise of Mass Communication Research*, Luton: University of Luton Press.

Pettigrew, A.M. (1990) 'Longitudinal field research on change: theory and practice', *Organization Science*, 1 (3): 267–92.

Rabbie, J.M. and Van Oostrum, J. (1984) 'Environmental uncertainty, power and effectiveness in laboratory organizations', in G.M. Stephenson and J.H. Davies (eds), *Progress in Applied Psychology*, vol. 2, Chichester: Wiley.

Rosen, M. (1991) 'Coming to terms with the field: understanding and doing organizational ethnography', *Journal of Management Studies*, 28: 1–24.

Sackett, P.R. and Larson, J.R. (1990) 'Research strategies and tactics in industrial and organizational psychology', in M.D. Dunnette and L.M. Hough (eds), *Handbook of Industrial and Organizational Psychology*, Palo Alto, CA: Consulting Psychologists Press, Inc.

Spradley, J.P. (1979) *The Ethnographic Interview*, New York: Rinehart & Winston.

Srivastva, S., Obert, S. and Neilson, E. (1977) 'Organizational analysis through group process: a theoretical, perspective for organizational development', in C. Cooper (ed.), *Organization Development in the UK and USA,* New York: Macmillan.

Stewart, D.W. and Shamdasani, P.N. (1990) *Focus Groups. Theory and Practice.* (Applied Social Research Methods Series, Vol. 20), Newbury Park, CA: Sage.

Steyaert, C. (1995) '*Perpetuating entrepreneurship through dialogue. A social constructionist view*', unpublished doctoral dissertation for the degree of doctor in psychology. Katholieke Universiteit Leuven: Department of Work and Organizational Psychology.

Steyaert, C., Bouwen, R. and Van Looy, B. (1996) 'Conversational construction of new meaning configurations in organizational innovation: a generative approach', *European Journal of Work and Organizational Psychology*, 5(1): 67–89.

Strauss, A. and Corbin, J. (1998) *Basics of Qualitative Research,* Thousand Oaks, CA: Sage.

Templeton, J.F. (1994) *Focus Group Revised: A Strategic Guide to Organizing, Conducting and Analyzing the Focus Group Interview*, New York: McGraw-Hill.

Vaugh, S., Schumm, J.S. and Sinagub, J.M. (1996) *Focus Group Interviews in Education and Psychology*, London: Sage.

(13)—— **Participant Observation** ————————————————————

David Waddington

The eminent American investigative social researcher Jack Douglas maintains that 'when one's concern is the experience of people, the way that they think, feel and act, the most truthful, reliable, complete and simple way of getting that information is to share their experience' (1976: 112). This is precisely the outlook subscribed to by proponents and practitioners of participant observation, the method described and evaluated in this chapter. The contents of the chapter are based on insights drawn from my own doctoral study of the 1981 Ansells brewery strike – a bitter five-month conflict involving opposition to redundancies and revised working practices which eventually resulted in the permanent closure of the brewery and the dismissal of the entire 1,000-strong workforce.

Here I intend to refer to my own experience of the strike, both as a practical illustration of participant observation, and as a demonstration of the hard-headed pragmatism and extemporization required when conducting fieldwork of this nature. I begin by outlining the essential features of the method, defining the type of circumstances to which it is best suited, the particular skills required of the practitioner, and the techniques by which data are accessed, recorded and analysed. I then indicate how far and how successfully these skills and principles were applied in my study, before using this experience as a basis for evaluating the method.

INTRODUCTION TO THE METHOD ————————————————————

According to Taylor and Bogdan (1984: 15), participant observation 'involves social interaction between the researcher and informants in the milieu of the latter', the idea being to allow the observer to study first-hand the day-to-day experience and behaviour of subjects in particular situations, and, if necessary, to talk to them about their feelings and interpretations.

The extent to which observers actually *participate* in the activities of the people they are studying may vary from one project to the next. Burgess (1984) discusses four possible research identities:

1   the *complete participant*, who operates covertly, concealing any intention to observe the setting;
2   the *participant-as-observer*, who forms relationships and participates in activities but makes no secret of an intention to observe events;
3   the *observer-as-participant*, who maintains only superficial contacts with the people being studied (for example, by asking them occasional questions); and
4   the *complete observer*, who merely stands back and 'eavesdrops' on the proceedings.

One key distinguishing feature of the method is that the observer's own experience is considered an important and legitimate source of data (Brewer, 2000: 59). In contrast to most other methods, participant observation uses an *inductive*, as opposed to a deductive, strategy (see also Johnson, Chapter 14, this volume). Thus the participant observer uses his or her initial observations as the starting point from which to formulate single or multiple hypotheses. These hypotheses may subsequently be discarded or refined in order to accommodate any unanticipated or contradictory observations which may emerge (Jorgensen, 1989).

Whilst it is highly likely that the participant observer will find the experience exciting and rewarding, he or she may also encounter any one of a host of practical pitfalls and emotional or ethical predicaments. Such issues will be comprehensively addressed in the course of describing my Ansells study, once full consideration has been given to the key skills and principles involved at the main stages of observational research.

Entering the field

Research settings inevitably vary in the extent to which they are open or closed off to public scrutiny, and sometimes incorporate private or 'backstage' regions (Goffman, 1959) which researchers may be especially keen to investigate. Such variables obviously have a bearing on the amount of preliminary negotiation required to gain access, and how far the participant observer must be prepared to conceal or declare his or her true objectives and identity. Most textbooks highlight the importance, at this initial stage, of creativity, common sense and interpersonal skills.

As Taylor and Bogdan explain, 'Getting into a setting involves a process of managing your identity; projecting an image of yourself that will maximize your chances of gaining access . . . You want to convince gatekeepers that you are a non-threatening person who will not harm their organization in any way' (1984: 20). These authors advocate an initial approach which guarantees confidentiality and privacy, emphasizes that the researcher's interests are not confined to any one particular setting or group of people, and gives a 'truthful, but vague and imprecise' summary of the research procedures and objectives to reduce the risk of eliciting defensive or self-conscious behaviour.

Conduct in the field

Once the researcher has gained access, he or she must concentrate on maintaining a positive and non-threatening self-image – ideally, that of the 'acceptable incompetent' (Fielding, 2001: 149). Key interpersonal skills are required at this stage:

> The primary one is to maintain the balance between 'insider' and 'outsider' status; to identify with the people under study and get close to them, but maintaining a professional distance which permits adequate observation and data collection. It is a fine balance. 'Going native' is a constant danger, wherein observers lose their critical faculties and become an ordinary member of the field; while remaining an 'outsider', cold and distant from people in the field, with professional identity preserved and no rapport, negates the method. (Brewer, 2000: 59–60)

Taylor and Bogdan (1984) recommend that fieldworkers should emphasize whatever features they may have in common with their respondents, take care to show sufficient interest in people's views, avoid being arrogant, and do favours or try to help people whenever possible. They further insist that fieldworkers must 'pay homage' to the routines of the persons with whom they come into contact – by not requiring them to depart from their usual schedules or contexts of interaction. Such ploys help to facilitate a 'bounded reciprocal relationship', based on mutual trust and co-operation (Roper and Shapira, 2000: 17).

Recording data

Due to the importance attached to direct observation as the principal source of data, participant observers are often anxious about the possibility of failing to be in the right place at the right time, or of having to cope with and make sense of a seemingly incessant stream of activity (Roper and Shapira, 2000). For this reason, experienced fieldworkers often recommend an initial period of acclimatization during which note-taking is suspended (Burns, 2000). Opinion is divided between those practitioners who advocate the open jotting down of fieldnotes at the earliest possible opportunity (on the grounds that subjects will soon become accustomed to and tolerant of this practice) and those who caution against conspicuous note-taking activity on the grounds that it may reinforce the researcher's 'outsider' status and undermine rapport (Emerson et al., 2001).

Since note-taking is the principal means of recording data, participant observers place a heavy priority on comprehensiveness and self-discipline, stressing that it is common for observers to devote up to six hours of writing up for every hour spent in the field. According to Taylor and Bogdan, this process

> should include descriptions of people, events and conversations as well as the observer's actions, feelings and hunches or working hypotheses. The sequence and duration of events and conversations are noted as precisely as possible. The fabric of the setting is described in detail. In short, the field notes represent an attempt to record on paper everything that can possibly be recalled about the observation. A good rule to remember is that if *it is not written down, it never happened.* (1984: 53, emphasis in original)

Although participant observation is chiefly concerned, as its name suggests, with the observation and recording of human activity, most practitioners of the method adhere to the principle of 'triangulation' – the use of more than one source or method of data collection (Denzin, 1978). Thus fieldworkers regularly rely on other forms of information, such as documentation (for example, diaries, minutes, letters and memoranda), mass media coverage and discussions with respondents, which may vary in formality from casual conversations to tape-recorded interviews and routinized surveys (Brewer, 2000; Jorgensen, 1989).

Analysing data

With participant observation, data analysis is seldom a 'one-shot' process. More typically, it involves a dialectical procedure, known as 'sequential analysis' (Fielding, 2001: 158–9) or 'analytic induction' (Burns, 2000: 413). According to this process:

> Data are dissembled into elements and components; these materials are examined for patterns and relationships, sometimes in connection to ideas derived from literature, existing theories, of hunches that have emerged during fieldwork or perhaps simply

commonsense suspicions. With an idea in hand, the data are reassembled, providing an interpretation or explanation of a question or particular problem; this synthesis is then evaluated and critically examined; it may be accepted or rejected entirely – or with modifications; and, not uncommonly, this process then is repeated to test further the emergent theoretical conception, expand its generality, or otherwise examine its usefulness. (Jorgensen, 1989: 110–11)

Whilst this may seem an incredibly taxing and complicated undertaking, it nevertheless ensures that the research problem becomes progressively more focused and susceptible to explanation – often in terms and concepts spontaneously introduced by the subjects themselves (Hammersley and Atkinson, 1983).

Of equal importance to the task of analysing field data is the process of critical self reflection, or *reflexivity*, that is considered such an essential feature of participant observation (Brewer, 2000). Here the researcher is required to consider the various ways that the character of the data may have been affected by such factors as the sensitivity of the research issues, their own individual identity and the quality of interaction between themselves and their respondents.

Leaving the field

Conducting fieldwork may well prove an extremely absorbing and time-consuming activity, making it difficult for the researcher to determine when to break off from further study. Ultimately, the decision to withdraw or depart from the field is likely to rest on a combination of practical imperatives (for example, time or research funds running out) or the fact that *theoretical saturation* (the point at which no major new insights are being gained) has occurred (Glaser and Strauss, 1967).

As authors like Taylor and Bogdan point out, leaving the field may often prove painful: 'It means breaking attachments and sometimes even offending those one has studied, leaving them feeling betrayed and used' (1984: 67). Sensations of joy and relief may be intermingled with feelings of sadness and regret (Jorgensen, 1989). Textbooks advise the researcher to 'ease out' or 'drift off' without terminating relationships too abruptly. Any negative impact on informants may be lessened by maintaining contact – even to the extent of inviting feedback on interview transcripts or draft reports – and keeping them informed about any publications arising from the research (Fielding, 2001; Taylor and Bogdan, 1984).

APPLYING THE METHOD: THE ANSELLS BREWERY STRIKE ──────────────

Participant observation studies of strikes have involved researchers occupying the full range of possible roles from complete observer to complete participant (compare Batstone et al., 1978; Fantasia, 1983). Closest in character to my Ansells project is the research undertaken by Green (1990), who adopted the role of participant-as-observer in order to study the changing political consciousness of residents in Ollerton, a Nottinghamshire mining village subjected to intensive policing during the 1984–5 miners' strike. As part of her research, Green lodged for over five months with the family of a striking miner, daily attending soup kitchens, picket lines, demonstrations and other strike-related activities.

My own study closely resembles Green's insofar as I spent the entire duration of the five-month Ansells strike in the role of participant-as-observer. In order to effectively recount my own experience as a participant observer, it is first necessary to provide a brief overview of the dispute.

The strike was precipitated when management disciplined a group of production workers for allegedly engaging in action calculated to disrupt the smooth running of a four-day working week which Ansells had recently imposed due to slack consumer demand. Three weeks into the strike, management delivered an ultimatum that, unless the employees agreed to accept a package of redundancies and revised working practices as the basis for an immediate return to work, they would be dismissed for breach of contract and the brewery would be permanently closed. Far from intimidating the workers, management's threat merely hardened their determination to win. A long battle of attrition followed, involving the 'secondary picketing' of other production units belonging to Ansells's parent company, Allied Breweries. Ultimately, the strike was defeated and the brewery stayed shut. The seemingly half-hearted support provided to the strikers by their union, the Transport and General Workers' Union (TGWU), provoked accusations of cowardice and betrayal by the disillusioned brewery men.

Fortunately for me, Ansells brewery was located a mere two miles away from Aston University, where I was conducting my doctoral research. In the strike's early stages, picketing was confined to the brewery. These factors were obviously advantageous and encouraged me to try to gain access. My first, nerve-wracking encounter with Ansells' pickets occurred when the strike was only a few days' old. Much to my relief, however, the pickets were overwhelmingly receptive towards my stated intention of exploring the 'feelings and experience of workers who were out on strike'.

Subsequently, I obtained the endorsement of branch officials, who told me that, while they were generally happy to lend their cooperation, they were only prepared to do so on condition that I promise not to 'interfere' in any activities or pass on information to other interested parties, such as management or the local press. Once I accepted these conditions, the branch secretary wrote out a letter, encouraging all members to support me wherever possible.

At the outset of the strike, I had no preconceived research strategy, other than a vaguely defined intention to administer some sort of attitude survey to a representative sample of the workforce. On entering the field, I quickly realized that such a preformulated approach would be incapable of probing the rich but often transitory layers of meanings underlying the strikers' actions. I soon found myself mesmerized by the ceaselessly unfolding activities of the strike and the corresponding attempts to interpret them. On the day I first arrived, most strikers I talked to confidently predicted that the dispute would be settled within a week. Ansells then threatened to close the brewery and, suddenly, every picket I met was adamant that management was out to smash their trade union organization and that the strike would drag on for months. I therefore realized that, in order fully to understand the strikers' beliefs and motives, it was imperative that I immerse myself in the distinctive culture of the participants and witness first-hand the manufacture and transmission of their ideas.

Consequently, I spent most of my research activity attending picket lines, mass meetings and policy-discussions, and accompanying the strikers on flying-picketing and intelligence-gathering manoeuvres. The objectives of such missions were to trace the suppliers of 'scab beer' or deter the delivery of essential brewing ingredients like sugar and carbon dioxide. Due to the long distances travelled, it was sometimes necessary to sleep rough on hostel floors or the back seats of cars, or spend whole nights walking rainswept streets.

In my everyday dealings with the strikers, I consciously projected an image of myself as an earnest, sympathetic, if slightly naïve, student who was grateful for the opportunity to learn from their experience. I set out to gain the strikers' affection and respect by spending long hours on the picket line and participating in such mundane, off-duty activities as gambling, drinking in pubs, sharing jokes and tall stories, and accompanying them into situations involving elements of physical or legal risk.

The fact that I am a working-class male with a pronounced northern accent undoubtedly influenced the strikers' willingness to accept me into their ranks. Rightly or wrongly, I assumed it necessary for me to demonstrate more personal commitment to the dispute than the majority of actual strikers in order to ensure their continuing trust and support. Picket organizers regularly exploited this attitude, knowing full well that they could always depend on me to 'make the numbers look respectable' whenever volunteers were scarce.

Much of the data I collected were derived from direct observation or the contents of informal interviews. I knew of no ready formula to indicate the type of informant I should preferably talk to, or where I should ideally locate myself to observe the most 'important' action. I merely settled in one location sufficiently long enough to engage in long conversations with separate gangs of pickets, or to watch a particular episode of activity run its course, before moving on to where I suspected, or had already been informed, that the next important round of activity was imminent.

My note-taking usually occurred in the lulls between major bouts of activity. Pickets soon grew accustomed to this practice and, in due course, helped to maintain its accuracy by cross-checking my recollection of events against their own (a form of voluntary triangulation). Far from resenting or objecting to this activity, many pickets seemed to regard my interest as a form of flattery and looked forward to reading the final chronicle. My notes most typically took the form of scribbled down words or phrases or, less commonly, verbatim quotes, which I expanded when entering them into my log book at the end of the day.

I supplemented this basic approach by collecting all forms of documentation issued during the strike (for example, letters, strike bulletins, propaganda leaflets), and selected local and national media coverage (including radio bulletins which my wife recorded on my behalf). I deliberately avoided any contact with management during the strike to offset any risk of jeopardizing my relationship with the strikers. I also decided not to inform full-time TGWU officials of my involvement until the strike was over because I was afraid they might consider me a meddler and instruct their members not to cooperate. Subsequently, however, I conducted interviews with representatives of Ansells management and the TGWU. As a result of these meetings, I amassed huge quantities of documentary material (for example, formal correspondence and minutes of union–management meetings spanning two decades).

By immersing myself so deeply in the strike, I found it possible to comprehend how the workers interpreted their situation, and how their collective definitions of reality had been shaped by their own subjective history. It was fascinating to observe, for example, how management's ultimatum to the strikers was collectively understood in terms of a shared, cognitive schema – the *BL script* – which characterized their behaviour as an imitation of the strategy used by Sir Michael Edwardes to undermine trade union power at BL Cars. According to this definition, the strike represented an all-or-nothing struggle for the survival of the trade union organization:

Ansells management is clearly trying to be the Michael Edwardes of our industry, both in job reductions and the destruction of union organization. Our fight to keep Ansells open is not just a question of saving jobs. For us it is a matter of trying to stop our employers going through our trade union organization like a dose of salts. WHAT IS HAPPENING TO US CAN AND WILL HAPPEN TO ANYONE. (Trade union correspondence)

By linking the everyday slogans, comments and anecdotes of the strike to material deriving from newspaper archives, company and trade union documents, letters and richly detailed minutes of trade union management meetings, I was able to develop a longitudinal-processual analysis. This demonstrated how the contemporary beliefs, values and attitudes of the workforce, and the mutual feelings of animosity and distrust between employees and management, were shaped by a sequence of historical events stretching back over 20 years.

Once I had collected all my data, I immediately delved into potentially relevant areas of social scientific literature (social psychology, sociology, political science, and so on), much of which I was previously unfamiliar with, in order to unearth a sufficient range of explanatory concepts to build my social–cognitive analysis of the entire dispute (see Waddington, 1986, 1987, for further details).

The termination of my fieldwork was something I had no control over; rather it was induced by the formal ending of the strike and all related picketing activity. My withdrawal from the field was a sobering experience. For several days afterwards I was affected by the feelings of bitterness and despondency which inevitably accompany a strike defeat. Long after such feelings had subsided, I continued to miss the companionship of the strikers and often worried about their fate. Worse still were the recurring feelings of guilt I suffered – based on the knowledge that I was one of the few people to come out of the strike with something tangible to show for the considerable anguish and hardship it entailed.

EVALUATING THE METHOD

Such was the character of my research. Later in this section, I argue that no other methodology could have given me such a penetrating insight into the cognitions and emotions of striking employees. It would be stupid to pretend, however, that any form of research undertaken in such a politically sensitive and emotionally charged environment could ever be expected to proceed entirely straightforwardly and unproblematically. My own research gave rise to a number of practical and ethical issues that require close examination.

Disadvantages of participant observation

It is evident from the wider literature that participant observers often find themselves confronted by ethical dilemmas involving such hard choices as whether or not to inform the authorities about illegal and potentially dangerous activities. For example, Westmarland (2001) was placed in the dilemma of having to decide whether or not to 'blow the whistle' on police officers subjecting prisoners to violent and unlawful abuse.

During my Ansells research I found myself confronted by a broadly similar ethical dilemma. This situation arose in the third month of the strike – shortly after the local press had started to concentrate on numerous allegations of sabotage, assault, intimidation and vandalism that were being levelled against the strikers. I can say, on the basis of personal observation and reliable hearsay, that at least some of these accusations were valid. Consequently, I found myself struggling to decide whether my personal commitment not to interfere with the 'natural course' of events should override what might be regarded as my moral obligation to complain about life-threatening activities or, where necessary, report them to the police.

Mercifully, the negative publicity associated with these activities discouraged their further use and thus rescued me from a dilemma I was finding practically impossible to resolve. None the less, this example emphasizes Taylor and Bogdan's assertion that 'one is not absolved of moral and ethical responsibility for one's actions or inactions merely because one is conducting research. To act or fail to act is to make an ethical and political choice' (1984: 71).

The possible risk of physical danger has been rigorously illustrated by commentators like Armstrong (1993), Punch (1998) and Angrosino and de Perez (2000), who catalogue numerous instances where researchers have found themselves threatened with violence, beaten up, arrested, stalked, harassed, and even raped while in the field.

There were numerous times during the strike when I could easily have been arrested, especially during picket-line mêlées, or when my personal safety was jeopardized. Once, for example, I was almost beaten up by Ansells pickets who suspected me of working for the Special Branch! This improbable development was the direct result of a *Daily Mail* article of 21 April 1981 which established that the Special Branch had been brought in to investigate 'an extreme left-wing terror campaign against pub managers and their families', allegedly perpetrated by 'Trotskyist hard men' who had recently infiltrated the strike. This represented a scurrilous attempt to attribute the strike violence to the influence of two Workers' Power activists (a slight, bespectacled man and a silver-haired woman) who had been distributing leaflets urging the strikers to form 'defence squads' against the police. Nevertheless, some strikers took the *Mail's* disclosure seriously and, shortly after the article appeared, I was seized and interrogated by three burly draymen who knew me only as a stranger. It was only after I had received a blow to the ear that two familiar pickets returned from the local fast-food restaurant to vouch for my identity and spare me from further injury.

One common criticism of participant observation is that people are likely to react to the researcher being present by engaging in untypical or extreme forms of behaviour. My own experience suggests that any exhibitionistic or unusual forms of behaviour excited by the researcher's arrival tend progressively to disappear the longer he or she remains part of the research setting. Nevertheless, I did find it extremely difficult to maintain a passive role in such a politically volatile and dynamic environment. This difficulty is best illustrated by the outcome of our week spent picketing Ind Coope's Romford brewery – a sobering episode in which we tried, unsuccessfully, to obstruct the delivery of essential supplies. When we returned to Birmingham, my erstwhile colleagues grossly exaggerated our achievements, having already appealed to me not to say anything which might contradict their story and thereby undermine rank-and-file morale.

Afterwards, I rationalized my part in this 'conspiracy' by convincing myself that it was the least obtrusive and contaminatory of all the available options. Much closer to the truth was the fact that I very much wanted the Ansells workers to succeed in their action and would not have said or done anything to weaken their commitment. In taking me for someone who was relatively detached from the strike, pickets often asked me for my prognosis of the outcome. Privately, I considered it extremely unlikely that the strikers could effectively resist such a powerful and well-prepared adversary as their multinational parent company; but this view was something I never publicly conceded.

Advantages of participant observation

During the course of my postgraduate studies, it was put to me by more established colleagues that I should regard my Ansells research as merely an exploratory 'pilot' study: that it would be 'courting disaster' as far as the outcome of my PhD was concerned to rely exclusively on such a soft methodology; and that I should perhaps 'hedge my bets' by carrying out a laboratory simulation of a strike. I now realize that I should have argued more assertively that some degree of researcher bias is not only inevitable in studies of social conflict, but can also prove extremely *beneficial* to the study; and that, whilst a researcher's presence is bound to have an impact on his or her data, it is preferable to address the possible effects head on than to merely pretend – as positivists do – that research can be carried out in a social vacuum.

For all my former diffidence, I have never had much difficulty emphasizing that the benefits to be gained from adopting a participant observation approach to an appropriate research issue will far outweigh any practical or ethical problems likely to be encountered. One of the most advantageous reasons for using this approach is that it promotes the development of confidence and trust between the researcher and his or her respondents – all the more so if the latter have reason to assume that the former is sympathetic towards them (Green, 1993: 16–17). I very much doubt whether the Ansells strikers would have been quite so confiding and willing to admit me to the 'backstage' regions of the strike, had they not been given adequate time to thoroughly appraise my character and detect my sympathetic attitude.

Participant observation also helps to reduce the likelihood of being deceived by one's respondents (Burns, 2000). During my research, I was able to assess the consistency of people's statements, moods and behaviour at different times and in contrasting situations, eliminating the possibility of being fooled by initial appearances. I was also in a position to witness sudden or progressive changes in people's definitions and emotions – something I could never have appreciated had I used a more conventional, 'one-shot' method. There is no doubt, either, that my chosen methodology afforded me an excellent opportunity to observe the creation and exchange of key social ideas. This is best illustrated by the build-up to a crucial mass meeting of 14 February 1981.

During this period, I observed the way that shop stewards systematically mingled among the pickets in order to innoculate them against the potentially damaging views of full-time TGWU officials who were preparing to tell them that it would be futile to prolong the strike. One steward after another reassuringly explained to his members that the TGWU were desperately looking for a strike victory in order to reverse a recent trend of humiliating defeats at the hands of local employers. District and regional officials were preparing to risk the union's remaining credibility by 'fully backing' the strike, but first they had to convince themselves that the Ansells men had sufficient determination to last out what might well prove a long and bitter struggle. For this reason, the TGWU officials were planning to convey an extremely pessimistic (though entirely bogus) impression of the strikers' chances at the forthcoming mass meeting.

As a 'member' of the picket line, I observed how one shop steward impressed the following message on his members:

We've got to show them that we're solid. If we do that, we'll have the full weight of the 'T and G' behind us. So, we want none of this 'orderly meeting' stuff. Say what you want and open your bloody mouths. Raise the roof off. (Quoted in Waddington, 1987: 86)

Thanks in no small measure to this preliminary activity, the members voted, virtually unanimously, in favour of continuing the strike. This meant that, notwithstanding their genuine misgivings about prolonging the dispute, the TGWU's full-time representatives were politically obliged to pledge their organization's financial and moral support.

By joining the brewery workers on strike, I found myself capable of empathizing with many of their cognitions and emotions. While it was clearly impossible for me to share the full extent of their material hardship and psychological anxiety, I none the less experienced a wide spectrum of mental states ranging from temporary euphoria to exasperation and despair. I see no need to apologize about the so-called softness and subjectivity of my approach; rather I take an immense pride in the 'thickness' of my data and analysis (Denzin, 1989), maintaining that no other methodology could have given me such an authentic insight into the strikers' subjective experience.

CONCLUSIONS

In this chapter I have used my own study of the 1981 Ansells brewery strike to examine some of the main features of participant observation, the principal methodology used in field research. We have seen how this method of investigation involves the researcher immersing him- or herself, within a distinctive culture or social setting in order to study at first hand the actions and experiences of its members.

The particular skills and abilities required of the participant observer are very different from those required in most other forms of psychological research. The majority of conventional psychological methodologies emphasize proficiency in sampling techniques, experimental design and statistics. Participant observation, however, places a priority on such personal qualities as an open and inquiring mind, tenacity and determination, and a chameleon-like capacity to adapt to different types of people and situations. As Van Maanen points out, 'There are no easy or preformulated answers to the dilemmas of fieldwork since one cannot know what one is getting into until one gets into it' (1982: 138).

There is a second reason why the researcher's personal attributes are likely to be important. I have already indicated that certain of my status characteristics (notably my gender and class location) appeared to make it easier for me to gain access and develop an easy rapport with the strikers. This emphasizes the crucial need for fieldworkers to be adequately reflexive, considering, for example, the various ways that structural variables like age, class and ethnicity can influence the research process and affect the 'reality perspectives' of the observer and respondents alike (Easterday et al., 1982).

When conducting my Ansells research in 1981, I tried to delude myself and others into believing that I was capable of remaining like a fly on the wall: unaffected by emotions, and having little or no impact on the people I was observing. Similarly, when writing up my research I carefully avoided any significant discussion of my personal feelings and loyalties, fearing that this might provoke charges of subjectivity and emotionality and detract from the perceived validity of my analysis. Now I have acquired the confidence to concede that, whilst participant observation is less tidy and more complicated than I formerly pretended, it is one of the surest ways I know of getting *directly to the heart* of human experience.

FURTHER READING

A useful overview of the main principles and techniques of participant observation is contained in Nigel Fielding's chapter on 'Ethnography' (Fielding, 2001). Longer and more comprehensive discussions of the epistemological assumptions underlying participant observation, as well as some key practical and ethical issues concerning the method, are provided by Jorgensen (1989) and Brewer (2000). Finally, the volume of readings edited by Hobbs and May (1993) includes several frank and illuminating chapters by fieldworkers reflecting on their experience of participant observation.

REFERENCES

Angrosino, M.V. and Mays de Perez, K.A. (2000) 'Rethinking observation: from method to context', in N.K. Denzin and Y.S. Lincoln (eds), *Handbook of Qualitative Research*, second edition, London: Sage.

Armstrong, G. (1993) '"Like that Desmond Morris?"', in D. Hobbs and T. May (eds), *Interpreting the Field: Accounts of Ethnography*, Oxford: Clarendon Press.

Batstone, E., Boraston, I. and Frenkel, S. (1978) *The Social Organization of Strikes*, Oxford: Basil Blackwell.

Brewer, J.D. (2000) *Ethnography*, Buckingham: Open University Press.

Burgess, R. (1984) *In the Field: An Introduction to Field Research*, London: George Allen & Unwin.

Burns, R.B. (2000) *Introduction to Research Methods*, fourth edition, London: Sage.

Denzin, N.K. (1978) *The Research Act*, second edition, New York: McGraw-Hill.

Denzin, N.K. (1989) *Interpretive Interactionism (Applied Social Research Methods Series*, Vol. 16), Newbury Park, CA: Sage.

Douglas, J. (1976) *Investigative Social Research*, Beverley Hills, CA: Sage.

Easterday, L., Papademas, D., Schorr, L. and Valentine, C. (1982) 'The making of a female researcher: role problems in fieldwork', in R.G. Burgess (ed.), *Field Research: a Sourcebook and Field Manual*, London: George Allen & Unwin.

Emerson, R.T., Fretz, R.I. and Shaw, L.L. (2001) 'Participant observation and fieldnotes', in P. Atkinson, A. Coffey, S. Delamont, J. Lofland and L. Lofland (eds), *Handbook of Ethnography*, London: Sage.

Fantasia, R. (1983) 'The wildcat strike and industrial relations', *Industrial Relations Journal*, 14: 74–86.

Fielding, N. (2001) 'Ethnography', in N. Gilbert (ed.), *Researching Social Life*, second edition, London: Sage.

Glaser, B. and Strauss, A.L. (1967) *The Discovery of Grounded Theory: Strategies for Qualitative Research*, Chicago: Aldine.

Goffman, E. (1959) *The Presentation of Self in Everyday Life*, Garden City, NY: Doubleday.

Green, P. (1990) *The Enemy Without: Policing and Class Consciousness in the Miners' Strike*, Buckingham: Open University Press.

Green, P. (1993) 'Taking sides: partisan research in the 1984–85 miners' strike', in D. Hobbs and T. May (eds), *Interpreting the Field: Accounts of Ethnography*, Oxford: Clarendon Press.

Hammersley, M. and Atkinson, P. (1983) *Ethnography Principles in Practice*, London: Routledge.

Hobbs, D. and May, T. (eds) (1993) *Interpreting the Field: Accounts of Ethnography*, Oxford: Clarendon Press.

Jorgensen, D.L. (1989) *Participant Observation: A Methodology for Human Studies*, Newbury Park, CA: Sage.

Roper, J.M. and Shapira, J. (2000) *Ethnography in Nursing Research*, London: Sage.

Taylor, S.J. and Bogdan, R. (1984) *Introduction to Qualitative Research Methods: The Search for Meanings*, second edition, New York: Wiley.

Van Maanen, J. (1982) 'Fieldwork on the beat', in J. Van Maanen, J.M. Dabbs and R.R. Faulkner (eds), *Varieties of Qualitative Research*, Beverly Hills, CA: Sage.

Waddington, D.P. (1986) 'The Ansells brewery dispute: a social-cognitive approach to the study of strikes', *Journal of Occupational Psychology*, 59 (3): 231–46.

Waddington, D.P. (1987) *Trouble Brewing: A Social Psychological Analysis of the Ansells Brewery Dispute*, Aldershot: Gower.

Westmarland, L. (2001) 'Blowing the whistle on police violence: gender, ethnography and ethics', *British Journal of Criminology*, 41: 523–35.

— **Analytic Induction** ————————————————

Phil Johnson

Usually analytic induction (AI) is defined as involving the intensive examination of a strategically selected number of cases so as to empirically establish the causes of a specific phenomenon. Intrinsic to the approach is 'the "'public'" readjustment of definitions, concepts, and hypotheses' (Manning, 1982: 283). However despite several notable exceptions (for example, Lindesmith, 1947; Cressey, 1953; Becker, 1973; Bloor, 1976; Lennon and Wollin, 2001), there seems to be few published examples of research, particularly organizational research, that use AI. Moreover, even in 'qualitative' methodology books, AI often appears to be ignored (for example, Bannister et al., 1994; Glesne and Peshkin, 1992) or limited to a short outline (for example, Silverman, 1993).

Given this situation, the aims of this chapter are to outline the rationale and procedures of AI through a brief discussion of its epistemological commitments and an illustration of its empirical application in an accountancy/industrial relations context. The chapter will then conclude with a discussion of some of the problems implicit in AI.

THE EPISTEMOLOGICAL COMMITMENTS OF AI —————————————

The term 'induction' refers to the processes by which observers reflect upon their experience of social phenomena and then attempt to formulate explanations that may be used to form an abstract rule, or guiding principle, which can be extrapolated to explain and predict new or similar experiences (Kolb et al., 1979). Hence AI is a set of methodological procedures which attempt to systematically generate theory grounded in observation of the empirical world. As such it sharply contrasts with deductive procedures in which a conceptual and theoretical structure is constructed prior to observation and then is ostensibly tested through confrontation with the 'facts' of a cognitively accessible empirical world (see Wallace, 1971: 16–25).

Although debate between rival proponents of induction and deduction is complex (see Johnson and Duberley, 2000), today the justification for induction in the social sciences usually revolves around two related claims. First, it is argued that in contrast to the speculative and a priori nature of deductively tested theory, explanations of social phenomena which are inductively grounded in systematic empirical research are more likely to fit the data because theory building and data collection are closely interlinked (Wiseman, 1978) and therefore are more plausible and accessible (Glaser and Strauss, 1967). Secondly, there is the argument that deduction's etic analyses, in which an a priori external frame of reference is imposed upon the behaviour of social phenomena in order to explain it, are inappropriate where the phenomena in question have subjective capabilities (see Shotter, 1975; Giddens, 1976; Gill

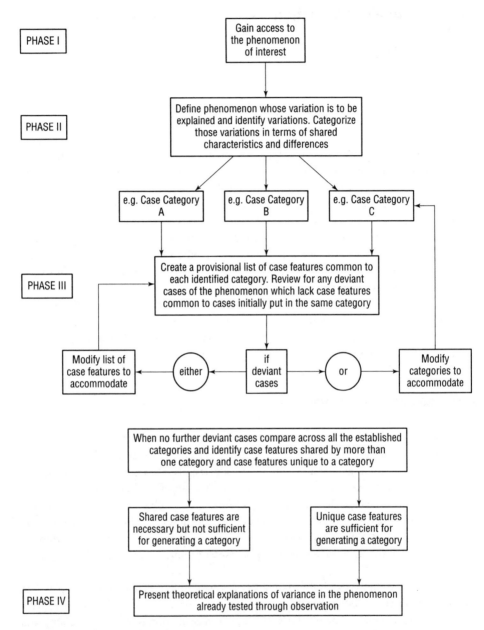

Figure 14.1   Adapted from Bloor's approach to Analytic Induction

Source: Gill and Johnson (2002: 156) with permission

and Johnson, 2002). It follows that social science research must entail emic analyses where explanations of human action are generated inductively from an a posteriori understanding of the interpretations deployed (namely cultures) by the actors who are being studied.

Hammersley and Atkinson (1995) argue that ethnographic fieldwork shares these inductive commitments. However, ethnographers' explanations of observed behaviour often remain at the level of a posteriori 'thick description' (Geertz, 1973; Denzin, 1978) of actors' interpretative procedures which goes beyond the '. . . reporting of an act (thin description) but describes the intentions, motives, meanings, contexts, situations, and circumstances of action' (Denzin, 1978: 39). In this, theorization is limited to providing a conceptual framework for understanding actors' cultures. While the theoretical aims of AI include such descriptive frameworks, AI avoids what Loftland (1970) has called 'analytic interruptus' by also trying to explain and predict through positing causal models as illustrated by Bloor (1976, 1978). The ontological and epistemological ambiguities this creates will be returned to later.

I shall now illustrate the application of Bloor's model by reviewing how it was used to describe and explain how senior shop stewards interpret disclosed accounting information in collective bargaining.

THE EMPIRICAL APPLICATION OF AI

The background to the research

The empirical focus of this research was to examine the significance of disclosed accounting information (DAI) in senior shop stewards' constructions of organizational reality and tentatively delineate the factors that engendered these propensities through the generation of grounded theory. Obviously there were different possible ways of pursuing these objectives. One could have been to observe and analyse actual collective bargaining processes in their everyday social contexts. However getting access to such events appeared unlikely, therefore a more viable strategy was pursued which entailed following Bloors' approach to AI and applying it to Life Histories collected by interviewing a sample of individual senior shop stewards. Below I shall give an account of this research, with each phase in data collection and analysis corresponding to those illustrated in Figure 14.1 above.

Phase I: gaining access

My initial contact with a selection of informants was facilitated by a friend I knew from my prior membership of a major blue-collar trade union. In many respects he was my equivalent of Whyte's 'Doc' (1955) since he acted as an intermediary and informal sponsor by mobilizing an extant social network by introducing me to senior shop stewards and vouchsafing for me. In this he unwittingly presented these potential informants with a rather vague description of my intentions since I had described the research as being concerned with 'plant-level industrial relations and how things had changed over the past few years'.

Although informants' initial compliance had been appropriated by the intercession of my sponsor, I was concerned to resolve any persisting anxieties. So an important element in my impression management was to make informants feel comfortable and gain their trust by interviewing them on their own 'turf' (Lyman and Scott, 1970) as well as engaging in initial 'interaction rituals' (Goffman, 1972) so as to establish feelings of 'mutuality' (Beynon, 1983) – that we had something in common in terms of interest and experience. Through these interaction rituals rapport was usually established and gradually I eased conversation around to their roles as senior shop stewards. Through the felicity of my sponsor, informants had an initial idea of what I wanted to talk about. I tended to reinforce this impression by stating my interest in their experiences as senior shop stewards and how their roles might have recently changed. Basically, I was using Douglas' 'principle of indirection' (1985: 137) to encourage their self-disclosure and then subtly manipulate dialogue towards my main focus – DAI.

Phase II: defining the phenomenon and identifying variations

As the term implies, processes of AI focus upon the analysis and interpretation of data. Except for induction, it does not specify how data should be collected. In principle it can therefore be used to analyse data that derive from any method of collecting data that has been applied in an inductive fashion, such as life histories, participant observation, repertory grids, and so on. In the research reported here data were collected through life history interviews. This was because life history research is regarded as having a primary concern with the '. . . phenomenal role of lived experience, with the ways in which individuals interpret their own lives and the world around them' (Plummer, 1983: 67). This allows access to how individuals 'create and portray' (Jones, 1983: 147) their social worlds. Significantly they are taken to avoid the problems that beset the 'brisk' interview (Bulmer, 1975) in which respondents are impelled, by the structured prompts of the interviewer to make statements which although fitting into the researcher's conceptual and theoretical pro forma, give little opportunity for them to articulate the ways in which they conceptualize and understand their own worlds.

Although life histories can be used to 'provoke, suggest and anticipate later theorizations' (Plummer, 1983: 124), a research strategy guided by AI procedurally formalizes this process and explicitly introduces theoretical concerns during fieldwork. But because AI entails sampling according to emergent theoretical criteria so as to enable comparison, inevitably some of the depth traditional in life histories is traded off. Essentially, these overt theoretical objectives militated against the orthodox use of life histories, as exemplified by Shaw (1966) and Bogdan (1974), in which the outcome is in the form of comprehensive biographies of single subjects. Thus I used life history interviews to generate and document informants' accounts of their lived-in organizational realities with an emergent focus upon how they perceived DAI in collective bargaining.

Where it was practical I had decided to interview each informant at least twice. The first round of interviews were aimed at gaining their confidence and eliciting descriptive data that could be used to generate dimensions of similarity and difference across the whole cohort (see Spradley, 1979) regarding their perceptions of, and orientations towards, DAI. By guiding the interview around pertinent issues through the use of various prompts and questions, the nature of which being contingent upon the 'state of play' in our interaction, I elicited and documented their perspectives. These processes necessitated some degree of skill and intuition on my part, especially in regard to when to remain silent or whether to follow up some comment immediately, or how to phrase mutually intelligible prompts which allowed informants' elaboration upon a significant issue without inadvertently fixing the terms in which they spoke, or the perspectives which they articulated. In some of the earlier interviews I suspect that I made blunders, but through reflection upon these mistakes I was able to learn how to unobstrusively guide informants to the issues of greatest interest to me at this particular stage of fieldwork.

As I proceeded in this fallible manner, I regularly reviewed my field notes and compared informants' accounts so as to identify the similarities and differences in their accounting orientations out of which I would establish an initial taxonomy of categories. Although this remained my main focus at this stage, I also attempted to identify possible relationships between these emergent orientations and other phenomena, identifiable in their accounts. These phenomena could constitute possible case features and thereby represent future areas of exploration in subsequent interviews. In sum I was at this stage following a process similar to what Glaser and Strauss call the 'constant comparative method', in that the researcher . . .

> . . . starts thinking in terms of the full range of types of the category, its dimensions, the conditions under which it is pronounced or minimized, its major consequences, its relation to other categories, and its other properties. (1967: 106)

After 13 life history interviews, each around three hours' duration, I began to perceive that I had constructed an initial taxonomy of 'observer-identified' (Loftland, 1971) categories and their conceptual properties while staying within the limits of the data (Glaser, 1978). This had entailed comparing informants' accounts so as to identify similarities and differences thereby constructing the uniformities underlying and defining the emergent categories. I then conducted a further three interviews so as to check the exhaustiveness of this taxonomy. Since no new accounting orientations or categorical properties emerged, I had to assume that I had reached the point which Glaser and Strauss call 'theoretical saturation' where 'no additional data are being found whereby the sociologist can develop properties of the category' (1967: 61).

Thus by the end of Phase 2 of AI it was possible to differentiate three types of accounting orientation articulated by senior shop stewards. These I called the 'financial realist' (six informants), the 'financial sceptic' (eight informants) and the 'financial cynic' (two informants). This last category was initially undifferentiated from the emergent 'realist' orientation. However as I accumulated more primary data, it became evident that there were deviant cases within the 'realist' category which were reassigned to constitute the 'cynic' category.

Initially I had begun this differentiation through my attention being drawn to how informants' perceived DAI either as providing an objective/veracious representation of organizational affairs, or as providing a fallacious and managerially contrived construction. These apparent differences in informants' life histories led to the initial construction of the 'realist' and 'sceptic' categories. However the data also suggested variability in the 'realist' category around how they made sense of social relationships in their work organizations. With regard to this characteristic, two of these shop stewards were closer to 'sceptics' – something which combined with a veracious view of DAI to produce an accounting orientation which was differentiable from both 'sceptics' and 'realists'. Thus the whole cohort were further differentiated according to their interpretations of intra-organizational relationships namely those informants who perceived there to be a conflict of interest between their constituents and management as opposed to those who perceived that there was no difference of interest between their constituents and management. This process of comparison enabled the subsequent differentiation and articulation of the 'cynic' category.

Unfortunately space prevents a fuller presentation of the primary data which illustrate the properties of each category. Instead they are presented in summary form in Figure 14.2.

Perception of
accounting information

		Veracious	Fallacious
Perception of intra-organizational relations	Unitary	Financial realist	A theoretically possible orientation encountered in the field
	Dichotomous	Financial cynic	Financial sceptic

Figure 14.2   Accounting orientations of senior shop stewards

Phase III: case features and causal analysis

Although the primary aim of the first interviews had been to gather data about variability in orientation and thereby construct a taxonomy of categories, a secondary aim was to provisionally elucidate case features so as to facilitate the development of an explanatory framework. This process entails movement down the 'funnel structure' of 'progressive focusing' (Hammersley and Atkinson, 1995: 206) with a shift of concern from description to the development of grounded theory regarding the categories by explicit reference . . .

> . . . to their involvement in a complex of inter-connected variables that the observer constructs as a theoretical model . . . which best explains the data . . . assembled. (Becker, 1970: 196)

From the data elicited it was possible to initially compare accounting orientation categories so as to identify which case features were unique to a category and which were shared by two or more. For Bloor (1976, 1978), case features shared by all three categories might be ruled out as influences upon their variability. Conversely, if case features appear to be randomly distributed between categories it is possible to infer that they are not exerting any systematic influence upon the categories. Some of the commonalties were outcomes of the research strategy adopted, while others serendipitously emerged during fieldwork; both types are described below.

Shared case features

All informants were men who defined themselves as 'lay' elected senior shop stewards and as skilled manual workers employed in private sector engineering. They all worked in organizations with between 600 and 1,000 employees. Trade union membership varied within each category, but since members of the (then) AEU, GMBATU and TGWU were to be found amongst both 'realists' and 'sceptics' while the two 'cynics' were members of the AEU and GMBATU, membership of a particular trade union did not seem to influence category membership. Moreover no pattern within or between categories emerged regarding subjects' ages or length of experience as a senior shop steward.

All informants worked in organizations with a lengthy history of trade unionism with management recognition often having been acquired after protracted and attritious campaigns. Thus it was unlikely that they belonged to managerially sponsored shop steward organizations (see Willman, 1980). As incumbents of very similar offices all had been involved in significant areas of negotiation including collective bargaining over domestic rates of pay, changes in working practices, the introduction of new technology, redundancies, grievances, and the enforcement of collective agreements as well as custom and practice norms.

During fieldwork, several informants had claimed that they had not been exposed to DAI, they were therefore excluded from the sample. The remaining 16 were all familiar with employee reports and said that management also provided plant level disaggregated information during collective bargaining. The latter included things such as output per worker (often juxtaposed with that of major competitors), plant operating accounts, costing information, state of the order book details, simplified balance sheets and predictions of future plant and company financial performance.

In this context, Jackson-Cox et al. (1984) have noted the significance of management's disclosure strategies in mediating the impact of DAI. They differentiate an 'integrated' strategy, with routine but selective provision of information, from an ad hoc strategy characterized by the piecemeal and intermittent provision of information. Of the informants in this research, two-thirds felt that management regularly provided information pertaining to specific issues with the remainder claiming that DAI was temporally intermittent and substantively haphazard. But since there was no pattern to the distribution of these phenomena between categories, I had to conclude that they exerted no systematic influence upon the development of the accounting orientations expressed by informants.

While they all had undergone some financial training through the education services of the trade union movement, a pattern between and within categories was apparent when I questioned them about in-company financial training provision. Only one 'sceptic' had admitted to some in-company financial training whereas all the 'cynics' and 'realists' did admit to this training. Although the form and content of these programmes varied, all the relevant informants remembered discussions and presentations of the missions and goals of their firm with a focus upon the current and future financial situation. All alluded to an emphasis upon issues such as the need to invest in current and fixed assets, sources of investment, profit and loss, value added, interest rates and the implications of these issues for the current and future financial management of the firm.

Therefore in-company financial training seemed to be an important case feature that might explain the development of informants' accounting orientations. But it was shared by two categories – 'realists' and 'cynics' and therefore could not account for their apparent differences. This implied that some unique case feature must account for this differentiation – but what?

During the first round of fieldwork I began to suspect that variations in informants' roles vis-à-vis constituents might constitute a battery of unique case features. These suspicions developed out of various comments such as that of a 'realist' who claimed . . .

I tell the lads the plain facts, its then their decision as to what we should do . . . it's only right to be democratic.

At this point I decided that it might be wise to obey Glaser and Strauss' (1967) injunction, regarding the application of the constant comparative method, to use the library to further develop what Blumer has called 'sensitizing concepts' or suggestions of 'directions in which to look' (1954: 7). While there were a variety of ideal-type categorizations of shop stewards' roles available, it was the one provided by Marchington and Armstrong (1983) which appeared most helpful for sensitizing concepts regarding shop stewards' roles, especially since it had developed out of a critique of earlier models (for example, Batstone et al., 1977). Their four-fold taxonomy of role ideal types is illustrated by Figure 14.3 below.

According to Marchington and Armstrong (1983) the 'leader' is highly committed to trade unionism and espouses wider political aims such as socialism or workers' control. In this s/he is willing and able to lead members. In contrast the 'populist' is neither committed to trade unionism and its wider political aims nor leading members, rather his/her role is perceived as the 'mouthpiece' or 'spokesperson' of constituents. 'Workgroup leaders' shared this parochialism, but they display strong leadership over constituents by agenda setting with reference to what they define as being in the best interests of their particular members. Finally the 'cautious supporter' was identified as a more transient role, containing various people who shared a wider commitment to trade unionism but were extremely cautious since they also perceived their role as being a delegate mandated by members. The potential for role conflict and ambiguity made this ideal type a stopping off point prior to a move into the 'populist' of 'leader' roles.

Senior stewards re-visited – the search for unique case features

Armed with the sensitizing concepts developed out of both primary and secondary data, I returned to the field with the aim of elucidating their status as case features. This entailed a shift from describing informants' accounting orientations to explaining their occurrence through exploration of their perceptions of their roles as senior stewards and their definitions of and commitment towards trade unionism. This entailed more structure during interaction so as to direct dialogue towards the themes identified as potential unique case features. This progressive focusing was facilitated by grounding each second interview in the informants' frames of reference and terminology elicited in the prior round of interviews. The increasing complexity of the comparative analysis of emergent case features sometimes necessitated

		Representative	Delegate
	High	LEADER	CAUTIOUS SUPPORTER
Orientation to Unionism			
	Low	WORK GROUP LEADER	POPULIST

Figure 14.3 Shop stewards' roles
Source: adapted from Marckington and Armstrong, 1983: 42 (with permission)

reinterviewing informants for a third time so as to check and develop elements of my emerging theoretical scheme. Space precludes a full rendition of the subsequent accounts, so below I will provide only some examples of the data elicited during progressive focusing which illustrate some pertinent aspects of case features.

Although informants were all senior shop stewards it emerged that relative to both 'cynics' and 'realists', 'sceptics' had appeared to be highly committed to a similar definition of trade unionism articulated as solidarity to 'fellow workers' in other work places. Typically one 'sceptic' claimed that . . .

> . . . many of the lads can't see beyond their own noses . . . If they think that something doesn't affect them then they're not interested . . . [but] . . . we're all in this together . . . us, the miners, nurses, dockers, teachers . . . we're all workers . . . I have more in common with a German steelworker or a French miner than I have with the plant manager . . . we share economic conditions, all I share with management is the English language.

All 'sceptics' emphasized being a representative in the sense of having a proactive role as protector and leader of their constituents in what they considered to be an continual struggle against the excesses and arbitrariness of management. This entailed much agenda setting so as to protect or advance what they perceived as their members' best interests . . .

> . . . some of the lads are not too bright . . . they read rubbish like the S** and listen to Radio H***** . . . when it comes to knowing what's best for themselves they need help . . . that's my job . . . If I didn't . . . and sometimes stop them from doing stupid things . . . management would twist them around their little fingers . . . most of the lads can't see beyond page three . . .

In contrast 'realists' were ambivalent towards the trade union principles of the 'sceptic' . . .

> One good thing that Thatcher has done for industrial relations is to stop secondary picketing . . . at one time my members were continually being laid-off because of disputes elsewhere – things that had nothing to do with us.

Meanwhile 'cynics' also displayed an ambivalence towards such trade union principles but this was overlaid by a highly combative parochialism . . .

> I'll only support the JSSC when it doesn't go against my members' interests – I have to fight to protect their interests sometimes from other unions and sometimes even from our own . . . in this world you have to look after yourselves – nobody else will.

What further differentiated between 'cynics' and 'realists' was how they arbitrated and defined constituents' interests. The former typically assumed a proactive representational role and perceived themselves as arbiters of what was best for their members whereas 'realists' adopted a delegate role vis-à-vis constituents, this emphasized being a spokesperson for constituents, passing on their views to management and communicating management's position to members.

From the interviews, no 'cautious supporters' appeared to be evident in my sample. I decided that this was hardly surprising given that all informants were experienced senior shop stewards and that the 'cautious supporter' role was seen to be a transient role often adopted by neophyte shop stewards.

In sum three important associations emerged, the populist-realist, the workgroup leader-cynic and the leader-sceptic. Although this covariance between unique case features and categories was important to any theoretical explanation, it was also important to explore what kind of rationale might underpin these apparent conjunctions in my data and elucidate the directions of causation.

Phase IV: theorization

POPULIST-REALIST ASSOCIATION

It was plausible that informant's populism might exacerbate their susceptibility to accounting renditions of reality since such apparently objective information enabled them to 'rationally' transmit the 'facts' to constituents and facilitated their avoidance of taking unmandated decisions. If constituents wilfully chose to ignore those financial 'facts' and adopt 'irrational' courses of action, he was personally divorced from any responsibility in his role as delegate. However it was plausible that 'realism' could cause 'populism'. For instance 'realism' might abrogate them from the responsibility for defining constituents' interests and engender the role of reactive messenger because DAI constituted immutable facts that had to be transmitted regardless of their palatability.

The only way I could test the direction of causation was to investigate whether or not 'realists' had been 'populists' prior to their exposure to in-company financial training. Despite one exception it appeared that financial training was a possible case feature that differentiated 'sceptics' from both 'realists' and 'cynics', but the varying use of accounting information by 'cynics' and 'realists' implied the influence of some further discriminating factor. Therefore in a third round of interviews, with all the 'realists' I attempted to elucidate whether they had always adopted a 'populist' role, particularly with regard to delegacy, and especially prior to their exposure to in-company financial training. From the resulting data it appeared that 'populism' preceded 'realism' – the statement below was typical . . .

> . . . I've always been a go-between . . . At first I didn't have much of an opinion about the messages . . . but since I've gained more experience I think that sometimes the lads won't face up to the [financial] facts . . . but that's up to them isn't it . . .

THE WORKGROUP LEADER-CYNIC ASSOCIATION

The 'cynic' shares the realist's assumptions about the veracity of DAI, moreover they have also been exposed to in-house training. But these factors do not explain their very different negotiating strategies with management. For the 'cynic', although veracious, DAI does not define constituents' interests – rather it is taken as a lexicon that might be applied in their furtherance or discarded when it appears to be incommensurable. While these artful bargainers share with 'realists' an ambivalence towards trade union notions of solidarity, this is overlaid by a combative and parochial image of the 'us', while the 'them' pertains to anyone outside that immediate constituency.

The 'cynic's' parochialism creates a perceived need to defend constituents from the ever present threats from other groups. This concern appears to override the immanent implications of their acceptance of DAI as veracious and their exposure to in-company financial training. Although DAI may be the harbinger of an immutable financial reality, the intercession of this imagery prevents the translation of these 'truths' into the attitudes and practices of the 'realist'. Instead the cynic's 'war' leads to their Machiavellian pursuit of perceived interest by any available means, regardless of the moral imperatives deriving from an accounting rendition of organizational reality. Such training therefore appears to provide the 'cynic' with one more tactically deployable weapon in his arsenal. His proactive representative predilections enable and legitimate the implementation of this strategy as they insulate him from the impediment of constituents' sanction.

THE LEADER-SCEPTIC ASSOCIATION

Excluded from the 'cynic's' conception of 'us' are broader constituencies of trade unionists. Although these 'others' are not necessarily perceived in the combative gaze that guides the 'cynic's' perception of management, there is a parochial ambivalence that coincides with the 'cynic's' orientation towards trade union principles of solidarity, and so on. In contrast the 'sceptic' invokes solidarity with groups, outside their immediate constituency, engaged in a shared 'class war'. However another factor unique to the sceptics, save for one subject, is a lack of exposure to in-company financial training. Hence, which of these case features was the most important in explaining the 'sceptic' accounting category?

Treasuring my exception, I carefully reanalysed the case of the one 'sceptic' who had experienced some in-company financial training and confirmed his original categorization. Unfortunately this subject refused to be interviewed for a third time, so from the data I had already collected, I left with the tentative conclusion that any exposure of 'sceptics' to in-company financial training would have little impact upon their view of DAI. Presumably the tenure of solidaristic trade union principles, and the radical imagery that this implies, could prevent the acceptance of the messages disseminated through such training. For instance this imagery led to a perceived association between accounting information, accountants and management. As one 'sceptic' typically argued . . .

> . . . they all in it together . . . [DAI] . . . tells us what they like so as to get us to do what they want us to — accountants and managers they all the same . . . con men with company cars out to screw us.

In sum, from the primary data inductively collected throughout this fieldwork, the social phenomena and processes that influence informants' propensity to refer to particular accounting orientations are diagramatically illustrated by Figure 14.4 below.

For Bloor (1976, 1978) AI will usually end at this stage – the proposal of a theoretical explanation inductively grounded in empirical data. However I decided to try to further test my grounded theory by interviewing six new informants. I reversed the data collection processes I had undertaken so far by first elucidating the shared and unique case features which, according to the above model, explain variation in accounting category. By analysing that data I then predicted which accounting category each subject would be in, and then I conducted a second round of interviews to elucidate the accuracy of those expectations. The aim of this process was to try to deal further with the criticisms levelled by Robinson (1951) of Cressey's approach. As Hammersley points out (1989: 196–7), it implies that AI should investigate cases where the conditions specified by the hypothesis hold and if the phenomenon does occur, AI may then stop.

For the six informants, data referring to their relationships with constituents, their commitment towards trade union principles of solidarity and exposure to in-company financial training suggested that three would be 'sceptics' and two 'realists'. However from his interview, the sixth informant displayed the case features of a 'cynic' except he had not been

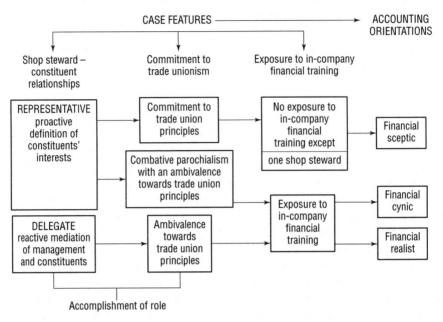

Figure 14.4 A summary of the influences upon senior shop stewards' propensity to hold particular accounting orientations

exposed to in-company financial training. During fieldwork he had expressed Machiavellian representative propensities and a combative parochialism couched in an ambivalence towards trade union principles. This suggested that his espoused accounting orientation would show a potential for 'cynicism' which could lie dormant until he was exposed to financial training.

In the subsequent round of interviews my expectations regarding the three sceptics and two realists were accurate. Meanwhile the potential for 'cynicism' in the sixth informant was confirmed and illustrated how factors that relate to the senior shop steward's accomplishment of his role mediate the potential impact of any in-company financial training intervention. Moreover, this data seemed to corroborate my earlier speculations about the significance of those factors for mediating the potential impact of such training upon 'sceptics'.

CONCLUSIONS

This example of the application of AI illustrates how it seeks to capture aspects of the social world from the perspective of actors and allows the revision of hypotheses and conceptual structures through the analysis and elimination of negative cases. In doing so it attempts to maintain a faithfulness to empirical data gathered from a relatively small number of cases as the research process moves from that data to the construction of categories and from the elucidation of their case features to theorization and generalization. However underlying these processes are a number of epistemological and ontological ambiguities which are worth outlining.

First, a criticism of AI argues that due to the small samples used, the method can rarely make claims about the representativeness of its samples and therefore any attempt at generalizing is tenuous. For Mitchell (1983) such a criticism shows a confusion between the procedures appropriate to making inferences from survey research and those which are appropriate to case study work. He argues that analytical thinking about survey data is based upon both statistical and logical (namely causal) inference and how there is a tendency to elide the former with the latter in that 'the postulated causal connection among features in a sample may be assumed to exist in some parent population simply because the features may be inferred to co-exist in that population' (Mitchell, 1983: 200). In contrast inference in case study research can only be logical and derives its external validity not from its representativeness but because 'our analysis is unassailable' (Mitchell, 1983: 200). Such analytical thoroughness is achieved in AI by eliminating exceptions and revising hypotheses so that statistical tests are actually unnecessary once negative cases are removed (Fielding and Fielding, 1986: 89). Thus in AI extrapolation is derived from logical inference based upon the demonstrated power of the inductively generated and tested theoretical model 'rather than the representativeness of the events' (Mitchell, 1983: 190).

Secondly AI's procedures entail the movement from the 'thick' description and categorization of actors' phenomenological worlds to propounding theoretical explanations of those categories. This entails an initial (re)presentation of actors' internal logics grounded in verstehen in order to formulate categories. However, in order to avoid analytic interruptus AI requires the researcher to shift to a form of analysis that entails his/her imposition of an external logic which exists independently of, and explains, the actors' internal logics. Clearly this shift entails an overt form of what Burrell and Morgan term 'ontological oscillation' (1979: 266) – the initial adoption of a subjectivist stance with the subsequent introduction of incommensurable objectivist assumptions. Now the question for AI is whether, as Burrell and Morgan claim (1979), such oscillation poses a contradiction which should be avoided, or as Weick (1995: 34–8) argues, such oscillation is a vital element in sensemaking that helps us understand the everyday actions of people. Basically the latter view would support AI as it is presented here, whereas the former would either necessitate the discarding of a phenomenological starting point for AI, or AI's dissolution through a limitation to phenomenological 'thick description'.

Finally there remains a basic question regarding the extent to which 'pure' induction is possible. Ironically, the claim that it is possible shares with logical positivism the implicit assumption that there exists a theory neutral observational language in which the researcher is construed as neutral conduit of cultural experience who can objectively elucidate and present the 'facts' of a cognitively accessible empirical world. For Hammersley (1992) such issues are especially problematic for any approach which is committed to accessing members' phenomenological worlds so as to reveal their subjectivities. It creates a contradiction between an objectivist impulse that emphasizes how phenomenological accounts should correspond with members' subjectivity and a phenomenological impulse that suggests that people socially construct versions of reality – culturally derived epistemic processes to which researchers are not immune. Perhaps a key task for any methodologist with a subjectivist agenda is to resolve the problems posed by these epistemological ambiguities while avoiding the spectre, and quagmire, of relativism (see Alvesson and Deetz, 2000).

FURTHER READING

Despite the famous contributions of scholars like Znaniecki (1934), Lindesmith (1947) and Cressey (1950, 1953) AI remains a very unusual approach to empirical research. Unfortunately there are even fewer examples of AI in organizational research. A recent exception is Lennon and Wollin's (2001)research into organizational learning and their approach can be compared to that put forward here and by Bloor (1976, 1978). For a discussion of many of the epistemological and ontological debates which have impacted upon the use of induction in organizational research see Johnson and Duberley (2000) or Alvesson and Sköldberg (2000) while Locke (2000) provides an accessible overview of grounded theory in management research. Obviously Glaser and Strauss' (1967) original work on grounded theory remains a key point of reference for reseachers interested in analytic induction. However it is worth comparing this work with the different directions taken by these authors in Strauss and Corbin (1990) and Glaser's defence of what he sees as the original tenets of grounded theory (1992).

REFERENCES

Alvesson, M. and Deetz, S. (2000) *Doing Critical Management Research*, London: Sage.

Alvesson, M. and Sköldberg, K. (2000) *Reflexive Methodology: New Vistas for Qualitative Research*, London: Sage.

Bannister, P., Burman, E., Parker, I., Taylor, M. and Tindall, C. (1994) *Qualitative Methods in Psychology: A Research Guide*, Buckingham: Open University Press.

Batstone, E., Boraston, I. and Frenkel, S. (1977) *Shop Stewards in Action*, Oxford: Blackwell.

Becker, H.S. (1970) 'Problems of Inference and Proof in Participant Observation', in W.J. Filstead (ed.), *Qualitative Methodology*, Chicago: Markham.

Becker, H.S. (1973) *Outsiders: Studies in the Sociology of Deviance*, London: Free Press.

Berreman, G. (1962) *Behind Many Masks: Ethnography and Impression Management in a Himalayan Village*, Monograph 4, Society For Applied Anthropology, Ithaca NY: Cornell University Press.

Beynon, J. (1983) 'Ways in and staying in: fieldwork as problem-solving', in M. Hammersley (ed.), *The Ethnography of Schooling Methodological Issues*, Driffield: Nafferton.

Bloor, M. (1976) 'Bishop Berkeley and the adenotonsillectomy enigma: an explanation of variation in the social construction of medical disposals', *Sociology*, 10(1): 43–61.

Bloor, M. (1978) 'On the analysis of observational data: a discussion of the worth and uses of inductive techniques and respondent validation', *Sociology*, 12(3): 545–52.

Blumer, H. (1954) 'What is wrong with social theory?', *American Sociological Review*, 19(1): 3–10.

Bogdan, R. (1974) *Being Different: The Autobiography of Jane Fry*, London: Wiley.

Bulmer, M. (1975) 'Some problems of research into class imagery', in M. Bulmer (ed.), *Working Class Images of Society*, London: Routledge and Kegan Paul.

Burrell, G. and Morgan, G. (1979) *Sociological Paradigms and Organizational Analysis*, London: Heinemann.

Cressey, D. (1950) 'The criminal violation of financial trust', *American Sociological Review*, 15: 738–43.

Cressey, D. (1953) *Other Peoples' Money*, Glencoe, IL: Free Press.

Denzin, N. (1978) *The Research Act: A Theoretical Introduction to Sociological Methods*, second edition, London: McGraw-Hill.

Douglas, J.D. (1976) *Investigative Social Research: Individual and Team Field Research*, London: Sage.

Douglas, J.D. (1985) *Creative Interviewing*, London: Sage.

Fielding, N.G. and Fielding, J.L. (1986) *Linking Data*, No. 4 in Qualitative Research Methods Series, London: Sage.

Geertz, C. (1973) *The Interpretation of Cultures*, New York: Basic Books.

Giddens, A. (1976) *New Rules of Sociological Method*, London: Hutchinson.

Gill, J. and Johnson, P. (2002) *Research Methods for Managers*, third edition, London: Sage.

Glaser, B.G. (1978) *Theoretical Sensitivity*, San Francisco: The Sociological Press.

Glaser, B.G. (1992) *Basics of Grounded Theory Research*, Mill Valley: Sociology Press.

Glaser, B.G. and Strauss, A. (1967) *The Discovery of Grounded Theory*, Chicago: Aldine.

Glesne, C. and Peshkin, A. (1992) *Becoming Qualitative Researchers: An Introduction*, London: Longman.

Goffman, E. (1969) *The Presentation of Self in Everyday Life*, Harmondsworth: Penguin.

Goffman, E. (1972) *The Interaction Ritual*, Harmondsworth: Penguin.

Hammersley, M. (1989) *The Dilemma of Qualitative Method: Herbert Blumer and the Chicago Tradition*, London: Routledge.

Hammersley, M. (1992) *What is Wrong with Ethnography?*, London: Routledge.

Hammersley, M. and Atkinson, P. (1995) *Ethnography: Principles in Practice*, second edition, London: Routledge.

Hansen, E.C. (1977) *Rural Catalonia Under the Franco Regime*, Cambridge: Cambridge University Press.

Jackson-Cox, J., Thirkell, J.E.M. and McQueeney, J. (1984) 'The disclosure of company information to trade unions', *Accounting, Organizations and Society*, 9 (3/4): 253–73.

Johnson, P. (1995) 'Towards an epistemology for radical accounting: beyond objectivism and relativism', *Critical Perspectives on Accounting*, 6 (4): 485–509.

Johnson, P. and Duberley, J. (2000) *Understanding Management Research: An Introduction to Epistemology*, London: Sage.

Jones, G.R. (1983) 'Life history methodology', in G. Morgan (ed.), *Beyond Method*, London: Sage.

Kidder, L.H. (1981) 'Qualitative research and quasi experimental frameworks', in M.B. Brewer and B.E. Collins (eds), *Scientific Inquiry and the Social Sciences*, San Francisco: Jossey-Bass.

Knights, D. and Willmott, H.C. (1993) 'It's a very foreign discipline: the genesis of expenses control in a mutual life insurance company', *British Journal of Management*, 4 (1): 1–18.

Kolb, D.A., Rubin, I.M. and McIntyre, J.M. (1979) *Organizational Psychology: An Experiential Approach*, London: Prentice-Hall.

Laing, R.D. (1967) *The Politics of Experience and the Birds of Paradise*, Harmondsworth: Penguin.

Lennon, A. and Wollin, A. (2001) 'Learning organizations: empirically investigating metaphors', *Journal of Intellectual Capital*, 2 (4): 410–22.

Lindesmith, A. (1947) *Opiate Addiction*, Bloomington, IN: Principia Press.

Locke, K.D. (2000) *Grounded Theory in Management Research*, London: Sage.

Loftland, J. (1970) 'Interactionist imagery and analytic interruptus', in T. Shibutani (ed.), *Human Nature and Collective Behaviour: Papers in Honour of Herbert Blumer*, Englewood Cliffs, NJ: Prentice-Hall.

Loftland, J. (1971) *Analysing Social Settings: A Guide to Qualitative Observation and Analysis*, Belmont: Wadsworth.

Lyman, S.M. and Scott, M.B. (1970) *A Sociology of the Absurd*, New York: Appleton-Century-Crofts.

Manning, P.K. (1982) 'Analytic induction,' in R.B. Smith and P.K. Manning (eds), *Qualitative Methods: Volume 11 of Handbook of Social Science Methods*, Cambridge, MA: Ballinger, pp. 273–302.

Marchington, M. and Armstrong, R. (1983) 'Typologies of shop stewards: a reconsideration', *Industrial Relations Journal*, 14(1): 34–49.

Mitchell, J.C. (1983) 'Case and situational analysis', *Sociological Review*, 31(2): 187–211.

Plummer, K. (1983) *Documents of Life: An Introduction to the Problems and Literature of an Humanistic Method*, London: Allen and Unwin.

Robinson, W.S. (1951) 'The logic and structure of analytic induction', *American Sociological Review*, 16(6): 812–18.

Rorty, R. (1979) *Philosophy and the Mirror of Nature*, Princeton, NJ: Princeton University Press.

Shaw, C.R. (1966) *The Jack Roller. A Delinquent Boy's Own Story*, Chicago: Chicago University Press.

Shotter, J. (1975) *Images of Man in Psychological Research*, London: Methuen.

Silverman, D. (1993) *Interpreting Qualitative Data: Methods for Analysing Talk, Text and Interaction*, London: Sage.

Spinelli, E. (1989) *The Interpreted World*, London: Sage.

Spradley, J.P. (1979) *The Ethnographic Interview*, New York: Holt, Reinhart and Winston.

Strauss, A. and Corbin, J. (1990) *Basics of Qualitative Research*, London: Sage.

Trice, H.M. (1956) 'Outsider's role in field study', *Sociology and Social Research*, 14 (1): 27–32.

Van Maanen, J. (1995) 'An end to innocence: the ethnography of ethnography', in J. Van Maanen (ed.), *Representation in Ethnography*, London: Sage.

Wallace, W. (1971) *The Logic of Science in Sociology*, Chicago: Aldine-Atherton.

Weick, K.E. (1995) *Sensemaking in Organizations*, London: Sage.

Whyte, W.F. (1955) *Street Corner Society: the Social Structure of an Italian Slum*, Chicago: University of Chicago Press.

Willman, P. (1980) 'Leadership and trade union principles: some problems of management sponsorship and independence', *Industrial Relations Journal*, 11 (4): 39–49.

Wiseman, J.P. (1978) 'The research web', in J. Bynner and K.M. Stribley (eds), *Social Research, Principles and Procedures*, London: Longman.

Znaniecki, F. (1934) *The Method of Sociology*, New York: Farrer and Rheinhart.

(15) —— Critical Research and Analysis in Organizations ——

Kate Mackenzie Davey and Andreas P.D. Liefooghe

Critical research aims to expose power relations. It challenges assumptions that are often taken for granted in other approaches, and while, in its broadest sense, it is applied to any work that goes beyond unquestioning description, critical research has more to contribute than finding fault. Critical research is concerned with the implications that social practices have for different groups and with making the exercise of power visible. Critical research in organizations examines the ways in which work practices serve to maintain or reinforce imbalances of power. It challenges the managerial view taken by much organizational research to consider how the least powerful are affected. In doing so it directs attention to the way common sense measures of success such as increased profitability are used to deflect attention from the human cost of organizational activities.

We examine the assumptions critical research makes about the importance of context and ideology; language; power and reflexivity and describe some classic and recent studies. We then discuss how we have applied this to research on bullying at work. In conclusion, we argue that, while there are tensions in critical approaches to research it contributes to our understanding of organizations and, more particularly, offers a platform from which to try to improve the experience of work for most people.

UNDERLYING ASSUMPTIONS

While critical research is interpreted in a number of different ways that both overlap and, occasionally, undermine each other, ultimately those who identify themselves as critical researchers use their work as social criticism, and are influenced by ideas of social construction. Kincheloe and McLaren (1998), for example, identify the following as assumptions likely to be shared by most critical researchers:

1 Thought is mediated by social and historical power relations.
2 Facts cannot be isolated from values.
3 The relation between concept and object or word and concept is never stable or fixed.
4 Language is central to awareness.
5 Certain groups are privileged.
6 Oppressed groups often accept their position as natural and inevitable.
7 Oppression has many facets, for example, class, race and sex that may be connected but cannot be collapsed.
8 Mainstream research (unwittingly) reproduces existing power relations.

While critical research uses postmodern tools of deconstruction to examine the ways in which language positions people, critical researchers reject postmodernist relativism (Parker, 1999). Critical researchers argue that there are real, identifiable differences in power between groups and that power differences influence what is taken for granted as true and right in ways that often oppress the less powerful. Kincheloe and McLaren's points can be summarized as a concern with context and ideology, language and power. Underlying these is a concern with reflexivity: as researchers are inevitably ideologically positioned they should acknowledge their role in the research and responsibility for its impact. There is a concern with ethical responsibility, both for the research process and for the social impact of research findings.

Context and ideology

Social and power relations influence thought and knowledge so it is impossible to achieve understanding without examining the context in which any action takes place. As there is no such thing as a neutral or value free position, in order to carry out critical research we must make our taken for granted assumptions explicit and see how they operate to legitimize power imbalances (Alvesson and Deetz, 2000).

Language

Words are not fixed in their meaning and the ways in which they are used will have an impact on our understanding of the world. This makes the interrogation of language central to many critical approaches, especially critical discourse analysis (see Dick, Chapter 17, this volume). Critical analysis demands a sensitivity to different readings of texts, to the contested nature of meaning and to the impact of these readings on different groups (for example, Mumby, 1993; Parker, 1992).

Power

Power is fundamental to critical analysis, and can be the thorniest issue. Postmodernism supplies the tools to dismantle established meanings, and to introduce voices previously unheard, but is uneasy with simple realist claims about power. Conversely, critical theorists argue that privileged groups can be identified. They draw links between power, knowledge and language claiming that the most powerful are most likely to be heard and that their interpretation of reality is more likely to be accepted. Fundamental to this link between power and language is the notion of voice. The powerful have voice: they are more likely to speak, to be heard and to be acknowledged.

Reflexivity

Crucial to the acknowledgement of context is the recognition of the researchers' own position and a critique of the research process itself. Since it is not possible to be neutral, it is important to be open about our ideological positions. Researchers are privileged. We are responsible for the impact of our work and we should not lose sight of our place in the social context in which the research takes place. Reflexivity involves both an openness and honesty about our own position, and serious reflection on our responsibility as researchers.

Critical research may challenge academic privilege by arguing for the role of the participant researcher (Denzin and Lincoln, 1998). Participation could be through action research in which employees themselves explore and challenge organizational practices (see Heller, Chapter 28, this volume), or through the acknowledgement of participants as co-researchers (see Hartley, Chapter 26, this volume). This is in sharp contrast to the traditional positivist psychological description of research subjects and to some degree, in conflict with Alvesson and Deetz's (2000) argument that only outsiders can make the familiar strange and so observe the subtle exercise of power.

Ethics

Ethical issues are fundamental to critical research and include not only a concern with research practices, but also critical awareness of whose interests the research serves. As critical researchers, we must be open about our own ideological position, concerned about the impact that we have within an organization and take responsibility for the wider impact of our research findings.

We must observe the normal ethical standards of sound research but also expose ourselves to criticism. In adopting such a position, we must be seen to practise what we preach (see for example, the debate between Wray-Bliss and Collinson in *Organization*, 2002). In other words, we must reflexively examine our own motives.

As critical researchers we position ourselves as speaking for the oppressed. This presents two ethical risks: one is the danger of misrepresentation and the second, more complex difficulty, is of the power structures and dominance inherent in the arrogance of claiming to speak for another.

Summary

Broadly, there are four areas we see as fundamental to critical analysis. First are issues of context and ideology. What is the social and historical context in which the research takes place and how does this influence what is accepted as true? Second is the focus on language. How are the research areas discussed within organizations, how are words used and defined and what alternative readings are there? Third is concern with power. Who is speaking and who is heard? What are the implications of these uses of language for privilege and oppression within this context? Finally, there is a responsibility to reflect on our own role and the ethical implications of our research. Where are we positioned as researchers and what is the possible impact of our work on other participants in the process? Critical research is concerned both with challenging research orthodoxy and challenging organizational practice.

PREVIOUS RESEARCH

Critical research has aimed to reveal both the subordinating processes that have an impact on underprivileged groups but also show the ways in which group members may recognize, subvert and resist domination. For example, early critical research was clearly focused on social class. Paul Willis (1977) in *Learning to Labour* challenges the extent of liberation through equality of educational opportunity by examining the socializing of working class boys into ideas of work. Christine Griffin (1985) in *Typical Girls?* follows Willis's analysis of class by focusing on gender and race through examining adolescent girls' recognition of patriarchy. This reflects the move away from the classic Marxist view to a broader approach to critical theory.

Recent approaches have taken a combination of methods and have focused on language and symbolic aspects of organizations. While many of these are influenced by post-structuralism, they reject theoretical relativism and take a realist approach to power. Philips and Brown (1993) look at different patterns of power and reflection of interests in an advertising campaign. They use the symbolic aspects of the organization as a way of examining how all organizational actors struggle, 'to reframe understandings in ways that enhance their positions and increase their power and influence' (Philips and Brown, 1993: 1572). Markham (1996) reveals the way vague instructions, for example, 'be creative', can be used to control and often to undermine, confuse and humiliate the less powerful. Ambiguity can be exploited by managers to reject work, for example, as not creative enough, without a clear explanation. Approaches may be more or less specific about the methodology. On the one hand, Witmar (1997) gives an exemplary, detailed account of the method in her structuration based approach to Alcoholics Anonymous examining the exercise of discipline and marginalizing of women. Others tend to use a broader brush approach. Parker (2000), for example, is cavalier in his dismissal of the need for details of method in his study of organizational identity.

Mumby and Stohl (1996) use deconstruction to undermine the monolithic managerial voice most often presented as legitimate in organizations by challenging the tradition of the invisible author and by offering different readings by others who may not have a voice. In this critical approach, rather than a single clear, apparently objective account, we have a series of partial and interested groups including managers but also employees lower down the hierarchy and researchers themselves. Such a deconstruction exposes the interests and power structures that underlie the right to be heard in organizations.

Alvesson (1996) examines different views by analysing a single meeting from three different theoretical approaches. He analyses the occasion as a culture constitutive event, as an expression of power (Foucault inspired) and following classic critical theory, as communicative distortion (Habermas, 1984). He goes on to examine what each of these interpretations contributes to our understanding of the meeting and how, as researchers, we cope with multiple interpretations. As he shows, good theories are extremely powerful: 'The theories influence what is perceived, what will be emphasized as the focal situation, and how it will be interpreted' (1984: 205). While he argues that few researchers can move successfully between theories rooted in different paradigms he demonstrates the ways that theoretical orientations and ideological background will change the focus of research.

ASSUMPTIONS AND PRACTICALITIES OF OUR METHOD

Our research examines bullying in organizations (Liefooghe, 2001; Liefooghe and Mackenzie Davey, 2001; Mackenzie Davey and Liefooghe, 2003). Our research questions concerned how bullying was defined and described within organizations and what the implications of these descriptions were in terms of power relations. Our ideological position was based in critical discursive psychology and so suspicious of any attempt to create a totalizing meta-narrative, but particularly concerned with the power of labelling and the use of individualizing discourse to depoliticize structural difference. We were also concerned that the use of the term bullying in organizations was a site of struggle between experts and that while this was presented as a problem suffered by employees, no one was asking employees how they experienced bullying. We aimed to give these employees a voice. Through doing this and feeding our research back to organizations we hoped to influence organizational practices and to alert academics to the limitations of focusing solely on expert derived measures without examining their meaning for participants concerned.

The context in which the research took place was a growing application of the term, bullying, to work. This appeared in both academic and in popular literature. The research began with discomfort at the wide application to work of a term previously used mainly in schools. We were suspicious, not only of the usefulness of applying the conventional measures derived from studies of school bullying to studying workers, but also with the faddish ubiquity of the term in the popular management press. We were concerned that individuals were being demonized in an attempt to deflect attention from some fundamental organizational issues. The focus on individual differences and, at the most, interpersonal interactions leads to an unpoliticized and undersocialized world view overemphasizing the role of individual agency (Henriques et al., 1984). Our concern was whether bullying is seen as due to the deviant behaviour of rare individuals in an organization or whether it is more fundamental to organizational culture.

Language was regarded as central to the area as a number of different groups sought to own and define the term (Ashforth and Humphries, 1997). Academics, managers, trade unions, and victim groups were amongst those concerned with establishing their own definitions. Power was fundamental, both within definitions of bullying and in the enthusiasm with which groups sought to close down alternate meanings. We investigated how a term (bullying) could suddenly be claimed by different groups and be attributed specific meanings that both challenged past use and exploited previous associations. The question was, 'Who defines bullying and what are the implications of this definition for subordinated groups in the organization?' The main aim of the research was to hear from workers themselves what they experienced as bullying at work.

MANAGING THE RESEARCH PROCESS

Liefooghe is the field worker who negotiated with the organizations and collected the data. His background is in psychology, group dynamics, counselling and, bullying. Mackenzie Davey had no contact with the organizations and was involved in the analysis of the transcript data and discussion of interpretation of other observations. Her background is in organizational communication, feminist research, and discourse analysis. While the data are clearly Liefooghe's the analysis is shared. This approach to critical analysis encourages the challenge of any position, prevents researchers from going native and analysis from becoming divorced from the organization (Alvesson, 1998). We argue that collaboration encouraged reflexivity as interpretations constantly had to be justified and examined.

The critical research agenda is not the most seductive for senior managers. As Alvesson and Deetz say, 'Why should corporate managers allow a valuable corporate resource – time – to be used against their own and maybe the company's interest?' (2000: 193). However, the popular press and management literature about bullying at work meant managers were concerned about the issue and in some cases keen to find out more. Even so, response to a letter to 40 companies was negligible and the organizations were recruited through personal networking. The material reported here is from the case of a bank that had undergone recent organizational change. The company had recently received survey results they described as worrying. In response to a questionnaire over half the employees claimed to have been bullied. It was not clear why the question had been asked, but once it had been raised the organization felt the need to respond. Formal consent for the research was obtained from the directors and from the union.

Gathering accounts

The research began with individual interviews with policy makers and the collection and analysis of the company's documents on bullying. The company offered a definition of bullying and issued videos that gave examples of bullying and how to respond to it.

Focus groups were used to encourage participation from a large proportion of employees and to allow participants to discuss and interrogate terms with minimal intervention from the researcher. The research was presented as a project on 'relationships at work' and bullying was introduced as a term used in the media to describe some work relationships. Participants were asked whether they would apply the term to any relationship in the workplace and how they would define it. The researcher did not offer a definition. The discussions were recorded and transcribed for discourse analysis (Potter and Wetherell, 1987). Participants are identified by sex and order in which they spoke (for example, F3 is the third woman to speak in this group). The researcher is identified by initials.

Analysing accounts

We will first examine the official company definition that was frequently referred to by managers and then draw on some of the material from the focus groups. Both researchers read all the organizational material. First, all mentions of the term bullying in the transcripts were identified in a broad, thematic content analysis. This allowed selection of sections of text where participants were using the term or discussing examples of use of the term. Each researcher read the transcripts independently, highlighting areas of interest.

The initial analysis of transcripts focused specifically on language and meaning. We examined how the term bullying was used, how different participants define bullying, and the examples that they give. Our approach examined both the consistencies and contradictions in the ways that participants use discourses of bullying. Employees draw on the same discourses identified by school researchers, but also apply the term in novel ways to describe their own experiences at work.

We went on to consider the implications of different definitions of bullying for power relations within the organization. We examined who was speaking and who was heard and interrogated the different interests that might be served by different accounts.

Finally, we were repeatedly returning to what the implications of the research were for all our participants and for our own role within it. We considered how material could be fed back to the organizations and what impact it may have on organization practices.

In practice, of course, the analysis jumped between levels and progressed erratically. We argued about interpretations, checked tapes, went back to the literature and to the transcripts again.

In the company policy, bullying is defined as:

> personal criticism or abuse, either in public or in private, which humiliates an individual and undermines self-esteem and confidence. It is therefore distinct from the way we all feel at times when we are under pressure for example to meet tight deadlines or particular targets or those occasions when we make a mistake and are legitimately called to account for this, in private with our supervisor or manager. The point about bullying behaviour is that it is not constructive criticism which will assist an individual in the future – it is quite the opposite.

Primarily, this definition legislates for what bullying is and is not. It seems to deny ambiguity. Secondly, it describes bullying as clearly negative. Thirdly, it is framed in terms of a manager's behaviour towards a subordinate. That is, it is defined as an interaction between two individuals in which one person has a negative impact on another. Normal acceptable behaviour by a manager or supervisor (legitimately calling to account, constructive criticism) is differentiated from the unacceptable. That this should be necessary suggests that there may be room for confusion. The implication is that bullying is likely to take place within this relationship and this is supported by research on incidence of bullying. The use of first person plural can be seen as distancing 'us' from those who bully, or indeed are bullied. A further message is that all of 'us' will be under pressure to meet deadlines at some point and that all of 'us' will be called to account when 'we' make mistakes. Managers are differentiated from the managed and simultaneously united as members of a group. Both bullies and the bullied are positioned as outside 'our' group.

The definition individualizes bullying, not only by stressing that it is personal criticism (not being *legitimately* called to account), but also by defining it in terms of an individual response. Bullying humiliates, undermines self-esteem and confidence and does not assist an individual in future; if individuals can overcome any such threat to self esteem, by this definition they have not been bullied. The bullied individual is differentiated from the 'we' who all feel under pressure and may be legitimately called to account by our superiors; these are normalized as legitimate.

Thus the definition claims to speak for all, manipulates meaning to defend organization power groups and legitimize management action, individualizes those who experience bullying and demonizes bullying by associating it with negative, unhelpful and illegitimate behaviour. In offering this kind of definition the organization appears to offer increased clarity but still allows great ambiguity.

Context: school or work

Focus group participants are sophisticated in the ways in which they examine the different approaches to bullying. In employee accounts, the meaning of bullying is not homogeneous or clear. Participants struggle between different interpretative frameworks in order to define and describe bullying. They interrogate such issues as whether bullying could be objectively defined by specifying behaviours or whether it is subjectively defined by individual response or intention.

Participants draw on the notion of bullying in a school in an attempt to define and explain what is happening in their work place. However, the repertoire is found to be of limited use. School bullying is regarded as clearly defined, whereas work bullying depends on perception:

F3: But surely it's . . . my immediate reaction when I think of bullying is in the school situation, having kids at school, and that I think we can all relate to, it's a bigger person picking on a smaller person, but I think once you get into the working environment it gets a lot more difficult because surely it becomes a matter of perception. Because what one person takes for bullying another one is quite comfortable with that working relationship, I just think it's a very hazy area out there . . .

The use of the term bullying in a school environment is seen as unproblematic, in contrast to the 'hazy area out there' in the work place. It calls for a subjective definition, rather than a definition that is clear, unambiguous and understood by all. Bullying offers a link between the two environments of school and work. School becomes a guiding framework participants draw upon to account for what is happening to them now in a work environment. Yet, when participants are asked to elaborate on this, and give examples of how these types of school bullying now manifest themselves in their organization, they clearly differentiate them.

F4: I think the old fashioned way of bullying is non-existent.
M1: Yes.
F4: Your school ground mentality-type bullying. There's more subtle bullying going on.
M1: And it's organizational.
AL: Can you think of examples of bullying happening between two people at work? Or even if they're colleagues or whether they're a manager and one person – on an interpersonal level rather than an organizational level.
F4: Not really, no. I mean, to me – I would class that as the old fashioned type of bullying and I don't think that happens anymore. It's the more subtle – like – speaking up damages your career. That's bullying because – I mean, our director said that speaking up won't damage your career and it has been proved that speaking up does damage your career, but it's done subtly.
AL: How . . .
F4: In the appraisal process.
M3: At the appraisal process.
F4: You can't prove a lot of it now because it's subtle. It's behind the scenes, and, erm, and it – not just affects individuals, it affects – it can affect a broad base.

When the researcher (AL) tries to lead them into considering interpersonal bullying at work, his suggestion is emphatically rejected. Their experience of bullying at work is linked to organizational systems.

Two issues linked to power are considered as bullying here: the lack of meaningful participation in negotiation and the dangers of speaking out. These are enforced through appraisal and performance related pay systems (PRP), which are viewed as unfair.

Language, power and voice

Being bullied is equated with being told rather than asked and being afraid to object for fear of reprisal. The notion that speaking up can damage your career is not focused on a single individual but seen as perpetrated by the organization against a group, or groups of employees. There is a dissonance between what the official line is (the director says speaking out won't harm you) to what happens in practice (in the appraisal process). In these negotiations, 'very subtle intimidation and bullying takes place' (F4). Rather than talking about bullying as something between two individuals, participants construct a collective (rather than an individual) identity (for example, union–management).

> F5: So, yeah, so when you say, have you experienced bullying in the Bank, yes we have experienced bullying and we are experiencing it now. Maybe not personally, individually, but the staff as a whole are experiencing bullying by the Banco management.

The lack of negotiation, being told what to do, forms the core of bullying. Bullying was widely used to describe not being heard. It was discussed both in traditional union–management negotiations and in individuals' daily experiences of work.

Discipline and surveillance

The appraisal process in Banco is linked with reward (PRP). This type of bullying is seen as 'subtle' – and this subtlety may be due to the fact that it does not operate at an individual level, but at an organizational one, as it is engrained into an organizational system:

> F1: I think, in a way, that there's some, kind of, like, really indirect bullying goes on and it's to do with all the PRP system and stuff that we have. And it comes from right from the top, the targets and they go right down the managers. If your manager's got a target that they're really trying to achieve, I don't think – I sometimes think I feel, kind of, like the overtime one and stuff. Putting me under a lot more stress and not really wanting to understand what I'm feeling now, but just more trying to, like, cut costs.
>
> M1: If your overtime's cut because your manager's got to make his targets, they say, you know, 10 per cent reduction in overtime. So he's telling you there's no overtime but your customers are saying, 'I need this and need it now.' You're then getting – effectively getting bullied in two directions.

F1 and M1 discuss here how an organizational system (PRP) is not just an environmental factor facilitating interpersonal bullying, but is bullying itself. The system itself is criticized – it is there to cut costs. Within this system, managers are put under pressure to increase staff performance, reduce overtime, and cut costs to meet their targets. M1 then introduces the element of customers bullying through putting extra pressure, leading to being bullied from both directions. Rather than positioning individual managers as bullies, however, employees acknowledge that they function within the constraints of a system that requires them to act in the way they do. They have to keep their budget down. Thus, the cause of bullying is not attributed to individuals nor to organizational groups or departments, but to the organizational systems within which they operate. These are the processes by which pay and performance are negotiated – the way targets are set – and the appraisal system and PRP function to discipline employees:

> M5: We're having the system imposed on us. And it still hasn't changed. We still get the system where you get given, er, you get given – targets which now, are not very, er, measurable because they've decided – you can't measure – too many of these things. They [HR] didn't want to know. They want to be able to say, we've got this bell curve, you're supposed to fit into it in each team. Now that's what I call bullying.

This participant challenges the objectivity of the system through questioning the measures and processes used to assess performance. There is no reward for 'an objective good performance' as it depends where an individual falls on the imposed bell curve within their team. In other words, a whole team can never be 'excellent performers' as performance is treated as normally distributed within a specific team. Measurement, or the lack of it, becomes bullying in two senses: the lack of appropriate measures, and imposing a technological artefact (normal distribution) that is regarded as being unfair.

In sum, employees acknowledge the roots of bullying at school but distinguish this from their experience at work. *Classic bullying*, the kind that occurs within schools amongst children, is seen to be interpersonal in its nature. *Organizational bullying*, they argue is less straightforward and more subtle. It consists of organizational practices such as ignoring employee voice in negotiation, target setting, performance management and the pay and appraisal system. These systems are seen as inherently unfair.

CRITICAL REFLECTIONS

Critical analysis concentrates on challenging forms of domination and revealing contradictions between rhetorics of equality and discrimination (Morrow, 1994). In attempting both to acknowledge different accounts and to highlight power imbalances we are oscillating between postmodern relativism and critical realism. The serious issue underlying these arguments is how, if you are subjecting everything to critique, you can justify a position that argues that 'real' social inequalities exist, that we can identify them and that we have a duty to challenge them (Edwards et al., 1995; Parker, 1999). For Habermas, clarifying the ways that language is used can reveal the operation of power and open systems to challenge. We positioned ourselves to represent those employees who were not heard in the organization. In doing so, we demonstrate that a term represented by management as protecting individual employee interests may be adopted by those employees to describe their own oppression by management as a group.

Throughout the analysis we were painfully aware of the implications of our reporting. First, we had to confront how we were going to report findings back to the managers in the organization who had sponsored the research. We had to balance issues of clarity and fidelity to the data with the need to preserve confidentiality. Our hopes of having an impact on material organizational practices, were disappointed when a director greeted our feedback with the words, 'Given our tremendous performance and profit over the last financial year, we must be doing something right. And if they call that bullying, perhaps we should do more of it.' This raises issues of how far critical researchers can challenge the organizations that they study.

Secondly, and of greater concern, is the issue of how to present our work without undermining the position of those who experienced an extremely abusive, threatening, interpersonal relationship at work. In describing how employees use language, we were sometimes seen as denying that 'real' bullying happened. Demonstrating how an emotional term is used by different interest groups can appear to belittle the experience.

In raising the profile of the mundane, there is a danger of deflating the value of the extreme. This dilution of emotive terms demonstrates the delicacy and significance of labelling and definition in creating meaning.

Thirdly, academic peers were concerned that we were appropriating the term bullying and neglecting existing research on definition, measurement and frequency of bullying. Our research however, was not concerned with owning a specific definition of bullying, but with the functions the term fulfils for different groups.

CONCLUSION

Our critical analysis highlights the messy and ambiguous use of a contested term, exposes the power relations inherent in definition and labelling, and demonstrates that research does not take place in a political vacuum. However, in attempting to raise the interests of a neglected group of employees we encountered two problems. First, we doubt that this specific research improved the position of the participants; secondly, in focusing on one group, we neglect others. This returns us to fundamental reflections on whose interest the research served and how far research can be liberating. In other words, while the critical agenda may serve the interests of researchers, it is less clear that it serves the interests of other stakeholders. Ultimately, our responsibility is to represent the position of those who have not been heard in this debate and who contributed to our research, that is, employees in organizations.

FURTHER READING

Alvesson and Deetz's (2000) guide to *Doing Critical Management Research* is the most useful general overview. The journals *Organization*, *Organization Studies* and the *Journal of Management Studies* are the most likely sources of critical research although they rarely give detail of method or analysis. Habermas (1984) is undoubtedly fundamental to critical theory, and is helpful to those wishing to explore the theoretical background of this chapter further.

REFERENCES

Alvesson, M. (1996) *Communication, Power and Organisations*, Berlin: Walter de Gruyter.
Alvesson, M. (1998) 'Gender relations and identity at work: a case study of masculinities and femininities in an advertising agency', *Human Relations*, 51 (8): 969–1005.
Alvesson, M. and Deetz, S. (2000) *Doing Critical Management Research*, London: Sage.
Ashforth, B.E. and Humphrey, R.H. (1997) 'The ubiquity and potency of labelling in organizations', *Organization Science*, 8 (1): 43–58.
Collinson, D.L. (2002) 'A response to Wray-Bliss: revisiting the shop floor', *Organization*, 9(1): 41–50.
Denzin, N.K. and Lincoln,Y.S. (1998) (eds) *The Landscape of Qualitative Research*, Thousand Oaks: Sage.
Edwards, D., Ashmore, M. and Potter, J. (1995) 'Death and furniture: the rhetoric, politics and theology of bottom line arguments against relativism', *History of Human Sciences*, 8 (2): 25–49.
Fournier, V. and Grey, C. (2000) 'At the critical moment: conditions and prospects for critical management studies', *Human Relations*, 53(1): 7–32.
Friere, P. (1970) *Pedagogy of the Oppressed*, New York: Herder and Herder.
Griffin, C. (1985) *Typical Girls? Young Women from School to the Job Market*, London: Routledge and Kegan Paul.
Habermas, J. (1984) *The Theory of Communicative Action, Vol. 1: Reason and the Rationalization of Society*, Boston, MA: Beacon Press.
Henriques, J., Hollway, W., Urwin, C., Venn, C. and Walkerdine, V. (1984) *Changing the Subject: Psychology, Social Regulation and Subjectivity*, London: Methuen.
Jackall, R. (1988) *Moral Mazes: The World of Corporate Managers*, Oxford: Oxford University Press.

Kincheloe, J.L. and McLaren, P.L. (1998) 'Rethinking critical theory and qualitative research', in N. Denzin and Y. Lincoln (eds), *The Landscape of Qualitative Research*, Thousand Oaks, CA: Sage, pp.260–99.

Liefooghe, A.P.D. (2001) 'Accounts of bullying in organizations: voice, power and discourse at work', unpublished PhD thesis, University of Surrey.

Liefooghe, A.P.D. and Mackenzie Davey, K. (2001) 'Accounts of workplace bullying: the role of the organization', *European Journal of Work and Organizational Psychology*, 10 (4): 375–92.

Mackenzie Davey, K. and Liefooghe, A.P.D. (2003) 'Voice and power: critically examining the uses of the term bullying in organizations', in A. Schorr, B. Campbell and M. Schenk (eds), *Communication Research and Media Science in Europe*, Berlin: Walter de Gruyter, pp.441–57.

Markham, A. (1996) 'Designing discourse: a critical analysis of strategic ambiguity and workplace control', *Management Communication Quarterly*, 9 (4): 389–421.

Morrow, R.A. (1994) *Critical Theory and Methodology*, Vol. 3: *Contemporary Social Theory*, Thousand Oaks, CA: Sage.

Mumby, D.K. (1993) (ed.) *Narrative and Social Control: Critical Perspectives, Vol. 21, Sage Annual Reviews of Communication Research*, Newbury Park: Sage.

Mumby, D.K. and Stohl, C. (1996) 'Disciplining organizational communication studies', *Management Communication Quarterly*, 10 (1): 50–72.

Reason, P. (1994) 'Three approaches to participative enquiry', in Y. Lincoln and N. Denzin (eds), *Handbook of Qualitative Research*, Thousand Oaks, CA: Sage.

Parker, I. (1992) *Discourse Dynamics. Critical Analysis for Social and Individual Psychology*, London: Routledge.

Parker, I. (1999) 'Against relativism in psychology, on balance', *History of the Human Sciences*, 12 (4): 61–78.

Parker, M. (2000) *Organizational Culture and Identity*, London: Sage.

Philips, N. and Brown, J.L. (1993) 'Analyzing communication in and around organizations: a critical hermeneutic approach', *Academy of Management Journal*, 16 (6): 1547–76.

Potter, J. and Wetherell, M. (1987) *Discourse and Social Psychology: Beyond Attitudes and Behaviour*, London: Sage.

Van Maanen, J. and Kunda, G. (1989) 'Real feelings: emotional expression and organisational culture', *Research in Organization Behavior*, 11: 43–103.

Willis, P. (1977) *Learning to Labour. How Working Class Kids get Working Kids get Working Class Jobs*, Farnborough, UK: Saxon House.

Witmar, D.F. (1997) 'Communication and recovery: structuration as an ontological approach to organisational culture', *Communication Monographs*, 64 (4): 324–49.

Wray-Bliss, E. (2002) 'Abstract ethics, embodied ethics: the strange marriage of Foucault and positivism in labour process theory', *Organization*, 9 (1): 5–39.

Young, E. (1989) 'On the naming of the rose: interests and multiple meanings as elements of organisational culture', *Organization Studies*, 10 (2): 187–206.

John McAuley

Lying at the heart of hermeneutics are issues of intuition, interpretation, understanding, the relationship between the researcher and the subject of research and the reader. In recent times, hermeneutics is understood as a philosophical take on interpretivist social science; an assertion that 'understanding *is* interpretation. . . . Thus reaching an understanding is not a matter of setting aside, escaping, managing, or tracking one's own standpoint, prejudgements, biases, or prejudices. On the contrary understanding requires the *engagement* of one's biases' (Schwandt, 2000: 194). However, the hermeneutic paradigm encompasses many positions. Ricoeur, for example, states starkly 'there is no general hermeneutics . . . but only disparate and opposed theories concerning the rules of interpretation' (1970: 26). Although it is hoped that there is much in what follows that casts light on the topic it is also acknowledged that much is left out.

This chapter begins with an interpretation of a number of texts on hermeneutics with the intention of showing how different perspectives bring useful insights into researching organizations. At one end of the hermeneutic paradigm is what Alvesson and Sköldberg (2000) refer to as objectivist hermeneutics that 'results in the understanding of underlying meaning, not the explanation of causal connections' (2000: 52). At the other end is what they characterize as 'alethic hermeneutics', which has 'its focus on truth as an act of disclosure, in which the polarity between subject and object – as well as that . . . between understanding and explanation – is dissolved in the radical light of a more original unity' (2000: 52). This represents the development of a social science 'in which the communicative relationship between subject and object is given full recognition' (Bleicher, 1982: 70). The second section is an exploration of the implications of the intellectual and emotional pre-understanding that the researcher brings into the research situation and the development of the hermeneutic circle. This leads to an exploration of a key aspect of the hermeneutic approach – the interpretive process and the role of intuition. This is linked to a brief discussion of the psychoanalytic encounter, which has been taken by some as representing hermeneutics as research method. This is extended into a discussion of some of the ways in which researchers have attempted to place hermeneutics into the arena of 'normal' social science. The chapter concludes with a discussion of research activities undertaken by the author (and colleagues) informed by the hermeneutic approach.

REACHING FOR THE TRUTH?

The interest in interpretation within the hermeneutic tradition comes from a particular version of scientific knowledge known as *Geistwissenschaften* which can be translated as '"sciences of the spirit", . . . the concept is deeply rooted in German idealist philosophy. . . . Hermeneutic-spiritual knowing and positivistic-pragmatic knowing are opposed to each other' (Bettelheim, 1983: 41).

The idealist thrust in hermeneutics may be illustrated through the work of Dilthey, who is the instigator of the development of modern hermeneutics (Blaikie, 1995). According to Blaikie, 'Dilthey insisted that the foundation for understanding human beings is in life itself, not in rational speculation or metaphysical theories. Life, by which he means the human world, provides us with the concepts and categories we need to produce this understanding' (1995: 32). As social scientist (or actor) the '"objectifications of life", or residues of our thoughts in cultural achievements and physical things, can be understood through an inner process of *verstehen*, of hermeneutic understanding' (1995: 32). This is related to the idea of hermeneutic phenomenology in which the 'aim is to construct an animating, evocative description of the human actions, behaviours, intentions, and experiences as we meet them in the lifeworld' (Van Manen, 1990: 19).

Whilst the contribution of Dilthey is important in the development of modern hermeneutics and clearly influences the legitimacy of hermeneutic approaches to understanding human behaviour he does not tell the whole story. Gadamer, for example, suggests that 'Dilthey's attempt to explicate the human sciences in terms of life, and to start with the experience of life, was never really reconciled with his firmly held Cartesian conception of science' (1985: 258) – the split between the outer and the inner aspects of life.

Gadamer, who may be seen as 'both the most forceful and coherent exponent of contemporary hermeneutics' (Grondin, 1995: xi) discusses a number of core principles that underpin the hermeneutic approach and that constitute the hermeneutic cycle. These include the idea that there can be a 'hermeneutical rule that we must understand the whole in terms of the detail and the detail in terms of the whole. . . . The harmony of all the details with the whole is the criterion of correct understanding' (Gadamer, 1985: 291). He then suggests that there is an objective and subjective aspect to this understanding. He discusses this in terms of looking at a text as an example of the unfolding hermeneutic cycle or spiral, the 'iterative process whereby each stage of our research provides us with knowledge' (Gummesson, 2000: 70).

When the researcher looks at a text 'objectively', that text needs to be looked at in the context of the writer's work, and that work has to be looked at in relation to the genre and tradition of the culture. From the perspective of the researcher, this assessment of the text can only be undertaken with an awareness of the researcher's own 'objective' circumstances. On the subjective side, he suggests, 'the same text, as a manifestation of a creative moment, belongs to the whole of its author's inner life' (Gadamer, 1985: 291).

An example of exploration of the subjective may be seen in the work of Saleh and Hassan (1999). They suggest that the professional activity known as financial audit is usually understood through the lens of positivist empirical research but that this approach alienates practitioners, researchers and academics from each other. They suggest that if audit is considered as an art, as a social phenomenon and exposed to the hermeneutic gaze greater understanding can be achieved. A different approach to the reconciliation of the objective and the subjective may be seen in Boland (1989). He claims, 'the hermeneutic turn appreciates that our understanding of accounting and organizations is not guaranteed by a method that separates the objective from the subjective. Instead, our knowledge of accounting and organizations is constructed through a social practice in which such distinctions are not meaningful' (1989: 591). In these readings of audit or accountancy, the objective aspect would include such social constructions as the codified rules of audit or accountancy, professional codes of practice, regulatory features that govern the relationship between the professional and the organizations in which they are undertaking the audit or accountancy practice. The subjective aspect would be such matters as the way the auditor or accountant, consciously or unconsciously, experiences the professional activity in relation to other aspects of being human and how the auditor or accountant understands his/her relationship with the self and with others. This subjective aspect may be individual or it may be a shared understanding or collusion. It may be seen that in this sense the subjective and the objective elide into one another. In this sense the research interest would be in understanding how the auditor or the accountant constructs and tells the story of the processes by which audit or accountancy is accomplished.

However the researcher is not looking at the experience of the subjects alone; there is also the position of the interpreter as the scene unfolds and in the process of interpretation. Gadamer suggests that the hermeneutic circle

> ... is not formal in nature. It is neither subjective nor objective, but describes understanding as the interplay of the movement of tradition[1] and the movement of the interpreter. The anticipation of meaning that governs our understanding of a text is not an act of subjectivity, but proceeds from a commonality that binds us to the tradition ... (Gadamer, 1985: 293)

The problem is, however, that this version of the hermeneutic circle 'can only serve to sanction prevalent use of language' (Bleicher, 1980: 161) because of the emphasis on commonality of tradition.

An extension of this to the exploration of patterns of communication that are fractured, where that commonality may be lacking, is suggested by Habermas who has an interest in hermeneutics but is also thought of as a critical theorist. In this tradition the hermeneutic aspect lies 'in the sense that it enables self-conscious reflection on the social conditions surrounding the production, dissemination, and reception of texts' and the critical element lies in an analysis of the contribution of these texts to 'the creation and maintenance of power differentials' (Phillips and Brown, 1993: 1547) where it is assumed that the language of power differentials leads to a distortion of communications.

Within the hermeneutic tradition this interest in meaning and understanding has the consequence (intended within the neo-idealist tradition) of an interest in improving communication and self-understanding in an essentially ameliorative way. This moral dimension can give an interesting edge to the research activity. Tillery, for example, wanted to explore 'the complex relationship of ethics, writing and power (which) continues to be a major concern for scholars and teachers of technical communication' (2001: 1970). In her research she is guided by Gadamer's assertion that: 'the practical science directed towards this practical knowledge ... must arise from practice itself and with all the typical generalizations that it brings to explicit consciousness, be related back to practice' (2001: 92). Tillery adds that hermeneutics can be a process of cultural critique that is crucial for understanding how ideology functions.

THE HERMENEUTIC CYCLE

In the above what is being suggested is that researchers inevitably bring (and positively embed) something of their objective and subjective selves to the feast of the research activity. Researchers also bring an intellectual pre-understanding. This may be illustrated by Ferch whose work on the relationship between physical touch and developing the ability to forgive follows the principles of hermeneutic phenomenology. He wrote: '*Because research indicates* appropriate levels of touch are related to consistent human development, and *because recent literature* presents forgiveness as an important part of personal and interpersonal growth, a study incorporating both touch and forgiveness was warranted' (my italics) (2000: 159). At a prima facie level, this could look like good old-fashioned hypothesis making. But it is not. Its status is quite different. When Dalton was undertaking his magnificent work that led to the production of his seminal study *Men who Manage* he wrote that although he eschewed explicit hypotheses he had 'hunches which served me as less exalted guides' (Dalton, 1964: 53) to the development of research.

The researcher can start the hermeneutic circle 'at one point and then delve further and further into the matter by alternating between part and whole, which brings a progressively deeper understanding of both' (Alvesson and Sköldberg, 2000: 53). In this case prior research and prior literature is bringing into the developing scene some loose boundaries, some steer into what is being explored. In this sense both the preunderstanding and the research itself go through iterations of interpretation. From this springboard, 'hermeneutic scientists interpret immediate events such as non-verbal phenomena; physical environment and unexpected events in the light of previous events, private experience and whatever else they find pertinent to the situation under investigation' (Gummesson, 2000). It is analogous to the ethnographic process of 'trying to read (in the sense of "construct a reading of") a manuscript – foreign, faded, full of ellipses, incoherences, suspicious emendations, and tendentious commentaries, but written . . . in transient examples of shaped behaviour' (Geertz, 1973: 10).

This process of reading, of iteration, of moving back-and-forth, of emergent interpretation may be illustrated by the work of Thompson et al. They were concerned to explore the 'everyday consumer experience of contemporary women with children' (1990: 346) through the lens of the hermeneutic approach. The transcripts of the interviews (which were formulated 'in concert with participant descriptions' (1990: 347)) were initially interpreted ideographically uncovering the internal logic of the data. The pattern of interpretation was widened as themes, common patterns, began to emerge from the interviews. It is important to note that these themes were those that came to the minds, intuitively, of the researchers. As the cognitive anthropologist Geertz points out 'the object of study is one thing and the study of it another . . . *we begin with our interpretations of what our informants are up to, or think they are up to and then systemize those . . .*' (author's italics) (1973: 15). At this stage the test of validity of the interpretation, according to Thompson et al., is that the individual 'text' will support the thematic interpretation. They further suggest that these themes should first be accessible to readers, and secondly be those themes that are 'consistent with the aims motivating the study, can be directly supported by reference to participant descriptions, and provides insight . . .' (1990: 347). This process of emergent thematic analysis, which they refer to as bracketing, allows 'for seeing the text from a phenomenological perspective without predefining participants' experiences in terms of the interpretative framework' (Thompson et al., 1990: 347).

INTERPRETATION AND THE HERMENEUTIC ENDEAVOUR

Bleicher (1982) suggests that hermeneutic theory represents a framework for the explication of meaning, for rendering explicit what has remained implicit, taken for granted or misunderstood. In this sense it is a 'reading', an interpretation of the self-interpretation of others within a context. There is additionally the requirement for dialogue (sometimes active, sometimes silent) between researcher, reader and the subject of research. This is the process known as *verstehen*. As Strati suggests *verstehen* is the

> device that releases people from their isolation. We understand human action on the basis of dynamic connections and in relation to purposes and values. We are enabled to do so by a process of inner experience. . . . It is a process, moreover, which frees us from the necessity of having directly lived the experience or emotion . . . (1999: 58)

The basis of the ability to undertake such interpretation lies, in part, on the notion that 'the capacity of another person, *or a professional observer*, to understand human objects is . . . based on a belief that all human beings have something in common' (my italics) (Blaikie, 1993: 33). Bleicher (1982) suggests that this shared humanity enables the work of the analyst to claim for the work an all-pervasive or universal character.

So, in coming to interpretation there is, on the one hand understanding of common humanity – that no matter how unlike the surface understanding of the world of the other human beings can access those experiences. On the other hand there is the notion that the professional observer is privileged in their access to understanding. For example, Alvesson and Sköldberg talk of the significance of intuition in hermeneutic understanding. In their view, intuition represents a 'privileged royal road to true knowledge of the world. This is achieved . . . at a stroke, whereby patterns in complex wholes are illuminated. . . . Knowledge is then often experienced as self-evident. Intuition implies a kind of inner "gazing" . . .' (2000: 52). And behind their gentle irony there lies a problem. Eco pithily suggests that 'While it is a principle of hermeneutics that there are no facts, only interpretations. That does not prevent us from asking if there might not perchance be bad interpretations' (1999: 48). Within hermeneutics there are two ways in which there is a legitimation of the hermeneutic approach as a mode of reaching truth. One of these lies in the professionalization of the hermeneutic researcher; the other in the methodic processes through which hermeneutic work is conducted.

PRIVILEGING HERMENEUTICS AS MANIFESTED IN THE PSYCHOANALYTIC ENCOUNTER

Dilthey wrote that 'the final aim of the hermeneutic procedure is to understand the author better than he has understood himself: a proposition which is the necessary consequence of the doctrine of unconscious creation' (1900: 116). One route into this is through the psychoanalytic process. Both hermeneutics and psychoanalysis are concerned with the restoration of meaning (Ricoeur, 1970) both to the researcher (through the development of understanding) and to the subject of research. Habermas took psychoanalysis as the theoretic lens, the pre-understanding through which distorted communication could be explored. At a different level, Ricoeur suggests, both hermeneutics and psychoanalysis are concerned with 'demystification, as a reduction of illusion' (1970: 26).

The alignment of psychoanalytic theory to the hermeneutic spirit, to the German understanding of what Renan (cited in Bettelheim, 1983) called *la science de l'humanité* may be illustrated at three levels. Psychoanalysis provides a theoretical basis for understanding both the objective and subjective aspects of the subject of research. Habermas, for example, suggests that Freud 'dealt with the occurrence of systematically deformed communication in order to define the scope of specifically incomprehensible acts and utterances' (1970: 349). At a second level, psychoanalytic theory provides an account of the relationship between the researcher and the subject of research. The theory of transference and countertransference (see, for example McAuley, 1989) shows how in the relationship the researcher and the subject of research create a relationship that can be explored reflexively by both parties in the situation. At a third level psychoanalysis provides an account of the setting (Malcolm, 1988) in which the hermeneutic research act can be conducted. Habermas characterizes the analytic setting as a 'special design of communication. The fundamental analytic rule . . . ensures a standard relationship . . . which meets quasi-experimental conditions' (1970: 352).

Some of the ways in which the hermeneutic tradition is manifested in the psychoanalytic encounter may be seen in these 'rules of conduct' (cited in Malcolm, 1988: 142). These were distilled by the psychoanalyst Winnicott (1958) from Freud's thinking. The key points, for present purposes, from Winnicott's ideas are in italics. They have been interpreted in relation to undertaking the research act not only for psychoanalytic framework but in the hermeneutic frame generally:

- *The analyst aims to get in touch with the process of the client, to understand the material and to communicate the understanding in words.* There is a key issue here of interpretation and the adequacy of the interpretation to capture and develop the ability to understand the situation. There is, however, additionally in this understanding and communication an emancipatory process whereby it investigates the communication between therapist and client (or in our case researcher and the subject of research) as 'an expression of an unconscious symbol-system' (Giddens, 1982: 86).

- *The analyst's method was one of objective observation*: on the one hand writers in the psychoanalytic tradition such as Bion (1970) write of the need, in the analytic encounter, to be able to suspend memory (for example of previous encounters), desire (for example that the subject 'likes' the researcher), understanding (in the sense of coming to an immediate conclusion) and intuitions that are based on a lay rather than professional understanding of the situation. The development of this objectivity comes, so it is claimed, after years of training and self-insight.

  On the other hand there are those who would claim that, given the nature of the hermeneutic cycle the researcher (whether in human or natural science (Ginev, 1999)) cannot escape from 'socialized pre-understandings . . . there is no observation free from the observer's interpretation based on the presuppositions that derive from their initiation into the 'know how' of a particular socio-historical culture' (Johnson and Duberley, 2000: 66). Contrary to this view, Habermas suggests that the analyst's (researcher's) preunderstanding 'is directed at a small sampling of possible meanings' (1970: 352) – in other words is highly focused and therefore amenable to tight control.

- *The analyst keeps out moral judgement, though he/she should not appear unaware of some universal shock.* What this refers to is that the researcher is not there to make moral judgements about the subjects' values or behaviours. In the case of a morally repugnant encounter the hermeneutic task is to understand what is causing the repugnance in the researcher's own inner life.

- *There is a clear distinction between fact and fantasy, so that the analyst is not hurt by an aggressive dream.* Again, this sounds rather odd – but it is crucial in the hermeneutic research situation. In the transference and countertransference relationship the researcher can sometimes get into a fantasy about the research situation. In the research which is discussed below one of the issues for us was that sometimes one of us would feel that somebody we interviewed was, to put it crudely, either hero – or villain – as we responded to them. This very response became part of our analysis – what was it that made x a villain or y a hero? But we had to be reflectively aware of the response so that we could deal with it, make it part of the analysis rather than a polluting element.

Psychoanalysis is only one of many approaches to the pursuit of hermeneutic truth. Bleicher, for example, suggested that ethnomethodology could be seen as a 'hermeneutically informed study of social phenomena' (1982: 185). Another approach (Riordan, 1995) is to link the hermeneutic tradition, with its potential for 'the idea of dialogue and coercion free communication . . . which would allow values and political commitments to be subjected to critical review' (1995: 12) to the undertaking of action science research in and beyond organizations.

PRIVILEGING HERMENEUTIC TRUTH – ALIGNING HERMENEUTICS TO 'NATURAL' SCIENCE

Although psychoanalysis represents, for the reasons cited, an important approach to hermeneutics there are other ways in which hermeneutics can underpin research activities in organizations. Traditionally, the relationship between hermeneutics and natural sciences has been one of opposition. However one way of making hermeneutics respectable to audiences who find its underpinning philosophical stance difficult to understand as 'proper science' is through what has been called 'objective hermeneutics'. This is an attempt to develop qualitative equivalents to quantitative criteria such as validity, reliability, generalizability and hypothesis testing (Denzin, 1989: 54). Denzin suggests that the hermeneutic approach could establish itself as methodically reputable through the establishment, through statistical means of the sample of subjects of research and the establishment of its representativeness. In objective hermeneutics there would be clarification of the extent to which generalization may be made from the data and the development of hypotheses (although these may well have the status of hunch). Within this approach, issues of truth and objectivity lie within the rigour of application of methodologies in the qualitative tradition. In this sense, scientific truth is represented by the concept of authenticity. The objective aspects are the external features of the subject's life that cannot be changed. In objective hermeneutics validity and adequacy are assessed on the basis of the researcher's ability to give an interpretation and understanding of the ways in which the subject's definitions are produced – the degree of rigorous adherence to the hermeneutic cycle.

This idea of objective hermeneutics is expressed in, for example, Forster (1994) who suggests a seven-stage model for the hermeneutic process. The first step is development of an understanding of the meanings of individual texts (or discourses) – getting to grips with the '"taken for granted" assumptions and viewpoints' of the actors. From this the researcher starts the process of identification of sub-themes, and then at the third stage begins to identify thematic clusters. Forster then discusses the need to triangulate documentary data. This is a 'critical' (1994: 152) stage. He suggests that at this stage what is involved is going back to the original research question. The data provides a commentary on those questions. He then suggests that there is a need to conduct reliability and validity checks. His suggestion is that this can be done through the collaboration of co-researchers to test the interpretation. Another way is to go back to the subjects of the research and test out the interpretation with them. The sixth stage is to recontextualize and retriangulate the data. That is to place the data into the broader context of the organization. Then the final stage is to use 'representative case material' (1994: 151) either in writing up the research or in presentation of research outcomes to clients.

HERMENEUTICS IN ACTION

The author had worked in a polytechnic and then a 'new' university over many years. As an observer of the passing scene (but not a *flaneur*) he had noticed the ways in which that scene was changing – the onset of strategic planning and the emergence of what, in the literature, was referred to as managerialism. He also worked with natural research scientists (employed within research institutes that were under the aegis of research councils) on management development courses. As the 1990s progressed the scientists began to explore topics such as business planning and other manifestations of the managerialist agenda. Their responses to this adventure varied from the dismissive through to the indifferent through to the enthusiastic.

The author's experience of what was happening to himself and within his institution and the experiences of the scientists *seemed* to be intertwined. He began to dream of a research project. A colleague joined me and we developed a project proposal. This had to be cunningly constructed so that although it was within the hermeneutic tradition we had to establish that the study would be rigorous in a more traditional scientific sense. Although we had not encountered it at the time our proposal had something of the shape of objective hermeneutics (Denzin, 1989) discussed above. Our proposal was accepted [2] and a researcher joined us.

Our approach to developing the research was intuitive in the sense that it was based on our own understanding of what it was to employees within a professional organization (McAuley, 1985). We prepared a very approximate list of issues, based on our preunderstanding, of what the issues might be. The preunderstanding was based on our own experience within the university, our understanding of what *at that stage* we had taken as the relevant literature, and the experience of the author in working with research scientists. This preunderstanding has objective and subjective aspects. Our list of issues represented our hunches (McAuley et al., 2000: 95).

In the event we interviewed some 58 scientists. As we did this the issues we discussed changed – some were clearly interesting to the scientists others were not. The interviews were, characteristically, conversations (in some cases therapeutic). There were interesting issues of transference and countertransference as the work progressed. For example some of the interviewees were quite hostile to us, others very friendly. By the same token there were some of the scientists that we engaged with, at emotional and intellectual levels, more than others. These issues were built into our analysis, our developing understanding.

Our analysis was thematic and attempted to reconcile the objective and the subjective both in the subjects of the research and in ourselves. One of the issues we explored (Cohen et al., 2001) was the ways in which the subjects constructed their understanding of what it is to be a scientist. What we found, to express a complex matter very briefly, was that scientists weave their own ways through changing discourses about the nature of science. They make choices in the light of their shared understandings of the nature of science and in the light of their understanding of the traditions of the particular scientific milieu in which they are placed. In conducting the research we started with the individual scientist's understanding, explored that understanding in the light of the understanding of others, and then attempted to understand that in the light of the shared understandings of the pluralist culture in which they live. The objective side is the understanding of the subject of study in its own terms. From our point of view we had to have an understanding of our own objective positions (as reflected in status, role, and so on) in our organizations.

In the research work referred to above (Cohen et al., 2001) it may be doubted that we ever penetrated too deeply into the subjective inner lives of the scientists with whom we worked. At the same time the material we gained from them evoked issues, for them, of the nature of their scientific identity and integrity as scientists. In other words we gained for interpretation a good enough version of their inner lives in relation to the theme under study. We gained an understanding of the inner meanings that they gave to their experience, their lives as scientists. At the same time, we had to examine those subjectivities in the light of our own subjective experience, our own pre-understanding of the situation. Our understanding and analysis arose from the issues they spoke about, the meanings they gave to such topics as the emergent managerialist milieu in which they lived (Cohen et al., 1999a), the relationships between the head office and the institutes (McAuley et al., 2000), the nature and purposes of science (Cohen et al., 2001; Cohen et al., 1999b) and so on.

The interpretative framework we brought to development of understanding of subjective experience was, for the most part, from the symbolic interactionist lens. Thus the understanding we brought to bear was that the members are capable of making their own thoughts and activities objects of analysis both for themselves and for others and that they were able, self-consciously, to direct their own activities. It underpinned our interpretation that social objects (for example, science, management, strategy, and so on) are constructs and that meanings are worked out and negotiated but become stabilized by members (Meltzer et al., 1975). The interpretative framework means that our work is characterized by an understanding that many (but not all) of the scientists that we research engage in shaping external environmental forces in ways that suit their understandings of science, that they are proactive in dealing with the tensions that are part and parcel of their work.

In our work we were trying to keep the hermeneutic faith, even though there were moments when we faltered. We were, in the research, guided by (but not bound by) preunderstandings, intuitions that we were obliged to explore in our development as reflexive researchers. We were engaged in the search for the understandings that members gave to their organizational situations. In order to explore these understandings and develop an analysis of them we used interpretive frameworks that seemed to create a dialogue between the data and the interpretation; the interpretation helped explore the data rather than constrain it. In this way we worked through the hermeneutic circle.

CONCLUSION: THE PRIVILEGED RACONTEUR

Gadamer has this concept of the 'dialectic of experience (which) has its proper fulfilment not in definite knowledge but in the openness to experience that is made possible by experience itself' (1985: 355). Lying at the heart of the hermeneutic approach is this notion of openness to the data, the artful development of the interplay between the intuition of the researcher, the data (text or whatever) of the subjects of study, the interpretive frameworks that are brought to bear on the analysis of the text and, ultimately, the reader. If this openness is undertaken in good faith then the product of the research is an account that is on the one hand truthful (authentic) to the data but is, on the other hand, not the only truth (authentic account) that could be produced. In this overview of hermeneutic understanding we have presented it as a way of approaching research that is based on the notion that research is a human, subjective activity but that this humanity is a crucial resource in the development of understanding.

NOTES

1 The word 'tradition' carries many meanings. In one sense it represents the past as captured in a text. In another sense the word can be used much more widely. It can be a text, or a conversation, or an ethnographic study or interviews that represent a particular group of people or research topic.
2 The author acknowledges support for this research from the Economic and Social Research Council Grant Number R000221639.

FURTHER READING

The chapter on hermeneutics in Alvesson and Sköldberg (2000) is a wide ranging and stimulating overview of the topic, which also asks some challenging questions about the hermeneutic approach. The chapter by Schwandt (2000) also provides an extremely useful overview of hermeneutics and places it into the context of other approaches to qualitative research. Although Gummesson (2000) is not solely concerned with the hermeneutic approach, his book includes a number of accessible insights into hermeneutics as an approach to qualitative methods. The books by Bleicher (1980 and 1982) both represent fine-grained studies of hermeneutics and locate the topic into general preoccupations about the nature of research in the social sciences.

REFERENCES

Alvesson, M. and Sköldberg, K. (2000) *Reflexive Methodology: New Vistas for Qualitative Research*, London: Sage Publications.
Bettelheim, B. (1983) *Freud and Man's Soul*, London: Chatto and Windus.
Bion, W.R. (1970) *Attention and Interpretation*, London: Tavistock.
Blaikie, N. (1993) *Approaches to Social Enquiry*, Cambridge: Polity Press.
Bleicher, J. (1980) *Contemporary Hermeneutics: Hermeneutics as Method, Philosophy and Critique*, London: Routledge and Kegan Paul.

Bleicher, J. (1982) *The Hermeneutic Imagination: Outline of a Positive Critique of Scientism and Sociology*, London: Routledge and Kegan Paul.

Boland, R.J. (1989) 'Beyond the objectivist and the subjectivist: learning to read accounting as text', *Accounting, Organizations and Society*, 14: 5 (6): 591–605.

Cohen, L., Duberley, J.and McAuley, J. (1999a) 'Fuelling discovery or monitoring productivity: research scientists changing perceptions of management', *Organization*, 6 (3): 473–97.

Cohen, L., Duberley, J.and McAuley, J. (1999b) 'The purpose and process of science: contrasting understandings in UK research establishments', *R&D Management*, 29 (3): 233–45.

Cohen, L., McAuley, J. and Duberley, J. (2001) 'Continuity in discontinuity: changing discourses of science in a market economy', *Science, Technology and Human Values*, 26 (2): 145–67.

Dalton, M. (1964) 'Preconceptions and methods in *Men Who Manage*', in P.E. Hammond, *Sociologists at Work: Essays on the Craft of Social Research*, New York: Basic Books Inc.

Denzin, N.K. (1989) *Interpretive Biography*, Newbury Park, CA: Sage Publications.

Dilthey, W. (1900) 'The rise of hermeneutics', in P. Connerton (1976) (ed.), *Critical Sociology*, Harmondsworth: Penguin.

Eco, U. (1999) *Kant and the Platypus*, London: Secker and Warburg.

Ferch, S.R. (2000) 'Meanings of touch and forgiveness: a hermeneutic phenomenological inquiry', *Counseling and Values*, 44 (April):155–73.

Forster, N. (1994) 'The analysis of company documentation', in C. Cassell and G. Symon, *Qualitative Methods in Organizational Research: A Practical Guide*, London: Sage Publications.

Gadamer, H.-G. (1985) *Truth and Method*, second edition, London: Sheed and Ward.

Geertz, C. (1973) *The Interpretation of Cultures: Selected Essays*, New York Basic Books. Reprinted 1993 London: Fontana Press.

Giddens, A. (1982) *Profiles and Critiques in Social Theory*, London: Methuen.

Ginev, D. (1999) 'On the hermeneutic fore-structure of scientific research', *Continental Philosophy Review*, 32: 143–68.

Grondin, J. (1995) *Sources of Hermeneutics*, New York: State University of New York Press.

Gummesson, E. (2000) *Qualitative Methods in Management Research*, second edition, London: Sage.

Habermas, J. (1970) 'Systematically distorted communication', in P. Connerton (ed.) (1976) *Critical Sociology*, Harmondsworth: Penguin.

Johnson, P. and Duberley, J. (2000) *Understanding Management Research: An Introduction to Epistemology*, London: Sage.

Malcolm, J. (1988) *Psychoanalysis: The Impossible Profession*, London: Maresfield Library.

McAuley, J. (1985) 'Hermeneutics as a practical research methodology', *Management Education and Development*, 16 (3): 292–99.

McAuley, M.J. (1989) 'Transference, countertransference and responsibility: their rôle in therapy and consultancy', *Journal of Contemporary Psychotherapy*, 19 (4): 283–87.

McAuley, J., Duberley, J. and Cohen, L. (2000) 'The meaning professionals give to management . . . and strategy', *Human Relations*, 53 (1): 87–117.

Meltzer, B.N., Petras, J.W. and Reynolds, L.T. (1975) *Symbolic Interactionism: Genesis, Varieties and Criticism*, London: Routledge and Kegan Paul.

Phillips, N. and Brown, J.L. (1993) 'Analyzing communications in and around organizations: a critical hermeneutic approach', *Academy of Management Journal*, 36 (6): 1547–76.

Ricoeur, P. (1970) *Freud and Philosophy: An Essay in Interpretation*, New Haven, CT: Yale University Press.

Riordan, P. (1995) 'The philosophy of action science', *Journal of Managerial Psychology*, 10 (6): 6–13.

Saleh, N.M. and Hassan, M.S. (1999) 'Consensus of audit judgment in the post-modern era', *International Journal of Management*, 16 (2): 266–75.

Schwandt, T.A. (2000) 'Three epistemological stances for qualitative enquiry: interpretivism, hermeneutics and social constructionism', in N. K. Denzin and Y. S Lincoln (eds), *Handbook of Qualitative Research*, second edition, Thousand Oaks, CA: Sage.

Strati, A. (1999) *Organization and Aesthetics*, London: Sage.

Thompson, C.J., Locander, W.B. and Pollio, H.R. (1990) 'The lived meaning of free choice: an existential-phenomenological description of everyday consumer experiences of contemporary married women', *Journal of Consumer Research*, 17 (December): 346–61.

Tillery, D. (2001) 'Power, language and professional choices: a hermeneutic approach to teaching technical communication', *Technical Communication Quarterly*, 10 (1): 97–116.

Van Manen, M. (1990) *Researching Lived Experience: Human Science for an Action Sensitive Pedagogy*, London, Canada: Althouse.

Winnicott, D.W. (1958) *Collected Papers: Through Pediatrics to Psychoanalysis*, New York: Basic Books.

Penny Dick

Discourse analysis is concerned with how individuals use language in specific social contexts. There are very many forms of discourse analysis, which range from quite descriptive techniques, aimed at understanding such conventions in speech as 'turn-taking', 'hedges' and grammatical structure, through to more analytic techniques, focused on understanding language use in specific social contexts, such as patient–doctor interactions.

This chapter is concerned with a particular form of discourse analysis, called critical discourse analysis, which shares in common many of the concerns of critical research, as discussed by MacKenzie Davey and Liefooghe, Chapter 15, this volume. It is a method that examines how individuals use language to produce explanations of themselves, their relationships and the world in general. It is critical in the sense that language is not seen as reflecting the *nature* of individuals, of relationships and of the world, but as actively *constructing* these domains. Furthermore, the constructions that are made of these domains are neither incidental nor arbitrary: they have distinct regulatory and ideological functions, and are hence productive of social practice. As a method, therefore, critical discourse analysis is underpinned by a social constructionist epistemology. A key focus is not only on understanding *how* individuals use language to construct themselves and the world, but also on understanding *why* they construct themselves and the world in particular ways. Critical discourse analysis assumes that the constructions individuals make operate not only to 'make sense', but also to reproduce or challenge ideological systems of belief that exist in society at large. Such systems are rarely monolithic but are generally contested. Foucault's work on discourse is used within critical discourse analysis to understand the complexity of ideological systems.

FOUCAULT AND DISCOURSE ANALYSIS ────────────────────────────

Foucault was concerned with knowledge production. In society, what constitutes knowledge is discursive in nature. That is, it is created in language, and is not necessarily related to the discovery of 'truth'. This is particularly the case when dealing with objects in the social world (such as people), but nevertheless applies also to objects in the so-called hard sciences (Mulkay and Gilbert, 1982). Foucault suggests that knowledge production, particularly as it pertains to social objects, is a consequence of the operation of *disciplinary power*.

From a Foucauldian perspective, power is not examined in terms of its properties or source, but in its *modus operandi*, *how* it produces compliance or resistance. Power operates by disciplining individuals, rendering them visible, and making their psychological and physical attributes salient. It is through *discourse* that disciplinary power exerts its effects at the level of the individual. The regulatory effects of discourse occur due to the production of 'normalizing judgements' (Foucault, 1977). That is, discourses *prescribe* appropriate behaviours and attributes across a whole range of social domains. In different epochs, certain domains of behaviour come under the scrutiny of the authorities of that period because they are deemed to be problematic for various reasons. It is when domains are scrutinized that discourses that construct these domains are both identified and produced. An example from Foucault's own work should help make these ideas easier to understand.

In his analysis of sexuality, Foucault (1981, 1988, 1990) argues that the Victorian era saw the attempt to regulate the sexual activity of the population by various authorities including the government and the medical profession. The aim was to confine sexual activity to the legitimate heterosexual couple, in response to a number of problems, including the health of the population, the capacity of the population to engage in economically productive work, and a general concern at the time with moral and physical hygiene. However scrutinizing the population to examine its sexual practices (in the form, for example, of medical and psychiatric interviews) resulted in an explosion of discourses on sexuality produced as a direct consequence of this scrutiny. Thus, far from successfully regulating the sexual activity of the population, the production of a plethora of discourses on sexuality meant that the establishment of 'norms' was impossible.

As this example should make clear, the production of discourse in any social domain is always uncontrollable and unpredictable. The upshot of this is that discourse is never unitary (there are never just one set of norms governing any area of social practice). Because of this non-unitary nature of discourse, disciplinary power never secures complete compliance – there are always alternative discourses available that enable different individuals and groups to resist the regulatory norms in any specific social domain.

Discourses effectively produce different versions of what counts as 'normal' social practice. Thus, at the present time, there are very many discourses that construct the social domain of 'employment', constructing norms of behaviour that are targeted at employees. Any individual employee will come to understand his or her own behaviour as an employee through the discourses that construct that domain. That is, discourses not only construct objects in the social domain – employees in general, but also produce subjects in that domain – I, the employee. Foucault is anti-essentialist. He does not believe that individuals possess innate characteristics. Instead he suggests that discourses make available 'positions' that we can take up in response to our own personal circumstances. Thus for example, being *un*employed is a term that someone might use about themselves if they are not in paid employment. This 'positioning' has distinct effects on how the individual views him or her self, as well as how they feel and act. However, the position 'unemployed' is only available through discourses in which employment is constructed as contributing directly to the economic activity of society (Grint, 1998). In the feudal epoch, this discourse was far less dominant, and therefore the position 'unemployed' with its attendant effects on the identity of the individual was available to relatively few people, and certainly would not have had the meaning (nor effects) that it has today.

THE PRINCIPLES OF CRITICAL DISCOURSE ANALYSIS

Utilizing Foucault's ideas, described above, Fairclough (1992) has developed an extensive and elaborate system of critical discourse analysis. The method set out in this chapter is based on

Fairclough's approach, but also draws on the discourse analytic methods of Hollway (1989) and Mama (1995).

Fairclough (1992) suggests that discourse constitutes the identity of individuals, the relationships between individuals and the ideological systems that exist in society. He refers to these as, respectively, the *identity*, *relational* and *ideational* functions of discourse. In order to identify how discourse constitutes these three domains, Fairclough recommends a three dimensional analytic framework in which discourse is analysed as *text*, as *discursive practice* and as *social practice*.

Text

This analytic level is very similar to that used in more traditional conversation and discourse analysis. The concern is with understanding how a piece of text (either written or spoken) is constructed. The key task for the analyst is to understand what the text is trying to achieve. Is it attempting to assert, persuade, justify, accuse, defend or explain? Fairclough (1992) refers to this as the *force* of the text. The next task is to examine how the text achieves its aims. What words and phrases are used and what propositions (statements that are treated as self-evident 'facts') are being made?

Discursive practice

Discursive practice is the analytic level that examines the *context* of text production. This is a very important level of analysis as it is this which enables the analyst to infer the types of interpretation that might be made of the text or parts of the text. For example, the question 'Do you drink?' is likely to be interpreted entirely differently if the question is asked by a medical doctor than if it is asked by a social science researcher. In turn, the interpretation that is made of the question will then have quite specific consequences on the nature of the text produced. For instance, if the question was asked by a doctor, it might account for the fact the response contains hedges (the question is not answered directly), and an attempt to defend the behaviour ('Only on social occasions').

Social practice

This level of analysis is most closely related to Foucault's ideas on discourse, discussed above. The key focus for the analyst is examining the propositions that are made in the text and the extent to which the text 'gets away with' using a specific proposition without being challenged, or anticipating being challenged. Propositions that are relatively easy to 'get away with' are probably ideological in origin. That is, they are taken from a dominant discourse that is generally taken as 'true'.

Propositions that are challenged or which are defended in the text are examples of *hegemony*, which Fairclough (1992) describes as the process through which contested views of reality are dealt with in order to secure ideological consent. Fairclough (1992) talks about 'hegemonic struggle' as a situation where different ideologies compete for dominance.

It is this dimension that bears most resemblance to Foucault's view of discourse as multiple and contradictory. As already discussed, discourses provide individuals with subject positions. However, because discourse is never unitary there are always alternative positions available that the individual could take up or in which other people could place that individual. The extent to which the text appears to defend or justify the position is an indication of hegemonic struggle (Fairclough, 1992), or more simply a sign that competing discourses exist in that particular domain.

IDENTIFYING DISCOURSES

In addition to analysing text in terms of the three-dimensional framework discussed above, it is useful in some research contexts to identify specific discourses, defined as 'sets of regulated statements' (Henriques et al., 1998) or, 'interpretive repertoires' (Potter and Wetherell, 1987) that are being used to construct certain accounts of reality. Hollway (1989) and Mama (1995) used this process in their work on adult heterosexual relations and the identity of black British females, respectively. More recently, this type of analysis has been applied in organizational settings, to examine the identities of call centre workers (Ball and Wilson, 2000); the career identities of British graduates (Coupland, 2001), and resistance to diversity initiatives in a UK police force (Dick and Cassell, 2002).

Identifying a specific discourse can be a difficult process, not least because of questions over what actually counts as a discourse. Strictly speaking, in critical discourse analysis, the researcher is seeking to identify social constructions that have regulatory effects, and which, to some extent, are presented as self-evident or common sense features of the social domain that is being researched. For example, Dick and Cassell (2002) identified a dominant discourse within a UK police force that was used to construct promotion practices. This discourse constructed promotion practices as being fair and objective, as utilizing job specific criteria to inform decision-making and of being based on principles of equal opportunities. This discourse could be used to construct subject positions. For example, a recently promoted officer could use this discourse to account for their success. Having identified the discourse in use, the text analysis then followed the three dimensional framework proposed by Fairclough to examine the ideological and hegemonic processes that were at play.

It is important that any discourse that is identified has validity. That is, the researcher needs to be able to demonstrate that the discourse exists as a resource within the specific context of the research. This might be achieved by demonstrating its use by a relatively large proportion of the respondents (for example, Ball and Wilson, 2000), by referring to instances of its use in other texts (referred to by Fairclough as *intertextuality*) (for example, Dick and Cassell, 2002); or simply by pointing out its dominance in any specific socio-cultural context (for example, Hollway, 1989). While this notion of validity appears, at face value, at odds with a social constructionist philosophy, it is, in fact, simply concerned with identifying those relative stabilities (Kilduff and Mehra, 1997) in the social domain under exploration. The focus in critical discourse analysis is not to present any such stabilities as objective features of that domain, but to carefully examine how those stabilities are reproduced or changed.

COLLECTING 'TEXT' FOR ANALYSIS

In Fairclough's system, any instance of language use can be used for discourse analysis. In his book, *Discourse and Social Change*, he uses a variety of 'texts' to illustrate his system, including newspaper articles, extracts from health care brochures, and transcripts of conversations. These are 'natural' texts in the sense that they are the products of mundane interactions or everyday text production. However, in the case of organizational research, while there are many opportunities to collect such everyday texts, such as in-house magazines and snatches of conversation, most often the researcher has a specific question in mind and will probably be collecting 'text' in the form of interview data.

Interview data needs to be fully transcribed for analysis. Some discourse analysts recommend the use of special notations to indicate pauses, overlap between speakers, and other paralinguistic features of the text. The method set out in this chapter does not require this amount of detail in the transcription, as the focus for analysis is on content, more than process (see Hollway, 1989 for a further discussion of this issue).

SAMPLE AND SAMPLE SIZE

If collecting text for discourse analysis via interviews, typically only a relatively small sample of respondents will be involved in the study. This is because the focus is on the text, not the individual and because the aim is to provide an in-depth analysis that is focused on explanation, rather than generalization. However, as has already been mentioned, if attempting to identify a specific discourse, it is important to be able to demonstrate that the discourse does exist as a set of regulated statements. If this is to be achieved through examining what respondents say, then it is advisable to use a grounded theory approach to sampling (Glaser and Strauss, 1967).

Thus, for example, if the researcher believed he or she had identified a discourse that was being used to construct a specific version of some particular social object (say nursing practice), he or she would then need to interview a number of other nurses, from different organizational and personal contexts (for example, age, seniority, role, ward type, and so on) in order to identify whether this discourse was also used by individuals in these groups, or whether different discourses were used. The contextual features of the text production can then be used in the analysis to explain any variations thus identified.

Analysing *how* a discourse is used to construct a certain version of reality and explaining *why* it is being used in this way can be carried out on one text or several, depending on the scope and scale of the research. In the application example below, for instance, the analysis is carried out on one extract, though the discourses used in the analysis were identified using a larger sample of 16 participants.

CONDUCTING AN INTERVIEW IN A DISCOURSE ANALYTIC STUDY

In critical discourse analysis, it is vital that the researcher realizes that no matter how informally they present themselves and no matter what their own epistemological stance is to the knowledge production process, the participant is likely to position the researcher according to their own personal beliefs. Simply put, the participant makes a social reading of the interview and the interviewer and this has a fundamental effect on the nature of the data produced, which needs to be accounted for within the analysis. This is illustrated in the application example below.

The use of structured and semi-structured interviews as well as unstructured conversations are all legitimate ways of collecting data for discourse analysis. Which technique is used depends on the nature of the research. Exploratory research looking at an open-ended issue may best be approached using unstructured conversations. In the application example below, the research aim was to explore issues around the management of diversity in the police service in the UK. Unstructured conversations were used to collect the data.

The disadvantage of this technique is that it generates a huge amount of data and transcribing and analysing such a quantity of data is thus very, very time consuming. A useful technique for dealing with this type of data was developed by Hollway (1989) and is called *data sampling*. The researcher initially listens to the taped conversations repeatedly in order to get a feel for what is being said. Once the researcher believes that he or she has identified a specific discourse that is of particular significance to the research aims, he or she transcribes only those parts of the conversation in which that discourse is used. The discourses used by the participant *and* the researcher are attended to.

Structured and semi-structured interviews are more useful where the researcher is interested in examining a specific issue, for example, graduates' career expectations (Coupland, 2001). However, it is important to account for the discourses used by the researcher to construct the interview questions and to build these into the analysis.

APPLICATION EXAMPLE: THE SOCIAL CONSTRUCTION OF POLICE WORK ──────────

Background to the research

The management of diversity within the UK police service is high on the agenda of most forces. Aside from the problem of recruiting and retaining racial minorities, police forces have an additional problem recruiting and retaining female officers. This retention problem makes the achievement of female representation in the senior ranks extremely difficult for most forces.

The key problem in retaining police women is that they tend to leave the job once they have families. This tendency is unproblematically attributed to the difficulties of combining motherhood with full-time police work. The reasons why the two appear incompatible is because policing is generally portrayed as being mainly concerned with crime fighting and as therefore being unpredictable and highly demanding. The practical consequences of this portrayal are that officers need to work a harsh rotating shift system; be prepared to stay on at work at the end of a shift in order to process a crime; and be prepared to be called in to work at very short notice in case of manpower shortage. This portrayal of policing has been subject to considerable debate over the last 20 or so years. Waddington sums this up as follows:

> There is little doubt that the occupational self-image of the police is that of 'crime-fighters' and this is not just a distortion of what they do, it is virtually a collective *delusion*. A mountain of research has indicated that police have little impact on crime rates, are responsible for discovering few crimes and detecting fewer offenders, do not spend much duty-time on crime related tasks and so forth . . . Indeed, it would be as accurate, if not more so, to associate policing with the provision of help and assistance . . . (1999: 299, original emphasis)

If policing is not that demanding and unpredictable, then why are officers so invested in maintaining this portrayal? This is a crucial question, as it is this portrayal that is largely responsible for maintaining the idea that policing is incompatible with motherhood. Using critical discourse analysis enables an examination and explanation of this issue. The application example that follows uses an extract of conversation from a research project that was focused on the position of women in the police. For the sake of brevity, details about the research project are omitted, but a fuller account can be read in Dick and Cassell (forthcoming).

Using the techniques described above in the section entitled 'identifying discourses', two particular discourses were identified that officers routinely used to construct the nature of police work. One of these discourses promoted the view that policing was mainly concerned with crime fighting and that as a consequence it involved a high level of conflict management, the necessity for a reliable team to support officers on the streets, and a high level of commitment from individual officers to the job. The other discourse promoted the view that policing was not about 'force' but about service and as such was mainly concerned with fostering and maintaining good public relations. Both of these discourses are discussed widely in the police literature (for example, Heidensohn, 1992; Morris and Heal, 1981; Reiner, 1992; Waddington, 1999).

Transcripts of the conversations were made whenever these discourses were used by either the participants or the author. This process reduced the data considerably. The data obtained from this process were then subjected to the three dimensional analytic framework discussed above. In the analysis which follows, the discourse that promotes the idea that policing is mainly concerned with crime fighting will be illustrated to show how the idea that policing and motherhood are incompatible is successfully reproduced.

REPRODUCING THE IDEA THAT POLICING AND MOTHERHOOD ARE INCOMPATIBLE ——————

Extract 1 Judy (probationer constable, aged 26)

```
1    Me:    Right. And do you want to go far (in your career)?
2    J:     I don't know, because my attitude's changed somewhat. When I joined
3           I wanted to go up the ladder and get as high as I can. But now, um my
4           values have probably changed and meeting somebody that I've got
5           engaged to and everything..and that I want to spend the rest of my life
6           with and have a family now . . . so it's . . .
7    Me:    You don't see the family and going up the rank structure as compatible?
8    J:     Well . . . we've talked about this and what I've said is...if we have a fam . . .
9           I mean we're going to get married sort of this time next year . . . so it's in
10          the future, after my  probation and everything . . . but what I've said
11          is . . . that I wouldn't mind going back part-time, but not on the beat.
12          Cos I don't think that's fair to my family to have two . . . two parents that
13          are both in a dangerous job . . .
```

APPLYING FAIRCLOUGH'S FRAMEWORK

At the level of *text*, the first question to ask is what is achieved by both of the individuals in this extract? In terms of *force*, therefore, the researcher has produced two accounting situations by implying that Judy ought to have aspirations associated with the modern woman: the desire for a career and the maintenance of that career following marriage and children (lines 1 and 7). In terms of *force*, Judy's response is an attempt to justify her aspirations.

What propositions have been made within the extract? The researcher's propositions are constructed through feminist discourse in which the notion that women should have careers even when they have children is promoted. The dominance of this discourse is indicated by the large number of hedges (statements that are not directly related to the questions asked) Judy makes (all her statements up to line 12 when she answers the question). This suggests that she feels the need to defend her aspirations by providing several lines of justification.

Judy's propositions are constructed through two key discourses. The first is a discourse of family that promotes the idea that the needs of children should be a mother's primary consideration. She imputes her change of aspirations (from initially wanting to climb as high as she could (line 3), to wanting to work part-time (line 11)), to her proposed marriage and family. The proposition here is that young single women are likely to be more career minded than older married women who have children. She justifies her desire to work part-time following the birth of her children by proposing that this will ensure that the children are guaranteed at least one parent (lines 12–13). Again the proposition here is that the mother is the best person to take care of the children.

The second discourse is that which portrays policing as crime fighting and it is this that enables the justification of her desire to work part-time to be both creditable and credible. She says that it is unfair (on the children) to have both parents in a *dangerous* job (line 13). The proposition here is that if both parents worked as full time beat officers then they might be at risk of death or debility, therefore depriving the children of one or both parents. This justification results in a further textual achievement: she persuades the researcher that the reasons for her wish to work part-time are not because she is an 'old-fashioned' woman who believes that a woman's place is in the home, nor because she is 'frightened' of the conflictual nature of police work (a further assertion of her 'modern woman' credentials), but are instead related to her concern for her future offspring.

At the level of *discursive practice* the relationship between the researcher and the participant has effectively produced the accounting situation discussed above. This illustrates the point made earlier about the difficulties of attempting to equalize the power relationship between the researcher and the participant. The large number of hedges in Judy's responses to the researcher's questions – lines 2 to 10 (indicating that Judy is anticipating disapproval from the researcher), and the nature of her justification, suggest that she has positioned the researcher as the more powerful party. The achievement of her self-construction as a modern woman who has a desire to be a 'good' mother, proceeds directly from the nature of the interaction. The researcher has raised the possibility that Judy could be positioned as a lackey to male power, by desiring to drop her career aspirations following the birth of her children.

At the level of *social practice*, there is evidence of *hegemonic struggle* illustrated by the competing ideologies of the feminist and family discourses discussed above. Despite the success (and dominance) of feminist ideology in promoting the idea that women are as entitled to a career as men, the perhaps more dominant ideology, that a woman is the best and 'natural' caregiver to children, competes with this. In the specific context of this extract, the gender of the author, the aims of the research and the nature of the questions asked have resulted in the need for Judy to cut a careful path between the two ideologies, as has been shown. The discourse of policing as crime fighting has enabled her to attribute her desire to work part-time not to any psychological failings of her own, but to the nature of the job itself. Thus at the level of identity, these discourses have enabled Judy to position herself as a modern woman and a good potential mother; at the relational level, she has maintained her credentials within the research relationship; and at the ideational level she has successfully reproduced elements of both feminist and family ideologies, though, as discussed, these two ideologies do compete in terms of their construction of what women's aspirations ought to be.

IMPLICATIONS

What has been achieved in this analysis? First, the analysis has treated the idea that policing *is* crime-fighting as a discourse that performs particular functions in the specific socio-cultural context of both the police institution and the research study itself. Within the specific context of the police institution, this discourse functions in a number of ways. It provides officers with a meaningful identity within a problematic occupation. Despite the fact that the police from their inception were heralded as 'citizens in uniform' (Reiner, 1992), they are able to exercise (or at least have the potential to exercise) coercive authority. The discourse of policing as crime-fighting therefore functions ideologically to legitimate the police to the public, and to themselves (Waddington, 1999). In turn, it justifies the working practices that constitute a key part of the officer's identity: working harsh shifts, working overtime on command, and being available for duty at any time are constructed as signifiers of a committed officer who sees the job as a vocation (Heidensohn, 1992). Within the context of the research study, the discourse has enabled the participant to avoid being positioned by the researcher in ways that might compromise her own identity.

Second, this analysis suggests that the position of women officers could be different. If policing is actually more to do with public service than fighting crime, then not only can the working practices that are accepted as 'normal', be challenged, but also the attributes that are taken as self-evidently essential for police officers can be opened up for scrutiny. Do officers need to be so committed to their jobs that they must subordinate home to work at all times? The increasing numbers of officers taking up part-time work is a site where the discourse of policing as crime-fighting might be most successfully challenged (Dick and Cassell, forthcoming).

Third, this analysis has shown that ideologies about the proper role for women in society are in continual hegemonic struggle. Discourses of family that position women as the best and most natural caregivers of children are disrupted and resisted by feminist discourses that promote women's rights to both career and family. These discourses have to be successfully navigated by women in certain contexts, as positioning the self fully within either can compromise the woman's subjectivity. However, this struggle has changed social practices within policing – the very *availability* of part-time work and job share illustrates this most clearly.

A final, contentious issue, relates to ethics. Some detractors (for example, Reed, 1998) suggest that the sort of approach outlined in this chapter, encourages an 'anything goes' mentality, whereby potentially harmful and certainly unethical 'acts' such as rape or discrimination are dismissed as 'discourses' that lack material reality. This is certainly a worrying criticism. However, proponents of the approach would argue that the existence of discourses that construct certain acts as 'rape' or 'discrimination' illustrate the unpredictable, imprecise and fragmented nature of the operation of disciplinary power. Such discourses have been produced by 'resistance' to social practices that could potentially be constructed as normal or harmless, thus illustrating one of Foucault's central ideas: power is rarely oppressive, but always productive. Critical discourse analysis does not deny a material reality to social practices such as sexual activity, but it suggests that our understanding of such practices is constructed through discourse and is therefore always open to change.

CONCLUSIONS

The key concern of critical discourse analysis is to understand language use as both constructing aspects the world, and as simultaneously reproducing and/or changing these aspects. The focus for analysis is the identification of how this reproduction or change occurs.

The advantage of critical discourse analysis is that it encourages researchers not to accept research data at face value. It takes nothing for granted and indeed is underpinned by the assumption that the world can be different (Burr, 1998). Its chief disadvantage is that it is excessively time consuming and is a technique that requires considerable experience before the researcher feels 'comfortable' with it.

A final point, as discussed in the section above, is that critical discourse analysis is a contentious method. Its social constructionist, and especially Foucauldian underpinnings are the subject of much academic debate and critique (for example, Reed, 1998; Newton, 1998). The 'relativist' criticism is particularly difficult to deal with. One potential ethical issue has already been discussed. However, there is a further, potentially worrying ethical issue. Researchers using critical discourse analysis are often concerned with political issues, seeking to explore situations that oppress or advantage certain groups in society. Not only is there a problem of researchers speaking on behalf of groups that may not perceive themselves to be oppressed or disadvantaged (Burr, 1998), but there is also a further, related problem. In seeking to subvert dominant constructions of reality and the social structures and institutions that are produced through them, there is a danger that the alternative constructions and structures that are produced could subordinate different groups to those whose lot researchers are seeking to improve. These are the sorts of issues that researchers using this method need to be prepared to engage with.

FURTHER READING

For an excellent account of the epistemological and ontological concerns of discourse analysis, see Hollway (1989). See Fairclough (1992) for a detailed account of the analytic framework outlined in this chapter. See Reed (1998) for a wide ranging and thoughtful critique of discourse analytic methods, especially those with a Foucauldian bent.

REFERENCES

Ball, K. and Wilson, D.C. (2000) 'Power, control and computer-based performance monitoring: repertoires, resistance and subjectivities', *Organization Studies*, 21 (3): 539–65.

Burr, V. (1998) 'Overview: realism, relativism, social constructionism', in I. Parker (ed.), *Social Constructionism, Discourse and Realism*, London: Sage.

Coupland, C. (2001) 'Accounting for change: a discourse analysis of graduate trainees' talk of adjustment', *Journal of Management Studies*, 38(8): 1103–19.

Dick, P. and Cassell, C. (2002) 'Barriers to managing diversity in a UK constabulary: the role of discourse', *Journal of Management Studies*, 39(7): 953–76.

Dick, P. and Cassell, C. (forthcoming) 'The position of police women: a discourse analytic study', *Work, Employment and Society*, 18(1).

Fairclough, N. (1992) *Discourse and Social Change*, Cambridge: Polity Press.

Foucault, M. (1977) *Discipline and Punish*, London: Allen Lane.

Foucault, M. (1981) *The History of Sexuality*, volume 1: *The Will to Knowledge*, London: Penguin.

Foucault (1988) *The History of Sexuality*, volume 2: *The Uses of Pleasure*, London: Penguin.

Foucault (1990) *The History of Sexuality*, volume 3: *The Care of the Self*, London: Penguin.

Glaser, B.G. and Strauss, A.L. (1967) *The Discovery of Grounded Theory: Strategies for Qualitative Research*, Chicago: Aldine.

Grint, K. (1998) *The Sociology of Work*, Cambridge: Polity Press (first edition 1991).

Heidensohn, F. (1992) *Women in Control? The Role of Women in Law Enforcement*, Oxford: Clarendon Press.

Henriques, J., Hollway, W., Urwin, C., Venn, C. and Walkerdine, V. (eds) (1998) *Changing the Subject: Psychology, Social Regulation and Subjectivity*, London: Routledge (first edition 1984).

Hollway, W. (1989) *Subjectivity and Method in Psychology*, London: Sage.

Kilduff, M. and Mehra, A. (1997) 'Postmodernism and organizational research', *Academy of Management Review*, 22 (2): 453–81.

Mama, A. (1995) *Beyond the Masks: Gender, Race and Subjectivity*, London: Routledge.

Morris, P. and Heal, K. (1981) *Crime Control and the Police: A Review of Research*, Home Office Research Study No. 67. London: Home Office.

Mulkay, M. and Gilbert, G.N. (1982) 'Accounting for error – how scientists construct their social world when they account for correct and incorrect belief', *Sociology*, 16 (2): 165–83.

Newton, T. (1998) 'Theorizing subjectivity in organizations: the failure of Foucauldian Studies?', *Organization Studies*, 19(3): 415–47.

Potter, J. and Wetherell, M. (1987) *Discourse and Social Psychology: Beyond Attitudes and Behaviour*, London: Sage.

Reed, M. (1998) 'Organizational analysis as discourse analysis: a critique', in D. Grant, T. Keenoy and C. Oswick (eds), *Discourse and Organization*, London: Sage.

Reiner, R. (1992) *The Politics of the Police*, London: Harvester Wheatsheaf (first edition 1985).

Waddington, P.A.J. (1999) 'Police (canteen) sub-culture: an appreciation', *British Journal of Criminology*, 39(2): 287–309.

— **Talk-in-interaction/conversation analysis** ————————

Dalvir Samra-Fredericks

Talk is at the heart of all organizations. Through it, the everyday business of organizations is accomplished. People in organizations talk all day, every day. (Boden, 1994:1)

If we take Chia's (1996) account of a 'postmodern science of organization' seriously, then his declared focus upon 'becoming' centralizes the micro-activities of organizational members interacting. When we observe these interactions what we see or hear is a lot of talk. However, taking naturally occuring talk as a topic for fine-grained analyses remains rare in management/organization studies. One possible reason for this absence may be due to problems in securing access, discussed later. Another reason may be unfamiliarity with approaches for analysing naturally occuring (and recorded) talk. This chapter introduces Conversation Analysis (CA) as one approach for the systematic description/analysis of naturally occuring talk. There is, though, the suggestion that the term CA is a misnomer which has given rise to the term 'talk-in-interaction', hence the title for the chapter (Psathas, 1995: 2; see also Schegloff, 1987), although the shorthand term 'CA' will be used here.

Since the publication of an earlier version of this chapter in 1998, continued interest in language use within the organization/management studies field has begun to explicitly consider CA and ethnomethodology's contribution (for example, see Richards, 2001[1]; also Putnam and Fairhurst's (2001) review chapter). Indeed, as Silverman (2000: 138) contends, both approaches can 'properly claim to be the major contemporary social science traditions oriented to . . . the aesthetics of the mundane', in other words, the everyday lived experiences of members. What this chapter aims to do is to illustrate aspects of CA from my research into the talk of 'managerial elites' (a term applied to senior managers, (non-)executive directors, MDs and CEOs by Pettigrew (1992) and referred to as elites here).

The important point to be emphasized from the outset is that CA is a rigorous and systematic method for examining social interaction (rather than language *per se*). This is easily lost in the belief that it is just about language and thus, a sub-branch of linguistics. The founder of CA, Harvey Sacks (1984: 26)[2], asserted that it was because social organization must be apparent at the level of mundane face-to-face interactions that he turned to conversation. CA, based as it is upon naturally occuring talk, explores 'social phenomena' to discover the form, structure, machinery and methodical procedures (Psathas, 1995) of *social actions*. Ethnostudies such as CA are characterized by a particular disposition to social phenomena and thus, to offer 'instructable features' (Psathas, 1995) for discovery. Analysis and description of talk is problematic since it presumes a range of 'beliefs' or assumptions carried by the researcher about the nature of the social world and the role of talk for its constitution. This inevitably raises problems concerning a neutral 'stand alone' rendering of 'the methods' or techniques of CA. In a simple but quite profound move, what both Garfinkel's (1967) ethnomethodology and Sacks' (1992) CA sought to do was to turn the 'problem of order' upside down. Boden (1994: 65) elaborates by stating that CA seeks to 'answer' an overriding

> question [which] is not one of how people respond to normative constraints, but rather how it is that order is produced as a situated social matter. . . . To understand the profound orderliness of social life requires not aggregation and abstraction but attention to the finegrained details of moment-to-moment existence, and to their temporal, spatial and profoundly sequential organization.

The chapter will consider just one small aspect of the 'moment-to-moment existence' of a group of elites to illustrate the 'hallmarks of all CA', namely, turn-taking. It is just one basic 'method' or procedure used for organizing conversation as a social activity. In addition, given space considerations, the debates between 'pure' and 'applied' CA (ten Have, 1999) or institutional talk (Heritage, 1997) are only briefly considered here together with issues arising from ethnographic fieldwork. Locating where I 'sit' in relation to various issues or concerns and the declared boundaries of CA and other approaches has been a challenge and I must state from the outset that, like Drew (1990: 34), 'I cannot claim to speak in any sense "on behalf of" conversation analysts, some of whom may demur at points I've made, or may have different priorities'.

In my case, to begin to grasp the complex nature of human interaction for 'organizing', I undertake ethnomethodologically informed ethnographic studies of managerial elites at-talk work. Part of the fine-grained analysis of the empirical materials draws upon CA where the focal interest is in the tacit 'methods' or implicit procedures – pauses, assertion, turn-taking, glosses, interruptions and so on – for doing social order/structure. This interest is firmly foundered upon the early CA studies conducted by Sacks (1972) and colleagues which explored the turn-taking system (Sacks et al., 1974), adjacency pairs such as questions/answers and procedures for opening and closing conversations (Schegloff and Sacks, 1973).

THE RESEARCH

My interest in talk and how organizational members go about their daily tasks began in the early 1980s whilst still an undergraduate. Since 1986, I focused upon organizational arenas and thereafter, upon groups of managerial elites. This interest continues today as I seek to understand and describe their basic ethno-methods and conversational/linguistic resources for 'doing social life' as we know it. The chapter will refer to one piece of research conducted into elites' routines and their resources for 'doing' (ethnomethodologically speaking, see Garfinkel, 1967 and Heritage, 1984) strategy in 'real time' and deemed to be a neglected area in management literatures (Samra-Fredericks, 1994, 1996). One central aspect alongside observation or work-shadowing was the audio-recording of everyday interactions such as board level meetings, departmental meetings, audit review sessions, chats in offices, corridors, car parks lifts and, so on as they happened (the only place I did not venture was the men's toilets!). Through doing so, a 'reasonable record' of what happened during a particular 'strip of social life' (Boden, 1994: 65) was made available for repeated access/analysis in order to discern, in my case, which conversational/linguistic resources and forms of knowledge had pragmatic utility for these elites as they sought to shape strategic direction (Samra-Fredericks, 1996, 2003).

The biggest problem was gaining access to such elites. As far back as 1986 initial attempts were made but the companies continued to express reservations since recording in 'real time' was perceived to be too invasive. Finally, after a series of protracted negotiations with another set of companies over several months, high level access was granted to two organizations. Armed with a tape recorder I finally entered the 'field' and as I write this chapter, two further talk-based ethnographies in the 'Technology, Media, Telecoms' sector are nearing their conclusion. In all cases, from just 'being there' over a period of time, elites' interests, goals, likes and dislikes and how they talked and presented themselves more generally was also being noted. It is because of this fieldwork component that the issue of 'transcript-extrinsic data' (Nelson, 1994) arises.

CA, evidence and transcript-extrinsic data

Given CA's 'strong bias against *a priori* speculation about the orientations and motives of speakers' (Heritage, 1984), what CA demands is that the analyst demonstrates that such matters were orientated to by the participants in some way. Yet, to 'warrant' the analysts' inferences and demonstrate how 'contextual' 'facts' are 'connected to a particular conversation' (see Zimmerman, 1988: 418; Jacobs, 1988) remains a challenge. Wieder (1988: 453) has suggested that the process of actual analysis can be seen as one of continually making the 'tacit explicit'. In terms of the analysts' tacit knowledge informing analyses, Zimmerman (1988: 449) adds that the 'initial purchase on some phenomena may be gained on intuitive grounds, but this is merely the beginning'. It is then 'worked up' through a process of searching across a number of conversations. The suggestion is that it is possible, through 'empirical control over inference', for the analyst to support the claim that the participants actually display particular understandings of a conversational event by presenting collections of conversational materials which can be compared. Whilst on one level, this process was broadly adopted in my research (see Samra-Fredericks (1998: 170–1) especially Table 9.1), concerns over CA having positivistic tendencies seem to arise from this apparent emphasis upon rigour/control to 'get at' what really happened, as well as the need for comparisons to warrant the analysts' claims. Inevitably, the indexical properties of language use and speakers' biography of prior dealings complicates matters further.

The inherent philosophical and methodological issues are not easily resolved, but a brief discussion on the role of 'transcript-extrinsic data' (Nelson, 1994) is called for. Moerman (1988) demonstrated that to identify and account for an action (during a turn at talk) we sometimes need to know speakers' intentions and this may have to be gleaned from 'transcript-extrinsic data'. Here, ethnography would provide the researcher with a 'local knowledge' (Geertz, 1993) which 'fills in' the gaps which is what speakers routinely do anyway. It is where participants' prior dealings or experiences do provide a 'frame' or a set of background expectancies which furnish meanings, knowledge about another's interests and so on and which are not always readily apparent or available to the analyst who is primarily focused upon 'transcript-intrinsic data'. Garfinkel's (1967) studies also showed that shared knowledges/experiences result in many things being left unsaid but known. I felt that access to this 'knowing' required immersion in the elites' everyday lived experiences. Consequently, I agree that:

[f]ixedness on the page and in collections [of segments of talk] must not make us forget the emergent and prospective character of talk . . . Turns, repairs . . . – all units of conversation analysis – are the locally occasioned products of ongoing interactive work: contingent, negotiated, defeasible, prospective . . . and always thoroughly, personally, and meaningfully contexted. When conversation analysis loses sight of this, it misleads us about those units and about processes of interaction. (Moerman, 1988: 46)

My purpose here is not to identify a 'flaw' in CA but to recognize the issues and challenges that face us *all* as social scientists. Recently, Alvesson and Karreman (2000) specifically proposed that the 'linguistic turn' within the social sciences for organizational analysis demands that we are able to defend three types of 'claims' crystallizing into an approach they term 'discursive pragmatism'. Fundamentally, one of these claims is foundered upon 'the level of talk' which demands 'conversational evidence' (2000: 147). It is here that the CA approach is, indeed, exemplary. The other two claims to be defended are at the 'level of practice with observational evidence' and the 'level of meaning with ethnographic evidence'. The crucial point is that analytical depth may be provided for through ethnographic evidence, but to 'answer basic questions about *how* people are constituting that setting through their talk' (Silverman, 1997: 15), approaches such as CA are called for, whilst also recognizing that they give rise to various practical issues.

Practical issues

The tape recordings of elites' talk-based routines were collected over a period of time with numerous reassurances of confidentiality and minimal disruption. I also soon discovered that the significance of the 'task' (for example, a sudden product failure in the market place mid-way through the research) was greater than any interest in me. In other words, the need to monitor their talk because of my presence was over-ridden by a need to track the conversation as a participant and to determine the implications (for them and their functions) of what was being 'done' as they talked. Furthermore, whilst entering the 'organization' and recording the talk for a relatively young woman, whose ethnic origins were 'unclear' posed some problems (and interest) – they were overcome as time progressed (Samra-Fredericks, 1995).

While it was also important to state that confidentiality and anonymity would be maintained, if any individual wanted an analysis or interpretation of their 'performance', then I would have provided that. I also emphasized that no one person was to glean 'information' (my interpretations) about any other person. I felt that this stance was important in order to build trust and to establish a clear and honest mode of operation since I would be 'in and out' of the organization over many months to come. They also expected to be consulted if and when the 'findings' were to be made public (published) – for example, prior to presenting at an international conference examples of what the transcribed talk would 'look/read like' in a conference paper were provided. It showed that all references to the organization, individuals or products and so on had been removed. All the tapes are coded and whilst I have played parts of the tapes to fellow academics and researchers in various settings, they are carefully selected so that any identifiable features are not voiced at that time. So, having collected an extensive set of recordings, what next?

Transcription

Transcribing any spoken 'text' is a time-consuming activity and this was multiplied many times since I was dealing with multi-party talk as opposed to two-person interviews. Equally, in terms of CA, the level of detail transcribed is demanding.[3] It is the intricacies of interaction and not just the 'content' of what is said that must be transcribed. In addition, as both Fairclough (1992) and Psathas (1995) observe, it is the objectives of the research which guides the employment of particular symbols or system of notations. Fairclough adds that depending upon the system of transcription it may 'take anything from six to twenty-hours or more to transcribe one hour of recorded speech' (1992: 229). Furthermore, recording clarity and the passion with which the elites spoke all impacted upon the hours invested to transcribe the talk. A foot and headset transcriber assisted the transformation of the talk into the written format as the tapes could be slowed down so that inaudible speech could be discerned. Yet, even then there were occasions where there were difficulties in discerning the utterance (Psathas, 1995; Psathas and Anderson, 1990). Analysts working with talk also acknowledge that the 'status of the transcript remains that of "merely" being a representation of the actual interaction' and that 'it is not the interaction and it is not the "data"' (Psathas and Anderson, 1990: 77; Zimmerman, 1988).

The transcripts generated from this particular company recorded false starts, hesitations and interruptions. However, and this is an important point which does *not* conform to CA, pauses were not recorded as tenths of seconds but were divided into two types: first, a short pause (less than a second) was marked by '(.)' in the transcript; and secondly, a longer pause (more than a second) represented as '[brief pause]'. This level of transcription detail varies from both CA studies where pauses are timed in a split-second fashion (Jefferson, 1989; Psathas and Anderson, 1990) and from those studies which include organizational talk (for example, Forester, 1992; Knights and Willmott, 1992; Mangham, 1986) but where pauses are not noted and/or timed at all. Whilst there are various transcription systems in use which encompass features such as laughter, coughs, tempo, intonation and so on, Psathas and Anderson (1990) offer a short but informed introduction to transcription generally. The key features to facilitate the reading of the transcripts here can be found in the Appendix (p.224).

In terms of the manufacturing company study, then, over a two-year period I repeatedly listened to the tape recordings (termed 'methodical listenings' – Psathas and Anderson, 1990), generated transcripts and sought to understand how social order is produced, decisions are made, meetings realized, role-identities assembled and 'organization' (re)created (one visual representation of this process is found in Samra-Fredericks, 1998: 170). Given the interest in how elites 'do' strategy when face-meets-face, talk recorded during the monthly day-long executive meetings, for example, was one type of bounded event selected for detailed analysis.[4] And one part of this overall analytical effort employed CA with details of other analytical routes outlined elsewhere (Samra-Fredericks, 1994, 1996, 2000, 2003). Inevitably only a minute proportion of the empirical materials (three brief extracts) are reproduced here and the discussion is further confined to illustrating the 'hallmark' of CA, namely, the taking of turns.

Illustrating conversation analysis

The analysis of elites' talk could not avoid turn-taking since it is the 'most fundamental unit of social action' which 'provide[s] a simple, economic and extraordinarily efficient way of allocating activities' (Boden, 1994: 66). Taking a turn at talk is so taken-for-granted that its close study may at first appear trivial and mundane. The turn-taking system initially forwarded by Sacks et al. (1974) was one where: one speaker speaks at a time; number and order of speakers vary freely; turn size varies; turn transition is frequent and quick; and there are few gaps and few overlaps in turn transition (see Boden, 1994: 67; Boden and Zimmerman, 1991: 9; Heritage, 1997: 163–73). Subsequent research in institutional settings has noted variants to this system – for example, in courtrooms, doctor/patient and teacher/pupil interactions (Atkinson and Drew, 1979; Atkinson, 1982; Greatbatch, 1992; Heritage, 1989; Mehan, 1979) where through taking specific types of turns, institutional identities are instantiated.

In terms of the elites' talk, Boden (1994) notes a variation in turn-taking for 'pacing topics' and 'spacing speakers' which the formal setting of the boardroom/TMT meetings also confirmed. It was where the ability to mitigate an interruption and/or to be able to suspend the 'normal' features of the turn-taking system through securing an extended turn (for example, by prefacing one's utterance through 'just three things/concerns/issues . . . ' and so on) were crucial 'methods' for 'pacing and spacing speakers' and more significantly, for framing others' attention. The three brief extracts reproduced here will simply illustrate the broad parameters of the turn-taking 'system' which characterized aspects of the formal boardroom/TMT meetings. The speakers are: managing director (MD), finance director (FD), sales and marketing director (SMD), quality manager (QM), purchasing manager (PM) and operations director (OD). Our focus will remain with the MD for analytical purposes whilst remembering that others are vital for instantiating roles and identities and 'organization'.

Extract 1

MD: OK [name of FD] do you want to take us through=
FD: =yes ok well the April results urm (.) UK operations . . .
    . . . [cont.]

Extract 2

MD: right [name of Qual Mgr]
SMD: ok =
MD: =you are on (.)
QM: right=
MD: =BS5750

Extract 3

MD: so (.) bit of a culture shock that I think [quietly spoken] err are we missing somebody?
    [brief pause]
SMD: =[no   [name of QM]
PM: =[no er [name of QM] was [er
L5 MD: [oh OK yeah fine 'Attendu'
FD: yeah=
MD: =you all got it
FD: um=
OD: =yep
[pause as they locate their copy amongst their papers and find appropriate pages]
L10 MD: err what we tried to do in that document is really to say . . . .
    . . . [cont.]

In extracts 1 and 2 the MD selects next speaker given the next item on the formal agenda. Overall, the agenda (circulated prior to the meeting) dictated the sequence of the topics or items discussed but transgression occurred if relevance could be (skilfully) demonstrated. In extract 1, the 'well' uttered by the FD in response to the MD's invitation to talk is an example of a 'pause marker' (Fraser, 1990; Schiffrin, 1987). This function has been differentiated from the use of 'well' as a turn-initial marker signalling forthcoming dissonance which became apparent during the conflictual encounters (Samra-Fredericks, 2003). In extract 2, the SMD's inserted 'OK' concludes a preceding extended turn by him and acknowledges the MD's right to move onto the next item/topic (at line 1 by naming the next speaker). In extract 3, after 'so' (line 1) the MD signals his move as concluding the preceding 'presentation' on securing quality standards.[5] The MD continues by 'self selecting' (line 5) but he still needs to 'tie' his talk to this agenda, announced through 'Attendu' (line 5, the budget). In this way, he 'marks' his talk as that of being a participant/presenter of an item. In other words he simply moves from one who regulates others' turns to one who is a participant and whose forthcoming talk was characterized by 'information dissemination' (not reproduced here).

It is also noteworthy that for the formal status of the meeting to continue particular individuals did need to be present. Here, for example, at line 2 in extract 3, the MD asks who is missing. Boden (1994: 89) observes that 'the essence of membership is marked by some kind of listing display' or the 'presence of a quorum' which is important if the meetings are to be organizationally and interactionally meaningful. Here, the absence of the QM is implicitly accounted for (it is shared knowledge, 'picked up' by the researcher from 'hanging around', where once an item has been presented/discussed by a senior manager, he may leave). Extract 3 also illustrates another feature of their talk. At line 10, the MD begins by stating – 'what we tried to do in that document is really to say . . . ' and through doing so, he implicitly ties prior talk-based events to the present. This is an important re-occuring feature for 'organizing' (Weick, 1979: also having links to Garfinkel's (1967) notion of prospective-retrospective mode of reasoning). The simple selection of 'we' against that of 'I' has also been subjected to detailed analysis by CA scholars (for example, see Drew and Sorjonen (1997) on personal pronouns and institutional identities; Samra-Fredericks, 2000). In this particular instance, the 'we' invokes a collective entity – 'an operating board' – who had apparently agreed to what was documented in writing before them. Given this initial 'staging' from line 10 onwards the MD secured an extended turn to select and reformulate the important parts of the budget. The listeners then tracked the 'multiplicity of conversational objects' (assessments, invitations to agree/disagree, to confirm and so on, (Boden, 1994) that followed.

Recognizing that these three extracts are too brief to illustrate the multitude of ways orderliness was achieved as well as numerous other features worthy of close analysis, what can be stated is that in the formal meetings there was an adjustment to the basic model of conversational turn-taking proposed by Sacks et al. (1974). It was where the initial allocation of turns was undertaken by the MD and in selecting the next speaker (director or senior manager), extended monologues were also expected. On only one occasion did I see an organizational member attempt to formally 'go through' the chair (the MD) although turns did regularly revolve back to him. The monologues, as a technical departure from the system proposed by Sacks et al. (1974), were 'warranted' as they made reports, statements and assessments about the state of the company and competitors. Interestingly, what Boden (1994) noted and was confirmed in my analysis of elites at-talk, was that during the routine long turns they also accomplished 'stories' and used them to 'construct positions and realize agendas' very much like in the courts or plea-bargaining settings (Maynard, 1984).

In contrast, during the 'discussion phase' (Bargiela-Chiappini and Harris, 1997), characterized by short economical turns secured through self-selection, Sacks et al.'s basic model appeared to be adhered to. Sacks et al. (1974) also note that as each speaker takes a turn they do have recipients in mind and listeners are 'motivated to "hear" a turn that is for them'. Boden (1994: 71) suggests that this gives 'talk its rather syncopated and agreeably collaborative quality' and in this manufacturing company, was characterized by interruption and 'latching on' (glimpsed in Samra-Fredericks (1998) together with the embedded use of adjacency pairs and the routine invoking of typified schema (Berger and Luckmann, 1967) to constitute a shared world). Given space considerations, other features of the turn-taking system not illustrated here was that departures from established procedures were always marked in some way. Even the MD marked his interruptions and waited to be granted a turn. Indeed, through consistently saying 'hang on hang on' as a turn-entry device during the conflictual encounters, he slowed down the turn-over in speakers and through doing so was deemed to not only instantiate his 'role' as 'chair', but also 'fine-tune' it to constitute neutrality (Samra-Fredericks, 1996).

TAKING A TURN TO TALK AND INSTANTIATING INSTITUTIONAL IDENTITIES ——————————

Theorizing speakers' 'role' or identity as constituted through talk is problematic for some CA scholars and space considerations mean that only a brief comment is possible here. Heritage (1989) observes that studies of institutional talk recognize that the 'creation and maintenance of institutional roles is ultimately realized through specific sequences of conversational actions' (1989: 36; Drew, 1990: 32; Drew and Heritage, 1992; Heritage, 1997). But there are critics. For example, Psathas (1995) has strongly warned against formulations that employ the 'vocabularies and theoretical perspectives' of organizational sociology such as roles, status, authority and so on. So what about my own study where the analysis of talk is elaborated against the more traditional sociological and organizational concepts? What remains crucial is that the status of speakers is not assumed to 'dictate the talk' although 'discourse identities and institutional roles . . . [were] surely instantiated *through* talk' (Boden, 1994: 77). In such cases, the challenge is to demonstrate that analyses of 'institutional interaction . . . demonstrate in the details of conduct, the "normatively oriented-to" (Heritage, 1984; Psathas, 1999) or interactionally relevant identities' (Boden and Zimmerman, 1991: 13) of speakers.[6]

In some settings clear statements concerning the types of turns available to particular speakers and the instantiation of an 'institutional identity' is possible. One example is news interviews where speakers confine themselves to asking or responding to questions (Greatbatch, 1992). Studies of court room questioning also confirm that, because of the types of turns available to professionals and witnesses, particular roles/identities are instantiated. Through the 'known-in-common' pre-allocation of specific types of turns to particular participants, some speakers (interviewer, lawyer, teacher and doctor) primarily ask questions and others provide answers (interviewee, witness, pupil, patient, for example, Atkinson and Drew, 1979; see also Dillon, 1990; Drew, 1992; Harris, 1995; Fisher and Todd, 1986). Through this initial deployment of such basic 'methods' or procedures speakers accomplish or 'talk into being' (Heritage, 1989, 1997) both institution and the identities of its representatives.

In my study of elites, though, the way in which the institutional context was recursively evoked and maintained through their talk was found to be more fluid and difficult to categorize into neat communication formats. In other words, identifying a relationship between roles/identities and tasks and the discursive rights and obligations (for example, the use of the turn-taking system) was not possible. These elites were not constrained by the types of turns taken and thus, unlike other CA studies, their organizational identities were not so easily assembled from the types of turns taken. The only role that appeared to necessitate 'occasioned obligation' (Goffman, 1983: 7) in any clear way was that of the 'chair' (the MD) and whilst limited, the three extracts do enable us to *begin* to glimpse how this was an 'achieved phenomenon'.[7]

SO . . ., TO BE OR NOT TO BE A CA SCHOLAR – CONCLUDING COMMENTS ────────

My prime objective here was to introduce CA/talk-in-interaction through a focus upon its central hallmark – the general parameters of the localized turn-taking system. Yet, this has not been a simple task knowing the CA stance and the issues, concerns, misunderstandings and debates it has generated since its inception. Indeed, shortly after the 1998 version of this chapter was published, a colleague who would describe themselves as working from the interpretive tradition exclaimed, 'you're not CA are you?!' What underpinned this outburst was a general and vague notion that CA has 'positivist' leanings, 'doesn't it?' This is a fundamental misunderstanding of much of CA studies, but in some ways understandable too. It is because of CA's emphasis upon: formal and systematic analysis; the need to demonstrate that 'extra-linguistic' features are relevant for, or orientated to by the participants in some way and evident in their talk, and; the explication of generic organization of practices, for example, the turn-taking 'model', that such beliefs and concerns have arisen. Yet, as one of the original founders of the turn-taking model (Sacks et al., 1974), Schegloff (1999: 415) explicitly stated, those who are critical of CA are 'mistaken' in thinking it 'entail[s] a systematic inattention to the contextual specifics and the lived reality of the events being examined – a kind of dry and scientist academicism'. He continues by stating that

> 'formal' accounts are like an inventory of tools, materials and know-how from which practicing research analysts can draw for their analytic undertakings because practicing *interactants* draw on them in concertedly constructing and grasping what transpires in interaction . . . .(Schegloff, 1999: 415)

In other words, and for example in relation to the turn-taking model considered here, there is available a systematic approach and an analytical tool or framework for examining how interactants deploy aspects of the model and make it work for them (given their goals and interests). It is the activities that get done therein that underlays the interest in the model and this orientation has revealed significant variation in institutional settings as noted in the prior section, enabling some understanding of how pre-allocation of turns, normatively invoked, instantiate institutional identities.

Disagreements over whether CA has 'positivist' tendencies removing it from ethnomethodology's 'phenomenological orientation' (Lynch, 2000a: 517) continue, but as the ethnomethodologist Lynch (2000b: 541) in a reply to Sharrock (2000) concluded, '(. . . our) differences with conversation analysis are embedded in long-standing respect for its achievements'.[8] I agree and CA continues to widen its net and challenge prevailing orthodoxies (Maynard and Clayman, 1991). Correspondingly, though, CA is challenged by those who move beyond 'transcript-intrinsic data'. The value and potential of 'transcript-extrinsic data' needs to be continuously and carefully considered and this chapter has sought to raise awareness on this issue. Moerman ((1988); see also Alvesson and Karreman, 2000; Miller, 1997) in particular mapped out the ground for those who see themselves, as I do, drawing upon both CA and the ethnographic traditions. When 'in the field' and listening to groups of elites, their goals, intentions and biographies of prior dealings inevitably adds further complexity to any fine-grained analyses of their talk. It is where

we never merely exchange turns of talk. In all conversation, people are living their lives, performing their roles, enacting their culture. The motives and meaning of talk are thick with culture. (Moerman, 1988: 22)

Yet, CA does have 'some promise of precisely locating and describing . . . how the experienced moments of social life are constructed, how the ongoing operation of the social order is organized' (Moerman, 1988: xi; also Nelson, 1994: 315; Silverman, 1997). This explains my move to CA and in part answers the question, 'to be or not to be a CA scholar?' If the interest is in the intricate and dynamic ways human beings skilfully deploy their forms of everyday knowledges and basic ethnomethods to simultaneously accomplish work tasks, identities and organization, then CA is indeed one rigorous and systematic approach, notwithstanding the debates and concerns touched upon here. It takes us beyond the classic studies of managers-at-work (for example, Mintzberg, 1973; Kotter, 1982) which rightly observed that talk was the most pervasive and noticeable feature of managerial work. My own research placed talk centre stage as a 'topic' for analysis in order to discern how elites do strategy, realize social and political relations of one sort or another whilst simultaneously co-constructing an artefact – the 'strategy document' handed to me during my 12 months in and out of this company. Yet, these same documents continued to be subject to re-interpretation and were made relevant or irrelevant during subsequent talk-in-interactions, all of which resided upon knowing and being able to, for example, suspend or stretch the 'normal' parameters of something so taken-for-granted and seemingly trivial as the turn-taking system.

NOTES

1 A conference on 'Ethnomethodology – a Critical Celebration' (2002) took place at the Management School, Essex.
2 Sacks sadly died in 1975, one year after his (and colleagues') landmark publication of *A simplest systematics* . . . (1974). Sacks' unpublished lectures from the mid-1960s to the early 1970s have been collected together and edited by Jefferson under Sacks (1992).
3 The various notation symbols to assist the transcription of different features of speech such as intonation, stress, pauses, tempo, overlap and so on have been added to since the original system developed by Jefferson (see Sacks et al., 1974; and also Atkinson and Heritage, 1984; Drew and Heritage, 1992; Boden, 1994; Psathas and Anderson, 1990; also Zimmerman, 1988: 413–5). The symbols seek to capture numerous phenomena that organize conversation.

4 Zimmerman (1988: 413) noted that tapes of conversation are 'not usually collected for specific purposes' enabling the means for 'encountering otherwise unnoticed features of talk'.

5 *So* signals 'of result' (Fraser, 1990) which Boden (1994: 96) notes is a standard topic transition marker.

6 More recently, Psathas (1999) discusses how Sacks' (1992) notion of membership categorization devices (MCDs) provide for a rigorous and systematic study of social structure or 'talk in institutional settings' whilst meeting Schegloff's insistence on the analyst demonstrating relevance. One example from my own research would be references to MCDs such as 'accountant' (Samra-Fredericks, 2003).

7 Heritage (1997: 164) further assists those interested in close studies of the local instantiation of institutional identity through outlining 'six basic places to probe the "institutionality" of interaction'. They are: turn taking; overall structural organization; sequence organization; turn design; lexical choice; epistemological and other forms of asymmetry.

8 What Lynch (2000b: 542) feels is missing within CA today is a development of Sacks' legacy in terms of the various topics which were 'animated by a radical vision of social order and scientific methodology'. Topics such as the 'narrative and sequential design of stories and jokes', 'poetics and punning as organizational resources', the 'pragmatics of proverbial expressions', 'categorizing', 'moral orders', etc.

APPENDIX

[	indicates overlapping/interrupted [speech [speech
=[	indicates simultaneous speech
(.)	indicates a brief pause (not consistent with CA)
=	continuous speech where speakers's utterance latches onto= =previous speaker's speech
::	elon::gated pronunciation of that word
italics	indicate emphasis
[word(s)]	indicate transcriptionist doubt and will say [inaudible] or state that the speech referred to either: the actual names of actors, or the organization, or the products, or to financial figures [to ensure confidentiality]

FURTHER READING

For a concise introduction to CA/talk-in-interaction with examples from empirical research set alongside the debates surrounding its phenomenological 'roots', see Boden (1994); Drew and Heritage (1992); Heritage (1984); Hutchby and Wooffitt (2001); Lynch (2000a, 2000b); Psathas (1995); Silverman (1998); ten Have (1999); van Dijk (1997). To appreciate the issues, concerns and points of contention between 'pure' CA scholars and ethnographers see Moerman (1988, 1992) and Nelson (1994). Both Alvesson and Karreman (2000) and Miller (1997) also address this issue more broadly. They both highlight the overlaps and gains to be made through a systematic study of naturally occuring talk while taking account of the ethnographic context to facilitate interpretation. In addition, given that some readers may be interested in or familiar with critical discourse analysis, the exchange between Schegloff (1997, 1998) and Wetherell (1998) would be a useful starting point for discerning the core points of contention, but also where overlaps may be located.

REFERENCES

Alvesson, M. and Karreman, D. (2000) 'Taking the linguistic turn in organizational research, challenges, responses, consequences', *The Journal of Applied Behavioural Science*, 36 (2): 136–58.

Atkinson, J.M. (1982) 'Understanding formality: notes on the categorization and production of "formal" interaction', *British Journal of Sociology*, 33: 86–117.

Atkinson, J.M. and Drew, P. (1979) *Order in Court: The Organization of Verbal Interaction in Judicial Settings*, London: Macmillan.

Atkinson, M. and Heritage, J. (1984) (eds) *Structures of Social Action, Studies in Conversation Analysis*, Cambridge: Cambridge University Press.

Bargiela-Chiappini, F. and Harris, S. (1997) *Managing Language – The Discourse of Corporate Meetings*, Amsterdam and Philadelphia: Benjamin.

Berger, P. and Luckmann, T. (1967, reprint 1985) *The Social Construction of Reality*, Harmondsworth: Penguin.

Boden, D. (1994) *The Business of Talk*, Cambridge: Polity.

Boden, D. and Zimmerman, D.H. (1991) (eds) *Talk and Social Structure: Studies in Ethnomethodology and Conversation Analysis*, Cambridge: Polity.

Chia, R. (1996) 'The problem of reflexivity in organizational research: towards a postmodern science of organization', *Organization*, 3 (1): 31–59.

Dillon, J.T. (1990) *The Practice of Questioning*, London: Routledge.

Drew.P. (1990) 'Conversation analysis: who needs it?', *Text*, 10: 27–35.

Drew, P. (1992) 'Contested evidence in courtroom cross examination: the case of a trial for rape', in P. Drew and J. Heritage (eds), *Talk at Work – Interaction in Institutional Settings*, Cambridge: Cambridge University Press.

Drew, P. and Heritage, J. (1992) (eds) *Talk at Work – Interaction in Institutional Settings*, Cambridge: Cambridge University Press.

Drew, P. and Sorjonen, M.L. (1997) 'Institutional dialogue', in T.A. van Dijk (ed.), *Discourse as Social Interaction. Discourse Studies: A Multidisciplinary Introduction*, vol. 2, London: Sage.

Fairclough, N. (1992) *Discourse and Social Change*, Oxford/Cambridge: Polity Press/Basil Blackwell.

Fisher, S. and Todd, A.D. (eds) (1986) *Discourse and Institutional Authority, Medicine, Education and Law*, Norwood, NJ: Ablex.

Forester, J. (1992) 'Critical ethnography; on fieldwork in a Habermasian way', in M. Alvesson and H. Willmott (eds), *Critical Management Studies*, London: Sage.

Fraser, B. (1990) 'An approach to discourse markers', *Journal of Pragmatics*, 14: 383–95.

Garfinkel, H. (1967) *Studies in Ethnomethodology*, Englewood Cliffs, NJ: Prentice Hall, paperback edition 1984: *Studies in Ethnomethodology*, Cambridge: Polity Press.

Geertz, C. (1993) *Local Knowledge*, London: Fontana Press.

Goffman, E. (1983) 'The interaction order', *American Sociological Review*, 48: 1–17.

Greatbatch, D. (1992) 'On the management of disagreement between news interviewees', in P. Drew and J. Heritage (eds), *Talk at Work – Interaction in Institutional Settings*, Cambridge: Cambridge University Press.

Harris, S. (1995) 'Pragmatics and power', *Journal of Pragmatics*, 23: 117–35.

Heritage, J. (1984) *Garfinkel and Ethnomethodology*, Cambridge: Polity Press.

Heritage, J. (1989) 'Current developments in conversation analysis', in D. Roger and P. Bull (eds), *Conversation: An Interdisciplinary Perspective*, Clevedon: Multilingual Matters.

Heritage, J. (1997) 'Conversational analysis and institutional talk: analysing data', in D. Silverman (ed.), *Qualitative Research: Theory, Method and Practice*, London: Sage.

Hutchby, I. and Wooffitt, R. (2001) *Conversation Analysis, Principles, Practices and Applications*, Cambridge: Polity Press.

Jacobs, C. (1988) 'Evidence and inference in conversation analysis', in J.A. Anderson (ed.), *Communication Yearbook II*, California: Sage.

Jefferson, G. (1989) 'Preliminary notes on a possible metric which provides for a "standard maximum" silence of approximately one second in conversation', in D. Roger and P. Bull (eds), *Conversation: An Interdisciplinary Perspective*, Clevedon: Multilingual Matters.

Knights, D. and Willmott, H. (1992) 'Conceptualising leadership processes: a study of senior managers in a financial services company', *Journal of Management Studies*, 29 (6): 761–82.

Kotter, J.P. (1982) *The General Manager*, New York: Free Press.

Lynch, M. (2000a) 'The ethnomethodological foundations of conversation analysis', *Text*, 20 (4): 517–32.

Lynch, M. (2000b) 'Response to Wes Sharrock', *Text*, 20 (4): 541–44.

Mangham, I.L. (1986) *Power and Performance in Organizations. An Exploration of Executive Process*, Oxford: Basil Blackwell.

Maynard, D.W. (1984) *Inside Plea Bargaining: The Language of Negotiation*, New York: Plenum Press.

Maynard, D.W. and Clayman, S.E. (1991) 'The diversity of ethnomethodology', *Annual Review of Sociology*, 17: 385–418.

Mehan, H. (1979) *Learning Lessons: Social Organization in the Classroom*, Cambridge, MA: Harvard University Press.

Miller, G. (1997) 'Toward ethnographies of institutional discourse: proposal and suggestions', in G. Miller and R. Dingwall (eds), *Context and Method in Qualitative Research*, London: Sage.

Mintzberg, H. (1973) *The Nature of Managerial Work*, New York: Harper and Row.

Moerman, M. (1988) *Talking Culture*, Philadelphia: University of Pennsylvania Press.

Moerman, M. (1992) 'Life after CA: an ethnographer's autobiography', in G. Watson and R.M. Seiler (eds), *Text in Context*, Newbury Park, CA: Sage.

Nelson, C.K. (1994) 'Ethnomethodological positions on the use of ethnographic data in conversation analytic research', *Journal of Contemporary Ethnography*, 23 (3): 307–29.

Pettigrew, A. (1992) 'On studying managerial elites', *Strategic Management Journal*, winter special edition, 13: 163–82.

Psathas, G. and Anderson, T. (1990) 'The "practices" of transcription in conversation analysis', *Semiotica*, 78: 75–99.

Psathas, G. (1995) '*Conversation Analysis, The Study of Talk-in-Interaction*', Qualitative research methods series 35, California: Sage.

Psathas, G. (1999) 'Studying the organization in action: membership categorization and interaction analysis', *Human Studies*, 22: 139–62.

Putnam, L.L. and Fairhurst, G.T. (2001) 'Discourse analysis in organizations. Issues and concerns', in F.M. Jablin and L. Putnam (eds), *The New Handbook of Organizational Communication: Advances in Theory, Research and Methods*, Newbury Park, CA: Sage.

Richards, D.S. (2001) 'Talking sense: ethnomethodology, postmodernism and practical action', in R. Westwood and S. Linstead (eds), *The Language of Organization*, London: Sage.

Sacks, H., Schegloff, E. and Jefferson, G. (1974) 'A simplest systematics for the organisations of turn-taking for conversation', *Language*, 50 (4): 696–735.

Sacks, H. (1972) 'An initial investigation of the usability of conversational data for doing sociology', in D. Sudnow (ed.), *Studies in Social Interaction*, New York: Free Press.

Sacks, H. (1984) 'Methodological remarks', in J.M. Atkinson and and J. Heritage (eds), *Structures of Social Action: Studies in Conversation Analysis*, Cambridge: Cambridge University Press.

Sacks, H. (1992) *Lectures on Conversation*, edited by G. Jefferson (2 vols), Oxford: Blackwell.

Samra-Fredericks, D. (1994) 'Organising the past in the present as a way of beginning to construct tomorrow – talking change and changing talk', paper presented to the Standing Conference on Organisational Symbolism, Calgary University, Canada.

Samra-Fredericks, D. (1995) 'The experience of being a 'single-case' woman (in a multi-case world)', paper presented at the British Academy of Management, Sheffield.

Samra-Fredericks, D. (1996) 'The interpersonal management of competing rationalities – a critical ethnography of board-level competence for "doing" strategy as spoken in the "face" of change', PhD thesis (access restricted) Brunel University/Henley Management College.

Samra-Fredericks, D. (1998) 'Conversation analysis', in G. Symon and C. Cassell (eds), *Qualitative Methods and Analysis in Organizational Research, A Practical Guide*, London: Sage.

Samra-Fredericks, D. (2000) 'An analysis of the behavioural dynamics of corporate governance – a talk-based ethnography of a UK manufacturing "board-in-action"', *Corporate Governance, an International Review*, 8 (4): 311–25.

Samra-Fredericks, D. (2003) 'Strategizing as lived experience and strategists' everyday efforts to shape strategic direction', *Journal of Management Studies*, 40 (1): 141–74.

Schegloff, E.A. (1987) 'Between macro and micro: contexts and other connections', in J. Alexander, B. Geisen, R. Munch and N. Smelser (eds), *The Micro-Macro Link*, Berkeley, CA: University of California Press.

Schegloff, E.A. (1997) 'Whose text? Whose context?', *Discourse and Society*, 8 (2): 165–87.

Schegloff, E.A. (1998) 'Reply to Wetherell', *Discourse and Society*, 9 (3): 413–16.

Schegloff, E.A. (1999) 'Discourse, pragmatics, conversation analysis', *Discourse Studies*, 1 (4): 405–35.

Schegloff, E.A. and Sacks, H. (1973) 'Opening up closings', *Semiotica*, 8 (4): 289–327.

Schiffrin, D. (1987) *Discourse Markers*, Cambridge: Cambridge University Press.

Sharrock, W. (2000) 'Where the simplest systematics fits: a response to Micheal Lynch's "The ethnomethodological foundations of conversation analysis"', *Text*, 20 (4): 533–39.

Silverman, D. (1997) 'The logics of qualitative research', in G. Miller and R. Dingwall (eds), *Context and Method in Qualitative Research*, London: Sage.

Silverman, D. (1998) *Harvey Sacks, Social Science and Conversation Analysis*, Cambridge: Polity Press.

Silverman, D. (2000) 'Routine pleasures: the aesthetics of the mundane', in S. Linstead and H. Hopfl (eds), *The Aesthetics of Organization*, London: Sage.

ten Have, P. (1999) *Doing Conversation Analysis, A Practical Guide*, London: Sage.

van Dijk, T.A. (ed.) (1997) *Discourse as Social Interaction. Discourse studies: A Multidisciplinary Introduction*, vol. 2, London: Sage.

Weick, K.E. (1979) *The Social Psychology of Organizing*, New York: Newbery Award Records Inc.

Wetherell, M. (1998) 'Positioning and interpretative repertoires: conversation analysis and post-structuralism in dialogue', *Discourse and Society*, 9 (3): 387–412.

Wieder, D.L. (1988) 'From resource to topic: some aims of conversation analysis', in J.A. Anderson (ed.), *Communication Yearbook II*, Beverly Hills, CA: Sage.

Zimmerman, D.H. (1988) 'On conversation: The conversation analytic perspective', in J.A. Anderson (ed.), *Communication Yearbook II*, Beverly Hills, CA: Sage.

19 —— Attributional Coding ——————————————————————

Jo Silvester

Causal attributions refer to the explanations we make for our own behaviour, the behaviour of other people and the events that we observe or hear about from others. One only has to consider how prevalent gossip is in everyday life to understand that causal attributions are a very common phenomenon. They are also very common in the workplace. Managers seek to explain the behaviour of the people who work for them – why Sally has performed especially well over recent months, or why Robert's team seem to be experiencing difficulty meeting targets. Employees may try to understand why a boss has become more supportive, why a particular colleague appears to be getting all the best jobs, or why the organization has announced a programme of organizational change. Similarly, we might try to work out why we were not put forward for an expected promotion, why a customer is being difficult, or why we are suddenly dissatisfied with our work.

According to attribution theorists we engage in a process of sense-making to identify the causes of novel, important, or potentially threatening events (Wong and Weiner, 1981), because by doing so we render our environment more predictable and therefore controllable (Heider, 1958). Organizational researchers have been particularly interested in these attributions because the way in which an individual explains an event can have an important influence upon how they choose to respond. Researchers have studied attributions made by sales people for successful and unsuccessful sales outcomes (Seligman and Schulman, 1986; Silvester et al., 2003); the relationship between attributions and job-seeking behaviour (Prussia et al., 1993); managers' attributions for employees (Knowlton and Mitchell, 1980); and the impact of causal attributions upon strategic decision making among CEOs and their senior teams (Gooding and Kinicki, 1995).

However, because causal attributions have traditionally been conceptualized as internal and private phenomena, researchers have typically relied upon quantitative research methods such as questionnaires, and behavioural vignettes to render them explicit. In fact, one might be surprised to find attributional research described in a book concerned with qualitative methods. Yet, the production of causal attributions is also a very public activity (Antaki, 1994). Whilst individuals are motivated to make sense of the world in order to aid mastery of their environment, they also need to share this understanding if they are to interact effectively with other people (Silvester and Chapman, 1997). Communicated attributions are one means by which people seek to persuade others to adopt their view of causal reality. Similarly, by listening to attributions produced by others, individuals can learn about different perspectives as well as the causes of events that they may not have observed. They can also learn why one might be expected to behave in a particular way by listening to attributions produced by senior individuals within an organization (Silvester et al., 1999). This chapter describes a method known as 'attributional coding' that enables researchers to extract, code, and analyse patterns of communicated attributions. Such attributions can be derived from interviews, conversations, team meetings, speeches, or in written material such as company reports, letters, and e-mail.

EPISTEMOLOGICAL BACKGROUND

As Cassell and Symon (1994) point out, research methods are not necessarily 'quantitative' or 'qualitative'; it is the epistemological assumptions underlying how the method is used that determines whether the research is best described as reductionist or constructionist. This is particularly pertinent in the case of attributional coding, which is unusual in being a method that can be used in both qualitative and quantitative research. Traditionally most attribution research has taken a reductionist perspective. For example, researchers have sought to identify stable differences in the way individuals typically explain outcomes. Much of my own research has also been reductionist. One area has been concerned with how applicants' spoken attributions during employment interviews act as cues for interviewers keen to determine likely future levels of motivation. I have also been interested in exploring managers' attributions for male and female performance. By conducting critical incident interviews with managers, and analysing and comparing the causal attributions they make, it is possible to detect subtle differences in discourse that are indicative of bias and stereotypes.

However, I have also been interested in how causal attributions come to be shared among members of a group or organization: in particular, the role of the leader in communicating a shared vision and shared understanding of how and why individuals must behave in a particular way. This focus on the communication and sharing of causal attributions fits more closely with a constructionist perspective that views communication as a dynamic and creative process. It also highlights an interesting tension between treating causal attributions as indicative of internal cognitions at an individual level, and also as a public mechanism for fostering shared cognition between individuals. Supporters of a radical constructionist approach argue that there is no fixed, measurable objective reality, and that it is language itself that shapes our world. Consequently, treating language and discourse as simply reflecting internal cognitions is seen as misleading and wrong (Edwards and Potter, 1993). My own perspective is somewhat different. I view communicated attributions as being both reflective of internal cognition *and* part of a dynamic process whereby individuals actively share their understanding with others and negotiate shared meanings (compare Silvester et al., 2002).

BACKGROUND TO ATTRIBUTIONAL CODING

Traditionally, the most common method of investigating causal attributions has been the questionnaire. Two examples include the Attributional Style Questionnaire (ASQ: Peterson et al., 1982) and the Occupational Attributional Style Questionnaire (OASQ: Furnham et al., 1992). Both require respondents to consider a series of hypothetical events (for example, 'You secured the promotion you were looking for'), identify possible causes for these events, and then rate them on a series of causal dimensions. From a research perspective there are clear advantages to using questionnaires: they are easy to administer and analyse, and they are consistent across subjects. Yet they also have important limitations. Attention is focused on topics that the researcher considers meaningful or important. The respondent therefore has little or no freedom to negotiate the meaning or relevance of the attribution with the researcher (Antaki, 1994). Similarly, causal events are often presented as isolated incidents with little, if any, contextual information to aid sense-making.

The focus of this chapter is on an alternative method that involves coding spontaneously produced spoken attributions using the Leeds Attributional Coding System (LACS: Munton et al., 1999). This system enables researchers to explore and code attributions made by one person about their own behaviour or the actions of other people or entities. The LACS was originally designed as an ecologically valid and less intrusive method for analysing the attributions produced by family members during therapy sessions. It has since been used in a variety of clinical (for example, Brewin et al., 1991; Leggett and Silvester 2003) and non-clinical contexts (for example, Silvester, 1997; Silvester et al., 1999). Given the sensitive nature of the original research context, ethical issues were an important consideration in the development of the LACS. For research purposes all participants are assured anonymity and, in the case of organizational research, no information about individuals is reported back to employers. However, the use of semi-structured and critical incident interviews allows participants considerable control over the content of the material to be coded.

The following section draws upon examples from recent research investigating candidates' attributions during selection interviews and managers' attributions for worker performance. The five stages to attributional coding as defined by the LACS are illustrated in Figure 19.1.

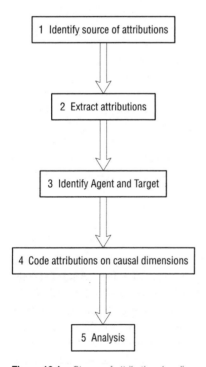

Figure 19.1 Stages of attributional coding

IDENTIFY SOURCE OF ATTRIBUTIONS

The LACS can be used to code attributions from a range of sources, for example: a speech by a chief executive officer, team meetings, semi-structured research interviews, or written archival material such as annual reports or letters to share-holders. Attributions can be found in a variety of materials, but certain sources may not be as rich as others. Experience suggests that technical descriptions, or interviews where factual or problem solving answers are requested, tend to generate fewer attributions than material where individuals discuss important events (for example, performance down-turn of an organization or group, failure to pass an exam) or justify decisions and behaviour (for example, promoting one individual and not another, choosing to study abroad). Typically, semi-structured or critical incident research interviews will generate 1–2 attributions per minute.

EXTRACT ATTRIBUTIONS

Attributions are extracted from verbatim transcripts of the material. Although attributions can be extracted by 'ear' simply by listening to audio-tapes (less time-consuming and costly), this can lead to a reduction in reliability. It also makes it difficult for coders to use the additional contextual information that is present in a transcript. An attribution is defined as: 'a statement that refers to a causal relationship where the speaker implies that a specific outcome (for example, 'I got the job') is a consequence of a particular cause' (for example, 'because I had friends in that company'). In general, the LACS makes no distinction between reasons, justifications, causal accounts or hypothetical outcomes. Finally, it is very important to remember that attributions are extracted and coded from the speaker's perspective. Therefore, all attributions made by the speaker, whether considered highly unlikely or even 'wrong' by the researcher (for example, 'I got the job, because I'm the best candidate they'll ever see'), are extracted for later coding.

It takes a little practice to identify attributions quickly and reliably. Some attributions are more obvious than others and many will include a causal connective such as 'because', 'so', 'therefore', 'as a result'. But there will also be causal attributions where the link is implied rather than stated explicitly. In the case of 'He's never been very good in cars, he had a bad experience when he was young' the bad experience (cause) results in not being very good in cars (outcome) but no link word is used. In selection interviews, interviewers often explicitly request a causal explanation (for example, 'Why do you think you are suited to this particular job?') and in doing so they provide an outcome (being suited to the job) and request one or more causes from the candidate (for example, 'Well, I've always been very good with people'). Similarly, although speakers do generate simple causal statements (for example, 'I will get a good grade if my lecturer gives me feedback'), in many instances causal statements are complex and may be best described as a causal sequence. Take the following example of a manager describing a good performing female:

Interviewer: Can you give me an example of someone you have managed who performed particularly well?

Manager: Yes well, I will talk about an individual who happens to be a lady. She was particularly successful because she was always willing to listen and learn. Um ... worked incredibly hard, was a team player. She was

> always willing to help others, which meant that she got back help from others when she needed it. She was able to analyse situations so that she didn't spend unnecessary time on the stuff that you shouldn't spend time on. Um . . . very personable and approachable so everybody was happy to ask for her help.

Rather than code individual causal statements, certain researchers (for example, Brewin et al., 1991) have chosen to extract causal paragraphs rather than causal sentences. While this can make extracting attributions easier, it does pose difficulties for later coding. For example, in the previous example, the speaker produces a number of different, even contradictory causes for the same outcome. The LACS suggests that in such cases the researcher should identify the outcome (for example, 'failing an exam') and then list each of the stated causes separately (for example, missing a bus, not revising enough, poor lecturer). These are treated as separate causal statements for later coding. A common convention when identifying causal attributions in transcripts is to use a pencil to underline a cause with an arrow pointing in the direction of the outcome, and a slash(/) indicating approximately where the outcome ends (in the case of an outcome following a cause) or begins (when the outcome precedes a cause). This is shown in the following example taken from a study of managers' attributions for performance (Silvester, Conway and Fraser, 2004) with extracted causal attributions.

> Manager: Yes well, I will talk about an individual who happens to be a lady. (1) /She was particularly successful ← because she was always willing to listen and learn. Um, (2) ← worked incredibly hard, (3) ← was a team player. (4) She was always willing to help others, → which meant that she got back help from others when she needed it/. (5) She was able to analyse situations → so that she didn't spend unnecessary time on the stuff that you shouldn't spend time on/. (6) Um very personable and approachable → so everybody was happy to ask for her help./

1   She was particularly successful <u>because she was always willing to listen and learn</u>.
2   (She was particularly successful because she) <u>worked incredibly hard</u>.
3   (She was particularly successful because she) <u>was a team player</u>.
4   <u>She was always willing to help others</u>, which meant that she got back help from others when she needed it.
5   <u>She was able to analyse situations</u> so that she didn't spend unnecessary time on the stuff that you shouldn't spend time on.
6   (She was) <u>very personable and approachable</u> so everybody was happy to ask for her help.

CODING AGENTS AND TARGETS

Once all attributions have been extracted, the first stage of coding is to identify the 'Agent' and 'Target' for each attribution. These distinguish between the person, entity or group causing an outcome to occur, and the person, entity or group to whom something happens. Agent-Target coding is essentially a content analysis of who or what are seen as causing events and who or what is being influenced. The LACS defines an 'Agent' as the person, group or entity nominated in the *cause* of the attribution, and the 'Target' as the person, group or entity which is mentioned in the *outcome* of the attribution. In order to simplify coding, Agent-

Target categories are usually restricted to individuals, groups or entities likely to be of interest in that particular investigation. For example, a researcher interested in family attributions might code each family member as a separate Agent and Target. Theoretically, any number of Agent-Target categories can be coded, but larger numbers have the disadvantage of reducing inter-rater reliability. I have used the following categories with material from selection interviews:

(1) Speaker
(2) Speaker's family
(3) Friends and work colleagues
(4) Education (may include teachers at school or university)
(5) Company or employer
(6) Other

So, in the attribution: 'I decided to study law <u>because several of my family are lawyers</u>', the Target or person involved in the outcome (I decided to study law) would be coded 'Self' (1) and the Agent would be coded 'Family' (2). Similarly, in: '<u>My school was very proactive in securing work placements</u>, several of my friends got work that way', Agent = 'Education' (4) and Target = 'Friends' (3). The second attribution illustrates an advantage that the LACS has over other similar coding schemes in that it allows the researcher to code attributions where the Speaker is neither Agent nor Target.

Agent-Target coding has a number of uses. By counting the number of times a speaker mentions different Agents or Targets, it is possible to explore the extent to which a speaker describes themselves as an Agent (namely causing events to occur) rather than a Target (being influenced by a particular cause). A simple count provides insight into the extent to which the Speaker considers or wishes to portray him- or her-self as influencing of, rather than being influenced by specific outcomes. It is also possible to identify the Agents that a Speaker views as most likely to influence different Targets and, third, whether particular Agents and Targets are associated with negative or positive outcomes. In recent work investigating CEO attributions, we found that customers were described more often as Agents than Targets, suggesting reactive rather than proactive customer relationships (Silvester, West and Dawson, 2002).

ATTRIBUTIONAL DIMENSIONS

The LACS codes attributions using five causal dimensions. They include: Stable–Unstable, Global–Specific, Internal–External, Personal–Universal and Controllable–Uncontrollable. Extracted attributions are coded on each of these causal dimensions and definitions of these dimensions together with examples are provided in the next section. It is important to note that attributions are coded, as well as extracted, from the perspective of the Speaker. The coder should use information present in the attribution or surrounding transcript to make a decision, rather than rely upon his or her own view of causal reality. Antaki (1994) describes this as 'hearable as', that it is the meaning that the individual wishes to convey which is important, irrespective of whether or not the listener believes or agrees with what is being said.

STABLE–UNSTABLE

This refers to how permanent or long-lasting the speaker believes the CAUSE of the attribution to be. 'Stable' causes are more likely to have an ongoing effect upon subsequent behaviour than 'Unstable' causes. A simple question to ask oneself when coding is 'does the speaker believe that this cause is likely to have an ongoing effect on this or other outcomes?' A Stable cause may also be a 'one-off' event that has continuing effects upon the Speaker. If the Speaker believes that the cause is likely to have an ongoing influence upon future outcomes, then code 'Stable' (3). If the cause appears to be relatively short-term or have a non-permanent effect upon subsequent outcomes, code 'Unstable' (1). Where there is insufficient information to determine whether the attribution should be coded Stable or Unstable, use (2).

Stable: 'I'm not particularly good in large groups of people, so I'm looking for a job which will allow me to work by myself' (the Speaker gives no indication that he believes the cause – a personal characteristic – is likely to change). Stable: 'I think the problem is more in women than men, it's the hard-nosed stuff like asking for customer commitment that they find difficult' (the cause is perceived by the Speaker to be an on-going influence upon developing relationships with customers). Unstable: 'I'm sorry I can't make the meeting because my car has a flat tyre' (there is no evidence to suggest that the cause will continue to have an effect). Unstable: 'I didn't do too well that year, because I had glandular fever' (having glandular fever could have had long-term repercussions on this individual's choice of university and subsequent job opportunities, but the coder must use what information is present in the attribution – here no such information is provided).

GLOBAL–SPECIFIC

This refers to the 'importance' or sphere of influence of the CAUSE of an attribution. A Global cause (3) is one that can affect a large number of other non-trivial outcomes. The Global and Personal dimensions are best defined with respect to the aims and context of the study. For example, in a study of organizational attributions 'Global' causes were defined as those that resulted in outcomes at a company rather than a group or an individual level. In the case of selection interviews, a 'Global' cause is defined as one that could reasonably be expected to influence later work opportunities or choice of career. A 'Specific' (1) cause is one that has a more limited and less important effect on outcomes: one that is unlikely to have a wide influence or is considered relatively unimportant by the Speaker. Again, if there is insufficient information for a decision to be reached, code (2). Global: 'I think managing to get into Cambridge University, has opened doors for me' and 'I think if you're going to be successful in this organization, you have to put your family second' (because both have, or are likely to, influence career opportunities). Specific: 'I go to quite a number of plays and films, because I belong to the university arts society' (because there is no evidence that belonging to the arts society has any influence over other outcomes), similarly: 'I do lots of sport, so I have to be organized'.

INTERNAL–EXTERNAL

In the case of the Internal–External, Personal–Universal and Controllable–Uncontrollable dimensions, each attribution can be coded separately for Speaker, Agent and Target when these involve different people or groups. For example, if a mother makes the attribution: 'she (daughter) doesn't like school, because the other children bully her' her daughter would be identified as Target and the other children as Agent. The cause could then be coded separately for Mother (Speaker), Daughter (Target) and Children (Agent) on these dimensions. This is particularly useful when exploring an individual's interpersonal attributions, that is their explanations for another person's behaviour. For example, in the following attribution Speaker would be coded External, but the employee who is both the Agent and Target would be Internal: 'He was lazy, he just wasn't prepared to work hard with the customer'. In order to keep things fairly simple in this chapter, however, I will focus on coding attributions for Speaker only. The reader is referred to Munton et al. (1999) for further information.

An attribution is coded 'Internal' (3) when the CAUSE originates in the person being coded, for example, their behaviour, a personality characteristic or a skill. Thus, 'The company took me on, because I knew about that particular system' would be coded 'Internal' (3) because the cause is the individual's knowledge, and 'I failed the exam because I didn't do enough preparation' would be coded Internal because the cause is the individual's failure to act. Alternatively, causes coded 'External' (1) originate outside the person being coded and may include the behaviour of someone else, situational constraints or circumstances in which the person finds themselves. For example, 'None of the class did very well on that particular exam, because the teacher gave us the wrong material to learn' would both be coded 'External' (1). As with the other dimensions, code '2' if uncertain or there is insufficient information to make a decision.

PERSONAL–UNIVERSAL

The Personal–Universal dimension was originally created as a way of identifying attributions where family members identified something 'different', special or unique to a particular person. This dimension can also be useful in a work context to distinguish between attributions where an individual seeks to set themselves apart from the group and attributions where they describe their actions in normative terms. Recent findings suggest that interviewers pay more attention to personal attributions produced by applicants in telephone interviews, possibly because of the increased anonymity of the applicant in that context (Silvester and Anderson, 2003). An attribution is coded 'Personal' (3) when either the cause or the outcome describes something unique or idiosyncratic about the person being coded and not typical of that particular referent group. I have used other graduates as the referent group in the case of graduate recruitment interviews. For example, 'They chose me, because I had captained the school hockey team' would be coded 'Personal' because the interviewee describes something about herself which she considers is distinct, or at least untypical of the majority of graduates applying for this job. Similarly, 'Backpacking through Africa gave me a rare insight into other cultures' would be coded Personal. In contrast, an attribution is coded 'Universal' (1) when there is nothing in the cause or outcome to indicate something distinctive about that person or where the cause or outcome might be typical of any other person in that referent group. For example, 'I wanted to do criminal law, I guess at that age you're rather naive and utopian' would be coded 'Universal' because the candidate associates their behaviour with a 'group norm', that is, anybody of that age might have been expected to act similarly.

Again, it is worth remembering that attributions are coded from the Speaker's perspective. Therefore, even though in the coder's opinion the action describes something highly idiosyncratic about the person, if the Speaker is describing the outcome or cause in terms which are 'normative', the attribution would be coded 'Universal'. In the following attribution: 'It was nothing special, my friends were taking soft drugs so I decided to get involved' the cause might be taken as indicating something Personal about the individual. However it would still be coded 'Universal' because the Speaker refers to the behaviour as being relatively normal.

CONTROLLABLE–UNCONTROLLABLE

According to Weiner (1986), the perceived controllability of a cause will influence an individual's motivation to act upon or change future outcomes. An attribution is coded 'Controllable' (3) if in the Speaker's opinion the cause could, without exceptional effort, be influenced or changed by the Speaker so as to produce a different outcome. For example, 'I failed Chemistry, because I spent too much time on my duties as Secretary for the Athletics Society' would be coded 'Controllable' because the Speaker could have been expected to have influenced the outcome. It was within their sphere of influence. Similarly, 'I went on writing letters and in the end they decided to offer me the place' would be coded Controllable. The following attribution would also be coded 'Controllable' because the Speaker was able to influence the outcome: 'They were renovating the school library, so I asked if I could use the one at the local college'. In contrast, an 'Uncontrollable' (1) attribution is one where the speaker perceives the outcome to be inevitable or not open to influence. For example, 'I missed the deadline for the application because I came down with flu' would be coded 'Uncontrollable' as would: 'None of my class did well in that subject because the teacher followed the wrong syllabus.' If there is not enough information to determine whether the individual considers themselves to have control over the cause or the outcome, code (2).

As a matter of convention when using the LACS all dimensions are coded on a three point scale, where, for example a 'stable' attribution would be coded '3' an 'unstable' attribution '1' and, in the case of each dimension when there is insufficient information for the coder to make a decision or the cause is somewhere in-between stable and unstable (for example) the attribution is coded '2'. As a rule of thumb, approximately 20 per cent of attributions will usually fall into this middle category. There is no reason why a researcher should not choose an alternative coding system, for example a 1–7 scale, although different systems are likely to have different consequences for inter-rater reliability.

VALENCY

There is evidence that people make different types of attributions for positive and negative outcomes, consequently these can be coded and analysed separately. Attributions referring to a positive, neutral or desired outcome are usually coded 'Positive' (2) and those referring to a negative or undesired outcome are coded 'Negative' (1).

CODED EXAMPLE

The following extract taken from an early part of a selection interview with a male applicant has been coded using the LACS. The interviewer has asked the applicant to discuss his experience of rowing at university. For all attributions the cause has been underlined and a '/' indicates the approximate end (or beginning) of an outcome:

> *I:*   I see that you mention rowing on your application form. Could you tell me /what motivated you to get involved with rowing?
>
> *C:*   I'm not too sure, rowing just kind of appealed to me (1) it just seemed like part of university life, you know, the Oxford and Cambridge boat race. Also (2) I wanted

to try a totally new sport it's very different from what we've practised in the south of Ireland where we had no chance really to row.

I: OK, right. Have you continued with it at all?

C: I have, yes. I rowed for my final two years as an undergraduate and then I rowed when became a postgraduate. /I gave it up after my first year for a few different reasons.

I: Like what?

C: (3) Well I didn't enjoy the club atmosphere that much. This will probably sound quite bad, but (4) not being from a public school made it quite difficult/. We were all asked where we came from and you know you'd have a guy saying 'Oh I rowed at Cambridge' or 'I rowed at Oxford' and it was 'Oh great a Cambridge man'. (5) Obviously where I studied was 'Oh OK'/. Also (6) there was no real structure in the club so I didn't see myself doing too well/. I got selected for the first crew initially but (7) the team didn't feel right, so I decided to give it up for a while/. (8) But now I kind of miss the structure in my life that rowing gave me so that's why I'm trying to get back into it at the moment./

Table 19.1 illustrates how these attributions have been coded. The first attribution is coded 'unstable' because there is little indication that Speaker considers that the cause (that rowing seemed like part of university life) is likely to operate again in future. Similarly, it is coded 'Specific' because there is no evidence in this attribution that the cause has influence over a large number of other important areas of the Speaker's life. It is coded 'External' because the cause originates outside the Speaker and 'Controllable' because the Speaker implies that he

Table 19.1   Coded examples of attributions from transcript

Attribution	Stable	Global	Internal	Personal	Control
1 (I got involved in rowing because) it just seemed like part of university life.	1	1	1	2	3
2 (I got involved in rowing because) I wanted to try a totally new sport.	1	1	3	3	3
3 I gave it up after my first year . . . Well I didn't enjoy the club atmosphere that much.	1	1	1	3	3
4 Not being from a public school made it quite difficult.	3	3	3	3	1
5 Obviously where I studied (they thought) was 'Oh OK'.	3	3	3	3	1
6 There was no real structure in the club so I didn't see myself doing too well.	1	1	1	1	1
7 The team didn't feel right, so I decided to give it up for a while.	1	1	1	1	3
8 But now I kind of miss the structure in my life that rowing gave me so that's why I'm trying to get back into it.	3	3	3	3	2

had influence over this particular outcome. The 'Uncertain' coding has been used for 'Personal' because it is difficult to establish whether the Speaker is implying that his view – that rowing is part of university life – is something unique to him, or widely shared by other undergraduates.

The second attribution is coded 'Unstable', 'Specific' and 'Controllable' for the same reasons as the first, but this time the cause is coded 'Internal' because it refers to the Speaker's wish to try a new sport. The attribution is also coded 'Personal' because there is more evidence that the Speaker is implying that the attribution refers to something which distinguishes him from other undergraduates. The third attribution is coded 'Unstable' because the cause 'not enjoying the club atmosphere' appears to be a 'one-off' occurrence and there is little indication that the Speaker believes that this will be typical of other clubs that he joins. It is also coded 'Controllable', because although the Speaker may not have been able to influence the club atmosphere, he was able to take the decision to leave the club. In the fourth and fifth attributions, the causes, both of which relate to not being from a public school, have been coded 'Stable' and 'Global', this is because not having attended a public school, in this Speaker's opinion, appears to have ongoing and potentially wide-ranging consequences. In addition, both of these attributions are coded 'Uncontrollable' because there is little to indicate that the Speaker believes that he could have influenced the outcome in either case, or changed either cause.

In attributions (6) and (7), the Speaker appears to externalize responsibility for having left the club by stating that there was 'no real structure' in the club and that 'the team did not feel right'. Neither of these suggests that the Speaker considers cause or outcome to reflect anything personal about himself. Attribution (6) is coded 'uncontrollable' because there is nothing to indicate that the Speaker considered himself able to influence cause or outcome. Attribution (7), however, is coded 'controllable' because the outcome refers to a decision to give up rowing. Finally, in the eighth attribution, the Speaker implies that rowing provides a structure to his life that is likely to have an ongoing and important influence. Hence the attribution is coded 'Stable' and 'Global'. It is also coded 'Internal' and 'Personal' because of the implication that the statement describes something that originates within him and is relatively idiosyncratic. However, the 'Uncertain' coding is used for control, because, while there is evidence that the Speaker is attempting to influence the outcome, he has not as yet succeeded.

ANALYSIS

Whilst there is no reason why an individual should not code their own attributions, researchers using the LACS have generally employed independent, trained coders to extract and code attributions. As such, emphasis is placed on the extent to which attributions convey a similar meaning to different listeners. Thus, consistent with qualitative research involving content analysis of discourse material, inter-rater reliability is defined as the extent to which two or more coders working independently code individual attributions in the same way.

Achieving good levels of inter-rater reliability is particularly important if the researcher's aim is to undertake a statistical analysis of coded attributions (an approach that is more compatible with a quantitative reductionist research paradigm). However the use of qualitative material of this type means that it is unlikely that the researcher will achieve levels of reliability similar to that achieved using structured questionnaires. Good reliability requires clearly defined dimensions and coders who have had sufficient training and practice. Reliability is calculated using Cohen's kappa (see Fleiss, 1971) for approximately 20–30 per cent of the attributions extracted for a study. In general, Fleiss (1971) suggests that kappas above 0.4 are considered acceptable, whereas those above 0.6 are good.

A further advantage of coding spoken attributions rests with the number of attributions it is possible to generate. In comparison with questionnaires which may rely on six positive and six negative attributions, the focus on spoken attributions for real events means that several thousand attributions can be generated from a single research study. Moreover, as attributions are coded on each dimension, the resulting data set can prove large enough to permit investigation of both nomothetic and idiographic patterns. By entering the data into an SPSS data sheet, it is possible to select certain types of attributions, for example where the speaker is Agent and outcomes are positive.

ADVANTAGES AND DISADVANTAGES OF THE METHOD

Researchers need to weigh the advantages and disadvantages of using any research method before determining which one best suits their particular research question. The potential disadvantages of attributional coding lie with its complexity – it can be more costly in terms of time and money than traditional questionnaire methodology. Moreover, it will take time before the newcomer feels entirely confident with the method, and able to achieve adequate levels of reliability. Attributional coding also depends upon transcribed material and, therefore the time or funds necessary to acquire such transcripts. However, a growing body of transcribed material is now available through outlets such as Qualidata sponsored by the ESRC in the UK (see Chapter 30). This should help to reduce costs and increase opportunities for qualitative researchers. Such issues aside, attributional coding can be a very rewarding method for exploring how individuals make sense of their world.

However, as mentioned previously, the analysis of public or spoken attributions sits somewhat uneasily between the two powerful camps of constructionist and reductionist research. This means that research is potentially open to challenge by advocates of both approaches and, unfortunately, there is still a tendency to mistake the method for a particular epistemological approach. I believe that a strong advantage of attributional coding is that it has the potential to be used by both qualitative *and* quantitative researchers. However, this does mean that the researcher needs to be absolutely clear about his or her assumptions when using the method and reporting their findings. Quantifying individual attributions according to a pre-specified coding framework fits with a reductionist perspective in that it enables the researcher to explore consistency and track change in the patterns of attributions produced by individuals or groups of individuals. But, as Marshall (1994) points out, the positivistic standpoint which accepts language as a transparent medium through which cognitions are transmitted unproblematically, and without distortion, is very much open to question. Indeed, when studying public or spoken causal attributions, it is difficult (and no doubt unwise) to ignore the importance of context in contributing to the type of attributions produced. Similarly, rather than assume that discourse is divorced from cognition, the greater challenge will be to determine how context, cognition, personality and skill interact when individuals communicate their causal understanding of the world to one another.

In conclusion, the advantages of attributional coding include a focus on naturalistic data: more specifically, the attributions that individuals produce themselves for real events rather than hypothetical scenarios created by researchers. The sensitivity of the method means that areas previously beyond the bounds of more intrusive research methods can be explored. The ability to quantify patterns of attributions also renders them open to further investigation and comparison, including how they change over time. Although attributional coding is not a technique that can be lifted from the shelf one day and applied the next, perseverance can be rewarded with a more detailed insight into the relationship between attributions and behaviour, such as the selection decisions reached by interviewers listening to candidates explain themselves. Attributional coding permits researchers a rich insight into the proactive and complex way in which people make sense of their surroundings as well as how they choose to communicate this understanding to others. Therefore attributional coding affords a way of contributing to the more typical empirical enquiries into causal sense-making.

FURTHER READING

Readers who would like to explore attributional coding further will find the book *Attributions in Action: Coding Qualitative Data* by Munton et al. (1999) useful (all reading in this section can be found in the reference section). This book provides a background to attribution theory and separate chapters explaining how the method has been used in clinical, marketing and organizational contexts. For readers interested in understanding how attributional coding has been used in research, the following references would be useful. First, Silvester (1997) looks at the spoken attributions produced by applicants in graduate recruitment interviews and how they relate to interviewer selection decisions. This work is extended in Silvester et al. (2002), which considers the role of impression management in the production of causal attributions. Using attributional coding to explore organizational culture and culture change is the focus of Silvester et al. (1999). Finally, Leggett and Silvester (2003) describe how nurses' causal attributions for violent incidents, reported on restraint forms, can be coded. This research demonstrates how spontaneous attributions can help to uncover the potential for gender bias in explanations and actions.

REFERENCES

Antaki, C.R. (1994) *Explaining and Arguing*, London: Sage.
Brewin, C.R., MacCarthy, B., Duda, K. and Vaughn, C.E. (1991) 'Attribution and expressed emotion in the relatives of families with schizophrenia', *Journal of Abnormal Psychology*, 100: 546–54.
Cassell, C. and Symon, G. (1994) 'Qualitative research in work contexts', in C. Cassell and G. Symon (eds), *Qualitative Methods in Organizational Research: A Practical Guide*, London: Sage. pp. 1–13.
Edwards, D. and Potter, J. (1993) 'Language and causation: a discursive action model of description and attribution', *Psychological Review*, 100: 23–41.
Fleiss, J.L. (1971) 'Measuring nominal scale agreement among many raters', *Psychological Bulletin*, 76: 378–82.
Furnham, A., Sadka, V. and Brewin, C.R. (1992) 'The development of an occupational attributional style questionnaire', *Journal of Organizational Behaviour*, 13: 27–39.
Gooding, R.Z. and Kinicki, A.J. (1995) 'Interpreting event causes: the complementary role of categorization and attribution processes', *Journal of Management Studies*, 32: 1–22.
Heider, F. (1958) *The Psychology of Interpersonal Relations*, New York: John Wiley.

Knowlton, W.A. and Mitchell, T.R. (1980) 'Effects of causal attributions on a supervisor's evaluation of subordinate performance', *Journal of Applied Psychology*, 65: 459–66.

Leggett, J. and Silvester, J. (2003) 'Care staff attributions for violent incidents involving male and female patients: a field study', *British Journal of Clinical Psychology*, 42: 393–406.

Marshall, H. (1994) 'Discourse analysis in an occupational context', in C. Cassell and G. Symon (eds), *Qualitative Methods in Organizational Research: A Practical Guide*, London: Sage. pp. 91–6.

Munton, A.G., Silvester, J., Stratton, P. and Hanks, H.G.I. (1999) *Attributions in Action: A Practical Guide to Coding Qualitative Material*, Chichester: Wiley.

Peterson, C., Semmel, A., Von Baeyer, C., Abramson, L.Y., Metalsky, G.I. and Seligman, M.E.P. (1982) 'The attributional style questionnaire', *Cognitive Therapy and Research*, 6: 287–300.

Prussia, G.E., Kinicki, A.J. and Bracker, J.S. (1993) 'Psychological and behavioural consequences of job loss: a covariance structure analysis using Weiner's (1985) attribution model', *Journal of Applied Psychology*, 78: 382–94.

Seligman, M.E.P. and Schulman, C. (1986) 'Explanatory style as a predictor of productivity and quitting among life insurance sales agents', *Journal of Personality and Social Psychology*, 50: 832–38.

Silvester, J. (1997) 'Spoken attributions and candidate success in the graduate recruitment interview', *Journal of Occupational and Organizational Psychology*, 70: 61–73.

Silvester, J. and Anderson, N. (2003) 'Technology and discourse: a comparison of telephone and face-to-face employment interviews', *International Journal of Selection and Assessment: Special Issue on Technology and Selection*. 11: 206–14.

Silvester, J., Anderson-Gough, F.M., Anderson, N.R. and Mohamed, A. (2002) 'Attributions, locus of control and impression management in the selection interview', *Journal of Occupational and Organizational Psychology*, 75: 59–76.

Silvester, J., Anderson, N.R. and Patterson, F. (1999) 'Organizational culture change: an inter-group attributional analysis', *Journal of Occupational and Organizational Psychology*, 72: 1–24.

Silvester, J. and Chapman, A.J. (1997) 'Asking "why?" in the workplace: causal attributions and organizational behavior', in C.L. Cooper and D.M. Rousseau (eds), *Trends in Organizational Behavior*, 4: 1–14.

Silvester, J., Conway, V. and Fraser, T. (2004), 'Managers' explanations for male and female performance'. Proceedings of the 2004 Annual Occupational Psychology Conference, Stratford: BPS.

Silvester, J., Patterson, F. and Ferguson, E. (2003) 'Comparing two attributional models of sales performance in retail sales: a field study', paper accepted for the *Journal of Occupational and Organizational Psychology. Special Issue on The Industrial, Work and Organizational-Cognition Interface*, 76: 115–32.

Silvester, J., West, M.A. and Dawson, J.F. (2002) 'CEO sense-making and discourse as a predictor of organizational performance: a longitudinal study', *Proceedings of the 2002 Annual Occupational Psychology Conference*, Leicester: British Psychological Society.

Wong, P.T.P. and Weiner, B. (1981) 'When people ask "why" questions and the heuristics of attribution search', *Journal of Personality and Social Psychology*, 40: 649–63.

Hannakaisa Länsisalmi, José-María Peiró and Mika Kivimäki

We are going to begin this chapter with a brief introduction to grounded theory, including a short history and description of its main components. After that we will briefly describe previous applications of grounded theory in organizational studies. We will then describe a case study, which illustrates how grounded theory can be applied when studying organizational phenomena, and finally, we close the chapter by discussing methodological considerations related to the application of grounded theory in the case study described.

INTRODUCTION TO GROUNDED THEORY

Grounded theory was developed by Glaser and Strauss (1967) when they observed that in sociological research, studies focusing on verifying existing classic theories flourished, while research on generating new theories hardly existed. Grounded theory is a kind of theory generated from the data collected. Grounded theory methodology, in turn, refers to a style of conducting qualitative data analysis. The aim is to discover what kinds of concepts and hypotheses are relevant to the area one wishes to understand. Grounded theory, therefore, provides new insights into the understanding of social processes emerging from the context in which they occur, without forcing and adjusting the data to previous theoretical frameworks (Glaser, 1995, 1998).

The basic elements of a grounded theory include conceptual categories and their conceptual properties, and hypotheses about or generalized relations between these categories and their properties. The researcher's task is not to produce a perfect description of the area he or she wishes to understand, but to develop a theory that accounts for much of the relevant behaviour. Grounded theory develops through constant comparative analysis, where a specific coding scheme is used to ensure conceptual development and density. With respect to data sources grounded theory often applies triangulation, namely combines different types of data collected by interviews, participative observation and analysis of documents. The data are gathered through theoretical sampling, which means that the selection of samples is guided by the development of the concepts. Once no additional data are to be found whereby one could further develop properties of a particular conceptual category, 'theoretical saturation' (see Glaser and Strauss, 1967) is achieved and the theory is 'ready'.

When comparing grounded theory to other qualitative approaches, such as template analysis, the major difference is perhaps the starting point. In template analysis the researcher has an initial coding template, which is then verified and/or modified through data collection (see King, Chapter 21, this volume). Grounded theory starts from uncovering the conceptual scheme in a contextual way without any predetermined theoretical or conceptual framework. When compared to discourse analysis, grounded theory focuses more on uncovering phenomena and processes, whereas discourse analysis goes deeper and in more detail in analysing specifically the language, discourses and discourse events as instances of sociocultural practice (for example, Fairclough, 1995).

GROUNDED THEORY IN ORGANIZATIONAL RESEARCH

Organizational psychology has recently been marked by a trend of moving from an individualistic point of view towards a more collective view based on social psychology, sociology and anthropology (Peiró, 1990; Rousseau, 1997; Schein, 1996). In this context, the application of grounded theory also has gained more popularity among organizational researchers. It has been applied in for example, studies focusing on organizational culture (Länsisalmi et al., 2000), organizational growth (Brytting, 1995), organizational change and innovation (Carrero et al., 2000; Lowe, 1995; Price, 1994), work teams (Gersick, 1988) and company survival (Lowe, 1995). Studies applying grounded theory in organizational research fall, roughly, into two categories: first studies focusing on generating new hypotheses around a specific theme (for example, Länsisalmi et al., 2000) and secondly studies that aim at revealing social processes producing a certain phenomenon (for example, Carrero et al., 2000).

Grounded theory is highly recommended in organizational research because it produces descriptions of organizational reality, which are easily recognized by the members of the target organization. Such descriptions may elicit positive discussions around important themes in the organization among the employees and, thus, form a basis for positive organizational development trends.

As for the ethical considerations of grounded theory, issues may rise in research settings that include secret observations (see, for example, Van Maanen, 1988) as a means for data collection. Also when collecting interview and observational data issues of confidentiality may rise. To avoid such issues, it is crucial to clearly communicate to the participants of the study before data collection who will listen to their interview tapes, transcribe them and analyse the data in written or audio-visual format. Furthermore, the researcher should also describe in detail how the research results will be presented and whether or not it will be possible to identify individuals' opinions and quotes in the reported research results. After receiving all the information available about the data analysis and its restoration the participants should also always have an option to withdraw from the study.

CASE STUDY: COLLECTIVE STRESS AND COPING IN THE CONTEXT OF ORGANIZATIONAL CULTURE

In this section, we describe a case study in which we utilized a grounded theory approach to explore and understand the phenomena of collective stress and coping.

In recent literature, the collective nature of stress experiences and coping has been emphasized (Handy, 1995; Newton, 1995; Semmer et al., 1996); evidence of relationships between individual stress-related behaviour patterns and organizational culture has been produced (Porter, 1996); and the universality of the traditional interpretation of individually experienced stress in different organizational contexts has been questioned (Barley and Knight, 1992; Meyerson, 1994).

Therefore, in our case study, we attempted to shed more light on the theme of stress and coping by applying an organizational culture perspective. More specifically, we examined the sources of collective stress in an organization and collective coping mechanisms that exist to alleviate such stress. We regard collective stress as a cultural artefact (Fineman, 1995) that results when members of a particular organizational culture as a group perceive a certain event as stressful. Collective coping, then, consists of the learned, uniform responses that members within the culture manifest when trying either to remove the stressor, to change the interpretation of the situation, or to alleviate the shared negative feelings it produces.

Since we were interested in developing, instead of testing, hypotheses about collective stress and coping within the context of organizational culture, we chose an inductive approach applying the grounded theory framework (see also Johnson, Chapter 14, this volume). We combined an ethnographic perspective, emphasizing the exploration of the nature of the social phenomenon with unstructured data, with a clinical descriptive perspective, which stresses interpretational aspects. Grounded theory methodology was justifiable, as the application of the above-mentioned perspectives often results in large amounts of unstructured data, accumulating in rather non-standard and unpredictable formats (Martin and Turner, 1986; Turner, 1981). Grounded theory provides a very systematic approach for the collection and analysis of such data by specifying clear procedures and rules to be followed throughout the entire research process (Glaser and Strauss, 1967; Strauss and Corbin, 1990). By applying such an approach we identified sources of collective stress and collective coping mechanisms in three divisions of a large multinational company.

Case description

The target organizations were three economically independent divisions (A, B and C) forming a company within a multinational corporation (total n = 850). They operated in the engineering industry. Until 1995, one year before the start of this study, these divisions formed part of the same Finnish subsidiary, after which they were separated and integrated into two different subsidiaries. This, in turn, resulted, among other things, in a restructuring of the organization. One work unit (X), originally forming part of Division B, was merged with Division C. Although the multinational company formed a common context to all the target organizations, these rather independent organizational units operated in very different business environments.

Methods in phase 1

FIELD DATA COLLECTION

To help in understanding the collective sources of stress and coping mechanisms, we analysed the organizational cultures of the three divisions by gathering descriptive data. The data were collected in 1996 by individual thematic interviews and complemented with observations at the work site, participant observations at meetings, and analysis of documents. A total of 63 informants were interviewed over a period of three months. The informants represented all the divisions, different professional groups, hierarchical levels, both sexes, and different age groups. The themes guiding the one- to two-hour interviews were: first the informant's own work and daily routines, secondly work-related values and company values, and thirdly the informant's career history within the company and important events in the organization during this career.

Although the themes guided the interviews, the interviewer (the first author of this chapter) did not ask exactly the same questions each time. In this way each successive interview was used to expand understanding of the organizational culture. After each interview, the interviewer summarized the emerging themes and these summaries served as a basis for the reformulation and development of questions and testing of the emerging hypotheses. All the interviews were recorded and extensive notes were taken during them. Based on these notes, 33 of the most informative interviews were transcribed, and the rest served as validation material in recorded form. Most informative interviews included several representative quotes describing different dimensions of a variety of themes. These interviews were selected due to their 'density' regarding both their descriptive strength and richness in referring to various themes.

ANALYSIS

An inductive analysis of the data was conducted following the basic principles of grounded theory methodology. The main aim was to generate a descriptive theory of the dominant organizational culture and/or subcultures present in the divisions, and to formulate preliminary hypotheses on how collective stress might be produced and coped with within these cultures.

The process of data analysis is illustrated in Figure 20.1. The data were, first, read and categorized into codes that were suggested by the data rather than imposed from outside, a procedure known as 'open coding' (Strauss and Corbin, 1990). These codes were then clustered into 'concepts'. Once all the data were examined, the concepts were organized by themes, which became candidates for a set of stable and integrative categories. Concepts represented the properties and dimensions of a particular theme. The identification of themes within each division and comparisons between divisions often required several rounds of analysis of the transcriptions. Once a particular theme had enough properties, namely no new properties related to a theme emerged in the transcriptions, a particular theme became an integrative category with a set of defined dimensions. Iteration between data, concepts and themes ended when enough categories and associated dimensions were defined to describe the cultures of the divisions, a situation Glaser and Strauss (1967) refer to as 'theoretical saturation'.

Constant comparative method was, thus, applied on three levels. First, we compared different codes and respective extracts of transcriptions, which resulted in the definition and selection of a set of concepts to be elaborated further. Second, we compared different concepts to one another, which resulted in the definition of a set of properties and dimensions describing each theme and, finally, an integrative category. Third, we compared themes and categories, which resulted in the definition of three main integrative categories describing and distinguishing the subcultures.

These integrative categories were found in all the subcultures, but had somewhat different content (namely, dimensions) in them. The first two categories represent what Schein (1990, 1996) describes as underlying basic assumptions and values and the third one observable artefacts, 'products' of and manifest behaviours of a certain culture (Table 20.1):

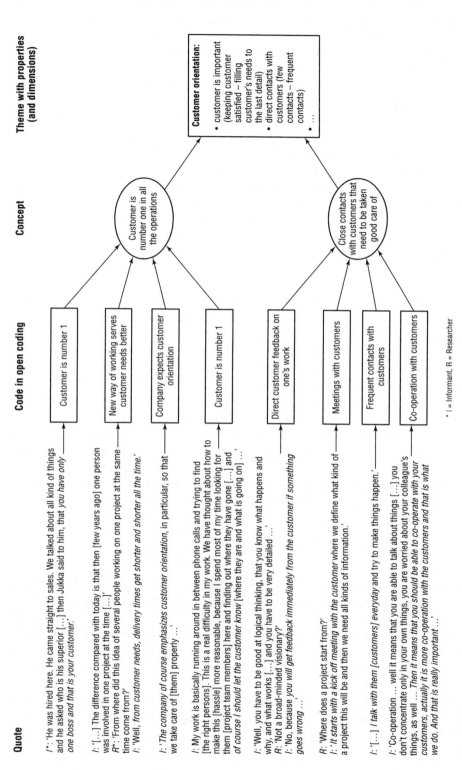

Figure 20.1 A worked example of data analysis

- fundamental recipe, that gives the 'gestalt' to the culture and includes the assumptions about the core task of each employee or the mission of the organization;
- guiding assumptions, consisting of assumptions, expectations, interpretations and myths that guide the work and daily life in the divisions;
- work-related emotions, namely how one is supposed to feel in relation to work and the organization.

As a result, four subcultures were identified and distinguished by the above-described categories, which were derived from themes, which had originally been derived from concepts and codes.

Table 20.1 Description of the four subcultures

	Division A	Division B	Division C	Work Unit X
Culture				
(1) Fundamental recipe	Jig-saw puzzle	Making money	Scattered islands	Making money
(2) Guiding assumptions	Hierarchy Working is performing Provide help when necessary	Client focus Time is money Myth of a salesman	Hierarchy Working is performing Provide help only when asked	Client focus Time is money Organized co-operation
(3) Work-related emotions	Foreman vacuum Fluctuation Insecurity Selfishness	Chaotic urgency Collective commitment Sense of belonging: humane leadership, pride Optimism	Powerlessness Inflexibility Isolation Alienation: mistrust, non-commitment	Hectisism Collective commitment Autonomy Equality Pride

Source: This table was first published in Länsisalmi et al. (2000), *European Journal of Work and Organizational Psychology*, 9(4). Reprinted with the permission of Psychology Press.

These categories were validated by comparing them with the information obtained through: first reading the summaries and listening to the tapes of the individual interviews not transcribed; secondly participant observations at the work site; thirdly analyses of divisional and company documents, and fourthly cross-checking the validity of the choice of categories with selected informants. Two additional procedures ensured that the data analysis was not relying on one researcher only: first, during data analysis the first author had hours of detailed discussions about the cultural models with three colleagues, two of whom acted as consultants in organization development activities in the divisions, and secondly a random sample of the collected individual interview data was blindly re-analysed by the third author of this chapter. The discussion confirmed the validity of the categories, and the first and the second analyses corresponded to each other. In total, the first phase of the study took one year to complete.

Methods in phase 2

FIELD DATA COLLECTION

Over a period of one month, in 1997, we conducted group interviews (n = 32) covering a total of 90 informants in groups of two or three people. The informants were representative of the entire population (compare Phase 1). Group interviews, instead of individual interviews, were preferred for two reasons. First, we wanted to increase the total number of informants used in order to confirm the validity of the cultural models in a wider sample of the target population. Secondly, by interviewing a group of persons at the same time, we created a situation of social control that would minimize the emergence of individual interpretations and maximize the emergence of collective interpretations, which were the main interest of the present study.

The critical incidents technique (see Chell, Chapter 5, this volume) was applied with the aim of specifying how collective stress is produced in the existing culture and what kinds of coping mechanisms are used to remove or alleviate collectively experienced stress. The specific themes guiding the interviews were: first definition of well-being and its components, secondly description of situations or events which result in the deterioration of employee well-being, and thirdly description of situations or events which result in enhanced employee well-being.

ANALYSIS

An inductive analysis was conducted, following the earlier described principles of grounded theory to confirm the validity of the cultural categories developed in the first phase, and to specify the relationship of these categories in each culture with collective stress and coping. Figure 20.1 and Table 20.2 illustrate this process.

The following two integrative categories emerged in the analysis: first collective stressors, defined as incidents and factors, interpreted by the members of the particular culture as stress-producing, and secondly collective problem-focused, appraisal-focused and emotion-focused coping mechanisms, defined as learned uniform reactions to collectively experienced stress. The integrative categories of coping mechanisms consisted of intentions to change the situation or the interpretation of the situation, and of efforts to manage the emotions that arose in response to threat (Lazarus and Folkman, 1984; Miller et al., 1988).

Overall results

Our research results confirmed that stress and coping had collective qualities (see Table 20.2). Collective stress emerged as a response to two types of situations across the different subcultures: first adaptation to the environment of the division or work unit was somehow imperfect and secondly there was friction inside the community (Table 20.3). Of the corresponding coping mechanisms a large proportion were also found to be collective in nature. Collective coping consisted of learned uniform responses to remove the collectively identified stressor, to change the interpretation of the situation or to alleviate negative feelings produced in the stressing situation (for more detailed research results see Länsisalmi et al., 2000).

METHODOLOGICAL CONSIDERATIONS

Regarding the strengths of the applied methodology, at least two advantages need to be raised here. First, the methodology enabled us to identify the rich contextualized detail of the characteristics of culture in different parts of the organization and to understand how these impacted on collective understandings of stress (see King, 2000). A quantitative survey would have missed the powerful way that current experiences were shaped by the organizational history, especially through myths and stories (Figure 20.1).

Second, our findings are also important for practitioners in the field dedicated in preventive stress management and stress interventions in organizations (compare Quick et al., 1998). The grounded theory approach revealed that we should be looking for collective responses that are significant for large groups of individuals and, from there, identify interventions that will have the maximum impact in a particular organization, instead of focusing on interventions derived from traditional individual-focused stress theories often verified with quantitative methods (for example, Lazarus and Folkman, 1984; Miller et al., 1988; Karasek and Theorell, 1990; Cooper, 1998).

Regarding the disadvantages of the method at least three issues need to be addressed. The first one deals with the generalizability of our findings. As the present comparative case study was conducted in three predetermined organizations of a multinational company, specific implications for other contexts are questionable. Case studies, in general, are sometimes accused of being anecdotal, testimonial and rather impressionistic accounts of events, which may inhibit theory accumulation in the field (Macy et al., 1989). A more general and 'formal' theory (see Glaser and Strauss, 1967) would perhaps have required more case organizations, so that the theoretical sampling process would have been enhanced (see Hartley, Chapter 26, this volume for further discussion of this issue). In practice, however, a researcher working with real organizations rarely has an opportunity to implement text-book theoretical sampling processes due to problems in gaining access to various companies and keeping up with deadlines set for a particular research project.

Second, the method is prone to a researcher bias on relying, normally, on one researcher as the primary analyst and creator of the essential categories of the grounded theory (for example, Rennie, 1994). This was the case in the present study as well. However, we tried to overcome this bias by triangulating several types of data, by negotiating differences among ourselves, and with anonymous third parties during later stages of the analyses and by conducting a blind re-analysis of a random sample of the data. An alternative would be to insist on initial group consensus in the generation of the categories (for example, Rhodes et al., 1993). We also tried to construct a somewhat 'negotiated joint reality' (see Henwood and Pidgeon, 1992) with the participants of the study, thus, enhancing the ecological validity of the findings. In the end, however, grounded theory puts the main researcher in a central role in the analysis and it is not surprising that Glaser (1977) emphasizes the researcher's theoretical sensitivity as an important ingredient for the successful application of the method (Carrero et al., 2000).

Third, in our case study, we focused more on generating hypotheses about the nature of collective stress and coping in organizational contexts instead of trying to generate a coherent theory about the social processes producing these phenomena in the context of organizational culture. Dachler (2000) points out that if qualitative researchers want to take a significant step ahead, instead of seeking to discover 'content', organizational researchers should focus more

Table 20.2 Examples of open coding, integrative categories, and dimensions of the categories (division A)

Examples of quotations	Code in open coding	Integrative category, memo notes and dimensions of the category
I [1]: What I did, was that I stepped on someone else's area of responsibility, but I wanted to take care of that issue. It was completely irrelevant, the matter. A piece of paper was missing a date. If you print out lists of prices and there is no date, then you have to go through an awful lot of trouble to find out which one is the newest list. So [this time] I went to take care of it [myself] and I got it done immediately, but then I ran into that guy who is supposed to take care of those things [normally]. So, I told him that I went to check this[date] . . . and I noticed immediately that this was an extremely negative thing that I had done, that what is it my business to get involved in that. So that's the attitude with people who have done the same job for a long time.	One should take care on his / her business only.	Integrative category: jig-saw puzzle Dimensions: • Specific jobs and tasks / person, work is divided into small pieces • Functions well, if all the pieces work well • Narrow, deep competence (source of professional pride), 'I own my piece' (sign of competence if you are able to master your own job) • The different work units have few contacts with each other (coffee breaks and other socializing events preferably with the own group) • 'Us' and 'them'
R [2]: So are these like defined areas of responsibilities?		
I: They are unwritten rules, that you should not put your nose in everything.		
R: How are those areas determined?		
I: They are not determined anyhow. Maybe somewhere it says that for example this guy takes care of development work.		
R: Do you have a Christmas party?	Preference of own group's parties.	
I: We would have had, but I didn't take part in it.		
R: Was it for the whole company?		
I: Yes. But I normally participate only in our own parties, I'm probably kind of cliquish, . . . in the events organized for 'our tube', as we usually call ourselves.		
R: Going back to the day you started working here . . . When was that?	Feeling proud about being so young when started working.	Quotation from the Memo notes: The organization is a machine like jig-saw puzzle. The work is divided by products / functions to different work units. The jig-saw puzzle works well, if every piece in the game takes care of his share of the work (mechanistic view of the organization). Professional competence develops over the years. Everyone deepens his expertise
I: 1962, the 18th of October. I was a young man then.		
R: How young?		
I: Just under 18. Yes after one week I became 18, but I can say that I was under 18 when I started!		

Table 20.2 cont.

Examples of quotations	Code in open coding	Integrative category, memo notes and dimensions of the category
R. Can you do that by heart? I: There are instructions for that, but I haven't really needed them. I have been [working here] for so long. Then the same jobs are repeated . . .	Professional competence develops over years of experience.	in his own job. A real professional is a person who skillfully fulfills his responsibilities, without errors.
[. . .]		
R: What kind of an employee is appreciated here? I: Well... depends on what you do, you have to be an expert at least, you have to know what you're doing. That's what I think, that at least and as I have been already here for a long time I think I am somehow competent in what I'm doing. That's one characteristic at least.		
I: The worst thing that can happen is that you make bad piece, it really feels bad, kind of 'hurts your pride'. Once you have been here as long as I have	Mastering your task as a source of pride.	
I: [. . .] Now we have this team thing here [messing things up], we have our warehouse there and it is so big that you can't be in all the places at the same time, it should be kept like it has always been, divided into areas. Then you know where you are and what there is, and that an 'outsider' does not go [and mess up] your things, that becomes a total mess, you can't find anything . . .	Work divided in to clearly defined areas of responsibility, everything works well if everyone takes care of his share.	
I: We have designers for this and designers for that, but then we have a 'no man's land', we have no one who would co-ordinate the whole.	Bits and pieces, no co-ordination.	

1) I = Informant, 2) R = Researcher

Source: This figure first published in Länsisalmi, et al. (2000), European Journal of Work and Organizational Psychology, 9(4). Reprinted with the permission of Psychology Press.

Table 20.3 Collective stressors and coping mechanisms in divisions A, B and C and work unit X

	Division A	Division B	Division C	Work Unit X
Stressors	– fluctuation – risk of unemployment – social undervaluation	– constantly changing customer needs combined with shortage of time – poor client satisfaction – intra-company competition	– risk of unemployment – social undervaluation, 'penal colony' reputation – implementation of group bonus system	– work overload – pressure towards more extensive autonomy (blue-collar workers) – culture shock due to a restructuring of the organization
Coping problem-focused	– collective responsibility – rotation of employees – rely on hierarchy	– 'workaholism' – providing and relying on getting help – active sharing of information	– rely on hierarchy – watching and controlling peers, labelling lazy ones	– weekly meetings – providing and relying on getting help – solidarity in dividing aversive week end work – clinging to 'own group'
appraisal- and emotion-focused	– climate (= few conflicts in the own group) – blaming others – storytelling ('good old days', 'bun eating')	– climate (= 'perfect', everyone gets along) – belonging to an 'all stars' division compensates for sacrifices – stress interpreted as normal and as an admired state	– climate (= few destructive quarrels in own work group) – gossiping, creating conflicts with other groups – pottering – enhancing isolation, attributing 'badness' outside of own division – storytelling ('good old days', 'we're better' measured by other indicators)	– climate (= people get along well) – belonging to a good work unit (pride) – high degrees of freedom in the own job – storytelling (good old days with no hurry) – 'making Porches'-metaphor

'Good old days' story

Man:	When you compare [this] with the old days, then . . . when there was no work to do, women were knitting socks for weeks. But the boss said that you have to be there, even though there was nothing to do.
Women:	You don't sit around anymore a lot. You have to look for a place to hide, if it looks like you have nothing [to do] in those days, you were allowed to sit around freely, to read the newspaper, to knit. I came here in 73.
Man:	We were cleaning windows.
Woman:	In the garden we raked dead leaves. That was fun.
Man:	And we worked, when there was work.
Interviewer:	Now, people get laid off if there is no work?
Man:	You wouldn't be knitting for long.
Interviewer:	Who decides on these layoffs?
Man:	I believe that the decisions come from up there [the head quarters of the multinational], there they just check this and that. The first impulse probably comes from there. These [managers] here are only messenger boys that obey the orders.
Woman:	Today it's like that.
Man:	There, they just deal with numbers. It is a hard game.

'Bun eating' story

In the old days life in the plant was like living in a prison. Even having a bun with coffee or listening to the radio at the workplace was considered a crime that would be severely punished, if detected by the foremen. Nowadays, the atmosphere at the plant resembles more that of a recreation park; the coffee-machines provided by the employer produce 5 litres of coffee a minute, the workers are eatiing buns, sandwiches, anything, whenever they feel like it, and rock 'n' roll is heard all day long.

Figure 20.2   Example of collective coping (appraisal and emotion-focused): the 'good old days' story and the 'bun eating' story

on discovering the social processes by which certain content is socially validated within a given community of understanding.

In conclusion, we applied grounded theory in our research mainly as a means to describe characteristics and generate hypothesis about the role of collective stress and coping in the context of organizational culture. In our opinion, grounded theory can be used both within an approach that is context-based (which represents the more traditional school of grounded theory) and one that applies *a priori* concepts. Our case study falls somewhere in between these two extremes. If thorough theoretical sampling is possible across units and organizations, grounded theory can be used to generate a formal theory about a certain phenomenon (see Glaser and Strauss, 1967). In our opinion, however, it can also be used as a methodology verifying *a priori* concepts. It could be applied in a similar fashion as template analysis starting from a loosely predetermined conceptual frame and verifying and/or modifying it through gathering and analysing data with grounded theory methodology. In such a context, grounded theory is powerful as it gives room for the interpretation of 'real' experiences of the participants and also provides a systematic means to efficiently analyse large quantities of unstructured qualitative data.

FURTHER READING

For an overview of grounded theory we recommend A. Strauss (1987) *Qualitative Analyses for Social Scientists*, Cambridge, UK: Cambridge University Press. If one is more interested in how to perform grounded theory analysis, in more detail, we recommend the following excellent guides: B. Glaser (1994) *The Constant Comparative Method of Qualitative Analysis*, Sociology Press, pp. 182–92; A.L. Strauss and J. Corbin (1990) *Basics of Qualitative Research: Grounded Theory Procedures and Techniques*, Newbury Park, California: Sage; and A.L. Strauss and J. Corbin (1998) *Basics of Qualitative Research: Techniques and Procedures for Developing Grounded Theory*, Newbury Park, California: Sage.

REFERENCES

Barley, S.R. and Knight, D.B. (1992) 'Toward a cultural theory of stress complaints', in M. Barry, B.M. Staw and L.L. Cummings (eds), *Research in Organizational Behavior*, Greenwich, CT: JAI Press, pp. 1–48.

Brytting, T. (1995) 'Organizing in the small growing firm: a grounded theory approach', in B. Glaser (ed.), *Grounded Theory 1984–1994*, Mill Valley, CA: Sociology Press, pp. 517–38.

Carrero, V., Peiró, J.M. and Salanova, M. (2000) 'Studying radical organizational innovation through grounded theory', *European Journal of Work and Organizational Psychology*, 9: 489–514.

Cooper, G. (ed.) (1998) *Theories of Organizational Stress*, Oxford: Oxford University Press.

Dachler, H.P. (2000) 'Commentary – Taking qualitative methods a (radical) step forward', *European Journal of Work and Organisational Psychology*, 9: 575–83.

Fairclough, N. (1995) *Critical Discourse Analysis. The Critical Study of Language*, New York: Longman Publishing.

Fineman, S. (1995) 'Stress, emotion and intervention', in T. Newton (ed.), *Managing Stress, Emotion and Power at Work*, London: Sage, pp. 120–35.

Gersick, C. J. G. (1988) 'Time and transition in work teams: toward a new model of group development', *Academy of Management Journal*, 31: 9–41.

Glaser, B.G. (1977) *Theoretical Sensitivity: Advances in the Methodology of Grounded Theory*, Mill Valley, CA: Sociology Press.

Glaser, B.G. (1995) *Grounded Theory: 1984–1994*, vol. 1, Mill Valley, CA: Sociology Press.

Glaser, B.G. (1998) *Doing Grounded Theory: Issues and Discussions*, Mill Valley, CA: Sociology Press.

Glaser, B.G. and Strauss, A.L. (1967) *The Discovery of Grounded Theory: Strategies for Qualitative Research*, New York: Aldine.

Graham, L. (1995) *On the Line at Subaru-Isuzu. The Japanese Model and the American Worker*, Ithaca, NY: ILR Press.

Handy, J. (1995) 'Rethinking stress: seeing the collective', in T. Newton (ed.), *Managing Stress, Emotion and Power at Work*, London: Sage, pp. 85–96.

Hatch, M.J. (1997) *Organization Theory. Modern, Symbolic and Postmodern Perspectives*, Oxford: Oxford University Press.

Henwood, K.L. and Pidgeon, N.F. (1992) 'Qualitative research and psychological theorizing', *British Journal of Psychology*, 83: 97–111.

Karasek, R.A. and Theorell, T. (1990) *Healthy Work: Stress, Productivity, and the Reconstruction of Working Life*, New York: Basic Books.

King, N. (2000) 'Commentary – Making ourselves heard: the challenges facing advocates of qualitative research in work and organizational psychology', *European Journal of Work and Organizational Psychology*, 9: 589–96.

Länsisalmi, H., Peiró, J.M. and Kivimäki, M. (2000) 'Collective stress and coping in the context of organisational culture', *European Journal of Work and Organizational Psychology*, 9: 527–59.

Lazarus, R.S. and Folkman, S. (1984) *Stress, Appraisal and Coping*, New York: Crowell.

Lowe, A. (1995) 'Small hotel survival', in B. Glaser (ed.), *Grounded Theory 1984–1994*, Mill Valley, CA: Sociology Press. pp. 589–612.

Macy, B.A., Peterson, M.F. and Norton, L.W. (1989) 'A test of participation theory in a work re-design field setting: degree of participation and comparison site contrasts', *Human Relations*, 42: 1098–165.

Martin, P.Y. and Turner, A.A. (1986) 'Grounded theory and organizational research', *Journal of Applied Behavioral Science*, 22: 141–57.

Meyerson, D.E. (1994) 'Interpretations of stress in institutions: the cultural production of ambiguity and burnout', *Administrative Science Quarterly*, 39: 628–53.

Miller, S., Brody, D. and Summerton, J. (1988) 'Styles of coping with threat: implications for health', *Journal of Personality and Social Psychology*, 54: 142–8.

Newton, T.J. (1995) *Managing Stress, Emotion and Power at Work*, London: Sage.

Quick, D.J., Quick, C.J. and Nelson, D.L. (1998) 'The theory of preventive stress management in organizations', in G.L. Cooper (ed.), *Theories of Organizational Stress*, Oxford: Oxford University Press, pp. 246–68.

Peiró, J.M. (1990) 'Expected developments in work and organizational psychology in Europe in the nineties', in P.J. Drenth, J.A. Sergeant and R.J. Takens (eds), *European Perspectives in Psychology*, vol. 3. Chichester: Wiley, pp. 21–38.

Porter, G. (1996) 'Organizational impact of workaholism: suggestions for researching the negative outcomes of excessive work', *Journal of Occupational Health Psychology*, 1: 70–84.

Price, J.L. (1994) Organizational turnover: an illustration of the grounded theory approach to theory construction', in B. Glaser (ed.), *More Grounded Theory Methodology: A Reader*, Mill Valley, CA: Sociology Press, pp. 323–34.

Rennie, D.L. (1994) 'Clients' deference in psychotherapy', *Journal of Counselling Psychology*, 41: 427–37.

Rhodes, R.H., Hill, C.E., Thompson, B.J. and Elliott, R. (1993) 'Client retrospective recall and resolved and unresolved misunderstanding events', *Journal of Counseling Psychology*, 41: 473–83.

Rousseau, D.M. (1997) 'Organizational behavior in the new organizational era', *Annual Review of Psychology*, 48: 515–46.

Schein, E.H. (1990) 'Organizational culture', *American Psychologist*, 45: 109–119.

Schein, E.H. (1996) 'Culture: The missing concept in organizational studies', *Administrative Science Quarterly*, 41 (June): 229–40.

Strauss, A.L. and Corbin, J. (1990) *Basics of Qualitative Research: Grounded Theory Procedures and Techniques*, Newbury Park, CA: Sage.

Semmer, N., Zapf, D. and Greif, S. (1996) 'Shared job strain: a new approach for assessing the validity of job stress measurements', *Journal of Occupational and Organizational Psychology*, 69: 293–310.

Turner, B.A. (1981) 'Some practical aspects of qualitative data analysis: one way of organizing some of the cognitive processes associated with the generation of grounded theory', *Quality and Quantity*, 15: 225–47.

Van Maanen, J. (1988) *Tales of The Field*, Chicago: University of Chicago Press.

(21)—— Using Templates in the Thematic Analysis of Text ——

Nigel King

WHAT IS TEMPLATE ANALYSIS?

Definitional and epistemological issues

The term 'template analysis' does not describe a single, clearly delineated method; it refers rather to a varied but related group of techniques for thematically organizing and analysing textual data. The essence of template analysis is that the researcher produces a list of codes ('template') representing themes identified in their textual data. Some of these will usually be defined a priori, but they will be modified and added to as the researcher reads and interprets the texts. The template is organized in a way which represents the relationships between themes, as defined by the researcher, most commonly involving a hierarchical structure.

As a set of techniques, rather than a distinct methodology, template analysis may be used within a range of epistemological positions. On the one hand, it can be employed in the kind of realist qualitative work which accepts much of the conventional positivistic position of mainstream quantitative social science. That is to say, research which is concerned with 'discovering' underlying causes of human action, and which seeks to achieve researcher objectivity and to demonstrate coding reliability (for example, Miles and Huberman, 1994; Kent, 2000). On the other hand, template analysis can be used within what Madill et al. (2000) call a 'contextual constructivist' position. Here, the researcher assumes that there are always multiple interpretations to be made of any phenomenon, which depend upon the position of the researcher and the context of the research. Concern with coding reliability is therefore irrelevant; instead issues such as the reflexivity of the researcher, the attempt to approach the topic from differing perspectives, and the richness of the description produced, are important requirements. Phenomenological, interactionist and some narrative approaches fall within this category.

Despite the variety of epistemologies which may support the use of a template approach, there are positions for which it is probably not appropriate. For those researchers seeking to combine qualitative and quantitative analyses, template analysis may appear to produce coded segments which could simply be treated as units of analysis for content analysis. This is highly problematic, however, because of the emphasis in template analysis on the flexible and pragmatic use of coding (see below) – the assumption that the frequency of a code in a particular text corresponds to its salience simply cannot be made. Template analysis is also inappropriate for methodologies taking a radical relativist position, such as discourse analysis, for two main reasons. First, discursive approaches require a much more finely grained analysis than it provides. Secondly, the attaching of codes to segments of text would be seen by a discourse analyst as limiting the possibilities for fully exploring the diversities of meaning – and especially the ambiguities – in the way that language is used to construct reality.

Why use template analysis?

Why should anyone about to embark on a qualitative research project choose to use template analysis? In particular, why should they choose it over other approaches which resemble it and for which there exists a more substantial literature, such as grounded theory (for example, Strauss and Corbin, 1990; Carrero et al., 2000) and interpretative phenomenological analysis (IPA: for example, Smith, 1996; Jarman et al., 1997)? In this section I will consider the advantages that template analysis may offer in relation to these two approaches.

Focusing first on grounded theory, for some researchers a preference for template analysis may be based on their philosophical position. While it may be argued that grounded theory is not wedded to one epistemological approach (Charmaz, 1995), it has been developed and utilized largely as a realist methodology. That is to say, its users have mostly claimed to be uncovering the 'real' beliefs, attitudes, values and so on of the participants in their research. Those qualitative researchers taking a contextual constructivist stance that is sceptical of the existence of 'real' internal states to be discovered through empirical research, may therefore feel that template analysis is more conducive to their position.

Template analysis may also be preferred by those who are not inimical to the assumptions of grounded theory, but find it too prescriptive in that it specifies procedures for data gathering and analysis that *must* be followed (Strauss and Corbin, 1990). In contrast, template analysis is, on the whole a more flexible technique with fewer specified procedures, permitting researchers to tailor it to match their own requirements.

When employed within a broadly phenomenological approach, template analysis is in practice very similar to IPA, in terms of the development of conceptual themes and their clustering into broader groupings, and the eventual identification across cases of 'master themes' with their subsidiary 'constituent themes'. The main differences between these approaches are the use of a priori codes in template analysis, and the balance between within and across case analysis. IPA tends to analyse individual cases in greater depth before attempting any integration of a full set of cases. The net effect of these differences is that template analysis is generally somewhat less time-consuming than IPA, and can handle rather larger data sets more comfortably. IPA studies are commonly based on samples of 10 or fewer; template analysis studies usually have rather more participants, 20 to 30 being common. Template analysis works particularly well when the aim is to compare the perspectives of different groups of staff within a specific context.

Defining codes

Put simply, a code is a label attached to a section of text to index it as relating to a theme or issue in the data which the researcher has identified as important to his or her interpretation. To take a hypothetical example, in the transcript of an interview with a work-based counsellor, the researcher might define codes to identify the points in the text where the interviewee mentions particular groups of staff ('senior managers', 'middle managers', 'clerical staff', and so on), or particular categories of presenting problems ('workload problems', 'relationships at work', 'relationships outside work'). Codes such as these are essentially descriptive, requiring little or no analysis by the researcher of what the interviewee means. Many codes will be more interpretative, and therefore harder to define clearly; in our hypothetical example, these might include codes relating to the counsellor's feelings about the mismatch between their own and clients' perceptions of their role.

Hierarchical coding

A key feature of template analysis is the hierarchical organization of codes, with groups of similar codes clustered together to produce more general higher-order codes. Returning to the workplace counselling example, separate codes relating to 'unrealistic client expectations', 'uncertainty about availability of resources' and 'confusion in relationships with outside agencies' might be incorporated into a single higher-order code, 'effects of lack of role clarity'. Hierarchical coding allows the researcher to analyse texts at varying levels of specificity. Broad higher-order codes can give a good overview of the general direction of the interview, while detailed lower-order codes allow for very fine distinctions to be made, both within and between cases. There can be as many levels of coding as the researcher finds useful, but it is worth bearing in mind that too many levels can be counter productive to the goal of attaining clarity in organizing and interpreting the data.

Parallel coding

Template analysis usually permits parallel coding of segments of text, whereby the same segment is classified within two (or more) different codes at the same level. Parallel coding is only likely to be problematic in research which is located strongly towards the positivistic end of the qualitative research spectrum, where researchers may wish to combine template analysis with elements of quantitative content analysis.

The study: managing mental health in primary care

The project I will be describing here examined general practitioners' decisions about the management of patients with mental health problems, with a particular emphasis on their understanding of service delivery and organization. This is an area that has long been recognized as problematic for primary care (for example, Freeling and Tylee, 1992). It was commissioned by the relevant health authority in the hope that it would inform choices about the mental health services purchased on behalf of GPs by the authority. The research was carried out by myself and Julia Maskrey. Two main research questions were posed:

1. What factors do GPs perceive to be influential in their mental health treatment/management decisions?
2. What are GPs' experiences of and attitudes towards mental health service providers?

The study district was largely urban, but with a very mixed population in terms of class and ethnicity. The 13 participating GPs were recruited with the assistance of local GP representatives to include a cross-section of practice areas. Three of the GPs were female and 10 were male. The average age of the GPs was 30 and the average length of time spent in the profession was nine-and-a-half years.

The method chosen for this study was that of focus group interviews. Focus groups are a valuable way of gaining insight into shared understandings and beliefs, while still allowing individual differences of opinion to be voiced. They enable participants to hear the views and experiences of their peers, and cause them to reflect back on their own experiences and thoughts. At the beginning of each focus group, each GP was asked to comment on one of six previously recorded cases, focusing on any particularly difficult or notable experiences. Discussion of particular cases then led into a wider consideration of issues relating to mental health services. The interviewers used a set of broad topic headings to guide the interviews, but tried as far as possible to allow the participants to lead the discussion. Each of the focus group interviews lasted for approximately one and a half hours, and was tape-recorded for later transcription.

DEVELOPING THE TEMPLATE

In this section I will describe the development of the analytical template, illustrating throughout with examples from the 'Managing mental health' study. It is crucial to recognize that development of the template is not a separate stage from its usage in analysis of texts. A useful contrast can be made with content analysis, where the researcher first constructs a coding scheme, then applies it to the texts to generate quantitative data for statistical analysis. In qualitative template analysis, the initial template is applied in order to analyse the text through the process of coding, but is itself revised in the light of the ongoing analysis.

Creating the initial template

As noted earlier, template analysis normally starts with at least a few pre-defined codes which help guide analysis. The first issue for the researcher is, of course, how extensive the initial template should be. The danger of starting with too many pre-defined codes is that the initial template may blinker analysis, preventing you from considering data which conflict with your assumptions. At the other extreme, starting with too sparse a set of codes can leave you lacking in any clear direction and feeling overwhelmed by the mass of rich, complex data.

Often the best starting point for constructing an initial template is the interview topic guide – the set of question areas, probes and prompts used by the interviewer. The topic guide itself draws on some or all of the following sources, depending on the substantive content and philosophical orientation of a particular study: the academic literature, the researcher's own personal experience, anecdotal and informal evidence, and exploratory research. Main questions from the guide can serve as higher-order codes, with subsidiary questions and probes as potential lower-order codes. This is most effective where the topic guide is fairly substantial and (in qualitative terms) structured, with the interviewer defining in advance most of the topics to be covered. In contrast, some research requires a more minimalistic approach to the construction of the topic guide, allowing most issues to emerge within each individual interview. This was the case in our 'Managing mental health' study; issues for discussion were identified during the first part of each group interview, where GPs described individual cases. We did produce a list of issues to raise ourselves if the participants did not bring them up, and this was added to as the study progressed, but it was not sufficiently detailed to serve as an analytical template in itself.

The approach Julia Maskrey and I used was to develop an initial template by each examining a sub-set of the transcript data (one group interview each), defining codes in the light of the stated aims of the project. We then considered each other's suggestions and agreed a provisional template to use on the full data set. This kind of collaborative strategy is valuable as it forces the researcher to justify the inclusion of each code, and to clearly define how it should be used.

1   CASE BACKGROUND HISTORY

    1   Illness category
    2   Treatment history
    3   Patient's personal history

2   THE CONSULTATION

    1   Presenting problem
    2   Treatment/management offered
        1   Prescription
        2   Advice
        3   Referral
    3   Factors influencing treatment/management
        1   Patient/GP interpersonal relationship
        2   The GP role
            1   GP's own perception of role
            2   GP workload/time pressure

3   SERVICE CONTACT

    1   Service(s) used
        Practice nurse
        Psychiatrist
        Clinical psychologist
        Community psychiatric nurse
        Social worker
        CAST (community assessment team)
        CRUSE (bereavement counselling)
        Relate
        Drug rehabilitation
        Other voluntary services
    2   Factors influencing GP use of service
        Role responsibilities of service
        Communication difficulties
        Availability of service
        Response time of service
        Personal familiarity with individual service provider
        GP knowledge about mental health services
        Flexibility of service
        Appropriateness of specific intervention(s)

4   POSSIBLE AREAS OF IMPROVEMENT

    1   Areas identified in course of discussion
    2   Priorities for investment (responses to specific question)

Figure 21.1   Initial template from the 'managing mental health' study

As can be seen in Figure 21.1, the initial template consists of four highest-order codes, sub-divided into one, two or three levels of lower-order codes. The extent of sub-division broadly reflects depth of analysis, with the second and third highest-order codes ('The Consultation' and 'Service Contact') covering the central issues of the study; patient management decisions in the selected target cases, and GPs' wider experiences of the various mental health services available to their patients. (For the sake of clarity I will henceforth refer to coding levels numerically, with the highest order codes being 'level one' and the lowest 'level four').

The first level-one code is 'Case Background History', which comprises three level-two codes: 'Illness category', 'Treatment history' and 'Patient's personal history'. It would have been entirely possible to further sub-divide these codes. However, as these biographical issues were tangential to the main research questions of the study, and as time and resources were tight, no further levels were defined.

The second level-one code ('the Consultation') relates to accounts of specific consultations with patients. Level-two codes index references to the particular problem the patient presented with on the occasion in question, the treatment or management offered, and factors influencing its choice. This area is of direct relevance to the study's aims, and therefore required a more finely-grained analysis than the first level-one code, hence the inclusion of four levels of coding on the initial template.

'Service Contact' is the third level-one code, and also encompasses key issues for the study. It is used to index accounts of mental health services used by the GPs in the study, mentioned either in the course of describing specific cases, or in the more general discussion of issues arising. The first level-two code here is purely descriptive, identifying sections of transcripts where references to services are made. Ten level-three codes specify particular services, or types of service used by the GPs. The second level-two code relates to factors influencing when and how they choose to utilize specific services.

Finally, 'Possible areas of improvement' is the fourth level-one code. While this was an important issue, it was secondary to the main aims of the study. Therefore, on the initial template the code was sub-divided only as far as two second-order codes, the first identifying areas for improvement emerging in the course of the focus group discussions, the second covering comments specifically about how GPs would prioritize future investment in mental health services.

Revising the template

Once an initial template is constructed, the researcher must work systematically through the full set of transcripts, identifying sections of text which are relevant to the project's aims, and marking them with one or more appropriate code(s) from the initial template. In the course of this, inadequacies in the initial template will be revealed, requiring changes of various kinds. It is through these that the template develops to its final form. Below I describe five main types of modification likely to be made whilst revising an initial template, illustrating with examples from our study:

INSERTION
Where the researcher identifies an issue in the text of relevance to the research question, but not covered by an existing code, it is necessary to add a new code. Arguably the most significant

insertion in this analysis was the definition of 'Inter-agency issues' as a level-one code, embracing a set of lower level codes which were either new themselves or had initially appeared elsewhere in the template. This was in recognition of our increasing awareness over the course of the analysis that inter-agency issues were a key theme in much of the GPs' discussion:

> Sometimes, when there's a large team and you contact a central point [pause] the case is allocated, you tend to lose a bit of control and you're speaking to someone who's nameless.

DELETION

An initially defined code may be deleted at the end of the process of template construction simply because the researcher has found no need to use it. Alternately, a code which had seemed to represent a distinct theme may be found to substantially overlap with other codes (perhaps as a result of re-definitions) and again will be deleted.

On our initial template, under the level-one code 'Possible areas of improvement' we distinguished between suggestions arising in the course of discussion, unprompted by us as interviewers, and suggestions made in response to a direct question about participants' priorities for additional investment. On reflection we decided that there was so much overlap in the kinds of comments arising in these two contexts that it did not make sense to keep these as separate level-two codes. We therefore deleted both and replaced them with two new codes, identifying whether the suggestions were related to particular services or general improvements (such as 'better communication').

CHANGING SCOPE

Where the researcher finds that a code is either too narrowly defined or too broadly defined to be useful, the code will need to be re-defined at a lower or higher level.

We used this kind of modification extensively in developing our template. 'GP Role' was initially a level-three code, defined narrowly as one of the factors influencing treatment/ management decisions in specific consultations. It very soon became apparent that this was an issue of much wider relevance to the study, and we consequently revised the template to include it as a level-one code:

> I think you've also got to bear in mind that people have got an individual responsibility, so, my feeling would be that patients have an individual responsibility for themselves, and they can't just bring all their woes and off-load them on their GP and expect them to give them answers.

At the same time, we decided to use 'the Consultation' code simply to index descriptive details about patients discussed by participants, and therefore reduced it in scope to a level two code, under 'Case background details'.

CHANGING HIGHER-ORDER CLASSIFICATION

The researcher may decide that a code initially classified as a sub-category of one higher-order code would fit better as a sub-category of a different higher-order code.

We used this modification in several places in our study's template, often in conjunction with other types of modification. For example, we initially included 'Communication difficulties with specialists' as a third level code, under 'Factors influencing service use'. We subsequently decided that it would be clearer if this second-level code was removed, and all the individual factors which had comprised it (including 'Communication . . .') were placed as third-level codes under each of the individual services identified. Later in the analysis, the higher-order classification of 'Communication . . .' was then changed again, as a second-level code under the newly-defined level-one code; 'Inter-agency issues'. It was also redefined as referring to all kinds of communication issues, and not just 'difficulties':

> What was good about the clinical psychologist is that you could grab her and say 'I've got this lady, or gentleman, this situation, which direction do you think I should be going and is it worthwhile you seeing them?' So you could actually relate an actual scenario, and that was very useful.

Thus the process of finding a suitable location in the template for this code involved all four of the types of modification I have identified; the *deletion* of 'Factors influencing service use', two *changes to higher-order classification*, the *insertion* of 'Inter-agency issues' and a *change in scope* from third to second level.

The 'final' template

One of the most difficult decisions to make when constructing an analytical template is where to stop the process of development. It is possible to go on modifying and refining definitions of codes almost ad infinitum, but research projects inevitably face external constraints which mean that you do not have unlimited time to produce an 'ideal' template. The decision about when a template is 'good enough' is always going to be unique to a particular project and a particular researcher. However, no template can be considered 'final' if there remain any sections of text which are clearly relevant to the research question, but remain uncoded. Also, as a rough rule of thumb, it is most unlikely that a template could be considered final if all the data have not been read through – and the coding scrutinized – at least twice.

Commonly most or all of the texts will have been read through at least three or four times before you begin to feel comfortable with the template. It is generally easier to make a confident judgement that the point has been reached to stop the development of the template where two or more researchers are collaborating on the analysis. A solo researcher might use one or more outside experts to help determine whether the template is sufficiently clear and comprehensive to call a halt to modifications.

Figure 21.2 shows the 'final' template from the 'Managing mental health' study.

Using software in template analysis

Recent years have seen major developments in qualitative research software, both in terms of the range of products available and their power and utility. Amongst the best known are NUD*IST and NVivo, both produced by QSR, and Atlas TI. Although the facilities offered by such programs vary, they generally enable the researcher to index segments of text to particular themes, to link research notes to coding, and to carry out complex search and retrieve operations. NVivo also has powerful tools to aid the researcher in examining possible relationships amongst themes (see Gibbs, 2002, for a detailed account of the use of NVivo). It is, of course, true that software can only aid in organizing and examining the data, and cannot by itself make any kind of judgement; however, computerization enables the researcher

1   CASE BACKGROUND HISTORY

    1   The consultation
        1   Presenting problem
        2   Treatment/management decision
            1   Prescription
            2   Advice
            3   Referral
    2   Management/treatment history
    3   Patient's personal history

2   GP ROLE AND RELATIONSHIP ISSUES

    1   GP Role
        1   GP perceptions of role
            1   Changing role
            2   Inappropriate aspects of role
        2   GP workload
            1   'Shifting' patients to other agencies
            2   Reduction in amount of advice provided for patients
        3   GP lack of mental health training
    2   GP/patient interaction
        1   Quality of GP/patient relationship
        2   GP perceptions of patient
            1   Need to 'protect' other services
            2   Somatisation
            3   Ethnicity
    3   Patient's co-operation/compliance
    4   Stigma of mental illness

3   INTER-AGENCY ISSUES

    1   Inter-agency communication
        1   Between GPs and other agencies
            1   Psychiatry
            2   Clinical psychology
            3   Community mental health team
            4   Practice-based counsellors
            5   Alternative therapists
            6   Voluntary agencies
            7   Other agencies in general
    2   Amongst other agencies
        1   Psychiatry
        2   Clinical psychology
        3   Community mental health team
        4   Practice-based counsellors
        5   Alternative therapists
        6   Voluntary agencies

Figure 21.2   Final template from the 'managing mental health' study

            7   Other agencies in general
    2   GP's personal familiarity with other agencies
    3   GP's knowledge/understanding of other agencies
            1   Effects of changes in mental health services
            2   Formal information provided for GPs

4   SPECIFIC SERVICES

    1   Psychiatry
    2   Clinical psychology
            1   Rapid access
            2   Other
    3   Community Mental Health Team
            1   CAST
            2   Community psychiatric nurses
            3   Social workers6
            4   Team as a whole
    4   Practice-based counsellors
    5   Alternative therapists
    6   Drug and alcohol services
    7   Voluntary agencies
            1   CRUSE
            2   Relate
            3   Drug rehabilitation
            4   MIND
            5   Others
    8   Child services
            1   Psychiatry
            2   Psychology
            3   Others

    1   Degree of use
    2   Specific skills
    3   Availability
            1   Via cross-referral
            2   Waiting times
    4   Flexibility of service
    5   Effectiveness of interventions
        Patient attitudes to service
    7   Comparisons between services
    8   Role responsibilities
    9   Appropriateness for particular problems
            1   Is appropriate
            2   Is inappropriate

5   POSSIBLE AREAS FOR IMPROVEMENT

    1   Specific services
            Clinical psychology
            Community mental health team
            Practice-based counselling
            Substance abuse services
            Child services
            Adult psychiatry
            Forensic psychology
    2   General areas for improvement
            1   Communication
            2   Definition of roles
                    1   GPs'
                    2   Others'
    3   Reduced frequency of organizational change

Figure 21.2 *cont.*

to work efficiently with complex coding schemes and large amounts of text, facilitating depth and sophistication of analysis. The time needed to prepare data and to learn to use packages effectively may deter some researchers, but the recent improvements in both software and instructional materials more than compensate for this in all but the smallest of projects. The central role of the template structure in template analysis makes it an approach which is particularly well-suited to computer-assisted analysis.

INTERPRETING AND PRESENTING TEMPLATE ANALYSIS

Interpretation

It is sometimes assumed that developing a template and using it to code a set of transcripts (or other textual data) constitutes the process of analysis *in toto*. All that is left is to report which codes occurred where in which transcripts. Such an approach leads to a very flat, descriptive account of the data, providing little more depth than would be gained from quantitative content analysis, but without the rigorously consistent definition of units of analysis required to properly carry out that method. The template and the coding derived from it are only means to the end of interpreting the texts, helping the researcher to produce an account which does as much justice as possible to the richness of the data within the constraints of a formal report, paper, or dissertation.

It would be inappropriate to set out any general rules for how a researcher should go about the task of interpreting coded data; a strategy must be developed which fits the aims and content of a particular study. I will offer some guidelines and examples which may serve as a useful starting point, but urge readers not to view these as the only permissible strategies.

LISTING CODES

I usually find it useful at an early stage to compile a list of all codes occurring in each transcript, with some indication of frequency. Most qualitative analysis software packages enable you to do this very simply. If coding is entirely by hand, it is important that codes are marked very clearly in margins, ideally with some colour-coding, to make it possible to list codes quickly and accurately. The distribution of codes within and across transcripts can help to draw attention to aspects of the data which warrant further examination. For example, if a theme occurs prominently in all but one of a set of interview transcripts, it may be revealing to look closely at the one exception and attempt to explain why the code was absent.

A word of warning about the counting of codes is required. While patterns in the distribution of codes within and across cases may suggest areas for closer examination, the frequency of codes per se can never tell us anything meaningful about textual data.

SELECTIVITY

Perhaps the opposite danger to that of drifting into a quasi-quantitative approach through counting codes is that of unselectivity, where the researcher attempts to examine and interpret every code to an equal degree of depth. Novice researchers fall into the trap of unselectivity for the best of reasons, heeding exhortations to keep an open mind and not allow the analysis to be limited by their own prior assumptions. This is valuable advice, but it has to be followed realistically, which means that you must seek to identify those themes which are of most central relevance to the task of building an understanding of the phenomena under investigation.

OPENNESS

The need to be selective in analysing and interpreting data must be balanced against the need to retain openness towards it. You must not be so strongly guided by the initial research questions that you disregard all themes which are not obviously of direct relevance. Themes which are judged to be of marginal relevance can play a useful role in adding to the background detail of the study, without requiring lengthy explication. More problematic are those themes that are clearly of great importance to participants, but that seem to lie well outside the scope of the study, and perhaps were even deliberately excluded from it. In such cases, you must carefully consider whether investigation of the 'excluded' theme casts any significant light on the interpretation of central themes in the study. If it does, then it should be included in the analysis.

RELATIONSHIPS BETWEEN THEMES: BEYOND THE LINEAR TEMPLATE

The standard template depicts the relationship between themes as a linear one; each code is listed in turn with its subsidiary codes next to it, down to as many levels of hierarchy as are identified. This simple structure has advantages in terms of clarity – an important point when it comes to presenting findings, as I discuss below. However, it may not reflect the kinds of relationships a researcher may want to depict in his or her analysis. Even in the example I have used here, the final template shows some deviation from a purely linear structure, with the group of fourth-level codes under 'Specific services' shown as applying to all other codes in this section of the template. Similarly, in a study of experiences of diabetic renal disease, my co-authors and I identified two 'integrative themes' which we felt permeated all the other themes coded on the template (King et al., 2002). Crabtree and Miller (1999) recommend the use of maps, matrices and other diagrams to explore and display template analysis findings. The researcher should feel free to use these kinds of strategies in building their interpretations, and not feel that analysis has to stop at the point where a full linear template is produced.

Presentation

The final task facing you is to present an account of your interpretation of the data, often in the limited space of a few thousand words in a report or academic paper. I firmly believe that writing-up should not be seen as a separate stage from analysis and interpretation, but rather as a continuation of it. Through summarizing detailed notes about themes, selecting illustrative quotes, and producing a coherent 'story' of the findings, the researcher continues to build his or her understanding of the phenomena the research project has investigated.

As with other stages of template analysis, it is impossible to define one single correct or ideal way to present findings. The researcher needs to consider the nature of the data, the type of document to be produced (including its word length) and, critically, the intended readership. All the same, it is possible to identify three common approaches to presentation; any one of which might prove useful, at least as a starting point.

(i) *A set of individual case-studies, followed by a discussion of differences and similarities between cases.* This gives the reader a good grasp of the perspectives of individual participants, and can help to ensure that the discussion of themes does not become too abstracted from their accounts of their experience. However, where there are a relatively large number of participants, this format can be confusing for the reader, and it does rely on there being sufficient space to provide an adequate description of each case.

(ii) *An account structured around the main themes identified, drawing illustrative examples from each transcript (or other text) as required.* This tends to be the approach which most readily produces a clear and succinct thematic discussion. The danger is of drifting towards generalizations, and losing sight of the individual experiences from which the themes are drawn.

(iii) *A thematic presentation of the findings, using a different individual case-study to illustrate each of the main themes.* This can be a useful synthesis of approaches (i) and (ii) above; the key problem is how to select the cases in a way which fairly represents the themes in the data as a whole.

Whatever approach is taken, the use of direct quotes from the participants is essential. These should normally include both short quotes to aid the understanding of specific points of interpretation – such as clarifying the way in which two themes differ – and a smaller number of more extensive passages of quotation, giving participants a flavour of the original texts.

ADVANTAGES AND DISADVANTAGES OF THE TECHNIQUE

Throughout this chapter I have alluded to a variety of advantages and disadvantages of using template analysis; I will draw them together here to present what I hope is a balanced summary. The greatest advantage of template analysis resides in the fact that it is a highly flexible approach that can be modified for the needs of any study in a particular area. It does not come with a heavy baggage of prescriptions and procedures, and as such is especially welcome to those who want to take a phenomenological and experiential approach to organizational research. At the same time, the principles behind the technique are easily grasped by those relatively unfamiliar with qualitative methods – in part because of the similarities to content analysis – and as such it can be a valuable introduction to the whole field. Template analysis works very well in studies which seek to examine the perspectives of different groups within an organizational context – for example, different professions working in a collaborative setting, or different grades of staff affected by a particular organizational change. Finally, the discipline of producing the template forces the researcher to take a well-structured approach to handling the data, which can be a great help in producing a clear, organized, final account of a study.

Regarding disadvantages, the lack of a substantial literature on this kind of technique, compared to that on grounded theory or discourse analysis, can leave the lone novice researcher feeling very unsure of the analytic decisions he or she has to make. This can result in templates that are too simple to allow any depth of interpretation, or (more often) too complex to be manageable. It can also result in the dangers of over-descriptiveness and of 'losing' individual participants' voices in the analysis of aggregated themes, which I discussed above. Networking with experienced researchers and with fellow novices is highly recommended to tackle such difficulties. The Internet is an increasingly useful tool for this, as there are several discussion lists devoted to issues around qualitative research.

CONCLUDING COMMENTS

A fundamental tension in template analysis (indeed in most qualitative research) is between the need to be open to the data and the need to impose some shape and structure on the analytical process. Too much openness and the product is likely to be chaotic and incoherent; too much structure can leave the researcher with all the drawbacks of quantitative research but none of its advantages. I have tried to offer guidance as to how the reader may cope successfully with this tension throughout this chapter. If anything, I have tended to veer towards an over-structured rather than under-structured approach, because in my experience newcomers to this type of research more often suffer from too much openness than too little. You must remember that there are no absolute rules here; in the end you must define an approach to analysis that suits your own research topic and the epistemological position you wish to take.

FURTHER READING

There is a large volume of literature which discusses thematic analysis in general, much of which can usefully inform the use of template analysis (for example, Flick, 2002; Silverman, 1999). Relatively little, however, deals specifically with the template approach. One exception is Crabtree and Miller's (1999) chapter, 'Using codes and code manuals: a template organizing style of interpretation'. Note that they include matrix analysis approaches within their remit, which are dealt with in Chapter 22 of the present volume (Nadin and Casell). The paper by King et al. (2002), although in a health rather than organizational psychology area, may be a useful example of applying the template approach in a phenomenologically oriented study. Finally, readers may find my website on template analysis a helpful resource: http://www.hud.ac.uk/hhs/research/template_analysis/

REFERENCES

Carrero, V., Peiró, J.M. and Salanova, M. (2000) 'Studying radical organizational innovation through grounded theory', *European Journal of Work and Organizational Psychology*, 9 (4): 489–514.

Charmaz, K. (1995) 'Grounded theory' in J.A.Smith, R.Harré and L. Van Langenhove (eds), *Rethinking Methods in Psychology*, London: Sage.

Crabtree, B.F. and Miller, W.L. (1999) 'Using codes and code manuals: a template organizing style of interpretation', in B.F. Crabtree and W.L. Miller (eds), *Doing Qualitative Research*, second edition, Newbury Park, CA: Sage.

Flick, U. (2002) *An Introduction to Qualitative Research*, second edition, London: Sage.

Freeling, P. and Tylee, A. (1992) 'Depression in general practice', in E.S. Paykel (ed.), *Handbook of Affective Disorders*, second edition, Edinburgh: Churchill Livingstone.

Gibbs, G. (2002) *Qualitative Data Analysis: Explorations with NVivo*, Buckingham: Open University Press.

Jarman, M., Smith, J.A. and Walsh, S. (1997) 'The psychological battle for control: a qualitative study of healthcare professionals' understandings of the treatment of anorexia nervosa', *Journal of Community and Applied Social Psychology*, 7: 137–152.

Kent, G. (2000) 'Understanding the experiences of people with disfigurements: an integration of four models of social and psychological functioning', *Psychology, Health and Medicine*, 5 (2): 117–29.

King, N., Carroll, C., Newton, P. and Dornan, T. (2002) '"You can't cure it so you have to endure it": the experience of adaptation to diabetic renal disease', *Qualitative Health Research*, 12 (3): 329–46.

Madill, A., Jordan, A. and Shirley, C. (2000) 'Objectivity and reliability in qualitative analysis: realist, contextualist and radical constructionist epistemologies', *British Journal of Psychology*, 91: 1–20.

Miles, M.B. and Huberman, A.M. (1994) *Qualitative Data Analysis: An Expanded Sourcebook*, Beverly Hills, CA: Sage.

Silverman, D. (1999) *Doing Qualitative Research*, London: Sage.

Smith, J.A. (1996) 'Beyond the divide between cognition and discourse: using interpretative phenomenological analysis in health psychology', *Psychology and Health*, 11: 261–71.

Strauss, A. and Corbin, J. (1990) *Basics of Qualitative Research: Grounded Theory Procedures and Techniques*, Newbury Park: Sage.

Using Data Matrices

Sara Nadin and Catherine Cassell

Data matrices are a way of displaying qualitative data in a format where they are readily accessible for the process of interpretation. Although the main purpose of matrices is as a way of presenting various types of data, they can also be used as part of the qualitative data analysis process. Matrices derive from the work of Miles and Huberman and their uses are outlined in detail in *Qualitative Data Analysis: An Expanded Sourcebook* (1994). In this chapter we will firstly describe what a matrix is and then outline some of the ways in which matrices can be used. We will then provide a case example from the first author's own research and conclude by evaluating some of the advantages and disadvantages of using matrices for analysing qualitative data.

WHAT IS A MATRIX?

'A matrix is essentially the "crossing" of two lists, set up as rows and columns' (1994: 3). It typically takes the form of a table, although it may also take the form of 'networks' – a series of nodes with links between them. Each row and column is labelled, with rows usually representing the unit of analysis – be it by site, if a between site analysis or comparison is being conducted, or by different individuals from the same site for a within site analysis. The columns typically represent concepts, issues or characteristics pertinent to the research questions. It is important to stress that deciding what the columns and rows represent is an integral part of data analysis and interpretation, informed by the research questions and what is important and what is not in relation to those questions. Another factor determining what the columns and rows represent is the function or purpose of the matrix which can range from providing a general description to providing an in-depth comparative analysis.

The actual information contained in the matrix can take a variety of different forms (for example, blocks of text, quotes, ratings symbolic figures and so on), though when using interview transcripts the use of direct quotations where possible is recommended. Again, selecting what goes into each 'box' is a decision grounded in an in-depth analysis of the data. As such, matrix construction is itself the result of an in-depth analytical process from which further analysis and interpretations can be made.

HOW CAN MATRICES BE USED?

Miles and Huberman (1994) distinguish between matrices which are *descriptive* and those which are *explanatory*. Descriptive matrices aim to make complex data more understandable by reducing it to its component parts. In doing so these can supply the basic material for explanations and therefore enable the theory generation or testing process. In explanatory matrices the concern is with trying to understand *why* specific things happen as they do, with the matrix enabling the display of explanations which seem relevant to a particular question. The boundary between describing and explaining is not always apparent and both are key stages of the qualitative data analysis process. Miles and Huberman suggest that:

> Naturally there is no clear boundary between describing and explaining; the researcher typically moves through a series of analysis episodes that condense more and more data into a more and more coherent understanding of what, how and why. (1944: 91)

The idea of *display* is central: the aim being to provide visibility to the process of data analysis. Miles and Huberman also point out that the key skill of constructing a data analysis matrix is to make a large amount of data 'accessible' and meaningful whilst doing justice to the complexity of the data by enabling cross site and within site comparisons – especially to the reader who is looking at the research for the first time. They argue that this is different from typical methods of qualitative data display where readers are often confronted with data that are dispersed over many pages, sequential rather than simultaneous, and often poorly ordered and bulky. Good displays have clear advantages for both the researcher and the reader, enabling them to absorb large amounts of information quickly.

A key advantage of matrices is their flexibility. They can be used at various points in a project for a range of different functions. Initially they may be used to get an overview of the data in an exploratory way or, later in the project, to carry out a more detailed analysis. Matrices can also be used for different levels of analysis. For example, for within site analysis they can be used for combining parallel data from a range of research methods. Alternatively they can be used for combining data from several cases for cross-site analysis.

STAGES OF MATRIX ANALYSIS

The first stage of creating a matrix is to create a synopsis of a case. Once data have been collected, Miles and Huberman suggest a 'contact summary sheet' be drawn up relating to each site:

> After a field contact (from one to several days) and the production of write ups, there is often a need to pause and ponder: what were the main concepts, themes and issues that I saw during this contact? Without such reflection it is easy to get lost in a welter of detail. (1994: 51)

A contact summary sheet is a single sheet with some focusing or summarizing questions about the contact. The field worker reviews the written up field notes and answers each question briefly to develop an overall summary of the main points in the contact. This summary can also draw on all the different data collection tools used and can provide a structure for the analysis as a whole.

The next stage of matrix analysis is coding of data. This is a key element in all qualitative data analysis. Inevitably at this stage of the process the researcher needs to make a decision about whether to code all data or not, and the extent to which the aim is to produce a 'thick' or 'thin' textured description (Geertz, 1973). Miles and Huberman detail a number of ways in which data can be coded and categorized. They emphasize that coding is analysis

(1994: 56). One of the problems of qualitative data analysis can be data overload. By beginning to code data in the early stages of a study, some of the problems associated with this can be compensated for. This is similar to template analysis (see King, Chapter 21, this volume) where the aim is to have an initial start list (pre-determined codes). The transcripts are then read, adding labels at the side thus generating further codes, with the codes then arranged into categories in the template.

Once an initial coding has been completed, revision of the codes is necessary. For example, some codes may have become redundant with the data now more appropriately categorized under a different label; others become too big and need breaking down further. Miles and Huberman use the four stages proposed by Lincoln and Guba (1985) to describe the most common types of revisions and modifications made as: filling in, extension, bridging and surfacing. They also offer some useful practical tips on entering data into matrix displays, warning against the *over-reduction* of data which may actually obscure understanding. They suggest it is important to keep note of the decision rules used when deciding what data went where and why. They also recommend that the type of table used in analysis should be the one used in the final report enabling the readers themselves to see how conclusions were drawn, rather than being handed study results to be taken on blind faith. This notion of an audit trail is one that is increasingly being used as a criterion for assessing the quality of qualitative research, for example the dependability of qualitative findings (Lincoln and Guba, 1990).

A completed matrix is not the end point of the analysis. This then has to be further interpreted and analysed with care, the aim of which is to produce meaningful conclusions which are then written up alongside the matrix. These conclusions are called 'analytic text' and are an integral part of matrix analysis. At this stage, having the data displayed in a matrix format is useful as the researcher can constantly refer between the matrix and original field notes. In this way, interpretations can be checked and clarified and information in the matrix can be added to or modified if necessary. (It is at this stage that one advantage of having thoroughly coded and categorized the interview material is realized simply in terms of locating the original section of text). Analysing the matrix usually involves looking for relationships or patterns – these may be points of contrast or points of similarity and can be either by row or by column label. The analytical process will be grounded in and guided by the research questions to which the matrices relate.

It is essential that the whole matrix is displayed on one page, regardless of how big it has to be. Having the matrix split over two or more pages such that it is not possible to view all the information at the same time defeats the object of matrix analysis, and arguably offers little advantage over attempting to analyse pages and pages of text.

Similarly, for the reader, it is essential for the analytic text to be presented alongside the matrix such that the reader is able to view both at the same time. Presenting the matrix without the analytic text or the analytic text without the matrix is of little use. As Miles and Huberman put it, 'the display does not speak for itself – and the analytic text does not stand alone without reference to the display' (1994: 100)

DIFFERENT TYPES OF MATRIX

As noted previously, one of the advantages of matrices is the diverse ways in which they can be used. Examples that have been used by the authors include time ordered displays where the researcher can order longitudinal data by time and sequence. This is useful in terms of the chronological flow and sequencing of events. The second author used matrices in this way for a series of longitudinal case studies that covered a two year period (Cassell, 1989). Other types of display are role ordered displays where information is ordered according to people's roles in a formal or informal setting, or conceptually ordered displays where the data are ordered around concepts or variables. In the example that follows the display focuses on different levels of analysis, and data are ordered around those different levels of analysis.

Matrices can also be used within a variety of epistemological approaches. Miles and Huberman define themselves as 'in the lineage' of 'transcendental realism' – the belief that social phenomena exist not only in the mind but also in the objective world – and that some lawful and reasonably stable relationships are to be found among them. They acknowledge the difficulty of attempting to explore such relationships given the complex social structures in which these relationships are embedded (structures which are often invisible but nevertheless real) – but it is not an impossible task. Miles and Huberman could be described as post positivists in that they share a desire for the traditional validity and replicability measures associated with more positivist approaches. However matrices can be used within a number of different epistemological stances. The case that follows for example comes from a constructivist perspective. Miles and Huberman themselves play down the importance of their epistemological position concluding that ultimately, it is pragmatic concerns which dominate:

> We just want to do good analysis, and we believe, perhaps less naively than the reader might think at first, that any method that works – that will produce clear, verifiable, replicable meanings from a set of qualitative data – is grist for our mill, regardless of its (epistemological) antecedents. (1994: 17)

A CASE EXAMPLE

Two matrices from the same research project will be presented. The focus of the research was the nature of the psychological contract within small businesses. A key research objective was to assess the relevance of mainstream theory on the psychological contract to small businesses. This was explored by conducting in depth, semi-structured interviews with 10 owners of small businesses. All of the interviews were tape recorded and later transcribed ready for analysis. Following each interview, first impressions and general feelings about each interview were recorded in a research diary. This was later used to complete a 'contact summary sheet' for each company. As well as a valuable source of data, the research diary provided the opportunity for the researcher to reflect upon their role in the research process, noting for example how they may have influenced, or may have been influenced themselves, by the interviewee. It was important for such reflections to be noted as soon as possible after the interview in order to capture the often emotional impact the interview had had on the interviewer.

During the research this diary played an important role as a reflexive tool. The process of leaving an interview and then filling the diary with reflections on that interview helped to shape how the researcher made sense of the data collected. Some of these reflections were quite factual, for example what the dominant themes were in the interview, but others were based on the experience of the interview as a social episode. So, for example, after one interview the researcher experienced an intense dislike for a male interviewee. She viewed him as a racist, sexist bigot and felt considerably patronized by the way he had shared his views with her. Afterwards when reflecting on her behaviour in the interview she felt concerned that at no point had she challenged any of his views, rather she felt she had colluded in the whole episode in terms of making reassuring noises and nods of the head. In contrast, another interviewee was experienced as a considerate man who could not do more for his employees but still considered himself as 'not a proper business' and indeed 'not worthy of studying'. The researcher on reflection felt angry that researchers may play a role in perpetuating what types of company are perceived as worthy of study and which are not. In this case, these reflections were not put into the matrix, but rather were used as a way of providing the researcher with the opportunity to examine her own experience of the interviews and how this might have impacted upon her analytical interpretations. In this way the research diary was used alongside the matrix analysis. In another study, however, such types of experiences could indeed be included in a matrix, depending on the aim of the study.

Initially, template analysis (see King, Chapter 21, this volume) was chosen as the method of analysis and an 'initial template' was constructed following the first three interviews. The main aim of this was to assess the appropriateness of the interview schedule before proceeding with the remaining interviews. An important realization at this stage was that whilst there were themes and issues common to all three interviews, the interviews were also very different from each other, and, that this uniqueness should be reflected in the analysis. Thus, whilst identifying themes common to all cases was very valuable, this should be complimented by an exploration of the differences between the cases, thus preserving the uniqueness of each case. This created a challenge analytically as it suggested analysis at different levels. Another important realization was the sheer depth and volume of the data generated in the interviews, little of which appeared to be redundant. Thus, even once the template analysis had been completed, the result was a weighty document of over 80 pages. A method was required of summarizing the data in a meaningful and relevant way in order to make it accessible both to the researcher (namely being able to step back from it and look at the wider picture) and also for the reader.

Faced with the problem of how to do this, *cross site matrices analysis* (Miles and Huberman, 1994) offered the ideal solution. Miles and Huberman comment upon the increasing trend towards multi-site (as opposed to single site) field research, a trend which they trace back to Glaser and Strauss (1967) in *Discovery of Grounded Theory*. Whilst Glaser and Strauss advocated the use of multiple comparison groups by ethnographers, as Miles and Huberman point out, they 'did not move on to the pragmatics of how one actually does multiple-case study work' further adding that 'developing a good cross-site synthesis is not a simple matter' (1994: 151). Such words are reassuring in so far as they confirm our initial perception of the analytical challenges faced as somewhat problematic. Matrix analysis offered a practical solution to the problem enabling the identification of common themes (or points of contrast) between the cases (a between group analysis), whilst allowing the uniqueness of each case to be preserved through the within-site analysis. Some may question whether an interview with one person from an organization is enough to form the basis of a cross site analysis. It is worth quoting Miles and Huberman in full on this point:

> Once again we remind the reader that we use the term 'site' by preference, to indicate a bounded context where one is studying something, but 'site' is for us equivalent to 'case', in the sense of 'case study'. So what we call 'cross-site' methods can actually be used in the study of several individual people, each seen as a 'case'. (1994:151)

Added to this is the fact that the focus of the research was on the employer, thus generating, by definition, a sample of one from each company.

Another important factor instrumental in the choice of matrix analysis was the similarity in the coding process described by Miles and Huberman and the technique of template analysis. Before any matrix construction can begin, the process of 'data reduction' is necessary, a process which involves 'selecting, focusing, simplifying, abstracting and transforming the raw data' (1994: 10), which is done, where interview transcripts are concerned, by coding. As mentioned earlier these are very similar to the stages of coding described by King for template analysis (King, 1998), as are their suggestions for making revisions and modifications. Also consistent with template analysis are Miles and Huberman's assertions that coding *is* analysis – the labelling and categorization of data involves interpretation and value laden assumptions about what the data actually mean. Finally, as with template analysis, Miles and Huberman acknowledge that the process of coding is an iterative one in which the researcher should be sensitive to the data before them and adapt the techniques accordingly. It is these shared characteristics that led to the conclusion that template analysis would dovetail effectively into matrix analysis both practically and theoretically. This is not however to undermine the strengths of template analysis in its own right. As will be discussed later, the two techniques do serve different functions.

DOING THE ANALYSIS

Having resolved the issues identified above, the remaining seven interviews were conducted, recorded and transcribed. These transcripts were then coded, using the initial template as a basic framework for interpretation. This process was broken down into the following stages:

1 Immersion in the data – reading and re-reading the transcripts, labelling at the sides to generate appropriate codes.
2 Arranging the codes into categories.
3 Collating the different sections of the different interviews into the appropriate category. This was done by cutting and pasting hard copies of the transcripts onto large sheets of paper.
4 Taking each category individually and 'making sense' of the data within it, further subdividing the information into sub-categories where necessary. Examples of 'sense making' included: noting any similarities in the comments made and whether this indicated a general trend; noting which points were emphasized by employers more than others; noting whether the issue was emotive or not and if so in what way; noting the different ways in which employers qualified their views and actions.

In total this resulted in an 18 category template, 13 of which were further sub-divided. So, for example, category 3 was 'employer's unmet expectations' which was sub-categorized as follows:

3. Employer's unmet expectations
    3.1 General comments
    3.2 Specific examples
        3.2.1 theft
        3.2.2 sub-standard behaviour
        3.2.3 loyalty
   3.3 No violations

Once the categorization process was complete, namely all revisions and modifications had been made, the 'final template' was transferred on to a computer. Each category began with a summary paragraph providing an overview of what was in that particular category along with interpretative comments to suggest possible implications and interpretations of the data. Interpretative comments were added throughout the categories where necessary. The result was a large dense document with the potential to overwhelm (or bore?) even the most tenacious of reader, simply due to its volume and the level of detail included in the template. Thus a key reason for using matrix analysis in this case was accessibility – to enable the reader and the researcher to absorb and understand a large amount of, otherwise potentially disparate, information. For this reason, matrices were used principally for categories which were large and dense (for example, employer's unmet expectations) and when selective information from different categories needed to be pooled (namely matrix 1 which provides an overview of the cases). Matrix 1 also drew on information from the contact summary sheets completed for each interview. Matrices were not used for those template categories which were simple and small enough to interpret as they were.

WORKED EXAMPLES

Two matrices are presented as illustrative examples. Matrix 1 (see Table 22.1) aims to provide a descriptive summary of four companies in terms of basic biographical details and dominant issues related to the research questions. (In the original research all 10 cases were included in matrix 1. Limited space means that only a sample of these can be presented here. This issue is returned to later.) Presented alongside the matrix is the 'analytic text' that offers further interpretation. This is divided into three sections. The first (1 Analysis by Column), summarizes the table column by column offering an overview of the companies in relation to that concept. However it is when the columns of 'management style' and 'dominant themes or issues' are considered that the need for the second section, (2 Analysis by Site), becomes clear and provides an alternative lens through which to regard information in the preceding columns relating to each site. So, for example, Ian's expectation for his staff to run the business for him as a result of his 'hands off' management style and lack of involvement is very different from the expectations of Debbie for employees to take on their role when they are not present. The third section (3 Emergent Findings), is a result of taking all of the information together which led to a number of key realizations. Important insights here emerge from the presentation of the data together. In our experience of using data matrices there is almost a process of absorption or osmosis that enables different insights to be made. This highlights one of the main strengths of the matrix as an analytical tool and not simply a presentation aid.

Matrix 2 (see Table 22.2) focuses upon incidents of theft and is what Miles and Huberman term a 'concept based' matrix. This is when the information is organized on the basis of concepts related to a particular issue or topic. So, when employers described what happened, often in great detail, they revealed important information about how they reacted and why, how it made them feel and also how it impacted on other employees.

Matrix 1 is the most complex of the two matrices, requiring more 'unpacking' in terms of analytic comment than matrix 2. This is probably because matrix 1 is largely descriptive and is drawing on data from across different categories within the template as well as the contact summary sheets, whereas matrix 2 is drawn from within the same template category

Table 22.1 Matrix 1: descriptive summary

Company	No. of employees	Age of company	Do they have a formal contract?	Is the psychological contract valid?	Main expectations of employer	Main expectations of employee	Violations	Management style	Dominant themes/issues
Andrew dental practice	7	17 years	Yes. Very simple, 'it just tells them how much notice they have to give me before they go on holiday.'	Yes	Flexibility to provide cover for holidays and sickness. '90% of success is that you find the right person you like in the first place ... people who take responsibility for things'.	Respect from employer – it was important for this to be reciprocal.	Senior dental nurse approached Andrew for the insensitive way he had dealt with another member of staff. The issue was discussed and resolved. One incident of theft which resulted in the individual being sacked.	Committed to being a good dentist, namely a profession as well as small business owner. He seemed 'in touch' with things going on and had good relations with his staff. He had 'key members of staff who kept him organized and informed'.	Commitment to the profession as well as the business. The future of NHS dentistry and the dilemmas faced deciding whether or not to convert to taking only private patients.
Ian dental practice	7	18 years	Yes. Basic one recommended by dental association.	Yes	That they ran the business for him. Skill shortages mean he can't afford to be choosy or expect too much. 'It's very much a case of taking what's out there ... it's a real problem, so you take them on and try and mould them to what you want'.	Couldn't answer the question: 'I don't know how to get a handle on it. They probably think I don't do enough and that I leave them to it too much'.	None to report.	Very much 'hands off'. Leaves the day to day running of the business to his staff and only gets involved when asked. Was happy for the business to tick over; he only worked four days; dentistry was a choice career; he too worked to live.	His lack of involvement in his business. He had difficulties talking about relationships, possibly because he didn't have any, and kept the discussion superficial and non-emotive.

Table 22.1 cont.

Simon pizza take away business	24	10 years	The drivers do for insurance purposes. The others don't.	Yes, 'definitely... there are very few formal contracts in the business'.	'Everyone's expected to do what's required'. Emphasis on the need to help each other out as well as the need to fit in socially 'people who don't gel with the group don't last long'. He can't have too many expectations as they would tell him to 'shove his job'.	To be there and hands on. To provide them with support for personal problems.	Employee caught stealing from customers – was sacked but later given job back because Simon was short staffed and 'can't afford to be fussy'.	Very much hands on working shifts, playing a key role keeping staff motivated and committed. Strong emphasis on social aspects of work, people has to enjoy it or else they wouldn't last – it was a demanding and dull job on minimum wage.	Insistence that it wasn't a proper job – people did it as a 'top up', which is why the social aspects were so important. The relationships had a regulatory effect too.
Debbie care home for the elderly	10	3 years	Yes. 'It's one that we actually sat down and put together so its for their benefit as well'.	Yes. 'I was going to say, it would be very hard to write a psychological contract'.	Loyalty. 'They need to be loyal to me and I need to know that when I walk out of here they are taking on the role of me'. Looking after vulnerable people requires compassion, reliability, caring approach and a sense of humour.	At first, nothing except to be paid. Now they expect a pleasant working environment, to have meals when working through, flexibility, loyalty from Debbie, to ask for subs.	Serious violation involving theft from residents. Covert surveillance operations set up to catch the thief, who when caught four months later was sacked. A difficult and stressful time for Debbie and her employees.	Very hands on often working shifts and is always available when not there. Close relationships with her staff are important and they socialize together. Open management style – staff know what she expects and that these standards will not be compromised.	She is proud of running a successful nursing home with a high standard of care. Having good working relationships is important and she recognizes the need for her to provide 'something extra' in order to keep staff. She is hoping to expand the business.

Table 22.1 cont

1.1 Analysis by column

The companies included two dentists, a pizza take away business, and a care home for the elderly. One of the businesses had been established for three years, the others for 10 years or more, with the number of employees ranging from seven to 24 people. Whilst all of the employers said they used formal contracts, they stressed how simple or basic this was and that it was not an accurate reflection of the job required. Debbie was the only employer to suggest the formal contract served a positive function for both her and her employees. All employers agreed that the notion of the psychological contract was useful, especially in light of the vagueness of the formal contract. Employers' expectations of their employees included: loyalty; flexibility; to use initiative; to take responsibility and to work to a high standard. Simon stressed the need for his employees to fit in socially and Debbie emphasized the need to be caring and compassionate as well as having a sense of humour. Detailing what employees expected of them proved more difficult to answer suggesting it was something they had given little thought (see Ian's comments). Reciprocating the expectations they as employers had of their employees was a strong theme, specifically in terms of mutual respect, flexibility, loyalty and support. Simon commented on the expectation his staff had for him to listen to their personal problems. Debbie noted that the expectations of her employees had increased as relationships with her staff had become more established. Three of the employers reported incidents of violation, all of which involved theft by an employee. All four employers had contrasting management styles which revealed a lot about their own personal motivations for running their business. Similar contrasts are revealed in the 'dominant themes /issues' column (see 1.2, analysis by site).

1.2 Analysis by site

Contrasts between the sites become very obvious when considering management styles and the dominant themes/issues. A useful way of summing up the differences was to label each site as a particular 'type' – in this way, the label acts as a heuristic device describing the 'character' of each site, for example, Andrew was labelled 'the professional dentist', whereas Ian was labelled 'the jobbing dentist'. Whilst Andrew was highly committed to becoming the best dentist he could and took an active involvement in the running of his business and staff welfare, for Ian dentistry was just a way to earn a comfortable living. He had as little involvement as possible in the running of the business and left his staff to sort themselves out. Two very different establishments which on paper, at first look very similar.

Debbie was described as 'committed to care'. She owned and managed a care home for the elderly and took a lot of pride in providing high quality care for vulnerable people. She was very 'hands on' and had close relationships with all her staff. She felt the need to provide her staff with 'something extra' making them less likely to leave. Debbie wanted to expand the business but was aware of the need to maintain the 'family atmosphere' of the home.

Simon was given the label 'not a proper job' as this was a recurrent theme in his interview. People were only there to earn extra money or to top up another income. The pay wasn't that good and the job unpleasant and it was difficult to find the right people for the job. When an employee was caught stealing, Simon gave him a 'chance' in order to avoid staff shortages. Simon stressed the need for his staff to fit in socially, also describing the regulatory effect of the social group in terms of establishing and monitoring the norms of expected behaviour.

1.3 Emergent findings

Insights were gained from 'stepping back' and looking at the matrix as a whole. In this way linkages between seemingly unrelated cells could be identified, further highlighting salient issues or themes. Two key issues were identified in this way, showing how the matrix is a useful analytical tool and not just a presentation aid.

Issue 1: the importance of relationships

Employers stressed the importance of having good social relationships within the workplace – people who got on together worked well together. Simon explained how having a positive social life at work compensated for the dullness of the job. Even Ian, who had very little to do with his employees, recognized the important function of positive relationships between his colleagues. Good relationships were the cornerstone of the implicit obligations employees had with their employer and with each other.

Issue 2: difficulties in finding and keeping good staff.

This was a problem identified by all four employers which they responded to in different ways. For Ian and Simon this limited the expectations they could reasonably have of employees. You simply had to take what was out there (Ian) and not expect too much of them because they would say 'shove your job' and go and work in a supermarket (Simon). Debbie and Andrew's response to this pressure was to minimize staff turnover. Debbie felt she had to provide her staff with 'something extra' to ensure they would stay. Andrew emphasized the importance of finding and retaining the right staff and was proud that many of his employees had worked for him a long time. He had recently recruited a new dental nurse by offering the job to one of his patients.

(namely 3.2.1 incidents of theft) and therefore has a much greater degree of conceptual coherency.

THE DIFFERENCES BETWEEN MATRIX ANALYSIS AND TEMPLATE ANALYSIS

Having stressed how complimentary the techniques of template analysis and matrix analysis are, it is worth commenting on their differences. Essentially they serve two different functions and in the research example given, matrix analysis was used to augment the template analysis in the light of the difficulties faced in doing multi-site research. The emphasis of matrix analysis is on data display and how this enhances the accessibility and interpretation of data. The final template itself was a large document and it would simply not be practical to present it in its entirety. This would result in information overload both for the researcher (potentially obscuring the interpretation process), and the reader (potentially inhibiting accessibility or understanding). However, it was not necessary to construct a matrix for every category in the template, with certain categories being simple enough to be presented as they were. Also, even for the categories that have been represented in a matrix, it would certainly be of great value to go back to the template if more detail is required about a particular issue. This is certainly recommended for the examples of theft presented in matrix 2 where the reductionism necessary to get the incidents into matrix format does not do justice to the depth and power of each incident when read in their entirety. Thus, template analysis and matrix analysis can be regarded as operating at different levels, the strengths of each technique compensating for the weaknesses in the other (namely too much detail versus too little detail). The decision to use matrix analysis in the current example was ultimately driven by a desire to do justice to the data and get the most out of it and reflects the complexity of doing multi-site research.

ADVANTAGES AND DISADVANTAGES OF THE TECHNIQUE

As already stressed, one advantage of matrix analysis is providing accessibility to large amounts of qualitative data. It may also be preferred by those who are more 'spatial' in terms of their cognitive orientation and find it easier to work with information that is physically laid out in front of them on one page as opposed to being stored serially on numerous pages or on a computer. One possible disadvantage of the techniques is that it is time consuming, especially if a template analysis alone may suffice. Hopefully such decisions about the suitability of matrix analysis will be based on methodological considerations rather than practical restrictions. It may also prove difficult to present a large matrix on one page such that all the information can be viewed at once. Whilst this can be overcome in the research stage simply by getting larger pieces of paper, the problem comes when attempting to present the matrix in say, academic papers or, indeed, in volumes such as this one! The solution preferred by Miles and Huberman is for their book to be A4 size. One final concern about matrix analysis is that it is too reductionist. However, the authors feel that these charges can be avoided if matrix analysis is dovetailed with template analysis, thus establishing a clear audit trail and enabling issues to be followed up in greater detail. Indeed this is one of the strengths of the technique in that it allows insights to emerge which had not previously been identified, which then necessitates going back to the template to explore these in more detail. This may result in

Table 22.2 Matrix 2: contract violation – incidents of theft

	Act	Reaction	Description	What does it violate	Rationale for action	Emotional response	Impact on other employees
Debbie	Employee caught stealing from purses of fellow employees.	Instant dismissal. 'Get your coat and leave'.	Debbie caught the employee in the act; the employee was dismissed immediately and no further action was taken.	Basic expectation of honesty.	'That's something I don't abide. If someone had come to me and said Debbie I've got no money, I've got problems then I'd sort them out'.	'Just go'.	None described.
Andrew	Employee took money from the till as a 'sub' and later denied having it.	Challenged the employee and dismissed her on the grounds of breach of formal contract. Other practitioners were informed about her conduct.	Andrew had identified a 'series of untruths' – a pattern of behaviours concerning bogus medical complaints. She was therefore considered untrustworthy. She'd had subs from her wages before but on this occasion took the money without asking.	Trust. In breach of formal contract. Violated expectation of reciprocal treatment.	Reasonable man: if only she'd asked, "I'm approachable"'. Reciprocity: 'I don't treat people like that and it shocks me.' It was a good excuse to get rid of her. 'It was good to feel that the rest of the staff were on my side'.	'Disappointed . . . taken for a mug', he describes being 'shaken' and 'shocked'. 'I don't treat people that way and it shocks me when somebody lets you down like that'. He describes his state when telling her she was being sacked: 'I was shaking...I could hardly speak, I was that upset about it'.	The other staff didn't trust her: 'It wasn't adding up for them. They knew it wasn't true'. It was a colleague who split on her and the rest of his staff were very supportive of his actions.

Table 22.2 cont.

| Debbie H | Care assistant caught taking money from a purse of one of the elderly residents. | Dismissed immediately once caught. Did not press charges as the amount taken was small. Informed social services. | Once aware that there was a thief a surveillance operation involving hidden cameras (and the police) was set up. Staff and residents were informed about the problem. After 4 months the thief was caught on camera, taken to the police station and later dismissed. | Trust – between Debbie and the thief, as well as the thief and her colleagues. Also, abuse of vulnerable residents. | The thief did have a record but nothing had ever been proven. Debbie wanted to stop her once and for all. Also reinforced to other staff that this would not be tolerated but would be dealt with fairly and thoroughly. It could have finished them as a business. A strong sense of responsibility towards her residents and their families. | 'It was terrible . . . terrible. When we actually did catch her I just burst into tears because I was so upset . . . I was in bits... in bits'. 'I was often in tears and they (her other staff) were very supportive of me'. | 'It was terrible, everybody suspected everybody. It just caused ill feeling, they couldn't wait to get off shift'. Once the thief had been caught Debbie described the reactions of her staff: 'there was relief . . . and anger, well sheer fury because she had made everybody's life a misery and she had ripped off these old people and they couldn't believe how hard faced she was'. They also blamed the thief for the later death of the resident who was at the centre of the investigation. |

Table 22.2 *cont.*

| Allan | Petrol scam | Warning was given but not dismissed. The value of the stolen fuel was repaid. | Trust. | 'I was watching him cos I suspected it. Well, we got this phone call one morning and found out what he was doing. He was meeting his wife at the petrol station who backed her car close up to his and he'd fill her car first before filling his own' – using the company card to pay the bill. | Allan could have sacked him: 'I mean I had a legal basis to put pressure on, but I had two views, if he left I'd never get my money back and it was over a thousand quid that had gone, and also if he kept his job I didn't have the inconvenience of finding another driver'. 'He did a good job. He's got an amoral wife and a son who's a junkie...I'm very reluctant to sack anyone unless they bugger the job up, but buggering me about I can tolerate for a bit...if he does it again he's for it'. | 'It's difficult now. I don't trust him now, I find I'm very formal with him now and he will insist on calling me mate or 'Al' and I don't like it cos once somebody has done that.' | None. |

Table 22.2 cont.

| Simon | Driver overcharging customers | Initially sacked but then taken on with the warning that he was being watched. | 'He wasn't stitching me up, he was overcharging customers, so you know every time there was an eight pound delivery he'd say it was nine. Well he delivered to one of the girls who used to work for me . . . well she rang us up to tell us'. | Trust. | 'So he was out straight away . . . . but we ended up short staffed and we needed another driver so we thought right, we'll give him another go, he knows that if he does anything wrong again it's definitely all over'. 'He'd thrown away quite a few quid a week so he's over the moon to be back'. | Commenting on his relationship now: 'I wouldn't get him to babysit or give him the keys to the safe or anything like that, but yeah I trust him to do the job OK'. | 'He's coming back here and he's working in an environment where he thinks everyone's looking over his shoulder and watching his every move'. 'When the tills are down or something you'll get like that core group who'll stay at night and they'll get really angry about it and pressure will come to bear on this person'. |

Matrix 2: Analytic comment

Employers were asked if they had any incidents where their employees had failed to meet their expectations, five of whom reported incidents of theft. Two incidents involved theft from the employer (Andrew and Allan); another two involved theft from the clients with one incident involving theft from fellow employees. In three of the cases the employee concerned was sacked, in one case they were initially sacked and later given their job back and in one case they were given a second chance. The basic expectation violated was trust. Most employers described the chain of events surrounding the incidents – how they discovered it, how they dealt with it and how it made them feel, revealing the often profound impact the incidents had had on them and other employees. Justifications were often offered for the action they had taken – for example, they should have asked if they had no money (Debbie G, Andrew); the need to stop the thief once and for all (Debbie H); strong sense of duty to vulnerable clients (Debbie H); sacking the culprit would have left them short staffed and they did do a good job, and, if they did it again they'd be straight out (Alan, Simon). Most employers had an emotional response to the incident – anger, feeling upset, disappointed. One interesting question raised is whether or not it matters who the victim of the theft is, namely whether it's the employer, clients or other employees. Looking at the incidents on a site basis provides an invaluable summary of each incident and the impact it had had on each individual employer.

modifications either to the template or the matrix and in this sense the two techniques could be considered iterative.

It is perhaps surprising to find that there are very few other published examples of matrix analysis – a literature search of three principal indexes generated zero 'hits'. One possible reason is that the technique has been used (for example, presenting qualitative data in table format), but not termed matrix analysis. Having said this, it is important to distinguish matrix analysis from the simple tabulation of data. As stressed earlier, construction of the matrix is an integral part of the analysis. Decisions about what the rows and columns are, and what goes into each of them, are an essential part of the interpretation process. Indeed, they are the foundations upon which the ultimate outcomes of the research are based. Having now conducted several matrix analyses, the authors are impressed by their scope and potential, both practically and theoretically. Their use enables both accessibility and thus insights into large amounts of qualitative data which may otherwise remain obscure or impenetrable. Hopefully this chapter will encourage other researchers facing the challenge of doing qualitative, multi-site research, to use the technique.

FURTHER READING

There is one key text in which matrices are described: M.B. Miles and A.M. Huberman (1994) *Qualitative Data Analysis: An Expanded Sourcebook*, second edition, Thousand Oaks, CA: Sage. In this text a whole range of data matrices are outlined.

REFERENCES

Cassell, C. (1989) 'The use of information technology in the community: an evaluation', University of Sheffield. PhD thesis.

Geertz, C. (1973) 'Thick description: toward an interpretive theory of culture', in C. Geertz, *The Interpretation of Cultures*, New York: Basic Books.

Glaser, B.G. and Strauss, A.L. (1967) D*iscovery of Grounded Theory: Strategies for Qualitative Research*, Chicago: Aldine.

King, N. (1998) 'Template analysis', in G. Symon and C. Cassell, *Qualitative Methods and Analysis in Organizational Research: A Practical Guide*, London: Sage.

Lincoln, Y.S. and Guba, E.G. (1985) *Naturalistic Enquiry.* Beverly Hills, CA: Sage.

Lincoln, Y.S. and Guba, E.G. (1990) 'Judging the quality of case study reports', *Qualitative Studies in Education*, 3 (1): 52–9.

Miles, M.B. and Huberman, A.M. (1994) *Qualitative Data Analysis: An Expanded Sourcebook*, second edition, Thousand Oaks, CA: Sage.

23 — Preserving, Sharing and Reusing Data from Qualitative Research: Methods and Strategies

Louise Corti, Paul Thompson and Janet Fink

In this chapter we explore methodological, ethical and theoretical considerations relating to the secondary analysis of qualitative data. There is a well-established tradition in social science of secondary analysis of quantitative data, and there is no logical intellectual reason why this should not be so for qualitative data.

We start by exploring the ways in which data materials from qualitative research can be made available so as to make them useful for the secondary analyst. Here we discuss issues relating to the preparation of research data for subsequent reuse, touching on the conduct of fieldwork, the organization and documentation of data materials, and the legal and ethical issues surrounding access to qualitative data such as confidentiality and informed consent.

Last we describe ways in which data sources can be used and have been reused and discuss the strengths and weaknesses of these various approaches. By drawing upon research material from *The Last Refuge* (1962), Peter Townsend's study of institutional care, we illustrate the potential which archived data holds for the analysis of such diverse topics as the power dynamics within institutions, the spatial organization of the workplace, and the relationship between research and policy.

THE CASE FOR THE REUSE OF QUALITATIVE DATA

Archived qualitative data are a rich and unique yet often unexploited source of research information that can be reanalysed, reworked, compared with contemporary data, and that will, in time, form part of our cultural heritage as historical resources.

For British sociological research the decades since 1950 have witnessed an unprecedented flowering: in the growth of its influence, in the spread of its themes, and in the development of its quantitative and qualitative methods. From the 1960s into the 1970s sociology was not only an exceptionally popular subject with students, but was also given more national research resources than at any time before or since. This enabled social researchers to carry out studies of a thoroughness unlikely ever to be equalled. Just one example is Peter Townsend's in-depth investigation into the nature and status of long-stay institutions in postwar Britain, *The Last Refuge* (1962).

This great wave of research activity has left us with a double heritage. The first is the development of crucial ideas – such as the role of the extended family in the cities, or of the 'moral panic' – which remain part of the mainstream of current sociological thinking. The second is a rich residue of original research data, much of which in the UK is now permanently archived as a resource for social researchers in the future.

The progress of social science has always been essentially cumulative, right from its origins in the eighteenth century. The building up of knowledge has been incremental, resting on the foundations of earlier findings, while interpretation has always depended upon comparisons: with other contexts, other periods of time, other social groups, and other cultures. It is only possible for comparison to be effective when there is sufficient data to enable convincing re-evaluations. It is fortunate that many social scientists grasped this relatively early. For example, in Britain the original returns of the population census were kept as public records, and have proved an invaluable basis for reanalysis in recent years. Similarly the Webbs (1894) on completing their pioneering study of British trade unionism, archived their notes on their interviews carried out throughout the country. These fieldwork notes, now held in the LSE's library, remain the principal source of information on trade unionism in the late nineteenth century.

However, in spite of the potential offered by accessible archived qualitative data, there has been a noticeable silence close to the heart of the qualitative research community. There are a large number of published texts describing different styles of interviewing, how best to use them, their potential and their pitfalls. There are also, although significantly fewer, excellent texts on how to analyse and interpret interview material. In the case of survey interviews, it is assumed that a researcher will be mainly interpreting interviews which were carried out by other researchers, and textbooks explicitly discuss the issues involved in the secondary analysing of survey material (Dale et al., 1988). But for qualitative researchers, the traditional assumption has been the reverse.

Qualitative methods handbooks typically advise new researchers to immerse themselves in the field, know their informants and their context, remember the gestures as well as the words of their interviews, savour them through the long process of transcribing, and out of that total immersion will emerge the original insights which they are seeking.

Why has there been a reluctance to draw on material created by other researchers? Is it simply an unspoken inhibition? Is it that it is a problem of epistemology, and the implicit nature of qualitative data collection and analysis techniques? Or are there likely to be such difficulties in using material created by other people that it is scarcely worth the time to try looking at it? How constraining is informed consent? And what about scientific verification – is there an insecurity about exposure of one's own research practice?

We attempt to answer these questions in the following sections by reviewing the pros and cons of secondary analysis of qualitative data and, providing examples which illuminate ways in which they can be sensibly reused in both research and teaching.

AVAILABILITY OF ARCHIVED QUALITATIVE DATA

The case of the UK: history

Throughout the world there are innumerable archives which collect (mainly historical) qualitative material, as well as a large number of sound archives and ethnographic archives, but there are few common descriptive standards, little integrated resource discovery and often access to collections is poor. One of the earliest and perhaps best known sources in the UK is the collection of papers resulting from the 1930s social research organization, 'Mass-Observation'. These were established as a public archive at the University of Sussex in the early

1970s. and since then have attracted a steadily increasing number of researchers (Sheridan, 2000).

It was also only from the late 1980s that any sustained concern with archival issues amongst oral historians developed. In 1987 Paul Thompson established the National Life Story Collection as an independent charitable trust within the oral history section of the British Library National Sound Archive. The intention was to launch a national autobiography in sound, aimed at providing a wider resource for other researchers, writers and broadcasters. The projects archived include, amongst others, lives of the book trade, the food industry, North Sea Oil, the financial elite of the City of London (Courtney and Thompson, 1996), and workers of British Steel (Dein and Perks 1993).

The Economic and Social Research Council (ESRC) had already recognized, very early on in 1967, the value in retaining the most significant social science machine-readable survey data from the empirical research which it funded by establishing a data archive. Thus crucial survey data could be reanalysed by other researchers, and the money spent on research became not only an immediate outlay, but an investment for the future. There was, however, a significant gap in this policy in that qualitative data was rarely acquired, in spite of much data being created in word processed form.

The 1990s saw a growing demand for access to digital texts, images and audio–visual material. When a small pilot study commissioned by the ESRC was carried out by Paul Thompson in 1991 (Thompson, 1991), it was revealed that 90 per cent of qualitative research data was either already lost, or at risk, in researchers' homes or offices. It was further calculated that it would cost at least £20 million to create a resource on the scale of that at risk. For the older material, moreover, the risk was acute, and the need for action especially urgent. This was subsequently borne, to name but a few, out by the destruction of research data on the classic UK community studies of Banbury (Stacey, 1974) and Sparkbrook (Rex and Moore, 1967).

It was to remedy this unnecessary waste of qualitative research resources that in 1994, the first qualitative data archiving project on a national scale, Qualidata was established with support from the ESRC. Housed within the Department of Sociology at the University of Essex, its objectives were to facilitate and document the archiving of qualitative data arising from research, whilst also drawing the research communities' attention to its existence and potential. Its first task was to conduct a rescue operation aiming to seek out the most significant material created by research from past years. The second was to work with the ESRC to implement a datasets policy (ESRC, 2002) to ensure that for current and future projects the unnecessary waste of the past did not continue. Qualidata was not set up as an archive itself, but as a clearing house and an action unit, its role being to locate and evaluate research data, catalogue it, organize its transfer to suitable archives across the UK, and publicize its existence to researchers and encourage reuse of the collections (Corti et al., 1995; Thompson and Corti, 1998).

In the mid-1990s Qualidata established procedures for: sorting, processing and listing both raw data and accompanying documentation (metadata); for systematically describing studies for web based resource discovery systems; for establishing appropriate mechanisms for access; and for promotion of and training in the reuse of qualitative data (Corti et al., 1995; Corti, 2000). From 2001, Qualidata began a new life as a specialist unit housed within the UK Data Archive (UKDA) at the University of Essex, with a focus on acquiring and distributing digital data. The service aimed to provide a joined up data service for social science data depositors and secondary analysts.

Across the Atlantic, there was a centre that had been systematically gathering qualitative research data in order to make it available to other social science researchers. The collections of the Henry A. Murray Research Center, based at Radcliffe College, Harvard have focused on the eastern USA and on themes related to women's studies. It is a multidisciplinary research centre and unusually it collects both qualitative and quantitative data, offering analysis in the reanalysis of both kinds of data. Established in 1976, the Center now holds over 225 data sets, with especially strong holdings on human development and social change (James and Sorenson, 2000).

The build up of a stock of qualitative data resources has thus encouraged the uptake of secondary analysis. As a result we have seen developments in the intellectual arguments for and against the reuse of data as well debates on the method. Before we explore these further it is useful to examine the resource stocks to see what is available for reuse and how they can be accessed.

TYPES AND SOURCES OF ARCHIVED QUALITATIVE DATA

Types of qualitative data

Qualitative data are collected using qualitative research methodology and techniques across the range of social science disciplines. Strategies often encompass a diversity of methods and tools rather than a single one and the types of data collected depend on the aim of the study, the nature of the sample, and the discipline. As a result data types extend to: in-depth or unstructured, individual or group discussion interviews, field and observation notes, unstructured diaries, observational recordings, personal documents and photographs. Qualitative research often involves producing large amounts of raw data although the methods typically employ small sample sizes. Finally, these data may be created in a number of different formats: digital, paper (typed and hand-written), audio, video and photographic.

By 2002, Qualidata had acquired, processed and catalogued some 140 datasets, and catalogued a further 150 already housed in archives across the UK. Surviving 'classic studies' data from key researchers was also rescued, including outstandingly well-known single projects such as Goldthorpe et al.'s *The Affluent Worker* (1968), the entire life's work of pioneering researchers such as Peter Townsend (*Family Life of Old People* (1957) and *The Last Refuge* (1962) and *Poverty in the UK* (1979), and Paul Thompson including the life-history interview studies of *The Edwardians* (1975) and *100 families* (1991, 1993 and 1995).

Archive collections of potential interest to those conducting organizational research might include: Richard Brown's 1970s study on Orientation to Work and Industrial Behaviour of Shipbuilding Workers on Tyneside; Hilary Wainwright's collection including her 1970s trades union study on Lucas Aerospace and Vickers (Wainwright and Elliott, 1982); Ray Pahl's and C. Wallace's 1980s study of Employers on the Isle of Sheppey; Chas Critcher et al.'s 1980s work on Split at the Seams?: Community, Continuity and Change after the 1984–5 Coal Dispute; and Jan Webb's 1980s research on New Technology and the Management of Expertise in Customer–Supplier Relations.

PREPARING QUALITATIVE DATA FOR REUSE

In order for a data collection to be reusable, collections must be 'processed'. This involves a range of activities that will enable a data set to be reusable including: checking, digitizing and optical character recognition (OCR), converting, anonymizing, organizing, creating metadata (information about data). Data deposited must also conform to ethical and legal guidelines with respect to the preservation of anonymity, if so, where requested. Information on the ethical and legal issues surrounding informed consent, confidentiality and copyright have been published by Qualidata (Corti et al., 2000), and the ESRC (1999).

Creating appropriate documentation that can help the user interpret raw data sources is a key task for data archives. Three pieces of documentation are crucial to both enable discovery of relevant data resources and informed reuse (Corti, 2002). The first is a systematic Catalogue Record that provides a detailed overview of the study, the size and content of the dataset, its availability and any terms and conditions of access (UKDA, 2002). The second is a User Guide that brings together key documentation from the research that contains information on how to use the data, how the data were collected, the original topic guides, personal research diaries, end of award reports, and publications. Qualidata User Guides which contain useful and often unique research and methodological information about the study are freely available online via the catalogue record. Finally, a Data Listing, detailing the key characteristics of the data or interviewees, is constructed to help users to identify particular types of interviews or transcripts (such as women of a particular age in the sample). In many ways these defining characteristics are analogous to 'variables' in quantitative datasets. Depositors are asked to consider that data are collected, prepared and documented in the course of conducting fieldwork or analysing data with an eye towards long-term preservation,

GAINING ACCESS TO DATA

Depending on the format of materials, data can be accessed through traditional library-based special collections or via a digital data archive set up to disseminate data to a distributed community of users. In the case of digital materials, data are available as word processing documents and accessed via web download facilities or burnt on a CD-ROM. Users accessing data are required to sign an agreement to the effect that they will not attempt to identify individuals when carrying out analyses.

In the field of qualitative data, innovative on-line data access and analysis tools are beginning to appear. Web-based multi-media resources including those with search and retrieve functions for text provide enhanced access and are of great value (Barker, 2002).

REUSING DATA

How can qualitative data be reused?

The reuse of qualitative data provides a unique opportunity to study the raw materials of the recent or more distant past research to gain insights for both methodological and substantive purposes. The ways in which qualitative data can be reused have much in common with those applicable to the secondary analysis of survey data. Data may be used for:

Description – describing the contemporary and historical attributes, attitudes and behaviour of individuals, societies, groups or organizations. Data created now will in time become a unique historical resource.

Comparative research, replication or restudy of original research – to compare with other data sources or to provide comparison over time or between social groups or regions, and so on. Also for substantiating results, although we have yet to see any evidence of reuse for this purpose.

Reanalysis – asking new questions of the data and making different interpretations to the original researcher. Approaching the data in ways that were not originally addressed, such as using data for investigating different themes or topics of study. The more in-depth the material, the more possible this becomes.

Research design and methodological advancement – designing a new study or developing a methodology or research tool by studying sampling methods, data collection and fieldwork strategies and topic guides. A researcher's personal fieldwork diary can offer much insight into the history and development of the research.

Verification – data can be scrutinized with scientific vigour to either support or challenge a set of findings or to appraise the method.

Teaching and learning – both older 'classic' studies and more contemporary focused sets of transcripts along with supporting documentation, can provide unique case material for teaching and learning in both research methods and substantive areas across a range of social science disciplines.

In support of these possibilities, Hammersley (1997) provides some arguments for the archiving of qualitative data and suggests that its contributions to the development of sociological research include 'facilitating the process of assessing research findings; and in providing the basis for secondary analysis both as a supplement to primary data and perhaps also as a basis for extensive historical and comparative studies' (1997: 140). Zeitlyn (2000) further argues that dissemination of field data from anthropology both enhances academic debate by enabling alternative analysis and provides rich resources for teaching.

How have qualitative data been reused?

As reuse of qualitative data is a relatively recent phenomenon, the literature is sparse. Since 1995, the patterns of reuse that Qualidata have witnessed tend to vary, although they are necessarily dependent on what data are on offer. The demand for reusing data is partly a result of the efforts invested by the data holders in promoting or re-packaging data collections according to researchers' wishes.

Sheridan (2000) observes that the Mass Observation collection has attracted a steadily increasing number of researchers not only from within the academic community but also from the wider community of broadcasters, writers, oral and local historians, teachers and school students. This more recent use of materials which were originally collected for other purposes at other times has been substantial. Use of the Mass Observation collection has taken three main forms: use of the material as historical sources; use of the papers to explore issues in relation to the research process; and use of the papers as a way of developing new projects.

James and Sorenson (2000) report that users of Murray Center data span a range of disciplinary perspectives which demonstrate the variety of ways in which qualitative data can be restructured for new research. In particular, creative approaches to the use of existing qualitative data have included seldom-used methods such as the use of multiple data sets for multi-cohort designs, follow-up cohort studies.

Although there are few published examples of experiences of reuse on the UK, Fielding and Fielding (2000) present an insightful account of their work on revisiting Cohen and Taylor's (1972) original analysis of long-term imprisonment of men in maximum security published as *Psychological Survival*. They are positive towards the applicability of 'old data' for reanalysis:

> Secondary analysis has a particular role in qualitative research addressing sensitive topics or hard to reach populations because researchers can best respect subjects' sensitivities, and accommodate restricted access to research populations, by extracting the maximum from those studies which are able to negotiate these obstacles. Secondary analysis can protect the sensitivities of subjects and gatekeepers by ensuring they are not over-researched, and can position further enquiries so that they ask what is pertinent to the state of analytic development, building on, rather than simply repeating, previous enquiries. (2000: 678)

In their findings, Fielding and Fielding further state how the reanalysis offered 'a means to extract further analysis purchase from research on a group seldom exposed to fieldwork' (2000: 688). Thompson (2000) reflects on his own personal experiences of reanalysing data from his pioneering large scale oral history, and on using other researchers' data to develop his own pilot work for a new study. Finally, during the 1990s there has been some discussion of reanalysing earlier qualitative research data in the field of health research, but this has been at a very preliminary level (Hinds et al., 1997; Thorne, 1990).

Arguments for and against reusing qualitative data

Since 1994, Qualidata carried out numerous surveys of and interviews with qualitative researchers at all levels of seniority across the UK, from principal investigators to postgraduate students. The responses obtained point to a small number of key concerns. Whilst there are strong feelings within the community, they are by no means homogenous. It is important to consider some of the reasons for which we believe qualitative researchers harbour scepticism about sharing and reusing qualitative data. The prime concern relates to questions of confidentiality and agreements made at the time of fieldwork. Researchers' worries about confidentiality are discussed in detail in other papers (Corti et al., 2000). However, other reasons are more to do with the assertion of intellectual property rights, methodological concerns and fear of criticism or 'exposure'.

INTELLECTUAL PROPERTY RIGHTS

Some researchers consider their data as private property, and seem almost bonded to their own ethnographic fieldwork notebooks or interviews. Anthropologists may have built a career around studying one particular remote region, and the data generated over the course of a professional career will be seen as unique, as a stock of intellectual capital that he or she can exploit in order to further their career. However, there still remains a strong case for avoiding duplication by making use of existing data in order to avoid unnecessary replication of research, and to gain a more informed approach or comparative perspective to a new topic.

METHODOLOGICAL CONCERNS

Sociologists are not used to consulting colleagues' data and the concept of 'secondary analysis' is still viewed by most qualitative researchers as pertaining to 'number crunching' activities. Some researchers believe that qualitative data cannot be used sensibly without the accumulated background knowledge, or rapport with the participant, which the original investigator acquired during its collection. Thus the essential contextual experience of 'being there' and the lack of being able to engage in reflexive interpretation is seen as a barrier. Mauthner et al. (1998) endorse this negative stance towards the practice of reusing data in asserting that 'data are the product of the reflexive relationship between the researcher and researched, constrained and informed by biographical, historical, political, theoretical and epistemological contingencies' (1998: 742).

While qualitative research uses reflexivity relating to experience of fieldwork as a means of enhancing data collection and forming new hypotheses in the field, the secondary analysis of data should not be dismissed that easily. Indeed, there are instances where research data is, in a sense 'reused', by the investigators themselves. For example, some principal investigators who write the final articles resulting from a project, have employed research staff or a field force to collect the data. Similarly, for those working in research teams, sharing one's own experiences of the research are essential. Both rely on the fieldworkers and co-workers documenting detailed notes about the project and communicating them to each other. Furthermore, the whole practice of social historians is based on understanding evidence created by other witnesses and indeed also of legal proof. Documentation of the research process provides some degree of the context, and whilst it cannot compete with being there, field notes, letters and memos documenting the research can serve to aid the original fieldwork experience. Audio and video tape recordings also augment the capacity to reuse data without having actually been there.

FEAR OF CRITICISM OR EXPOSURE

Generally, qualitative social 'scientists' are not used to making their findings accountable. Therefore some feel vulnerable about others seeing their data, and the possibility of criticism. However, accepting the label of a social 'scientist' does imply a willingness to adopt the scientific model of offering our data to scrutiny, and the testing of reliability and validity. Indeed, such practice should lead to better quality, more transparent research.

CASE STUDY: REVISTING PETER TOWNSEND'S DATA COLLECTION

Peter Townsend's decision in 1996 to deposit his life's work in The National Social Policy and Social Change Archive at the University of Essex has proved to be an invaluable illustration of the potential for reuse which archived qualitative data sets offer to researchers. The Peter Townsend Collection, as it has become known, comprises more than 80 boxes of archived papers, which contain not only diverse forms of qualitative material as personal correspondence, interview transcripts, photographs and diaries, but also span a period of some 50 years. The richness of the data is augmented still further by Townsend's punctilious approach to the organization and preservation of all contextual material relating to his work. Moreover there is another, more recent layer within this collection which further enhances its reuse potential. Between 1997 and 1999, Paul Thompson conducted a series of in-depth interviews with Peter Townsend about his life and research. These provide additional opportunities to explore how and why particular research projects were devised and conducted and how different projects relate to each other, and to consider the ways in which conceptual and methodological interests have shifted over recent years.

For those working in the fields of organizational and institutional research, at least four of the data sets within the collection offer much of value in reuse terms. Three of these relate directly to Townsend's own political and lobbying commitments and the fourth to an in-depth research project, *The Last Refuge*, in which Townsend investigated the nature and status of long-stay institutions in postwar Britain. Each of the data sets is rich in both the quantity and quality of their primary and contextual materials. So, for example, private correspondence, committee papers and newspaper reports, stemming from Townsend's long involvement with the Labour Party and his role as member of the party social policy sub-committee, form one discrete set of materials. These exemplify how archived data can throw light upon a range of different organizational practices and processes, such as the collection and use of evidence in decision-making, the building of alliances between committee members, and the effective formulation and dissemination of policy initiatives.

Data sets originating from Townsend's position as a founding member of two influential lobbying groups, the Child Poverty Action Group and the Disability Alliance, offer another perspective on the ways in which the reuse of data might be employed in organizational research. Investigation of correspondence, committee papers, reports and press releases relating to the origins of these organizations open up opportunities to analyse the ways in which their aims were first conceived and enacted and how, in turn, promotion drives drew upon the media to publicize and circulate information about their motives and objectives. The data can thus be used to explore the strategies deployed to develop the social and political influence of their lobbying campaigns. And, at another level, the records of these two groups can be analysed to illuminate issues of growing concern in contemporary Britain, not least the negotiation and management of the relationship between the state and voluntary sector organizations and the ways in which organizations acknowledge and address the diverse and, at times, competing demands of their clients and users.

The fourth data set within the collection which holds much potential for reuse in institutional research is related to Townsend's investigation of long-stay homes for elderly people which was conducted between 1957 and 1961. A team of four research officers worked alongside Townsend undertaking visits, interviews and statistical analyses across a wide range of institutions and homes. The data collected is extensive. It includes notes and reports of interviews, questionnaires with residents, correspondence, photographs of homes and residents, interviewers' notes, diaries, press cuttings and other contextual material. Its reuse offers insights, therefore, into a range of different institutional processes and relationships.

Interviews with professional staff such as matrons, wardens and county welfare officers, include information about the local provision of care, management of homes, regulations, duties of staff and general issues relating to care in the homes. Such data illustrate the hierarchical nature of employment within institutions, particularly the constitution of professional identities and the ways in which boundaries between professional and non-professional staff were constructed and maintained. These shifting and contested power dynamics are also demonstrated in the descriptions of relationships between staff within the homes and local authority personnel.

Visual materials, such as photographs and drawings of the layout of particular homes, provide a powerful and highly effective resource for analyses of the spatial organization of care and employment in long-stay institutions. The photographs provide a sense of the sharp contrast between the institution's public presentation of itself, with imposing frontages and well-tended, attractive gardens, and its private face, characterized by stark, anonymous rear views of grim yards and dilapidated out-buildings. In turn, photographs of the homes' interiors evoke the lack of privacy and absence of personal space experienced by residents in long-term care whose lives were lived out in shared bedrooms and small, cramped communal rooms. They are equally revealing about the working conditions of staff and the difficulties of managing the provision of care in environments without adequate facilities for washing, the preparation of food and recreational activities.

The Last Refuge was considered a pioneering piece of research when it was published in 1957 and attracted much publicity for its focus on an important and hitherto neglected area of policy. It has been the subject since then both for its methodology and its policy recommendations, but it remains a rich, multi-layered resource for institutional research which seeks to explore the meaning and nature of institutional life across both micro and macro levels of analysis.

Our particular approach to the reuse of archived data is focused upon three possibilities. The first and arguably, to date, most popular is reuse wherein the researcher revisits deposited research materials relating to a particular project in order to better understand the themes and issues which structured its production and to gain insights into its social, political and economic context. Revisiting cannot only throw light upon the origins of a particular piece of research but is also a useful tool in evaluating the effectiveness of the theoretical framework and conceptual tools that were used in the analysis of the data. One of its advantages is that it provides the means by which researchers can set their own work within a broader comparative or historical context thereby addressing the impact and effects of socio-economic change, cultural diversity and shifting policy and political objectives.

The second possibility for reusing data addresses the issue of methodology. Although researchers generally explain and justify their research methods in published outcomes relating to projects, there are considerable advantages to examining the primary data in their original state and to assessing the validity and merits of the research methods deployed. Where researchers have also retained contextual material relating to projects, this can be particularly fruitful. It thus becomes possible to learn more about how projects were developed, funded and conducted, how various projects (by the same researcher and in comparison with other researchers) relate to each other, and also how the methods deployed were devised and implemented. In the case of The National Social Policy and Social Change Archive, where social scientists have archived either their life's work or key individual projects, there are opportunities to trace the ways in which qualitative methodologies have been drawn upon and developed by the social science community over the past 40 years. Such archived material, and especially that from the most recent research, is also a significant learning resource providing students and researchers with first-hand knowledge of the interviewing process and examples of how to record field-notes, keep diaries and organize large collections of primary data.

Reanalysis offers a third possibility in the reuse of data. Such an approach acknowledges that researchers not involved in the original research may find different potential in data sets than that envisaged when they were originally collected. Different questions may be posed of the materials: new themes may be traced or alternative interpretations of the research findings may be proposed. Reuse allows researchers, therefore, to exploit more fully the potential of existing data by extending and developing existing analyses. But, more importantly, the reuse of qualitative sources presents researchers with invaluable opportunities to explore how 'knowledge' about particular issues was constructed, understood and acted upon and how, in turn, that 'knowledge' has become a crucial factor in our own understanding of the importance of research to the exploration of contemporary society.

REUSING DATA FOR LEARNING AND TEACHING

Key qualitative data sets, such as those of Townsend's, are prime targets for exploitation for learning and teaching. Using these materials in a learning environment, students benefit from examining data collected using sociological and anthropological research methods, and from comparing this with historical data collected in the late nineteenth century. Particular research issues can be examined, such as kinship patterns in both Townsend's interview material, questionnaires and notes, and Webb's detailed notes on the tenants (Qualidata, 1999). In examining critically the methods used and the outcomes of the research students can consider the merits of these methods and whether they may have approached the research differently. There is also scope to examine different issues in greater depth.

Learning about the work of researchers who have made a significant impact in their field, and enabling participants to take the best practice elements from this work and further develop them in their own research work is equally valuable. Moreover, the kinds of discussions arising out of group learning that Qualidata has run, underline the value of data confrontation workshops in encouraging an imaginative approach to archiving and reuse. Whilst hands-on exercises have obvious immediate benefits to students in terms of their current research activity there will doubtless be other long term benefits as their careers as researchers evolve, for example, illustrating the importance of preparing data for reuse so that researchers themselves will be more inclined to archive and share their own data.

CONCLUSION

There are, in short, many very important gains from reanalysis. At the start of a research project, it can be invaluable in providing a sense of the topics which can be successfully covered in interviewing, and therefore make the pilot stage of the new project both more effective and also much swifter. At a later stage a comparable interview set may also provide a crucial wider sample base for testing the interpretations which are emerging. Finally, by making research data available to reanalysis by others, the investigator may strikingly multiply the outcomes from this initial research through the publications of others from the same material.

In terms of data provision to support reuse, we have identified a number of critical issues for qualitative data archives. First, a culture of sharing in research practice needs to be encouraged with appropriate user support for data creators. Secondly, appropriate collection priorities need to be developed that assess the reusability of data. Thirdly, procedures and standards for the deposit, processing, description and provision of access to data must be established. Fourthly, a programme of promotional work, user support and outreach activities, such as training provision and the creation of web-based resources for teaching and research should be put in place. Finally, in view of long-term stability, major national funders of social research should be encouraged to implement archival policies so to add value to the empirical research they support.

FURTHER READING

Qualidata Web site (2002) at http: //www.qualidata.essex.ac.uk/This web site contains relevant and up to date information on the availability of sources of data and issues concerning reuse.

K. Mruck, L. Corti, S. Kluge and D. Opitz (eds) (2000, December) Text . Archive . Reanalysis. *Forum: Qualitative Social Research* [Online Journal], *1*(3), Available at: http://esds.ac.uk/qualidata. This is a whole issue of the journal devoted to the sharing and reuse of qualitative data, and comprising some 40 papers on the topic.

REFERENCES

Barker, E. (2002) *Edwardians Online Pilot Resource*, Qualidata, UK Data Archive.

Brown, R.K. 'Orientation to work and industrial behaviour of shipbuilding workers on Tyneside [collection]. Colchester, Essex: UK Data Archive [producer], Q141/QDD/Brown 1. Modern Records Centre (MRC), University of Warwick Library UK [distributor].

Brown, R.K.. Brannen. P., Cousins, J. and Samphier, M. (1973) 'Leisure in work: the occupational culture of shipbuilding workers', in Michael Smith, Stanley Parker and Cyril Smith (eds), *Leisure and Society in Britain*, London: Allen Lane, pp. 97–110.

Cohen, S. and Taylor, L. (1972) *Psychological Survival: The Effects of Long-term Imprisonment*, London: Allen Lane.

Corti, L. (2000) 'Progress and problems of preserving and providing access to qualitative data for social research – the international picture of an emerging culture', *Forum Qualitative Social Research* [online journal], 1(3): (December).

Corti, L. (2002) *Qualilitative Data Processing Guidelines*, Qualidata UK Data Archive.

Corti, L. and Ahmad, N. (2000) 'Digitising and providing access to social-medical case records: the case of George Brown's works' [19 paragraphs], *Forum Qualitative Social Research* [online journal], 1 (3).

Corti, L., Day, A. and Backhouse, G. (2000) 'Confidentiality and informed consent: issues for consideration in the preservation of and provision of access to qualitative data archives', *Forum Qualitative Social Research* [online journal], 1 (3).

Corti, L., Foster, J. and Thompson, P. (1995) 'Archiving qualitative research data', *Social Research Update*, Issue 10, Department of Sociology, University of Surrey.

Corti, L. and Thompson, P. (2000) *Annual Report of Qualidata to the ESRC*, University of Essex.

Courtney, C. and Thompson, P.R. (eds) (1996) *City Lives*. London: Methuen.

Cousins, J. and Brown, R. (1975) 'Patterns of paradox: shipbuilding workers' images of society', in M. Bulmer (ed.), *Working-Class Images of Society*, London: Routledge and Kegan Paul, pp. 55–82.

Critcher, C., Waddington, D. and Jones, K. 'Coal and community: a comparative study of three mining communities after the strike [collection]. Colchester, Essex: UK Data Archive [producer], Q140/QDD/Critcher. Modern Records Centre (MRC), University of Warwick Library Acquisition no. MSS:371/Coal [distributor].

Dale, A., Arber, S. and Procter, M. (1988) *Doing Secondary Analysis*, London: Unwin Hyman.

Dein, Alan and Perks, Robert (eds) (1993) *Lives in Steel*, audio compilation, British Library: London.

ESRC (1999) *Guidelines on Copyright and Confidentiality: Legal Issues for Social Science Researchers*, ESRC: Swindon.

ESRC (2002) *ESRC Datasets Policy*, ESRC: Swindon.

Fielding, N. and Fielding, J. (2000) 'Resistance and adaptation to criminal identity: using secondary analysis to evaluate classic studies of crime and deviance', *Sociology*, 34 (4): 671–89.

Goldthorpe, J., Lockwood, D., Bechhover, F. and Platt, J. (1968) *The Affluent Worker: Industrial Attitudes and Behaviour*, Cambridge: Cambridge University Press.

Hammersley, M. (1997) 'Qualitative data archiving: some reflections on its prospects and problems', *Sociology*, 31(1): 131–42.

Hinds, P., Vogel, R. and Clarke-Steffen, L. (1997) 'The possibilities and pitfalls of doing a secondary analysis of a qualitative data set', *Qualitative Health Research*, 7(3): 408–24.

James, J. and Sorensen, A. (2000) 'Archiving longitudinal data for future research. Why qualitative data add to a study's usefulness [59 paragraphs]', *Forum Qualitative Social Research* [online journal], 1 (3).

Mauthner, N., Parry, O. and Backett-Milburn, K. (1998) 'The data are out there, or are they? Implications for archiving and revisiting qualitative data', *Sociology*, 32(4): 733–45.

Mruck, K., Corti, L., Kluge, S. and Opitz, D. (eds) (2000) Text. Archive. Re-Analysis. *Forum: Qualitative Social Research* [online journal], 1(3): December, Available at: http: //qualitative-research.net/fqs/fqs-eng.htm

Pahl, R.E. (1984) *Divisions of Labour*, Oxford: Blackwell.

Pahl, R. and Wallace, C. 'Isle of Sheppey' [collection]. Colchester, Essex: UK Data Archive [producer], Q015/QDD/Pahll/HWS PIL, SS81; HWS; HWS83: Q012/QDD/Pahll/YE80. National Social Policy and Social Change Archive [distributor].

Qualidata (1999) *Teaching Pack The Last Refuge: A Qualitative Research Study by Peter Townsend*, Colchester: University of Essex.

Rex and Moore (1967) *Race, Community and Conflict*, Oxford: Oxford University Press.

Sheridan, D. (2000) 'Reviewing mass-observation: the archive and its researchers thirty years on', *Forum: Qualitative Social Research* [online journal], 1(3): December.

Stacey, M. (1974) 'The myth of community studies', in C. Bell and H. Newby (eds), *The Sociology of Community*, London: Frank Cass.

Thompson, P. (1975) *The Edwardians: The Remaking of British Society*, London: Weidenfeld and Nicolson.

Thompson, P. (1991) 'Pilot study of archiving qualitative data: Report to ESRC', Department of Sociology, University of Essex.

Thompson, P.R. (1993) 'Family myth, models and denials in the shaping of individual lifepaths', in P.R. Thompson and D. Bertaux (eds), *Between Generations*, Oxford: Oxford University Press.

Thompson, P. (2000) 'Experiences of re-analysing data in qualitative research', *Forum: Qualitative Social Research* [online journal], 1(3).

Thompson, P. and Corti, L. (1998) 'Are you sitting on your qualitative data? Qualidata's mission', *Social Research Methodology: Theory and Practice*, 1 (1): 85–90.

Thompson. P.R., Itzen, C. and Abendstern, M. (1991) *I Don't Feel Old, Understanding the Experience of Later Life*, Oxford: Oxford University Press.

Thompson, P.R. and Newby, H. (1991, 1993 and 1995) 'Families, social mobility and ageing: an intergenerational approach', (100 families) [collection]. Colchester, Essex: UK Data Archive [producer], Q209/QDD/Thompson 7/100 FAM. The British Library National Sound Archive, London Accession No. C685 [distributor].

Thorne, S. (1990) 'Secondary analysis in qualitative research: issues and implications', in J.M. Morse (ed.), *Critical Issues in Qualitative Research Methods*, London: Sage, pp.263–79.

Townsend, P. (1957) *The Family Life of Old People*, London: Routledge.

Townsend, P. (1962) *The Last Refuge, A Survey of Residential Institutions and Homes for the Aged in England and Wales*, London: Routledge.

Townsend, P. (1979) *Poverty in the UK, a Survey of Household Resources and Standards of Living*, London: Penguin Books.

UKDA (2002) 'Cataloguing and indexing guidelines', UK Data Archive, University of Essex.

Waddington, D., Wykes, M. and Critcher, C. (1990) *Split at the Seams? Community, Continuity and Change after the 1984–5 Coal Dispute*, Milton Keynes: Open University Press.

Wainwright, H. and Elliott, D. (1982) *The Lucas Plan. A New Trade Unionism in the Making*, London: Alison and Busby.

Wainwright, H. and Elliott, D. 'Lucas aerospace 'open door project' [collection]. Colchester, Essex: UK Data Archive [producer], Q151/QDD/Wainwright 4. National Museum of Labour History [distributor].

Webb. J. 'New technology and the management of expertise in customer–supplier relations' [collection]. Colchester, Essex: UK Data Archive [producer], Q048/QDD/Webb, .J. Archives and Business Records Centre. University of Glasgow Accession no. ACCN1594 [distributor].

Webb, J. and Cleary, D. (1990) *Organisational Change and the Management of Expertise*, London: Routledge.

Webb, S. and Webb, B. (1894) *History of Trade Unionism*, London: Longman, Green.

Zeitlyn, D. (2000) 'Archiving anthropology', *Forum: Qualitative Social Research* [online journal], 1(3). (December)

Michael Rowlinson

There are increasing calls for a historical perspective in organization studies. The hope is that a 'historic turn' might help to make the study of organizations less deterministic and more ethical, humanistic and managerially relevant (Clark and Rowlinson, forthcoming). In this chapter I use the example of my own research on the extensive collection of historical documents held by Cadbury, the British chocolate company, to explore issues to be considered when analysing company documents from a historical perspective. My intention is to address the question of why historical analysis of company documents is rarely pursued as a research strategy by organizational researchers. The discussion is organized around the theme of exploring the differences between organization studies and business history, starting with a series of misconceptions concerning archival research on the part of organizational researchers. Then I contrast the problem of periodization in business history with the focus on everyday life in qualitative organizational ethnography and how this affects writing strategies in history and organization studies.

ORGANIZATION STUDIES AND BUSINESS HISTORY ————————————

Considering their common interest in business organizations, dialogue between qualitative organizational researchers and business historians concerning theory and methods is relatively limited. This is partly because business history, which can be defined as 'the systematic study of individual firms on the basis of their business records' (Tosh, 1991: 95; Coleman, 1987: 142), and is virtually synonymous with the historical analysis of company documentation, is characterized by a lack of methodological reflection. This is a characteristic of history in general, as Hayden White, one of the most influential philosophers of history, observes:

> History is rather a craftlike discipline, which means that it tends to be governed by convention and custom rather than by methodology and theory and to utilize ordinary or natural languages for the description of its objects of study and representation of the historian's thought about those objects. (1995: 243)

Qualitative researchers in organization studies are expected to justify their methodology, whereas business historians do not have to contend with a high expectation that they can and will account for their methodological approach. Business history remains resolutely empiricist and atheoretical in the sense that its conceptualizations and claims are relatively unexamined and, unlike organization studies, it lacks an ostentatiously theoretical language. Business historians verge on assuming that their interpretation of company documents is common sense, and therefore their procedure needs no explanation (Rowlinson, 2001: 15).

The preference in qualitative organization studies, especially organizational culture studies, is for interviews and observation, which I refer to as organizational ethnography (for example, Ott, 1989; Van Maanen, 1988, see Brewer, Chapter 25 this volume), as opposed to the historical analysis of documents. Organizational researchers obviously prefer what they know and do best. However, for organizational researchers considering a historical perspective I would like to address what I see as a series of misconceptions in organization studies concerning archival research. These misconceptions can be summarized as follows (distilled from Strati, 2000: 158–9; see also Martin, 2002: 348, 352): (1) history consists of a repository of facts that can be used to confirm or refute organizational theories; (2) historical analysis of company documentation does not interfere in the dynamics of an organization; (3) company documents have already been collected and organized by companies before a researcher can analyse them; (4) archival research is not a proper method of empirical organizational research because instead of being directly generated in the course of organizational research, historical data is merely collected; (5) the validity and reliability of company documentation must be questioned more than other sources, since it has been collected and processed for the purpose of legitimating a company; (6) history is synonymous with the organizational memory shared by members of an organization.

History as a repository of facts

Organizational researchers tend to regard history as a repository of facts, or else they castigate historians for holding such a naïve view of history. However, philosophers of history have long recognized the ambiguity of history. As Hegel wrote:

> the term *History* unites the objective with the subjective side . . . it comprehends not less what has *happened,* than the *narration* of what has happened. (quoted in White, 1987: 11–12)

As a result of this inherent ambiguity, history has always had to tackle epistemological questions such as: 'How can we know about the past? What does it mean to explain historical events? Is objective knowledge possible? (Fay, 1998: 2). However, historians often evade such questions by practising a

> sleight of hand . . . hiding the fact that all history is the study, not of past events that are gone forever from perception, but rather of the 'traces' of those events distilled into documents and monuments on one side, and the praxis of present social formations on the other. These 'traces' are the raw materials of the historian's discourse, rather than the events themselves. (White, 1987: 102)

Historians seek to 'reconstruct the past' mainly by studying its documentary 'traces' (Callinicos, 1995: 65), whereas for organizational ethnographers, 'The history that counts is . . . embedded in the daily practices and symbolic life of the group studied' (Van Maanen, 1988: 72). What passes for history in organization studies usually consists of interpretations of studies that have already been carried out by historians rather than original historical research. This reinforces an impression that historical 'facts' come ready-made, and detracts from appreciating 'the historian's almost alchemical gift of transmuting old records in archives into the struggles and passions of the once-living human beings of whom these documents are the traces' (Callinicos, 1989: viii).

Historical analysis and organizational dynamics

If history is merely required to frame contemporary research on an organization then access to company documentation is probably not required. Sufficient information can often be found in publicly available sources such as: published company histories; annual reports; prospectuses; newspapers; trade directories; house journals; trade press; trade catalogues; and parliamentary papers (Orbell, 1987: 9). Most of these sources can be consulted without having to contact companies being researched and they are a mainstay for comparative historical surveys of companies (for example, Whittington and Mayer, 2000). But if history is to provide more than background information, and if the company being researched is still in existence, then access will probably be required to the historical documents held by the company itself. The situation facing researchers who propose to use company documentation is one that business historians are all too familiar with:

> Many firms are conservative in their access policy . . . and normally they will insist on vetting any publication which results before it goes to press. This is understandable, for the records are the private property of the company, and businesses need to ensure customer and employee confidentiality – some, such as banks, especially so. (Armstrong, 1991: 25)

A small number of companies in the UK have archivists, but the majority have 'no formal in-house provision for the care and administration of their historical records' (Orbell, 1987: 9, 12). The *Directory of Corporate Archives*, produced by the Business Archives Council (Richmond and Turton, 1997), lists 88 British businesses that 'offer access to their archives on a quasi-formal basis', most of which employ an archivist. However, non-inclusion in the Directory should not be taken to mean that a company does not possess a significant collection of historical documents, or that access will automatically be denied. Cadbury, for example, does not appear in it.

In 1983 Sir Adrian Cadbury, then Chairman of Cadbury Schweppes, granted access to the historical documents held by the company at its main Bournville site in south-west Birmingham, UK, to a team of organizational researchers from Aston University in Birmingham. The purpose of the archival research was to provide an historical orientation for a case study of changes in work organization at Cadbury (Smith et al., 1990). As the doctoral researcher in the team I was assigned to the historical research and spent much of my time from 1983 to 1987 poring over documents in the Cadbury library (Rowlinson, 1987). In retrospect I have come to realize that this was a rare opportunity for an organizational researcher to conduct a detailed historical study of company documents. Few researchers are ever allowed the level of access I was granted to such an extensive private collection of company documents without being commissioned to write an authorized history of the company concerned (Coleman, 1987).

As with ethnographic research (Turner, 1988: 114), my historical research at Cadbury was the product of a relationship between me, as a researcher, and members of the organization. The staff in Cadbury's company library made access to documents a reality on a daily basis, allocating me space to work and often providing an understanding of the documents I was studying based on their long service with the company. It is inevitable that a researcher comes to identify with an organization and its members, and subsequently I have often felt duplicitous for disclosing an interpretation of my data that is critical of Cadbury. The ethnographic researcher who criticizes an organization can hide behind anonymity by using a pseudonym for the organization in which research took place. But the historical researcher is answerable to the organization members who granted access if, as is expected in business history, the company is named when the research is written up.

Collection and organization of company documentation

Business historians warn that the state of many collections of company documents is unlikely to match the expectations of organizational researchers. For an organizational researcher my first sight of the historical documents held by Cadbury was daunting. The documents were stored in various places around the factory. Two large cupboards in a corridor in the basement were stuffed full of papers and files. If there was any organization in these cupboards, it was not apparent. I was allowed to rummage through the documents, which mostly consisted of large bound annual volumes containing minutes of committee meetings. When I found volumes that looked interesting I could take them to the Cadbury library to read through.

One set of documents was set apart from the rest. These were the Cadbury Board Minutes and accompanying files, which were kept in a room of their own on the top floor of the main office block, adjacent to the directors' offices, which symbolized a reverence for the firm's history. The minutes start from 1899, when Cadbury converted from a partnership to become a private limited company. Each annual volume of board minutes has an accompanying volume of the Board File, containing correspondence and reports. In the earliest years the Board Minutes and documents in the files were hand written in an impressive style, which I often found difficult to decipher. The historical documents held at Cadbury are best described as constituting a 'collection' rather than an 'archive', as the term archive carries connotations, for historians, of documents having been organized and catalogued by an archivist.

Generation of historical data

Organizational ethnographers maintain that they 'face the problem that their texts . . . taken from the field must first be constructed', whereas the texts used by historians and literary critics come 'prepackaged' (Van Maanen, 1988: 76). But historians maintain that their sources are *not* the same as literary texts, since historical texts have to be constructed (Evans, 1997: 110). Although the term 'text' can be taken to mean any written document, qualitative organizational researchers usually take historical documents to consist of published material, such as books, magazines and newspapers (Denzin and Lincoln, 2000: 375). Qualitative documentary research is equated with a deep and detailed analysis of a small sample of such publicly available texts (Silverman, 2000: 42–3). But this does not correspond to the task that faced me when I was confronted with the historical documents in the Cadbury Collection.

Just as the organizational ethnographer faces choices over what to record in the field, so the historian has to decide which documents to consult and how to take notes from them. After seeing the extent of the Cadbury Collection, I decided to restrict my 'primary' research to the documentation it contained and to forego documentary research in other libraries, such as the Birmingham public library. There were two pragmatic reasons for this decision. First, it limited my 'archive' to manageable proportions. Second, in case access to the Cadbury collection was not extended beyond the duration of the research project, it seemed sensible to make the most of the access I had been granted while it lasted.

From the vast array of documents in the Cadbury Collection, I selected for consultation those which appeared most likely to shed light on the management of labour. The procedure I followed, if it can be called that, was to take a volume of minutes, such as the Board Minutes or the Works Council Minutes, and to flick through the pages trying to spot any item of interest. For later volumes of the Board Minutes and some other committees there was an index, and I could note any entries in the index that looked as if they might be of interest. For each item of interest I made notes on a five by eight inch record card. It was also possible to photocopy particularly interesting documents. What I now refer to as my 'data' from the research on Cadbury consists of four boxes containing approximately 4,000 record cards and four lever arch files full of photocopies which I can consult when writing about Cadbury without revisiting the Cadbury Collection. The record cards contain all my hand written notes on the documents I consulted during the research. In addition to the board minutes I examined various volumes of minutes for other management committees, minutes for the separate Men's and Women's Works Councils, from their inception in 1918, and the *Bournville Works Magazine*. Of course some of the cards have only a few lines, whereas others are filled with verbatim notes of what appears in the documents. My most detailed notes are from the board minutes. I have one full box of nearly 1,000 record cards in chronological order for all volumes of the Board Minutes from 1899 to 1929. To take one year as an example, in 1916 Board meetings were more or less weekly and over 800 minutes were taken. Out of these my data consists of notes on 55 minutes from 35 meetings.

As with other qualitative methods in organization studies only a small proportion of my data is ever likely to be utilized in published outputs. However, the versatility of the enormous volume of data I generated in the craft-like fashion of a historian, rather than a narrowly prescribed procedure, means that I have been able to use the data to address a range of historiographical debates of relevance to organization studies, namely: the early application of scientific management by Cadbury in 1913 (Rowlinson, 1988); the symbolism of the Cadbury centenary celebrations in 1931 in the company's corporate culture (Rowlinson and Hassard, 1993); the relationship between the corporate culture and the adoption of a multidivisional structure by Cadbury in 1969 (Rowlinson, 1995); the nostalgic historiography of Quaker firms (Rowlinson, 1998), and the heritage view of history presented by Cadbury World, the firm's visitor attraction that opened in 1990 (Rowlinson, 2002). I have also shared my data with other historians.

Validity and reliability of company documentation

From a business historian's point of view interviews are seen as supplementary to documentary research, since:

> Without extensive research in corporate records it is all too easy to accept one's informants' statements at face value or to mistake an external façade for an internal reality. Documentary research provides an excellent means to test the accuracy of different images and perceptions of the organization and to compare espoused and actual values. It may also furnish an alternative to the official version of the firm's history. (Dellheim, 1986: 20)

In contrast to the historian's confidence in documentary research, the view of organizational researchers seems to be that the problems of meaning and understanding in history are best overcome by qualitative, in-depth interviewing. This consigns 'the analysis of documentary materials' to a supplementary role of 'providing background information about an organization and those who belong to it' (Strati, 2000: 158). Even research that is noted in strategy and organization studies for its use of historical documents mainly does so in order to supplement long semi-structured interviews (for example, Pettigrew, 1985: 40).

It may be the case, as organizational researchers allege, that 'official publications such as brochures, annual reports, and press releases . . . typically reflect only what a team of executives and public relations people want to convey publicly' (Ott, 1989: 109). But the value of such publications as historical documents is that they can reveal what *past* executives wanted to be publicly conveyed, which may well be different from present executives. Commemorative company histories, for example, reveal much about the concerns of companies at the time they were commissioned (Rowlinson and Hassard, 1993: 306). Unpublished, private company documents, such as the minutes of meetings, are *not* composed, collected and processed for the purposes of subsequent social legitimation, but to provide a record of decisions taken. As such they are the outcome of a political process. The value of such archival materials is that they have not been collected, or concocted, for the benefit of the researcher, unlike stories (see Gabriel and Griffiths, Chapter 10, this volume) and reconstructed memories elicited in interviews (see King, Chapter 2, this volume).

Historians do face the problem that the records of businesses that are no longer in existence are difficult to locate, and even the records of some companies that are still in existence may be very thin (Armstrong, 1991: 25). This tends to bias historical research towards companies such as Cadbury, where the importance attributed to the company's history results in a degree of reverence for historical documents which ensures their preservation. But I found little evidence to suggest that the documents collected by Cadbury had been continually or systematically edited in the light of current concerns for the company's public image. The biggest fear for historical researchers is that masses of documents are likely to be unsystematically discarded by companies. Historical documents may be discarded, but it is difficult for them to be systematically doctored. If a mass of documents have been preserved, as at Cadbury, then one of the most difficult tasks for the historical researcher is selecting documents from the sheer volume available.

History and organizational memory

In organization studies there is a tendency to conflate history and memory, as in Karl Weick's wry contention that every manager is a historian, and 'any decision maker is only as good as his or her memory' (1995: 184–5). David Lowenthal (1985: 200–14), a historian concerned with representations of heritage, has elaborated a distinction between history and memory that can be extended to distinguish between organizational history and organizational memory. Lowenthal maintains that memory, and by extension we can also say organizational memory, is *not* a repository of knowledge about past events. Instead it consists of recollections of past events that express organization members' feelings about those events. Insofar as these feelings summarize organization members' sense of 'past experience' (Weick, 1995: 111), they cannot be gainsaid, which means that there is necessarily a tension between memory and history, since history consists of a dialogue in which the past is continually, and deliberately, reinterpreted.

Through an interpretation of documentary sources, a historian can contradict the past that organization members remember, which may be discomfiting.

Academic business historians may be wary of accepting a commission to write the history of a company in case it is seen as 'a form of inferior journalistic hack-work' (Coleman, 1987: 145), and companies are advised that 'book reviewers and the general reader are inherently sceptical about the objectivity and balance in "management-sanctioned" corporate histories' (Campion, 1987: 31). But despite conceding that 'corporate sponsorship usually means the loss of a critical stance', business historians still maintain that 'good history is good business' (Ryant, 1988: 563), that it can help managers by 'getting things, events and facts into shared memory' (Tedlow, 1986: 82), 'encourage investor interest and, not insignificantly, spark employee pride' (Campion, 1987). Hence the proclamations of independence and objectivity on the part of business historians who do accept a commission to write a company history can be questioned. But even without doubting the integrity of business historians, it can be argued that the process of commissioning a company history favours a particular kind of historian writing a distinctive type of history (Rowlinson, 2000; Rowlinson and Procter, 1999).

My view is that, if companies are wary of letting historians rummage around in their archives, it is not because they know what is in the archives, but because they *do not know* what is in them. Companies are right to be fearful of what documents a historian might find in the archives and how a reinterpretation of history might undermine their organizational memory and adversely affect their public image. Once found, a historical document becomes part of the historian's data. Even if the original document is destroyed, the knowledge of its existence resides with the historian and may become public knowledge if published. A problem for companies is that their preference for commissioning uncritical historians to write their histories has often produced unreliable as well as dull tomes that remain unread. But letting critical researchers comb their archives for contentious events with relevance for contemporary historiographical debates has the potential to be damaging for companies.

PERIODIZATION AND WRITING STRATEGIES

I now turn to the problem of periodization that confronts a historical researcher if chronology is to be used as a framework for analysing and presenting historical data. Periodization involves the identification of suitable places to start and stop, as well as significant turning points in a narrative. It is barely noticed in qualitative organizational research, but the various procedures used for analysing data, such as coding interviews or categorizing stories, represent alternatives to a chronological ordering of events. For example, a small sample of the volumes of Cadbury board minutes could be coded according to various criteria, such as the terminology used. Instead I consulted all volumes of the board minutes from 1899 through to 1940, as well as from 1966 up to 1969, when Cadbury merged with Schweppes, taking note of any interesting items. I store the record cards on which I recorded the data in chronological order. The stored historical data could be said to constitute a chronicle, a chronologically ordered sequence of events (White, 1987: 16–20). In order to construct a narrative I needed to identify themes and connections between the events recorded. The procedure I used for this resembled coding for interviews (see King, Chapter 21, this volume), in that I read through the record cards, marking the cards pertaining to a particular theme, such as the application of scientific management, and listing them. Not the least of the difficulties in this was identifying connections between the records from various sources, such as the Board Minutes and the *Bournville Works Magazine*, in order to reconstruct events. The more the data is processed and interpreted the less the final narrative will appear to be a mere chronicle, a purely chronological, day-by-day, year-by-year, ordering of data.

Periodization in the history of a company can come in various forms. The approach I used for Cadbury entailed identifying the origins of a series of institutions that developed in relation to the management of labour (Rowlinson, 1987; summarized in Rowlinson and Hassard, 1993: 310–14). My periodization emerged from examining the data for Cadbury rather than external events in wider society, such as wars or changes in government. In other words I did not assume that periods such as pre- or post-World War One would necessarily correspond to periodization within Cadbury. This meant that I collected a lot of data on the company from before and after the period I decided to write about in order to identify the period itself. My focus on the period 1879 to 1919 starts with the move to a purpose-built factory on a greenfield site at Bournville in 1879; followed by the founding of the Bournville Village Trust in 1900 and the building of a 'model village'; the development of welfare for employees, the introduction of sophisticated personnel management techniques, and the formalization of a rigid sexual division of labour during the 1900s; the introduction of significant elements of scientific management from 1913; and finally the implementation of the Works Council scheme in 1918. By 1919 the major labour management institutions associated with Cadbury were in place. As a result of my theoretical orientation I traced the sources of ideas for each of these institutions to contemporary social movements rather than the inspiration of individual members of the Cadbury family.

My approach to periodization, which could be called an institutional approach, can be contrasted with that of Charles Dellheim, who has studied Cadbury from a corporate culture perspective. Dellheim's account of the Cadbury corporate culture is bounded by symbolic events:

> The period explored ... begins in 1861, when George [1839–1922] and Richard [1835–1899] Cadbury took over the family business. It ends in 1931, when capitalist and worker celebrated the firm's values at its centenary. A historical approach to company cultures begins with the guiding beliefs of the founders. (1987: 14)

Dellheim attributes the development of the Cadbury corporate culture to the religious beliefs of the Cadbury family, namely their membership of the Religious Society of Friends (Quakers).

Periodizing events through the use of company documentation tends to obscure the everyday experience of organizational participants that is constituted by regularities which are not recorded because they are taken for granted. Dellheim concedes that:

> The historian who examines a firm exclusively from the viewpoint of founder-owners or managers runs the risk of naively assuming that the official view they put forth is accurate. Hence, it is also necessary to study company cultures from the perspective of workers. .... The major obstacle to understanding workers' attitudes is the relative scarcity of source materials. (1986: 14)

But the methodological problem of studying everyday life through company documentation does not merely arise from the hierarchical privileging of senior management records in the preservation of documents. Even if they are preserved, the minutes of workers' representatives' meetings, no less than board minutes, generally fail to record the stories from everyday life that can be interpreted to reveal the meanings which workers and board members attach to their experiences. I could find little in the way of personal correspondence, diaries, or unofficial newsletters, which might be more revealing, among the official company documents in the Cadbury Collection.

Periodization emphasizes the singularity of historical events. My periodization of Cadbury, for example, emphasizes the firm's singularity in its adoption of scientific management ahead of most other British companies (Rowlinson, 1988). According to Dellheim, Cadbury 'was not a typical British firm', although it is representative of the Quakers in business (1987: 14). By contrast the focus on everyday experience in organizational ethnography is usually predicated upon demonstrating typicality rather than singularity. The more singular and significant a company is deemed to be for business history, the less usefully typical it becomes for an organizational ethnography of everyday life.

The emphasis upon periodization of events and singularity, as opposed to everyday life and typicality, has implications for the writing strategy in business history. As Barbara Czarniawska observes, organizational ethnographers are able to present findings for an organization which 'may not exist, and yet everything that is said about it may be true . . . that is, it may be credible in the light of other texts' concerning similar organizations. In an effort to preserve anonymity for informants, and as a result of the stylization which suggests that findings can be generalized, the texts of organizational ethnographers tend towards 'fictionalization' (Czarniawska, 1999: 38). Revealing the unique periodization of an organization through narrative history derived from company documentation would undermine this fictionalized typicality.

However, the fictionalization which is permitted in organization studies would be anathema to historians. It is taken for granted by business historians that the organizations they write about have actually existed in history, and that their interpretations refer to the documentary traces of past events that can be verified through extensive footnotes citing sources. Verification becomes increasingly important if the interpretation of an organization's past emphasizes its singularity rather than typicality. Footnotes are part of the rhetoric of history (Hexter, 1998). In contrast to organization studies, historians frequently relegate actual debate with other historians to the footnotes. But more importantly for my argument here, it is in the footnotes that the nature and interpretation of the evidence is laid out. If non-historians, including organizational researchers, read historical writing without reference to the footnotes, then they will miss the implicit debate about sources. The discourse of history can be described as debate by footnote. Each historian marshals her evidence to support an argument, hoping to bury her opponent under a barrage of footnotes citing superior sources.

CONCLUSION

Qualitative researchers using company documentation face a choice of whether to research and write in the genre of business history or organization studies. Business history requires an extensive trawl through a mass of documentation whereas in organization studies an intensive analysis of a limited selection of documents is likely to be acceptable (for example, Forster, 1994). In organization studies, an account of the research methodology is required, whereas such an account would be unusual in business history. Reflection on the nature of history itself is likely to be indulged in organization studies, as in the emerging field of organizational history (Carroll, 2002). But such reflection, no matter how well informed, is rarely required in business history. In organization studies, periodization tends to be subordinated to theory and macro-historical generalizations. In business history periodization is a perennial problem as the data is chronologically ordered, which means that turning points and end points tend to be identified from the data themselves rather than imposed from prior theoretical postures. Paradoxically, the scientistic pretensions of organization studies facilitate fictionalization through a demonstration of the typicality of everyday life presented in qualitative research. In business history, conscious fictionalization would not even be considered as a writing strategy. The implicit commitment to verisimilitude through verification makes writing in business history immensely satisfying as it can reinforce a naive sense of realism. Unfortunately, the different criteria for assessing truth claims has meant that hitherto organizational researchers and business historians have had little appreciation of each other's genres. I hope this chapter will help to rectify that.

FURTHER READING

Scholarly historical research of the highest quality with numerous footnotes citing company documents can be found in the long-established journals *Business History* (UK) and *Business History Review* (USA). In recent years journals such as *Enterprise and Society* and *Journal of Industrial History* have encouraged more explicitly theoretically oriented articles but still with extensive footnotes citing company documents. Alfred Chandler's *Strategy and Structure* (1962) remains by far the most influential book in strategy and organization studies that is written by a business historian and based on company documents. Andrew Pettigrew's *Awakening Giant* (1985), along with Richard Whipp and Peter Clark's *Innovation and the Auto Industry* (1986), are outstanding examples of strategy and organization researchers who have used extensive collections of company documents. Richard Evans' *In Defence of History* (second edition 2001) provides an accessible introduction to the outlook of contemporary English-speaking practising historians. Theoretical writing by historians and philosophers of history is to be found in the journal *History and Theory*. The best theoretical articles from that journal over many years, dealing with issues such as the status of narrative, which is increasingly receiving attention in organization studies, has been put together by Fay et al. in their edited collection, *History and Theory* (1998).

REFERENCES

Armstrong, J. (1991) 'An introduction to archival research in business history', *Business History*, 33 (1): 7–34.
Callinicos, A. (1989) *Making History*, Cambridge: Polity Press.
Callinicos, A. (1995) *Theories and Narratives: Reflections on the Philosophy of History*, Cambridge: Polity Press.
Campion, Frank D. (1987) 'How to handle the corporate history', *Public Relations Journal*, 43: 31–2.
Carroll, C.E. (2002) 'Introduction "The strategic use of the past and the future in organizational change"', *Journal of Organizational Change Management*, 15 (6): 556–62.
Chandler, A.D. (1962) *Strategy and Structure: Chapters in the History of the Industrial Enterprise*, Cambridge, MA: MIT Press.
Clark, P. and Rowlinson, M. (forthcoming) 'The treatment of history in organization studies: toward an "historic turn"?' *Business History*.

Coleman, D. (1987) 'The uses and abuses of business history', *Business History*, XXIX (2): 141–56.

Czarniawska, B. (1999) *Writing Management: Organization Theory as a Literary Genre*, Oxford: Oxford University Press.

Dellheim, C. (1986) 'Business in time: the historian and corporate culture', *Public Historian*, 8 (2): 9–22.

Dellheim, C. (1987) 'The creation of a company culture: Cadburys, 1861–1931', *American Historical Review*, 92(1): 13–43.

Denzin, N.K. and Lincoln, Y.S. (2000) 'Strategies of inquiry', in N.K. Denzin and Y.S. Lincoln (eds), *Handbook of Qualitative Research*, second edition, London: Sage. pp. 367–78.

Evans, R.J. (1997) *In Defence of History*, London: Granta.

Fay, B. (1998) Introduction, in B. Fay, P. Pomper and R.T. Vann (eds), *History and Theory: Contemporary Readings*, Malden, MA: Blackwell.

Forster, N. (1994) 'The analysis of company documentation', in C. Cassell and G. Symon (eds), *Qualitative Methods in Organizational Research*, London: Sage. pp.147–66.

Hexter, J.H. (1998) 'The rhetoric of history', in B. Fay, P. Pomper and R.T. Vann (eds), *History and Theory: Contemporary Readings*, Malden, MA: Blackwell.

Lowenthal, D. (1985) *The Past is a Foreign Country*, Cambridge: Cambridge University Press.

Martin, J. (2002) *Organizational Culture: Mapping the Terrain*, London: Sage.

Orbell, J. (1987) *A Guide to Tracing the History of a Business*, Aldershot: Gower.

Ott, J.S. (1989) *The Organizational Culture Perspective*, Pacific Grove, CA: Brooks/Cole.

Pettigrew, Andrew M. (1985) *The Awakening Giant: Continuity and Change in Imperial Chemical Industries*, Oxford: Blackwell.

Richmond, L. and Turton, A. (1997) *Directory of Corporate Archives: A Guide to British Businesses which maintain Archive Facilities*, fourth edition, London Business: Archives Council.

Rowlinson, M. (1987) 'Cadburys' new factory system, 1879–1919'. PhD thesis, Aston University, Birmingham.

Rowlinson, M. (1988) 'The early application of scientific management by Cadbury', *Business History*, XXX (4): 377–95.

Rowlinson, M. (1995) 'Strategy, structure and culture: Cadbury, divisionalization and merger in the 1960s', *Journal of Management Studies*, 32 (2): 121–40.

Rowlinson, M. (1998) 'Quaker employers', review essay, *Historical Studies in Industrial Relations*, 6 (Autumn): 163–98.

Rowlinson, M. (2000) 'Review of N. Ferguson "The World's Banker: The History of The House of Rothschild, *Human Relations*"' 53(4): 573–86.

Rowlinson, M. (2001) 'Business history and organization theory', *Journal of Industrial History*, 4(1): 1–23.

Rowlinson, M. (2002) 'Public history review essay: Cadbury World', *Labour History Review*, 67(1): 101–19.

Rowlinson, M. and Hassard, J. (1993) 'The invention of corporate culture: a history of the histories of Cadbury', *Human Relations*, 46: 299–326.

Rowlinson, M. and Procter, S. (1999) 'Organizational culture and business history', *Organization Studies*, 20(3): 369–96.

Ryant, C. (1988) 'Oral history and business history', *Journal of American History*, 75(2): 560–66.

Silverman, D. (2000) *Doing Qualitative Research: A Practical Handbook*, London: Sage.

Smith, C., Child, J. and Rowlinson, M. (1990) *Reshaping Work: The Cadbury Experience*, Cambridge: Cambridge University Press.

Strati, A. (2000) *Theory and Method in Organization Studies: Paradigms and Choices*, London: Sage.

Tedlow, R.S. (1986) in A.M. Kantrow (ed.), 'Why history matters to managers', *Harvard Business Review*, January-February: 81–8.

Tosh, J. (1991) *The Pursuit of History*, second edition, Harlow: Longman.

Turner, B.A. (1988) 'Connoisseurship in the study of organizational cultures', in A. Bryman (ed.), *Doing Research in Organizations*, London: Routledge. pp. 108–22.

Van Maanen, J. (1988) *Tales of the Field: On Writing Ethnography*, Chicago: University of Chicago Press.

Weick, K. (1995) *Sensemaking in Organizations*, London: Sage.

Whipp, R. and Clark, P. (1986) *Innovation and the Auto Industry*, London: Pinter.

White, H. (1987) *The Content of the Form: Narrative Discourse and Historical Representation*, Baltimore: John Hopkins University Press.

White, H. (1995) 'Response to Arthur Marwick', *Journal of Contemporary History*, 30: 233–46.

Whittington, R. and Mayer, M. (2000) *The European Corporation: Strategy, Structure, and Social Science*, Oxford, Oxford University Press.

John D. Brewer

Sociologists understand the term 'organization' in very broad terms to mean any structure by which social life and behaviour are managed. The term is more narrowly understood to mean formal organizations with a bureaucratic structure. Some formal organizations process 'clients', like schools and police stations, where the principal purpose is the management of people and their needs. Others are involved with the management of work, such as factories, where the principal purpose is the work itself. In the first case the people employed within the formal organizations still experience it as work, but this work involves the management of people in non-work settings. In the second, people are still being managed, but it is the employees themselves whose behaviour is being organized in the work setting. The reason for this clarification is to limit the boundaries of this chapter. Ethnography has contributed significantly to research on organizations in both the loose and strict meaning, but this chapter will focus on ethnographies that have been done on work in formal organizations and only on ethnographies done in people-processing organizations where the research focused on how employees experience it as work.

DESCRIPTION OF THE METHOD ————————————————————

Ethnography is a style of research rather than a single method and uses a variety of techniques to collect data. This style of research can be defined as:

> the study of people in naturally occurring settings or 'fields' by means of methods which capture their social meanings and ordinary activities, involving the researcher participating directly in the setting, if not also the activities, in order to collect data in a systematic manner but without meaning being imposed on them externally. (Brewer, 2000: 10; for other explications of ethnography see: Atkinson et al., 2001; Burgess, 1984; Davies, 1999; Fetterman, 1998; Hammersley and Atkinson, 1995)

The methods used must therefore permit access to people's social meanings and activities and involve close association and familiarity with the social setting. This does not necessarily mean actual participation in the setting, so ethnography's repertoire of techniques includes in-depth interviews (see King, Chapter 2, this volume), discourse analysis (see Dick, Chapter 17, this volume), personal documents and vignettes (on vignettes see Barter and Renold, 1999) alongside participant observation (see Waddington, Chapter 13, this volume). Visual methods, like video, photography and film (see Pink, 2001) and the Internet (Hine, 2000) are now also joining the list. These methods are also used in non-ethnographic research and what distinguishes their application in ethnography is that they are employed to meet the objectives that distinguish it as a style of research – the exploration of the social meanings of people in the setting by close involvement in the field. One other feature of these methods when used in ethnographic research is that they are not employed in isolation from each other. Ethnography routinely builds in triangulation of method because it involves the use of multiple methods of data collection.

One further complication is that there is an interpolation of method and methodology in ethnography. As well as presupposing certain methods of data collection, ethnography is closely associated with a particular philosophical framework that validates its practice. This framework is called naturalism (also the humanistic, hermeneutic or interpretative paradigms). Naturalism is an orientation concerned with the study of social life in natural settings as they occur independently of experimental manipulation. It is premised on the view that the central aim of the social sciences is to understand people's actions and their experiences of the world, and the ways in which their motivated actions arise from and reflect back on these experiences. Once this is the central aim, knowledge of the social world is acquired from intimate familiarity with it and in capturing the voices of people who inhabit it, something ethnography is suitably equipped to achieve.

APPLICATIONS OF METHOD TO ORGANIZATIONAL RESEARCH

Ethnographies of work in organizations have a central place in the genre (see Smith, 2001 for listings of this work). It is useful to order this research into three categories: a focus on occupational careers and identities as mechanisms by which organizations maintain themselves; managerial control in organizations; and practical reasoning in bureaucratic and formal organizational settings. In first establishing ethnography in sociology, the Chicago School used it to illustrate the processes by which social life reproduced itself (on the School's use of ethnography see Deegan, 2001) and their preoccupation with work derived from an interest to show how specific social institutions maintained themselves through workers' careers and identities (on which see Barley, 1989). 'Natural histories' of various occupations were undertaken by means of ethnographic research, often with a focus on the unusual occupations found on the margins of urban industrial society. This trait has survived into the contemporary period where the intent remains to capture the experience of workers in organizations whose perspective and identity result in the maintenance of the particular social institution. Everett Hughes gave a name to this focus when he called it 'dirty work' (1964; also see Hughes, 1958) and ethnographers have toiled as nightclub hostesses (Allison, 1994), train locomotive repairers (Gamst, 1980), police officers (Brewer, 1991; Holdaway, 1983), prison warders (Jacobs and Retsky, 1975), lorry drivers (Hollowell, 1968), assembly line workers (Chinoy, 1955), machine operators (Burawoy, 1979), massage parlour trainees (Chapkis, 1997), and many more besides.

This kind of research often only incidentally addresses the organizational setting within which the work takes place, but this focus is the main attention of ethnographies that address control within organizations. The well-known Hawthorne studies in the 1920s established a tradition of ethnographic research that blended with developments in human relations management theory to focus on informal social interaction in the workplace. The research pointed to the existence of an informal organization alongside the formal one and showed how the pace of work and job satisfaction are regulated by informal sets of norms and rules (classic studies include Roy, 1952, 1953, 1954). Besides the obvious impact in revising our understanding of bureaucracy (for classic studies on which see Blau, 1955; Gouldner, 1954; Jacobs, 1969), this ethnographic research sensitized us to the role of informal social organization in coping with boredom (Roy, 1960), the problems inherent in coercive control (Burawoy, 1979) and the dynamics of worker resistance (Beynon, 1975). Some of this ethnographic work later went in a neo-Marxist direction with Braverman's study of deskilling (1974) and Willis's ethnography of dead-end work (1977).

A third category of ethnographic organizational research addressed the practical reasoning skills of people coping at the bottom of bureaucracies. Ethnographies conducted within the framework of ethnomethodology (on which see Pollner and Emerson, 2001) focused on the way workers understood the bureaucracy's formal rules and invoked them informally in accounts of how they achieved the organization's goals (see Bittner, 1964; for an application to prisons see Weider, 1974). This often focused on the work of professionals and semi-professionals, such as doctors (Becker et al., 1961), nurses (Chambliss, 1996) or psychotherapists (Schwartz, 1976), the thrust of which was to show how complex jobs are ordinary in that they involve practical reasoning skills. Other ethnographies had the opposite effect and alerted us to the tacit knowledge possessed by workers and only by means of which the pressure of work at the bottom of the bureaucracy could be accomplished. They uncovered the operation of discretion, decision making and the complexity of knowledge required for routine jobs (for examples see Brewer, 1991; Finlay, 1988; Juravich, 1985; Paules, 1991).

These strands of ethnographic research on work persuaded qualitative sociologists to reconceptualize their notion of organization. It is not just that bureaucracy has dysfunctions or that alternative sets of informal norms exist, ethnography enables qualitative sociologists to see bureaucracy differently. Organizations are symbolic social institutions entirely rooted in people's practices for reproducing them. There is a recursive relationship between the formal and informal organizational structure and rules in which its formal character is seen to be the result of the ad hoc negotiation processes and practical reasoning of its workers. Workers often try to follow the formal rules but have to engage informally in practical reasoning and ad hoc practices to operationalize them when the formal rules are incapable of meeting the job at hand, such that fulfilment of the organization's formal goals requires informal organizational rules, tacit knowledge and discretion. However, workers have to make it look as if the formal rules were followed as part of the organization's coercive control, so engage in further ad hoc practices to ensure the paperwork conforms to procedures. Organizations have no reality other than that given them by people who reproduce the appearance of formal structure in their informal practices and lay reasoning. This reformulation is the culmination of ethnography's long-standing application to the study of work and owes all to ethnography's special approach as a method: its focus on the naturally occurring activities and social meanings of workers employed in real life organizations, captured in their own words and understood in their own terms.

ETHNOGRAPHIC RESEARCH IN POLICE ORGANIZATIONS

It is instructive to highlight some features of the practice of ethnography by reference to my own study of one police organization, the Royal Ulster Constabulary (RUC). The research was conducted in 1987 and I employed Kathleen Magee, a young, female Catholic as the

ESRC-funded research assistant. This fact is interesting for two reasons. It was an early example in British sociology of multiple researcher ethnography, something that was more common at the time in social anthropology; secondly, it gave a high profile to gender and sectarianism within the organization, both highly controversial issues for the RUC (the results are discussed in Brewer, 1990, 1991; Magee, 1991). It is impossible here to accent all features of the research design but some points are worth consideration.

The research was overt, thus access was negotiated and permission obtained from the gatekeeper, the Chief Constable. Hornsby-Smith (1993: 53) makes a useful distinction between 'open' and 'closed' access, the latter involving fields where controls are likely to be imposed and barriers erected. Anticipating the RUC to exemplify the latter, it was essential beforehand that attention be given to what the gatekeeper thought sensitive, so the research was presented to him in such a way that permission might be granted. This strategy involved an important ethical compromise, for the interests of the gatekeeper were allowed to affect the conduct of the research, although the ethical problems around covert ethnography are just as great (see Bulmer, 1982). But there are different levels of gatekeeping and once in the field informal gatekeepers tried to restrict the access given on their behalf by the head. The permission of the chief constable was a disadvantage in the field because it raised doubts in the minds of people lower down in the organization about why the management had agreed to the research (for similar experiences in police organizations see Fox and Lundman, 1974). Retrenchment from below in organizational research is as much a problem as limitations from above.

The selection of cases and planning for the possibility of empirical generalizations to other police organizations also needed careful thought before entry into the field (see also Hartley, Chapter 26, this volume). Stake (1998: 88–9) identifies three kinds of case study. The intrinsic case studies address one instance (perhaps the only instance) of the phenomenon; collective case studies focus on several instances of the same phenomenon to identify common characteristics; while instrumental case studies focus on the phenomenon because it facilitates understanding of something else. Collective cases permit empirical generalizations; instrumental cases theoretical inferences. Empirical generalizations involve application of the data to a wider population and there are two ways this can be done ethnographically. It is possible to design the project as a series of parallel ethnographic studies with different cases or with the same case in different fields, perhaps using multiple researchers (for example see Brewer et al., 1997), or to design the single project in the mould of similar ones in different fields so that comparisons can be made across them and a body of cumulative knowledge built up. This option was adopted in the study of the RUC. The project was designed deliberately to follow the pattern of ethnographic studies of police organizations in socially homogeneous societies without communal conflict so as to add to this cumulative knowledge the dimension of studying a police organization in a divided society. This allowed us to explore the impact of civil unrest in routine police work.

Effective sampling of cases is critical to the aspiration to engage in empirical generalizations. To sample means to select the case or cases for study from the basic unit of study when it is impossible to cover all instances of that unit. In some cases it is possible to cover all instances of the unit and sampling is unnecessary – this is possible when the unit of study is a specific organization interesting in its own right. But where there are many instances or where the ambition is to engage in empirical generalizations, sampling becomes necessary. The RUC research involved what Glaser and Strauss (1967) call 'theoretical sampling', in which an optimal case is selected as the fieldwork site where the processes being explored can be expected to happen. With our intent to study the way in which police work was affected by communal conflict, in order to link up with those studies on routine police work in police organizations operating in socially homogeneous settings, we needed to select a site where routine policing took place. 'Easton' was selected as a police station purposely because it was in an area of Belfast where routine policing was possible. Sampling of cases was not the only consideration, for we needed to sample by time and event (on sampling in ethnography see Burgess, 1984: 61ff). The time frame spent in the field and the events and people encountered in the organization needed to be representative of the organization: too little time and the events and people encountered can be abnormal and unusual. We asked police officers to complete time budget diaries to determine our sampling of the time to spend in the field and we initially restricted the fieldworker's contact to a few hours a shift once a week, gradually building up to a full shift, including nights, twice a week for a whole year. This was done not only to ensure a representative cross section of people and events in the organization but also to facilitate the development of a fieldwork role for the researcher in which rapport could be established.

Ethnographers are viewed differently as a relationship is built up and trust developed. This bond of trust is premised on the same qualities people bring to all social relationships – honesty, friendliness, reciprocity, openness, communication and confidence building. Trust is rarely instantaneous and normally builds slowly. The RUC fieldwork shows that it is also sometimes not a one-shot process: trust continually needs to be worked at and reassurances given. Over a 12-month period in the field, a fieldworker's persistent inquisitiveness is bound to become something of an irritant, and van Maanen (1982: 111) warns that ethnographers must not expect to be liked by everyone. But leaving aside moments of irritation, most informants in the organization became confident enough of Magee's presence to express what were widely held fears about the research, mostly by humour but once by anger. Toward the end of a long and tiring night shift, when news was coming through of the murder of another member of the RUC, one policeman in particular decided to put the fieldworker through a gruelling test of trust that was something like a rite of passage that she needed to pass before she could be trusted (outlined in Brewer, 1991: 21–4 and discussed further in Brewer, 2000: 86–7).

Getting people to talk to you when trust has not been established is difficult; it is so even when this bond has been established. The problem can be compounded where people in the organization are suspicious of the management's motives in permitting access. People can be reluctant to talk to ethnographers and avoid one-to-one contact (see Westley, 1970 for his experiences in a police organization in the USA). In this case it is necessary to hang around long enough to force people to talk. With respect to the RUC, we used those naturally occurring moments when sensitive topics came up in conversation naturally or could be artfully manufactured to appear as if casual by use of props. We used as props artefacts like events seen on the television the night before or as they appeared on screen in the television room of the station, things read about in the daily newspapers and relayed by computer as they happened in police stations elsewhere. Our experience shows that recording data when people do talk needs to be handled sensitively too. The ethnographer's conventional notepad can be obtrusive, yet when the time in the field is extensive it is impossible to do without this aid. To recall events in detail in the evening or when in private is difficult and results in general impressions. Sometimes a tape recorder or video camera can be used to record data but these are even more obtrusive. If note taking is the main form of recording data, one way of allaying fears is by taking notes as unobtrusively as possible. This can be achieved by reducing the visibility of the pad and the physical activity of note taking, occasionally foregoing it when the situation seems appropriate, and by emphasizing that the notebooks are not secret. In the RUC research, the fieldworker was instructed to consider certain spaces in the station as private (the recreation and television rooms) where note taking was not done *at the time* (but left to later), and to leave the notebook around the station so that people could read it and thus know it was not secret. We occasionally reiterated this point by showing respondents extracts of the data. However, irrespective of what occasion the ethnographer decides to record the data, writing up the field notes from the notebook in a more legible form is essential. The sooner this is done after recording the data the better. In our research, writing up of notes was done before the next venture into the field so that points of clarification at the next visit could be identified and new issues addressed. This was essential given the involvement of two ethnographers in the project.

The data collected was voluminous, containing over half a dozen large box files of typed notes. With this bulk, computer-assisted analysis packages for managing and organizing the data are very useful (on which see Fielding and Lee, 1998), although these packages were in their infancy at the time and were not used. This bulk also meant that field notes had to be carefully maintained. While notes are a running description of events, people and conversations, we kept a note of the time, date, location and identities of the people involved, and of other circumstances (Burgess, 1982: 192 calls these 'methodological field notes'). We recorded notes of many conversations and identified whether they were verbatim or précis. Records of what is seen and heard (called 'substantive field notes') were kept separate from our interpretation of it (called 'analytic field notes'). Analysis was not a separate process from fieldwork and the initial tentative interpretations occurring while in the field were recorded but kept separate from the data. We also kept a diary separate from the field notes in which I asked the fieldworker to record her impressions, feelings and emotions, reflecting on such things as the developing relationships in the field, the emotional costs and problems in the field and other exigencies that affected the research. This was used later as the basis of the reflexivity that contextualized the results. Finally, we made duplicate copies of the notes once they were written up and we kept them in different places for security reasons.

The final issue to be highlighted here concerns the handling of the ethnographer's identity in the field. It is a myth to see ethnographers as people without personal identity, historical location and personality who would all produce the same findings in the same setting. Because gender is perhaps the primary identity for most people, feminist ethnographers were amongst the first to deconstruct ethnographic practice and identify the ways in which identity influenced fieldwork relations (for an excellent overview see Warren, 1988). Attention has been given to the special problems of female ethnographers in obtaining entrée, the problems around establishing rapport and trust, and sexual politics in the field. Van Maanen (1981: 480) once argued that researchers on the police had to be male in order to be able to participate fully in masculine occupational cultures, although this is no guarantee (for the difficulties of a male researcher in establishing rapport in the police see Warren and Rasmussen, 1977: 358). However, while female ethnographers have discussed their treatment as sex objects, their gender ensured they were seen as a light relief from the demands of the job, seen as less threatening than males (Hunt, 1984), and treated as 'acceptable incompetents' (Lofland, 1971: 100), resulting in informants giving them more time and taking more care to explain (for example see: Easterday et al., 1977; Hunt, 1984). The downside is that young female ethnographers can be subject to sexual hustling, fraternity and paternalistic attitudes from male respondents, and treated as gofers, mascots, or surrogate daughters. Although some of these roles may be useful in establishing rapport with men, female ethnographers can receive the unwanted sexual attention of male informants. Magee, for example, was asked for a date by several policemen, and it was only after some time spent in the field when her presence became routine that we were sure she was being talked to as a person rather than a sex object. Nonetheless her experience shows that female ethnographers should not risk over-personalized interaction and should be on guard for the sexual hustle disguised as research cooperation. Yet her identity proved a distinct advantage in another way, in that it pushed onto the research agenda issues normally glossed over by the organization – gender and religion. In some settings gender is not the primary identity, although there is very little methodological debate about other biographical features. As a Catholic, Magee's religion was assumed by us to be problematic and we first tried to conceal it, which reflected our naivety in under-estimating the skill the Northern Irish have in telling identity from various subtle cues (for a discussion of how we managed the effect of her religion on fieldwork see Brewer, 1991: 24–7). Instances like this reinforce the importance of ethnographers being reflexive when writing up the results but also of ensuring that fieldwork is sufficiently prolonged and intensive so that relationships of trust can be built up in the field.

ASSESSMENT OF THE METHOD ————————————————————

The interpolation of method and methodology that characterizes ethnography has proved problematic. Within naturalism, ethnography was privileged as the principal method and weaknesses overlooked in exaggerated claims for its efficacy, while critics of naturalism as a theory of knowledge rejected ethnography more or less out of hand. This has led to two sorts of criticisms of ethnography. The natural science critique condemns ethnography for failing to meet the canons of natural science methods as applied to social life (for a modern example see Goldthorpe, 2000). Some principles it offends have to do with the role of the researcher. The natural science model of research for example, does not permit the researcher to become a variable in the experiment yet ethnographers are not detached from the research but are themselves part of the study or by their obtrusive presence come to influence the field. If participant observation is used in data collection, ethnography can involve introspection, or what Adler and Adler (1998: 97–8) call auto-observation, whereby the researcher's own experiences and attitude changes while sharing the field become part of the data. Another principle ethnography offends concerns methods of data collection. Methods that are unstructured, flexible and open-ended can appear to involve unsystematic data collection, in which the absence of structure prevents an assessment of the data because differences that emerge can be attributed to variations in the way they were collected. The rationale behind the highly structured methods of the natural sciences is to minimize extraneous variations in order to isolate 'real' differences in the data. This is why methods within natural science models of social research are designed to eliminate both the effects of the researcher and of the tool used to collect the data. Ethnography also breaches dearly held principles about the nature of data. The natural science model of social research seeks to describe and measure social phenomena by assigning numbers to the phenomena. Ethnography also describes and measures, but it does so by means of extracts of natural language and deals with quality and meaning (see Bryman, 1988). As Dey indicates (1993: 12), meanings may seem shifty, unreliable, elusive and ethereal.

The other set of criticisms constitutes what can be called the postmodern critique. This attacks the exaggerated claims made by some ethnographers who fail to recognize its weaknesses in the light of postmodern deconstruction of science as an intellectual enterprise. In this respect, all knowledge is relative, so there are no guarantees as to the worth of the activities of researchers or the truthfulness of their statements. This 'moment' in the development of ethnography is referred to by postmodern critics as the 'double crisis' (Denzin and Lincoln, 1998: 21–2; for greater detail see Brewer, 2000: 38–54). The first is the crisis of representation. This challenges the claim that ethnography can produce universally valid knowledge by accurately capturing the nature of the social world 'as it is' – a view described as 'naïve realism' (for this critique in anthropology see Clifford, 1988; Clifford and Marcuse, 1986; in sociology see Atkinson, 1990; Atkinson and Hammersley, 1998; Denzin, 1997; Hammersley, 1990, 1992; Hammersley and Atkinson, 1995; van Maanen, 1988). All accounts are constructions and the whole issue of which account more accurately represents social reality is meaningless (see Denzin, 1992).

The second is the crisis of legitimation. In as much as ethnographic descriptions are partial, selective, even autobiographical in that they are tied to the particular ethnographer and the contingencies under which the data were collected, the traditional criteria for evaluating ethnography become problematic, as terms like 'validity', 'reliability' and 'generalizability' lose their authority to legitimate the data. 'Validity' refers to the extent to which the data accurately reflect the phenomena under study (also sometimes called 'internal validity'), 'reliability' the extent to which measurements of it are consistent, and 'generalizability' the applicability of the data to other like cases (also sometimes called 'external validity'). The postmodern critique challenges that there is an objective and knowable 'real' world that can be accurately described and this undermines all evaluative criteria.

These crises have implications for how we should understand ethnographic accounts: ethnography does not neutrally represent the social world (but, then in this view, nor does anything else). There are implications for the claims ethnographers are able to make about their account: ethnography is no longer a privileged description of the social world from the inside (once called 'thick description' in order to emphasize its richness and depth). There are also implications for the written text, which attempts to represent in writing the reality of the 'field', for ethnographers should no longer make foolish authority claims in order to validate the account as an accurate representation of reality but be 'reflexive'. That is, reflect on the contingencies that bore upon and helped to 'create' the data as a partial account. Thick descriptions, therefore, do not represent 'reality as it is' because such descriptions are selective from the various competing versions of reality that could have been produced and end up presenting a partial picture: if ethnographers see themselves as cameras 'telling it like it is', the picture is blurred because there is more than one image on the lens.

CONCLUSION

So whither ethnography? Ethnography is not left in the postmodern state of complete scepticism and relativism in which 'anything goes'. Some ethnographers have rescued it from the worst excesses of postmodernism while still accepting some of the more valid criticisms of naïve realism. As Seale argues, quality in qualitative research is possible (1999: 17), and a number of sets of guidelines exist by which the practice of ethnography is codified and can be made rigorous (Brewer, 1994; Hammersley, 1990, 1992; Silverman, 1989; Stanley, 1990). What one might call 'post postmodern ethnography', advocates the possibility and desirability of systematic ethnography and remains rooted in weaker versions of realism. Martyn Hammersley's account of subtle realism (1990: 61, 73ff, 1992), for example, makes it clear that he believes in independent truth claims that can be judged by their correspondence to an independent reality. 'Post postmodern ethnography' contends that while no knowledge is certain, there are phenomena that exist independent of us as researchers and knowledge claims about them can be judged reasonably accurately in terms of their likely truth. This shares with naïve realism the idea that research investigates independently knowable phenomena but breaks with it in denying that we have direct access to these phenomena. It shares with anti-realism recognition that all knowledge is based on assumptions and human constructions, but rejects that we have to abandon the idea of truth itself. This is the best ethnography can claim but it is more than enough.

FURTHER READING

For a general introduction to the method for beginners see Brewer (2000). This mounts a strong defence of ethnography against various contemporary critics. For a view of the method's limitations and potential by a leading quantitative researcher see Goldthorpe (2000). The handbook collated by Atkinson et al. (2001) contains chapters on various aspects of the history, methodology and practice of the method written by some of the world's leading ethnographers.

REFERENCES

Adler, P.A. and Adler, P. (1998) 'Observational techniques', in N. Denzin and Y. Lincoln (eds), *Collecting and Interpreting Qualitative Materials*, London: Sage.
Allison, A. (1994) *Nightwork*, Chicago: Chicago University Press.
Atkinson, P. (1990) *The Ethnographic Imagination*, London: Routledge.
Atkinson, P., Coffey, A., Delamont, S., Lofland, J. and Lofland, L. (2001) *Handbook of Ethnography*, London: Sage.
Atkinson, P. and Hammersley, M. (1998) 'Ethnography and participant observation', in N. Denzin and Y. Lincoln (eds), *Strategies of Qualitative Inquiry*, London: Sage.
Barley, S. (1989) 'Careers, identities and institutions: the legacy of the Chicago School of sociology', in M. Arthur (ed.), *Handbook of Career Theory*, Cambridge: Cambridge University Press.
Barter, C. and Renold, E. (1999) 'The use of vignettes in qualitative research', *Social Research Update*, no. 25.
Becker, H., Geer, B., Hughes, E. and Strauss, A. (1961) *Boys in White*, Chicago: Chicago University Press.
Beynon, H. (1975) *Working for Ford*, Harmondsworth: Penguin.
Bittner, E. (1964) 'The concept of organization', *Social Research*, 3: 239–55.
Blau, P. (1955) *The Dynamics of Bureaucracy*, Chicago: Chicago University Press.
Braverman, H. (1974) *Labour and Monopoly Capital*, New York: Monthly Review Press.
Brewer, J.D. (1990) 'Sensitivity as a problem in field research', *American Behavioral Scientist*, 33: 578–93.
Brewer, J.D. (1991) *Inside the RUC: Routine Policing in a Divided Society*, Oxford: Clarendon Press.
Brewer, J.D. (1994) 'The ethnographic critique of ethnography: sectarianism in the RUC', *Sociology*, 28: 231–44.
Brewer, J.D. (2000) *Ethnography*, Buckingham: Open University Press.
Brewer, J.D., Lockhart, B. and Rodgers, P. (1997) *Crime in Ireland 1945–95*. Oxford: Clarendon Press.

Bryman, A. (1988) *Quantity and Quality in Social Research*, London: Allen and Unwin.

Bulmer, M. (1982) *Social Research Ethics*, London: Macmillan.

Burawoy, M. (1979) *Manufacturing Consent*, Chicago: Chicago University Press.

Burgess, R. (1982) *Field Research*, London: Allen and Unwin.

Burgess, R. (1984) *In the Field*, London: Routledge.

Chambliss, D. (1996) *Beyond Caring*, Chicago: Chicago University Press.

Chapkis, W. (1997) *Live Sex Acts*, London: Routledge.

Chinoy, E. (1955) *Automobile Workers and the American Dream*, Urbana: University of Illinois Press.

Clifford, J. (1988) *The Predicament of Culture*, Cambridge, MA: Harvard University Press.

Clifford, J. and Marcuse, G. (1986) *Writing Culture*, Berkeley: University of California Press.

Davies, C.A. (1999) *Reflexive Ethnography*, London: Routledge.

Deegan, M. (2001) 'The Chicago school of ethnography', in P. Atkinson, A. Coffey, S. Delamont, J. Lofland and L. Lofland (2001) *Handbook of Ethnography*, London: Sage. pp. 11–25.

Denzin. N. (1992) 'Whose Cornerville is it anyway?', *Journal of Contemporary Ethnography*, 21: 120–32.

Denzin, N. (1997) *Interpretive Ethnography*, London: Sage.

Denzin, N. and Lincoln, Y.S. (1998) (eds) *Collecting and Interpreting Qualitative Materials*, Thousand Oaks, CA: Sage.

Dey, I. (1993) *Qualitative Data Analysis*, London: Routledge.

Easterday, L., Papademas, D, Schorr, L. and Valentine, C (1977) 'The making of a female researcher', *Urban Life*, 6: 333–48.

Fetterman, D. (1998) *Ethnography*, London: Sage.

Fielding, N. and Lee, R. (1998) *Computer Analysis and Qualitative Research*, London: Sage.

Finlay, W. (1988) *Work on the Waterfront*, Philadelphia: Temple University Press.

Fox, J. and Lundman, R. (1974) 'Problems and strategies in gaining access to police organization', *Criminology*, 12: 52–69.

Gamst, F. (1980) *The Hoghead*, New York: Holt, Rinehart and Winston.

Glaser, B. and Strauss, A. (1967) *The Discovery of Grounded Theory*, Chicago: Aldine.

Goldthorpe, J. (2000) 'Sociological ethnography today: problems and possibilities', *On Sociology*, Oxford: Oxford University Press.

Gouldner, A. (1954) *Patterns of Industrial Bureaucracy*, Glencoe: Free Press.

Hammersley, M. (1990) *Reading Ethnographic Research*, London: Longman.

Hammersley, M. (1992) *What's Wrong with Ethnography?* London: Routledge.

Hammersley, M. and Atkinson, P. (1995) *Ethnography: Principles in Practice*, London: Routledge.

Hine, C. (2000) *Virtual Ethnography*, London: Sage.

Holdaway, S. (1983) *Inside the British Police*, Oxford: Blackwell.

Hollowell, P. (1968) *The Lorry Driver*, London: Routledge.

Hornsby-Smith, M. (1993) 'Gaining access', in N. Gilbert (ed.), *Researching Social Life*, London: Sage.

Hughes, E. (1958) *Men and their Work*, Glencoe: Free Press.

Hughes, E. (1964) 'Good people and dirty work', in H. Becker (ed.) *The Other Side*, Glencoe: Free Press.

Hunt, J. (1984) 'The development of rapport through the negotiation of gender in fieldwork among the police', *Human Organization*, 43: 283–96.

Jacobs, J. (1969) 'Symbolic bureaucracy', *Social Forces*, 47: 413–22.

Jacobs, J. and Retsky, H. (1975) 'Prison guards', *Urban Life and Culture*, 4: 5–29.

Juravich, T. (1985) *Chaos on the Shop Floor*, Philadelphia: Temple University Press.

Lofland, J. (1971) *Analysing Social Reality*, Belmont: Wadsworth.

Magee, K. (1991) 'The dual role of the RUC in Northern Ireland', in R. Reiner and M. Cross (eds), *Beyond Law and Order*, London: Macmillan, pp. 78–90.

Paules, G. (1991) *Dishing it Out*, Philadelphia: Temple University Press.

Pink, S. (2001) *Doing Visual Ethnography*, London: Sage.

Pollner, M. and Emerson, R. (2001) 'Ethnomethodology and ethnography', in P. Atkinson, A. Coffey, S. Delamont, J. Lofland and L. Lofland (2001) *Handbook of Ethnography*, London: Sage, pp.118–35.

Roy, D. (1952) 'Quota restriction and goldbricking in a machine shop', *American Journal of Sociology*, 57: 427–42.

Roy, D. (1953) 'Work satisfaction and social reward in quota achievements', *American Sociological Review*, 58: 507–14.

Roy, D. (1954) 'Efficiency and the fix', *American Journal of Sociology*, 59: 255–66.

Roy, D. (1960) 'Banana time: job satisfaction and informal interaction', *Human Organization*, 18: 156–68.

Schwartz, H. (1976) 'On recognizing mistakes', *Philosophy of the Social Sciences*, 6: 55–73.

Seale, C. (1999) *The Quality of Qualitative Research*, London: Sage.

Silverman, D. (1989) 'Six rules of qualitative research: a post-Romantic argument', *Symbolic Interaction*, 12: 215–30.

Smith, V. (2001) 'Ethnographies of work and the work of ethnographers', in P. Atkinson, A. Coffey, S. Delamont, J. Lofland and L. Lofland (2001) *Handbook of Ethnography*, London: Sage, pp: 220–33.

Spencer, J. (1989) 'Anthropology as a kind of writing', *Man*, 24: 145–64.

Stake, R. (1998) 'Case studies', in N. Denzin and Y. Lincoln (eds), *Strategies of Qualitative Inquiry*, London: Sage.

Stanley, L. (1990) 'Doing ethnography, writing ethnography: a comment on Hammersley', *Sociology*, 24: 617–28.

Stocking, G. (1983) *Observers Observed*, Madison: University of Wisconsin Press.

Van Maanen, J. (1981) 'The informant game', *Urban Life*, 9: 469–94.

Van Maanen, J. (1982) 'Fieldwork on the beat', in J. van Mannen, J. Dabbs and R. Faulkner (eds), *Varieties of Qualitative Research*, London: Sage.

Van Maanen, J. (1988) *Tales of the Field*, Chicago: Chicago University Press.

Warren. C. (1988) *Gender Issues in Field Research*, London: Sage.

Warren, C. and Rasmussen, P. (1977) 'Sex and gender in fieldwork research', *Urban Life*, 6: 359–69.

Weider, D. (1974) *Language and Social Reality*, The Hague: Mouton.

Westley, W. (1970) *Violence and the Police*, Cambridge, MA: MIT Press.

Willis, P. (1977) *Learning to Labour*, Farnborough: Gower.

Jean Hartley*

Case studies are widely used in organizational studies and across the social sciences, for example, in sociology, organizational psychology, anthropology, employment relations, political science. There is some suggestion that the case study method is increasingly being used (for example, Yin, 1994; Robson, 2002), and a number of publications examine the approach (for example, Yin, 1994; Stake, 1995; Eisenhardt, 1989; Abrahamson, 1992; Hamel, 1993). There is growing confidence in the case study as a rigorous research strategy in its own right.

Case studies can be theoretically exciting and data rich so it is important to analyse their strengths and weaknesses as well as provide a practical guide on how to conduct and manage them. This chapter examines what case studies are, the circumstances in which they are most valuable, the design of case studies and the relation of method to theory.

WHAT IS A CASE STUDY? ────────────────────────

Case study research consists of a detailed investigation, often with data collected over a period of time, of phenomena, within their context. The aim is to provide an analysis of the context and processes which illuminate the theoretical issues being studied. The phenomenon is not isolated from its context (as in, say, laboratory research) but is of interest precisely because the aim is to understand how behaviour and/or processes are influenced by, and influence context. There is an increasing interest in understanding context (for example, Rousseau and Fried, 2001) as an explanatory factor in organizational behaviour. A number of methods can be used to address this, but case studies are a key way. The case study is particularly suited to research questions which require detailed understanding of social or organizational processes because of the rich data collected in context. In organizational research, the case study is likely to be one or more organizations, or groups and individuals operating within or around the organization (for example, particular departments, types of employee, customers or clients). Case studies can focus on other levels of analysis, from public policy (for example, Allison's 1971 study of the Cuban missile crisis) to individual psychodynamics (for example, Freud's famous studies; Bromley, 1986). The overall approach is similar – generally inductive analysis focusing on processes in their social context. Yin (1994) adds the use of multiple methods as part of the definition of case study research. In this chapter, I focus on the use of case studies in organizational (and inter-organizational) research.

A case study is not a method but a research strategy. The context is deliberately part of the

* Jean Hartley would like to acknowledge the support of the ESRC/EPSRC Advanced Institute of Management Research under grant number Res-331-25-008 for this research.

design. As such, there will always be too many 'variables' for the number of observations made and so the application of standard experimental or survey designs and criteria is not appropriate. Issues of reliability, validity and generalizability are addressed, but with different logics and evidence.

Within this broad strategy a number of methods may be used – either qualitative, quantitative or both. Case studies generally include multiple methods because of the research issues which can be best addressed through this strategy. Participant observation, direct observation, ethnography, interviews (semi-structured to relatively unstructured), focus groups, documentary analysis, and even questionnaires may be used, or in combination. A case study researcher is also likely to be sensitive to opportunistic as well as planned data collection. Many case study researchers, in their pursuit of the delicate and intricate interactions and processes occurring within organizations, will use a combination of methods, partly because complex phenomena may be best approached through several methods, and partly deliberately to triangulate data and theory (and thereby improve validity).

A case study, therefore, cannot be defined through its research methods. Rather, it has to be defined in terms of its theoretical orientation. This places emphasis on understanding processes alongside their (organizational and other) contexts. The value of theory is key. Although a case study may begin with only rudimentary theory or a primitive framework, the researcher needs to develop theoretical frameworks during the course of the research which inform and make sense of the data and which can be systematically examined during the case study for plausibility. The theory needs to provide not only a sense of the particular circumstances of the case but also what is of more general relevance and interest. In some situations, grounded theory (Glaser and Strauss, 1967; Länsisalmi et al., Chapter 20, this volume) may lead to emergent theory, while in other situations researchers may enter the case study organization with clear propositions to examine. Either way, without a theoretical framework, a case study may produce fascinating details about life in a particular organization but without any wider significance.

Case study theory-building tends, generally (but not exclusively), to be inductive. The opportunity to explore issues in depth and in context, means that theory development can occur through the systematic piecing together of detailed evidence to generate (or replicate) theories of broader interest. The method, Yin (1994) suggests, is akin to that of the detective who must sift evidence (some of it relevant and some of it not) to build inferences about what has happened, why and in what circumstances. This detective work is undertaken not only to understand the particular features of the case(s) but also to draw out an analysis which may be applicable on a wider basis.

Case study research design is therefore flexible (see Robson, 2002), in that it is able to adapt to and probe areas of planned but also emergent theory. This requires a rigorous approach to the research design, the formulation of research questions and the data collection. 'Most researchers find that they do their best work by being thoroughly prepared to concentrate on a few things, yet ready for unanticipated happenings that reveal the nature of the case' (Stake, 1995: 55).

Research case studies must be distinguished from teaching case studies, which are widely used particularly in business and law schools. Teaching case studies are written, sometimes quite vividly, with the intention of highlighting particular issues for teaching and learning and to encourage seminar debate. By contrast a research case study aims to examine research questions and issues, by setting these in a contextual and often causal context. Yin (1994) notes that a high quality case study is characterized by rigorous thinking, sufficient presentation of evidence to reach appropriate conclusions, and careful consideration of alternative explanations of the evidence.

QUESTIONS WHICH CAN BE ADDRESSED USING CASE STUDIES

Case studies are useful where it is important to understand how the organizational and environmental context is having an impact on or influencing social processes. Case studies can be useful in illuminating behaviour which may only be fully understandable in the context of the wider forces operating within or on the organization, whether these are contemporary or historical. For example, examining job insecurity in the context of a case study of organizational decline enabled a thorough exploration of what job insecurity is and means to different employees and how it is inadvertently increased or ameliorated by organizational actions (Hartley et al., 1991).

Case studies can be useful for exploring new or emerging processes or behaviours. In this sense, case studies have an important function in *generating* hypotheses and *building* theory. The initial identification of research questions and theoretical framework will work best where it is tentative – with a recognition that the issues and theory may shift as the framework and concepts are repeatedly examined against the data which are systematically collected. Eisenhardt (1989) notes that although a common stereotype of case studies is that researchers find what they want to find in fact the opposite may be the case: the realities which conflict with expectations 'unfreeze' thinking and allow for the development of new lines of inquiry.

Case studies can be used where the intention is to explore not typicality but unusualness or extremity with the intention of illuminating processes. The exaggerated example may suggest processes which occur in more mundane or common settings (where they may be harder to observe). For example, Pettigrew et al. (1992), in research on health authorities, chose deliberately to focus on 'high change' rather than 'average change' organizations, partly because managerial actions would stand out in sharper relief under such conditions.

Case studies can be useful in capturing the emergent and changing properties of life in organizations. A survey may be too static to capture the ebb and flow of organizational activity, especially where it is changing very fast. The establishment of a totally new organization to prosecute the steel strike in Rotherham (Hartley et al., 1983) or the weekly changes in organization due to distributed leadership in a women's campaigning organization (Brown and Hosking, 1989) can probably only be captured through contemporaneous case study methods.

Case study is also a useful technique where exploration is being made of organizational behaviour which is informal, unusual, secret or even illicit. While exploration of such issues is not confined to case study method, the trust which develops over a period of time between researcher and organization members means that gradually information may be provided which would not be given to the researcher in a one-off interview.

Case study can also be used to understand everyday practices and their meanings to those involved, which would not be revealed in brief contact. For example, Barley (1990) analysed attitudes and actions in connection with technological change in a hospital radiology department. Indeed, Barley (1990) notes of his year-long study that 'one reason for pursuing fieldwork longitudinally is that it actually enables researchers to get beyond presentational shows. People simply find it difficult to monitor their behaviour or to dissemble for an entire year' (1990: 241).

Finally, detailed case studies may be essential in cross-national comparative research, where an intimate understanding of what concepts mean to people, the meanings attached to particular behaviours and how behaviours are linked is essential. Pettigrew and Fenton (2001) examined networks within and between organizations in a number of countries. They used case studies to ensure a detailed understanding of culture and context, to triangulate with data collected through a survey.

CASE STUDIES: RESEARCH DESIGN

Research design is the argument for the logical steps which will be taken to link the research question(s) and issues to data collection, analysis and interpretation in a coherent way. Yin (1994) sets out some important theoretical issues to consider in research design, and Stake (1995) illustrates some of these issues practically.

It is helpful to consider whether the case study is, or is likely to be, exploratory, descriptive or explanatory (Yin, 1994) as this will affect the focus of the research questions and the degree to which the aim of the case study is to analyse particular, unique circumstances or to focus on generalization. Stake (1995, 2000) suggests that case studies can be either intrinsic or instrumental, which addresses the degree to which the focus is on the unique or the generalizable features of the case research. There are occasions when a solely intrinsic case study can be useful (for example, certain types of programme evaluation), though even in those circumstances, funders and participants are likely to want to know how far the case is typical.

A key decision to be made is whether the research will be based on a single case study or on multiple (two or more) cases. A single case study, the result of weeks or years spent by a researcher in one organization, can provide valuable information about the research question. Such a study may be the only feasible option where access difficulties, resources or the rarity of the phenomenon precludes a wider study. In single case studies, the challenge is to disentangle what is unique to that organization from what is common to other organizations. The research may be strengthened by the addition of a second case. Alternatively, the researcher can develop contrasts within the case. For example, in our study of the Rotherham strike organization (Hartley et al., 1983) we spent a few days at both the Sheffield and Scunthorpe strike committees. These were particularly informative contrasts, because we were able to tease out, from a similar geographical location and prior level of union organization, that the form of organization and decision-making in Rotherham arose from the presence of key officials prior to the strike and to the dynamics of the strike committee during the strike.

Multiple case studies can be valuable, although attention needs to be paid to the quantity of data which must be collected and analysed, especially where data are collected by different members of a research team. The choice of case studies is particularly crucial in multiple-case design, to ensure illuminating contrasts and similiarities across the contexts and processes (for examples, see Pettigrew and Whipp, 1991; Brown and Eisenhardt, 1998).

In either design, consideration also needs to be given to whether the case study focus is the whole unit (for example, the organization or set of organizations) or whether the focus is in contrasting cases which exist within the whole unit. Some case studies may utilize both elements. For example, in the study of a county council facing uncertainty (Hartley, 2000), the principal focus was on the whole organization, but the case also examined the contrasting ways in which the politicians and managers responded to uncertainty.

Case study research design can be used with other research strategies to address related research questions in different phases of a research project. For example, a study of inter-organizational learning through a national government award scheme started with a national survey of English local councils, but followed this with 12 case studies of councils which had been particularly distinctive from the survey (Downe et al., 2002). A further strategy is to start with exploratory case study research, testing the emerging findings in wider survey-based research.

UNDERTAKING CASE STUDY RESEARCH

This section looks at some of the practical steps and plans which are needed in case study research.

Choosing the case study

An initial issue is how to select the case study organization. First, what kind of organization is the researcher looking for? Is it intended to be typical of the phenomenon to be studied? Or an extreme example? Has the researcher the resources and interest in undertaking more than one case? How might the cases contrast each other? The researcher needs to be clear about what kind of organization would fit the criteria for the research.

Using contacts in government and industry, academia and friendship circles can be helpful, first, in establishing what the *population* is of organizations you might draw the case study from, and second, how to select the case(s). Interviews with informed experts (for example, government officials, employers' representatives, trade unions nationally or locally, academics) can be useful in finding out about certain organizations before you make a direct approach. Reading the specialist and trade press is informative too.

Gaining and maintaining access

Particular attention has to be paid to this element of the research, both because you will need repeated access to the case study organization and also because the organization is likely to want to safeguard its reputation in allowing you access. Deciding on who are the critical 'gate-keepers' to organizational research is important. These are the people (there may be several) who are influential in deciding whether you will be allowed access, for how long, and who can introduce you to useful informants. Whoever the initial gatekeeper is, you need to establish quickly who are the other significant people in the organization. Mapping the stakeholders inside the organization can be useful initial work. There may also be valuable external stakeholders and commentators to consider interviewing as part of the case study. Sometimes, setting up a working party in the organization to sponsor and oversee the research can be a way of ensuring that it is supported by the organization. Clearly you need to have a keen (and continuing) sense of the politics of the organization. A number of writers have commented on access issues in organizational research (for example, Buchanan et al., 1988; Bryman, 1988; Stake, 1995).

Choosing an initial theoretical framework

Depending on the depth and range of the extant literature, the initial focus of the case study may be quite focused or broad and open-ended. Even in the latter case, some focus is needed to structure the study to avoid the twin dangers of being overwhelmed by data and being drawn into narrative at the expense of theory-building (Gomm et al., 2000). Because the case study strategy is ideally suited to exploration of issues in depth and following leads into new areas or new constructions of theory, the theoretical framework at the beginning may not be the same one that survives to the end.

Stake (1995) argues that the research issues may evolve over time, but need to be organized around a small number of research questions. They may be quite simple but generally focus on 'how' and 'why' questions (namely, processes). They may vary according to how much they are focused on issues recognized in the literature and how much they reflect issues as experienced by the case study participants. Skilled researchers will link the latter issues to a wider literature by the end of the case study.

COLLECTING SYSTEMATIC DATA

Given the variety of sources of data potentially available to the researcher – documents, observation, interviews, attendance at meetings – and the variety of people who might be suitable informants for the research, how do you start?

The first strategy might well be to get a general overview of the structure and functioning of the organization. This might consist of half a dozen 'orientation' interviews in which the researcher learns something of the history and present functioning of the organization. Obtaining an organization chart (if available) is useful in ensuring that you are aware of the work of the principal departments. Mapping external partnerships and stakeholders can be important. It can be valuable to be 'walked round' the organization following the workflow and observing the work being undertaken. In this way you can map out where you think the principal sources of data are likely to be. You will probably also gain an idea of when are the best (and worst) times and occasions on which to talk to people and this will help you plan your work.

Having gained an overview, you can plan out the people and the groups you want to talk with/observe and the research methods you want to use. Yin (1994) argues that it is helpful to prepare for data collection by setting up a research protocol. This makes explicit the theories being tested, the propositions being explored, the data to be collected, through which methods and with which informants, over what time period, and with what sampling of organizational events and meetings.

The use of the research protocol will be helpful in ensuring that you look for multiple informants and evidence. The protocol may be tentative in that the strategy may be modified in line with new sources of information or new constructs developed in the course of the research. However, the emphasis, despite flexibility and opportunity, is to develop research evidence systematically. This includes an emphasis on multiple and triangulated methods where possible: is the theory supported by evidence gained in different ways, from different groups, in different situations or with different researchers in the research team? The search, as with all systematic inquiry, is for a broad array of evidence which looks for and takes into account disconfirming as well as confirming data. Checking evidence includes ensuring that plausible alternative explanations for the data are dealt with systematically, not dismissed as inconvenient.

The data collected need to be systematic rather than ad hoc. It is useful to ask yourself certain questions as you set up interviews and observation periods: have I sampled this behaviour/process from a wide enough set of informants? Are there other people who might have a different view or explanation of this? Are there any data which do not support my current hypothesis?

There is *some* place for ad hoc or opportunistic data collection; a conversation with a receptionist as you walk in one morning, or a chance meeting by the coffee machine may give you new ideas which then need to be incorporated into your research design and investigated more thoroughly. This can be a spur to further systematic investigation. Can someone else shed light on the phenomenon? Are there documentary records you can check? An observation may crystallize into a proposition which can then be examined.

Managing data collection

While it is tempting in a case study to go on collecting more data, thought has to be given to the opportunity costs and to the management of the data collected. Will a further interview or period of observation add significantly to what you already know? Does it allow you to be reasonably certain there is no disconfirming evidence in the organization? At some point you have to decide to stop collecting further data.

I will not discuss in detail the recording of data because that is covered elsewhere. However, thought must be given to how you will record data and how you will prevent yourself being overwhelmed by the data. In many organizations, as an observer, tape-recording will be both impractical and inadvisable for a variety of reasons and it is likely that recording by notebook will be best. Impressions, insights and theoretical musings need to be noted, as well as observed and elicited data about the organization and its members.

Unless you are a full participant observer, continual presence in the organization is unlikely to be beneficial. Considerable time needs to be given to writing up notes of interviews and observations and this needs to be done as soon as possible after the event. Some distancing from the organization is also advisable so the researcher is not overloaded with impressions and does not get so close to the data that he or she is unable to see their wider significance.

Analysing the data

Data collection and analysis are developed together in an iterative process in a case study (a contrast with experiments and surveys). This can be a strength as it allows for theory development which is grounded in empirical evidence. However, a danger is that the researcher reaches premature closure, having been unduly influenced by particularly vivid, unusual or interesting data. There are several ways to guard against such tendencies.

The first is careful description of the data and the development of categories in which to place behaviours or processes. The data may be organized around certain topics, key themes or central questions. Then the data need to be examined to see how far they fit or fail to fit the expected categories. Use of tables to search for patterns, or grouping of similar topics may help to examine certain types of data. Initial interrogations of the data may lead to unexpected or unusual results which may mean that the categories need refining or that events need to be interpreted differently. One method may suggest one interpretation while this is not confirmed by another method. Questions lead to further questions. All the time the researcher must be alert to the need to draw on disconfirming data and possible alternative explanations of the phenomenon. These can be welcomed (however initially inconvenient) as indicating that further theory-building and/or refinement is required.

Yin (1994) notes that final explanations should fit several criteria. The explanatory case study should be an accurate and complete rendition of the features and 'facts' of the case, there should be some consideration of the possible alternative explanations of these, and a conclusion drawn based on the explanation which appears most congruent with the facts. There should be a chain of evidence which allows the reader of the case study 'to follow the derivation of the evidence from initial research questions to ultimate case study conclusions' (and vice versa) (Yin, 1994: 98). Eisenhardt (1989) concurs, suggesting that the writing up of the research should provide enough evidence for each construct used to allow readers to make their own assessment of its fit with theory.

A mistake in writing up case studies is to believe that the narrative is the most interesting aspect of the study. Narrative alone is unlikely to be of interest to those outside the organization and every effort has to be made to draw out the wider implications of the study while giving a strong sense of the particular circumstances of the case. Sometimes a brief description of the main events – perhaps in a tabulated diary form – can set the events chronologically in a succinct way so that the writing can then pursue themes. Yin (1994) suggests that an antidote to time-based rather than issue-based analysis is to write the later elements of the case first, and work backwards to the beginning.

The careful checking of constructs and theory against various sources of evidence helps prevent being biased by early impressions. Other means of increasing the internal validity of the research exist too. The use of research teams can help, with the similarities in data – but also the contrasts – being carefully explored (for example, Pettigrew et al., 1992). In addition, there may be other researchers who can act as devil's advocate and provide critical questioning for your analysis. During the steel strike research, our data collection and interpretation were enhanced by having two researchers in the field and one researcher who rarely visited the field. This supported the combination of closeness and distance which is essential to good research.

Checking the findings with the case study participants can be a valuable part of the analysis and can enhance validity. As a researcher, you bear responsibility for the interpretation of the findings, but participants should be able to agree with the verifiable facts you present.

Finally, the analysing of data is enhanced by reference to the existing literature and using this to raise questions about whether the researcher's findings are consistent with or different from extant research. Sources of difference need to be examined and can be the source of creative theory development.

Leaving the case study

When you have collected enough data (or when the issue under study has ended), you will have to leave (see also Buchanan et al., 1988). Paying careful attention to completing the case study relationship can be important both for you and for your informants (see Barley, 1990). It is advisable to remind the key liaison person for the study (or working group) about your plans for analysing and writing up the case study, when results will be available, and agreements about confidentiality of data or any required anonymity. You may choose to offer feedback in recognition for the help you have received, for example, a short report or a seminar to discuss the findings and policy recommendations. It is valuable to give the organization the opportunity to check that it is satisfied that it has been sufficiently disguised in any publications. Care needs to be taken with information which was offered to you 'off the record' – are individuals disguised or in other ways protected?

GENERALIZING FROM CASE STUDIES

Over the last decade there have been considerable advances in assessing how case studies can be used to understand phenomena beyond the immediate case. More rigorous and explicit research design has been developed and methods of data collection and analysis have improved (see especially, Yin, 1994). There is also greater clarity about the logic of the limits and opportunities of generalizing in both quantitative and qualitative studies.

For a quantitative researcher, generalization is achieved through such techniques as sample size, sampling frame and so on. The idea is to be able to sample cases (respondents, organizations) which are typical (in specified ways) of the population. If the sample is correctly drawn, then the results are deemed to be applicable (generalizable) to the specified population. This is statistical generalization (Yin, 1994). However, it is a mistake to base the robustness of case studies on this approach, as there will never be enough cases, even in a multiple cases research design (Gomm et al., 2000).

Rather, case studies need to focus on analytical generalization. The detailed examination of processes in context can reveal processes which can be proposed as general or as specific to that organization. The detailed knowledge of the organization and especially the knowledge about the *processes* underlying the behaviour and its *context* can help to specify the conditions under which the behaviour can be expected to occur. In other words, the generalization is about theoretical propositions not about populations. Thus the basis of the generalization is not primarily about the typicality of the organization (cases may have been chosen deliberately to be untypical in order to bring to the surface processes hidden in more usual settings). Rather, the argument is about the existence of particular processes, which may influence behaviours and actions in the organization. Understanding the contingencies (context) in which those processes occur is important.

There are certain actions which a researcher can take to ensure that generalizations are as strong as possible. Clearly, the techniques for ensuring the construct validity of operational measures, the internal validity of the research, the reliability of phenomena (namely that the data are capable of being repeated with the same results in the same or a similar context) are important so that the case study itself is well argued, presented and examines alternative explanations of the data.

In generalizing from the case study, using existing literature to assess the extent of generalizable findings is important (see Eisenhardt, 1989). The aim of writing with a clear conceptual framework rather than a narrative will also help to relate theory to the literature and aid generalization. Where the researcher has been able to undertake more than one case study, this clearly increases confidence in the findings, by enabling cross-checking and comparison (for example, Brown and Eisenhardt, 1998). However, even a single case study can be the basis of generalizing, and it may later be tested through replication or additional studies.

CONCLUSIONS

Case study research is a heterogeneous activity covering a range of research methods and techniques, a range of coverage (from the single case study through carefully matched pairs up to multiple cases), varied levels of analysis (individuals, groups, organizations, organizational fields or social policies), and differing lengths and levels of involvement in organizational functioning.

However, the key feature of the case study approach is not method or data but the emphasis on understanding processes as they occur in their context. Research questions about 'how' and 'why' rather than 'what' or 'how much' are best suited to the case study strategy. The emphasis is not on divorcing context from the topic under investigation but rather to see this as a strength and to explore the interactions of phenomena and context. Much case study research, because of the opportunity for open-ended inquiry, is able to draw on inductive methods of research which aim to build theory and generate hypotheses rather than primarily to test them. However, some case study analysis, especially where linked with other research approaches such as surveys, can provide theory-testing.

Case studies are demanding in both intellectual and emotional terms. Intellectually, the need to create clear links between theory and data collection, and between data analysis and theory, means that the researcher needs to be able to deal with theory and method concurrently rather than sequentially. In particular, generalization requires systematic attention to theory. The opportunity to refine and develop the research as new events and issues come to light through intensive study provides flexibility which must be handled carefully and rigorously. In addition, the researcher needs to be skilled in a range of methods and be aware of when each may be most useful. Emotionally, the demands of working closely with a variety of informants in their organizational setting means attention to one's own behaviour and its possible effects on others. Yin (1994: 55) notes that 'the demands on a person's intellect, ego and emotions are far greater than those of any other research strategy'. Ethically, one may gain information about activities which are illicit, illegal, or out of line with one's own values. A researcher may hold privileged information, given in interview, which could be damaging if made public, either directly or in response to others in the organization. Stake (1995: 60) argues that 'the researcher should leave the organization having made no one less able to carry out their responsibilities'.

Despite the daunting responsibilities, case study research can be engaging, rewarding, stimulating and intellectually challenging. There are likely to be surprises and sense-making throughout the case study, right up to the last page of writing. It can be helpful to learn the craft through working as part of a research team, and to continue to be supported by colleagues in critical enquiry even when working alone. The case study has a long history and an optimistic future.

FURTHER READING

The definitive book on case studies is Yin (1994), which is rigorous in the use of logic and design to draw appropriate conclusions from data. A companion book (Yin, 1993) provides examples of case study research. Stake has written a book (1995) and a summarizing chapter (Stake, 2000) about case studies, focusing particularly on the use of creativity to draw patterns out of experience. The book by R. Gomm, et al. (2000) takes a sociological view of case studies, and is widely used.

REFERENCES

Abrahamson, P. (1992) *A Case for Case Studies*, London: Sage.

Allison, G. (1971) *Essence of Decision: Explaining the Cuban Missile Crisis*, Boston: Little Brown.

Barley, S. (1990) 'Images of imaging: notes on doing longitudinal fieldwork', *Organization Science*, 1: 220–47.

Bromley, D. (1986) *The Case Study Method in Psychology and Related Disciplines*, Chichester: Wiley.

Brown, S. and Eisenhardt, K. (1998) *Competing on the Edge*, Boston: Harvard Business School Press.

Brown, H. and Hosking, D. (1989) 'Organizing activity in the women's movement: an example of distributed leadership', in B. Klandermans (ed.), *Organizing for Change: Social Movement Organisations in Europe and the United States*, Greenwich, CT: JAI Press.

Bryman, A. (1988) *Doing Research in Organizations*, London: Routledge.

Buchanan, D., Boddy, D. and McCalmam, J. (1988) 'Getting in, getting on, getting out and getting back', in A. Bryman (ed.), *Doing Research in Organizations*, London: Routledge.

Downe, J., Hartley, J. and Rashman, L. (2002) 'Networking among public service organizations: learning and change through the Beacon Council Scheme', Conference paper, Academy of Management, Denver, August.

Eisenhardt, K.M. (1989) 'Building theories from case study research', *Academy of Management Review*, 14: 532–50.

Glaser, B. and Strauss, A. (1967) *The Discovery of Grounded Theory: Strategies for Qualitative Research*, Chicago: Aldine.

Gomm, R., Hammersley, M. and Foster, P. (2000) *Case Study Method*, London: Sage.

Hamel, J. (1993) *Case Study Methods*, Thousand Oaks, CA: Sage.

Hartley, J. (2000) 'Leading and managing the uncertainty of strategic change', in P. Flood, S. Carroll, L. Gorman and T. Dromgoole (eds), *Managing Strategic Implementation*, Oxford: Blackwell. pp 109–22.

Hartley, J., Kelly, J. and Nicholson, N. (1983) *Steel Strike: A Case Study in Industrial Relations*, London: Batsford.

Hartley, J., Jacobson, D., Klandermans, B. and Van Vuuren, T. (1991) *Job Insecurity: Coping with Jobs at Risk*, London: Sage.

King, E. (1996) 'The use of the self in qualitative research', in J. Richardson (ed.), *Handbook of Qualitative Research Methods for Psychology and the Social Sciences*, Leicester: British Psychological Society.

Pettigrew, A. and Fenton, E. (2001) *The Innovating Organization*, London: Sage.

Pettigrew, A.M. and Whipp, R. (1991) *Managing Change for Competitive Success*, Oxford: Blackwell.

Pettigrew, A., Ferlie, E. and McKee, L. (1992) *Shaping Strategic Change*, London: Sage.

Robson, C. (2002) *Real World Research*, second edition, Oxford: Basil Blackwell.

Rousseau, D. and Fried, Y. (2001) 'Location, location, location: contextualising organizational research', *Journal of Organizational Behavior*, 22: 1–14.

Stake, R. (1995) *The Art of Case Study Research*, Thousand Oaks, CA: Sage.

Stake, R. (2000) 'Case studies', in N. Denzin and Y. Lincoln (eds), *Handbook of Qualitative Research*, second edition, Thousand Oaks, CA: Sage.

Yin, R. (1993) *Applications of Case Study Research*, second edition, Thousand Oaks, CA: Sage.

Yin, R. (1994) *Case Study Research: Design and Methods*, second edition, Thousand Oaks, CA: Sage.

27

——— **Soft Systems Analysis: Reflections and Update** ———

Susan Walsh and Chris Clegg

Soft systems analysis (SSA) is a method developed by Peter Checkland and colleagues (Checkland, 1981) for investigating complex problems. The method is used to plan change in existing systems, as well as to design new ways of working. The method has a strong pragmatic focus and can be seen as a practical working tool. It can also be used in applied research. As we will describe below, the method is organized in a series of relatively formal and well-structured stages through which its users work. In practice, considerable iteration can take place.

Systems thinking represents an overarching meta-theory for examining and understanding the behaviour of complex entities. The underlying notion is that a system is composed of parts or elements which are themselves interconnected to form some whole. To try to convey what 'soft systems' thinking is about, it is easiest first to discuss the meaning of 'hard systems'. Hard systems logic embraces the assumption that one can develop a model of the system under analysis, and that this is non-problematic. The system has a definable set of objectives or goals. There are some identifiable alternatives to reach the goals, and it is logically possible to identify optimal solutions. Implicit in hard systems thinking is the idea that there are objective truths about the system, that reality is independent of the actors (namely not subject to separate and independent interpretation). Hard systems abound in everyday life – consider for example, lighting, heating, and plumbing systems. Engineering disciplines typically study hard systems of this kind. One of Checkland's central arguments is that thinking about systems in this way is dominant, reflecting dominant values and epistemologies within our education and training. This is not to argue that hard systems thinking is wrong, but rather that it may not always be appropriate.

So what do we mean by 'soft systems'? A central assumption is that people see and interpret the world differently. Discrepancies in the views held by individuals are not sources of invalidity or 'noise' in the data; rather, differentiation reflects the nature of reality. People hold different interpretations; pluralism is the norm. Especially in complex systems, individuals or groups are likely to construct quite different views on how the system works, what may be wrong with it, and how it should be improved.

Checkland also argues that change in complex human activity systems is best achieved by debate and the pursuit of agreement, rather than by edict and the use of power. He argues for analysis in an open, public and participative manner. As such SSA emphasizes participation in the method by the actors working in the system under consideration.

The (soft systems) analyst is part of the situation. S/he is not a domain expert, but acts more as a therapist working with clients, helping them analyse and address their problems. The role is similar to that of the change agent in the tradition of action research, where the researcher is a participant in the process (as opposed to a disinterested 'scientific' observer) with a dual commitment to improvements in practice and advances in theory. Using Burrell and Morgan's

(1979) distinctions, soft systems analysis can be located within an interpretivist perspective, assuming an ontological commitment to order and an epistemological concern for the subjective nature of reality.

Checkland stresses that hard and soft modes of thinking are complementary and their appropriateness is dependent on the situation and the questions being asked. In his view soft systems thinking is especially relevant to human activity systems. Otherwise, the method has generic applicability; it is not limited to particular sorts of systems or problem domains. Indeed SSA has been used in a wide variety of contexts for a variety of problems (see Further reading).

The aims of this chapter are to:

- describe the method;
- provide a practical example of its application;
- review practical and epistemological developments; and finally
- consider some of the strengths and weaknesses of the method.

HOW IT WORKS

Whilst recognizing that SSA can be used in a variety of ways, it is easiest to describe in the first instance in its most straightforward format. The analyst initially gathers data about the problem situation, and this is represented in pictorial form. The users of the method, namely the analyst and the system participants, then try looking explicitly at their system in a number of different ways, searching for views which add some new light. They select a new perspective on the problem situation, and develop a model of what the system would logically have to do to meet the requirements of this new view. This model is then compared with the existing problem definition to see if there are any lessons for change. These are then discussed by the participants to decide which should be implemented. If the new view does not appear to offer help to the participants, another perspective is tried.

SSA has a number of essential characteristics. Thus, in its various stages, the method incorporates:

- participation by actors in the system;
- structure and organization of the process;
- imagination and innovation; and
- analysis and logic.

The method can be most easily visualized in seven stages as represented in Figure 27.1.

Stage 1

This stage involves a preliminary examination of the problem situation under analysis. The situation is typically a complex human activity system. It can be large scale, as in the case of a multi-national company or a government department, or quite small scale, for example involving a small working group. At this point the analyst resists the temptation to impose (or indeed accept) a premature understanding about the situation or its characterization as a problem of a particular type with an identified set of causes. This is more easily said than done,

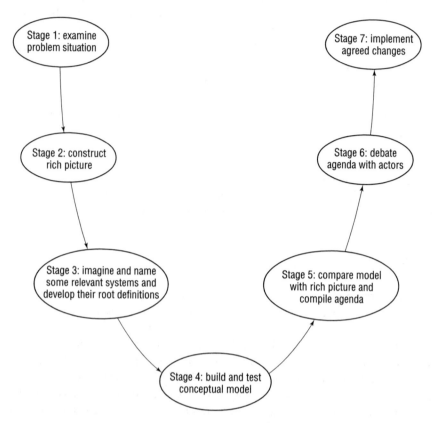

Figure 27.1　Stages of Soft Systems Analysis
NB: Stages 1,2,5,6 and 7 are 'real world' activities; Stages 3 and 4 are conceptual activities.

given the predilection for 'experts' to view the world in a particular way and to have a fairly specialized set of interests. Furthermore, there is a strong likelihood that actors in the system will describe it as a problem of a particular kind. Of course, there may be several alternative and conflicting versions.

During this stage the analyst begins to identify the scope of the system under review, and also negotiates arrangements for collecting data, along with 'contracts' about anonymity and confidentiality. The analyst should identify key roles at this time, especially regarding who is the client of the study ('Who caused the study to happen?'), the problem-solver ('Who hopes to do something about the problem situation?'), and the problem-owner ('Who "owns" the problems under investigation?'). These roles are important since these people need to be involved in agreeing the terms of reference and methods of working for the study, but also later, in debating what changes are appropriate.

Stage 2

This stage entails gathering a wide range of relevant data which are represented in a 'rich picture' and presented to study participants. Data gathering at this stage can take a variety of forms. The data should be broad-based, encompassing all those individuals (or an appropriate subset of them) who have inputs to, and interactions with, the system under study. This stage will normally incorporate the collection of 'hard' data (for example, regarding outputs and performance of the system) as well as the 'soft' data (for example, including attitudes and emotions).

The rich picture is a cartoon-like picture of the problem situation and includes a wide range of information, of both qualitative and quantitative kinds. The picture includes information on the tasks that the system must perform and also data on the issues that people raise, namely topics of concern or dispute. Also included may be elements of structure, process and climate, namely important aspects of the system. But this picture is not a systemic representation of the problem domain, and nor is it a characterization of a problem type. Thus the analyst still refrains at this stage from constructing an explanatory model of the problem situation, either in the form of a systems diagram or by describing it in a particular way (for example, that this is a problem of employee morale caused by an inappropriate reward system). The output of stage 2 is a rich picture which includes tasks and issues which are relevant to the system under study.

Both these first two stages are concerned with the present day reality: Checkland labels them as 'real world' activities. In contrast, the next two stages (3 and 4) are predominantly intellectual and conceptual.

Stage 3

In this stage the analyst and participants search for new ways of looking upon the existing problem situation. These new ways of looking at these complex interrelationships, are called 'relevant systems'. In essence, the analyst says 'let's try looking on this situation like this'. This is the imaginative part of the method. For example, a pub can be visualized in a number of alternative ways (based on Naughton, 1984). Thus it can be seen as a system for:

- providing drinks;
- initiating adolescents into adulthood;
- providing employment;
- entertaining customers;
- dispensing drugs;
- integrating a community;
- producing customers for taxi firms;
- scheduling work for the police; and so on.

These views are 'relevant' insofar as they cast light on the situation. Relevant systems can be task-based (for example, viewing a pub as a system for dispensing drinks) or issue-based (for example, a system for initiating adolescents into adulthood). This part of SSA is critical to its success. The analyst selects views (relevant systems) which s/he believes may be fruitful for uncovering aspects of the problem situation. The process of selection is informed by what makes most sense to the analyst and/or the participants, and by what promises to take their level of understanding further. This process is iterative as the formulation can always be modified later as understanding deepens. Thus the function of the relevant system is to provide 'an alternative way of viewing the problem situation which, when developed further in succeeding stages of the methodology, will provide the analyst with a sharp comparison between it and what is observed to go on in the real world situation' (Naughton, 1984: 36).

For each of these views, the analyst derives a root definition. Thus for every relevant system that is examined in detail, a root definition is developed. The root definition should follow logically from the choice of relevant system. The root definition is a precise verbal description of what is implied by the choice of relevant system. Normally speaking such a definition will include a statement of each of the following: the customers of the relevant system; the actors in the system; what the system transforms; the underlying *Weltanschauung* or worldview; the owners of the system; and its environmental constraints. These can be remembered using the mnemonic CATWOE. Checkland stresses that CATWOE is intended as a useful way of thinking about the definition, but not all definitions need all these components and other elements may be added to help provide a definition. The only mandatory element in a definition is a statement of what the system transforms.

A key point is that the root definition and its constituent parts will vary according to the chosen relevant system. For example, in the case of viewing the 'pub as entertainment system', it is transforming people who are not entertained into people who are, whereas the 'pub as community integrator' is transforming a community that is not well integrated into one that is. The output of stage 3 is a set of relevant systems and their associated root definitions.

Stage 4

This is also a conceptual stage. Here the analyst (perhaps with the help from the participants) develops a model of what the system would logically have to do to meet the requirements of the chosen relevant system and its accompanying root definition. This model is derived using deductive logic and is abstract. At this stage it does not necessarily bear any relationship with the real world. This model is explicitly a systems model and is described using transitive (namely active) verbs. The verbs are arranged in a logically coherent order. Naughton (1984) advises that such models should contain around six to 12 main activities, and that they should be simple rather than complex. A key point is that the model is concerned solely with 'what is done'. The conceptual model has no interest in 'how something is done' nor in 'who does it'.

For example, in the case of 'the pub as entertainment system', key activities in the conceptual model might include the following:

- gathering information on what existing (and potential) customers want;
- gathering information on what entertainment services and products are available;
- booking/hiring of various services and products;
- advertising and marketing the services/products;
- providing the services/products;
- maintaining quality control of these services/products; and
- evaluating customer reactions.

The core of SSA lies in stages 3 and 4 and these should be very tightly coupled one to another. Thus if the relevant system is changed, then the root definition will need alteration, as will the conceptual model. There may be many iterations between these two stages in particular as the analyst and the participants try out different relevant systems to see whether or not they lead to definitions and models that seem useful. A great deal of the craft skill in using SSA lies in developing and trying out alternative ways of looking at the system and then following through the logic of that view. The output of stage 4 is a conceptual model of a chosen relevant system.

Our experience is that conceptual modelling is a difficult activity. Whereas most participants willingly and productively engage in stage 3 (generating new views), they can find it harder to develop the logically derived conceptual models.

Stage 5

This stage involves a comparison between the new conceptual model (from stage 4) and the rich picture (from stage 2). This comparison may identify things which are part of the conceptual model but which do not happen in the real world, and also activities in the real world which are not included in the conceptual model. Any such differences are noted and discussed in the next stage. This stage can be handled in a relatively unstructured way, by simply comparing the conceptual model and the real world. Or this can be undertaken in more structured ways, for example by examining each part of the conceptual model (perhaps each verb) and then asking: does this happen in the real world? Such comparisons lead to the identification of possible changes in the system under analysis. The output of this stage is an agenda of possible changes in the form of a series of topics for discussion. The agenda is concerned with identifying what activities are present, absent, problematic or questionable. The focus remains on 'what' not 'how'.

Stage 6

In this stage the agenda is debated by the actors working in the system, along with the clients, problem-owners and problem-solvers (as identified in stage 1 of the method). The purpose of the debate is to identify those changes that are agreed as both systemically desirable and culturally feasible. Systemically desirable means that the change must make sense in system terms. For example, this could mean that all parties agree that the changes will improve the operation of the system in some way. Culturally feasible focuses on whether or not a particular change is feasible to the actors concerned. Only if both criteria are met should a change be implemented. Where such agreement is not reached, it may be that the analyst needs to accept that 'no change' is the chosen solution, or alternatively that s/he needs to try to develop another relevant system to see if a way forward can be found, namely work through the method again seeking new ideas. The output of stage 6 is an agreed set of changes, or an agreement not to change.

Stage 7

This stage involves the implementation of changes that have been agreed as both feasible and desirable. For example, changes may involve new structures, procedures, policies or processes.

We now describe one example of the application of soft systems analysis.

IMPLEMENTATION OF A CADCAM SYSTEM

In this instance, SSA was used in a research and development project examining the implementation of a Computer Aided Design Computer Aided Manufacturing (CADCAM) system in an engineering company. The researchers worked with the company from 1988 until 1990, making two sets of recommendations (in 1989 and 1990). A follow-up visit was undertaken in 1996. (A fuller account of this study is given in Symon and Clegg, 1991.) The researchers used SSA as a means of organizing and integrating some complex data, and as a vehicle for recommending how the implementation process could be better managed. For illustrative purposes the project is described chronologically using the stages of SSA.

Stage 1: the problem situation or 'mess'

The study was undertaken in an aerospace engineering company employing around 2,000 people. The company is part of a multi-national corporation and has a good reputation for the design and manufacture of high precision, small batch, engineering products. The company has a complex organizational structure. Of particular relevance here are three major functions: design, manufacture and corporate engineering. The design function is split into different product groups. The manufacturing department has a traditional organization based on machining process. It manufactures for all the design product groups, and the products flow through the production process from one machine area to another. The corporate engineering function is a central head office group which provides specialist engineering support to the whole company. Historically the company has been good at innovative engineering. Typically the design engineers take pride in designing new products to meet the needs and specification of their customers. They then hand over the design to the manufacturing department who are responsible for making the product. These two functions operate relatively autonomously and there has been little success at improving integration between the two functions.

Senior managers in corporate engineering decided to invest in an advanced CADCAM system. The main objectives for this investment included: reduced lead times for meeting customer demand; improved quality; reduced cost; increased integration between design and manufacture; and improved design for manufacturability. The initial direct cost of the new system was around £3m and this included 55 CADCAM terminals.

To manage the purchase and implementation of the new system, the director of engineering set up a project management team supervised by a project board. The project team was led by a full-time project manager from corporate engineering (whose title was project manager of computer aided design). He was assisted by a specialist in information technology (on part-time secondment from the management services department, also located in head office). The project board was chaired by a senior manager from corporate engineering and included representatives from engineering, management services, design and manufacture (all on a part-time basis).

The role of the researchers was to investigate the implementation process and to make recommendations for improvement from an organizational (as opposed to technical) perspective.

Stage 2: the rich picture

Symon and Clegg gathered data using a variety of research methods over 18 months, including interviews, participant observation, a tracer study, and questionnaires. They found that the implementation of the CADCAM was led by headquarters staff in corporate engineering and

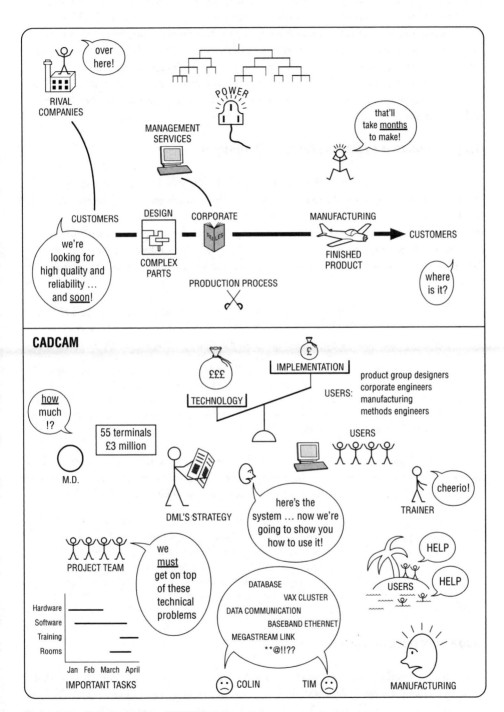

Figure 27.2 Rich picture of the CADCAM implementation

that the main concern was with getting the technology implemented at the minimum cost. Very little attention was paid to the wider organizational impact of the CADCAM, or indeed to the opportunities that were open to reorganizing and restructuring the work to improve the levels of integration between design and manufacturing. The CADCAM was not seen as a catalyst for organizational change; rather it was seen as a change in 'medium'.

A simplified version of the researchers' rich picture of this problem situation is given in Figure 27.2 for illustrative purposes. (For information Colin and Tim are the Project Manager and his assistant.)

Stage 3: relevant systems and root definitions

The researchers decided it would be useful to describe the existing relevant system that they believed (from the data collected) was guiding the implementation process. They also developed its associated root definition. This was then compared with an alternative relevant system and root definition. Symon and Clegg argued that the project was seen and managed as a 'technology implementation project'. This was the underlying 'relevant system'. Accordingly, they described the existing root definition guiding the project in the following terms:

> The company are replacing an existing, largely manual system for design and manufacture with a CADCAM system (transformation); this represents a change in medium and this process is owned (owners), led and managed (actors) by corporate engineering, with some help from management services, product designers and manufacturing. The clients are primarily the corporate engineers and the designers in the different product groups (customers). The emphasis is heavily on technical issues and problems, and the view is that organizational issues can be addressed later (*Weltanschauung*). This process is being undertaken using the minimum of scarce company resources (constraints).

Symon and Clegg argued that a useful alternative relevant system in this case would be to regard this process as an organizational (rather than technical) change. As such they developed a new root definition to guide the implementation process. This is described below:

> The key task is to design an organizational system integrating design and manufacturing, assisted by the use of CADCAM (transformation). This process is owned and managed by both design and manufacturing with help from management services, and with a strong emphasis on end-user participation (owners, actors and customers). The project involves joint consideration of technical, strategic and organizational issues (*Weltanschauung*). The process should be undertaken cost effectively using appropriate resources (constraints).

Stage 4: conceptual model

Using this root definition, the researchers developed a conceptual model of what needed to be done to meet the needs of this definition. This model is shown in Figure 27.3. This was then used as a basis for making a first set of recommendations to the company.

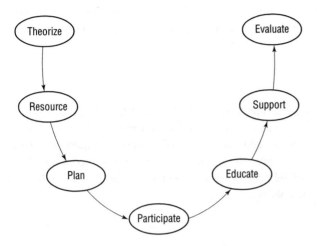

Figure 27.3 Conceptual model of an organizational change

Stage 5a: comparison and agenda

The researchers compared their new model with what was happening in the real world and identified some major gaps. These stemmed from use by the company of an inappropriate relevant system. Consideration of a new relevant system and its associated root definition led the researchers to generate an agenda for change. The key items were recommendations that the company should:

1 adopt a new view (or theory) of the implementation, placing more emphasis on organizational and end-user aspects of change;
2 invest more resources in the change programme;
3 formulate a plan which recognizes the strategic importance of CADCAM as a catalyst for change and examines the wider organizational opportunities it presents;
4 allow for and encourage more participation by end-users;
5 place more emphasis on wider education, awareness and communication for end-users and others;
6 develop an infrastructure to support end-users during the introduction and operation of the CADCAM system;
7 evaluate the introduction and operation of CADCAM, not just in financial and engineering terms, but also covering the human and organizational issues.

Stage 6a: debate

An open report describing the findings, relevant systems, root definitions, conceptual model and agenda for change was presented to all the interested parties. Two presentations were also given, one to the end-users and one to senior managers. Reactions were divided. The users were 'satisfied with the outcomes and acknowledged the perception of the implementation as technology-led, under-resourced and lacking an organizational strategy. They were keen to see the recommendations implemented, but suspected that senior managers would not agree with the conclusions reached' (Symon and Clegg, 1991: 282). They were right, indeed the director of engineering called the feedback 'a moaning minnies' charter'. Further debate followed.

Stage 7a: implementation

Some of these recommendations were accepted and implemented. A CADCAM user group was set up to address some of these issues, in particular concerning resources, end-user participation, education and training, and infrastructural support (namely covering recommendations 2, 4, 5 and 6 above). Also the researchers were invited to continue their work, including further evaluation of the human and organizational impact of the CADCAM (namely covering recommendation 7 above).

Stage 5b: a new agenda

The changes were implemented from March 1989 onwards. The researchers continued working in the company until April 1990, gathering further data using participant observation, tracer and questionnaire techniques (as described earlier). These data were used to compare how the process of change was now being managed with the conceptual model offered by the researchers. Thus the researchers maintained their proposed relevant system and root definition (stage 3) and their associated conceptual model (stage 4).

This work culminated (in April 1990) in the presentation of a second report including a further agenda for change. These recommendations included the following:

1   senior managers develop a strategy for the organizational and technical integration of the design and manufacturing functions – some specific suggestions were made for how this could be achieved;
2   the project management infrastructure should become more integrative (of design and manufacture); for example by
3   changing the roles of the existing CAD manager and CAD trainer into those of manager and trainer of the complete CADCAM system;
4   and rotating the chairmanship of the CADCAM user group so that representatives from manufacturing act in that role.

Stage 6b: debate

Presentations based on the researchers' second report were made to two groups of people, the end-users and the board of directors. The end-users were in broad agreement with the second report, though some were concerned that it appeared critical of the manufacturing function. The board of directors also approved the report ('what I have been saying for the past 8 years' according to the director of corporate engineering). The managing director (new in the role) stressed that the benefits of integrative technologies can only be achieved with organizational changes. 'The brick walls between design and manufacture have to come down'.

Stage 7b: implementation

Over the following months some of the second set of recommendations were implemented, in particular regarding a more integrative approach to project management (recommendations 2, 3 and 4 above). But no progress was made with a more strategic plan to integrate design and manufacture organizationally, as well as technically (recommendation 1). The researchers continued to visit the company regularly for 9 months after the second report. They reported that the CADCAM users group 'continued to operate very successfully addressing "bottom-up" issues . . . (but that) Little changed from a "top-down" perspective' (Symon and Clegg, 1991: 285).

Postscript

One of the researchers was able to revisit the company six years later (in 1996). The CADCAM project has been a success in the sense that the technology is fully operational, is widely used and is well liked. The CADCAM user group continues to function, seven years after its inception in March 1989. It continues in its role handling important 'bottom-up' issues. Just as interesting however, there remain problems of integration between design and manufacture. 'Design for manufacturability' has not been achieved. The investment in CADCAM (total cost by now around £12m) has not delivered the level of organizational integration that was required. Design and manufacture still operate separately. The project failed to address some major strategic and political issues that would have fostered structural change and increased integration within the company. Unfortunately this is not an unusual scenario for technical change of this kind. In the language of soft systems analysis, the organizational integration of design and manufacture was not 'culturally feasible' to certain very powerful people in the company.

Changes in the method

Mingers (2000) has identified three stages in the development of SSA since its inception. The first period in the 1970s charts the practical and philosophical development which culminates in the 'seven stage method' detailed herein (Checkland, 1981). The second period in the 1980s is marked by further development in the epistemological rationale, and a more flexible use of the SSA framework. Rigidly following the seven stage model of SSA was considered to be unnecessary and constraining. SSA now became defined as two streams of enquiry. The first was the stream of *cultural analysis*. This appears at one level to have been an attempt to integrate political and social considerations which underpin any potential successful change. The second (and in which were located the traditional SSA processes and tools) was the stream of *logic-based enquiry*. Here the relevant systems are compared with the real world. There was also discussion about the need to judge success on the basis of three criteria: efficacy, efficiency, effectiveness.

There was also increasing debate (and concerns about), the way in which SSA was being used and this led to the establishment of Mode 1 and Mode 2 usage (Checkland and Scholes, 1990). *Mode 1* was the traditional way in which SSA had been used by the authors and many others, working as external consultants using the seven stage model in order to tackle problems in organizations. In contrast, *Mode 2* is described as a differential use of SSA; for example, internal users taking up aspects of SSA to make sense of organizational issues by providing a 'thinking framework' (Flood, 2000). These are labelled respectively as the prescriptive and internalized SSA (Checkland, 1999).

In the 1990s the seven-stage model and the two-streams were supplanted by the four-activities model (Checkland and Scholes, 1990; Checkland, 1999). As described by Checkland (1999) the four activities are: exploring a problem situation; formulating the relevant systems of purposeful activity; debating the models generated and comparing them with what is possible in the real world; and finally taking action that will lead to improvement. The cultural stream of analysis was integrated across all the activities.

Although the reader needs to be aware of the changes in SSA, the developments detailed above represent a change in emphasis and a move towards increasing depth, rather than substantive change. In essence, they encourage a greater flexibility of analysis whilst bringing to the foreground the need to enact real change in the systems under study.

SSA: epistemological and ontological concerns

SSA encourages a way of exploring and revealing the discontinuities inherent in systems. Learning and change, theory and practice are actively connected. Change in the subjective meanings created by participants in a system is viewed as possible and desirable. In more detail:

- SSA assumes that social reality is continuously recreated by the participants and that the social world is fluid and both persists and changes.
- SSA utilizes interpretive-based systemic theory. Thus it is necessary to explore the meanings and perceptions of individuals within a given cultural context (Flood, 2000).
- In order to analyse social processes reflection based upon the interdependency of both soft and hard systems thinking is required.
- SSA connects subjectivity with intellectual rigour via an organized set of principles (methodology).
- SSA applies action research principles to systemic theory (Mingers, 2000; Flood, 2000; Checkland and Holwell, 1998). Collaboration, critical inquiry, change in practice and self-reflective learning are key.
- SSA advocates the value of an inherent learning cycle in which users reflect upon their world and where debating difference leads to change.

STRENGTHS AND WEAKNESSES OF SSA

In this section we consider some of the apparent strengths and weaknesses of SSA, recognizing that these may vary with the situation in which usage is planned.

Strengths

In our experience the major strengths of SSA are sixfold, recognizing that these benefits in use can be interconnected. First, the method provides structure and organization to the process of investigating complex systems and managing change. Such structure can be helpful to all the actors in the process who can see what they are doing, where they are going and how they are getting there. SSA offers a 'grammar', a set of rules but without being too restrictive for its users.

Second, the method is broadly participative, and stresses the inevitability, and thereby the legitimacy, of different views and perspectives. As such these are not aberrant behaviours to be ignored, worked around or smoothed over. These differences become part of the process. The underlying assumption is one of pluralism, a refreshing antidote to many more managerially oriented perspectives which stress more unitary outlooks.

Third, a great strength of SSA lies in its explicit requirement that its users spend time looking for different views of the problem situation. To provide possible alternatives to these well worn paths can provide a sense of liberation. Our experience is that groups of people, with practice, enjoy this activity and can become skilled at it. Groups can become highly innovative in this situation.

Fourth, SSA seems to us a very powerful analytic tool. The emphasis on tracing the logical implications of adopting a particular view of the problem situation is potentially a very rigorous and useful, albeit difficult, discipline.

Fifth, we have found that the thinking underlying SSA does become internalized with use. This applies especially to stages 3 and 4 which are the conceptual heart of the method. Thus we have found ourselves using the ideas of relevant systems, root definitions, CATWOE and conceptual models in our professional work, especially when working in complex systems and with a range of people who hold quite different perspectives and views. In this way parts of SSA have become personal professional tools, providing a useful addition to our skill set.

And finally, we need to reflect on the academic contribution of SSA. Holwell (2000) argues that one of its primary contributions has been the introduction and dissemination of interpretive thinking into the management and information systems literature.

Weaknesses

We draw attention to four potential weaknesses, accepting that these may well reflect our own particular experiences.

First, it is certainly the case that the 'language' and terminology of the method can get in the way. Central constructs such as rich pictures, relevant systems, root definitions and conceptual models are not easy to convey to others, nor necessarily easy to use. The method is difficult to learn and there is some considerable craft skill in its use. This can make it very hard to 'sell' the technique to people in organizations who may be experiencing problems and difficulties. They may already be uncomfortable with accepting 'outsiders' to help analyse their problem situation, without the additional problem of learning what can appear to be some arcane jargon that does not have immediate face validity. One irony here is that these very elements may also be one of the strengths of the approach.

Second, the method has been criticized for the conservative results it helps achieve. This appears due to a number of reasons. In part this is due to the inherent coupling within SSA of a participative methodological framework to a means of providing a rationale and tools for organizational change. Sometimes the two do not necessarily follow one from the other. Thus whilst it can be used to develop and enlarge upon quite radical perspectives and ideas, the method does suggest that change is only made where agreement is reached, in particular that the changes are both desirable and feasible. However, powerful stakeholders can resist and veto change, and this was certainly evident in the case study described above, where the senior managers responsible for key functions effectively blocked further attempts at organizational integration.

Third, the process of bringing about real change in organizations reveals a possible tension between analysis and facilitation and implementation. SSA requires that the researchers have some awareness of skills in organizational change and development. Thus, the success of the endeavour will, in part, be influenced by how the researchers manage the management of change process, for example, selling the method and the research process to the identified stakeholders. This can be difficult at times for the reasons previously identified. Until the stakeholders get used to the terminology and the use of diagrammatic forms of data representation, SSA can feel very alien and disconnected from personal experience. Direct reflection upon not only the method but one's skills to implement the method is invaluable.

Finally, SSA and Checkland's work have many passionate devotees, and there is a theme present within the literature of 'people doing it wrong' (Holwell, 2000; Checkland, 1999). This is interesting and potentially contradictory given first the method's complexity and second the refrain present in the literature about the need to capture diversity and that differences in understanding and application will inevitably emerge. We suspect that it may be very easy to 'do SSA incorrectly' but that seeing how participants differentially take up the method is one of the pleasures of using it.

CONCLUSIONS

SSA is primarily a method for analysing, discussing and planning change in complex systems involving human activity. It is highly pragmatic and organized in a series of iterative stages. The method is broadly participative, provides a structure for managing and coping with complexity and change, encourages the use of imagination and innovation, and requires logical analysis. It is also a useful research tool, especially for those working in an action research mode. Thus, it helps organize complex research projects, especially when incorporating different forms of data from different sources. SSA is not theory specific. Overall, it can be a very powerful and a useful addition to the skill set of people involved in research and development.

REFERENCES

Burrell, G. and Morgan, G. (1979) *Sociological Paradigms and Organizational Analysis*, London: Heinemann Educational Books.

Checkland, P.B. (1981) *Systems Thinking, Systems Practice*, Chichester: John Wiley and Sons.

Checkland, P. (1999) 'Soft systems methodology: a 30 year retrospective', in P.B. Checkland and J. Scholes (1999) *Soft Systems Methodology in Action*, Chichester: John Wiley and Sons.

Checkland, P.B. and Holwell, S. (1998) *Information, Systems and Information Systems*, Chichester: John Wiley and Sons.

Checkland, P.B. and Scholes, J. (1990) *Soft Systems Methodology in Action*, Chichester: John Wiley and Sons.

Flood, R.L. (2000) 'A brief review of Peter B. Checkland's contribution to systemic thinking', *Systemic Practice and Action Research*, 13 (6): 723–31.

Holwell, S. (2000) 'Soft systems methodology: other voices', *Systemic Practice and Action Research*, 13 (6): 773–97.

Lehaney, B. and Ray, J.P. (1996) 'The use of soft systems in the development of a simulation of out-patient services at Watford General Hospital', *Journal of the Operational Research Society*, 47: 864–70.

Mingers, J. (2000) 'An idea ahead of its time: The history and development of soft systems methodology', *Systemic Practice and Action Research*, 13 (6): 733–55.

Naughton, J. (1984) *Soft Systems Analysis: An Introductory Guide*, Milton Keynes: Open University Press.

Symon, G.J. and Clegg, C.W. (1991) 'Technology-led change: a study of the implementation of CADCAM', *Journal of Occupational Psychology*, 64: 273-90.

28

—— **Action Research and Research Action:**
A Family of Methods ————————————

Frank Heller

Action Research is not a single method of knowledge acquisition and change. It can be described as a family of methods distinguished by having several identifiable objectives and characteristics. However, the term became so diversified that it is difficult to evaluate its usefulness. One of this chapter's objectives is to restrict the variety of concepts that parade under this name and stress certain core elements as a way of giving the method a degree of coherence and provide a boundary within which the central family of Action Research methods retains a recognizable identity. This should open the way for this methodology to be more widely used in research. It may also overcome the problems that have led some funding bodies to exclude Action Research as a valid methodology for which they are prepared to provide funds (Heller, 1997).

The chapter starts with making a distinction between Action Research (AR) and Research Action (RA). It goes on to describe seven core attributes that can be applied to both AR and RA and the reasons for excluding certain projects from this family of methods. This leads into a short analysis of the origin and early work of AR/RA and some epistemological considerations and aspects of validity. I end the chapter with two short cases. One is a diagnostic AR using the socio-technical model, the other is a RA project which extends the previous research into new territory. These AR/RA projects easily accommodate with Rapoport's (1970) description: 'action research aims to contribute both to the practical concerns of people in an immediate problematic situation and to the goals of social science by joint collaboration within a mutually acceptable framework' (1970: 99).

DISTINGUISHING ACTION RESEARCH (AR) FROM RESEARCH ACTION (RA) ————————

Within this family of action-oriented methods there are two fairly distinct and legitimate approaches. In recent decades, the term Action Research has been used to describe projects that are based on a body of social science knowledge derived from earlier research, for instance from the socio-technical tradition and from theory and evidence in support of semi-autonomous job design and democratic decision making in organizations. This applies to a great deal of the important Scandinavian work research programmes (Qvale, 1976; Engelstad and Gustavsen, 1993). The emphasis in these AR programmes is on facilitating change based on readily available and reasonably validated evidence and theory. In these circumstances, putting the word *action* in front of *research* is fully justified. Nevertheless these projects have a research role. For instance supporters of Karl Popper (1992) would explain that the function of AR is to question the validity of previous findings and, perhaps, suggest a better explanation. There is also the opportunity to explore the relevance of the work for new contingencies and, of course, the change process itself will produce new knowledge about the phenomenon under scrutiny. Hence, the function of AR can be said to include an evaluation and extension of existing knowledge, an appreciation of the past and an assessment of potential futures (Chandler and Torbert, 2003).

However, as I will demonstrate later in the section on history, Kurt Lewin and others used the term AR to describe projects where the acquisition of new knowledge was a primary concern because little evidence or experience in this area of social science was readily available. This preoccupation with knowledge and experience did not diminish but integrate the use of action as part of the learning process (Sanford, 1976). Currently, there are large areas in social science that need to be explored and for which no knowledge and no theory is available (Drenth and Heller, 2004). Furthermore, in recent decades the complexity and speed of socio-political-economic change has increased and with it the need to put forward new hypotheses and develop new knowledge. Given that, in the current literature, the term AR is used primarily with projects that emphasize change, the term Research Action (RA) is put forward to describe projects for which change is a consequence of achieving new knowledge and developing new models of thinking.[1]

The two case examples at the end of this chapter reflects one way of distinguishing between AR and RA.

THE CORE ATTRIBUTES

While keeping the distinction between AR and RA clearly in mind, there are seven characteristics that illustrate an important degree of homogeneity in the family of action oriented methods:

- The core element of AR/RA is the close relationship between knowledge acquisition and action. Knowledge and action derives from research and diagnostic. Action, as an integral part of field methodology, differentiates AR/RA from traditional research.
- Knowledge acquisition and implementation is for the benefit of the client and participants as much, or more than, for the researcher and her/his community.
- Validation is through the learning-action process itself and, whenever possible, through co-interpretation of outcomes with the participants.
- The knowledge-action, or the action-knowledge process may be contingent on specific circumstances, but must not exclude a degree of generalizability within similar contingencies.
- The results of the AR/RA process must be available and widely shared between clients and researchers. This differentiates it from many forms of consultancy.
- There is always an ethical dimension to the AR/RA process with a degree of shared values and reflexivity between client and researcher.
- AR/RA tends to call on more than one scientific discipline and more than one knowledge acquisition method.

There will always be room for debate over demarcation and overlap at the boundaries of these categories. In particular, it is not possible to assign precise weights between the extent of learning compared with action, but AR/RA taken together exclude change agency on its own and consulting projects that are not substantially concerned with the acquisition of new knowledge or with testing the validity of existing knowledge.

For various reasons, based on the variability of client needs and environmental conditions, several of the seven categories will not always be fully implemented. For instance, it is not always appropriate or necessary to use more than one discipline. At the same time, some projects will extend the scope of a category or add new considerations. For instance, the relation between participants and researcher(s) can be usefully extended by jointly involving them in designing the project. It is important to recognize that, unlike traditional research, the design of which is the prerogative of the researcher, AR/RA has to be carefully planned with various stakeholders and take account of their legitimate interests. It is, therefore, not feasible to pre-specify all conditions. Similarly, it is inappropriate to establish a hierarchy of AR/RA methods by relegating projects with single organizations to a lower status than projects working with groups of companies or whole communities (Senge and Scharmer, 2000). At the same time, at each system level, the aim is to achieve critical mass diffusion by whatever resources are available.

INSIDE AND OUTSIDE THE FAMILY

I started the chapter by saying that the term Action Research has been used to describe an excessively diverse range of methodologies and this has made for unnecessary controversy and led to inappropriate critique. To achieve cohesion it is necessary to exclude some practices that use the term AR. While most social scientists now reject the idea that research should always discover basic principles and universal truths, there is no need to go to the extreme of restricting oneself to the discovery of local knowledge (Elden and Chisholm, 1993: 127). A different term, perhaps action-consultancy, could be used for projects that are of benefit only to a single client and have no generalizabilty whatsoever. The aim of AR/RA is to work with contingency theory that is to say the discovery of conditions or regularities that apply in defined circumstances (Kast and Rosenzweig, 1973). Perhaps as a reaction against the emphasis on discovery of new knowledge by pioneers like Kurt Lewin, projects have been called AR that are concerned almost exclusively with change (Reason, 1999). To use the term 'research' in what is really a 'change agent method', is misleading and should be avoided.[2]

Finally, there is an extension of change agency projects that have attracted a great deal of attention in recent decades. It is alleged that AR aims at nothing less than to call 'forth a world worthy of human aspirations' (see, for example, Bradbury and Reason, 2001: 449). While socio-political change projects can be very successful in empowering oppressed and underprivileged groups and in achieving a better standard of social justice (Fals Borda, 2001; Park, 2001), there is no reason why they should operate under a name occupied by a different social science tradition. These socio-political projects are often called the 'Southern form of AR' to differentiate them from the 'Northern form'. Brown (1993) describes the difference succinctly: 'the Southern tradition is committed to community transformation through empowering disenfranchised groups; the Northern tradition is concerned with reforming organizations through problem solving' (1993: 249). I see no advantage in using the term Action Research to describe these two very different approaches. Social activism is a much more appropriate term to describe the Southern form; it has its own legitimacy, but in line with our description of core attributes, must be excluded from the AR/RA family (see also Eden and Huxham, 1996). Diversification has continued with the journal *Action Research*, launched by SAGE in 2003. For instance, one article describes an approach on experiential play acting to bring out deep emotions like fear, pain and distress as a way of strengthening the capacity for action (Bradbury, 2003) The reasons for drawing a boundary around AR/RA will be become clearer when we look at how these methods came about.

A BIT OF HISTORY

Most social scientists trace the origin of Action Research to the period of the Second World War and its aftermath (Cunningham, 1993). Kurt Lewin and his colleagues at the Center for Group Dynamics at the Massachusetts Institute of Technology are usually associated with the early use of the term Action Research. The Tavistock Institute in London was equally interested in using social science to facilitate action and introduce change. In America as well as in Britain, the need was to understand new problems and then introduce the necessary change potential. In Britain there was the need to find new methods to select senior officers and rehabilitate prisoners of war. Social psychiatrists, psychologists and anthropologists were encouraged to combine their skills to deal with these issues and in this way 'a new action-oriented philosophy of relating psychiatry and the social sciences to society had become a reality in practice'. This was described as 'the social engagement of social science' (Trist and Murray, 1990: 1–34). Action was based on the discovery of new ways of engaging with groups in a variety of circumstances. This applied to group-based selection procedures that were successful during the Second World War and consequently carried over to the selection of senior civil servants (Murray, 1990: 45–67). Different experiences led to the discovery of group methods that were used to design therapeutic communities (Bridger, 1990: 68–87) and the re-settlement of prisoners of war (Curle, 1947: 42–68).

In the USA, even before Pearl Harbor precipitated America into the war, there was a need to send meat and butter to the European allies and this could be facilitated by persuading housewives to substitute beef hearts, sweetbreads and kidneys for conventional cuts of meat, and margarine for butter. There was no clear evidence for the superiority of different change methods like dialogue or lecture over more participatory methods of facilitating action. Hence, Kurt Lewin and colleagues embarked on a series of experiments to discover the most effective way of changing the behaviour of critical gatekeepers, in this case housewives, who make food purchasing decisions. The same content of argument and the same amount of time was devoted to matched groups who listened to lectures or took part in participative group discussions that ended with a request to indicate their decision by raising or not raising their hand. In a range of well-documented examples the group-decision method was about three times more effective in producing changes in purchasing behaviour (Lewin, 1947, 1953).

These early classical studies provide perfect examples of what I have called Research Action (RA). The initial purpose of the research was discovery. Action followed once reasonably adequate knowledge had become available. During the last decade many researchers have shifted their emphasis from knowledge acquisition towards the achievement of change and this legitimates the term Action Research or Participative Action Research [3] (see, for instance, Whyte, 1991). However, as I argued earlier, in social science there remain many issues that require extensive clarification, experience and knowledge before action can be safely recommended. This was clearly the position taken by Lewin and colleagues and the argument remains valid today and justifies the term Research Action.[4] Gustavsen (1998) is now keen to distance himself from the classical methodology of Lewin, in part because early Scandinavian fieldwork did not diffuse very successfully. There is no doubt that he is correct to draw attention to this problem and experiment with more intensive diffusion methods such as networking, dialogues and specially designed conferences (Emery and Purser, 1996). The aim of Gustavsen and his colleagues is to achieve a critical mass through co-ordinated large-scale projects that involve substantial numbers of co-researchers (Gustavsen, 2003). However, RA is as capable as AR to intensify diffusion under appropriate circumstances.

In reviewing the early work it is worth drawing attention to the fact that, from the beginning, action oriented research rejected the physical and pure science model and its positivistic assumptions.

> In the natural sciences, the fundamental data are reached by abstracting the phenomenon to be studied from their natural contexts and submitting them to basic research through experimental manipulation in a laboratory. It is only some time later that applied research is set under way. The social scientist . . . on the whole has to reach his fundamental data (people, institutions etc.) in their natural state and his problem is how to reach them in that state. His means of gaining access is through a professional relationship which gives him privileged conditions . . . and he can earn these privileges only by proving his competence in supplying some kind of service. (Trist, 1976: 46)

Trist sums up his position by saying that nothing could be more misleading than the view that treats the applied social sciences as comparable with the natural sciences. The same position is taken by Argyris (1993) who is very careful to differentiate between inappropriately following theoretical positivism and accepting the need for rigour in applied research.

SOME EPISTEMOLOGICAL CONSIDERATIONS

The above quotation from Trist is a useful way of starting a discussion of epistemological considerations relevant to AR/RA. In recent decades the discussions on the appropriate theory of knowledge have become emotional and polarized (Dachler, 2000). For instance, the claim has been made that 'knowledge without action is meaningless' (Elden and Chisholm, 1993: 122). This would eliminate nearly all philosophy and history as fields of knowledge. A number of ontological arguments are based on exaggeration, misunderstanding or error. For instance, the world is not divided only into phenomena that are completely subjective or completely objective. There are important examples of 'quasi objectivity', for instance, the description of hierarchy in an organization. The postmodern position on objectivity can serve as an example of the tendency to create unnecessary oppositionalism and divisiveness. It starts by claiming that 'modern' in contrast with 'postmodern' research identifies with objectivism, that is to say the view 'that things exist as meaningful entities independently of consciousness and experience, that they have truth and meaning residing in them as objects . . . and that careful (scientific) research can attain that objective truth and meaning' (Crotty, 1998: 6). I believe that today few applied social scientists would endorse such a narrow position. A more acceptable view is that from the *Oxford Companion to Philosophy*, which explains the difference between objectivism and subjectivism in simple terms: 'Fish have fins is an objective claim, its truth or falsity is independent of what anyone thinks or feels about the matter'. However 'raw fish is delicious is a subjective claim: its truth or falsity is not thus independent and indeed arguably it is neither true nor false'.[5] Several other divisive arguments relating to causality, rationality, value freedom and universality are examined by Heller (2001a). For the most part they are not what critically distinguishes traditional research from AR/RA. Two tendencies in traditional research are more questionable: one is discipline specialization, the other is cross-sectional design. The experience and resource of a single discipline is becoming increasingly inadequate for dealing with the complexity of modern problematics. It is therefore worth supporting the movement towards the integration of the social sciences (Heller, 2001a). Nearly all life experiences are meaningful only if looked at over time; research therefore should be longitudinal. Important factors in favour of AR/RA are their tendency to use more than one discipline and to be longitudinal. These are important epistemological considerations in support of validity.

The validity of results

Here I argue that in many ways AR/RA research is at least as valid as traditional research. I start from the position that most single methodologies have some strengths and some weaknesses. An important consideration therefore is to assess the balance between strength and weakness. In this chapter it is only possible to make a very limited analysis of this large topic. Recognizing the weakness of traditional methods is an essential point of departure (for instance, Speak, 1967 and Payne, 1975/76; Argyris, 1968, 1993). Payne, drawing extensively on Campbell (1976) exposes the limitations of scientific criteria of reliability, validity and the utility of correlation coefficients. Susman and Evered (1978) add a powerful historic and philosophical critique. Sommer et al. (2000) describe a research that demonstrates the weakness and implausibility of self-report questionnaire data. Payne and Pugh (1976) reviewed studies in which employees categorized structural dimensions of their organization and concluded that they were mostly inaccurate. Starbuck and Mezias (1996) used this type of evidence in a broader exposure of the weakness of research based on managerial perceptions. Even when these perceptions were allegedly objective, in most cases they were simply aggregations of subjective and inaccurate judgements. Yet most traditional research on management and organizations is based on such measures (Mezias and Starbuck, 2003). Drenth and Heller (2004) show that the limitations of traditional methods prevent the investigation of important societal issues. Ichniowski et al. (1996) list the kind of conditions that would produce high internal and external validity and then point out that, in field studies, this is hardly ever achieved. They go on to list problems with omitted variables, various selection and response biases and different measurement issues. Less frequently, we are reminded of the 'social desirability distortions' in most questionnaire-based research. The limitations of the pervasive cross-sectional design and a single discipline application to multi-dimensional problems has already been pointed out.

Given these severe limitations of traditional research, it is appropriate to point out that AR/RA tends to avoid many of these problems as indicated earlier. For instance, qualitative in-depth assessments that minimize social desirability responses (Cassell and Symon, 1994). Furthermore, AR/RA combine quantitative with ethnographic material (Heller, 1969). Undoubtedly the most important distinction and advantage of AR/RA is the validity test of action (action validity). Conventional research may produce statistically significant results, but in most cases then leaves it to others to see whether the findings work in practice.[6] Conventional research is often repeated by the same or other researchers on the assumption that similarity of findings adds reliability; this may be so, but it tells us nothing about validity in action, that is to say, in the implementation of results in real life conditions.[7] A very important improvement in validity occurs when participants become co-interpreters of the results. In conventional projects, the researcher monopolizes the interpretation of the results even when she/he has no information about the history and background of the data or any competence in the activities under investigation. This frequently leads the researcher to make vague suggestions for the possible meaning of the discovered statistical relationships. In AR/RA it is possible to make respondents into co-interpreters.[8] After all, researchers obtain data from certain categories of people because they value the quality of their judgement and consider them to have knowledge and experience in the area under study. However, when it comes to interpreting the data, traditional research is content to leave these knowledgeable respondents out of the picture. Co-interpretation produces important improvements in validity (consensual validity).

Taking all this into account, I would argue that, on balance, AR/RA results have at least as good a claim to scientific validity as traditional methods.

Finally, within the limits of a short chapter, I want to describe two interrelated action projects: first, an AR project that drew on existing socio-technical theory, secondly, a RA project that had to test new relationships for which no previous experience was available.

ACTIVELY SAFEGUARDING THE ENVIRONMENT: AN AR/RA PROJECT ——————————————

Saving the environment became a major area for public discussion towards the end of the twentieth century. The challenge now is to convert discussion and intentions into action. One way of approaching this problem is through the next generation of energy users: school children, whose attitudes and habits are not too rigid. An opportunity to work in this field occurred when Essex County Council approached the Tavistock Institute to look at a problem that they had with heating schools. Essex had been chosen by the European Union to test a new computer technology that could control the class room temperature of a large number of schools from a single central location. Internal and external sensors were installed. The central computer would start up the boilers of each school at a certain time of the morning depending on the outside temperature surrounding that particular school. The computer would then adjust the heating throughout the day based on internal sensors in each school. To maximize the use of technology, windows were bolted down and individual thermostats removed. The cost-benefit from this system was calculated to be considerable.

During the first winter, the Architecture Department of Essex, which was in charge of the system, was faced with irate headmasters who threatened to close their school unless the computer was disconnected. Some classrooms were freezing while others were quite warm. This is how the project started. Interviews with a sample of teachers, heads of schools and the department of architecture, led us to the conclusion that, on its own, the automated technology was unable to take account of important contingencies. The computer could not accommodate: weather patterns (changing prevailing winds), temperature differences for classrooms facing north or south, the body heat generated from different numbers of pupils in a given class, the number of windows in a classroom, the use of kitchen stoves in cookery classes and kilns in art rooms, and so on. From this diagnostic we concluded that this is a classic case where socio-technology solutions could be applied without further research. The automated technology had to be jointly optimized with human intervention (Trist, 1993: 580–98). Teachers and pupils had to obtain a greater measure of control. Thermostats were reinstated and windows unbolted (for variability of summer weather) to keep temperatures at the government-recommended 19 degree level. The new joint optimized, computer/school, self-help design was popular; it balanced temperature variations and reduced energy consumption and cost (Heller, 2001b).[9] The important conclusion is the recognition that only a short diagnostic, but no further research was necessary.

The situation with the next project was different. No theoretical model and no research experience was available to guide us. The Energy Directorate of the European Union supported a project to discover whether schools could be a suitable conduit to reduce the emission of carbon dioxide (CO_2) in line with government policy and international agreements. We formulated our research objectives in two stages. The first was to create *Active Energy Awareness* in pupils. *Active Energy Awareness* differs from awareness and favourable attitudes to saving energy, by being clearly associated with consistent changes in energy saving behaviour. Secondly, we had to try and demonstrate that this changed energy behaviour could be related to significant savings of CO_2. New knowledge had to be obtained and tested.

Oxford County Council collaborated in this project and facilitated our entry to ten secondary schools. In line with the funding body's requirement, we designated five schools operational and five as controls. The diagnostic phase was similar to the Essex project and involved heads of schools, teachers and discussion with groups of pupils. We explained, in non-technical terms, that unlike the Essex project, we were not now concerned with jointly optimizing technology for the comfort of school pupils. Instead, we wanted to jointly optimize technology for the comfort of the population in general through CO_2 reduction.[10] The diagnostic research led us to concentrate on lighting rather than heating and to use and amend the existing energy content in syllabuses in science, technology and geography to unify and strengthen energy awareness. The mathematics syllabus was also used to allow students to carry out calculations that converted energy saving to CO_2 emissions and to make graphs to plot progress.

The method to motivate and inform pupils was Group Feedback Analysis (GFA) which will only be described in outline (but, see Heller, 1969 and 1970). The method begins by creating dissonance between what pupils know and what they should know about energy. This links up with what is expected from their syllabuses in science, geography and technology. Later, regular feedback is used to show what each class achieves and how their energy saving can be translated into reducing CO_2 emission (this is part of the mathematics syllabus). Pupil energy monitors are appointed and asked to control lights in classes and corridors during breaks in the morning, afternoon, lunch and when lessons finish in the afternoon. With the permission of teachers, lights can also be switched off in classes where additional light is not really necessary. The monitors kept records of the number of quarter hours they saved. Regular feedback of results created considerable motivation. Everybody was astonished at the amount of electricity and CO_2 that could easily be saved. Head teachers and governors were particularly interested to see the calculations of cost saving, but teachers and pupils were much more motivated by translating kilowatt hours of electricity into CO_2 emission (Heller et al., 1997; Heller, 2001b).[11] Comparative graphs were produced for each term and for each school, further increasing motivation.

A considerable amount of knowledge and experience had accumulated in the two years of the RA project. The research experience was summarized in a multi-coloured booklet for distribution to the European Union and Oxfordshire County Council. The difference in energy saving behaviour between the control and operational schools was substantial. Teachers and pupils in the operational schools had progressed from a general interest in energy to active energy saving behaviour that was carefully documented in tables and graphs. Clear benefits in terms of cost saving and reduction in CO_2 emissions were achieved, although more in some schools than in others. Significant aspects of the RA project had been co-designed with teachers and influenced by boards of governors. Pupils as well as teachers helped to interpret the results. There is evidence that four of the Oxford schools have continued to use the procedure developed in the RA project, and Essex as well as Oxford schools have continued their socio-technical collaboration to stabilize classroom temperatures. There is no evidence that other counties in England have yet adopted these methods.

These two projects illustrate the difference between AR and RA. In the Essex project action could be based on previous research which had led to the formulation of the socio-technical model. Only a simple diagnostic was needed. No new knowledge had to be acquired. Hence this is an example of AR. The Oxford project however, had to establish a joint optimization relationship between an organization and its environment. It was necessary to demonstrate that *Active Energy Awareness* could be created and translated into behavioural changes that affected the external environment. Three methods were used and combined. Syllabuses in different subjects were integrated to highlight the use of energy. This integration was more effective in predisposing pupils to action than the previous independent teaching. Feedback of results to groups based on various stages of the project was an effective motivator. Energy monitors were effective in saving CO_2 emission from schools through regular demonstration of the relationship between switching off lights and reducing CO_2. The fieldwork research took two years. This is an example of Research Action.[12]

CONCLUSIONS

The term Action Research has become ambiguous. Researchers and social activists with a variety of ideological agendas and learning and change objectives have used the term to describe an excessive variety of activities. This chapter aims at reducing the heterogeneity of approaches and thus allows this methodology to be more widely used in social science research.

There are two usefully distinct approaches that combine learning with action. One method concentrates on action and change and is called Action Research (AR); it does not ignore learning but is most appropriate when reliable research evidence is already available but may need to be refined and/or extended. Research Action by contrast emphasizes acquisition of knowledge and applies where social science issues are problematic and need to be explored before change can be useful. In both cases it is accepted that the change process itself adds to the acquisition of knowledge; this is a major distinction and advantage of AR/RA. The Kurt Lewin research on changing the purchasing behaviour of women was given as an example of what I call RA. The Lewin research provided evidence that one change method was more effective than others. It then makes good sense to refine and test the new method through AR in different situations and groups.

The family of AR/RA methods share at least seven core characteristics which have to be applied flexibly. At the same time the core characteristics determine which methods cannot be accommodated within the family. The exclusion applies particularly to projects concentrating entirely or largely on change and social activism which many publications are content to group under A/R (for instance, Reason and Bradbury, 2001).

Having drawn a boundary for the family of methods, it is possible to enter the epistemological argument about scientific validity. Given the extensive and well-documented limitations of traditional methods, it is possible to concentrate on the complementary advantages of AR/RA and redefine certain validity criteria. Two in particular, *action validity* and *consensual validity*, are singled out as significant criteria that are not used in traditional research. I conclude that, for those research tasks to which AR/RA can be applied,[13] its validity is at least equal to that of conventional methodologies. Moreover, the kind of learning possible through AR/RA is on a deeper level than traditional social science research and leads to a firmer base for making sense of phenomena and facilitating change.

NOTES

I am grateful to George Strauss and Catherine Cassell for very helpful comments which in no way avoids my responsibility for any remaining problems.

1 The absence of such a distinction has made it easier for traditionalists to attack Action Research and deny it a useful role in social science. There will, neverthless, be examples where AR and RA overlap. Argyris came to a similar conclusion and has found it necessary to differentiate his Action Science from Action Research (Argyris et al., 1985) similar to my description of Research Action.

2 Change agents may claim that they and their clients learn from the experience; that is obviously so, but it is not the same as research. Stretching the meaning of terms creates unnecessary ambiguity.

3 The term 'participative' draws attention to the difference with traditional research that treats the people who provide information as subjects rather than as collaborators or joint interpreters of data. I have included the participative approach in the description of the core attributes. Hence, Research Action could also be called Participative Research Action. It must be admitted, however, that the early classical AR projects did not use participants in the way we now believe is appropriate.

4 The use of the term Research Action does not preclude the idea that knowledge can be acquired during an ongoing change process, that is to say, during action.

5 Of course I recognize that some philosophers will say that the judgement that fish have fins is based entirely on our visual and/or tactile perception and is therefore subjective in that sense. I think such arguments are appropriate for philosophy, but add nothing useful to applied social science.

6 There are exceptions. Selection tests, for instance, are used and validated in many practical situations and often suitably amended if the results are equivocal.

7 Conventional research is rarely tested in action, but see Wilkins, 1986; Latham, 2001; Drenth, 2001; Dunnette, 2001.

8 An early example of the systematic use of co-interpretation is Group Feedback Analysis (Heller, 1969). A version of this method was used in the case example at the end of this chapter.

9 Technology is now available, particularly for new buildings to adjust temperatures in each room with individual thermostats. It is unlikely that this costly degree of automation will be introduced in British schools for many years.

10 The classic socio-technical model has been tested only in relation to intra-organizational joint optimization. The extension of the model to cover the impact of technology on people in the external environment has only begun (Heller, 2001b).

11 In consultation with maths teachers we used a simple formula that students aged 10 years and more could use.

12 Both projects are different from traditional research which would investigate the relationship between dependent and independent variables, for instance, the effect of energy syllabus integration with changes to attitudes to energy awareness.

13   There are many research tasks to which AR/RA cannot be applied, for instance, where very large numbers have to be handled as in cross-national surveys, etc.

FURTHER READING

Colin Eden and Chris Huxham (1996) 'Action research for the study of organizations', in Steward Clegg, Cynthia Hardy and Walter Nord (eds), *Handbook of Organizational Studies*, London: Sage. pp. 526–40.

REFERENCES

Argyris, Chris (1968) 'Some unintended consequences of rigorous research', *Psychological Bulletin*, 70: 185–97.

Argyris, Chris (1993) 'On the nature of actionable knowledge', *The Psychologist*, 6 (1): 29–32.

Argyris, C., Putnam, R. and Smith, D. (1985) *Action Science: Concepts, Methods and Skills for Research and Intervention*, San Francisco, CA: Jossey Bass.

Bradbury, Hilary (2003) 'Sustaining the heart of action research(ers): an interview with Joanna Macy', *Action Research*, 1 (2): 208–223

Bradbury, Hilary and Reason, Peter (2001) 'Conclusion: broadcasting the bandwidth of validity: issues and choice-points for improving the quality of action research', in Peter Reason and Hilary Bradbury (eds), *Handbook of Action Research: Participative Enquiry and Practice*, London: Sage.

Bridger, Harold (1990) 'The discovery of the therapeutic community: the Northfield Experiments', in Eric Trist and Hugh Murray (eds), *The Social Engagement of Social Science*, London: Free Association Books. pp. 68–87.

Brown, David (1993) 'Social change through collective reflection with Asian non-governmental development organizations', *Human Relations*, 46 (2): 249–73.

Campbell, J.P. (1976) 'Psychometric theory', in Marvin Dunnette (ed.), *Handbook of Industrial and Organizational Psychology*, Chicago: Rand McNally, pp. 185–222.

Cassell, Catherine and Symon, Gillian (1994) *Qualitative Methods in Organizational Research: A Practical Guide*, London: Sage.

Chandler, Dawn and Torbert, Bill (2003) 'Transforming inquiry and action: Interweaving 27 flavours of action research', *Action Research*, 1 (2): 133–152

Crotty, Michael (1998) *The Foundations of Social Research*, London: Sage.

Cunningham, J. Barton (1993) *Action Research and Organizational Development*, Westport, CT and London: Praeger.

Curle, Adam (1947) 'Transitional communities and social re-connection: a follow-up study of the civil resettlement of British prisoners of war', part 1, *Human Relations*, 1947 (1): 42–68.

Dachler, Peter (2000) 'Taking qualitative methods a radical step forward', *European Journal of Work and Organizational Psychology*, 9 (4): 573–83.

Drenth, Peter (2001) 'Verity or applicability?' *Applied Psychology*, 50 (2): 212–21.

Drenth, Peter and Heller, Frank (2005) 'The dangers of resource myopia in Work and Organizational Psychology: a plea for broadening and integration', *Applied Psychology: An International Review* (accepted).

Dunnette, Marvin (2001) 'Science and practice in applied psychology: a symbiotic relationship', *Applied Psychology*, 50 (2): 222–34.

Easterby-Smith, Mark and Malina, Danusia (1999) 'Cross-cultural collaborative research towards reflexivity', *Academy of Management Journal*, 42 (1): 76–86.

Eden, Colin and Huxham, Chris (1996) 'Action research for the study of organizations', in Stewart Clegg, Cynthia Hardy and Walter Nord (eds), *Handbook of Organization Studies*, London: Sage. pp. 526–42.

Elden, Max and Chisholm, Rupert (eds) (1993) 'Emerging varieties of action research', *Human Relations* (Special Issue), 46 (2).

Emery, Merrelyn and Purser, Ronald (1996) *The Search Conference: A Powerful Method for Planning Organizational Change and Community Action*, San Francisco: Jossey Bass.

Engelstad, Per H. and Gustavsen, Bjorn (1993) 'Swedish network development for implementing national work reform strategy', *Human Relations*, 46: 219–48.

Fals Borda, Orlando (2001) 'Participation (action) research in social theory: origins and challenges', in Peter Reason and Hilary Bradbury (eds), *Handbook of Action Research*, London: Sage. pp. 27–37.

Gustavsen, Bjorn (1998) 'From experiments to network building: trends in the use of research for reconstructing working life', *Human Relations*, 51 (3): 431–48.

Gustavsen, Bjorn (2003) 'New forms of knowledge production and the role of action research', *Action Research*, 1 (2): 153–164.

Heller, F.A. (1969) 'Group feedback analysis: a method of field research', *Psychological Bulletin*, 72: 108–17. Reprinted in: D. Graves (ed.), *Management Research: A Cross Cultural Perspective*, London: Elsevier Scientific Publishing Co.(1973) 49–69. German translation *Gruppendynamik*, 1972 (2): 174–91.

Heller (1970) 'Group feedback analysis as a change agent', *Human Relations*, 23: 319–33.

Heller, Frank (1997) 'Is action research real research? Yes and no' A contribution to The Tavistock Institute's 50th Anniversary Seminar, 11–12 July. TTI Document No. 2T-720.

Heller, Frank (2001a) 'On the integration of the social sciences', *Human Relations*, 54 (1): January (Millennium Special Issue).

Heller, Frank (2001b) 'Towards a Socio-oecotechnology', *Journal of Engineering and Technology Management*. Special Issue: *Beyond Sociotechnical systems*, 18: 295–313.

Heller, Frank, Hammond, Kim and Hattingh, Pamela (1997) 'Creating active energy awareness in secondary schools'. Report to Energy Directorate, European Union, Tavistock Institute Paper.

Ichniowski, C., Kochan, T., Levine, D., Olson, C. and Strauss, G. (1996) 'What works at work: overview and assessment', *Industrial Relations*, 35 (3): 299–333.

Kast, F.E. and Rosenzweig, J.E. (1973) *Contingency Views of Organization and Management*, Chicago: Science Research Associates.

Latham, Gary (2001) 'The reciprocal transfer of learning from journals to practice', *Applied Psychology*, 50 (2): 201–11.

Lewin, Kurt (1947) 'Group decision and social change', in Theodore Newcomb and Eugene Hartley (eds), *Readings in Social Psychology*, New York: Henry Holt and Co.

Lewin, Kurt (1953) 'Studies in group decisions', in Dorwin Cartwright and Alvin Zander (eds), *Group Dynamics: Research and Theory*, London: Tavistock Publications. pp. 287–301.

Lewin, Kurt, Lippitt, Ronald and White, Ralph (1939) 'Patterns of aggressive behavior in experimentally created "social climates",' *Journal of Social Psychology*, (x): 271–99.

Mezias, John M. and Starbuck, William H. (2003) 'Managers and their inaccurate perceptions: good, bad or inconsequential?' *British Journal of Management*, 14 (1): 3–17.

Murray, Hugh (1990) 'The transformation of selection procedures: the War Office selection board', in Eric Trist and Hugh Murray (eds), *The Social Engagement of Social Science*, London: Free Association Books. pp. 45–67.

Park, Peter (2001) 'Knowledge and participatory research', in Peter Reason and Hilary Bradbury (eds), *Handbook of Action Research*, London: Sage. pp. 81–90.

Payne, Roy (1975/76) 'Truisms in organizational behaviour', *Interpersonal Development*, (6): 203–20.

Payne, Roy and Pugh, Derek (1976) 'Organizational structure and climate', in M.D. Dunnette (ed.), *Handbook of Industrial and Organizational Psychology*, Chicago: Rand McNally. pp 1125–73.

Popper, Karl (1992) *Unended Quest*, London: Routledge.

Qvale, Thoralf U. (1976) 'A Norwegian strategy for democratization of industry', *Human Relations*, 29 (5): 453–69.

Rapoport, Robert (1970) 'Three dilemmas of Action Research', *Human Relations*, 23: 499–513.

Reason, Peter (1999) 'Integrating action and reflection through cooperative enquiry', *Managerial Learning*, Col. 30 (2): 207–26.

Reason, Peter and Bradbury, Hilary (eds) (2001) *Handbook of Action Research: Participative Inquiry and Practice*, London: Sage.

Sanford, Nevitt (1976) 'Whatever happened to action research?', in Alf Clark (ed.), *Experimenting with Organizational Life*, New York: Plenum Press.

Senge, Peter and Scharmer, Otto (2000) 'Community action research: learning as a community of practitioners, consultants and researchers', in Peter Reason and Hillary Bradbury (eds), *Handbook of Action Research*, London: Sage.

Sommer, Stephen, Welsh, Dianna and Gubman, Boris (2000) 'The ethical orientation of Russian entrepreneurs', *Applied Psychology, Special Issue*, 49 (4): 688–708.

Speak, Mary (1967) 'Communication failure in questioning: errors, misinterpretations and personal frame of reference', (Chairman's address to Occupational Psychology Section of British Psychological Society, January 1965), *Occupational Psychology*, 41: 169–79.

Starbuck, William and Mezias, John (1996) 'Opening Pandora's box: studying the accuracy of managers' perceptions', *Journal of Organizational Behavior*, 17 (2): 99–117.

Susman, Gerald and Evered, Roger (1978) 'An assessment of the scientific merits of action research', *Administrative Science Quarterly*, 23 (4): 582–603.

Trist, E. (1976) 'Engaging with large-scale systems', in Alf Clark (ed.), *Experimenting with Organizational Life: The Action Research Approach*, New York: Plenum Press. pp. 43–57.

Trist, E. (1993) 'A socio-technical critique of scientific management', in Eric Trist and Hugh Murray (eds), *The Social Engagement of Social Science: A Tavistock Anthology, The Socio-Technical Perspective* vol. II, Philadelphia, University of Pennsylvania Press. pp. 580–98.

Trist, E. and Murray, H. (eds) (1990) *The Social Engagement of Social Science, The Socio-Technical Perspective*, vol. I. London: Free Association Books.

Whyte, William F. (ed.) (1991) *Participatory Action Research*, London: Sage.

Wilkins, Leslie (1986) 'Three projects involving prediction', in Frank Heller (ed.), *The Use and Abuse of Social Science*, London and Beverly Hills: Sage Publications.

29 ——Co-research: Insider/Outsider Teams for Organizational Research ——————

John Benington and Jean Hartley

There are both opportunities and difficulties in conducting collaborative research (Bartunek and Louis, 1996). Academic researchers and practitioners collaborate with different emphases. Academics often aim to produce general or nomothetic theories, whereas practitioners may be seeking theories which are context specific (ipsative theories). Practitioners may want to place more emphasis on understanding the immediate and direct consequences of actions, while academic researchers may emphasize more indirect and longer-term causal links.

Such differences in perspective can be productive of high quality collaborative research when recognized and addressed. Diversity in a research team can contribute to both efficiency and effectiveness where trust exists between the parties and there is a willingness to explore and use difference (Northcraft and Neale, 1993). Innovations by teams can flourish in conditions of heterogeneity and constructive conflict (West, 1994). Sensemaking can be more robust where challenged by competing interpretations of phenomena (Weick, 1995). Bartunek and Louis (1996: 9–10) also take this view: 'the deliberate and extensive harnessing of multiple, diverse perspectives to the task of inquiring and making sense of complex social phenomena can substantially enhance contributions to knowledge and practice'.

Some researchers aim to address difficulties in academic and practitioner perspectives by developing knowledge based on a close and collaborative research relationship with those in the research setting. There are a number of approaches. For example, action research has a long and productive history in both the USA and UK (for example, Elden and Chisholm, 1993; Lewin, 1951; Heller, Chapter 28 this volume). Participative enquiry (for example, Reason, 1994; Smith and O'Flynn, 2000) emphasizes that the people who are the focus of research should collaborate as equal partners in the research process. Interpretive approaches have been developed which take account of the perspectives of those inside and outside the organization (for example, Bryman, 1989; Evered and Louis, 1981). A distinction has been made between Mode 1 and Mode 2 knowledge production (Gibbons et al., 1994). Mode 1 is traditional, expert research, often generated within a disciplinary context. By contrast, Mode 2 knowledge production takes place in broader, trans-disciplinary contexts and includes a range of stakeholders to guide problem-solving research. Gibbons et al. (1994) argue that quality control in Mode 2 knowledge production includes not only professional peer-based review, but also wider criteria related to the social usefulness and applicability of outcomes.

The co-research approach described here falls within the Mode 2 range of research in that it recognizes and builds on the perspectives of both academics and practitioners in the production of research about organizations. Through collaborative networks within and across organizations, knowledge can be not only transferred but also jointly created between academics and practitioners, using dialectical processes of enquiry based on different interests and perspectives (Benington and Hartley, 2003). Nonaka (1994) has suggested a 'spiral' of knowledge creation based on social interaction loops within teams and organizations.

There are a number of arguments for a co-production approach, such as co-research, in developing organizational theory. First, organizations are complex phenomena that require some 'insider' knowledge if they are to be navigated in ways to produce theory and knowledge with high reliability and validity (Easterby-Smith and Malina, 1999). The size and complexity of many organizations means that a research study often requires help from individuals within the organization who can identify and locate appropriate informants for the study and who can work with the researchers to translate the organizational phenomena into the conceptual categories of the study (Buchanan et al., 1988).

Second, academics are increasingly recognizing and analysing organizational complexity. The instability, flux and change of organizations means that 'mono-method monopolies' (Martin, 1989) have to be replaced by multi-methods, including qualitative methods (see also Langley, 1999). Thus, there is a growing interest in collaborative research which reflects this type of epistemology.

CO-RESEARCH METHODOLOGY

Co-research is a methodology based on inter-organizational collaboration between academics and practitioners. It aims to establish a dialectical process of enquiry by drawing on the complementary, and sometimes conflicting perspectives, interests, skills and knowledge bases of both academics and practitioners. The research is designed and developed under the overall direction of the academic team leader and deliberately uses insiders and outsiders, theorists and practitioners, within the research team.

It is particularly relevant where the research requires a case study design, which emphasizes the study of organizational processes in context (Hartley, Chapter 26, this volume; Yin, 1994). Co-research employs a range of methods familiar to the social sciences, such as interviews, observation, questionnaires and analysis of documents.

CO-RESEARCH ROLES IN THE RESEARCH TEAM

There are three different research roles within a co-research team: the academic, the host officer and the co-interviewer (see Figure 29.1). First, there is the academic, who takes overall responsibility for the research and leads the research team. There may also be other academics in the team. The academics contribute an initial conceptual framework and help to shape, develop and modify this with the whole co-research team. The academics also provide expertise in research design and methods. Inevitably, the academics are 'outsiders' to the organization which is being studied. The research leader manages the overall project, including the preparations for the study, the analysis and the writing up (though unlike some other collaborative methodologies, the co-researchers are also expected to engage in all these activities).

Second, there is the 'host officer' who is employed by the organization being researched. This person is in a relatively senior and generally corporate position. He or she arranges the interviews (according to the research design) and also amasses the relevant organizational

Figure 29.1 Co-research methodology: research roles

documentation and contextual data required by the team, both prior to and after the field work phase. This person brings an 'insider' perspective on the organization for example, its history, context, processes and culture. They do not see the notes of the interviews undertaken in their own organization, so that they do not influence the direct observations and data. Therefore, the research can be seen as independent, and also their own role in the organization is not compromised by being responsible for research findings. The host officer may also comment on the interpretations of organizational and inter-organizational processes analysed by researchers in the other two roles. They are not involved in writing up the research and their name appears as an acknowledgement, not as an author, in the published report from the research.

Third, there is the 'co-interviewer' who is from a different organization from the one being studied but in the same service sector. This person is similarly in a fairly senior and generally corporate job in their own organization. The co-interviewer is a researcher in the research team, working alongside the academic(s) in the case study organization. Between one and six co-interviewers have been involved in our case studies. The co-interviewer is trained by the academics in case study research and interview techniques before undertaking the research. He/she is an 'insider' in that they are familiar with the type of organization (in our research this is the public service sector) but an 'outsider' to the extent that their own organization may have a different environment, structure, resources, set of challenges, culture and so on. The initial interviews are carried out jointly with the academic but over the course of the case study, some interviews may be carried out separately by the co-interviewer, using the interview schedule.

Where a research study involves more than one case study, the co-interviewer may also be a host officer of a case. Thus, a co-researcher may have two different roles in the course of a multi-case research programme.

SOME EXAMPLES OF CO-RESEARCH IN ACTION

We developed the co-research methodology initially in a study of the changing role of the corporate core in UK local authorities (Hartley et al., 1994) namely a study of how and why the political leadership, strategic management, policy unit and central services contribute to the corporate direction of the organization, and the tensions that arose between the corporate core and the service delivery departments of the organization (compare Goold and Campbell, 1987 for the private sector). In that study, after several meetings (across months) of co-research team planning, we examined three local authorities in England, in a team of two academics and three practitioners, spending several days in each organization and conducting interviews throughout the organization. We started with a case study of Nottinghamshire County Council, where the host officer was a manager in the chief executive's department. The interviews were carried out by one of the academics, working with the head of quality for North Tyneside Council as co-interviewer. The research team then studied the corporate core in Kirklees Council, where the Nottinghamshire manager became the co-interviewer, with the host officer being the head of organization development for Kirklees. Finally, the Kirklees manager joined the team to research North Tyneside Council (where the host officer was the manager who had been a co-interviewer in the first case study). The three organizations were very different in size (one of Nottinghamshire's service departments was larger than the whole of North Tyneside for example); in structure (North Tyneside had no chief executive, while Kirklees was an innovator in having strategic directors with no line management responsibility for services, and Nottinghamshire had a more traditional, for that time, chief officer structure); and in culture (Nottinghamshire was quite formal and relatively stable; North Tyneside was recovering from major job losses, and Kirklees was encouraging an experimenting and open culture). The differences across the case studies were very fertile in elucidating the role of the various elements of the corporate core. The practitioner researchers became fascinated by the differences they found in the organization they researched compared with the organization they worked in. As the team worked together, there were discussions not only of the data, but also of personal reactions and questions, based on the surprises they had encountered, as different from their own organization. There was considerable questioning across the whole research team as to how each organization 'worked'. Each case study was written up by the interviewers and an overview comparative report was also written. The overview report was able to address some contemporary organizational and policy debates about the role of the corporate core in organizational and cultural change. In particular, it examined how these public organizations dealt with the contradictory organizational tensions of fragmentation and integration, centralization and decentralization, stability and flexibility, and managing structural and cultural changes. It was able to reflect debates on these issues in private sector organizations but show how the pressures were somewhat different in the context of providing local democracy and public services.

A second use of the co-research method was in the study of the role of leadership and the management of influence in four contrasting local authority organizations (Devon, Hertfordshire, Knowsley and Warwick), which had each been engaged in a major change initiative (Hartley and Allison, 2000). The research team consisted of four academics and eight practitioners (seven managers and one councillor). On this occasion, the host officers participated in research in one or more of the other case studies, but other co-interviewers came from organizations not engaged in the research (though part of the wider network of organizations working with the academics in a Consortium – see later section). Practitioners participated to the extent that they had interest and time – from one case study only to being involved in three of the four. Two of the academics participated in all four case studies in this research, providing continuity and consistency across the cases. The research team wrote up four published reports (one on each case) and the whole team produced an overview report. In each report, the authors were the interviewers (whether academic or practitioner) in alphabetical order. The reports and academic publications were able to address quite subtle conceptual notions of political, managerial and distributed leadership and trace the impact of each of these types of leadership (and their interaction) on organizational processes of innovation and change.

Co-research is not appropriate for all research questions or contexts. From our experience, it seems to be most effective in research questions about the whole organization, and in the analysis of organizational and inter-organizational processes in a case study approach.

DETAILED DESCRIPTION OF CO-RESEARCH METHOD

Preparations for co-research and selecting co-researchers

The context for the co-research which we have carried out is the Warwick University Local Authorities Research Consortium, a long term partnership between academics and a network of 30 UK local authorities (see Benington and Hartley, 2003). The consortium has been in existence for over a decade and produces a collaborative research agenda and set of activities (annual conference, quarterly working groups, traditional research and co-research). Over time, we have developed a shared understanding of research (although different perspectives about it). A climate of trust and learning has been cultivated in the network. This provides important preconditions for the co-research methodology. It may be possible to engage in co-research without these particular working relationships. However, our experience of using co-research suggests that it is certainly helpful to have had some experience of working together prior to the co-research, in order to have the confidence to explore differences in perspective within the team.

Preparation for co-research includes the joint development of the research project through a working group of practitioners and academics, meeting on a number of occasions prior to the fieldwork. In the corporate core research, the team met on six occasions prior to fieldwork. This preparatory work enables the research framework and focus to be explored, scoped, widely discussed, and modified, so that by the time the empirical work is undertaken, at least two enabling conditions for co-research have been achieved. First, there is a shared understanding of the focus of the research and its conceptual underpinnings. Second, the academics and the practitioners have worked together in framing and developing the research so each knows each other well enough to work together productively.

In inviting co-researchers to take part in the research, the academics look for practitioners who have a strategic overview of their own organization (which will be useful both for hosting into the research and also for researching another organization) and who have the intellectual interest to take part in the research. Collaborative research often recruits those who are curious about their environment (King, 2000) and who have fair levels of confidence (Smith and O'Flynn, 2000).

The research focus on whole organization themes means that we select co-reseachers who have corporate and often senior positions in their own organizations. Most have first degrees and many have postgraduate degrees. For their part, co-researchers and host managers become involved in co-research not only for intellectual curiosity but also because it provides useful insights and sources of comparison with another organization. Some see co-research as a personal management development opportunity, as well as a development opportunity for their organization. They have already become familiar with academic research through the consortium.

King (2000) has questioned the validity of the co-research approach because of the choice of co-researchers in senior positions. He suggests that it would be more useful to include co-researchers from all levels of the organization. We argue our 'elite' approach is justified for the research questions we are trying to address. There are a number of reasons for using those in senior or strategic roles (incidentally, not just managers but also councillors and policy staff). In part, this is because our co-research extends throughout the whole research enterprise, as opposed to participatory or emancipatory research (Smith and O'Flynn, 2000; Oliver, 1997), where participant researchers are traditionally engaged for part of the research process (often data collection) and not the whole process. Involvement in conceptualizing the research and in writing it up requires a high level of skill and confidence. Even highly educated co-researchers can feel daunted – by the writing-up in particular. For example, 'Claire' worked as a host officer and a co-interviewer for the leadership research, and although she was a third tier manager in an education department, she admitted to feeling unsure of herself when it came to academic writing. Second, the focus on organizational strategy and cultural change means that it is helpful to have an overview and understanding of strategic and corporate issues, not just a particular departmental view (we do, of course, include stakeholders from all levels in the organization as informants). Finally, it helps that the co-researchers have different skills but are broadly equivalent in status to the academics, creating a team which can engage in dialectical enquiry, rather than the practitioner feeling overpowered by the language and practices of the academics.

The co-research team not only prepares the research focus and questions but also trains for the fieldwork. A day is spent by the academics with the co-researchers and host officers as a group, in interviewing purposes and skills, including interview analysis. Co-researchers are generally already experienced interviewers in their own professions (for example, personnel officer, head of policy) but interviewing for an academic research project requires working within a research framework. The academics also help the research team prepare by producing a case study pack, containing background data on the case study organization. (Some information is provided by the host officer and includes documentary material on the location, size, strategic priorities, workforce, organization structure, and so on). The pack also contains the interview schedule, background reading on carrying out and analysing research interviews, the draft report headings, advice on writing and editing, and the timetable for completing the research. In the preparation period, we also reiterate the importance of research confidentiality. We explore and gain agreement to the principle that discussions in the team are based on the 'Chatham House Rule'. This is a widely recognized code of conduct in UK government and policy circles for confidentiality in attributing sensitive information. Other safeguards of confidentiality used in case study research are used.

Fieldwork and 'sense-making'

Interviews are arranged so that co-researchers who are new to the team will work with an academic for the first few interviews in order to ensure comparability and consistency. Interviews are done in pairs where feasible but each member of the research team may need to work alone where the availability of informants demands this.

The research team meets up at the end of the first day to share information and compare observations and impressions of the organization so far. Sharing in this way (and in later analysis meetings) is an important part of the work. As well as sharing information gained through fieldwork, the researchers are engaged in 'surprise and sense-making' (Louis, 1980). In particular, a key feature of the co-research approach is tapping the surprise factor involved in comparison between different organizations, which can be highly informative. For example, 'Iain', from Gloucestershire County Council, was a co-interviewer in Hertfordshire County Council in the leadership study. He was surprised at the degree of informality found in the change team at Hertfordshire. We used this initial perception to tease out in discussion how 'Iain' had noticed other differences in the way that the major change was being conceptualized and implemented in the two organizations. This helped to elucidate the organizational processes in the Hertfordshire case. His reflections, and the team's curiosity, were a useful springboard to exploring and expanding questions on themes and issues in the data collected. The co-research method produces many such reflections, contrasts and insights. The academics take written notes of key points and bring these forward to the analysis stage.

The case study research typically lasts two to three days. Between 20 and 30 interviews (individual or group) may be carried out with internal and external stakeholders. In addition, the research team may attend meetings as observers (for example, a council meeting), or may engage in workshops or other discussions while on site. Interviews are tape-recorded.

Each researcher writes up their interviews, and these are circulated in strict confidence among the interviewers. Each researcher also attends a full day of case study analysis at the university, which involves discussion of interviews, observations and documentary data. Only the research team for each case study attends its own analysis day. However, this includes the host officer for that case study, who acts as the 'local guide', adding history, political background or other contextual data which helps the research team. However, the host officer does not take part in the analysis of interview notes or in the writing up of the report. On the analysis day, key themes for the research report are examined, tested and discussed, with the emphasis on disconfirming as well as confirming data. The triad work together to research and piece together the information gained in the case study, using their different sources of data and their different perspectives. The analysis day helps to model how to interpret data, look for patterns, seek disconfirming data, and relate data to the conceptual framework. Further analysis is undertaken later by researchers in their own time, as they work on their allocated sections of the report.

Notes from the analysis day are written up by the academic researchers and distributed to the research team (excluding the host officer). Co-researchers are expected to write as well as to interview, and sections of the report are allocated across the team, with the academic leading and guiding as appropriate. A draft is circulated to the full research team (including the host officer) and amendments or additions suggested by the team. Changes are made by the person responsible for the editing of the report (in the corporate core research this was the practitioners, while in the leadership research it was both practitioners and academics). The academic leader takes overall responsibility for the final structure and content of the report, agreeing it with the team. The research report becomes a working paper of the university, publicly available. The academic will also write an academic version of the report for publication in refereed academic journals (sometimes with the co-researchers depending on their interest in academic publication).

There are two further processes which help the quality of the case analysis. First, all the researchers working on the case studies in a research project meet at the end of their case analysis report-writing to compare the findings across the cases and to contribute to the summary report which analyses the data across the set of cases. Second, while the research is in progress, the emerging themes are explored by the consortium working group from which the co-research team has been drawn. This enables the research to engage in a further dialectical process between insiders and outsiders beyond the immediate research team. The working group may raise questions or request clarifications, thereby helping the co-research team refine its analysis and report.

Outcomes from co-research

There are three main outcomes from co-research. First, there is the production of reports and academic papers which, we suggest, are strengthened through this co-production methodology, because the richness and complexity of organizational processes can be shown. Second, the commitment to the research partnership means that the knowledge and understanding has a practical benefit to participating organizations. The research team offers workshops and seminars to the case organizations, in order to explore and elaborate issues arising from the research. This is not always taken up, but the opportunity is appreciated by the organization. An advantage of co-research is that it can build practitioner commitment to the research and thereby contribute to knowledge not only being generated but also being applied.

Third, practitioners value co-research as providing personal and organizational development benefits. It is an opportunity to research and learn in conjunction with academics. It also contributes to a 'magpie effect'. The co-interviewer may notice examples of good practice in the case study organization and may take ideas back to their own organization. Working links between the different organizations may also be established. For example, in the research on leadership, a mentoring relationship was established. Co-researchers report that they value these opportunities to learn from another organization as well as from the research.

STRENGTHS AND LIMITATIONS OF THE CO-RESEARCH METHODOLOGY ————————

Co-research can be highly productive and, under certain circumstances, has a number of advantages over traditional, 'academic as expert' research. First, interviewees are aware that both academics and practitioners are undertaking the research and some are reassured that their own culture and terms of reference are understood. In some cases, we have gained fuller, more textured responses. For example, in the research on the corporate core, an interview with a director of education about corporate financing of projects was aided by a co-interviewer who understood the nuances of local government finance. Technical language and jargon can be understood without interrupting the flow of the interview. We have also found it useful for interviewing elite actors, such as senior councillors or chief executives, where an insider's knowledge is appreciated by the interviewee. On the other hand, care has to be taken in matching co-researcher to interviewee. Although the research team is introduced as primarily working for the university, acknowledgement is given to their other, 'home organization', role. For example, in the case study of Knowsley, 'Martin' was a senior councillor working as a co-interviewer and it was considered inappropriate that he interview middle managers and junior staff, who might be overawed by such status. Instead, he interviewed senior staff and councillors, where a political analysis was particularly beneficial.

Second, practitioner knowledge aids the interpretation of data, especially where the financial, legal or organizational context is important or where informal processes underpin the issue under study (compare Brown and Duguid, 1991 on non-canonical processes in organizations). In case study research, contextual influences on organizational processes cannot always be fully specified in advance. Practitioners working alongside academics means that contextual influences can be identified during the fieldwork.

Third, the 'surprise and sense-making' (Louis, 1980) which occurs as newcomers enter unfamiliar organizational settings can be harnessed for clues, information and meanings not only about the organization currently being researched, but also about the organization that the co-interviewer comes from (where it is also a case study site in the research). As the academics and the co-interviewers work together to analyse and reflect on the data they have gathered, some of the similarities and differences between two organizations that the host officer and the co-interviewer come from can be shared, sorted and used to build the case study.

Fourth, the surprise and sense-making, which continues from fieldwork into the analysis and writing up, is also helpful in teasing out the degree to which the findings are generalizable to other processes and settings and in identifying particular contextual or organizational contingencies. The co-researchers use their organizational experience to raise questions about analytical generalizability (Yin, 1994), though they might not use this term.

Like all methodologies, co-research is relevant to some research questions and contexts but not others. In particular, it is a methodology suited to addressing process rather than variance theories of organizations (Langley, 1999; Weick, 1999), because practitioners' insights come from their experiences in working within organizations rather than from their experience of variance-based (largely quantitative) methodologies.

This can be effective in research which requires case studies, because they are most suited to the examination of processes in organizational context (Hartley, Chapter 26, this volume; Yin, 1994). Other types of data collection (such as questionnaire analysis) are more suitable for academics trained in detail in these techniques. Co-researchers, in any case, are less concerned with learning about 'pure' academic methodologies than in using their participation in research to extend their conceptual and practical understanding of organizations.

Co-research also requires commitment from the academics to managing a research team which is not entirely under their control and where they need to exercise research leadership through influence not hierarchy. The other members of the research team are senior organizational members in their own right, with sources of expertise and experience which are different from those of the academics. Co-research seems to work best where there is a close, productive and constructive dialogue between the academics and the practitioners, built on a foundation of common interest in wanting to find out more about the subject under study. In co-research, academics cannot be the experts directing research 'assistants'. The academics have a solid basis of expertise in academic theories and frameworks, and in research design and methods, but this has to be harnessed to the curiosity, practical wisdom and managerial and organizational experience and insights of the co-researchers. On the other hand, it takes confidence to direct a research team with members who may have their own interests, to manage tensions dialectically not oppositionally, and to steer a course which is both academically rigorous and engages with the research team in a collaborative way (see also Robson, 2002, on participatory research). While it may be argued that the overall power and influence lies with the academics, who are on the home ground of university research, we suggest that the power relations are more explicit than in traditional, Mode 1, research. In addition, power has to be exercised for collaboration as well as research direction (in a process of leadership and the management of influence).

The academics also have to take care to ensure that the team understands that the purpose of the research is to enlarge understanding of organizational processes and not to evaluate or judge the case study organization. For example, 'Colin', a co-interviewer from a well-managed organization started to deplore what he saw as a more chaotic state of management and systems in a smaller, less well-resourced authority. He commented that he believed that his own organization managed change in a superior way. By contrast, another co-interviewer, 'Alan' lionized the chief executive of the organization he was researching, and came to feel that his own organization would work much better 'if only' they had someone of the same calibre. These views are not frequent but they have to be guarded against and deflected into curiosity about organizational processes. That curiosity can then be harnessed as part of the sense-making.

The co-research method requires detailed preparation and also commitment from the academics and practitioners. The research has benefited during the interview and analysis stage of the research but it has, on some occasions, proved more difficult to maintain collaboration during the writing-up stage of the research. Geographical dispersion combined with demanding workloads back in the home organization have sometimes made it difficult for co-researchers to find the time for the reflection which aids writing and re-drafting. Some have lost confidence at the writing stage and need further support from the academics. From this experience, we have learnt to allocate more time to the writing up, to maintain close contact during the writing period and to ensure that the co-researchers are aware that the project involves not only interviewing but also analysis and writing up the research.

The role of academics within co-research also has some tensions. There is intellectual leadership in trying to stimulate a continuing dialectic between theory and practice, and between action and reflection (see also Benington and Hartley, 2003). There is also tension in writing for both practitioner and academic audiences. While the aim is to write for both audiences with the same research material, in practice there are conflicting pressures and expectations between the rhythms, time-scales and styles of discourse in the two communities and in practice, two different versions of papers have to be written. Gibbons et al. (1994) note that Mode 2 knowledge production is usually generated for a wider range of stakeholders and is disseminated through action as well as through reports to peers and this is also reinforced by Lawler et al. (1998) and Pettigrew (1995). The challenge for academics is that they are required in Mode 2 research to be both good researchers and good communicators. There is also the risk of overload in meeting two sets of demands from practitioners and from academic peers. On the other hand, the rewards of both conducting research and achieving high quality case studies and exploring their practical use can be enhanced through co-research.

ANNOTATED BIBLIOGRAPHY

Co-research methodology was first described by Hartley and Benington (2000), and that article is commented on by King (2000). An example of research using co-research is Hartley and Allison (2000). Bartunek and Louis (1996) address some interesting issues of methodology, practice and ethics about insider/outsider research teams, though they write about two roles in research in single organizations not the three roles of co-research. Gibbons et al. (1994) explain the pressures, challenges and opportunities of Mode 2 research, on which epistemological foundations co-research is laid.

REFERENCES

Bartunek, J.M. and Louis, M.R. (1996) *Insider/Outsider Team Research*, Thousand Oaks, CA: Sage.

Benington, J. and Hartley, J. (2003) 'Democratic dialogue: knowledge creation in public sector organizations', conference paper, Academy of Management, Seattle, USA, August.

Brown, J.S. and Duguid, P. (1991) 'Organizational learning and communities-of-practice: toward a unified theory of working, learning and innovation', *Organization Science*, 2: 40–57.

Bryman, A. (1989) *Research Methods and Organization Studies*, London: Routledge.

Buchanan, D., Boddy, D. and McCalman, J. (1988) 'Getting in, getting on, getting out and getting back', in A. Bryman (ed.), *Doing Research in Organizations*, London: Routledge.

Easterby-Smith, M. and Malina, D. (1999) 'Cross-cultural collaborative research: toward reflexity', *Academy of Management Journal*, 42: 76–86.

Elden, M. and Chisholm, R. (1993) 'Emerging varieties of action research', *Human Relations*, 46: 121–42.

Evered, R. and Louis, M.R. (1981) 'Alternative perspectives on the organizational sciences: "Inquiry from the inside" and "inquiry from the outside"', *Academy of Management Review*, 6: 385–95.

Gibbons, M., Limoges, C., Nowotny, H., Schwartzman, S., Scott, P. and Trow, M. (1994) *The New Production of Knowledge*, London: Sage.

Goold, M. and Campbell, A. (1987) *Strategies and Styles: The Role of the Centre in Managing Diversified Corporations*, Oxford: Blackwell.

Hartley, J. (2001) 'Strategic aid or hand grenade: employee surveys in organizational change', *International Journal of Public Sector Management*, 14: 184–204.

Hartley, J. and Allison, M. (2000) 'The role of leadership in the modernisation and improvement of public services', *Public Money and Management*, April: 35–40.

Hartley, J. and Benington, J. (2000) 'Co-research: a new methodology for new times', *European Journal of Work and Organizational Psychology*, 7: 1–16.

Hartley, J., Benington, J., Allison, C., Clark, A. and Stansfield, A. (1994) 'The role of the corporate core in organizational change', Consortium Paper Number 2, Local Government Centre, University of Warwick..

King, N. (2000) 'Commentary – making ourselves heard: the challenges facing advocates of qualitative research in work and organizational psychology', *European Journal of Work and Organizational Psychology*, 9: 589–96.

Langley, A. (1999) 'Strategies for theorizing from process data', *Academy of Management Review*, 24: 691–710.

Lawler, E. et al. (1998) *Doing Research that is Useful for Theory and Practice*, San Francisco: Jossey-Bass.

Lewin, K. (1951) *Field Theory in Social Science*, New York: Harper and Row.

Louis, M.R. (1980) 'Surprise and sense-making: what newcomers experience in entering unfamiliar organizational settings', *Administrative Science Quarterly*, 25: 226–51.

Martin, J. (1989) 'Breaking up the mono-method monopolies in organizational analysis', in J. Hassard and D. Pym (eds), *The Theory and Philosophy of Organizations*, London: Routledge.

Nonaka, I. (1994) 'A dynamic theory of organizational knowledge creation', *Organization Science*, 5: 14–37.

Northcraft, G.B. and Neale, M.A. (1993) 'Negotiating successful research collaboration', in J.K. Murnighan (ed.), *Social Psychology in Organizations: Advances in Theory and Research*, Englewood Cliffs, NJ: Prentice-Hall. pp. 204–24.

Oliver, M. (1997) 'Emancipatory research: realistic goal or impossible dream?', in C. Barnes and G. Mercer (eds), *Doing Disability Research*, Leeds: Disability Press.

Pettigrew, A.M. (1995) 'The double hurdle for management research', Distinguished scholar address to the US Academy of Management, Vancouver, August.

Reason, P. (1994) *Participation in Human Enquiry*, Thousand Oaks, CA: Sage.

Robson, C. (2002) *Real World Research*, second edition, Oxford: Blackwell.

Smith, B. and O'Flynn, D. (2000) 'The use of qualitative strategies in participant and emancipatory research to evaluate disability service organizations', *European Journal of Work and Organizational Psychology*, 9: 515–26.

Weick, K. (1995) *Sense-Making in Organizations*, Thousand Oaks, CA: Sage.

Weick, K. (1999) 'Theory construction as disciplined reflexivity: tradeoffs in the 90s', *Academy of Management Review*, 24: 797–806.

West, M.A (1994) *Effective Teamwork*, Leicester: British Psychological Society.

Yin, R.K. (1994) *Case Study Research: Design and Methods*, second edition, Thousand Oaks, CA: Sage.

30 —— The Future Conference

Fran Ryan

The first manifestation of the Future Conference (FC) as a method was in 1960 when Fred Emery and Eric Trist from the Tavistock Institute used it as a participative planning method to enable two diverse groups to agree a strategic plan for their joint future (Emery and Purser, 1996: 293). At that point, Emery and Trist's interest was not research as such, but in the dialogue that was needed for effective leadership and decision making particularly with respect to future (strategic) planning. Since then, their method has been used and developed and is now used all over the world in both private and public organizational settings as a means of creating effective proposals and plans for action. It has not been used widely as a research method per se and this chapter suggests that it has a place in the toolkit of those who need to use research as a basis for planning policy or practice in work or community settings.

In this chapter, I will cover first the question of the inclusion of the FC as a valid action research method, second a description of the process of the FC, its history, and its principles, third an illustrative case study, and fourth strengths and weaknesses of the method. I will conclude with suggesting why it should be given serious consideration as a legitimate action research method.

Because the Future Conference has to date mainly been used for future planning, and not as a research method per se, there is a question as to the appropriateness of its inclusion in a book about qualitative research methods. If it is to fit in anywhere, its focus on action would situate it within the family of action research methods. Elsewhere in this book (Chapter 28) Heller usefully articulates seven characteristics that identify action research (p. 350). After describing the FC in terms of both process and principles, and describing some case studies, I would like to return, in the concluding section, to Heller's criteria, to demonstrate that the FC fits quite neatly, with one possible exception, within his criteria. The exception is also addressed.

WHAT IS A FUTURE CONFERENCE?

The term 'Future Conference' will be used to cover both the Search Conference and Future Search which are sufficiently similar in terms of both lineage and practice to be treated as one for the purposes of this chapter. For more detail on the differences see Emery and Purser (1996) and Weisbord (1992). A Future Conference (FC) is a method for enabling diverse groups of people to create a set of proposals or a plan based around their common future. They usually, but not invariably, implement the plan themselves. The method focuses on ensuring that all stakeholders with an interest in the subject are represented, and on enabling meaningful dialogue to take place between them. The approach is always billed as a working conference or a workshop, with the explicit objective of producing a specific output, either a set of proposals or a plan.

HISTORY OF USE IN ORGANIZATIONAL RESEARCH

As noted already, the FC has not previously been used as an explicit tool for organization research. It is usually undertaken in the pursuit of a specific output rather than in pursuit of knowledge. Fred Emery and Eric Trist first used it in Barford, UK in 1960 to enable a merger between two hostile organizations. They believed a traditional 'talking heads' conference would have re-enforced the passive or destructive behaviour of the group (Emery and Purser, 1996: 294). Drawing on findings by psychologists Bion (1952) and Asch (1952) (see below) they designed a week long conference where they would use dialogue to establish trust and would use this to enable the group to work effectively together on a new strategic plan. Since then the search conference has been developed by Fred and Merrelyn Emery in Australia, and Marvin Weisbord and Sandra Janoff in the US. It has been used extensively in corporate, public, voluntary and community sector environments. (See Emery and Purser, 1996: Weisbord and Jaroff, 1995; and Rehm et al., 2002 for more detail and many organizational case studies.)

DESCRIPTION OF THE METHOD

Before the FC

Before the FC itself, the participants (up to 70 people, large enough to get diversity but small enough to enable good dialogue) will have been carefully selected for their key stake in the task: between them they need to have all the knowledge and power to make the best possible decision based on the best available data. This includes those with formal and informal leadership roles, those who hold the purse strings, those who will be affected (positively or negatively) by the outcomes and those who work in the area and have expert knowledge of the subject. If key people are not present, key pieces of data or power may be missing, and a successful result is less likely.

All participants will have had detailed information well in advance about why they are meeting, what will happen during the conference and what generic outcomes are expected (for example, a set of proposals or a plan and an implementation group or some other governance structure). They come willingly as the subject will be compelling for them. Conference preparation will usually be undertaken by a design team which includes people from the different parts of the system. This preparation includes:

- deciding on the specific focus and time line for the conference;
- identifying the stakeholders, the system and its boundaries;
- devising criteria and process for participant selection;
- providing briefings, handouts, information on the FC;
- arranging good conference location, with healthy working conditions, where interruptions will not interfere.

During the FC

The FC itself works around a series of dialogue sessions, some in small groups, some with the whole group. Small group discussions are always based on a specific task and have a specific output which is reported back to the whole group. The outputs provide a rich source of data from which conclusions are drawn (not always agreed), and on which the future possibilities and actions are built. Outputs of all of these sessions could legitimately count as 'research'. They are usually no different than the sorts of outputs collected by many questionnaire-based surveys. The difference here is that they have come as a result of dialogue and they do not have the empirical weight of coming from an unbiased representative sample.

PHASE 1: MAPPING THE ENVIRONMENT

The first exercise starts with looking at the context within which the system or organization operates. This is a plenary brainstorm during which people report their perceptions about what's happening in the world. This starts off the process of people getting to know each other's views and usually different people have different pieces of information. When it's all collected together it amounts to a complex jigsaw of significant information. The output from this session is usually a prioritized list of significant trends which represent both threats and opportunities for the organization or system.

PHASE 2: SYSTEM ANALYSIS

The second phase turns attention to an analysis of the system itself: past, present and future. First, a look at the system's past will generate a rich tapestry of different perspectives from many different people having different pieces of information. The second step of system analysis looks at strengths: things to keep and continue, weaknesses: things to stop and drop, and gaps: new things that need to be created.

Then participants spend a significant proportion of the time in small groups, discussing and producing ideas for their most desirable future. Small group outputs are presented back to the whole group, sometimes as a list of key strategic goals, sometimes as creative sketches, a song, a poem, a play depicting what they want to see in the future. Small groups then discuss what they have seen and heard and report a list of common goals. These goals are consolidated into a list of common ground which forms the basis for planning.

PHASE 3: ACTION PLANNING

The third phase of the FC is action planning. During this phase people identify and sign up for the action areas that they are committed to delivering or make happen. They also identify and plan to manage any blockages or constraints that may be in the way. Also included at this stage is the planning to disseminate the information to (and enlist help of) significant others not present. Participants also start to plan how to organize and manage themselves during the implementation. In some (especially complex) cases they may even

Table 30.1 Overview of the FC showing data outputs or findings and conclusions

Phase	Dialogue session	Findings and conclusions
Phase 1	Mapping the environment	Key changes identified
		Key changes prioritized in terms of significance for the planning task
Phase 2	System analysis	Stories or visual representation of significant events in the history of the system
		Lists of strengths, weaknesses and gaps in the current system
		Ideas for possible futures
		Common ground goals and values for the future
		Goals and ideas about which there is some disagreement
Phase 3	Action planning	Action groups formed
		Actions towards common ground defined and first steps planned
		Communication plans formed
		Next steps identified (e.g. meetings to check progress and review, etc.)

use another workshop to participatively design how best to structure themselves to get their work done.

EPISTEMOLOGICAL ASSUMPTIONS

From the description so far, it will be clear that the FC is situated very much outside a natural sciences or experimental perspective. I will now try to make explicit the characteristics that reflect a distinctive epistemological approach.

The goal is to produce a plan: knowledge is a necessary prerequisite

The goal of the FC is a proposal or plan of action. The research is an essential part of the journey but takes on less significance once the plan has been arrived at. The data and knowledge that emerge during the FC are therefore treated as a means to an end, rather than an end in itself. This focus on a clear task is a consistent trait of the FC. Emery used the findings of Bion to arrive at this. Bion had identified various ways in which groups avoid doing their work (through developing dependency on their leader, through flight or fight or through forming sub-groups) (Lawrence et al., 1999: 31) so Emery set out to minimize the conditions under which this unhelpful behaviour would happen. Emery therefore gave the group clear tasks and used a democratic leadership style (see below) and managed the group in such a way as to reduce the probability of unhelpful behaviours.

People can know and can learn about their environment and don't need experts to tell them

The question here is 'Who can know'? or 'Whose knowledge counts?' In the FC, the epistemological assumption is that the people who make up the system, between them, have sufficient knowledge, which, when it is gathered and analysed, allows them to decide what is significant, what is not, and how they want to use it to build their future plan. Fred Emery believed that ordinary people could work things out for themselves and did not need experts to tell them (Emery, 1993: 40–83). He wrote at length about his reading of the works of early perception psychologists such as Gibson and Heider, and the concept of 'direct learning' where people can directly see patterns and trends in data and information without the benefit of a teacher or mediator. Both Heider and Gibson believed that the environment was 'an orderly structure of information that we (humans) are adapted . . . to direct, unmediated knowing . . . This system is attuned to the invariances or unchanging patterns evident in the constant flow of events and movement in the environment' (Emery, 1993: 28). This is more like common sense or the Aristotelian concept of *phronesis*, practical wisdom which included intuition, emotion and imagination. Emery called it 'ecological learning'. His starting point was that people know what is going on. They know what the issues are in their own community or organization; they can research options and ideas that might be useful and therefore, they can devise the best solutions.

Another epistemological question under this heading is 'What counts as knowledge?' In the FC, peoples' perceptions are collected as 'data'. No attempt is made to quantify or verify them, which is sometimes difficult for participants from a traditional scientific or research background. It is not usually difficult for participants, who welcome the trust in, and hearing of, their perceptions. Because the emphasis in a FC is on understanding, there may actually be diametrically opposed perceptions which are all logged and even welcomed as examples of how people can 'agree to differ' but still maintain dialogue. So the data may have conflicts within it, but the people who own the data will decide what to do about such conflicts. As the knowledge or data refers to 'their' system or a system in which they have a compelling stake, the participants are the arbiters of whether the data is sufficiently valid or reliable.

There is a fundamental concern with empowerment

From what has already been described, it will be evident that the FC has a fundamental and explicit commitment to self management and empowerment. This is consistent with, but predates feminist thinking and so-called feminist approaches to research. In the first search conference, Fred Emery borrowed ideas from Kurt Lewin's research into leadership styles (Lewin, 1948: 71–83). Briefly Lewin demonstrated that autocratic, laissez faire and democratic leadership styles had profoundly different effects on the followers. He showed that groups that were led democratically were more collaborative, productive and less destructive than autocratically led groups. Democratically led groups could also get on with productive work in the absence of their leader. From this Emery sought to design the first search conference at Barford where the style of the conference would enable productive and creative work, and not passivity, dependence, varying degrees of learned helplessness, or at worst, destructiveness. This democratic leadership style also served to reduce the likelihood of passive or dependent behaviour as identified by Bion (Lawrence et al., 1999: 31). Emery called this approach 'the democratic design principle'. It states that people need to be involved in the decisions that affect their lives. This became the guiding principle of his work and has far reaching consequences for how social systems, large and small, are structured.

So in the FC the power (to collect data and determine what is significant, what decisions are to be made, what actions are to be taken, and so on) is explicitly situated with the group itself. Were the 'facilitators' or process managers to retain power over the content, this would reduce the likelihood of the group taking responsibility for the decisions, particularly about what happens afterwards. This is another significant point of departure from the traditional research paradigm where the 'expert' researcher collects and analyses the data and 'objectively' analyses it and reports significant trends and proposals deriving from them, back to the sponsors.

In the FC, people attending (who are a microcosm of the system and therefore cover all the different perspectives within the system) do the analysis and make decisions about what is critical, what is unimportant and what to take as the basis for decision-making.

There is no role for the traditional researcher

The corollary of the position above is that there is no place for a traditional researcher within this paradigm. Anyone using the method will be doing so effectively to enable people to do their own research as a prelude to making changes in their lives or social system (be it work or community based). The role of the manager/facilitator is to manage the process, structure the enquiry along pre-agreed lines, and help people stick with the task particularly when the going gets tough (for example, when there are disagreements about what the data means).

Validity and reliability are not concerns

This has been covered to some extent in the paragraphs above, but it is worth underlining it as another major source of difference with traditional approaches to research. As stated above, there is not much emphasis on reliability and validity of the data. However, there is a kind of validity that comes from the variety of perspectives. This helps to 'triangulate' the data to ensure that a single loud voice does not unfairly dominate the group (Pretty et al., 1995: 59).

The participants deal with complexity

This is a result of the assumption about 'who can know'. An extension of what Emery called 'ecological learning' (Emery, 1993: 83) is the ability of ordinary people to deal with complexity: in a rapidly changing world, it is virtually impossible for anyone to know everything that is going on. The FC has a simple and pragmatic way of dealing with this: once key people from any system get together, there will be a view from every part of the system, each with their unique perception, knowledge, and experience, and this enables complexity both within the system and immediately outside it to be quickly mapped. Done this way, the picture that emerges stands a better chance of being up to date, and reflecting what is actually happening both inside and outside the system.

Emery's wife Merrelyn, has added a useful concept to this, 'puzzle learning'. The analogy is the jigsaw where the shape of the next piece cannot be known until the last one is down. This is the kind of complex data gathering and assembly that people are good at. With complex multiple layered systems, is it also impossible for any single person to have the full view (Emery and Purser, 1996: 95–6).

OTHER PRINCIPLES AND THEORY UNDERLYING THE FC

Three other significant principles, two derived from other areas of the social sciences and the third from his practice, have also informed Emery's approach to the search conference.

Open systems theory

Open systems theory provides a hugely important principle underpinning for the FC, and contributes much to its potential effectiveness for enabling the research, design and implementation of sustainable change in our uncertain, turbulent world. Emery used the work of biologist von Bertalanffy (1950) as his starting point. Bertalannfy's basic premise of open systems is that the world is made up of systems and environments. For any system to be successful, it needs to have an open, adaptive relationship with its environment which is defined as everything outside its boundary. In order to survive and prosper, a system needs to open itself to learning from its environment. Based on what the system learns about its environment and what it knows about itself, the system plans for a future in which it will both adapt to its environment but may also change its environment. Adaptive in this sense means the system and environment are in a constantly changing relationship in which the system is learning from and is affected by the environment and, likewise, the environment is also affected and changed by the system. It's a two-way street of mutual impact.

This has much in common with the interpretation of 'system' in Walsh and Clegg's soft systems analysis (Chapter 27). The main difference is that in the FC 'adaptive' means more than just accommodating to change. In the FC people are trying to get a better grip on their environment and see what can be done to *change it* for the benefit of the system.

Creating the conditions for open dialogue

For the first FC at Barford, Emery and Trist's primary concern was how to create the conditions for dialogue (Emery and Purser, 1996: 134). They turned to the work of psychologist Solomon Asch's research on the conditions it takes for trust and open dialogue to occur among people. Asch's view (1952: 78–131) was that trust starts to develop when three conditions are fulfilled: when discussion is open and all views are welcome, when people feel they share similar perceptions of the world and when they feel they share the same hopes and fears about the future. As this trust develops, relationships strengthen and deepen, increasing the likelihood of mutual learning and community building. This is the rock on which effective planning is based. In a nutshell, the FC sets out to build the planning community.

Rationalization of conflict and common ground

Fred Emery added this aspect some time after the Barford conference. He discovered it while running another Search Conference in 1965, in Malaysia: focus energy on similarities and what is agreed (usually the greater percentage) and *agree to disagree* about the rest (Emery and Pursuer, 1996: 140–5 and 299). The Emerys took the view that consensus decision-making was overrated, particularly as some differences are so deep they cannot be reconciled. Emery's intervention was in a territorial dispute between Singapore, Malaysia and Indonesia – all part of the British Empire at that time. All efforts at mediation had failed. He found that resolution of the conflict occurred once the parties shifted their attention to what they agreed on.

Other research which adds to the understanding of avoiding conflict comes from futurist Edward Lindaman (cited in Weisbord, 1992: 49). Lindaman discovered that conflict is less likely when people in strategic planning exercises focus on developing a preferred future and then plan how to make it happen. Instead of breaking a problem down and trying to solve it logically, they asked people to imagine a preferred future and that proved to be a powerful guiding force attracting people towards it. Recent work in psychology also supports the notion that planning how to get to a desirable future is a more potent approach than planning how to solve current problems: Solution Focused Therapy is based on the notion that improvement is more likely when it focuses on the positive aspects of a situation and the preferred future and how to move towards it, rather than analysis of what has gone wrong in the past (de Schazer, 1988). In publicity for De Bono's latest book, he talks about 'the huge need to move away from "judgement thinking" to "design thinking"' (De Bono, 2003).

CASE STUDY1

How can sport contribute to the development of communities?

This question could have led to a piece of academic or consultancy research where the expert researcher used questionnaires, focus groups, literature searches and so on, to develop an understanding of the problem and some recommendations for action. Instead the sponsor, Sport England, took the view that an action research approach would produce adequately evidenced-based thinking but more importantly, would produce more energy for change and implementation.

The conference drew together a carefully selected group of people who had a stake in the outcome: young people, people who worked as volunteers in sport, people who used and did not use sports facilities, people who worked in sports-related business, people from education, health, crime prevention and community groups, as well as local authority officers and people from regional bodies. For 48 hours (starting on Wednesday afternoon and finishing mid-afternoon Friday) people talked in different combinations, formally, as well as informally over lunch and dinner, to find their common ground for action.

The conference ended with an outline action plan that identified eight areas that everyone agreed were key for the future. Further development of the chosen areas was to be taken forward at a meeting attended by a representative from each action planning group in the weeks following the conference.

What follows below is a sample of the outputs from some of the sessions which were captured verbatim on flip charts or by a documenter on a laptop.

Phase 1 mapping the environment

After producing a complex mindmap of the environment, stakeholder groups voted, using dots, to identify the most significant trends for the conference task. The votes were counted and those clusters with the greatest number of votes were listed on a separate piece of flip chart paper. The prioritized results on this occasion were as follows: more pressure on young people; too many short-term initiatives; more meetings/less action; more facilities needed for sport; national curriculum does not allow for sport as it did; increasingly complex society; increasing cost of sport tuition; need to change transport habits; reduced number of volunteers; increasing influence of legislation, for example, health and safety, child protection.

Phase 2 system analysis

THE PAST

During this phase, groups created a collective timeline of sport and how it contributed to communities in the past. This was interpreted by small group discussions. What follows is one example of this.

Table 30.2

Significant events in the history of sport and what we can learn from them

Story: More emphasis on school sport in 1970s and 1980s, no mention of school sport in 1990s and 2000s. Discovery of new sports. Traditional sports in 1970s, more diverse sports in 1990s. Less team sport, more individual. Participation has moved to administration, passion to professionalism – people now want some financial reward for helping out in sport, no money issues in the 1960s and 1970s.

What we have lost:	Enjoyment, innocence, voluntary commitment
What we have gained:	Red tape, industry – professionalism
Implications:	Dilution/lack of focus, loss of performance – two-edged, greater diversity/new activity – expectations

THE PRESENT: OUTPUTS FROM CURRENT SYSTEM ANALYSIS

In this session participants brainstormed what they thought was good and needed to be maintained, what needed to be dropped, what needed to be created. Sometimes, as all perceptions are accepted as equally valid data, the same thing appears on different lists.

Table 30.3

Keep	Drop	Create
Volunteers	Too much paperwork	Create more volunteers
Simple funding	Competition from the sports field	A more integrated policy
Fun	Separate initiatives	A wider definition of sport
Our motivation towards sport	Top-down approach to national	New mechanisms for
Keep sport on local authority	policy	promoting co-operation
agenda	Short-termism	More opportunities for participation, especially for girls

THE FUTURE: OUTPUTS OF COMMON GROUND SESSION

During this session, small mixed groups first presented their vision for the future of sport's contribution to communities and then they extracted common themes and ideas. This produced a list of common themes for action planning as follows:

Table 30.4

Common themes for action planning

Time (having more time for sport)
Health (enabling sport to be used to promote health)
Fun and enjoyment (must be fun)
More sport in schools
Access to sport for all (easily accessible for everyone)
Easily accessible information
Distrust of government bodies and bureaucracy which became 'community influence and keeping it simple'
Integrated complexes
Make school central to community
Range of new and different sports/choice
Cost of sport – low/free /accessible
Value of sport/community engagement

Phase 3 action planning

Eight areas were chosen from the list above for action planning. All action areas attracted a range of people who wanted to take it forward into action. Each of these areas had a more detailed action plan underneath produced by people at the conference who were also expecting to become involved in implementation.

Table 30.5

Action planning subject areas

Access for all: making access easier
Value of sport: promoting the value of sport
Health and crime: sport as a vehicle to improve health/crime situation both physically and mentally/socially
Keep it simple: getting a simpler organization structure
More sport in schools: PE and sport as physical activity for children and young people throughout the whole day on the school site
Increasing choice: international exchange sport/sport swap to promote more choice
Community sport in schools: schools as community centres of sport
Fun and enjoyment: sport needs to be fun

STRENGTHS AND WEAKNESSES OF THE METHOD

The FC offers a pragmatic approach to research and action, which has some significant benefits: the FC is more likely to produce an acceptable plan. There is a huge literature both in psychology and business about change programmes that do not work (for example, Robbins and Finley, 1996) because of the so called 'not invented here' scenario. When people have not devised something for themselves, it is less likely to be accepted by them. Traditional expert-led and usually externally produced recommendations, however objective and well meaning and well done, are frequently met with resistance and lie on the shelf gathering dust (see, for example, Devane's introduction to Rehm et al. (2002)). There is no guarantee with the FC but, because people have made the plan themselves, they are more likely to implement it. Although not yet rigorously evaluated, there is a growing body of evidence that supports participative planning as being both speedier and more appropriate (Bishop, 1994; Oels, 2000).

Inevitably, there are some problems with the approach. Much of the so-called benefits are still hypotheses, and have only anecdotal evidence to support them. The area is not without its critics and there is certainly room for improvement. Cooke has mounted a significant attack on participative methods that masquerade as empowerment and participation (particularly Participatory Rural Appraisal which is used extensively in developing countries) but which may in fact be anything but and in fact are tantamount to tyranny in his view (Cooke and Kothari, 2001).

In addition to that there are some practical considerations which can be challenging. On the face of it there is significant cost in both time and money. Not everyone will want to commit the time and budget to doing the pure method. Forty-eight hours over three days is a significant chunk of time in busy diaries. However, the payback comes during implementation which usually goes much better because there is less resistance.

Some leaders are threatened by the openness, and are worried about losing power and control. This is a legitimate fear. They could lose some power and control as this process aims to be democratic and to share out power appropriately, in a way that is optimal for the system. However, they are just as likely to gain a different sort of power, in that they may gain more control over their environment: if the system organizes itself to be more effective it may impact its environment for the organization's benefit. Progressive and innovative leaders can see the benefits of pushing responsibility to where it needs to be for effective work thus freeing up successive layers of management for more strategic and higher added-value work.

CONCLUSIONS

What potential does the FC have as a research method?

Heller (Chapter 28) comments briefly and usefully on the problems with traditional approaches to social science research so there is no need to repeat that here. Other critical commentators are Sandercock (1998) and Chambers (1997) both of whom suggest that alternatives to the traditional largely positivist approach are needed in the social sciences. Sandercock mounts a strong case for the inadequacy of traditional approaches to planning research. She questions the dominance of positivist approaches to 'who can know' and 'what counts as knowledges' as limiting, particularly to those who are traditionally not included. Her criticisms are equally valid for current social science and organizational research methods. She suggests that other forms of knowing are accepted such as knowing through dialogue ('To whom should we listen?' 'To what should we listen?'), that it should be more acceptable to use knowledge that comes from experience, that local people's knowledge should be used to discover locally appropriate solutions, and that music, painting, poetry and theatre should be acceptable alternative media for people to learn about complex and conflict-ridden issues. She speaks of the fact that the creation of symbolic forms are not validated by society and draws the contrast between learning in western culture where positivism reigns supreme, with Native American or Aboriginal culture where knowledge may not be based on questions and answers, but by suggestion, example, divining, showing and storytelling. Finally Sandercock suggests (making a link to social learning theory) that action is the only way to know (Sandercock, 1998: 57–83).

The fundamental point at the basis of these critiques is the question of power: whose interests are being served by the outcomes of the research? For researchers who are genuinely interested in using knowledge to empower people, the FC offers a pragmatic, tried and tested method that warrants further serious attention as a research tool. Although not in the least concerned with scientific method as such, Emery's search conference and its more recent manifestations would fit in with the requirements for more people centred approaches to research and decision making.

I have already called the FC 'action research' but to support my view will briefly cover it in terms of Heller's seven criteria: close relationship between knowledge acquisition and action, knowledge and action are for the benefit of the participants not the 'researcher', validation through the learning process itself, ability to generalize findings, shared values between researcher and client, using more than one discipline and more than one knowledge acquisition method, the FC meeting the criteria for action research. The only point where there might be some disagreement is whether the findings from a FC are widely available. This really depends on the situation. In public sector research, the findings are usually in the public domain, however, within formal organizations, research may not be so widely available. Here, the FC could be seen as a consultancy approach which in Heller's terms is defined as one where the results might not be openly available. My concern here is to discover appropriate and optimal methods to do research whether it is conducted by consultants or academics (and many if not most, do both). I suggest that both groups need to have in their toolkit a pragmatic approach to social science research that situates change (plans or other outcomes) at the heart of the method. When research is undertaken as a forerunner to decision making and action, whether that be new policy on a national scale or new practice at a local level, the FC offers a method that should be considered. It may also be more effective in terms of appropriateness of solution and speed of implementation.

A final comment about the FC method is the fact that it does not need those who are trained researchers to conduct it, an altogether different set of skills is needed. In conclusion, the FC seems to offer a pragmatic approach which also has the added benefit of meeting current government requirements for participation in situations where the research is needed as a prelude to developing new policy or planning guidelines, new community, or local plans.

Further research is needed as a matter of urgency to test the approach in such settings to see if it is genuinely more effective (in terms of solution) and speedier (in terms of delivery timescale) than traditional approaches.

FURTHER READING

Readers are directed to three books that capture most of the important material for this method, first of all, Merrelyn Emery and R. Purser's book (1996) *The Search Conference* which offers the best overview of the principles underlying the method as well as a detailed and extensive bibliography. Second is Weisbord and Janoff's book (1995), *Future Search* which offers many excellent hints and stories and finally *Futures that Work* a practical guide, also with many stories (Rehm et al., 2002).

REFERENCES

Asch, Solomon (1952) *Social Psychology*, Englewood Cliffs, NJ: Prentice-Hall.

Bion, W. (1961) *Experiences in Groups*, London: Tavistock.

Bishop, Jeff (1994) *Community Involvement in Planning and Development Processes*, London: HMSO.

Chambers, Robert (1997) *Whose Reality Counts*, London: ITDG Publishing.

Cooke, Bill and Kothari, Uma (eds) (2001) *Participation the New Tyranny?*, London and New York: Zed Books.

De Bono, E. (2003) *Why So Stupid*, Dublin: Blackhall.

De Shazer, S. (1988) *Clues: Investigating Solutions in Brief Therapy*, New York: Norton.

Emery, M. (ed.) (1993) *Participative Design for Participative Democracy*, Canberra: Centre for Continuing Education, Australian National University.

Emery, M. and Purser, R. (1996) *The Search Conference, a Powerful Method for Planning Organizational Change and Community Action*, San Fancisco: Jossey Bass.

Lawrence, W. Gordon, Bain, Alaistair and Gould, Laurence (1999) 'The fifth basic assumption', Free Associations, Vol. 6, Part I, 37.

Lewin, Gertrud Weiss (ed.) (1948) *Resolving Social Conflicts*, New York: Harper.

Oels, Angela (2000) 'The power of visioning, evaluation of Future Search conferences in England and Germany', Unpublished thesis. University of East Anglia, School of Environmental Sciences.

Sandercock, L. (1998) *Towards Cosmopolis*, Chichester: John Wiley.

Pretty, Jules, Gujit, Irene, Thompson, John and Scoones, Ian (1995) *A Trainer's Guide for Participatory Learning and Action*, London: IIED Participatory Methodology Series.

Rehm, Cebula, Ryan, F. and Large, M. (2002) *Futures that Work*, Stroud, UK: Hawthorn Press.

Robbins, Harvey and Finley, Michael (1996) *Why Change Doesn't Work*, London: Orion Business Books.

Von Bertalanffy, L. (1950) 'The theory of open systems in physics and biology', *Science*, 3: 23–9.

Weisbord, Marvin (1992) *Discovering Common Ground*, San Francisco: Berrett-Koehler.

Weisbord, M. and Janoff, S. (1995) *Future Search*, San Francisco: Berrett Koehler.

Index